WOMAN

WOMAN

The American History of an Idea

•

LILLIAN FADERMAN

Yale
UNIVERSITY PRESS
New Haven and London

Published with support from the Fund established in memory of Oliver Baty Cunningham, a distinguished graduate of the Class of 1917, Yale College, Captain, 15th United States Field Artillery, born in Chicago September 17, 1894, and killed while on active duty near Thiaucourt, France, September 17, 1918, the twenty-fourth anniversary of his birth.

Copyright © 2022 by Lillian Faderman.
All rights reserved.

This book may not be reproduced, in whole or in part, including illustrations, in any form (beyond that copying permitted by Sections 107 and 108 of the U.S. Copyright Law and except by reviewers for the public press), without written permission from the publishers.

Yale University Press books may be purchased in quantity for educational, business, or promotional use. For information, please e-mail sales.press@yale.edu (U.S. office) or sales@yaleup.co.uk (U.K. office).

Designed by Sonia L. Shannon
Set in Electra by Westchester Publishing Services
Printed in the United States of America.

Library of Congress Control Number: 2021944804
ISBN 978-0-300-24990-3 (hardcover: alk. paper)

A catalogue record for this book is available from the British Library.

This paper meets the requirements of ANSI/NISO Z39.48-1992 (Permanence of Paper).

10 9 8 7 6 5 4 3 2 1

For Phyllis,
who has been making everything possible for fifty years

CONTENTS

	Introduction: Tyranny and Mutability in the Idea of Woman	1
1.	Woman in Seventeenth-Century America	11
2.	Woman, Lady, and Not a Woman in the Eighteenth Century	36
3.	Daughters of Liberty: Woman and a War of Independence	62
4.	Woman Enters the Public Sphere: The Nineteenth Century	86
5.	Nineteenth-Century Woman Leaves Home	115
6.	Woman Goes to College and Enters the Professions	142
7.	The Struggle to Transform Woman into Citizen	168
8.	The "New Woman" and "new women" in a New Century	198
9.	"It's Sex o'Clock in America"	224
10.	Woman on a Seesaw: The Depression and World War II	249
11.	Sending Her Back to the Place Where God Had Set Her: Woman in the 1950s	276
12.	A New "New Woman" Emerges (Carrying Baggage): The 1960s	302
13.	Radical Women and the Radical Woman	332
14.	How Sex Spawned a New "Woman": The 1990s	360
15.	"Woman" in a New Millennium	384
	Epilogue: The End of "Woman"?	414
	Notes	425
	Acknowledgments	535
	Illustration Credits	537
	Index	539

Illustrations follow page 248

Introduction

•

TYRANNY AND MUTABILITY IN THE IDEA OF WOMAN

I grew up in the 1950s, surrounded by images of woman that had nothing to do with me or most of the girls who were my classmates at Hollenbeck Junior High School in East Los Angeles. Radio and TV images of middle-class wives and mothers like Harriet Nelson and June Cleaver, always in the bosom of their tidy families, did not apply. Nor did the few commercials that featured a working woman—usually a well-groomed blonde secretary. Nor did the ubiquitous warnings to girls to avoid premarital sex, lest they become damaged goods. The girls I went to school with were mostly from immigrant families. Many of them were pachucas (gang girls) who wore short, tight skirts and see-through nylon blouses and engaged in petty outlawry: that was their answer to the stifling mores their parents had brought with them from Mexico and to the white world that disdained them. They were often in trouble as "juvenile delinquents." I, one of the few white girls at Hollenbeck, was also the daughter of an immigrant, an unwed Jewish woman from Eastern Europe who made a living sewing dresses in a downtown LA garment factory. I too was a juvenile delinquent of sorts, because I had already discovered my outlaw sexuality and would soon be going to gay-girls bars, flashing a fake ID that said I was an adult. The dominant images of woman that I and my pachuca classmates could not avoid knowing about—through radio, TV, movies, billboards, magazines, sermons, laws, textbooks, and teachers—had no resonance for us, yet their effect on us was inescapable.

It was not unusual for my pachuca classmates to fall into the juvenile justice system and be sent to "juvi," as they called LA's Juvenile Hall. If their crimes were bad enough (burglary, serious assault, or prostitution, for example), they were sentenced to the Ventura School for Girls—which, despite having a name that sounded like a posh boarding school, was a reform school for what the staff psychiatrist called "prize recalcitrants." But throughout the 1950s, the school's "enlightened" methods were intended not only to discourage antisocial behavior but also to reform the girls by inculcating in them the dominant culture's ideal of womanhood. To that end they were visited by wholesome-looking Hollywood starlets (the studios' idea of a publicity stunt, perhaps) who modeled twirly feminine frocks. They were given "charm classes" and classes in office skills. They were taken by volunteers, citizens of Ventura, to church services to hear sermons on good morals. The indoctrination often did not work: students scaled the wall and escaped the Ventura School for Girls so often that finally a security fence had to be built. However, they could not escape knowing the dominant culture's idea of woman and that they had fallen short of it.[1]

As for me, I could easily have been caught in a gay-bar raid and ended up at the Ventura School for Girls, too. Instead, by a lucky encounter in the nick of time, I ended up in a PhD program at the University of California, Los Angeles. It was not where a young woman was supposed to be in 1962, but the long-forgotten women's righters of the previous century had made a space in PhD programs for women like me who could not go along with the feminine mystique. I entered the program gladly—yet as aware of myself as a fugitive from the ideal of woman as were my pachuca classmates.

How, when, and why had that ideal of woman been created? Why had its grip been so tenacious as to reach even into our poor and neglected little world? And how did it become possible to contest it and to live a life outside of it?

•

WOMAN BEGAN AS A PERSONAL QUEST to answer those questions. As someone who has been writing about history for a half-century, I naturally looked to the past—the twentieth century leading me backward to the nineteenth, then to the eighteenth, and finally the seventeenth, when Europeans first began to populate this country. I wanted to know who had had a hand in formulating the dominant idea of woman that I had been so aware of, even as I rebelled against it. Who had dared to rebel against it in other centuries? What were the forces that finally brought about seismic changes in the concept "woman"? And why have traces of the early concept stubbornly remained, even into the present?

For centuries it seemed that an unchanging idea of woman prevailed. In colonial America the men with the loudest megaphones, standing at church lecterns or sitting in the Massachusetts General Court, purported to define who woman is by nature, what her proclivities are, and how she is to behave. Though women's lot shifted from the seventeenth century to the eighteenth and then to the nineteenth, though it had reference to where they lived and the class to which they belonged, and though possibilities opened to them that were inconceivable earlier, the idea of woman among the megaphone holders often seemed not to budge.

Roger Williams, for instance, who on most subjects was so liberal that he was cast out of Puritan Massachusetts, observed in the seventeenth century, "Reason and Experience tell us that Woman is the weaker Vessel, that she is more fitted to keep and order the House and Children." In the eighteenth century, the enlightened Thomas Jefferson praised American women as "too wise to wrinkle their foreheads with politics" and "contented to soothe and calm the minds of their husbands returning from politic debates." In the nineteenth century, Thomas Roderick Dew, president of the College of William and Mary (but insensible to the struggles of Emma Willard and Mary Lyon to promote education for women), offered that woman's "inferior strength and sedentary habits confine her to the domestic sphere," where "grace, modesty, and loveliness are the charms which constitute her power."[2] Even into the twentieth century (and, in surprising ways, the twenty-first century), those ideas of woman continued to have currency. However, as megaphones proliferated—through forces such as population shifts, economics, education, and media—the old notions, while not vanishing completely, have had to live side by side with ideas of woman that challenged virtually everything that had been held as immutable truths.

For centuries, the men with the megaphones did not simply describe woman, they prescribed who she must be. They left out of their prescriptions those who were beneath their concern. The enslaved female, for instance, as Angela Davis has observed, was "annulled as woman." Almost nothing that signified "woman" to the megaphone holders applied to her; she had to forge her own meanings as best she could. Other women the megaphone holders coerced to fit their definition: "Your wives and daughters can soon learn to spin and weave," President George Washington told the men of the Cherokee Nation in 1796, naming pursuits more appropriate to women than agriculture, which had traditionally given Cherokee women power over food growth and distribution. Their old role would change, the president of the new United States promised in vowing to "procure" for Cherokee females "all the apparatus necessary for spinning & weaving, & hire a woman to teach the use of them." The dominant definers were still wielding their idea of woman like a cudgel over Indian women in 1839, when the commissioner of Indian affairs, T. Hartley Crawford, told Congress that Indian females must be "made good and industrious housewives, and taught what befits their condition," so that "their husbands and sons will find comfortable homes and social enjoyments, which, in a state of society, are essential to morality and thrift."[3]

As for the white women idealized as woman, those who balked openly against following prescriptions that circumscribed their agency risked paying a price from banishment, whipping, or, worse, to public shaming as hens that crow, as Ben Franklin called them in 1734. Some eventually found more subtle ways to exercise agency, and in doing so they expanded the parameters of woman. For instance, women's apparent collaboration in notions of woman's innate "modesty" or her "fitness" to keep house paradoxically served as their visas out into the world. "Intemperance has made [woman's] home desolate," they complained in the nineteenth century, and they organized temperance groups all over the country, posses of housewives raiding saloons or agitating for the passage of prohibition laws. It was men who dragged women into prostitution and defiled their natural modesty, women moral reformers complained. Bent on stopping men from trampling "on the honor of [woman] with impunity," they raided houses of prostitution to shame the customers and rescue the sex workers, and they convinced state legislatures to pass laws against the seduction of innocent women. Ultimately, they made reform into paying jobs for women, convincing governments that cities needed women social workers and policy makers because, as Clinton Woodruff, a Pennsylvania legislator, wrote in 1915, "Women by natural instinct as well as long training have become the housekeepers of the world, so it is only natural that they should in time become municipal housekeepers as well."[4] It was as "housekeepers" for the public good that nineteenth- and early twentieth-century women were finally able to claim a voice in the public square.

But women have also been complicit in maintaining the tyranny of the old ideas of woman, even mounting angry campaigns against attempts to change them. In 1913 women of the anti-suffrage movement pleaded with men as they were about to go to the voting booths: "Keep mother, wife, and sister in the protected home. Do not force us into partisan politics. Put a cross before the word 'No' on April 7 and win our gratitude." Three generations later, in the 1970s, the most impassioned fight against the Equal Rights Amendment was waged by STOP (Stop Taking Our Privileges) ERA, which represented tens of thousands of "homemakers," asking, "What about the rights of the woman who doesn't want to compete with men on an equal basis? Does she have the right to be a woman?"[5]

The tyranny of old notions about woman continued even as droves of women left the home to pursue careers. By the 1980s, women were beginning to outnumber men among college graduates and were entering professions in unprecedented numbers. But when some of them became mothers and faced child-care problems, they went home again while their husbands remained in the workforce. Ignoring the structural inequities facing working mothers of all classes, the media seemed to gloat that feminist fever had apparently broken, and things were getting back to normal. Throughout the 1980s, the *New York Times*, for instance, featured headlines such as "Many Young Women Now Say They'd Pick Family over Career" and "Professional Women Do Go Home Again." Much the same thing happened at the start of the new millennium. Women had begun approaching parity with men in professional schools and were accounting for one-third of the students in business schools. But the media reported, again seeming to gloat, that women were "opting out" of high-powered careers. They were deciding to "swing to a place where we enjoy, and can admit we enjoy, the stereotypical role of female/mother/caregiver. I think we were born with those feelings," a former lawyer proclaimed in the paper of record.[6]

But despite the tyranny of the old notions of woman that reassert themselves periodically, the shifts in a woman's lot have inarguably been momentous. Men's muscles stopped being vital to tame the wilderness, and women's incessant toil stopped being vital to the running of the home. The proliferation of mills in the early nineteenth century called laboring-class women out of their houses and into industry. Urban problems that followed the growth of cities opened a panoply of new professions to women. The legalization of contraceptives permitted women to control the number of children they would bear and rear. The eighteenth-century idea that the bourgeois white woman should be educated so she would be able to educate her sons for the new republic metamorphosed two centuries later into the idea that women of all classes and races had a right to go to college, and they did.

Wars too have had major, if contradictory, impacts on ideas of woman. In the eighteenth century, when presumptive fitness for combat was posited as a requisite for citizenship, women were officially disenfranchised— in good part through men's sentiment that woman's "delicate nature" made her unfit to engage in "the hardy Enterprises of War." But in the twentieth century, following women's frustrating seventy-year battle for the vote, they were finally enfranchised—in good part through men's sentiment that "we have made partners of the women in this war [World War I]; shall we admit them only to a partnership of suffering and sacrifice and toil and not to a partnership of privilege and right?"[7]

Communities of women with little ostensible power have also effected shifts in the possibilities for women and notions about woman. In the early twentieth century, for instance, young working-class women, white and Black, left their homes to find work in big northern cities where, unchaperoned, they created new subcultures. They asserted their right to be out on the streets at night for fun and even to frequent the newly established dance halls. Middle-class Black reformers complained about "half-naked Negro girls danc[ing] shameless dances with men in Spanish costumes" to the tune of "St. Louis voodoo blues" and about the dance-hall atmosphere of "unrestrained animality." Middle-class white reformers warned young white women that the dances they were inventing in the dance-hall "dens of iniquity" (the shimmy, the bunny hug, the grizzly bear) were nothing but simulations of sex acts and that "no girl who wishes to retain her virtue should visit these public traps of sin."[8] Yet not only did the working girls persist in having their fun, but the freedoms they took—wandering about when respectable girls were supposed to be fast asleep, displaying their bodies any way they pleased—became a direct inspiration for the middle-class flappers of the 1920s.

But it would be a mistake to believe with whiggish optimism that changes in the idea of woman have been linearly progressive. Given certain circumstances, the old dominant notions can and have asserted themselves tyrannically. After World War II, for instance, returning soldiers needed the jobs that women had been filling; heterosexual women were tired of the loneliness and celibacy that war had imposed on them; the zeitgeist was yearning, just as it had been after World War I, for a "return to normalcy." And much of the linear progress toward women's agency made in the first part of the twentieth century was erased. By the 1950s, women (some by choice, some by coercion) fell under the tyranny of the version of woman that had been current a hundred years earlier. Even those far outside the ideal of woman—as my pachuca classmates and I were—could not escape the knowledge of how a woman was supposed to behave.

The term "woman" had long conflated anatomical sex and gendered behavior, as in Roger Williams's assertion that "Woman is the weaker

Vessel . . . more fitted to keep and order the House and Children." Such conceptions of woman left no space for women who did not fit. They were called "monsters," "unsexed," "unnatural," "manly," and "Amazons" (an appellation not intended as a compliment). In the seventeenth century they were controlled by beatings or banishment. In later centuries they were controlled by contempt and pathologizing. As the physician William Lee Howard wrote in 1900 in the *New York Medical Journal*, the violation of the gender behavior deemed natural to a woman was tantamount to sickness: "The female possessed of masculine ideas of independence, the viragint who would sit in the public highways and lift up her pseudo-virile voice, proclaiming her sole right to decide questions of war or religion, . . . and that disgusting anti-social being, the female sexual pervert, are simply different degrees of the same class—degenerates."[9] The efforts to coerce women to stop trying to "act like men" and to perform "woman" as of old remained unrelenting.

Simone de Beauvoir's famous observation that "one is not born, but rather becomes, a woman" spoke to exactly the imperative that women faced to make prescribed gender behaviors match their anatomical sex. De Beauvoir was the first to articulate what Judith Butler has observed, that "'being' female and 'being' a woman are two very different sorts of being." In the 1980s, feminists of the second wave, such as Monique Wittig, inspired by de Beauvoir's ideas, called woman a "myth, an imaginary formation," conceived to make women weak and subservient. Wittig proposed the killing off of woman to free women. Second wave feminists wrote of androgyny as the ideal that would "liberate the individual from the confines of the appropriate"—that is, confines that prescribed gender behavior based on anatomical sex. Gender theorists of the 1980s and 1990s pointed out that "Sex-related differences between bodies are continually summoned as testimony to social relations and phenomena that have nothing to do with sexuality."[10] Such ideas spawned widespread examinations in the new millennium of the differences between gender and sex, which have illuminated how woman has been a social construct.

The most radical challenge to the illusion that woman signifies any inevitable or immutable set of characteristics has been fostered in recent years by an expanded understanding of "transgender" and "nonbinary" people. Americans in earlier eras were bemused when confronted with such a challenge, as a story that grabbed headlines all over the country in 1883 illustrates: a person identified in newspapers as "Mrs. Della Hudson" (a wife and the mother of two little girls) had lived in a small town in Illinois prior to fleeing to Waupun, Wisconsin, where "Mrs. Hudson" became "Frank Dubois" and married Gertie Fuller. Samuel J. Hudson—in hot pursuit of his wife, the little girls in tow—alerted the press as well as the police. A manhunt was on. Newspaper reporters located Frank Dubois before the marshal and the deputy sheriff did. "You insist that you are a man?" a reporter who sold his story to the New York Times and the Boston Weekly Globe claimed to have asked Dubois. "I do. I am. As long as my wife is satisfied it is nobody's business," was Dubois's brave response. But the reporter disagreed, focusing in his story on Dubois's broad hips, full chest, and a voice "that could not be mistaken for that of a man."[11]

Members of the general public, having no comfortable way to understand the story of an anatomical female wishing to marry another female, made up a story they could understand. "The mystery has at last been cleared up," the Atlanta Constitution reported with relief, explaining that "it is the general belief that Miss Fuller was betrayed by someone, and the mock marriage was hatched to cover up the disgrace." That is, having been seduced and abandoned by a man, Gertie Fuller found herself pregnant, and Della Hudson, pretending to be a man, married Gertie to help her save face. Despite the public assumption of Dubois's "innocence," he was taken into custody by the deputy sheriff. Apparently frightened, Dubois gave in: newspapers were soon reporting that "she" vowed to "return to her husband and family, and promised to live with them hereafter."[12]

Today, Dubois's story surely would have ended differently. He could have taken his place alongside trans men, trans women, and genderqueers. Far from being victimized by a hostile or vacuous press, he could have had his own megaphone through social media. He could have joined the big chorus of voices that, more than ever before, are complicating connections between sex and gender.

A new language has now emerged to recognize the various complications. In 2019, "they," used to indicate the refusal to call oneself either "he" or "she," became the "Word of the Year," according to the dictionary makers at Merriam-Webster. According to Dictionary.com, the "runner-up" Word of the Year was "nonbinary," meaning "relating to a person with a gender identity that does not fit into the male/female divisions." Dictionary.com also announced that among the "most salient additions" to the dictionary were terms such as "womxn," to be "inclusive of trans and nonbinary people." And according to a Pew Research Survey, 35 percent of teens and people in their early twenties said they knew at least one person who preferred that others refer to them with gender-neutral pronouns.[13] Notions about women that have long had a tyrannical hold are being seriously complicated and destabilized in brand-new ways as the millennium advances.

Of course, as history has shown, there is no guarantee that the present challenges will be impermeable to a reassertion of old ideas. The new understandings have little meaning for women such as the former lawyer who, sounding very much like Roger Williams in 1676, reveled in 2003 in being able to "swing to a place where we enjoy, and can admit we enjoy, the stereotypical role of female/mother/caregiver. I think we were born with those feelings."

Nevertheless, the megaphone holders—whose number has been greatly expanded by the internet—now include those who reify the proof that biology is not destiny, that the sex to which one is assigned at birth can be mutable, and even that the number of genders exceeds two.

1.
Woman in Seventeenth-Century America

On July 10, 1637, soon after colonists attacked a Pequot Indian village and burned alive hundreds of men, women, and children, Roger Williams, who acted as an intermediary between the Pequot and the colonists, wrote to John Winthrop, governor of the Massachusetts Bay Colony, to report that representatives of the Pequot had on three separate occasions come to beg for peace and mercy. The first time, a "squaw" came. She was decked out with numerous strings of beads made of white seashells, which symbolized her status and spiritual power. The second time, too, a "squaw" came, her dress set thick with white seashell beads. Both women were "questioned much for their Truth," Williams wrote. The colonists' leaders did not find them credible: as women, who could they possibly represent? They were dismissed. The third time, the Pequot sent five women and an old man. The colonists were now willing to listen—to the man.[1]

WOMAN IN THE MASSACHUSETTS BAY COLONY

"the place where God had set her"

—JOHN WINTHROP, *Winthrop's Journal* (1645)[2]

Governor John Winthrop was expressing a common Puritan sentiment in 1645 when he blamed the man who was governor of the Connecticut colony, Edward Hopkins, for the "sad infirmity" of his young wife, Ann. She had lost her "understanding and reason." She was barren in a community in which women typically had upward of six children, but Mr. Hopkins had been loving and tender to her. He had not wanted to grieve her, and he allowed her freedoms. However, Winthrop wrote in his journal with some satisfaction, Hopkins "saw his error, when it was too late." Instead of controlling his wife as was necessary for a husband to do, and making her tend to woman's duties, Hopkins had permitted her to "give herself wholly to reading and writing" and had even let her write books. And that was the cause of Mrs. Hopkin's destruction. "For had she attended to household affairs, and such things as belong to women, and not gone out of her way and calling to meddle in such things as are proper for men, whose minds are stronger, etc.," Winthrop opined, "she had kept her wits and might have improved them usefully and honorably in the place where God had set her."[3] The idea of woman for Winthrop and for most of his contemporaries was unbending: the sex a female had been assigned at birth defined her and dictated what her behavior should be, no matter her individual proclivities. Deviations meant trouble.

Winthrop's wives apparently gave him no such trouble. His first one, Mary, bore him six children before she died in childbirth in the tenth year of their marriage. His second wife, Thomasine, died in childbirth when they had been married for just one year. His third wife, Margaret, bore him eight children. Margaret assured her husband in letters she signed "your obedient wife" that like the biblical Abigail, wife of David, the future king, she would happily be to him "a servant to wash the feet of my lord" and she would do "any service wherein I may please my good husband." Margaret would never challenge the idea that, as Winthrop proclaimed in a speech to the General Court of Massachusetts, a true woman and wife understands that her man "is lord and she is subject to him." She submits willingly to her husband's authority; she has no desire to be anywhere other than in "the place where God had set her."[4]

Margaret died in 1647. The governor was almost sixty years old by then, but six months after Margaret's death he took his fourth wife, Martha, a thirty-year-old widow. They had one child before the governor died, in 1649.

The strictures on women could be less rigid outside of the New England colonies, but most Puritan ministers and magistrates echoed Winthrop's sentiments concerning woman. In sermons, laws, and imagination, they conceived of men as diverse, but all women in their society they subsumed under the single category of "woman." The ministers told women that they must never concern themselves with outside affairs or be "a rash wrambler abroad." A woman's role was to keep the home, "be helpful in the propagating of mankind," and "yield Subjection to [her husband] as her Head."[5] The magistrates made first a woman's father and then her husband legal despots over her, too. The laws of coverture said that husband and wife had one voice under the law—and that voice was his. Of course, there was no law saying that a woman must marry—but a woman who did not marry had few ways to support herself; even worse, in a small and insulated society she bore the pains of being deemed an unnatural creature. However, as a married woman she was as powerless as a child. She could not make contracts or sue in her name. Her possessions belonged to her husband. Even her children were under his authority.

Puritans had come to the New World with their religious inheritance intact, believing even, as the English divine Richard Greenham had preached, that regardless of a woman's virtues, "if she be not obedient [to her husband] she cannot be saued [saved]." In the New World, disoriented by the howling wilderness that surrounded them and strange beings that to them seemed as wild and unknowable as the wilderness, anomie threatened. As they sought order in divine guidance, they became even more rigid than they had been in the mother country, where Puritan women could find ways to temper patriarchy and claim a modicum of agency for themselves.[6] In America, the Old Testament provided for the Puritans an unquestionable literal truth about woman. Eve, foolish yet wily, had led her husband astray. Now man must recoup what Adam had lost by exercising a firm grip. Woman, Eve's daughter, also had her role to play in righting the ancient wrong. She must admit that she was the "weaker vessel"—in physical strength, intellectual power, moral understanding—and behave accordingly.

She could not speak in church because, as Eve had proven, she was prone to error and to seducing others to err. She must not even sing in church, lest she tempt the new Adam. She could not hold office. She could not participate in public affairs, regardless of her rank. A gentlewoman might be given deference by those socially beneath her, but she was no less subject to the authority of the men in her life than a servant girl would be. As the seventeenth century progressed, men were defined more and more by their work. They might be tradesmen or artisans or merchants. But with few exceptions, women continued to be only women and wives. Those who tried to be more courted grief.[7]

Even the most enlightened of the Puritans upheld the reigning notions of woman. Roger Williams, an advocate for religious freedom, believed in the separation of church and state. He was so progressive that the magistrates of the Massachusetts Bay Colony expelled him for harboring "new and dangerous ideas." He was one of the few seventeenth-century leaders who thought that the colonists ought to deal fairly with the Indians. He was also America's first abolitionist, beseeching Governor Winthrop in 1637 not to hold captive Indians in indefinite slavery. He even pleaded, in the midst of a war between the colonists and the Pequots, in favor of the Indians' reasonable right to their own land.[8]

Yet with regard to woman, Williams was an orthodox Puritan, believing even that "the holy spirit of God . . . commands the veiling of women"—especially in Christian meetings, where their hair might be a disturbing distraction to men. Williams had founded the colony of Rhode Island, where religious tolerance was encouraged. But upon learning that in Pennsylvania the Quakers permitted women to preach, he was repelled. He censured Quakers for not understanding what he knew to be obvious: "that the Lord hath given a covering of longer Hair to Woman as a sign" that she is to be modest, bashful, silent, and retiring, and that she is not "fitted for Manly Actions and Employments." When a woman dared question Williams's public pronouncement that scripture prohibited women from preaching, he dismissed her, snapping that he "would not Countenance so much the Violation of Gods Order in making a Reply to a woman in Publick."[9]

Yet surely not all colonial men were tyrants. The variability of human personalities suggests that some husbands and fathers must have been lenient, fair, and even democratic. But even if that were so, under the precepts of church and state almost all women suffered from the limitations imposed on woman. With limited exceptions, enjoyed mostly by wealthy widows, all agency and all positions of power were reserved for men.[10]

The first known Puritan poet in America was a female. Anne Bradstreet grew up in the home of the Earl of Lincoln, where her father was a steward, and she had free rein on the earl's estate and in his library. But at sixteen she was married, and in 1630 her husband and father decided that the family would join the migration of Puritans who were escaping persecution by Charles I and his Anglican bishops. She later wrote, in a letter addressed "To My Dear Children," that in the Massachusetts Bay Colony where they settled she "found a new world and new manners" at which her "heart rose" in horror, so unaccustomed was she to its roughness—to which she reconciled herself by accepting her new life as God's will.[11] But she also wrote poems, an evocation of the genteel hours she had spent in the earl's library.

As the story goes, her brother-in-law, John Woodbridge, abducted a sheaf of her poems, unbeknown to her, and took them to London. There they were published in 1650 under the title *The Tenth Muse Lately Sprung Up in America*. Woodbridge wrote an introduction to the volume, avowing that Anne Bradstreet, a wife and the mother of eight who was esteemed for her womanly qualities and pious conversation, had taken no time away from her true duties in order to be a poet. "These Poems are the fruit but of some hours, curtailed from her sleep," he testified. Indeed, Bradstreet had such womanly modesty, Woodbridge insisted, that had he himself not brought her poems "to publick view" they never would have gotten there because, with a reticence befitting woman, "she resolved [they] should never in such a manner see the Sun."[12]

Woodbridge's story of his secret abduction is belied by many of the poems themselves, in which Bradstreet directly addresses the readers she very clearly hoped to have. But had her brother-in-law not taken her poems to England, they would indeed never have "see[n] the Sun," because it would have been impossible for her to publish her book. Sermons, tracts, and religious books were being published in abundance in mid-seventeenth-century New England—but never a word written by a woman. When Thomas Parker, the pastor of a Newberry, Massachusetts, church, discovered that his sister, Elizabeth Avery, had dared publish a book in London in 1647, Parker wrote his errant sister an open letter, so that all his fellow Puritans might understand he had nothing to do with the business. "Your printing of a book, beyond the custom of your sex, doth rankly smell," Parker declared with horror.[13] Bradstreet escaped contumely by caution.

Anne Hutchinson, who also lived in Puritan Massachusetts, was not so gifted in the art of caution. Governor Winthrop described her as "a woman of haughty and fierce carriage, of nimble wit and active spirit, and a very voluble tongue, more bold than a man."[14] It was this boldness, this usurpation of traits appropriate only to men, that condemned her.

In 1634, the forty-three-year-old Hutchinson, her husband, and their eleven children (she would eventually have fifteen) had left Lincolnshire to follow their charismatic minister, Rev. John Cotton, to Boston. In England, Hutchinson had been a midwife and herbalist. In Boston, she started a healing group for a few women, which turned into prayer meetings that she held in the large common room of her home. Rev. Cotton initially approved because Hutchinson encouraged the women to join his congregation. But she was as charismatic as her minister, and the women, as well as a few men eventually, preferred attending her prayer meetings.

Hutchinson's teachings—that redemption came through the gift of grace and that personal prayer superseded ministerial intercession—were offensive to orthodox Puritans. But most offensive of all was that she was a woman who had overstepped, interpreting and teaching God's word as though she were a man. She had turned topsy-turvy the hitherto unquestioned authority of the religious and civil hierarchy. Hutchinson was soon in dire trouble. As one of her accusers, Rev. Hugh Peter (a Salem pastor who with virtually his last breath would urge his own daughter to "meekness"), complained at Hutchinson's excommunication trial, "You have stept out of your place. You have rather been a Husband than a Wife and a Preacher than a Hearer, and a Magistrate than a Subject."[15] She had unnaturally subverted her role as woman.

Because church and state were virtually inseparable, the magistrates complained too. It is "not fitting for your sex" to teach men, Governor Winthrop lectured Hutchinson at her trial. She was forty-six years old, pregnant again, and made to stand on her feet during the entire two days of the trial. When she spoke to defend herself, the governor shut her up. "We do not mean to discourse with those of your sex," he hissed at her.[16]

Even John Cotton, the minister whom Hutchinson had followed to America and who had encouraged her early prayer meetings, distanced himself from her transgressions of gender. Cotton proclaimed in a public meeting after Hutchinson had had a late-term miscarriage and was "delivered of a monstrous birth" that her suffering and the loss of her child signified God's punishment for her "error in denying inherent righteousness." In 1638 she was excommunicated and banished from Massachusetts Bay Colony. Winthrop, supposing perhaps that she would try to run to nearby Plymouth Colony, warned Plymouth's governor, William Bradford, about her.[17] Hutchinson fled to Rhode Island and then, in 1643, moved to New Netherlands, to an isolated area that later became the Bronx, New York. Nearby, the Dutch had massacred 120 Indian men, women, and children in their villages. A band of Siwanoy Indians staged a retaliatory attack. Among those killed were Hutchinson, five of her children, and several other members of her household.

But generations after her death, Hutchinson continued to haunt the Puritan imagination. Rev. Cotton Mather, writing in 1702, spoke of her as "the most Remarkable of Seducers" who led "Captive Silly Women" astray at her prayer meetings ("gossipings," he dubbed them). At those "gossipings," Mather declared, Hutchinson's errors and "damnable doctrines" infected the women in her presence and then "crawled like vipers about the country."[18]

Hutchinson's defiance left an indelible mark on the Puritan leaders. They were more determined than ever to control who a woman could be. But Hutchinson had triggered the first American rebellion among colonial women. Soon after her banishment, Jane Hawkins, another midwife and healer who had been an ardent follower of Hutchinson, was ordered to leave the colony. The magistrates gave Hawkins two months to go, and if she did not, they threatened, they would "dispose of her." "In the meane time," they ordered, "shee is not to meddle in surgery, or phisick, drinks, plaisters, or oyles, nor to question matters of religion." Hawkins left, but three years later she returned to see her children. The magistrates decreed that she must depart immediately, "upon paine of severe whipping and other punishments." Her sons were commanded "to carry her away according to order."[19] All such disruptive women were ungently silenced or exiled from Massachusetts Bay.

Yet more kept cropping up, like the Hydra's heads. Governor Winthrop declared in his *Journal* that the devil would not "cease to disturb our peace, and raise up instruments one after another"—in the form of troublesome women. Mary Oliver was thrown in prison for rising in church to question doctrine. When she reproached the church elders she was whipped, and a cleft stick was put on her tongue. Katherine Finch was whipped "for speaking against the magistrates, against the churches,

& against the elders" and for not "carry[ing] herself dutifully to her husband." Philipa Hammond was excommunicated for being "a slaunderer and revyler both of the Church and Common Weale." Among Hammond's sins was that after her husband's death she resumed her maiden name, she opened a shop in Boston, and she argued in public that "Mrs. Hutchinson neyither deserved the Censure which was putt upon her in the Church, nor in the Common Weale."[20] The ministers and magistrates feared, with good reason, that Hutchinson had planted the seeds of rebellion.

The most troubling seed was Mary Dyer, the wife of a wealthy colonist and a young mother of six children. A friend and follower of Hutchinson, Dyer was described by one of her contemporaries as having "a piercing knowledge in many things" and "so fit for great affairs that she wanted nothing that was manly, except only the name and sex."[21] Those were not qualities to endear her to ministers and magistrates. To compound the counts against her, when Hutchinson was expelled from the church, Dyer rose and walked by her side out of the building.[22]

Winthrop's hatred of her "very proud spirit"[23] became obsessive, as he revealed in his recording of a tragedy that befell her. In the seventh month of her next pregnancy, Dyer gave birth to a stillborn baby who probably had anencephaly and spina bifida. In his journal Winthrop declared (as he did of the baby Hutchinson miscarried after her trial) that the baby had been a monster, proof that the mother was not a natural woman. He described the dead baby, which he called a "woman child," in fantastical images that echoed the apocalyptic Book of Revelation. The passages testify to how unhinged Governor Winthrop could become when a woman violated gender prescriptions. The stillborn baby, he wrote,

> had no head but a face, which stood so low upon the brest, as the ears (which were like an Apes) grew upon the shoulders. The eyes stood farre out, so did the mouth, the nose was hooking upward, the breast and back were full of sharp prickles, like a Thornback, the navel and all the belly with the distinction of the sex, were where the lower part of the back and hips should have been, and those back parts were on the side where the face stood . . . and above the eyes, foure hornes.[24]

These "facts" about the "woman child," he claimed, had been forced out of Jane Hawkins, the midwife who was later banished.

Six months after the stillbirth, Winthrop, still obsessed, desired to see the monster for himself. He ordered the baby girl's body exhumed. "Though it were much corrupted, yet most of those things were to be seen, as the horns and claws, the scales, etc." he claimed. He amplified his fantasy with images of the mother's demonic possession. When the she-monster was born, Winthrop declared, the bed on which Dyer lay shook, and the stink was so terrible that the women who were there to assist with the birth "were taken with extreme vomiting and purging" and were forced to run from the room.[25]

Such wild imaginings continued long after both Hutchinson and Dyer had left Winthrop's territory. They attest to how unsettled Winthrop's contemporaries too were by women who slipped from their idea of woman. Rumors kept affirming that Hutchinson and Dyer had violated all womanly decencies and even committed terrible sexual sins. In 1667, state papers repeated the tale that the two women had been in a ménage à trois with Sir Henry Vane (who was governor of the colony in 1636 but lost a 1637 election to John Winthrop). Amplifying the already outrageous stories of the women's miscarriages, the report said that Vane had "debauched both, and both were delivered of monsters."[26]

Dyer wisely moved from the Massachusetts Bay Colony with her husband and eight children. For a while they lived in England, where she became a Quaker. But her story with the Puritans was far from over. Twenty years after leaving Massachusetts Bay, Dyer returned to protest Puritan cruelty to the Quakers, who were now being imprisoned or hanged if they set foot in the colony. The magistrates—determined to keep Quakers, especially obstreperous Quaker women, out of Massachusetts Bay—banished Dyer. But she kept coming back. On her third return she was thrown in jail and then led to the gallows along with two Quaker men. A noose was placed around each of their necks. The men were hanged from a large elm tree on Boston Common. Dyer watched and waited for the same fate, but the noose was taken off her neck, and she was told that if she left Boston she could live. She answered that she would not accept "the Mercies of the Wicked."[27] But they rode her on horseback out of town anyway.

Dyer had found a cause in whose name she could express her disdain for the ministers and magistrates. She demanded that the Puritans annul laws that persecuted Quakers. If they did not, they could hang her, she told them—and her martyrdom would force them to annul the laws because it would awaken a storm of indignation.

A few months later she returned again to Boston, and again she was imprisoned. Her husband begged the governor to spare her life, have mercy on him and her children, and forgive her for her "inconsiderate madness."[28] But she again would not accept "the Mercies of the Wicked" nor the characterizing of her protests as "madness." On June 1, 1660, she was hanged from the elm tree on Boston Common. Assistant Governor Humphrey Atherton, who four years earlier had overseen the hanging of Ann Hibbins as a witch, now watched Mary Dyer's death throes. "She hangs there like a flag for others to take example by," he said.[29] Atherton meant, of course, that Dyer's fate would scare renegades, but she became a "flag" that stood for resistance against Puritanism and its strictures on woman.[30]

Witch hysteria overtook the colony for the first time in the 1640s. Elizabeth Johnson just missed it. Johnson, an indentured servant, was brought up before the law for violations of piety and womanliness. Not only had she "stopped her ears with her hands when the Word of God was read"—a sure sign that she was visited by the Devil—but also, it was discovered, she was party to "unseemly practices betwixt her and another maid." (Hers was the first court case in America dealing with what would later be called lesbian behavior.) Had she been charged a few years later, Governor Winthrop would surely have found her to be a witch and sentenced her to death. But in 1642, Johnson was sentenced only to be "severely whipped and fined."[31] Witch hysteria, first addressed in English by the Witchcraft Act of 1542, had reemerged with a fever epidemic that started in 1645 in Puritan-dominated East Anglia and quickly swept across the ocean to the Massachusetts Bay Colony, where Winthrop and the other magistrates took it up. Women who stepped out of the character that befit the woman were periodically controlled by accusations of witchcraft.

In 1648, Margaret Jones, like Anne Hutchinson a midwife and healer, was damned first because she had told her patients that "if they did not make use of her physic they would never be healed, and accordingly their diseases and hurts continued." Then at her trial "her behavior was very intemperate," Winthrop recorded in his journal. She dared to "rail upon the jury and witnesses." Still railing and protesting her innocence, she was taken to Gallows Hill on Boston Neck, where she was hanged from an elm tree—the first woman to be executed as a witch in Massachusetts Bay Colony. Jones's status as a witch was confirmed, according to Winthrop, because "the same day and hour she was executed, there was a very great tempest at Connecticut, which blew down many trees, etc."[32]

Midwives and healers, women who had a measure of power, were often among the accused. Those who turned domestic skills into profitable enterprises that competed with men's businesses were also likely to be under suspicion. For example, Mary Hale ran a boardinghouse-cum-infirmary where she took in sick people and treated their illnesses, and Elinor Hollingsworth was a successful brewer who ran the Blue Anchor, a popular Boston tavern. Both were tried for witchcraft. Women who never married were particularly likely to be executed, but married women who lost their husband's protection were also vulnerable. Ann Hibbins was disliked for her unwomanly behavior even while her powerful husband, a wealthy Boston merchant and church elder, was alive. She had argued with a carpenter who made furniture for her home. He had cheated her, she complained. She went all over Boston and neighboring Salem, inquiring of other workmen whether she had been overcharged and grousing about the carpenter even to strangers. The elders of the First Church of Boston were scandalized. It should have been her husband who dealt with a workman, they advised her, and she must stop making a spectacle of herself. But she persisted. She was combative, lacking in meekness. She was called up by them to be admonished for having displayed "great pride of spirit."[33]

Hibbins's husband came to her defense, testifying that he had been too busy to deal with workmen and had "given her leave to order and carry on this business to her own satisfaction." But that did not satisfy the churchmen, who accused her of making "a wisp" of her husband.[34] She had acted on her own, she had been a rambler abroad, and she had disturbed the peace of the community.

Rev. John Cotton, Anne Hutchinson's betrayer, pushed to excommunicate Hibbins. She had exalted herself "against your guide and head—your husband I mean—when you should have submitted yourself," he lectured her. "You have scorned counsel and refused instruction, and have like a filthy swine trampled those pearls under your feet." He called her "an unclean beast, unfit for the society of God's people."[35] At this point it might have been prudent of Hibbins to hold her tongue against such fury, but she could not contain herself. Instead of bowing her head in womanly shame, she conducted a defense of herself. She was excommunicated.

Because Hibbins had behaved like a termagant and not their idea of a woman, she was on the ministers' and magistrates' watch list. After her husband lost much of his fortune, she became even more turbulent and quarrelsome. Then her husband died, and she was without his protection.

She was accused of being a witch. She was inspected for teats on her genitalia and under her arms, because the devil's familiars always suckled from teats located in those areas of a woman's body. No record exists as to whether extra teats were found, but evidence that she was a witch was provided by her neighbors. They said that she knew they were talking about her though she could not possibly have heard what they were saying without supernatural powers. The Massachusetts General Court found her guilty, and in 1656 she was hanged on Boston Common.[36]

Throughout the rest of the century, the magistrates and ministers continued to respond to women's violations of their idea of woman with tight controls. In 1672, the General Court passed a law saying that women who forgot womanly modesty and were "scolds or railers" were to be mortified in public by being "gagged or set in a ducking stool and dipt over the head and ears three times."[37]

Yet even such mortifications could not stem the tides of change. War was one spark for change, as it would be over and over again in subsequent centuries. From 1675 to 1676, during King Philip's War between colonists and Indian tribes led by a Wampanoag chief known as King Philip, men were frequently off fighting. Women were left to manage on their own, even to perform tasks that had been strictly in men's purview. In 1676, for example, women in Boston, fearing an imminent invasion by King Philip's warriors while their husbands fought elsewhere, began to build a fortification. A mock-heroic poem written that year by Benjamin Tompson, ridiculing the women's serious efforts as self-aggrandizing and silly, reveals Puritan anxiety at women's usurping men's work, no matter that it was done in desperation:

> A Grand attempt some Amazonian Dames
> Contrive whereby to glorify their names....
> A tribe of female hands, manly hearts,
> Forsake at home their pastry crust and tarts...,
> The pickax one as Commanderess holds,
> While t'other at her awk[ward]ness gently scolds.
> One puffs and sweats, the other mutters why
> Can't you promove your work as fast as I?[38]

Despite men's evident discomfort, however, women began making small claims to a presence outside the home. Massachusetts' burgeoning growth made that possible: in less than fifty years, the population more than tripled, from 15,000 inhabitants in 1643 to 50,000 by 1690. The colonists were no longer a tiny group living in the fearsome, howling wilderness. Opportunities for a woman to earn a living on her own were still far from abundant, but they were increasing. For example, before 1643, there were no women innkeepers in the colony, but by the 1690s, women accounted for over half the innkeepers in Boston and about 20 percent of the innkeepers in the rest of New England. Educational opportunities were gradually increasing, too. From the start of the Massachusetts Bay Colony, Puritan mothers had been teaching their daughters to read, beginning with a hornbook and then moving in turn to a primer, a psalter, and the end goal of the project—the Bible. A few girls were sent to dame schools, usually held in the home of an unmarried young woman or of a widow, where they would learn how to write. Then, between 1665 and 1689, nine private schools opened in Boston at which girls could go a little deeper into learning. Seeds were being planted for a proliferation of schools for girls in the next century.[39]

In a city like Boston, where 70 percent of the colony's population lived by 1690, a woman might even find some anonymity that allowed her to step outside the boundaries of proper behavior, as she could not in a small village where she was under the watchful eyes of neighbors. Ministers kept admonishing women that they must not violate the boundaries, but as the population grew and new influences emerged, the ministers' control weakened.[40] It was even becoming possible to pursue a modicum of worldly pleasure without being threatened with the pillory or stocks. This was so because the port cities of the colony, regularly in touch with England, were influenced by what was happening in the mother country, where the social tenor changed radically in the 1660s.

Charles I had been executed in 1649, and the monarchy had been replaced by a commonwealth: Oliver Cromwell, a Puritan, led England. That had reinforced Puritan style in America, including austerity of dress—which was already austere under a 1634 decree of the General Court that banned "immodest fashion" such as lace, clothing worked with gold or silver thread, and silk laces. Women were to wear drab kirtles and simple head coverings.[41] But austerity in dress broke down in 1660, when Charles II, who loved magnificence, ascended to the throne. With the Restoration, the somber style of Puritanism was decidedly over in England. The new taste was reflected in dramatically changing fashions in Boston.

A generation earlier, the General Court had decreed that women who violated the ban on fancy dress be sentenced to ten lashes with a multistranded whip or to time in the stocks, where they would be laughingstocks. But by the 1670s the ministers and magistrates were learning that they had little control over what a woman might wear. Increase Mather, a son-in-law of Rev. John Cotton, lamented bitterly in 1679 that "proud fashion" was coming into the country from England, and "the haughty Daughters of Zion" were "taking it up" and "infecting" the whole land with it.[42] But he could not stop the infection.

Fashions were not the only imports from across the ocean. A woman wandering around Boston might have stopped at a bookseller's shop and found a book that had been written in French by Francois Poulain de la Barre and translated into English that year with the title *The Woman as Good as the Man, or the Equality of the Sexes*. A few years later, in 1683, a woman stopping off at a Boston bookseller's might have found on display among the imports from London *Haec et Hic, or the Feminine Gender More Worthy Than the Masculine, Being a Vindication of that Ingenious and Innocent Sex from the biting Sarcasms, bitter Satyrs, and opprobrious Calumnies wherewith they are daily, though undeservedly, aspersed by virulent Tongues and Pens of malevolent Men, with many Examples of the rare Virtues of that noble Sex*. That same year she might also have found at that Boston shop *The Wonders of the Female World, or a General History of Women. Wherein by many hundreds of Examples is shewed what WOMAN [sic] have been from the first Ages of the World to these Times . . . to which is added a Plesant [sic] Discourse of Female Pre-Eminence, or the Dignity and Excellency of that Sex above the Male*.[43] Whether or not a Puritan woman would have dared bring such books home, their titles alone, spied at the bookseller's, would have made her think about women in ways she had never heard mentioned in church.

Witch hysteria came at a time when the devil seemed to have been loosed upon the Massachusetts Bay Colony. The Puritans had already been destabilized by bloody frontier wars with the Indians. Then came encephalitis and smallpox epidemics, followed by a serious economic downturn. On top of all that, social forces were altering the lives of women, who were becoming increasingly bold in stepping from the place where God had set them. Wars, diseases, and the vagaries of the economy all were ostensibly beyond man's control, but with a few exceptions, women had always seemed controllable. Cotton Mather, who succeeded his grandfather John Cotton and his father Increase Mather as the colony's most prominent minister, was in the forefront of the panicked efforts to regain control of women in the midst of troubled times. Mather's *Ornaments for the Daughters of Zion: Or The Character and Happiness of a Vertuous Woman* (1692) was the first conduct book for women written in America. Published at the start of Salem's witch hunt fever, it was, in effect, a series of instructions to women on how not to be subject to accusations of witchery. Woman had lost her way, Mather believed. She was indulging in frivolous pastimes such as dancing. She was painting herself and using other artificial methods to enhance her beauty. Instead of spinning and weaving for the sake of the family, she spent her time being "fashionable" and engaging in diversions such as card playing. Mather was frantic to redirect her. "The Cards at which many Gentlewomen Play wickedly with their Hands, are far more Debasing, than those Cards which fit the Wool for the Wheel," he carped.[44] He advised the married woman that if she loves her husband she will practice "a Cautious Diligence never to Displease him." She will call him "Her Lord, and though she do's not Fear his blowes, yet she do's Fear his Frowns." The "vertuous woman," Mather argued, relinquishes independent action and thought: "In every Lawful thing, she submits her Will and Sense to [her husband]."[45]

When such admonitions proved insufficient, the remedy of the previous generation was revived. The obverse of the virtuous woman was the witch. In the most sweeping witch hunts, which started in Salem in 1692, over two hundred people, mostly women, were accused and tried: twenty people were hanged and four more died in "witch jails," awaiting execution. In 1693, in the midst of the Salem hysteria, Mather published *The Wonders of the Invisible World*, about witches who had been outed. Among the signs that a woman was a witch, Mather declared, were that she led a "lewd and naughty kind of Life." However, unfeminine comportment also raised suspicion—and even served as proof—that she was in cahoots with the devil. Rachel Clinton "scolded and railed," Bridget Bishop was insubordinate to her husband and went around "muttering and menacing," and Sarah Good's own husband said that "either she was a witch or would be one very quickly" because of her "bad carriage" to him. Bishop and Good were hanged for their behavior. Clinton barely escaped hanging but died in misery in 1694.[46]

Poor and friendless women were likely to be accused, but wealthy women were accused too if they took on roles unbefitting to woman. Mary Bradbury, for instance, ran a butter business that was so successful that she became a main supplier for outgoing ships. The many charges against her reveal the hysterical fears triggered by woman's worldly success: Bradbury sold large batches of butter to a ship's captain, which she then caused to go rancid to sicken the crew. She unleashed a storm, making the ship lose its mainmast and rigging, and killing fifteen horses. She turned herself into a blue boar to wreak havoc on men and animals. The magistrates would have sentenced her to be hanged as a witch were it not for her prominent husband, a respected elder in the community. He delivered an emotional speech on her behalf, calling her "my beloved wife" who "hath been wonderfull laborious diligent & industrious in her place and imployment about the bringing up o'r family (w'ch have been eleven children)."[47] His heart-wrenching testimony, which proved she was a true woman after all, saved her from the gallows.

WOMAN IN NATIVE AMERICAN TRIBAL NATIONS

"By her Natural Right of Liberty."

—BARON DE LAHONTAN, *Nouveaux voyages dans l'Amerique* (1703)[48]

The colonists were baffled by the concepts of woman among the Indians, which were so different from European and colonial concepts. In Virginia the colonists saw the Pamunkeys, and in Rhode Island the Algonquins: both matrilineal tribes in which the women ruled the family, and the children's social standing was tied solely to that of the mother. In South Carolina the colonists might have seen that Cherokee women held prominent positions in tribal politics. An honored woman leader among the Cherokee was called Beloved Woman, and it was believed that the voice of the Great Spirit spoke through her. The women's council could even override the male chiefs. If the British trader Alexander Longe can be believed, Cherokee women were the dominant, and domineering, heads of their households. "The woman rules the roost and wears the breeches," Longe observed with astonishment, "and sometimes will beat their husband within an inch of their lives. The man will not resist their power if the woman was to beat his brains out [sic]."[49]

In the Massachusetts Bay Colony, the Puritans managed to exercise some control over local Indians and their unorthodox ideas about women. In 1654, the Puritans established several Praying Indian Villages for Indians who were willing to convert to Christianity. Members of several tribes such as the Ponkapoag professed to convert, which gave them certain practical advantages. Christian Indians were favored over heathens in trade, for example, and they were allowed to defend their land legally. But they also came under the jurisdiction of Massachusetts Bay Colony law, which altered the power dynamic between men and women. A Christian Ponkapoag woman and mother of four, Sarah Ahhaton, had been beaten by her husband, a Christian convert, who accused her of adultery. Under Puritan law, adultery was a crime punishable by death. Sarah Ahhaton was handed over to Captain Daniel Gookin, the superintendent of Indians, who took her to jail in Boston. She pleaded through an Indian interpreter for her husband's forgiveness, and she promised that henceforth "although he should beat her againe and suspect her of falseness to him without cause, yet shee doth acknowledge it to bee her duty to suffer it and to pray for her husband, & to love him still." At her trial, the General Court spared her from hanging—a possible sentence for adultery under Puritan law—but ordered that she "stand on the gallows . . . with a roape around her neck one hower, and that then the marshall generall shall cause her to be tooke doune & returned to prison, and committed to the Indian constable who . . . shall severely whip hir, not exceeding thirty stripes, & that she pay all charges for the prosecution."[50]

But the colonists could not control the tribes everywhere. Among the Cree in Georgia, warrior women went into battle alongside men, and among the Delaware Indians of New York and the Penobscot Indians of Maine, elderly matrons known as peace women had the power to stop a war chief from engaging in what the women judged to be unnecessary bloodshed. The colonists might have discovered that Delaware and Penobscot women chiefs were in charge of planting and feasts, and any man who displeased them did not eat. Or they might have learned from the travel memoirs of a Frenchman, Baron de Lahontan, who lived with Algonquin Indians in the 1680s, that among them a young woman was her own person, and neither father nor mother controlled her: she was "Master of her own Body, and by her Natural Right of Liberty is free to do what she pleases."[51]

In the colonists' view, all such elevation of woman was against the natural order. If they learned too that in many Indian tribes one did not even have to be born male to be a man, or born female to be a woman, they would have been outraged. In those tribes, if an individual was assigned one sex at birth and announced that they belonged to the other, their claim was honored—as it had never been in America outside of Native communities until the transgender movement of the current century. The entire community could participate in a ceremony that officially recognized and celebrated the person's public transition to his or her stated gender. Someone who had been identified as female at birth could, after announcing manhood, assume a man's role: hunting, trapping, fighting in battles, and even taking a wife. In some Indian cultures, such individuals were thought to have special powers and were held in high esteem—revered as spiritual healers, seers, prophets, and medicine men or medicine women.[52]

If they had lived among the colonists, it is unlikely that they would have survived. The fate of one seventeenth-century individual who was assigned female at birth but assumed a social role reserved for men presents a stark contrast to Indian flexibility about gender. Dressed in men's garb, the person became a sailor on a ship docked in Massachusetts Bay. At sea the other sailors discovered the individual's anatomical sex. "She" was ceremoniously dropped three times from the yardarm and then stripped naked to the waist and made to run the gauntlet. The sailors, armed with lashes and switches, were ordered to strike "her" with force. Barely alive, the "imposter" was also tarred and feathered.[53]

The Iroquois—five tribes that occupied the area from Niagara Falls to the Hudson River throughout the seventeenth century—were matrilineal and matrilocal. In fact, they were more matriarchal than any society outside of legend. Their creation story hints at why the Iroquois woman was elevated, just as the creation story about foolish and wily Eve hints at why the Puritan woman was denigrated. In the beginning, the Iroquois myth went, the mother goddess Sky Woman was ejected from her home in the heavens by her tyrannical husband, who threw her down to a bottomless sea in the world below. But birds and other animals came to her rescue by forming land for her from watery mud. Standing on the land, Sky Woman sprinkled dust in the air, creating the sun, moon, and stars. She then gave birth to a daughter, Breath of Wind (who in turn gave birth to boy twins, one good and one evil: quintessentially male, they warred with one another). Breath of Wind died, but she continued to nourish her children even after death. She was buried in the earth, and three sisters grew from her grave, Corn, Squash, and Beans—the fundamental staples of the Iroquois diet, which nourished them and allowed them to flourish.

The mythic powerful woman—mother and nurturer without whom there would be no life—thus defined the idea of woman for the Iroquois. Women were dominant in the family and at least equal to men in the community. Paternity had far less significance in Iroquois culture than in European culture, since it was the mother who gave the child its place in the social hierarchy. The fields for planting were passed down to women by their mothers. Men, whose physical strength was undeniably greater than that of women, cleared the land. But women cultivated and harvested it, and a woman elder decided how the food should be distributed. Men helped build the longhouse where the extended family lived, but the longhouse belonged to the women.[54]

Great political power belonged to them, too. Joseph-François Lafitau, a French ethnologist who lived among the Iroquois, observed that the women "possess all actual authority." On political questions, Lafitau wrote: "Women are always the first to deliberate. They hold their council apart, and as a result of their decisions, advise the [sachems]." Women did not often fight in battles, but they had a loud voice in whether a battle would be fought. The clan mother selected and confirmed the war chiefs, who served at her pleasure. It was the clan mother who had power over the life or death of the enemy, deciding whether captives would be killed or adopted into the clan.[55]

Among the colonists, marriage kept a woman in a passive position. She waited first for a man to propose and then for him to make the major decisions about where and how they would live. If her husband wished to get rid of her, she lost not only him but their children, too. If she had a child without a husband, she was punished for breaking the bastardy laws. Among the Iroquois it was the woman who proposed marriage, and if she wanted to have several husbands, she could. If she wanted to rid herself of them, she could do that, too: a wife initiated divorce by merely placing her husband's belongings outside the door of her family's longhouse, where they had lived together.[56]

Even into the eighteenth century, when Colonel Thomas Proctor led his artillery regiment in a deadly attack against the Seneca (one of the Iroquois tribes), it was the women who came to plead for peace. They believed that they had a right to address Proctor because they, the women, owned and planted the land. Their argument must have been puzzling to him. Their poignant plea—"Hear us for we speak of things that concern us and our children"—fell on deaf ears.[57]

It would take a very long time before American women of European descent could begin to enjoy status and freedoms approaching those of the seventeenth-century Iroquois woman or to move through the world "by . . . Natural Right of Liberty," as Baron de Lahontan observed of the

Algonquin woman. Long before that would happen, the Indian woman would be robbed of her "natural right of liberty," too.

THE WHITE WOMAN IN THE OTHER COLONIES

"Because I am a woman, forsooth."
—MARGARET BRENT, *Proceedings and Acts of the General Assembly, Maryland, January 1637/8–September 1664*[58]

In none of the colonies during the seventeenth century could a woman be entirely free, but the restrictions on her differed from region to region.[59] Most of the early settlers in the southern colonies (Virginia, Maryland, Georgia, and the Carolinas) had been single men who came without families. Women came later, some of them thrown out of England for bad behavior. For example, Narcissus Luttrell, a member of Parliament, recorded in his diary in November 1692 that a ship had just left Leith harbor bound for Virginia, with a cargo of deportees—fifty "lewd women" from the house of corrections and thirty more women found guilty of walking the streets after ten at night.[60]

Some women were recruited as mail-order brides. In Virginia, such recruitment began as early as 1620, when the treasurer of the Virginia Company of London observed that the colony, whose population was largely male, would not grow if the female share could not be expanded because men would stay only long enough "to gett something and then return for England."[61] The Virginia Company began offering women free transportation across the Atlantic as well as a sizable dowry once they got to Virginia: a plot of land, furniture, and even a trousseau.

Before slavery proliferated, some women with few resources came not as mail-order brides but as indentured servants, who were often at the mercy of the men who could afford to pay for their transportation and upkeep in return for four or five years of their labor. As court records indicate, it was not unusual for young women in such a position, alone and dependent on strangers, to become pregnant out of wedlock. But whether a pregnant woman had been a willing sex partner or had been raped (often by her employer), she was in trouble. She would be charged with violating the bastardy laws, which were intended to discourage immorality and protect the state from having to support illegitimate children. The penalties against the woman could be heavy. For example, Virginia's 1662 "Against Fornication Act, for restraint of the ffilty sin of fornication," ordered that "in regard of the losse and trouble her master doth sustaine by her haveing a bastard, she shall serve two years after her time by indenture is expired or pay two thousand pounds of tobacco to her master."[62] Of course, an indentured servant could not possibly pay two thousand pounds of tobacco, so her term of service without wages was extended.

That was not the end of the penalties levied against a woman who gave birth to an illegitimate child. Diana Jones, an indentured servant on a Virginia plantation, was brought to court for "fornication & bastardy" and ordered to give her master two extra years of service. In addition, for her "filthy sin of fornication," the sheriff was ordered "to take her into his custodie & give her 30 lashes on the bare back well laid on." But not even such cruelty lessened the number of out-of-wedlock births among indentured servants: in some southern towns between the mid-seventeenth century and the early eighteenth century as many as 20 percent were brought to court on bastardy charges.[63]

A few wealthy women in the early southern colonies escaped some of the sternest strictures on woman's life. In 1687, when Sarah Harrison, a colonel's daughter, was seventeen years old, she married James Blair, a thirty-two-year-old Anglican minister. Asked by the clergyman who officiated at the wedding to vow that she would "love, honor and obey" her husband, Sarah responded, "No obey." The officiate repeated the question a second time and then a third. Harrison's answer was firm and unchanging: "No obey." The ceremony finally continued. The marriage lasted until her death twenty-six years later. Sarah Harrison Blair apparently said no to having children, too, at a time when most women were either pregnant or nursing for much of their adult lives.[64]

Other women who claimed a modicum of freedom for themselves were unmarried. Had they lived in New England, some of them might have gone to the gallows for their boldness, while in the South they could flourish as exceptions. If they had inherited wealth, they were independent since, unlike married women, they were not subject to the coverture law that gave a husband complete control over a wife's property and person. In Virginia, court records show that some unmarried women owned plantations, had control over indentured servants, and went before the court to sue for the collection of debts. They even engaged in the terrible business of buying and selling slaves.[65] In Maryland, Margaret Brent, a noblewoman who had immigrated from England in 1638, received a land grant of thousands of acres. If she had been married, the property would have belonged to her husband, but she never married. Brent became the first woman landowner in the colonies. She named the property, where she lived with her sister, Mary, Sisters Freehold.

Brent was shielded by class and wealth, and she conducted her life as though she were not a woman. She was astute at business (probably the first American woman to whom the appellation "businesswoman" might apply) and was able to buy up even more land as well as several houses and a profitable mill. She was a self-taught lawyer, and between 1642 and 1650 she appeared in court 124 times to sue for the collection of debt on her own behalf. She even took care of her brothers' legal business, being more adept than they were.[66] She was widely thought to be brilliant and shrewd. In 1647, Leonard Calvert, Maryland's governor and her friend, made her the executrix of his will as he was dying. It was the first time in the history of the colonies that a woman who was not the decedent's wife was given such a position.

Yet as Brent discovered, there were limits to what even she could do. Calvert had hired mercenaries to protect Maryland's Catholic settlers from a Protestant attack, and he had taken on a personal obligation to pay them. But as his executrix, Brent found that there was not enough money in Calvert's estate to honor that obligation. She went before the Maryland Assembly, hoping to get it to pass a tax to compensate the soldiers. She argued that as one of the biggest landowners in Maryland, she should be able to vote on the issue. Brent had always succeeded in transcending the limitations imposed on woman, and she was demanding to do so again. In view of all her past victories, her request must have seemed to her perfectly reasonable.

To the men present, however, it seemed grotesque. Despite all the ways that Brent had broken precedent, a woman did not vote. Brent persisted: "I've come to seek a voice in this assembly. And yet because I am a woman, forsooth, I must stand idly by and not even have a voice in the framing of your laws."[67] But the assemblymen and Thomas Greene, the new governor (who, ironically, had been handpicked by Calvert to succeed him), were adamant. No matter who she was or what she had done, the men made it clear that she was a mere woman and at the mercy of the rules they wished to impose.

Brent had had reason to think that, transcending the usual limitations, she had forged a new meaning of woman, for herself at least. It must have been very disturbing to her to learn that she had not. Maybe that disillusion helps explain her puzzling last will and testament, which seemed to confirm woman's insignificance. Brent left most of her extensive property to her male relatives and gave her beloved niece, namesake of her sister, "all my silver spoons which are six."[68]

For the Quakers who settled in Pennsylvania in the 1650s and 1660s, church was no less dominant than it was for the Puritans, but Quaker women were less suffocated by their church. "May not the spirit of Christ speak in the female as well as in the male?" George Fox, the prophet of Quakerism, had asked. Not only could Quaker women speak, but they could also be elders and preachers. In enlightened contrast to Cotton Mather's description of women's prayer meetings as mere "gossipings," William Penn, founder of the colony of Pennsylvania, believed that women must lead their own prayer meetings because their "bashfulness" keeps them from speaking up when men are present, but "when by themselves [they] may exercise their gifts of wisdom and understanding."[69]

Women elders and preachers were freed from the seventeenth-century white woman's narrow domestic life by their role in the world outside. They counseled new wives and mothers, and they organized assistance for orphaned children and women who had been deserted or widowed. They cultivated the most unwomanly skills: speaking in public and organizing for the public good. Because a call from God trumped all familial obligations, they could travel on their own, usually two women together, going in (pious) high adventure to spread the word of Quakerism. They were also subject to the same cruelty with which their enemies treated Quaker men. Traveling ministers Elizabeth Hooten and Joan Brooksop left husbands, children, and all domestic duties to spread their religion in the Massachusetts Bay Colony and were there imprisoned, as Brooksop recorded, "in a stinking dungeon where there was nothing to lie down or sit on" before they were "deported into the wilderness, among wolves and bears."[70]

The Quaker woman's position was inarguably higher than that of the Puritan woman. Quaker women were not blamed as daughters of Eve who led men astray. Their marriage ceremony said nothing about the sacred obligation of the wife to obey her husband. Yet their freedoms had limits. Once married, they suffered under feme covert laws just as much as Puritan women did. And while equalitarian marriage was an ideal in Quaker theology, in practice it was elusive. Despite Fox's championing of women's freedoms, he proved himself to be ambivalent. His 1676 epistle about a wife's duty was, oddly, not much different from what Cotton Mather might have advised: "to be chaste and keepers at home, and good, obedient to their own husbands."⁷¹ He did not address the contradiction of having women be "keepers at home" with his encouragement of women to work as traveling ministers who proselytized for Quakerism. Nor did he ever go so far as to assert that women ought to have a place in the church hierarchy or a presence in the polity. Seventeenth-century Quaker women, even those who would be martyred for their cause, seem not to have even imagined asking for such things.

Nowhere in the colonies—or in the world, for that matter—were women an equal member of the polity. But for a while, in the settlement of New Amsterdam, which was under the jurisdiction of the Netherlands, they had a wide array of freedoms. A woman in New Amsterdam could inherit equally with her brothers, just as she could in Holland. She could, and often did, establish in a prenuptial agreement that the property she owned before marriage would continue to belong to her alone. She could go to court and sue someone. She could be appointed by the court as an official arbitrator in cases involving other women. She even had the authority to eject her husband from their home if he drank too much or smoked or cursed. And no matter how successful a woman was in business, or how cantankerous she was with her neighbors, she ran no risk of being accused of witchcraft. She could even sing in church.⁷²

Margaret Hardenbroeck, a burgher's daughter, had spent her formative years in the Netherlands, where women of her class could learn to read and write and keep accounts. She came to New Amsterdam in 1659 as an agent for a cousin in the import-export business. In New Amsterdam there were already hundreds of women like Hardenbroeck who worked outside their homes in responsible occupations as traders, real estate speculators, brickyard operators, and so-called she-merchants. Hardenbroeck—brash, ambitious, and pipe-smoking, with a commanding presence and forceful speech—had landed in the right place: In Massachusetts Bay those attributes would have made her suspect. In New Amsterdam she flourished.

At the age of twenty-four she married Peter de Vries, a trader and property owner, who was thirty-two years her senior. When he died two years later, he left her wealthy. Through her business acumen she multiplied that wealth. Hardenbroeck was soon running several businesses with skill, shrewdness, and amorality. She bought up properties from Indians in Manhattan. She bought numerous ships and directed a fleet back and forth across the Atlantic, exporting furs and importing cooking oils and vinegars. As ruthless as the male shipowners, she even participated in the slave trade, bringing human cargo from Angola to the plantations of Barbados. She was the first woman in America to build herself an empire.[73]

But when the English took over New Amsterdam in 1664 and it became New York, she no longer had free rein. Laws like those governing women in the Massachusetts Bay Colony were immediately adopted, and Hardenbroeck was reduced to woman. After her first husband's death, she had married Frederick Philipse, who had become her helper in her business enterprises. Now, as a married woman, she was suddenly a feme covert. She could no longer represent herself in a court of law; and she could no longer purchase land in her own name. All her property belonged to her husband.

Since hers was the talent in the family, she continued to run the businesses, though Philipse was their nominal head. Like Margaret Brent, Hardenbroeck became bitter about the disturbing reality of her position: regardless of her ships and houses and masculine command, according to the law she was a mere woman. Naturally peremptory, her disappointment in having to relinquish ownership in her name made her even more prickly and volatile. (Had she lived in Massachusetts Bay Colony she would most surely have been hanged.) When her husband implored the ministers of the Dutch Reformed Church to intercede for him in calming his wife's hot temper, she greeted the men in black at her door, as they reported, using "very prophane and godless language." A Dutch missionary who had been a passenger on board one of her ships detailed in his diary his horror at her "arrogance and nasty temper" and her "miserable covetousness," as well as his suspicions that she had a lover on board.[74] She did not hold back from expressing her anger at her lot or her unwomanly disdain for the womanly. But there was nothing she could do to stop the legal restrictions on her as a woman.

2.
Woman, Lady, and Not a Woman in the Eighteenth Century

In middle age, Benjamin Franklin corresponded with several young women, including Polly Stevenson, whose mother was the owner of a London boardinghouse where Franklin lived when he was a lobbyist for the colonies. When Polly and Franklin first met, in 1757, she was a bright eighteen-year-old. She called Franklin her "preceptor"; he called her "my dear little philosopher." She was flattered and delighted by his letters: he seemed to take her intellect seriously. He wrote her about his experiments with electricity, gave her scientific explanations illustrated with his own diagrams about tides in rivers, sent her a phonetic alphabet he had devised, and shared with her stories of the political events of the day. So enamored was Polly of the knowledge Franklin had opened to her that when she was twenty-one she decided, as she informed him, to "live single" and devote herself to learning.

Franklin was deeply disturbed. That was not at all what he had intended in sharing his cogitations with bright young girls such as Polly. He wrote her immediately to correct her misapprehension. She must not "neglect the knowledge and practice of essential duties," he emphasized. The most essential duty of woman was to marry and have children. Polly followed Franklin's advice. In her fourth year of marriage, while she was pregnant with her third child, her husband died. She devoted the rest of her life to the children's upbringing.[1]

WOMAN

> "Women are not formed for great Cares themselves, but to soothe and soften ours."
> —"Animadversions on the Affectation of Ill-Suited Characters of the Female Sex" (1745)[2]

The hysteria of the Salem witch hunts was emblematic of the desperation of Puritan leaders to wrest back control of their world that was tormented by disease, wars, a bad economy, and not least, as Cotton Mather wrote, women who played at cards instead of carding wool. The witch hunts ended in 1693. Lady Mary Phips, the wife of the new royally appointed governor of Massachusetts Bay, Sir William Phips, had signed a warrant in her husband's absence freeing a so-called witch from prison. When Lady Mary was accused of being in cahoots with the imprisoned woman and thus herself a witch, Sir William ordered the court that tried witches to be disbanded. His action was like a slap in the face of a hysteric. Finally, contrition set in, particularly for Salem's cruelty to women, who accounted for more than 80 percent of those convicted of witchcraft. In 1697, the General Court of Massachusetts deemed the witch hunts a grievous error and declared a day of fasting in repentance. Samuel Sewall, one of the foremost hanging judges during the witch trials, asked his minister to read to the congregation an apology that Sewall had written, in which he accepted "Blame & Shame" and begged God's forgiveness for sending innocent women to the gallows. Thomas Fisk, the foreman of Salem's witch-trial jury, and all eleven of his fellow jurors issued another apology, confessing that they had been "sadly deluded & mistaken." In 1711 the Commonwealth of Massachusetts paid restitution to the families of the victims.[3]

Sober realization of the horrors perpetrated on so many innocent women helped cast doubt on Puritanism's tyranny over them. In 1645, John Winthrop had summed up the colony's position on woman by declaring to the General Court that her husband "is [her] lord, and she is subject to him," just as man is subject to God. In 1712, in a sermon on "Duties of Husbands and Wives," Benjamin Wadsworth, minister of the First Church of Boston—which had been established by Winthrop's Puritan settlement—promoted a revised conception of woman and wife. Wadsworth continued to maintain that man is the head of his family and its governor, but in place of woman's subjection, he emphasized the "mutual duty" that husband and wife have toward one another. They must "unite in their prudent counsels and endeavors," he proclaimed. Woman had not become man's equal in Wadsworth's schema, but she was at least a consulting partner.[4]

However, though women may have been granted more agency within the New England family, they were begrudged even a cameo spot in the public square, as a minor uproar in Boston's Special Court of Admiralty demonstrated. Pirates had been rampant off the coast of New England, and their trials (melodramatic and sensational, they were the soap operas of their day) attracted an audience whose members would come to see justice at work or simply to gawk. In the beginning, trial watching was a man's sport, but as the population of ladies of leisure grew, they too began coming to the trials, for the same reasons the men came. That was not all right with the men. In 1724, a writer for the *New-England Courant*—possibly Benjamin Franklin, who was then a young apprentice at the *Courant*—let the women know that their invasion of men's turf was sharply resented. Justice cannot prevail in a court trying to do serious business when ladies are present, the writer complained. Ladies had no notion of how to conduct themselves. They chatted away despite the bailiff's shouts for "Silence in the Court." "Will you give me a pinch of snuff?" they asked one another. "This is a mighty pretty lace of yours. What did it cost a yard?" "My hoop will be squeez'd to pieces." They nattered on while a man's life hung in the balance. The moral of the satire was that women were out of place where men conducted important affairs.[5]

The sentiment was echoed whenever women pushed into places that had been men's purview. An essay in the *American Magazine and Historical Chronicle*, a major periodical of the era, declared in 1745 that nature had constructed women to be "confined within the limits of Domestick Offices," and that "when they stray beyond them, they move excentrically [sic] and consequently without Grace." The writer was especially outraged that women were claiming their right to follow intellectual pursuits. When women try to talk about politics and metaphysics, he complained, they "mangle the terms of each." They read "just enough of all Things, without comprehending any one," and so "they talk absurdly on every Thing." But their fault was not that they lacked deeper learning; rather, it was that they had no business having any learning whatsoever. "If a woman should ask what Province I leave to their Sex," he concluded grandly, "I answer that I leave whatever has not been assign'd by *Nature* to ours. I leave 'em a mighty Empire, Love."[6]

A new reason had arisen to keep women in their place: nature. Nature invested men, not women, with the power to direct "the more difficult and important Affairs of Life," the author of *Reflections on Courtship and Marriage* wrote in 1746. It was no longer Eve's foolishness but nature's law that demanded that "subordination [be] made a Rule of Conduct by the woman." However, the writer observed, nature also implanted in the woman an array of disagreeable traits that man must extirpate if he desired felicity in marriage: her "childish, little narrow-spirited Way of Thinking," her "mean and Injudicious Distrust," her "low and pitiful Artifices," and her "lurking Sort of Cunning."[7]

Woman could not win among the pundits. Bad as nature made her, she was even worse if she transgressed nature and became "unnatural": "Ill thrives that hapless Family that shows / A Cock that's silent and a Hen that crows. / I know not which lives more unnatural lives, / Obeying husbands or commanding wives," Franklin wrote in the guise of Poor Richard in the *Almanac* of 1734. All women in antiquity who were learned or heroic were not really women: they were "hermaphrodites," the *American Magazine and Historical Chronicle* declared in 1745, "and as for the Heroines of modern Date, we have more than Suspicions of their being at least of the Epicene gender."[8] This would be a line of attack used to keep women in their place for 250 years or more: those who wanted privileges belonging to men were deemed hermaphrodites, epicenes, Amazons, hens that crow, unnatural, unsexed, manly, lesbians.

Women of various Indian nations entered the eighteenth century with their "natural right of liberty" still intact. By the end of the century, that was no longer so. The missionaries' persistence in eradicating what they fantasized to be the Indians' sinful ways accounts for some of the transformation. Father Mathurin Le Petit, a French Jesuit stationed among the

Natchez Indians of New Orleans in 1730, wrote home to the procurator of the missions in North America, delineating how far from Christian morality the Natchez were. The reigning chief of the Natchez was succeeded not by his own son but by the son of his sister, Le Petit observed, inventing the reason why: it was because of the "knowledge the Natchez have of the licentiousness of their women. They cannot be sure that the children of the Chief's wife are of the blood Royal. Whereas the son of the sister of the chief must be of the blood Royal, at least on the side of the mother." Le Petit was also horrified at the wicked behavior of the Indian "Princesses," as he called Natchez women with power: "They have the right of dismissing their husband whenever it pleases them, and of choosing another from the Nation."[9]

Even worse, the missionary continued, "if the husband has been guilty of infidelity, the Princess may have his head cut off; but she is not herself subject to the same law, for she may have as many lovers as she pleases without the husband having any power to complain." And the husband, instead of trying to wrest control, "in the presence of his wife acts with the most profound respect, never eats with her, and salutes her with howls, as is done by her servants," the scandalized Le Petit informed the procurator.[10]

Efforts to transform what the Europeans found impossible to comprehend were already underway when Le Petit wrote his letter. It was essential, the missionaries believed, that Indian women be inculcated with white notions of what befits woman: modesty, purity, and submission. But the efforts were complicated by Indian resistance and white contempt. The Sisters of the Order of St. Ursula arrived in New Orleans in 1727 and founded the Ursuline Academy, the first Catholic girls' school in North America. Most of the students were white, but the Sisters, adhering to their order's "universalist missionary spirit," took in a few Indian and enslaved girls.[11] They were to be taught the catechism, as well as how to read, sew, and be chaste. The nuns were unnerved by their Indian pupils, though they persisted in trying to teach them—with unhappy results.

Marie-Madeleine Hachard, a twenty-three-year-old novice who would eventually become the abbess of the Ursuline order, arrived with the first boatload of Ursulines in 1727. She was soon writing letters to her father in Rouen that betrayed how ill suited the young French nuns were to work with Indian girls. She told him about her pleasure in teaching her white charges. Even the "Naigres [sic]" were easy to instruct in morality. But the Indians—"Sauvages," she called them—were "impossible to baptize without trembling since they have a penchant for sinning." Her distaste for them was palpable: "Under the air of modesty they hide the passions of beasts," she wrote.[12] As she knew, it was the job of Christians like herself to break the "beasts" and, in doing so, to refashion Indian women into their notion of woman.

That refashioning was advanced by other circumstances as well. The position that Indian women held in various tribes—as matrilineal ruler of the family, peace woman to whom the war chiefs yielded, or Beloved Woman through whom the Great Spirit spoke—all were eroded in contacts with the white world. The Europeans found it bizarre and disturbing that Indian men lived "under petticoat government," as James Adair wrote of the Cherokee in his 1775 *History of the American Indians*. Petticoat rule led to the untenable, Adair declared, reiterating European men's great obsession about what happens if men lose control over women: Cherokee men were so powerless that they were forced to allow women "full liberty to plant their brows with horns, as oft as they please, without fear of punishment."[13]

White leaders refused to honor "petticoat government" in any form. The demeaning lesson the Pequot women had learned a century earlier—when they came to beg an end to war and were turned away until they brought a man to negotiate—was relearned by women leaders from other Indian nations. In 1781, for instance, Nanye'hi, a Cherokee Beloved Woman, tried to negotiate peace and beg for a halt to white expansion after Cherokee villages in Georgia were destroyed by a militia led by Colonel John Sevier. "We are your mothers, you are our sons. . . . Let your women's sons be ours, our sons be yours. Let your women hear our words," Nanye'hi begged her hearers.[14] Her gynocentric plea had no meaning for Sevier, nor could he understand why the Cherokee would send a woman to represent them. The so-called peace treaty to which he agreed resulted in more takeover of Cherokee land. To subsequent negotiations with Sevier, the Cherokee sent men (who were no more successful in halting the landgrabs than the women had been).

White encroachment played the biggest role in changing the concept of woman for the Indian tribes in which women had been in charge of agriculture and livestock and men had been hunters. As white settlers took over more of the wild land, it became impossible for Indian men to hunt. What was there for them to do? In a 1796 address to the men of the Cherokee nation, President George Washington proposed a solution to their growing idleness: They must become the farmers in their families. In lieu of hunting, they could raise cattle and hogs and sheep. They must also grow cotton and flax, Washington told them, "to be sold to the neighboring white people, or made into cloathing for yourselves. Your wives and daughters can soon learn to spin and weave"—just as the white woman does. To that end, Washington promised to direct his agent to the Cherokee, Silas Dinsmoor, "to procure all the apparatus necessary for spinning & weaving, & to hire a woman to teach the use of them." Needless to say, the president did not address or consult the Cherokee women about the plan that would upend their lives.[15]

Other Indian nations, also robbed of their hunting grounds by white settlement, followed the solution imposed on the Cherokee. Indian women's communal importance had been connected, in many tribes, to their control of the production of food. Now they became as powerless as their white counterparts. They would learn to be housewives, economically dependent on their men, who would be the planters as well as the unequivocal heads of their individual households. Among the Six Nations Iroquois Confederacy, the transition was enforced by a Seneca religious leader named Handsome Lake, who claimed to be a messenger from the spirit world. He had died, he told his followers (historians suggest that he had passed out in an alcoholic stupor), and he had been resurrected, charged with bringing divine-inspired change to the Iroquois. It was a change that President Thomas Jefferson had proposed to Handsome Lake, urging him to "persuade our red brethren" to cultivate their lands and their women "to spin and weave for the family." With the power of the American presidency behind him, Handsome Lake carried out the reforms: Iroquois women had used wooden hoes to cultivate the soil, but now the men would take over, and they would use iron plows, like the white men did. And the women would ply their needles, like the white women did.[16]

Handsome Lake codified the radical changes he imposed on his people in an 1803 document titled the "Code of Handsome Lake," in which he revised even the Iroquois story of creation that had imagined Sky Woman as the creator of the sun, moon, and stars and her daughter, Breath of Wind, as the source of the life-giving staples: corn, squash, and beans. In Handsome Lake's creation myth there was a single god—male, the creator of everything, and very much like the Old Testament God. Old women, who in traditional Iroquois culture had been thought venerable and wise, were dishonored in the code, which depicted them as vicious destroyers of the new nuclear family's domestic happiness as well as sinners against the new monotheistic god. The code declared,

> Now it may happen that the girl's mother discovers she is very happy with her husband. Then she endeavors to make her daughter angry with her husband when he returns from a journey. But when the husband returns the young woman forgets the evil advice and greets him lovingly. Now the older woman, the mother, seeing this, speaks again, hoping to stir up an ill feeling. Says the old woman, "My daughter, your spirits are dull, you are not bright. When I was young I was not so agreeable." Now the Creator is sad because of the tendency of old women to breed mischief. Such work must stop. Tell your people it must stop.[17]

Old women were sent even deeper into disrepute by Handsome Lake's suggestion in his code that they might be witches, who "make disease and spread sickness to make the living die." Old women brewed witch powders too, which caused men to lose their minds. The Iroquois's own version of Salem ensued, and several women were executed.[18] Through Handsome Lake's code, the Iroquois matriarchate received its coup de grace.

"WOMAN" INTO "LADY"

"Needlework is the most important branch of female education."

—Alice Shippen to her daughter, Nancy, 1777[19]

The preamble to the Declaration of Independence, which states that "all men are created equal," was by no means a challenge to long-standing class distinctions, hereditary or otherwise. In colonial America there had been wealthy farmers, planters, and merchants, who constituted the "better class" (in the phrase of the day) and who strove to emulate the luxury and leisure of their wealthy British counterparts. Though as the eighteenth century progressed, the very rich got richer and the very poor got poorer, the number of well-off individuals who saw themselves as being in the "better class" expanded, as did the number of those who hoped to emulate them.[20]

In the early years of the colonies most women's days were filled with chores such as milking cows, making butter, feeding chickens, planting and cultivating a kitchen garden, and spinning and weaving. In the eighteenth century many women were free of such chores. More people had moved to cities, where they could buy essentials in convenient markets. On farms and plantations, too, as personal wealth grew for many colonists, they could purchase indentured servants or enslaved people to do the work that most colonial wives and daughters had once done. If a family was well off—particularly if the paterfamilias was a successful merchant or landowner, or a prominent government official—the wife and daughters of the household had no grueling domestic duties whatsoever. A woman of the "better class" could spend her time doing little other than being a lady. Those with "middling" status often aspired to do the same.

What did a lady do? She wrote letters and kept a diary. She read novels, engaged in social chitchat, and tended to whatever might enhance her beauty. If she did needlework, it was for her own pleasure. She learned to paint, dance, and make music. There were surely women of the upper classes who resented ladydom—who lived (as Kate Chopin wrote of an elite woman much later) an "outward existence which conforms [and an] inward life which questions"—but the outward conformity was virtually inescapable. Elite men required their wives and daughters to acquire the genteel refinements of a lady because their gentility signified that their domestic labors were not needed. A lady helped affirm to the world that the man of the family had achieved success.[21]

But even men whose achievements needed no further affirmation wished the women who represented them to be ladies. "With respect to the distribution of your time, the following is what I should approve," Thomas Jefferson wrote to his eleven-year-old daughter in 1783. He took time off from creating Jeffersonian democracy (which despised aristocratic behavior in the British) to give his child explicit instructions on how she must prepare herself to (in effect) emulate British aristocracy by becoming a lady:

From 8. to 10. o'clock practice music.
From 10. to 1. dance one day and draw the other.
From 1. to 2. draw on the day you dance, and write a letter the next day.

From 3. to 4. read French.
From 4. to 5. exercise yourself in music.
From 5. till bedtime, read English, write [that is, practice penmanship], &c.... Write also one letter a week.... Take care you never spell a word wrong. Always before you write a word, consider how it is spelt, and, if you do not remember it, turn to a dictionary. It produces great praise to a lady to spell well.[22]

Mothers could be as anxious as fathers to train up their daughters to be ladies. In 1777, in the midst of the Revolutionary War, Alice Shippen was detained in Philadelphia with her husband, a doctor who was head of the Continental Army Hospital. She wrote an urgent letter to her fourteen-year-old daughter, Nancy, who was in boarding school in Trenton, New Jersey. "There is an alarm here[. T]he enemy are said to be coming this way," she informed the girl. Fearing that her own life was in imminent danger, she gave her daughter breathless instructions—a critical legacy she was determined to leave her child, even with her dying breath. "Needlework is the most important branch of female education," she proclaimed, "and tell me how you have improved in holding your head & shoulders, in making a curtsy, in going out or coming in to a room, in giving and receiving, holding your knife & fork, walking and sitting. These things contribute so much to a good appearance that they are of great consequence."[23]

Just as a woman of the lower classes could never be a lady, a woman whose father or husband had fallen on hard times could be cast from ladydom. Her demotion might cause her chagrin, but the man of the family would feel it as a huge disgrace. Robert Morris—a signer of the Declaration of Independence and the U.S. Constitution, and a financier who constantly found himself in financial straits—was eternally fretful about his wife and daughter maintaining their status as ladies. If they could not do that, he rightly feared, his money troubles would be obvious to everyone. In the midst of the financial woes he faced throughout the 1780s, he instructed his wife to get a harpsicord and a music teacher for their daughter, Maria, as well as to take delivery of a "new Chariot" and be seen in it. He wrote her about his monetary "vexation, mortification, and struggles." However, he also gave her explicit directions on how to entertain a wealthy family who would be visiting when he was absent:

she must serve them a vintage wine that he treasured and "some of the best Fish and excellent Butters"; and to show that she shined in ladydom, she must introduce the visiting wife to the impressive "Ladies of your acquaintance."[24]

Morris was finally sent to debtors' prison, but even from there, he encouraged Maria to follow the habits that their class demanded of ladies: keep company with other ladies who "form an agreeable society," partake of "the pleasures of social life," study a musical instrument, and read books—though, he hastened to add, she must be careful in her book reading. "The customs of the world do not require that Ladies should be learned or deeply read," he warned, admonishing her against becoming "an affected learned lady."[25]

Women who were ladies could not fail to understand that to appear to be overly learned was antithetical to genteel refinement and anathema to the men of their class. *A Father's Legacy to His Daughters* was published in England in 1761 by John Gregory, a Scottish doctor, and was reissued in Philadelphia in 1775. It remained one of the most popular books in America well into the nineteenth century. "If you happen to have any learning," Gregory seriously advised his daughters, "keep it a profound secret, especially from men, who generally look with a jealous and malignant eye at a woman of . . . cultivated understanding."[26]

The message was strongly impressed upon a girl in training to be a lady. The books typically made available to young ladies put them in no danger of having to keep their learning a "profound secret" from men. Hannah Callender, a young daughter of a wealthy merchant, admitted in 1759 to having read only "fulsome Romances." Ladies and aspiring ladies had at their reading disposal primarily "ladies books," which gave advice about how a lady must behave. They bore titles such as *The Ladies Calling, The Ladies Library,* and *The Ladies New Years Gift.*[27]

To express political opinions was as unbecoming in a lady as to have too much learning. Jefferson, ambassador to France in the year before the French Revolution, professed to be repelled by Parisian women because they talked politics. "Amazons," he called them, a term that held the same disturbing connotation of unnatural behavior as did "lesbian" in the twentieth century. Jefferson wrote: "Our good American ladies, I trust, have been too wise to wrinkle their foreheads with politics. They are contented to soothe and calm the minds of their husbands returning from political debate. They have the good sense to value domestic happiness above all other, and the art to cultivate it beyond all others."[28]

Young women from the "better class" had little choice but to comply with the urging of fathers and mothers to eschew whatever would "wrinkle their foreheads" and to learn the arts of gentility instead—which is not to say that many did not relish learning those arts. The arts included not only needlework, French, and penmanship but also how to dress and dance well, as Anna Green Winslow wrote in her adolescent diary of 1771–1773. For her education, Anna was sent to Boston to live with her aunt in a three-story mansion, whose second floor was devoted to a ballroom where the elite gathered for soirees—the men in perukes with velvet breeches and matching waistcoats, and the women dressed in elegant hooped gowns with ruffled sleeves. In her letters to her parents, Anna described animatedly her own dress at the balls, "ruffels" [sic], black feathers and silver plumes, and "my best silk shoes," as well as her "dansing, danceing, I mean [sic]" the minuet. She would have learned the cotillion and minuet from a fashionable dancing master, one of those who announced themselves in newspapers with advertisements such as "Martin Foy, just arrived from Europe," who promised he could teach what he had "acquired from the most eminent Professors, the true movement of a Minuet with proper Graces and most exact Time."[29]

The culmination of ladydom training was marriage, often based less on sentiment than on affirmation of the family's social status—which could make the "domestic happiness" that Jefferson saw as the chief goal of "our good American ladies" sadly elusive. Alice Shippen's daughter, Nancy—to whom she had written when Nancy was fourteen about the importance of needlework and curtsies and holding a knife and fork properly—fell in love four years later with a French diplomat who had no great fortune. Nancy's father, then surgeon general of the U.S. Army, could not let Nancy make such a social mistake. He married her off to Colonel Henry Beekman Livingston, whose family owned one of the largest landed estates in New York.

A shibboleth of the era—as an essay on "Female Influence," published in *New-York Magazine* suggested—was that in courtship, young ladies would discourage "coxcombs and libertines," and in marriage they would steer their husbands "to virtuous habits and paths of rectitude." But how could eighteen-year-old Nancy Shippen, with all her genteel refinements, prevail over her father's choice of a fabulously wealthy libertine, a man thirteen years her senior? Her charms did nothing to discourage her new husband from keeping mistresses and having children by them. Nor could she do anything to stop Livingston's "ungovernable fits of rage," which began soon after their marriage. It was not long before she lamented to her journal, "What is my unfortunate situation! A wretched slave doom'd to be the wife of a Tyrant I hate."[30]

After four years, Nancy took her little daughter and fled back to her parents' home. Hoping to get a divorce, she wrote Arthur Lee, her maternal uncle and a prominent Virginia lawyer, and asked for his help. He responded with sarcasm, saying he had received her "letter of a fine Lady [which] talks of a Divorce with as much nonchalance as of a discarded lover." Lee thought it preposterous that his niece would leave a mansion on one of the largest estates in New York and compromise her "honor and interests."[31] However, he suggested, if she was really serious about a divorce, her father should talk to lawyers for her. He himself would do nothing.

But her father sided with her husband, though the husband threatened to take their daughter from her. Nancy declared herself "deprived of all hope of ever being happy in this world." She was twenty-two years old. What would she do with the rest of her life? In her journal she left a bitterly ironic record of the tedium of her days as a young woman who had been fashioned into a lady:

> Let me see, how have I employed my time today? The same way that I employed it yesterday, & the day before, & the day before that[. I]ndeed there is such a sameness in my life that the particulars of it are hardly worth setting down. . . . This morn'g I gave orders to the servants as usual for the business of the day, then took a little [needle]work in my hand, & set down before the fire just to think how I should dispose of myself in the evening. . . . I concluded to go to the concert. Then I considered what I would dress in, and having determined the important part, I felt light and easy.[32]

WOMAN IN THE SOUTHERN SLAVE STATES

"Show your neck, Betsy! There's a breast for you."
— "A Charleston Vendue in 1812" (1869)[33]

Measured by the idealized attributes that the colonists and their offspring ascribed to woman—delicacy, modesty, innocence, and virtue—no slave was to them a woman. This was especially true in the South, where exaggerated veneration of womanhood served as a purposeful contrast to southern men's contempt for the Black female. The white woman needed to be esteemed for her lovely fragility and natural purity, they reasoned, but the Black female was her polar opposite: physically strong and naturally lustful and abandoned. This meant that enslaved women could be worked and used with none of the considerations due to womanhood. It was convenient to the southern economy, moral and otherwise. Enslaved females were treated as equal to enslaved males—that is, their labors were often just as hard, and the mistreatment they suffered was just as callous and cruel.[34] And the women endured a double burden: They suffered not only on account of their skin but also on account of their sex. No slave was a woman in the colonists' meaning of the word, but women slaves were abused as females.

Girlhood among eighteenth-century whites in America signified a time when females of the "better" and "middling" classes were separated from boys and carefully trained in the attributes of womanhood. Poor girl children too were segregated by sex through their duties in the family, and they were taught the role of the woman of their class through their mothers. Among slaves, little girls were, ironically, less constrained in that they were not treated differently from little boys. Before they were old enough to work, they were sometimes watched by a "granny" who was too ancient to labor in the fields, but feminine roles were not imposed on them. They were as free to run through the woods, climb trees, hunt rabbits, and get as dirty as their boy counterparts. However, that freedom did not last long. By the time they were eight years old, girls, like boys, were put to work at jobs such as weeding, carrying water, or cleaning up as part of the "trash gangs" that trailed adult workers.[35]

Nor did overseers make distinctions between girls and boys in harsh punishment. In 1777, Elizabeth, an enslaved eleven-year-old Maryland girl, was separated from her parents and siblings and sold to another master, who immediately put her to work. When Elizabeth begged the overseer for leave to visit her mother, he refused. She went anyway, but her mother, knowing that runaway slaves and their abettors could be killed, sent the child back to her owner. "You have nobody in the wide world to look to but God," were her mother's parting words. When Elizabeth returned to her new place, the overseer tied her with a rope and beat her so badly that she was in pain for weeks. Despite her frenzied weeping and deep depression, and though she was weak because she could not eat, she was forced to work until close to death.[36] She was the same age as Jefferson's daughter had been when he instructed her to prepare to be a woman by spending her days in learning to dance, draw, make music, and speak French.

The work of an enslaved woman varied, depending on whether she lived on a farm, near a city, or on a large or small plantation, but her tasks were often no different from, or easier than, those of an enslaved man. Only about 5 percent of enslaved women were domestic servants. The rest worked in the fields. On a farm an enslaved woman might be assigned to clearing land, cutting timber, or burning brush. Sometimes she did those jobs in addition to domestic duties, such as tending to the poultry. On some plantations she might plow, hoe, spread manure, thresh wheat, and clean out swamps. On others she might be assigned jobs that required less muscle, such as beating grain or spinning and weaving wool and flax. Though her inferior strength was sometimes considered in the type of work required of her, slave owners honored no other aspect of woman in her, not even if she was pregnant. If a pregnant woman working in the field did something to anger the overseer, he might dig a hole in the ground big enough to contain her stomach, force her to lie face down, and then beat her—in that way protecting the unborn child, which was the master's property.[37]

Enslaved women's gender was unacknowledged most of the time: none of the qualities attributed to the woman was attributed to them. But slave owners were obsessed by enslaved women's sexual functions as breeders and objects of lust. Intent on increasing their assets, slave owners sometimes forced mating between slaves. A 1737 North Carolina account claimed that it "frequently happen[ed]" that when enslaved women had no children after cohabiting with one man for a year or two, "the Planters oblige them to take a second, third, fourth, fifth or more Husbands for Bedfellows: a fruitful Woman amongst them being very valued by the Planters." Those who made a business of slaves were pitiless in touting a woman's breeding capacities at slave auctions, as a Charleston, South Carolina, observer reported in the early nineteenth century. The auctioneer, he wrote, ordered a woman on the block to "show your neck, Betsy! There's a breast for you; good for a round dozen before she's done childbearing. Well, gentlemen, shall I say twenty-five hundred?"[38]

Enslaved women on southern plantations were encouraged to be often pregnant because the offspring would "yield at some future date." But motherhood did not excuse a woman from work. As one man who had been a slave later observed, "A white man start out wid a few womenfolk slaves, soon him have a plantation full of little niggers runnin' round in deir shirt tails and a kickin' up deir heels, whilst der mammies was in deir field ahoeing and geeing at the plow handles, workin' lak a man." Enslaved women who could bear many children became especially valuable after 1809, when the slave trade, though not slavery, was outlawed throughout the United States. The institution could only continue through the fertility of enslaved women, bolstered by a law which said that all children born of enslaved women were slaves, no matter who the father.[39]

No slave was a woman to the whites who defined the term in the eighteenth century, though enslaved women struggled to make their own meaning of the word. Motherhood was central to the eighteenth-century ideal of woman among whites, but enslaved women had no control over how they could be mothers to their children. The historical record is rife with accounts such as one from Wilmington, North Carolina, in which the writer described "a heart-rending spectacle" of a mother and her child "driven in from the country, like swine for market." The writer witnessed as the mother "clung to a little daughter, and implored, with the most agonizing supplication, that they might not be separated. But alas, either master or circumstances were inexorable—they were sold to different purchasers." Given such horrors, it was virtually an act of political resistance for an enslaved woman to cherish motherhood.[40]

Some enslaved women succeeded in that resistance and were even able to build some semblance of family. They frequently had to do it without the aid of their mate, because if a couple did not belong to the same slave owner, they could not live together, and the father could not play a daily role in his child's life. Enslaved men were likely to be sold without any regard to family, though a mother could often live with her children until they were at least ten years old. Sometimes women were able to hold together a network of kin—an extended family including aunts, uncles, cousins, and even grandparents who worked on neighboring plantations.[41]

But that was not always possible. As the sad story of Elizabeth, whose mother told her "You have nobody in the wide world to look to but God," suggests, even motherhood, a crucial definer of the eighteenth-century white woman, could be and often was snatched from enslaved women.

Some white women were themselves slave owners. Through a prenuptial marriage contract that could permit a woman to escape coverture laws, the slaves that she had received as a gift or through inheritance might remain her exclusive property and under her control. It is a paradox that a white woman's independent ownership of enslaved people was one of the few ways she might claim agency as well as freedom from the total economic dependency in which most of her white female contemporaries were imprisoned. Yet her position as a slave owner could be an ironic contradiction to the cherished image of the Southern white woman as delicate and pure, a "fragile flower." The historian Stephanie Jones-Rogers has written that female slave owners sometimes "personally orchestrated acts of sexual violence against enslaved women" because the resulting pregnancies meant more slaves for their owners.[42] If a slave-owning woman were pregnant, she might even force one of her enslaved woman to become pregnant at the same time, by any man on the plantation—white or Black—so that the enslaved mother could be put to work as a wet nurse for the white mistress's baby.

Male slave owners were cavalier and callous about paternity. By the nineteenth century, as historian Brenda Stevenson found in her work on Loudoun County, Virginia, perhaps one-third or more of enslaved people were "mulatto." If the snide observation of Mary Boykin Chesnut (a diarist who came from a long line of South Carolina slave owners) can be believed, the practice of plantation owners siring children by enslaved women was virtually universal, though some plantation mistresses maintained the pretense that their own menfolk were innocent. Chesnut wrote that any plantation mistress "is ready to tell you who is the father of all the mulatto children [on everybody's plantation] but her own. Those," Chesnut quipped in her *Diary from Dixie*, "she seems to think, drop from the clouds."[43]

Sexual exploitation was in fact endemic to slavery. Harriet Jacobs, who had been born into slavery in 1813, observed that "the slave girl is raised in an atmosphere of licentiousness" from the time she is fourteen or fifteen, subjected to the advances of "her owner, or his sons, or the overseer, or perhaps all of them." Slave owners added to their number of slaves by rape or even by promising an enslaved woman that she would be treated better if she gave her sexual favors. Louisa Picquet's firsthand account in an anti-slavery pamphlet about her, *The Octoroon*, is a dramatic confirmation of Jacobs's claim. Born in 1829 to a fifteen-year-old enslaved girl and her owner, a Columbia, South Carolina planter, Picquet was separated from her mother and sold at the age of fourteen to a forty-six-year-old man. He brought her to New Orleans and forced her to be his "concubine." Picquet had a child by him every year, until he died in 1847.[44]

Male slave owners may not have discussed their sexual exploits with their wives, but, as Josiah Quincy, a Boston lawyer traveling through the

South in 1773, recorded in his journal, they relished boasting to one another. Quincy claimed that "their enjoyment" of the black women over whom they had power "is spoken of as quite a common thing: no reluctance, delicacy or shame is made about the matter." Their fantasies of enslaved women as Jezebels stoked their enjoyment. It was an opportunistic delusion that let them believe that all African women not old enough to be "mammies" were amoral and hypersexual—the polar opposite to the pure and innocent white woman.[45]

Male slave owners violated the vaunted innocence of their wives and daughters if—as Chesnut claimed—the ladies all knew the paternity of the light-skinned enslaved children in the community. But in any case, the myth of universal sexual innocence among the slave owners' wives and daughters, which served to reassure husbands of their wives' prized purity and the legitimacy of their children, sometimes collapsed in the stark reality of individual women's sexual appetites. Harriet Jacobs wrote of a slave owner "whose head was bowed down in shame, for it was known in the neighborhood that his daughter had selected one of the meanest slaves on the plantation to be father of his first grandchild." Jacobs suggested that this was far from an isolated incident of sexual relations between slave-owning women and enslaved men.[46] Court records from the seventeenth century through the nineteenth bear out her point. Some slave-owning women defied the myth of their natural woman's purity and innocence, seized sexual agency for themselves, and satisfied their erotic appetites with men who were enslaved.

In 1680, for example, Katherine Watkins, the wife of a Virginia slave owner, may have been pregnant by a slave when she accused him of raping her, but her ploy did not work. The neighbors testified that they knew that several enslaved men were her paramours and swore to witnessing various incidents that showed she was the sexual aggressor. For example, when Dirke, an enslaved man, passed her one day, "she took up the tail of his shirt, saying 'Dirke, thou wilt have a good long prick.'" Some sexual relationships between slave owners' wives and enslaved men involved genuine affection. In 1824, Dorothea Bourne was sued by her husband, the owner of a small plantation, because Edmond, an enslaved man on a large neighboring plantation, had fathered several of her children. Louis Bourne did not want to be financially responsible for those children. Neighbors testified that they had caught Dorothea in flagrante delicto on a bed with Edmond, that everyone knew he was the father of her children, that she dwelled with him in a corner of her husband's property, and that she regularly washed and mended Edmond's clothes. One of the neighbors offered insight into the triangle, testifying that Edmond was much younger and handsomer than Louis Bourne, who was abusive and even violent with Dorothea.[47]

NOT A WOMAN: THE EIGHTEENTH-CENTURY SPINSTER

> "Everyone is not fitted for the single Life, nor was I ever moulded for the wed[d]ed one."
> —HANNAH GRIFFITTS, c. 1750[48]

In a society in which "woman" and "wife" were practically synonymous, an unmarried woman was considered pitiable. She was a woman manqué, a failed woman, since the meaning of "woman" was so tied to her function as wife and mother. Unmarried women were, in effect, excluded from womanhood.

An unmarried woman without money was in a particularly unenviable position. Few jobs were open to her, and there was little she could do to expand her opportunities. While a young man might become an apprentice in all sorts of artisanal occupations, a young woman might be an apprentice to a seamstress, spinner, or weaver—and not much else. While women who were married might learn trades from their husbands such as blacksmithing or barbering, an unmarried woman had no one who might teach her such income-producing skills. By the 1760s, women were even being squeezed out of the two "professions" they had dominated in earlier eras, when they could become midwives and healers by apprenticing to other women in those positions. Those possibilities were nearing an end because healing and midwifery were coming to be considered not knowledge that women handed down to one other, but complex technical skills that required training in medical schools, and women were not allowed in those schools.[49] An unmarried woman was called a spinster because spinning was one of the few jobs open to her.

For those who did not chose spinsterhood, it was a painful state. If a spinster had no trade or resources, she might be taken into the home of relatives, where she would usually pay for her room and board by doing much of the housework and caring for the family's children. The wife and mother of the household, the real woman, would serve as a daily reminder of the spinster's anomalous condition.

With a little bit of capital, an unmarried woman could set up a shop in the city, selling glassware perhaps, or candles or tea. But doing so had its own disheartening problems. As an angry petition from she-merchants to the New York City government shows, they were made to feel their inferior status. "[We] pay our Taxes, carry on Trade . . . contribute to the Support of the Government," they complained in 1733. "We ought to be intitled to some of the Sweets of it, but we find ourselves entirely neglected." They were given neither the respect nor the perquisites enjoyed by male merchants, they protested. But their doleful petition brought no results.[50]

Even a spinster who had a well-paying trade and was appreciated by her community might see herself as a failure at a time when woman's chief identity was derived from the married state. The diary of Rebecca Dickinson, a Massachusetts seamstress born in 1738, shows how she internalized the terrible stigma of spinsterhood, despite her external successes. Dickinson made gowns for the wealthy and fashionable. She was beloved in the small town of Hatfield, where she was affectionately called Aunt Beck and considered a "Saint on Earth." She was clearly proud of her independence. In one diary entry, for example, she wrote of being visited by an old friend with whom she had grown up, Patte Graves: "We went together to learn the trade of goun making, which has been of unspeakable advantage to me but of no Servis to her," Dickinson declared. She compared her own freedom to the domestic imprisonment of her friend, who had "married a man seven and thirty years older than her Self [and] has six children living."[51]

Yet many of Dickinson's diary entries reveal her secret shame that she had not done what a woman was supposed to do. Despite her neighbors' evident admiration of her, she imagined that they "hissed and wagged their heads at me by reason of my Solotary life." She asked herself in despair "how it come about that others and all the world was in Possession of Children and friends and a hous[e] and homes while I was so od[d] as to sit here alone." Over and over in her diary, Dickinson castigated herself as "od[d]," an outcast from womanhood because she had failed to become a wife.[52]

Dickinson's ambivalence about marriage was not unusual, though there were of course many happy marriages. For instance, Abigail Adams's numerous love letters to her husband, John, present a poignant story of enduring love. In 1782, when they had been married for eighteen years, Abigail wrote John, whom she addressed as "My dearest friend," acknowledging her loneliness during his frequent absences in service to the new country but also relishing her assurance in their mutual devotion:

> With an indiscribable pleasure I have seen near a score of years roll over our Heads, with an affection heightened and improved by time—nor have the dreary years of absence in the smallest degree effaced from my mind the Image of the dear untittled man to whom I gave my Heart. . . . The unbounded confidence I have in your attachment to me, and the dear pledges of our affection, has soothed the solitary hour.[53]

But regardless of whether or not a woman "gave [her] Heart," most married if they had the chance to do so. Marrying was what a woman did. And if she did not understand her obligation to marry, her parents would force that understanding upon her. Hannah Callender, for example, filled the pages of her journal in 1758–1759, when she was twenty-one years old, with defiance at the idea that a woman must be a wife. She declared that "elderly maidens are of service in the creation, notwithstanding Calumny," and that "History as well as our own time furnishes many Instances, of worthy Single Women." But three years later, her wealthy father ("Daddy," as she called him)—chagrined that his daughter at twenty-four was not yet a woman—bestowed a large dowry on her and then pushed her to marry a man neither she nor her mother liked. Callender became a wife, though the role clearly did not suit her. She wrote resentfully in her diary that she had begun "the Important Affair of Housekeeping, in which the woman's care is to make the house agreeable to her husband, and be careful of his Interest," noting that "in the Married State, you shall know trouble if you have been strangers to it before." Some women who had married because they were urged to by a parent, or because the single state was painful, learned to love their husbands and accept the place that had been set for women. Callender never did.[54]

But there were women who managed to disregard the parental or social pressures that defeated Callender. Some had the wherewithal to fashion for themselves a space in which to thrive, or they had the encouragement of like-minded friends. If "woman" was practically synonymous with wife and mother, they chose to drop out of womanhood. They assented—tacitly or not—to being "not a woman."

Jemima Wilkinson, much too large a personality to be contained by the woman's sphere, found a unique way to evade it. Wilkinson had grown up in a wealthy Rhode Island family, the sixth daughter among twelve children. Raised as a Quaker, she felt that she had a religious calling and intended to become a Quaker preacher. But in 1776, when she was twenty-three, she attended a Baptist church where she witnessed the passionate sin-and-repentance preaching inspired by George Whitefield, who had sparked the evangelical revivalist movement known as the first Great Awakening. Wilkinson was roused, and this left her in a quandary. Quaker women had always been accepted as preachers, but the Quaker preaching style had none of the intense emotional drama that appealed to her. Yet she could not be a Baptist preacher because Baptists did not license she-preachers. And then word reached the leaders of her Quaker congregation that Wilkinson had been flirting with another religion, and she was cast out: she no longer had even the option to be a Quaker preacher.

Wilkinson's solution to her quandary, now compounded by religious homelessness, was unique. A short while after being enthralled by Baptist preaching and being excommunicated from Quakerism, she had a fever. One of her brothers later claimed that her illness was slight and that she had quickly recovered, but Wilkinson presented a very different story to explain her metamorphosis after the fever. She announced that the fever had killed her and she had gone to heaven. There she had communed with the angels and been possessed by the spirit of God, who sent her back to earth, where she was to make His will known to the sinful world through her preaching. Her first step in her new mission was to disavow Jemima Wilkinson and assume a manly form.

Whether s/he had always had a self-conception that more recent times have identified as transgender is impossible to know. "Transgender" was, of course, not a term in the eighteenth century, though Wilkinson might have been an individual whom nineteenth-century sexologists would have dubbed a man trapped in a woman's body. However, one of the leading sexologists, Havelock Ellis, included Wilkinson not in his study "Female Sexual Inversion" (1897) but only in his book *Man and Woman* (1894), in his chapter on "The Intellectual Woman," where he presents her simply as a religious charlatan.[55] The historical record has no indication of Wilkinson's awareness of a masculine identity before the fever incident. But s/he now created a persona to be able to preach even to those who could never envision a woman preacher.

S/he was no longer a woman, Wilkinson insisted. S/he refused to be referred to as "she" or "her" and asked followers to use the address "Publick Universal Friend" instead. S/he dressed in men's clothes and sported a man's hairstyle. One person who saw Wilkinson preach in 1787 jotted down his memories: Wilkinson wore "a light cloth Cloake with a Cape like a Man's.... Man's shirt... purple handkerchief or Neckcloth tied round her neck like a Man's... wears a Watch—Man's Hat." Wilkinson's preaching combined Quaker tenets, such as the knowability of God's will through "inner light," with Baptist beliefs about sin and repentance, all delivered in masculine, fiery Baptist style. As one spectator remarked, "She do preach up terror alarmingly."[56]

S/he garnered large audiences and a sizable following of both men and women, many of wealth and high social position. Some believed Wilkinson to be "the Messiah Returned," quite forgetting that s/he had been assigned the female sex at birth and had lived before "death and resurrection" as a woman. Hundreds of adherents followed Wilkinson into the wilderness of western New York, where s/he established a town called Jerusalem and a community of the faithful. "Shun the conversation of the wicked world," s/he told them. Followers built Wilkinson a baronial mansion big enough to require nine fireplaces.[57]

Having been brought up as a Quaker, s/he was adamantly antislavery. A Rhode Island judge who owned eleven slaves freed them after hearing Wilkinson preach. S/he also advocated celibacy as a higher state of grace—though Wilkinson's detractors spread rumors about the preacher's "hypocrisy." (The French author of *Travels Through the United States of North America*, for instance, claimed with innuendo to have found in "her" chamber "Rachel Miller, a young woman of about twenty-eight to thirty years of age, her follower and admirer, who is entirely devoted to her. All the land which Jemima possesses is in the name of Rachel Miller.")[58]

Despite detractors, Wilkinson's disciples were dedicated and faithful. S/he was the first female born in America to have founded what was in effect a new religion, the "Universal Friends." S/he was also the first person we know of to have been assigned female at birth who successfully and permanently escaped the prison of "woman" by claiming not to be one. But Wilkinson's achievements, larger than life while s/he lived, died with Wilkinson's death: most of the followers had adhered to Wilkinson's preaching on celibacy, and because few children were born into the community, the sect s/he had founded soon disappeared.[59]

Though most women married in the eighteenth century, 18 percent of Quaker women were still single by the time they were forty. Perhaps there were so many Quaker women who never wed because they had been raised in a church that preached egalitarianism between men and women, and Quaker women came to expect it. But they saw that egalitarianism was not often practiced in marriage—even in Quaker marriage, men still ruled and women obeyed.[60] Disliking the roles of woman and wife, they chose other ways to live. In the previous century, in some colonies, they would have been likely targets for those who were eager to see a witch in any woman who diverged from the role of woman. In the eighteenth century, however, with enough pluck, money, and a supportive social circle, women who voluntarily dropped out of womanhood were able to thrive.

One of the most prominent of these marriage resisters, Susanna Wright, was from an influential and affluent Pennsylvania Quaker family. As the oldest daughter, she managed her father's household after the death of her mother; and because she was needed by the family, no pressure was put on her to marry. Not long after her father's death she was bequeathed a life interest in a mansion in the Susquehanna River area. She was now an independent woman. An intellectual at a time when a woman was advised, as Gregory wrote his daughters, "if you happen to have any learning, keep it a profound secret," Wright, known as the "Bluestocking of Susquehana," collected a large library that contained neither *The Ladies Calling* nor "fulsome Romances." She was proficient not only in French, but in Italian and Latin too. She conducted scientific experiments in botany and horticulture. And she produced such high-quality silk through the silkworms she raised that her friend Benjamin Franklin gifted a length of it to England's Queen Charlotte.[61]

Wright was also a healer and a dispenser of herbal medicines to her neighbors as well as to members of the neighboring Susquehannock Indian tribe. She gave legal advice, too, and was even called on by the community to arbitrate disputes. Though as a woman she could not vote, she campaigned for candidates in Pennsylvania's 1742 assembly elections. One local politician, whom she did not support, publicly reproached her for behaving like a man. "Could anyone believe," he wrote, "that Suzy could act so unbecoming and unfemale a part as to be employ'd [in distributing campaign propaganda]?"[62] But his criticism did not shame her. Wright was not a lady despite her family's social position, and she refused to be a woman.

She was not alone. Wright had a circle of friends who were marriage resisters, and she aimed to expand that circle. In 1750, she wrote a poem that celebrated the single state and presented an argument to all women about why they too ought to refuse to conform to the role of woman and wife. She questioned "when or where that law was made" that permitted men to "assert their right to govern womankind." She angrily dismissed the old justification for men's dominance in Eve's foolish mistake, telling women that men had absolutely no "superior virtue." She incited them not to let men "reign tyrant" over them.[63]

Elizabeth Norris, one of Wright's bluestocking friends, is presented in this poem as the model of how to fight the idea of woman that kept women down: Wright wrote that Norris declined "to yield obedience, or to wear the chain." Norris abandoned the dictates of ladydom over which men held sway. She established her own idyllic world at Fairhill, one of the largest country estates in Pennsylvania Owned by Norris's family, Fairhill was for many years governed by Elizabeth Norris. She invited other spinsters of her class, women who would not accept the role of woman, to live with her there in a gorgeous multistoried manor surrounded by a private park and flowered paths. Norris provided everything to nourish body and mind: lavish feasts, brilliant conversation, and—as Deborah Logan, who had lived there, recalled—even a detached library that made a "most delightful retreat for contemplative study," with "beautiful specimens of fine arts and many curiosities . . . [and] shelves filled with the best authors, and materials for writing and drawing at hand." At Fairhill, there was no "Important Affair of Housekeeping, in which the woman's care is to make the house agreeable to her husband," about which the newly married Callender had bitterly complained. Spinsterhood in Norris's little utopia signified resistance to the gender hierarchy that still kept woman "in the place where God had set her." Nor did the women of Fairhill suffer the pangs of devastating loneliness that Dickinson had agonized over. As another resident, Elizabeth Hudson, characterized it, the women of Fairfield had "Jonothen & david" [sic] friendships with one another.[64] "Thy love to me was wonderful, passing the love of women," David had declared of Jonathan. "My love for you is wonderful, surpassing the love of men," these women could declare.

Another of the marriage resisters at Fairhill was Hannah Griffitts, also from a wealthy and prominent Quaker family. Griffitts had been a poet since she was ten years old, when she promised God that she would write on "no trifling themes." Her poems, serious in content but often models of British-style eighteenth-century wit, were circulated mostly among her women friends, though a few (unbeknown to her, she claimed) were published in periodicals. It is not hard to understand why, though a serious poet, she did not seek publication. A handful of women did publish books in the mid-eighteenth century, but their reception was dispiriting. Martha Wadsworth Brewster, for instance, published *Poems on Divers Subjects* in 1757—for which she was roundly accused of plagiarizing from the hymnist Isaac Watts and other male writers. Publication by a woman was still almost as provocative as it had been a hundred years earlier, when Rev. Thomas Parker upbraided his sister that "your printing of a book, beyond the custom of your sex, doth rankly smell."[65]

The fact that Griffitts did not publish books is no indication that she ran from controversy. She was just the sort of female that Jefferson disparaged at the dawn of the French Revolution when he spoke of the Parisian "Amazons" who butted into men's sphere by chattering about politics. In the decade before the American Revolution, Griffitts decidedly showed herself to be an "Amazon" in Jefferson's sense of the word. She scoffed at the men of America for being "Supinely asleep" while the British stripped them of their freedoms and robbed them of their rights. Because the men had shown that they would not stand up for themselves, Griffitts wrote in her 1768 poem "The Female Patriots," it was time that the "Daughters of Liberty" take over: through their sharp tongues and militant boycotts of British goods, they would do what men could not figure out how to do; the women would know how to make the British hurt.[66] In "The Female Patriots," as in her life, she was passionate and vehement in her rejection of the notion of women as "weaker vessels."

Griffitts was militant in her protofeminism but she refused to be a woman, particularly as "woman" was linked with "wife." She claimed that she had nothing against marriage—for other women. As she explained to her married friend Milcah Moore, "There are many of you wed[d]ed ones who I believe are Placed in your [proper] Sphere [and] I sincerely wish you increase of Hap[p]iness in it without envying you one atom. . . . Everyone is not fitted for the single Life, nor was I ever moulded for the wed[d]ed one." She dismissed with good humor but a touch of defiance a friend who nagged her that as a woman she must wed, telling the friend in her poem "To Sophronia": "Leave me to enjoy the sweet Freedom I love / And go marry—as soon as you please."[67] Griffitts, like her friends at Fairhill, was glad to stand outside woman's proper sphere and be not a woman.

3.
Daughters of Liberty

•

WOMAN AND A WAR OF INDEPENDENCE

From 1775 to 1781, Azariah Grant, though already in his fifties, was a soldier in the Revolutionary War. During one crucial battle, purportedly, he failed to perform his duties so shockingly that his commanding officer complained to Azariah's wife; and Abigail Grant wrote her husband an impassioned letter: "I hear by Captain Wm Riley news that makes me very Sorry for he Says you proved a Grand Coward when the fight was at Bunkers hill, [throwing away your cartridges] so as to escape going into battle. If you are afraid pray own the truth & come home & take care of our Children & I will be Glad to Come & take your place, & never will be Called a Coward, neither will I throw away one Cartridge but will exert myself bravely in so good a Cause."[1]

WOMAN AT WAR

"All trifling discourse of fashions, and such low little chat was thrown by."

—*Letters of Eliza Wilkinson* (1780)[2]

The Founding Fathers of the United States, like women's own fathers, did not seriously question that nature had established woman's inferior place. Thomas Paine's pamphlet *Common Sense*—the clarion call to the War of Independence—attacked the injustice of political hierarchy: one man had no natural right to rule over other men. The personal hierarchy of man over woman, however, was inherent in the "distinctions of Nature," Paine wrote. John Adams agreed. Busy as he was drafting the Declaration of Independence in 1776, Adams took time out to write his friend James Sullivan, the future governor of Massachusetts, saying that a woman could be given no voice in government—because Nature made her "delicate." She was unfit for "the great Business of Life, and the hardy Enterprises of War, as well as the arduous Cares of State."[3] Since she was useless in those important areas, she was to be relegated to the same civil status as a child.

Women were complicit, even internalizing men's views of feminine frailty—or at least that was what they pretended when dealing with men. Sarah Jay—whose husband, John, would become the first chief justice of the United States—had been famous in her own right as a premier society hostess. She maneuvered diplomats, members of the nobility, and the Founding Fathers with finesse. When her husband was too busy to tend to personal business matters, she was a shrewd manager of the family fortune. Outside observers such as Diego de Gardoqui, a Spanish dignitary, observed that she dominated her husband: "Her opinion prevails." Yet Sarah's letters to John are peppered with lines such as "the weakness of my sex," "so weak & imperfect a creature as woman," and "you know we [women] are but weaker Vessels."[4] Whether or not she believed it, that was the prevalent idea of woman, and she reiterated it often, even against the evidence of her own accomplishments.

Despite the adoption of such retiring rhetoric, women shared fervid political opinions with one another. Adams's wife, Abigail, wrote her friend Mercy Otis Warren at the dawn of the Revolutionary War, quoting from the Twenty-Seventh Psalm ("Tho an hoste should encamp against us, our hearts will not fear") and declaring, "We know too well the blessings of freedom, to tamely resign it." But to men, she spoke very differently. She dared, for instance, to butt into the business of men by writing an urgent letter to a Massachusetts member of the Continental Congress, in which she knowledgably discussed threats to the credibility of the Congress. But she interrupted herself in the midst of her concerns to apologize: "I intreet your pardon for touching upon a subject more appropriately belonging to your sex."[5]

Yet the colonies' revolt against British control raised hopes in some women that the War of Independence might serve to change the parameters of woman. They threw themselves into the war effort in novel and imaginative ways that were not always welcomed by male leaders. Like Abigail Grant, many became superpatriots, even sometimes outdoing men to show how committed they were to the cause of freedom. For the first time, they dared to wax political, discussing among themselves and sometimes even in print what needed to be done in the fight against British tyranny, as though the outcome would actually affect them personally. Those who hoped their patriotic commitment and good efforts would be rewarded with a revolutionary reconception of the notion of woman were disappointed. But although women did not become first-class citizens of the new country, the Revolutionary War triggered small renegotiations that would eventually pave the way for bigger changes in the idea of woman.

In the spring of 1780, Eliza Yonge Wilkinson, daughter of a wealthy planter, gathered with her fashionable young lady friends in a house outside of Charleston, South Carolina. Balls and beaux had been their topics of conversation, but the British army had invaded and now occupied Charleston, and the young ladies' obsessions had been transformed overnight. The men were all off fighting (except for a few "skulking varlets" who were too cowardly to fight, Wilkinson complained in a letter to one of her friends). The women were on their own, and they had much to worry about: "Cruelty and Oppression" perpetrated by the British, as Wilkinson wrote; whether the colonists could really defeat the enemy; and the fact that the troops were "in a starving condition." "Never were greater Politicians" than these young ladies who had now gathered together, Wilkinson declared. "All trifling discourse of fashions, and such low little chat was thrown by, and we commenc'd perfect Statesmen. . . . If we had taken a little pains [sic], we should have been qualified for prime ministers, so well could we discuss several important matters in hand," she quipped facetiously, yet also with unwonted pride in the new seriousness of her sex.[6]

As the war dragged on, Wilkinson's facetiousness ceased. She became even more political and was "enchant[ed]" with liberty. "The land of Liberty! How sweet the sound!" she exclaimed in a letter. She was incensed about the contradiction between the ideal of liberty and woman's fettered state, in which a woman was thought "good for nothing except . . . domestic concerns." Men, she wrote, "say we have no business with [political matters], it is not our sphere!" But she was living through a war, making sacrifices, enduring losses. She felt emboldened to challenge men seriously about woman: "Our thoughts can soar aloft, we can form conceptions of things of a higher nature; and have as just a sense of honor, glory, and great actions as these 'Lords of Creation.' What contemptible *earth worms* these [men] make us," she angrily declared.[7] It was a sentiment that had not been much expressed before by the wives and daughters of wealthy southern planters.

The war encouraged such sentiment in all the colonies, as women set about proving their worthiness through their patriotism. Not permitted to fight themselves, women thrust their men into battle as a kind of "surrogate enlistment." Urban legends arose of women so patriotic that they would even sacrifice a beloved husband for their country, such as the New Jersey woman who, like the Roman matrons of old, was reported to have told her spouse as he was going off to war, "I would rather hear that you were left a corpse on the field than that you had played the part of a coward!"[8] Such stories, whether apocryphal or not, were presented as proof of woman's capacity to think on a scale larger than that of the welfare of her family—which, she had been told in earlier eras, was her only responsibility.

Women were actively invested in the war. Though they generally did not fight, thousands of them were voluntarily present at the fighting, following the troops, for whom they did woman's work as nurses, cooks, laundresses, water carriers like the legendary Molly Pitcher, and sex workers—though there was some attempt to ban the last group. Alexander McDougal, the Continental Army colonel in charge of troops stationed in New York City, issued a decree in 1775 stating, "No Woman of Ill Fame Shall be permitted to Come into the Barricks on pain of Being well Watred under a pump." But whatever their position as camp followers, the daring of the women in the proximity of battle did not change men's notions of woman as a timid, weak, and fainthearted creature. The worst thing that could be said of a man in the midst of war was that he was like a woman. A soldier who showed cowardice would not only be cashiered: he might also be forced into a woman's dress and made to march out of camp as the other soldiers threw dung at him.[9]

But a woman who defied the image of womanly weakness by wanting to fight like a man also usually met with outrage. When a "female" from Elizabeth, New Jersey, donned men's clothes and enlisted in the army, Colonel William Barton, suspecting her ruse, forced her to submit to a public examination. The "truth" was discovered, the colonel reported with hilarity, by the examiner "pulling out the Teat of a Plump Young Girl, which caused Great divertion." Barton, unimpressed by the soldier's patriotism, "ordered the Drum to beat her Threw the Town with the whores march."[10]

It is impossible to know how many other individuals who had been assigned female at birth tried to escape the limitations imposed on a woman's patriotism and to become a soldier during the Revolutionary War. It is tempting to speculate in our contemporary parlance that those who did may have been transgender or gender nonbinary, but since such concepts and terms were not available in their day, they were seen only as "women disguised as men." One of them, Deborah Sampson—who at five feet nine inches was taller than most men of her day—served for seventeen months under the name Robert Shurtleff. Sustaining multiple battle wounds, Shurtleff kept secret the musket ball lodged in a thigh and thus evaded detection as a woman by the doctor who treated the head wound. Falling ill months later, Shurtleff was discovered by another attending physician to have bound breasts. More fortunate than Barton's victim—perhaps because of having been wounded in combat and having served heroically for well over a year—Shurtleff was dismissed with an honorable discharge and was even eventually awarded a federal pension: but only after no less a personage than Paul Revere convinced a congressman to sponsor Shurtleff's cause by pointing out that "she had returned to a more feminine role as wife and mother," marrying Benjamin Gannett and bearing him three children.[11]

Most women did not go to the war, but the war came to them. Margaret Hill Morris, the widow of a dry-goods merchant who was raising their four children alone, recorded the six months of occupation and fighting (from December 1776 to June 1777) in her small city of Burlington, New Jersey. "I felt myself quite Sick I was ready to faint. I thought of my own lonely situation, no husband to cheer with the voice of love, my Sinking spirits. My little flock too without a father to direct them how to Steer," she wrote when she heard that soldiers had marched into town. Much of her journal is about the frights and fog of war: the commandant of the Hessians ordering his men to pillage houses in which arms or ammunition were concealed; the commodore of the Continental Army troops "order[ing] up 4 Gallies to fire on the town wherever 2, or 3 persons shoud be seen together"; rumors that the whole city would be set on fire; a deafening cannonade of heavy gunfire that continued for hours and lit up the sky like a shower of falling stars; and Morris and her children fleeing to the cellar of their home until the firing stopped.[12]

Her fright was mixed with feeling for the suffering all around her. As a Quaker she did not take sides in the war. But she hid a Loyalist in a secret room in her home because she knew that the Patriots, possessed by "the spirit of the Divil [that] rove[d] through Town in the shape of Tory Hunters," would kill him. On a cold night in January 1777, running across exhausted soldiers sleeping in the house next door, Morris wrote, "My heart melted to see such a number of my fellow creatures lying like swine on the floor, . . . many of them without blankets to cover them." When the soldiers marched out of Burlington her first thought, very different from the thoughts she had when they marched in, was that "my heart sinks when I think of the numbers unprepared for death who will probably be sent in a few days to appear before the Judge of heaven."[13]

Such experiences made women feel deeply implicated in the war. Yet they had no voice to make their feelings known. Women could not deliver lectures to a mixed audience. They were excluded from political meetings. They could not publish political editorials under their own names. Yet voiceless as they were, they were encouraged to send a message to the British that, as William Tennent III, a southern preacher and politician, wrote in the *South Carolina Gazette*, "American patriotism extends even to the Fair Sex."[14] For virtually the first time in the history of the colonies, women were being invited by men to play a public role. They were called on to protest the American Revenue Act of 1764 and the Stamp Act of 1765, through which the British levied taxes on sugar, wines, cambric, calico, and even playing cards. Women did the shopping for their family. They could be patriots through boycotts.

They embraced their task. In Boston they formed the Daughters of Liberty, an auxiliary organization to the Sons of Liberty, which had been started in 1765 by merchants in that city to protest British taxation. "Let the Daughters of Liberty nobly arise," Hannah Griffitts rallied "female patriots" in her 1768 poem. The Daughters of Liberty spread from Massachusetts to Connecticut, Rhode Island, Pennsylvania, and New Jersey. In southern states women formed groups such as the Edenton Ladies Patriotic Guild of North Carolina.[15] The organizations gave women an unwonted public presence.

However, as newspaper stories suggested, men took care to present the women's activities as no great departure from woman's sphere. "Eighteen Daughters of Liberty, young ladies of good reputation, [gathered] to declare as a body that the Stamp Act was unconstitutional, and that they would purchase no more British manufactures until it was repealed," one newspaper reported—emphasizing that the young ladies were mindful of their truest feminine "power": they had vowed to "spurn any suitor who refused to oppose [the Stamp Act]."[16]

Women were encouraged to take action again by the Townshend Act in 1767, which taxed items such as glass and tea, and the Tea Act in 1773, which further increased the tax. If women bought tea, Tennent dramatically warned them, it would be "paid for by the blood of your sons." Though tea had been not only a staple in the family diet but crucial to women's "tea parties," women wrote pledges swearing off imported tea. Newspaper editorials heaped praise on those who "made their breakfast upon rye coffee," which the housewife could brew from roasted rye, and those who, "to their great honour, preferred the balsamic Hyperion," concocted from raspberry leaves.[17] Red clover, chamomile, and goldenrod too were used to brew "Liberty Teas," as they were called. Women of all classes and generations claimed their patriotism through the issue of tea. The journal *The Spy* published a poem by a seamstress, touted by the editor as "an aged and very zealous Daughter of Liberty":

> Look out poor Boston make a stand
> Don't suffer any tea to land
> For if it once gets footing here
> Then farewell Liberty most dear.[18]

Women recognized that they had been given a rare opportunity to make a public and political statement, and they took advantage of it with fervor. Women's boycotts extended to all British imports. To avoid buying imported clothing, spinning once again became a chief activity of colonial women. They held spinning bees everywhere, spinning cloth while venting their anger at British oppression. The *Providence Gazette* gushed with approbation for the young women of a local Daughters of Liberty group who "exhibited a fine example of industry, by spinning from sunrise until dark and displayed a spirit for saving their sinking country rarely to be found among persons of more age and experience." In the summer of 1775, when it was announced by the army that 13,000 warm coats would be needed by the soldiers that winter, women got to work. As a young Connecticut woman wrote in her diary, they "spun short thread. . . . Spun linen. . . . Hatchelled flax . . . carded two pounds of whole wool, and felt Nationly [sic]." Their response to British tyranny was the first time that large numbers of American women had the opportunity to feel "Nationly." They were demonstrating that though they could not carry a gun or fire a cannon in the Continental Army, they could do battle in their own way. As a New York woman proclaimed, they would be "a fighting army of amazones . . . armed with spinning wheels."[19]

Even upper-class ladies, unaccustomed as they were to work, rolled up their sleeves. In 1780, in the midst of the war, Esther de Berdt Reed, wife of the governor of Pennsylvania, penned a broadside titled "The Sentiments of an American Woman," in which she declared women to be as committed to patriotism as men were. Reed had been a model of domesticity, having had six children in eight years, but she envisioned a heroic public role for women too. She pointed to Judith and Deborah in the Old Testament, Joan of Arc, and the matrons of Rome—all patriots who stepped out of woman's habitual role for the good of their country. She reminded her readers of the "famous sieges where the women have been seen forgetting the weakness of their sex, building new walls, digging trenches with their feeble hands," and even "darting the missile weapons on the enemy." American women too longed to prove their patriotism in the war against the British, Reed claimed.[20]

She was not asking that women literally be allowed to "dart the missile weapons on the enemy," of course. But she did want women to be able to step outside the confines of woman's sphere to show their patriotism. Her idea was to form the Ladies Association of Philadelphia, an organization of upper-class ladies who would go door-to-door in both rich and poor neighborhoods, distributing copies of Reed's "Sentiments of an American Woman" and asking for money to help the soldiers. It was not exactly like "digging trenches with their feeble hands," but it was a significant departure from what upper-class ladies did. Within a few weeks they had received contributions from 1,600 donors. Other Ladies Associations formed in New Jersey, Maryland, and Virginia and raised thousands more dollars by knocking on doors. It was a remarkable achievement—ladies breaking out of the rigidity of their roles, mixing with all classes, and working for a common good.

Reed hoped to use the money to bolster the spirits of the battle-weary soldiers by giving each one of them two dollars in gold or silver to use as they liked. Ready to hand over the impressive bounty that the various Ladies Associations collected, Reed went to the commander in chief of the Continental Army, General George Washington, whom she knew well because her husband had been his aide-de-camp. Washington told her he thought that making a gift of money to each soldier was a bad idea. He suggested that the ladies did not understand these men. The soldiers would squander their two dollars on drink.

Washington proposed that the ladies do something much more ladylike: they could make shirts for the soldiers. Each woman could personalize the shirt she made by embroidering her name on it.

Reed tried again on behalf of the women of the Ladies Association, who were hugely disappointed that Washington had quashed their initiative. This time she politely argued with the general in a letter:

> An idea prevails among the ladies that the soldiers would not be so much gratified by bestowing an article to which they look upon themselves entitled from public funds as in some other method which would convey more fully the idea of Reward for past Services & incitement to future Duty. Those who are of this opinion propose the whole of the money to be changed into hard dollars [gold or silver], and giving each soldier two, to be entirely at his own disposal.[21]

But Washington could not be budged from his conviction that he knew his men better than naïve ladies could possibly understand. The women deferred; Washington was after all the commander in chief. The ladies bought linen and made thousands of shirts for the soldiers.

Seven weeks after Reed wrote her letter to Washington, she died of dysentery at the age of thirty-four. The work was carried on by the daughter of Benjamin Franklin, and in February 1781, the soldiers got their shirts, with the name of each maker (whether she was a married woman or not) flirtatiously embroidered on the garment she had made. After the shirts were delivered, Washington thanked the women. Their work demonstrated, he wrote, that their "love of country is blended with those softer domestic virtues, which have always been allowed to be more peculiarly your own."[22]

But disappointing as the outcome of the Ladies Association project was, it represented the first large instance in which women, working across several colonies, shook off the concept of woman as belonging only to the home and family. They had organized in a common pursuit for the state. Their story suggests that in responding to British oppression, women were beginning to imagine themselves in roles that stepped outside the prevailing notion of woman. They wanted a place in public life. It also suggests that what that place might be beggared the imagination of the men who guarded the gates.

Women were still far from being able to formulate anything that approximated what would eventually be called a feminist movement. Rudimentary as it was, however, their involvement in protesting the status quo of British authority and their ambition to be actors in winning liberty can be seen as analogous to the later movement: Women began in the turbulent, radical 1960s by joining protests against the authority that denied Black people civil rights and involved the country in an unwinnable war. But soon they were also challenging the attitudes and laws that kept them down as women. In the same way, at the birth of the founding of the United States, women began by protesting the authority of the tyrannical British, but soon they were also challenging the authority that kept a woman in her place. Their eighteenth-century woman's voice would not permit them to shout a challenge—how could they have garnered the confidence to be vehement against the authority of Washington, Adams, and Thomas Jefferson? But their murmur was distinct.

WOMAN AFTER THE WAR OF INDEPENDENCE

"Whence arises the right of men to govern women?"
—JOHN ADAMS, *Papers of John Adams* (1776)[23]

The War of Independence triggered social changes because the moral justification for hierarchies had been called into question: first, the hierarchy that demanded the citizen's deference to the crown; and then by analogy, the hierarchies that demanded the apprentice's slavish service to the master and the child's absolute obedience to the parent. Yet two hierarchies continued to be considered legitimate: those rooted in race and gender.[24]

Unlike many white colonial women, enslaved people had little illusion that the Patriots would liberate them if they were victorious in the war against the British. In fact, a British victory seemed more promising to the slaves, because they shared a common enemy: the white colonists. In 1774, a delegation of enslaved men in Boston urged General Thomas Gage, the British military governor of Massachusetts, to help set them free. They addressed Gage with a man-to-man plea they believed would cut through differences of race and condition of servitude. Slavery destroyed the Black family: How can a husband cleave to his wife if he is subject to the will of the slave master? they asked. And "how can a wife submit themselves to there husband in all things?" [sic].[25] (Gage was too busy making sure that the Port of Boston would stay closed, in retaliation for the 1773 Tea Party, to concern himself with granting Black men the same rights over women that white men might assume.)

In the South, the Earl of Dunmore, who was the Crown's representative in Virginia, appealed to enslaved people to join the British cause. Dunmore issued a proclamation in November 1775 pledging that all "Negroes" willing to bear arms for King George would be freed from slavery. About eight hundred enslaved people seized the opportunity and were outfitted in military garb that included a sash with the inscription "Liberty to Slaves." Their numbers included enslaved women, who may have hoped to serve in the same capacities as white women did in the Revolutionary army—as cooks, laundresses, nurses, and so on. Thousands more slaves stole behind the British lines, hoping to be set free. In December 1775, when nine enslaved people (including two women) tried to reach Dunmore in Norfolk, they were captured by the Patriots. The *Virginia Gazette* reported that the Patriots would be "ma[king] examples" of them—that is, the enslaved women and men were to be hanged, as was everyone caught siding with the British. A fifteen-year-old enslaved girl who had run off to join Dunmore's regiment was captured by her owner, who beat her with eighty lashes and poured hot embers on her wounds.[26]

With the British defeat, Dunmore's promise went untested. Enslaved women in the South were soon even worse off than they had been before the War of Independence. The invention of the cotton gin in 1793 meant that most enslaved women—since they were "equal" to enslaved men—would now be enduring backbreaking labor in the cotton fields together with the men.[27]

Slavery was gradually abolished in the North, beginning with Vermont in 1777 and everywhere in the northern states by the early nineteenth century. But though northern Black women were no longer enslaved, they suffered on account of race (just as Black men did), and they suffered on account of sex (just as white women did). If they had to support themselves, they suffered from both the restrictions imposed on Blacks and those imposed on women. A Black woman could be a cook, a washerwoman, a domestic worker, a waitress in a tavern, or a seamstress. Even if she was the only one bringing money into her home to support her family, if she had a son over the age of sixteen and no husband, census takers listed her son as head of the household.[28]

Wherever free Blacks might emulate the society around them, Black women—no longer "equal" to Black men—were likely to be reduced to the dominant culture's idea of woman. Some pushed back, but their victory was hard won and only partial. Jarena Lee, a free-born Black woman, had been a live-in maid in New Jersey when, as she wrote in her autobiography, she had a visitation: she experienced first an "impressive silence" and then heard a voice demanding of her, "Go preach the Gospel!" She answered, "No one will believe me," because women did not preach. When the voice promised to put the words in her mouth, she feared that Satan had gotten into her head. However, her next vision (of a pulpit with a Bible on it) convinced her that her calling was genuine. Lee belonged to the newly formed African Methodist Episcopal (AME) Church, which had grown out of the Free African Society, a mutual-aid organization established by free Blacks in Philadelphia in 1787. When she told Richard Allen, the bishop, about her visions, his response was that the church "did not call for women preachers."[29]

In earlier eras, women—Black or white—might have had more difficulty challenging a male authority figure. Lee did not hesitate. "Unseemly" as a woman preaching might appear to Allen, she argued, "if a man may preach because the Savior died for him, why not the woman, seeing he died for her also?" The bishop was not swayed by her logic. Eight years later, however, he watched her jump to her feet and deliver an impromptu sermon when a visiting minister failed to show up. The spellbound parishioners were enthralled. Allen "now as much believed that [Lee] was called to that work as any of the preachers present," and he authorized her henceforth to preach.[30]

Yet the bishop would not go so far as to give her a pulpit. As an itinerant minister for the AME Church, Lee traveled mostly by foot, walking twelve miles or more a day, all over Pennsylvania, New York, and New Jersey, and later Michigan, Ohio, and even Maryland (though it was a slave state and thus risky for her to be there). She preached, as she wrote in her autobiography, to "well-behaved congregations both coloured and white," who sometimes "fell to the floor under the influence of God's power." Lee claimed to have convinced even those "who had come from curiosity to hear the woman preacher"—such as "a great slave holder" who had previously doubted that Black people had souls. He "had been very cruel, thinking nothing of knocking down a slave with a fence stake." But after hearing her preach, Lee boasted, the slave holder "became greatly altered in his ways for the better." Yet despite her success, as a woman she got no salary from the church and had to pass the plate to subsist. At the end of her life she was forced to rely on charity. The Pennsylvania Abolition Society reported in an obituary that she died wishing she "were done with begging."[31]

Those who harbored the hope that the American Revolution would bring about a huge rethinking of the idea of woman were soon corrected. In March 1776, while John Adams was busy discussing independence from Britain at the Continental Congress in Philadelphia, Abigail, back home in Braintree, Massachusetts, was taking care of their children. She was also supervising the family farm and continuing to manage their finances, making shrewd and judicious investments that would bring the Adams family considerable wealth. It was during this time that Abigail famously wrote to her husband, "In the New Code of Laws which I suppose it will be necessary for you to make, I desire you would Remember the Ladies, and be more generous and favorable to them than your ancestors. Do not put such unlimited power into the hands of the Husbands. Remember all Men would be tyrants if they could."[32]

John answered her half-jokingly, but revealing the fear that many white men must have felt that the rebellion against the British, which upended the status quo, was triggering other upendings. Adams referred in his letter to Indians "slighting their guardians" and "Negroes grow[ing] insolent to their masters." And now, he added, Abigail was giving him "the first intimation that a tribe, more numerous and powerful than all the rest, were grown discontented." It would be "the Despotism of the Petticoat," he quipped.[33]

Yet John did give Abigail's exhortation some serious thought, as his letter to his friend James Sullivan suggests. "Whence arises the right of men to govern women, without their consent?" he asked. The question proved to be rhetorical. Adams concluded that women had to be excluded from the polity and kept under the rule of men for incontrovertible reasons (which were belied by the accomplishments of his own wife): Women were unsuited for dealing with "the great business of life." They were "fittest for domestic cares." To give them a say in government by allowing them to vote would charge them with a duty unnatural to them and would distract them from their innate calling.[34]

Abigail was not the only woman Adams knew who gave the lie to his assumptions about women. He was a great admirer of the intellect of a family friend, Mercy Otis Warren. Warren, whose father, brother, and husband were all leading Patriots, wrote serious political commentary about the tyranny of the British, the Revolutionary War, and even the U.S. Constitution. She also wrote acerbic satires about the Loyalists who sided with the British. She wrote political poetry and personal poetry too. She often published anonymously to forestall critics who thought a woman had no business with political subjects. When she did write using her real name, she felt compelled to be diffident. In her three-volume *History of the Rise, Progress, and Termination of the American Revolution*, she begged the reader's indulgence "in consideration of her sex." In her letters to Adams that touched on political subjects, she was apologetic, telling him, "I ask pardon for touching on war, politicks, or anything . . . so far beyond the line of my sex."[35]

But Adams discounted her modesty, calling her "the most accomplished woman in America." At another point, quite forgetting what he had proclaimed about women in his letter to Sullivan, he gushed further superlatives about her: "Of all the geniuses which have yet arisen in America, there has been none superior." However, his enthusiasm had its limits. Disgruntled with Warren's treatment of him in the final volume of her history of the American Revolution, he retracted his lavish praise in one swoop and sent her back to the sphere of mere woman. As he groused in a letter to his fellow politician Elbridge Gerry, "History is not the province of the ladies."[36]

The U.S. Constitution, which John Adams helped draft, reified women's lowly status. Any young man, barely bearded, as long as he had some property and was white, could vote. He was a full citizen—superior to Abigail Adams, Mercy Otis Warren, and any other woman, no matter her age or sagacity or wealth. There was only one exception to women's disenfranchisement, and it had been established in 1776 by New Jersey's first constitution. The law said that "all inhabitants of this colony" who were adults, had been residents for at least a year, and had wealth of at least fifty pounds could vote in New Jersey elections: "all" meant women too. In 1790, the law was made more specific: women were included in a reference to eligible voters as "he or she," but woman suffrage was limited to unmarried women property owners. A married woman could not vote because her property generally belonged to her husband—in any case, it was assumed that a married woman did not need to vote because her husband represented her at the polls.

Limited though the law was with regard to women's enfranchisement, it was still unpopular, as a 1797 satirical ditty titled "Freedom of Elections" suggested. Published in a Newark newspaper and illustrated with comic scenes of mobs of women parading to the polls ("cheek by Jole [jowl], Sir!"), the piece derided women who were "now the oracles of the laws" and no longer followed "woman's occupation." Instead of "direct[ing] the wheel and loom," they dared "direct the nation." The horrors of enfranchised (and therefore masculinized) women were summed up in poetic lines about man's worst fear:

> To Congress, lo! Widows shall go,
> Like metamorphos'd witches!
> Cloth-ed in the dignity of state,
> And eke! In coat and breeches![37]

In 1807 the New Jersey law was amended to limit suffrage to white male property owners. By 1856, the requirement of property ownership for suffrage had been abolished in every state. All white men, even the poorest, could exercise their rights of citizenship and vote. In 1870, the Fifteenth Amendment gave any man, regardless of color, full citizenship and the right to vote. Women, white and Black, continued to be as excluded from the polity as were children, felons, and lunatics.

Women also continued to suffer under the old law of coverture that remained unchanged. Grace Growden, daughter of one of the richest men in Philadelphia, was one of the first victims under the law in the newly established republic. In 1758, her father, upset when her eye was caught by a young man from the middling class, married her off to Joseph

Galloway, an up-and-coming lawyer from a prominent family. Since Grace's father had no sons, he bestowed on her a huge dowry, to sweeten the match for his prospective son-in-law. Growden demanded no prenuptial agreement to reserve any part of his gift to his daughter in her own name—a sign of his total faith in the groom. The dowry made Galloway very wealthy, since under coverture laws all assets that the wife brought into a marriage, unless stated otherwise in a prenuptial contract, belonged to the husband.

Galloway eventually became a well-known figure in Pennsylvania: speaker of the Pennsylvania House of Representatives, friend of luminaries such as Ben Franklin, and a delegate to the First Continental Congress. There he argued fervently that rather than sever ties with the British, the colonists should try to reconcile with them. It was not a popular position. When his proposal for a compromise was rejected, Galloway broke with his old colleagues and became a Loyalist. The British appointed him superintendent of police during their occupation of Philadelphia. Naturally his position made him a pariah to the rebel Patriots, some of whom placed a box on his front porch containing a noose and a note that said, "Hang yourself or we shall do it for you."[38] Galloway was officially deemed a traitor, and with the British defeat, the General Assembly of Pennsylvania convicted him of high treason. He fled for his life to England.

Grace acquiesced to his plan to take with him Elizabeth, their daughter and only surviving child. Grace offered to remain in Philadelphia to protect the properties she had been given in her dowry and the large inheritance she had received after her father's death in 1770. But Grace was a lady, oblivious to the nuances of law; and no one—not even her lawyer husband—had made clear to her that the property was not hers but his.

She did not fare well alone in Philadelphia. She learned that the Patriots were merciless in their confiscation of the wealth of all Loyalists, and when she heard they were coming for her, she locked herself in her house. They broke in and found her hiding, as she wrote in a letter to her husband: "I have been taken by the Arme & led out of my own House[.] All my inheritance taken from me[.] My Father's House in the Country in possession of Strangers[.] Left without Friends or Relatives to take me in." To her daughter she wrote of her determination to be brave though she was dependent on the kindness of strangers for food and shelter: even her "chariot," as she called her carriage, had been taken from her. She was mortified by want and degradation. She had been sick for months, her body broken and her "nerves very weak," she wrote Elizabeth in disjointed sentences that revealed her anguish. One evening, coming home to her lodging, "in such a Storm of Rain as I was never out in before in my Life and just as I got home, my own Chariot Drove by me this made me feel but I drove it of [sic] in a moment knowing that all Sublunary things have their vicissitudes."[39]

Grace soon discovered that her project to save her fortune was hopeless. As she recorded in her diary, when she attempted to reclaim what she thought she owned, she learned from a lawyer, for the first time, that she owned nothing: "When a lady marries (unless by a special reserve of her lands in the hand of Trustees, made before the [marriage] contract)," the lawyer wrote her, "the use and profits and the real estate belonging to her rests in her husband. . . . This estate acquired by wedlock the gentleman can sell. It may be seised by creditors and applied to their relief. It may be lost by attaint," by which was meant that if a man committed a serious crime, the property that had automatically become his by marriage could be confiscated by the state and be forever lost to his wife.[40]

Grace died alone and in poverty in 1782. Joseph Galloway remained safe in England until his death, twenty-one years later. It would be another century before all U.S. states passed married woman's property acts, which protected the property that a woman brought into a marriage from being seized for her husband's debts or crimes.

EDUCATING FUTURE MOTHERS OF SONS OF THE REPUBLIC

"A peculiar and suitable education."

—BENJAMIN RUSH, *Thoughts Upon Female Education* (1787)[41]

Despite the persistence of the old laws that kept women in their place and the new laws that confirmed women were not worthy of citizenship, the role of women during the revolutionary years did spark some change in the idea of woman, most notably with regard to their education in a republic. Eliza Southgate, daughter of a wealthy doctor in Scarborough, Maine, was sent to Massachusetts to study at one of the many schools for young ladies that were being established in the years after the Revolutionary War. She was fourteen years old and had not been away from her parents and eleven siblings before. She wrote them that she suffered from homesickness but nevertheless wished to extend her time at school, to "drink freely of the fountain of knowledge" and "possess more useful knowledge than I at present do." Despite her eagerness to learn, she was allowed only fifteen months at school before her father called her home. He had sent her to school, after all, only to be "finished," as was the new fashion. As she later wrote in frustration, she was forced to leave school precipitously, "with a head full of something, tumbled in without order or connection." For the next two or three years, her days were taken up with the usual routine of young ladies of her class: the "toil, bustle, and fatigue," as she half-complained, of "parties, plays, balls, etc.," the purpose of which was to catch a suitable husband.[42]

Eliza Southgate, still rankled by her lot several years later, protested to her cousin, Moses Porter, that nature had not implanted great differences of intellect and personality between men and women and that the differences seemed to exist only because all woman's "strong, energetic qualities [were forced] to sleep in obscurity . . . and at last die for the want of exercise." She particularly resented the fact that woman's pursuit of knowledge was considered "infringing the prerogative of man." Women must be allowed to "cultivate the qualities with which we are endowed," Southgate argued.[43] But aside from exercising her intelligence in her letters, she had little opportunity in her short life to "infringe the prerogative of man." She married when she was nineteen and died, probably of puerperal fever, after the birth of her second child at the age of twenty-five.

Women's protests about their limited sphere were met with vexed counterprotests. The "prerogative of man" that Southgate wished to challenge was jealously guarded by men who tried to shame women for "infringing." The essay "Animadversions on the Affectation of Ill-Suited Characters of the Female Sex" had ranted in the mid-eighteenth century about the growing phenomenon of the female who "lays aside [her] natural Character" and lets "Rage of Ambition or Pride of Learning agitate and swell those Breasts, where only Love, Friendship, and tender Care should dwell." Panic that learning might defeminize women continued into the postrevolutionary years when a new worry emerged that, as John Adams suggested, the idea of revolution might expand to the revolt of women. A 1788 *American Magazine* article, "An Address to the Ladies," warned readers that a woman's "strong attachment to books [will keep] a man from approaching her with the offer of his heart." Alphonzo, the article's pseudonymous author, reminded females, "To be lovely you must be content to be women [and] leave the masculine virtues, and the profound researches of study to the province of the other sex." The obsession with the idea that a woman would become like a man if she were educated spread to the pulpit. John S. J. Gardiner (the most influential Episcopal clergymen of Boston and rector of Trinity Church) sounded very much like Alphonzo when he claimed in a sermon that "women of masculine minds"—that is, those who claim for themselves what should be the prerogative of men—"have generally masculine manners." And, he warned, "a robustness of person is ill calculated to inspire the tender passion."[44]

New concerns were sparked when a few women failed to follow those warnings and began formulating a radical idea: women should be allowed to pursue higher education. "To a Lady, Who Expressed the Desire of Seeing an University Established for Women," a scolding poem published in 1792 in the popular *American Museum, or Universal Magazine*, was indicative of the anxieties such desires elicited. Despite its playful tone, the author had serious admonitions—hinting, yet again, that a woman would turn into a hermaphrodite (or worse) and be destroyed as a so-called natural woman if she fell prey to the perversely "tempting arms" of science (personified in the poem as female). "For shouldst thou feel her strict embrace / Farewell to ev'ry winning grace," he cautioned. He ended by advising women how to avoid that terrible fate:

> Keep the station heav'n design'd,
> And reign triumphant o'er mankind;
> Nor ever wish, perverse to see
> A FEMALE UNIVERSITY.[45]

However, in the postrevolutionary years a competing dialogue appeared that presented female education as a patriotic necessity. Far from masculinizing a woman, it would permit her to better fulfill her womanly responsibilities while also serving her country. As a mother, proponents of female education argued, a woman was her sons' first teacher and hence made a lasting mark on them. An educated woman could play her part in the democracy by helping her sons become educated citizens.

It was a novel idea, and it had to be sold to the doubting. The proponents bolstered its justification with careful assurances that a woman's education would not interfere one whit with her other domestic duties. Not long after Jefferson advised his young daughter to prepare for ladydom by minding her music, drawing, letter writing, and French, a spate of "female schools" or "Young Ladies Academies" with more serious curricula began to proliferate. They were often geared toward girls of the middling class whose parents were somewhat less concerned than Jefferson or Southgate's father had been with fashioning a lady.

When Benjamin Rush, a medical doctor and one of the signers of the Declaration of Independence, opened the Young Ladies Academy of Philadelphia in 1787, he presented the argument that would become the standard justification for female education: America was now a democracy, which meant that every (white) male citizen had an equal share in its liberty and might be called to help govern the country. Those facts necessitated that "our ladies should be qualified to a certain degree by a peculiar and suitable education, to concur in instructing their sons in the principles of liberty and government." To prepare her for "Republican Motherhood," a young lady must therefore be taught serious subjects: history, geography, and math. She should also learn bookkeeping, for the sake of the family she will have—in case her husband needed her assistance or she became widowed and had to be the executrix of his will.[46]

Rush dismissed the fears of detractors that it was "unfit to [a woman's] domestic character" to educate her. He called such fears "the prejudice of little minds," and he was careful to make clear that the character of a woman would not be changed by this learning because he had built in a safeguard: in addition to academic instruction, she would be given "regular instruction in the Christian religion"—which, Rush declared in 1787, would inject her with a "sense of religious and moral obligation" and so "the government of [her] will be easy and agreeable." That is, she would continue to know her place, and despite her education she would not venture into man's domain and usurp his prerogatives. Indeed, Rush was no radical revolutionary. He genuinely believed in woman's knowing her place, as he made clear in a letter of advice to a bride-to-be in 1792, in which he sounded very much like Cotton Mather writing in 1692. "Don't be offended when I add that from the day that you marry you must have no will of your own," Rush wrote. "The subordination of your sex to ours is enforced by nature, by reason, and by revelation."[47]

Rush's ideas about female education influenced other founders of schools for girls during those years. In 1789, when William Woodbridge opened the Young Ladies Academy in Medford, Massachusetts, he declared that he hoped to inculcate in the pupils "true discipline of mind, and application to the solid branches of knowledge," which would be necessary for them as future mothers raising their sons in a democracy. His detractors, Woodbridge said, had asked him, "When girls become scholars, who is to make the pudding and pies?" He responded by contending that "science would never reach its acme, while the influential half of our race, to whom the training of the rising generation is committed, were left in ignorance of it." However, like Rush, he also felt compelled to avow unambiguously that the essential female character would not be changed by his educational principles. Young ladies could engage in serious study, he assured the worried, "without disqualifying themselves for domestic [duties]."[48]

The anxiety to justify the education of women was palpable in many of its proponents, who sometimes even modulated the education part by emphasizing the domestic-training part. Rev. John Cosens Ogden, an Episcopal rector who ministered to the Female Academy of Portsmouth, New Hampshire, declared at the opening of the academy in 1791 that educating girls in the use of "the needle and distaff" would "go hand in hand with the important branches of reading, writing, arithmetic, accounts, geography, history, and poetry." To emphasize further that he was not advocating the masculinization of woman through education but rather sought to make her not only ready for Republican motherhood but also more fit for her mate in a democracy, Ogden proclaimed: "Every man, by the Constitution, is born with an equal right to be elected to the highest office. And every woman is born with an equal right to be the wife of the most eminent man."[49]

Discussion about female education in the eighteenth century centered on young white ladies of the middle and upper classes. Lower-class women were generally left out of talk of Republican motherhood: it was assumed that they would not be educating sons for full citizenship because only property owners could vote. Black women, even those who were free, were also outside consideration since their sons could not vote either. Not until the nineteenth century was there any concern about offering education to Black females. Early attempts were met with mean resistance. In 1832, Prudence Crandall, a Quaker who founded an academy for young ladies in a prosperous corner of Connecticut, admitted to the school a twenty-year-old Black woman named Sarah Harris, the daughter of free parents who were respectable farmers near the village of Canterbury. Harris had done well in a district school and now hoped to prepare for teaching Black children. But the white parents of Crandall's students, judging that no Black girl could be a young lady, withdrew their daughters from the academy and had Crandall arrested. Crandall became a cause célèbre.

"What! Imprison a woman for keeping a grammar school!," an outraged editorial in the *Vermont Chronicle* exclaimed. "Much as we impugn the doctrines of the abolitionists, we cannot but feel indignation at proceedings not only so ungallant and so savoring of a barbarous age, but withal so unconstitutional."[50] Crandall spent just one night in jail.

She closed the school and then reopened it, pointedly renaming it an academy for Young Ladies and Little Misses of Color and announcing that she would be offering as serious a curriculum as that in other young ladies' academies (history, geography, philosophy, chemistry, and so on). Twenty students—not only from Connecticut towns but also from Boston and New York—signed up. The townspeople held numerous protest meetings, harassed the pupils, broke the school windows, and poisoned its well with manure. Crandall, forced to give up, left town.[51]

The American revolution may have served as inspiration for upper- and middle-class white women who hoped to escape the strictest confines of their place in society, but it seemed impossible for them to envision a truly revolutionary transformation in the idea of woman. Change had to be slow and incremental. Even women who wrote fervently in favor of female education exercised caution in not asking too much. It was radical enough to imagine a woman being allowed a serious education.

As a girl, Judith Sargent Murray—born in 1751 into a wealthy merchant family in Gloucester, Massachusetts—made extensive use of the family library to educate herself. Her father was so charmed by the precocious poems she wrote as a nine-year-old that he read them aloud to the family. He even permitted her to sit in on the lessons of her younger brother, Winthrop, while a tutor prepared the boy to enter the elite Boston Latin School and later Harvard College. But it would not have occurred to Judith's father to hire a tutor just for her: in the 1760s there was, of course, no Boston Latin School or Harvard for girls.

Judith fulfilled all that was expected of her by marrying a man of her class, a sea captain named John Stevens. She was then eighteen; he was ten years her senior. It appears that they were not well suited. She later wrote, reflecting on her unhappy marriage, that she had been too "hasty to dawn my matrimonial lot." In a 1784 essay, the first she published, she drew on autobiography to observe that if girls could be taught in childhood to value their "mental accomplishments," they would not accept the first proposal they received out of fear of "being stigmatized with that dreaded title, an Old Maid."[52]

But her status as Mrs. John Stevens did not squelch her intellectual longings. She dabbled in writing poems and essays, though for many years she did not dare to publish them. In 1779, in the midst of the Revolutionary War and the ubiquitous discourse about liberty, she wrote an essay (not published until 1790) about women's lack of liberty, to which she gave the revolutionary title, "On the Equality of the Sexes." Without revealing the autobiography behind the essay, Judith Sargent Stevens poured out the sadness of her own experiences as a girl. The opportunity to acquire knowledge is denied females, she said, but their ignorance is no proof that they are inferior in reason or judgment. Man and woman are by nature equal, she bluntly proclaimed—perhaps the first time such a claim was made in a published document (her ideas foreshadowed Mary Wollstonecraft's highly influential A *Vindication of the Rights of Woman*, published in 1792). The observable differences between boys and girls are largely the result of the differences in the customary treatment of them, she wrote: boys are glorified, but girls are denigrated. That treatment forms their "second nature": man enjoying "*apparent* superiority," and woman suffering a "mortifying consciousness of inferiority."[53]

Though she wrote from the deep bitterness of her own experience, she nonetheless felt obliged to reassure her readers that a woman could be educated and still not neglect her domestic duties. Seeming to understand the limits on what women might aspire to, in "On the Equality of the Sexes" she concluded that women could have ideas that are "worthy of rational beings" and at the same time "pursu[e] the needle, or the superintendency of the family."[54]

Judith Stevens was widowed in 1786. Two years later she married John Murray, a liberal preacher and founder of the Universalist Church in America. His encouragement of her intellectual pursuits made her far happier and optimistic than she had ever been before, and her changed personal circumstances were at least in part responsible for the euphoria of her later writing. In a 1798 essay about the "Future Prospects of Women in this 'Enlightened Age,'" she enthused over the "happy revolution which the past few years has made" in the position of woman. The bad old days when "the use of the needle was the principal attainment which was thought necessary for a woman" were finally over, she declared. There were now numerous schools for young ladies where they could spend their time in serious studies, which would have been inconceivable when she was a girl.[55]

But despite Judith Sargent Murray's celebration of progress, she understood that ideas about a woman's primary function and her fundamental limitations remained unchanged from what they had been in the earliest colonial days. She even felt obliged to assure her readers in 1798, just as she had in "On the Equality of the Sexes" in 1779, that even if a woman spent time on studies "more elevated and elevating" than the use of the needle, her children, spouse, and home would not be neglected. Woman, she wrote, would always "assume with alacrity [her] arduous employment" with regard to her duties as wife and mother.[56]

Though Murray exulted that "in this enlightened age" women were being permitted "to share the blessings of equality," she still could not envision women's freedom from "arduous" domestic responsibilities. Nor could she envision equality in polity. She was passionately interested in politics and wrote often on political subjects, but her political essays were published under pseudonyms—the Reaper, the Gleaner, or Mr. Virgilius—that hid her sex, lest her ideas be discounted as coming from a woman. Female pseudonyms such as "Constantia" or "Honora" she reserved for her nonpolitical essays. As deeply as she thought about political questions, and as much as she desired a voice (though a pseudonymous one) in political dialogue, she never dreamed of demanding that women be given the right to vote or to hold political office. It remained impossible even for her to imagine "equality" as signifying such a departure from the place where women had long before been set.

4.
Woman Enters the Public Sphere

•

THE NINETEENTH CENTURY

Nature made woman too delicate for "the Great Business of Life," John Adams had written. But nature also played a role in elevating her to new importance in the rhetoric of the republic. Nature had made woman less susceptible than man to raging desires. Not driven by uncontrolled appetites as men often were, women alone could fix men's manners and morals. "In what an exalted rank in the scale of existence has the God of Nature placed the lovely sex?" the author of "Female Influence" asked in *New-York Magazine* in 1795. Woman's glorious role was to "banish vice and folly from the earth," he grandiloquently declared.[1] No matter that the Constitution denied her first-class citizenship—the part she had to play was much greater than that of a mere citizen.

WOMAN AS MAN'S MORAL SUPERIOR

"The reformation of the world is in her power."
— "Female Influence" (1795)[2]

The very soul of the new nation was in women's hands, men would now have them believe. As the influential Unitarian preacher Joseph Buckminster of Boston declaimed to the women in his congregation in 1810, "We look to you, ladies, to raise the standard of character in our own sex." Women's role, Buckminster said, was to "guard and fortify" society against all manner of vice. They were to be the preserver and enforcer of the pubescent country's morals. This was the lofty notion of woman that was promulgated in the next decades, and women—especially those of the growing middle class, whites as well as free Blacks—embraced the task, often with a vengeance.[3] It was an opportune proposition. An army of women reformers arose. Men in the new republic were busy in their ever-expanding sphere of business and politics. Now woman's sphere might expand, too. She would remake the new country in her own morally pure image.

Mary Ann Brigham Brown, wife of a Baptist preacher and editor of *The Golden Rule*, one of the many female reform journals that emerged in the first half of the nineteenth century, exhorted women to become moral leaders because even the church had failed though it had lifted its voice against men's wickedness. Now was woman's time to show her mettle. She must consider herself "inferior by nature to no man," Brown declared. It was the woman who must teach men to be good. She must fight drunkenness, prostitution (blamed solely on men), and especially slavery because it forced enslaved women to endure from men "the most lawless and shameful system of licentiousness."[4]

Women gave each other permission to articulate raw anger that they would have felt compelled to suppress in the past, before they were deemed man's moral superior. An 1838 editorial in *Friend of Virtue*, another journal of the female moral reform movement, told women that the fight against licentiousness was woman's work and could not be left to men, who were innately untrustworthy on sexual matters. "Can we expect the wolf, ravenous for his prey, to throw up a barrier to protect the defenseless sheep? As well might we expect this, as to expect that men as a body will take measures to redress the wrongs of woman," the author declared. Men had always gotten away with their misbehavior toward women, but now women, united in moral power, would end men's wicked privilege. "A new era has commenced. Woman has erected a standard, and laid down the principle, that man shall not trample on her rights, and on the honor of her sex, with impunity," the author told the female moral reformers, exhorting them to "combine their strength and exert their influence."[5]

Free Black women too used militant rhetoric to exhort one another to take action. Mary Still, a teacher in Philadelphia, declared in an earnest pamphlet addressed to "the Females of the African Methodist Episcopal Church" that "the moral or degraded condition of society depends solely on the influence of woman." In grand verse she urged Black women of the church to perform their soldierly duty in the battle against social evils:

> Awake, ye Daughters of Bethel,
> No longer in idleness repose,
> Gird on the armor of bold resolution,
> And go forth to meet your foes.[6]

Women all over the country, in both cities and towns, heeded these calls to fix men's morals. They flocked to reform movements that were aimed at getting rid of all the social depravities. They undertook to clean house on a large scale. It was a task both familiar and revolutionary. Woman's sacred duty would be not only to police immorality and other bad behaviors in her own family, but also to steer the entire American family in the right moral direction. Here was a role that allowed her to combine the old notion of woman with a new one. She could acquiesce to the prevailing idea that woman's responsibility was the welfare of the family, while at the same time—ostensibly for the sake of the family—she could assert her right to make her voice heard in the public square.

From the Puritans to the Patriots, men had claimed that God or nature had made woman different from man and set her in an inferior place. Now women dedicated to reform could boast that, yes, of course God or nature had made woman different: but that difference—so far from signifying her inferiority—was her moral superiority. It was a heady notion. For middle-class women particularly, this new consciousness created a common identity and a solidarity among them.[7] They bonded together ardently to wage passionate battles against all of America's moral ills. If women were not allowed a role in running the country, at least they would run its morals.

GETTING RID OF LUST

"Woman alone can make [promiscuous man] tremble like a criminal on the gallows."
—BERIAH GREEN, address to the organizational meeting of the New York Female Moral Reform Society, 1834[8]

The oldest profession flourished in the new republic, along with its cities. Prostitution made a mockery of the widely cherished notion of woman's innate modesty and purity—but if loose women were no longer to be put in stocks as they once had been, how could they be controlled? The early efforts to reform sex workers were run by churchly men who were dedicated to "relieving and reclaiming unhappy females who have Swerv'd from the paths of virtue." However, "virtue," as defined by reformers, was a luxury that was irrelevant to the hard realities of many of these women's lives. As one woman said when asked why she sold her body, "No work, no money, no home."[9]

The first "Magdalen" asylum, sponsored by Quaker, Presbyterian, and Episcopal clergymen, was opened in Philadelphia in 1807. The clergymen announced that they planned to replace the prostitute's habit of vice with values of chastity and industry. They had few takers. At the most, a few dozen prostitutes a year agreed to seek shelter in the Philadelphia Magdalen Asylum, and many of them left before they were reformed. In some years, up to one-third managed to break out of the locked building where they were lodged, scale the high fence that surrounded it, and return to their more familiar life.[10]

Their escape was surely in good part their response to the drudgery for which they were being trained, since jobs such as seamstress, domestic servant, or laundress were virtually the only respectable occupations available to women of the lower class. As one lady of the night who worked in a luxurious brothel scoffed at her would-be rescuer's hope of placing her in a Magdalen asylum, "Do you suppose I would leave a life of splendor and ease?" That would be a poor bargain, she claimed. In her present life she was visited by some of the most distinguished men in New York City, and some weeks she took in as much as $400—more than a respectable servant, washerwoman, or seamstress could make in a year.[11]

Magdalen asylums seldom had much success in rescuing prostitutes. The New York asylum opened in 1812 but, being able to boast few triumphs, shut down in 1818. In 1830, a Presbyterian reformer, Rev. John R. McDowall, founded the House of Refuge for New York's fallen women. However, his efforts were short-lived. McDowall fell out of favor with his church and the politicians who had supported him when he published a shocking report in which he included detailed case histories of prostitutes. Even worse, he claimed that of the 100,000 women who lived in the city, fully 10 percent were "public harlots."[12] New Yorkers were outraged, and McDowall was accused of writing pornography. In the wake of the scandal, he stepped aside in favor of women reformers.

The reclamation of fallen women would seem to be an undertaking from which ladies of modesty and virtue would flee. It required not only acknowledging in broad daylight that people had sex, but also plunging deep into opulent bordellos reeking of perfume and shame or squalid little rooms connected to seedy saloons—places where "devils would blush to look." Yet proper ladies took up the challenge with gusto in cities and rural areas, and in New England, the Mid-Atlantic states, and the upper Midwest. Astonishingly, after the various failures of male-led Magdalen societies, ladies were even urged to undertake the work by respected churchmen. "Woman alone can make [promiscuous man] tremble like a criminal on the gallows. . . . It remains [with woman] to say whether licentiousness shall still triumph over the wrecks of female virtue, or hide its head forever," the Congregationalist minister Beriah Green proclaimed in 1834, increasing the already great enthusiasm of women reformers.[13]

They were also spurred on by an evangelical revivalist movement that attracted millions. The Second Great Awakening encouraged campaigns to eradicate social evils and make the world ready for the imminent second coming of Christ. In the 1820s and 1830s, at the height of the Second Great Awakening, women accounted for two-thirds of the new converts. Charles Finney, the most prominent of the revivalist ministers, urged the female multitudes to step out of their houses and carry on crusades that would bring the message of salvation to everyone. In the all-women prayer groups that the revivalists encouraged, women led prayers, testified to their spiritual experiences, supported one another, and plotted how to save the world.

Lydia Finney, Charles's wife and the mother of his six children, was the perfect model for the new evangelical womanhood: a pious wife and a fiery moral reformer who was vitally concerned with the welfare of her own family and also that of the larger American family. Lydia Andrews had been barely twenty years old when she met the charismatic Charles Finney, who was twelve years her senior and floundering in his faith. It was she who encouraged him to convert. They married in 1824, and she immediately began organizing the women of his church to go door-to-door distributing religious tracts. She led the women's prayer meetings, too, and she eventually convinced her husband that the women of their church must be invited into the men's prayer meetings and be allowed to speak and even to lead mixed meetings. She was ready to lead an entire movement, and the right one soon came along.

In 1834, Charles Finney became the minister of the Chatham Street Chapel in Five Points, an area of New York City that boasted more houses of prostitution than anywhere else in the country. His wife no sooner settled in than she helped found the New York Female Moral Reform Society, whose purpose was to banish the sin of licentiousness from the world. Lydia Finney opened each meeting of the society by reading lurid or condemnatory verses from the Bible about lust, fornication, or adultery, such as:

> "Amnon felt sick for his sister Tamar . . . and he took hold of her and said unto her, come lie with me, my sister."
> "From his roof David saw a woman bathing. Then he sent messengers to get her. She came to him and he slept with her."
> "When lust hath conceived, it bringeth forth sin: and sin, when it is finished, bringeth forth death."

She warned of the terrible dangers of seduction, and she admonished the ladies of the society to be wary on steamboats, in hotels, and at all the other places where immorality thrived.[14]

But the greatest raison d'être of the New York Female Moral Reform Society was to bring purity back to those who had lost it. The society's constitution expressed the group's urgency: "Whereas the sin of licentiousness has made fearful havoc in the world, corrupting all flesh, drowning souls in perdition, and exposing us to the vengeance of a holy God . . . it is the duty of the virtuous to use every consistent moral means to save our country from utter destruction."[15] The ladies would begin to eradicate sin by rescuing the prostitutes who worked in Five Points. Finney and other members of her society descended on the bordellos at dawn on Sunday mornings, waking startled residents and their overnight male guests with thunderous hymns, prayers, and readings from the Bible—bringing church to those who would not go on their own.

But what was unique about Finney's society was that it laid the blame for prostitution not on prostitutes, where blame had always been laid, but on men: the seducers and buyers of flesh. If women were "passionless," without sexual urges, as middle-class women were taught that they were supposed to be, it was inconceivable that a female could have willingly gone into prostitution. In the imagining of the New York Female Moral Reform Society, the prostitute was usually an innocent country girl who had been promised marriage, seduced, and then brought to the city "for the purpose of supplying the market of sin." In other cases, her anxious country parents might have entrusted her to some gentleman in the city for protection, and he had given her "the protection the vulture does the dove." Always after being seduced, she was abandoned to infamy and had no choice but to enter those doors "whose house is the way to hell, going down to the chambers of death."[16]

Men were the guilty ones, "deliberate destroyers of female innocence." It was they, not their victims, who must be punished and publicly shamed if prostitution was to be eradicated: "Impunity in guilt prepares the stronger sex to prey upon the weaker," the female reformers proclaimed in their society's journal, *Advocate of Moral Reform*. The stories of seduction that they published (generally some variation on the same tale of a virgin ruined by a "moral vulture") were written in melodramatic language. For example, one story reported, "In a few short months, this cup of joy was dashed from her trembling hand, and her soul made to pant even for the darkness of the grave. . . . He took an artless girl, ignorant and confiding—and, regardless of consequences, poisoned her mind, and led her on in this polluted way to hell."[17]

The *Advocate of Moral Reform* prevailed upon readers everywhere, particularly in small towns and rural areas, to submit the names of seducers. Prostitutes, too, were bidden to name the names of the men who had first led them astray. The men's names were exposed in the periodical, inviting scorn upon these perpetrators of vice. Always before, woman's social standing had been at the mercy of men. The periodical's campaign against seducers may be the first instance of women's organized revenge in a sex war (a nineteenth-century version of the twenty-first-century Me Too movement). Man's standing in society was now at the mercy of women.[18]

The New York Female Moral Reform Society was lily-white, but its members urged the formation of auxiliary female moral reform societies for free Black women. In 1835, they helped establish an auxiliary at the "colored" Zion's Church in New York. It quickly acquired 138 members, but it soon floundered. After two years its spokeswoman confessed, "We have not been able to accomplish much as yet." Despairing of the slow progress toward moral reform in the free Black community, the New York Female Moral Reform Society resolved at its next annual meeting that it would help. Members pledged that the pages of the *Advocate of Moral Reform* would now "be open to the cry of our suffering colored sisters, and we will recognize them as women, whose dearest interests [that is, sexual purity] are like our own."[19]

The society sent members of a visiting committee to Black neighborhoods, to rescue fallen women. But the white ladies had far less patience and sympathy with the women they found there than they had with white prostitutes, whom they imagined they could re-form into their own image. The visiting committee reported in the pages of *Advocate of Moral Reform* that the Black prostitutes they called on had seemed to be swayed by their message about the sin of sexual impurity and had even "listened with attention and apparent concern to our remarks." But, the ladies quickly concluded, it was all an act. The Black women, unlike the white prostitutes they hoped to save, could not be redeemed. "All those individuals, notwithstanding their fair pretenses, are sinners of the worst character, and the lowest grade," the ladies of the visiting committee ranted about the Black prostitutes, embracing the prevailing notion of Black women as inherently hypersexual and immodest.[20]

Another endeavor to rescue Black prostitutes, in Philadelphia, was somewhat more successful. Its driving force was Hetty Reckless, a free Black woman who had once been a runaway slave. Reckless not only ran an Underground Railroad safe house and established "colored" Sunday schools, but she also helped found and was the matron of the Moral Reform Retreat for Black "victims of vice." She shared the values of her white counterparts in that she wanted to save the fallen Black women from the "lowest haunts of vice and intemperance" and "restore [them] to decent habits." But unlike the ladies of the New York Female Moral Reform Society, who abandoned their efforts when they could not transcend their prejudices, Reckless was persistent. She worked with other Black women such as Sarah Mapps Douglass, a headmistress of a school for Black girls, to raise money to provide shelter and job training for the prostitutes they hoped to save. She also won the support of Philadelphia Quaker women such as the philanthropist and minister Rebecca Singer Collins, who were less quick to resort to toxic stereotypes. Collins visited the retreat to hand out to the women there books such as the abolitionist Abigail Mott's *Biographical Sketches and Interesting Anecdotes of Persons of Colour*, which told stories of Black people learning to read and write despite white opposition. During the first two years of the Moral Reform Retreat's endeavors, the organization boasted that "respectable places in the country" were found for several dozen women, who exchanged their employment in sin for work as cooks and laundresses.[21]

The vision of the women reformers, Black as well as white, was limited. They could not recognize that not all prostitutes were miserable in their trade: some prostitutes felt that they truly had agency and were not mere victims; some had made a reasoned choice between drudgery for subsistence wages and living decently, even opulently; some had dependents to support; and some felt loved and nurtured by friends who shared their trade. The female moral reformers lumped them all together. As "virtuous" women who professed horror at sex outside the conjugal bed, the reformers saw the prostitutes largely through their own narrow lens. Nevertheless, the moral reform movement spread. The *Advocate of Moral Reform* had almost 17,000 subscribers. In 1839, the New York Female Moral Reform Society renamed itself the American Female Moral Reform Society and absorbed the 445 female moral reform societies and auxiliaries around the country. It became the first national organization of women, working together on one cause: the eradication of male licentiousness.

Naive or unfairly punitive as some of their efforts may have been, the female moral reformers did provoke something of a shift in the idea of woman and the boundaries of her proper sphere. Women who had previously acquiesced in their confinement to domestic life learned about organizing, leading others, and working with one another. They presided over meetings, wrote constitutions, raised and distributed money, and published newspapers and newsletters. They demanded and got a public voice that went far beyond a whisper.

They even developed some political savvy. They had hoped to change men by shaming them into moral behavior, but they understood the value of getting the law on their side, too. They could not vote for laws, of course—it would not even have occurred to them to ask for suffrage. But though women could not vote, they had the right to petition lawmakers. For more than a decade, that was what the New York Female Moral Reform Society did: its members gathered tens of thousands of signatures on petitions until finally, in 1848, the State Legislature passed a law that made seduction "a crime against society," punishable by up to five years in prison and a $1,000 fine.

Other states followed suit. Iowa, for instance, deemed a man guilty if he seduced a woman "by some promise or artifice, . . . by his flattery or deception." But, as in New York, if a man could prove that the woman "had previously prostituted herself to the embraces of other men," he would be exonerated. By 1885, twenty-seven of the thirty-eight states had seduction laws. In some states, seduction was punishable by up to twenty years in prison. But almost all states required the woman to prove (usually by "character" witnesses) that—as the Iowa law specified—"she has yet preserved that priceless jewel that is the peculiar badge of the virtuous unmarried female." Seduction laws were thus only a partial victory for the female reformers who had wished to "erect a standard" to protect woman, as the *Friend of Virtue* declared in an 1838 editorial. [22] Juries everywhere in America consisted only of men, who had the right to decide whether a plaintiff's case was worthy based on whether or not she was a "virtuous" woman—according to the standards erected by the jury of men.

GETTING RID OF DRUNKENNESS

"Intemperance has made woman's home desolate."
—AMELIA BLOOMER, "To the Patrons of the Lily" (1849)[23]

Drunkenness was another of the social evils targeted by evangelicals as they awaited the second coming of Christ, as well as by Quakers, whose tenets demanded that they take action to relieve human misery. Alcohol consumption truly had become a problem in the United States by the 1830s. In the midst of a corn glut, midwestern farmers were distilling corn, the base of whiskey, into liquid assets and flooding the market. Hard liquor became so cheap that its annual consumption was over seven gallons per capita. (By way of comparison, the annual alcohol consumption among Americans in the twenty-first century has been about 2.3 gallons per capita.)[24]

Saloons proliferated. Public drunkenness became rampant. Temperance activists lamented that working men were drinking up their wages while their wives and children starved and froze in hovels. A writer for a laboring-class temperance journal complained that among the upper classes, ladies were making alcohol consumption fashionable. They were even serving it in such enormous quantities that gentlemen guests had to be "assisted home . . . or put to bed" by their hosts.²⁵ Troubled by the ubiquity of drunkenness, Americans made an 1854 novel about the ravages caused by intemperance—Timothy Shay Arthur's *Ten Nights in a Bar-Room and What I Saw There*—the best-selling book ever published in the United States to that date.

Woman, as the designated moral authority of her family, was deemed instrumental in the fight against drink. It was her duty to teach her children the ideals of sobriety by modeling sobriety in the home and eschewing alcohol in any form: never serving it to her husband or guests and never using it in cooking or even in medicinal remedies. A temperance movement spread across America, with young women everywhere vowing that "lips that touch liquor shall never touch mine." Twenty-two-year-old Emily Hawley, a Michigan farm girl and member of a rural temperance society, had been enamored of a young man whose only flaw, as she noted in her diary, was that "he drinks intoxicating drink. Though he says he's sorry and weeps about it—promises to never taste it again—yet I fear." She had vowed "to never marry the best man that lives if he is addicted to strong drink," and she sent her handsome suitor away.²⁶

Beyond such personal dramas, the fight against drunkenness opened larger vistas to woman. In fighting intemperance, she was caring for the welfare of her family—and at the same time making her voice heard in the public square. She was, she could claim, doing housekeeping on a large scale, because alcohol was destroying the families of the republic.

Male temperance leaders initially encouraged women's struggle for a public voice, as long as they did not claim too much. "In the cause of humanity, she may labor, and in the spirit of a moral heroine battle with vice and misery successfully," a Rhode Island Baptist minister acknowledged in 1843 about women in the temperance movement. But he added a caveat: "at the same time [she must] never step out of the position in which God has placed her, never assume the control of affairs in which she is the 'dependant' on man." Even women temperance leaders were initially careful in their claim of a public voice. Amelia Bloomer announced in 1849, in the first issue of her temperance journal, that "it is Woman that speaks through *The Lily*." But, conscious of the old taboo about woman speaking aloud at all, Bloomer was defensive. Because men's intemperance had "made [woman's] home desolate and beggared her offspring," Bloomer argued with a verbal quaver, "surely [woman] may, without throwing aside the modest retirement, which so becomes her sex, use her influence to lead her fellow mortals away from the destroyer's path."[27]

Such timidity did not last (not even in the pages of *The Lily*). Women became increasingly bold within the temperance movement, believing that as man's moral superiors, they had a right to lesson him about his moral failures. They invaded male spaces without apology. They fought to speak at temperance rallies. They entered saloons (where no respectable woman had ever before dared go), praying for the inebriates, lecturing them on their evil ways, and shaming them into putting down their glasses and wending their way home. They even wielded unwomanly hatchets to hack open kegs and casks, spill the demon drink, and shut down the saloon—all in the name of putting a stop to the drunkard's misbehaviors that brought misery to woman and child. Here, in the front lines of the temperance battle, was where God had set woman now, as they announced in women's temperance publications such as *The Pearl: A Ladies' Weekly Literary Gazette*: "We are engaged as a band of sisters; enlisted in the heaven-directed work to ameliorate the condition of society." The sisters were not shy about expressing their determination to wage their campaign independent of men. *The Pearl*'s editor, Virginia Allen, sniped: "One of the most annoying and discouraging things our Female Temperance Societies have ever had to contend with, has been the impertinent interference of the men in [our] affairs. The 'Lords of Creation' cannot be persuaded that women are capable of attending to their own affairs."[28]

The Pearl's idea of a "band of sisters" was focused on white women, but free Black women in the North formed their own sisterly temperance groups. In April 1833, male and female members of the First African Baptist Church in Boston, believing that tippling was a serious problem in their community, voted to dedicate themselves to the "promotion of temperance." The men at the meeting claimed the large meetinghouse for themselves so they might discuss forming their temperance organization. They sent the women off to the church's school room. The women leaped at the rare chance of starting an organization that would give them a voice. The group they formed quickly acquired a hundred members (the men's temperance group sluggishly grew to about half that size). Word got to *The Liberator*, the premier anti-slavery newspaper, which reported, "We have reason to rejoice and be elated at the noble example of the ladies."[29]

That June, at the Third Annual Convention for the Improvement of Free People of Color in Philadelphia, Black women got a chance to claim an even more public role. Convention delegates declared that temperance must be a major concern for Blacks because intemperance fueled the antiabolitionist cause. Apologists for slavery, delegates said, justified their belief that slaves in the South were better off than free Blacks in the North when they beheld "degraded [Black] men, clustering around those fatal corners, where *liquid fire* [sic] is dispensed." The men who led the convention, impressed by *The Liberator's* shout-out to the "ladies" and acknowledging the Black woman's influence over her family, encouraged the formation of "Female Societies" to fight in the forefront of the temperance battle.[30] By 1842, in Pennsylvania alone there were fourteen Black chapters of the Daughters of Temperance, totaling fifteen hundred members.

Upwardly striving and intent on promoting what has been called the "politics of respectability," Black temperance women were passionate in their conviction that colored people could not afford to be associated with drunkenness. They demanded a public voice in their community, claiming, as did their white women counterparts, that by fighting intemperance they were doing housekeeping on a large scale. One of the most widely read Black authors of her day, Frances Harper—who would later head the Colored Section of the Women's Christian Temperance Union—declared women to be indispensable in the movement for temperance. Harper wrote often against the evils of drink and the Black woman's power to fight drunkenness. The moral voice in her novel *Trial and Triumph*, Grandmother Harcourt, chastises a woman who sends her grandchild on an errand to a saloon to buy beer, lecturing the woman that "she ought to be ashamed of herself, not only guzzling beer like a toper, but to send anybody's child to a saloon to come in contact with the kind of men who frequented such places.... Women who sent their children to such places were training their boys to be drunkards and their girls to be streetwalkers." The imprudent woman yields to Harcourt's good sense and becomes a teetotaler. Harper reiterated in essays that it was up to Black women to keep their families sober, to fulfill their most important duties as mothers who are "character builders, patient, loving, strong and true," and make their homes "an uplifting power."[31]

There was a dual purpose in these temperance messages. Upwardly striving Black people needed to show that they valued sobriety as much as upright white people did; but temperance activism was also a chance for the Black woman (as it was for the white woman) to play a role outside her home. It was her right and her responsibility to demand temperance for the sake of respectability, not only for her own family but also for the larger Black American family.

Among Indians in the East, alcohol was unknown until European traders offered it to Indian fur trappers in exchange for pelts. Drunkenness became common in many tribes. Even tribal leaders such as Handsome Lake succumbed. Some made heroic efforts to get the white man's government to intervene. "You Yourselves are to Blame very much," the leader of the Catawba Indians accused North Carolina officials. "You Rot Your grain in Tubs out of which you take and make Strong Spirits You sell it to our young men and give it to them, many times; they get Very Drunk with it this is the Very Cause that they oftentimes Commit those Crimes that are offensive to You and us."[32] But the trade continued uninterrupted.

Indian women, who still played an active role in their world in the eighteenth and early nineteenth centuries, also carried on commerce with traders and were sometimes paid with firewater. Among the Indians of the Great Lakes, women initially used alcohol in mourning rituals, to enhance their efforts to enter the spirit world where their departed had gone. But eventually it was misused, as German Moravian missionaries who invaded the region recorded. Complaining of the rampant drunkenness among the Delaware Indians, the missionary Abraham Luckenbach noted in his diary of 1803 the sad story of an Indian woman who had been baptized but slipped from grace: "She sold all her eleven bushels of corn and all her belongings to buy whiskey. She then sat down and drank so long that, during her drinking, she gave up the ghost and fell over dead."[33]

There were no Indian equivalents of the large temperance societies among white and Black women, but Indian women who were still spiritual leaders did sometimes make efforts to control drinking in their tribe. In his 1805–1806 diaries, Luckenbach recorded the story of Beate, a woman prophet among the Delawares. She had been baptized by the Moravian missionaries but (in violation of the customs of the church) she continued to present herself as a spiritual leader. Luckenbach deemed her a babbling old woman and scoffed that "she went so far as to make the Indians believe she had actually seen the angels and even God himself, who had given the Good Spirit into her hands . . . and now he is inside her and telling her everything that God wanted the Indians to do." Beate had announced to the Delawares that she had had a vision in which two beings appeared to her and said, "God is not satisfied with you Indians. . . . You

Indians will have to live again as in olden times." And she asked her tribe to promise "to drink no more whiskey."

"This last thing would be well," Luckenbach wrote. But he groused that the same Indians had promised the same thing the year before and "unfortunately failed to keep their word and drank more than ever."[34] The Moravians were no more successful than Beate had been in spreading temperance. But they did manage, among the Indians they converted to Christianity, to undercut Beate and all women spiritual leaders.

White women on the lower social rungs also flocked to the temperance movement, believing that laboring-class females were especially victimized by the "waters of death." The cause gave working-class women too an unaccustomed public voice. The largest of their temperance organizations was the Martha Washingtonians, which proliferated all over the Northeast and the Midwest. Started in 1841 by women who were proud that their "earthly comforts are derived mainly from the labor of their own hands," the "directresses" of the chapters made their living as dressmakers, corset makers, and boardinghouse keepers. A butcher's wife led a large New York chapter. Other leaders were married to artisans and day laborers.[35]

They distrusted the Lady Bountiful methods of groups whose membership was solidly middle class, such as the Women's New York State Temperance Society, to which Bloomer belonged, and the Daughters of Temperance, the organization to which Susan B. Anthony would give her first public speech. Despite the limited finances of Martha Washingtonian members, each pledged to contribute a small sum of money every month to be used for the cause. Even more important, they met to sew clothes and take the fruits of their labor "into dark corners of our towns and cities, into the damp cellars and open garrets," where they would seek out dipsomaniacs and their rag-clad families. But they made clear to these unfortunates that their largesse was intended not to improve the drunkard's position but rather his character. They prided themselves on providing laboring-class tough love. "Change your habits and your company, leave your haunts of dissipation, and we will aid you," they lectured. They contrasted themselves to their "social betters," who gave aid condescendingly, never thinking to bring the recipient up to their level. "Come into our society, be one of us, and assume your claim to respectability again," the Martha Washingtonians demanded before they bestowed clothes and money.[36]

In their ideas about woman, they were not so different from either their wealthier white counterparts or Black women temperance workers—or, for that matter, from the ideal of previous centuries: woman as chaste, domestic, and "virtuous." Drunkenness among their own sex was especially distressing to the Martha Washingtonians because a drunken woman could not fulfill her responsibilities to her husband and children. A major focus of the group was to restore in women who imbibed their womanly nature. "Alcohol, the foe of humanity, is the demon curse of the domestic sphere," they declared in the lead article of the first issue of their journal, *Olive Plant and Ladies' Temperance Advocate*, lamenting that drunkenness was destroying "countless wives and mothers" by robbing them of all that is sacred and appropriate to woman.[37]

The Martha Washingtonians soon gave up on female imbibers who persisted in violating the image of woman to which the Marthas—respectable members of the laboring class—adhered. When in a single week in 1846 two hundred women in New York City were arrested for public drunkenness, the Marthas paid no attention. An article in *The Pearl* cried out for help from the Martha Washingtonians, to bravely search as they used to in the lowest places for female inebriates and again encourage them "in the pure joys of the paths of temperance." But the Martha Washingtonians, distinguishing firmly between their own lower-middle-class womanly respectability and the hopelessly low lower-class women drunkards who violated all ideals of womanhood, had already shifted their focus. Instead of pursuing the thankless task of scouring lowly places to rescue intemperate females, the Martha Washingtonians turned into a female mutual-aid society, providing sick benefits as well as death benefits to needy women of their class.[38]

The modus operandi of the female temperance movement had been moral suasion. Temperance women reprimanded drunken men for ruining their own children by modeling bad morals and for wasting their wages on drink while their family went cold and hungry. They scolded drunken women for violating the tenets of delicacy, purity, and womanliness. When visiting homes to upbraid the inebriates proved ineffective, temperance women invaded saloons. They went in bands to pray loudly at the patrons in their cups. They told the saloon keepers that they must stop destroying lives and instead destroy their stock and shut down their businesses. They had some success, but mostly they failed. As Bloomer complained in *The Lily*, the temperance groups were only occasionally able to "relieve the wants and sufferings of the drunkard's children" or rescue a woman "from the drunkard's path."[39] It mattered little what temperance women did, as long as alcohol continued to flow almost everywhere in the country, Bloomer wrote. They needed to find other solutions.

What worked when moral suasion did not was political action. In 1851, Maine passed the Act for the Suppression of Drinking Houses and Tippling Shops, prohibiting not only the sale of alcohol but also its manufacture. In one fell swoop, the problem of drunkenness in the state seemed to come to an end by an act of the legislature. It dramatized for temperance women the fact that they were powerless, having no political voice and no ability to choose their legislators. Bloomer proposed a remedy to women's helplessness: They must work "towards the attainment of the power of which they are wrongly deprived." They must demand their political rights.[40]

The very idea that women should have a real political voice seemed far-fetched, even to most women. In 1848, when Susan B. Anthony's social reformist father told her excitedly about the first women's rights convention in Seneca Falls, New York, she replied that she thought the women "were getting a good deal ahead of the times." However, Anthony changed her mind after she was made to feel powerless within the temperance movement. She was elected to be a delegate, representing the Daughters of Temperance, to the New York Sons of Temperance convention in 1852. Raised as a Quaker, she had been used to speaking at women's meetings, and since 1849 she had spoken in public on temperance—but only to audiences of women. Now she rose to speak to a mixed audience. She was stopped by the male moderator, who informed her that "the sisters were not invited to speak but to listen and learn." When Anthony stormed out and three or four other women went with her, the other women delegates, well-schooled in behavior suitable to woman, were as shocked as were the men. They deemed the protestors "bold, meddlesome disturbers."[41]

Anthony's feeling that she ought to fight to get rid of the restrictions on women—no matter that the battle would be "a good deal ahead of the times"—was confirmed for her in the following year, 1853. She attended an organizing meeting for the World's Temperance Convention, where she was nominated to be a member of the business committee. In response, the mayor of Providence, Rhode Island, who was officiating at the meeting, made an enraged speech, which the press declared "too indecent to be reported." The mayor also threatened to resign as chair if

Anthony were put on the committee. He "would never sanction ladies leaving their legitimate position in society," he proclaimed. A Rev. Dr. Hewitt, who had opened the meeting with a prayer, added that he too was "strongly against ladies taking part in public discussion." The reverend even proved from scripture that woman was to be silent. At that point, a little group of men was appointed to adjourn to another room and decide who should be permitted to participate in the proceedings. The men left, returned fifteen minutes later, and declared that "the call for this meeting was not intended to include female delegates, and [as] custom has not sanctioned the public action of women in similar situations, their credentials should be rejected."[42]

The editor of the *New York Sun* had been at the meeting, and he weighed in on the subject of the sort of female who would violate the ideal of woman by claiming a place in a man's world:

> The quiet duties of daughter, wife, or mother are not congenial to those of hermaphrodite spirits who thirst to win the title of champion of one sex and victor over the other. What is the love of one manly heart to the woman whose ambition it is to sway the minds of multitudes. . . . What are the tender affections and childish prattle of the family circle, to women whose ears itch for the loud laugh and boisterous cheer of the public assembly? . . . Could a Christian man, cherishing a high regard for woman and for the proprieties of life feel that he was promoting woman's interests and the cause of temperance by being introduced to a temperance meeting by Miss Susan B. Anthony, her ungainly form rigged out in bloomer costume? . . . Would he feel he was honoring the women of this country by accepting as their representative women whom they must and do despise?[43]

Anthony was stunned by the hysterical fear that was aroused by her mere service on a committee. But it confirmed her in her resolve. She organized a rival temperance convention, pointedly called the Whole World's Temperance Convention, meaning that it would be open to everyone, regardless of sex and even of race. That convention was held on September 1 and 2, 1853, a few days before the opening of the World's Temperance Convention from which women had been excluded. After her convention, Anthony left the temperance movement. She would thereafter devote herself to overturning the old ideas of woman.

But women who stayed in the movement also overturned some of those ideas. In the 1850s, they found a new way to deal with intemperance: they organized into bands and invaded local saloons, not to pray but (decades ahead of the infamous Carrie Nation) to destroy the liquor supply by actions that were not at all womanly. In 1854, for instance, Amanda Way, a twenty-six-year-old spinster who made her living as a seamstress and milliner, led fifty women armed with hatchets through the town of Winchester, Indiana, in what came to be called the "whiskey riots." The women burst into saloons, demanding that proprietors take the pledge and go out of business. Those who refused were put out of business. The women scared off the customers and then wielded their hatchets on the liquor stock. When a man in one saloon asked if he might finish his drink before he left, Way's unwomanly answer was, "I would rather brain you with this axe, so you can die sober."[44]

The largest whiskey riot took place in 1856, in Rockport, Massachusetts, a small fishing town on the eastern shore of Cape Ann. Hannah Jumper, a tall and rawboned spinster of seventy-five, led a hatchet gang of women on a five-hour rampage in and out of all the places in town where liquor was sold. Jumper had a big following among the women of Rockport. Not only was she the town's best herbalist, but she also opened her home to meetings of women whose husbands drank up their paltry fishermen's wages, which were desperately needed by hungry children and wives.

Jumper's hatchet gang had been meeting since the winter to plan the summer raid. On the morning of July 8, sixty women gathered in the town square with hatchets, as well as hammers and tomahawks, hidden under their shawls. They marched through town behind a large unbleached cotton sheet that was held aloft, announcing itself as "The Ladies' Temperance Banner." Below that phrase was painted a hatchet. The procession grew to include two hundred people. As one eyewitness reported, the participants were "almost all the women in Rockport,—all who could walk or move on crutches."[45] Joined by a handful of men, they systematically sought out the offending businesses; entered them, by force if necessary; seized barrels, kegs, and casks; and rolled them into the street. There they smashed over fifty vessels, whooping and cheering as the liquor seeped or gushed out. The saloon owners did not dare attack a bunch of ladies, and the gathering male residents of Rockport, rather than jumping in to protect private property, greeted the anarchy as a hilarious spectacle.

One of the saloon owners sued for damages. Temperance supporters raised the princely sum of $1,500 to hire lawyers for the accused. The case was heard in Massachusetts Superior Court, where the rioters prevailed, perhaps because by the 1850s, the temperance movement was popular and powerful in Massachusetts, and a hundred towns had chosen to prohibit the sale of alcohol within their borders. The chief justice of the court declared that "intoxicating liquors kept for sale and the vessels containing them [were] a common nuisance." Therefore, it was "lawful for any person to destroy them." It was even justifiable, he wrote, to use force to break into an establishment so that the common nuisance could be obliterated. The saloon owner was ordered to pay all the court costs.[46]

The justices never once castigated the unladylike behavior of the hatchet gang. Perhaps their concern about cleaning up the "common nuisance" permitted the justices to justify the women's actions as large-scale housekeeping. However the justices may have explained the women's militance to themselves, the escapades of Jumper's hatchet gang were a remarkable departure from the tactics of earlier women's temperance groups, such as the Martha Washingtonians with their "delicate and refined sensibility, modesty of feeling and manner, gentle and unassuming tenderness."[47]

FREEING SLAVES AND FREEING WOMAN

"Since I engaged in the investigation of the rights of the slave, I have necessarily been led to a better understanding of my own."
—ANGELINA GRIMKÉ, 1837[48]

William Lloyd Garrison—editor of *The Liberator*, the most influential anti-slavery newspaper in America—reminded free American women in 1832 that a million of their sisters were slaves and "liable to be sold or used for the gratification of lust or avarice." With that shocking fact, he called on women to form female anti-slavery societies, telling them that they must have no "misconception of duty" in thinking that their only moral responsibility was to their own family. Garrison extolled the women of Providence, Rhode Island, who had stepped outside their female sphere to start an anti-slavery society two weeks before.[49]

The women of Providence were not the first. Garrison did not know that five months earlier, in February 1832, free Black women had begun the Female Anti-Slavery Society of Salem in Massachusetts. (They apprised him of their society's existence after he touted the Providence group as unique.) The Female Anti-Slavery Society of Salem was founded by middle-class Black women such as Nancy Remond—the mother of eleven children and the wife of a successful caterer known as the "Colored Restaurateur"—whose home had been part of the early Underground Railroad. The group's mission was not only to help the enslaved and relieve the needy but also to "remove the monster prejudice from the minds of many in regard to free people of color." They were very aware of themselves as women actors, and they resolved in their society's constitution that they would take each other's ideas seriously: "Any member who wishes to speak is allowed the privilege: when any member speaks, there shall be no interruption"—a hint that in mixed groups that had not been the case for women.[50]

Other female anti-slavery societies—Black, white, and integrated—were soon started. However, sisterhood did not always prevail, and in the integrated groups white women tended to think of Black women as wards rather than as adult women seeking agency for themselves as well as for the enslaved, just as the white women were doing. Sarah Forten, a daughter of the wealthy Black Forten family and one of the founders of the integrated Philadelphia Female Anti-Slavery Society, complained: "Even our professed friends have not yet rid themselves of [prejudice]. To some it clings like a dark mantle, obscuring and choking up the avenues of higher and nobler sentiments." Nevertheless, by the time the first Anti-Slavery Convention of American Women was called, in 1837, there were already seventy-five female anti-slavery societies in ten states. By the 1840s, there were over a hundred societies in the Midwest alone, including Ohio, Indiana, Michigan, Illinois, and Wisconsin.[51]

Female anti-slavery societies drew in women reformers from the temperance and moral reform societies, as well as women who had never before ventured into the public sphere. The societies' members were troubled by all aspects of slavery, but the part that they found the most horrifying was that slavery invited a desecration of female sexual modesty, which they believed was innate to woman, her priceless pearl. Anti-slavery women issued a clarion call. The enslaved woman was "allowed to have no conscientious scruple, no sense of shame," the reformer Lydia Maria Child, an abolitionist who became a women's rights activist, wrote in "An Appeal in Favor of That Class of Americans Called Africans" in 1833. "Among our slave sisters in the South, the most lawless and shameful system of licentiousness prevails," Mary Ann Brigham Brown, editor of the

Golden Rule, a reform magazine, wrote in 1839. If an enslaved woman did not cooperate with the obscene demands of the slave owner, Brown explained, she was "made to endure a worse than living death, till she will yield her priceless virtue to the foul destroyer."⁵²

Women who joined the anti-slavery movement because they were enflamed by the plight of enslaved woman had more to be enflamed about within the anti-slavery movement. At the 1833 convention of the American Anti-Slavery Society, the members passed a resolution declaring that the organization would encourage the establishment of more female auxiliaries. They had just had an excellent experience with four women, sympathetic to abolition, who had attended the convention as observers. The women had been quiet and womanly. One of them, Lucretia Mott, had asked if she might make several brief amendments to the society's manifesto. She was permitted to speak, and though women had almost never before spoken to a mixed audience, Mott managed to do so without violating the rules of woman that the delegates cherished. One man later observed of her performance: "I had never before heard a woman speak at a public meeting. She said but a few words, but these were spoken so modestly, in such sweet tones, and yet withal so decisively, that no one could fail to be pleased. . . . She apologized for what might be regarded as an intrusion."⁵³ Mott was a licensed Quaker preacher and knew well how to speak forcefully. However, she also knew how to perform "woman" in front of her male listeners—who already had plenty to adjust to, just in seeing a woman at the podium.

Mott was not happy about being constrained to perform "woman." Nor was she happy a few weeks later when she and several others tried to start a female anti-slavery group. As she later recalled, none of the women present had had any experience in chairing a meeting, so they asked the assistance of James McCrummel, a Black man who was an orator and knew the rules of parliamentary procedure. "Negroes, idiots, and women were in legal documents classed together," Mott quipped sarcastically, "so that we were very glad to get one of our own class to come in and aid us in forming that Society."⁵⁴

Many of the Black women abolitionists in the North had first learned to organize when they joined female literary societies. Such groups, like the Philadelphia Female Literary Association, were formed for the "mental improvement [of] respectable colored females." In Boston, the constitution of the Afric-American Female Intelligence Association dedicated the group to "the diffusion of knowledge, the suppression of vice and immorality, and [the] cherishing [of] such virtues as will render us happy and useful to society." Most of the members were from the middle class. Some were even wealthy, such as the wife and daughters of James Forten, a businessman who was one of the richest men (Black or white) in Philadelphia. Their concept of woman and womanly virtues were very much like those of their white counterparts. The organization kept out the riffraff through charging yearly dues of $1.50—too steep for poor Black women. As Sarah Mapps Douglass (daughter of a wealthy Black family who had been educated by private tutors) confessed, it was possible for free Black women of her class to live in an insulated world, "not car[ing] to move beyond its precincts." By "its precincts," Douglass meant her sheltered Black society that mirrored the customs and values of bourgeois white society, especially in regard to womanly propriety. However, when the Afric-American Female Intelligence Society turned its attention from literary matters to the anti-slavery movement, womanly propriety became a distant secondary concern. Douglass recalled in a speech that after she finally learned through the anti-slavery movement about the horror of slavery, "I started up, and with one mighty effort, threw from me the lethargy which had covered me for years; and determined . . . to use every exertion in my power [to help] my wronged and neglected race."[55]

Such impassioned sentiment was not received well by many Black men in the anti-slavery movement. The Black woman, like her white counterpart, was not supposed to deliver impassioned speeches or commit herself to public "exertions." According to Rev. Samuel Cornish, leader of the free Black community in New York and a founder of the American Anti-Slavery Society, the Black woman should exercise her influence in the domestic sphere. If she participated in the anti-slavery movement at all, Cornish proclaimed, it should be by raising money to support the activities of the men. Women might, for example, hold fairs where they could sell needlework and baked goods. But they must not pursue "masculine views and measures." About Fanny Wright, a white person who was one of the first women in the United States to give a public lecture to a "promiscuous audience" (that is, one made up of both men and women), Cornish declared in America's first Black newspaper, *Freedom's Journal*: "This woman ought to get into pantaloons immediately. She is a disgrace to the fairer part of creation."[56]

Cornish was far from alone in his disgust with women who stepped out of their role, no matter the cause. In 1837, when several Black women in New York banded together to beat up a slave catcher who was about to capture two fugitive slaves, an editorial in *The Colored American Magazine*, published for free Blacks, opined about their unwomanly behavior: "Everlasting shame and remorse seize upon those females that so degraded themselves yesterday. We beg their husbands to keep them at home and find some better occupation for them."[57]

The Black woman who was unwomanly, even in the worthy cause of abolition, could be punished by her community. Maria W. Miller Stewart, described as "beautiful and lovely" (before she transgressed), was born free in New England but had lost both parents by the time she was five years old. She spent most of her youth as a servant in the home of a clergyman, where she educated herself through the books in his library. In 1826, Stewart married a man who was the only Black shipping agent in Boston, and she became part of the city's small Black middle-class community. Three years later, when she was only twenty-six, she lost her husband. She never remarried. With no children to occupy her, Stewart turned her energies to writing and publishing about her passions—Christianity, abolition, and the advancement of Black women—and, unwomanly as it was, to being a "warrior" for "the cause of oppressed Africa."[58]

In 1832, known now as "a highly intelligent colored lady," Stewart delivered addresses to the Afric-American Female Intelligence Society of Boston and an audience of abolitionists who came to hear her in Franklin Hall, in predominantly white South Boston. She called her Franklin Hall lecture "The Disadvantages Which the Free People of Color Labor Under in the New England States." She did not hold back in her criticism, calling out prejudice even among those whites who professed to be on the side of Blacks yet refused to hire Black "girls," justifying themselves by claiming that if they did so, their business "would be in danger of losing the public patronage." Stewart's eloquence in her plea for "equal opportunity for black girls," as she named it, was highly praised if not acted upon.[59]

But she got into trouble the next year, when she addressed another "promiscuous audience" of all Black people at the African Masonic Hall. Stewart gave a lecture billed as "African Rights and Liberty." Those men who assumed with Cornish that the Black woman's place was in her home might have come to hear Stewart in the spirit of Samuel Johnson's quip about woman's public speaking: it was "like a dog walking on his hind legs. It is not done well; but you are surprised to find it done at all."[60] In any case, they did not like what they heard.

Using her customary tone of rebuke and hoping to "fire the breast of every free man of color," Stewart dared to say that Black men had not much exerted themselves to "alleviate the woes of [their] brethren in bondage." She seriously overstepped in demanding to know, "Is it blindness of mind, or stupidity of soul, or the want of education that has caused our men . . . never to let their voices be heard nor their hands be raised in behalf of their color?" Even worse, Stewart fervently exhorted the audience, "If you are men, convince them that you possess the spirit of men."[61]

Cornish had warned the Black women readers of *Freedom's Journal* just a few years earlier that they must "support the cause of reason with all the graces of female gentleness" and observed that "a woman who would attempt to thunder with her tongue . . . is disgusting." Stewart, who had been used to being praised as "lovely" and "highly intelligent," triggered a small riot. The men in the audience erupted, rising to their feet and shouting and jeering at her. By some accounts they even threw rotten tomatoes. Stewart was rushed from the hall. The experience was so unsettling that she gave only one more speech, a farewell address defending woman's right to speak and decrying the men's fury. "What if I am a woman?" she asked defiantly. She reminded her audience that God had made Deborah a judge in Israel and chosen Queen Esther to save the lives of the Jews: "If such women once existed, be no longer astonished, then, that God at this eventful period should raise up your females to strive." Then she fled from Boston, never again to speak in public.[62]

White women abolitionists who challenged the idea of woman by assuming a public voice were no less reviled than Stewart. Sarah and Angelina Grimké were born into an aristocratic slave-holding family. As Sarah later wrote of her years of ladyhood in Charleston, South Carolina, her "lot [had been] cast among the butterflies of the fashionable world," in which women of her class were brought up to have vacuous minds and be "mere instruments of pleasure."[63] But when she accompanied her ill father, Judge John Grimké, to Philadelphia in his search for medical treatment, she made friends with Quakers, the opposite of the "butterflies of the fashionable world." They were active in the Underground Railroad and articulate about the wrongs of slavery, and they grounded her amorphous feelings of revulsion about the peculiar institution. After the judge's death, Sarah and her younger sister Angelina freed the family's slaves.

Eventually both sisters settled in Philadelphia, joined the Quaker church, and became active abolitionists. The Grimkés' early anti-slavery writing spoke directly to their Southern sisters back home, reminding them of woman's "moral superiority" and her duty to "overthrow this horrible system of oppression and cruelty, licentiousness and wrong," as Angelina wrote in 1836 in her *Appeal to the Christian Women of the South*. "Arise and gird yourself for this great moral conflict, with the whole armour of righteousness upon the right hand and on the left," she exhorted women who, like the Grimké sisters, had been raised to be fashionable butterflies.[64]

Because the Grimkés had seen slavery up close in their daily lives, they had a unique story to tell. Sponsored by the American Anti-Slavery Society, they went out to tell it—to "promiscuous audiences" as well as to all-female audiences—all over the country, in churches and to anti-slavery societies. In all they reached over 40,000 listeners. Some members of their audiences could not get past the shock of an orator wearing a dress. They "sit sometimes with 'mouths agape and eyes astare' [in] perfect amazement to witness a woman speak in the churches," Angelina wrote to the abolitionist leader Theodore Weld, who had become her betrothed.[65]

Weld, an iconoclast in all things (for example, two ministers—one white and one Black—officiated at his and Angelina's wedding), cheered the Grimké sisters on. The General Association of Congregational Ministers in Massachusetts did not. Though the association's members were among the most steadfast abolitionists, they fulminated in an 1837 pastoral letter that it was a particular outrage that the Grimké sisters lectured to audiences that included men. The Grimkés' offense "threatened the female character with widespread and permanent injury," the pastoral letter said. It accused the two women of perverting the essential attributes of woman. "The power of woman is in her dependence," the ministers carped to the faithful. "When she assumes the place and tone of man as a public reformer, our care and protection of her seem unnecessary."[66]

The Grimké sisters were as unsettled by such attacks as Stewart had been, especially because the attacks came from those who were ostensibly on the same side in the fight for justice. But the Grimkés were not silenced. They expanded their fight to include the liberation of women—and their foes to include not just slave owners but men like the Congregational ministers. "Since I engaged in the investigation of the rights of the slave, I have necessarily been led to a better understanding of my own," Angelina wrote in *The Liberator*. Sarah made the same point with more heat: "All I ask of my brethren is that they take their feet from off our necks, and permit us to stand upright." She attributed the forced subservience of women to men's "lust of dominion." It was that same "lust of dominion," she said, that explained the origin of slavery.[67]

The Grimkés were not the only women to liken woman's position to that of the slave. "Free" women may not be in literal manacles as slaves were, some began to argue, but they were not "free" either. Margaret Fuller, the leading antebellum female intellectual, even went so far as to suggest that the anti-slavery party ought to plead for women's rights, too—because, like slaves, women were kept in bondage by civil law, custom, and patriarchal abuse.[68] It was an emboldening insight.

Elizabeth Cady, daughter of a prominent New York lawyer, had had fantasies when she was eleven years old of leading a life of scholarship and self-reliance. Her goals were sharpened when she became fascinated by the law books in her father's library, and she decided to become a lawyer. But she soon learned that no matter how bright and studious she might be, a woman could not lead a life of scholarship or be self-reliant, and she certainly could not follow her father into the law because women did not become lawyers. In 1840, when she was twenty-five years old, she married Henry Stanton. Elizabeth Cady Stanton's new husband was an abolitionist, and he proposed that they go on their honeymoon to London, where he would be a delegate to the World's Anti-Slavery Convention. Before sailing the couple stopped off in New Jersey, so that Henry Stanton might introduce his new bride to his best friend, Theodore Weld, and to Weld's wife of two years. Angelina Grimké Weld was "very much pleased" with Henry Stanton's bride, as she later wrote. The feeling was mutual. "Woman has too long rested satisfied in the circumscribed limits which corrupt custom and a perverted application of the Scriptures had marked out for her," Grimké had said in an 1837 speech to the Anti-Slavery Convention of American Women. Those were Cady Stanton's sentiments exactly.[69]

At the World's Anti-Slavery Convention in London, which Cady Stanton attended with the intention of sitting beside her husband, women delegates and observers were immediately barred from taking their seats. The first day of the convention was devoted not to discussions of how to rid the world of slavery but to a heated debate about whether women delegates should be allowed to participate in the convention at all. The nays had it. Stanton sat in Freemason's Hall, outraged that so many "remarkable women"—devoted workers in the anti-slavery movement, many of whom were speakers and leaders among the Quakers—"were all compelled to listen in silence to the masculine platitudes on woman's sphere."[70]

The women delegates and all the other women who came as observers were sent to the spectators' gallery. From there the women could listen and watch, but they could not utter a word. Stanton found herself sitting next to Lucretia Mott, the woman who had been praised at an abolitionist meeting for speaking "so modestly, in such sweet tones." Now both women seethed. As Stanton later wrote, "It struck me as very remarkable that abolitionists, who felt so keenly the wrongs of the slave, should be so oblivious to the equal wrongs of their own mothers, wives, and sisters, when, according to common law, both classes occupied a similar legal status."[71]

Would Stanton have become the militant she did after the World's Anti-Slavery Convention if she had not been primed by the stories of Angelina Grimké Weld's mistreatment by male abolitionists? Or if Stanton could have sat with her husband and all the other delegates on the convention floor? Or if she had not been relegated to the spectators' gallery with Mott—who, as Stanton would write, had thought broadly about politics, religion, and all questions of reform, and soon opened to her "a new world of thought"? At the end of the first day, Stanton and Mott walked back to their lodging house arm in arm, talking about their indignation and disgust. They resolved to "hold a convention as soon as we returned home, and form a society to advocate the rights of women."[72] Thus began the first organized movement formed specifically to change the concept of woman and her circumscribed life.

For some women, the past decades had been leading inexorably to such a movement. The contradiction was too blatant to ignore: popular sentiment deemed woman morally superior to man while perpetually reminding her of the inferiority of her place. Women had been given, both expressly and tacitly, the responsibility to "guard and fortify" the country against man's poor moral choices. Yet they were allowed no tools to "guard and fortify" except moral suasion, which proved to be entirely ineffective. Women in the moral reform, temperance, and abolitionist movements had internalized the notion of woman's moral superiority. Many of them had come to believe that their sex did indeed need to save the country from the horrors perpetrated primarily by men: vice, intemperance, and slavery. The outrages visited on women every day—even when they were engaged in trying to do their job, to "guard and fortify"—were now added to the panoply of men's misdeeds.

Women had also learned to organize and lead in those movements. The questions some of them began asking were inevitable: If men were such moral miscreants and if women were their moral superiors, why did the law treat women as men's inferiors? And why were women not allowed a strong voice in how the country was run?

5.
Nineteenth-Century Woman Leaves Home

Thomas Roderick Dew, staunch defender of slavery and president of the College of William and Mary, worried about the ladies of the South. He admonished southern white women not to emulate the northern woman who was slipping from her place and avoiding her duties. In an 1835 diatribe—which could easily have been written 100, or even 200 years earlier—Dew urged women readers of the *Southern Literary Messenger* to remember that they belonged to the weaker sex, and that without man's protection they could not hope to survive "the great strife" of life. Dew's admonition was merely preemptive: white women in the South were not invading brothels, taking axes to saloons, or holding forth to mixed audiences. Nevertheless, he warned that man would not continue to be woman's protector if she failed to uphold her part of the bargain by "conform[ing] to that character which circumstances demand for the sphere in which she moves." Woman's business was still to cultivate appealing feminine qualities—Dew stressed grace, modesty, and loveliness—because that was how "to win over to her side" man, on whom she must depend.[1]

WOMAN GOES OUT TO WORK

> "I felt that I belonged to the world, that there was something for me to do in it."
> —LUCY LARCOM, *A New England Girlhood* (1889)[2]

The new consciousness about the wrongs of woman, and how those wrongs ought to be righted, was rousing, but it did not affect most women. There was anxiety, however, that it might. Conveniently ignoring the coarsening effect on white southern women of the institution of slavery, southern men were concerned that the carryings-on of northern females, which pushed at traditional concepts of woman, would spread below the Mason-Dixon line. In 1849, Charles Thiot, a twenty-seven-year-old Georgia planter, wrote his fiancée, Anna Charlton, about a dinner party he attended for a "yankee girl." He had never seen such a "repulsive countenance," Thiot said. It was not that she was ugly, but that when she talked she was fierce. "I could not help contrasting her, dear Anna, to your gentle self. And in drawing that contrast, that *striking* contrast of manners and expression, I could not help but feel how happy I could be with one, and how perfectly miserable with the other," Thiot declared, letting Anna know that he valued her as an old-fashioned southern belle.[3]

Southerners were not alone in their disapproval of the budding new idea of woman. From its inception in 1830 to its demise forty-eight years later, the most popular women's magazine in the United States, the Boston-based *Godey's Lady's Book*, promoted the ideal of woman as the angel in the house. This was in spite of the shifts that were taking place in many women's consciousness and conditions, which Sarah Josepha Hale, the magazine's "editress" (the term she preferred), ignored. She spoke to the larger masses, the women who had not yet been touched by those shifts. She not only reflected back to her women readers their static idea of woman, but she also promoted it even further. In January 1851, three months after the first National Woman's Rights Convention met in Worcester, Massachusetts, to demand equal rights for women, Hale responded to the meeting by warning her readers against "becoming like a man, doing man's work, or striving for the dominion of the world."[4]

Hale herself was phenomenally successful in "doing man's work." She was the first woman in America to be the editor of a major magazine, a job she held for forty years. In fact, most of Hale's own life contradicted her advice to her readers. She was widowed at the age of thirty-four, and though she lived for another fifty-six years, reaching the ripe age of ninety, she never remarried. Yet she told her women readers that their very lives depended on marriage; that a woman belonged in the home and must be content to rely on a husband "for protection and support"; that "she should look up to him with reverence as her earthly guardian"; and that she should be obedient to him, even if he is "not worthy of this honor," because his office as her husband was ordained by God.[5] Hale was among the first in a very long line of women who stepped far beyond the home but had phenomenal success in telling other women that the home was where they belonged.

Yet despite Hale and her readers, the concept of "true womanhood" (according to which women should be submissive, pious, pure, and domestic) was being challenged not only by women swinging hatchets or decrying woman's wrongs and demanding her rights.[6] New external conditions were pulling women—some of whom were willing and ready and some of whom were not—out of the domestic sphere and into the world.

Young women of the laboring class in the early nineteenth century had contributed to their family's income by working at home in what was called a "putting out" system. A merchant would provide the women with the materials for weaving or spinning, for example, and pay them for each piece that they completed. But in Waltham, Massachusetts, in 1813, Francis Cabot Lowell initiated a system of mass production that made such work obsolete: he used water-powered machines to turn cotton into cloth. Scion of a prominent New England family, Lowell was an idealist. In his vision, he would not be taking jobs away from the young women spinners. Rather, he would be creating new jobs for many more of them.

He would be revolutionizing their work. He would hire women, mostly between the ages of sixteen and twenty-two, and would have them well-housed, well-fed, and well-supervised in factory-owned boarding houses. His factory system would be different from that of the much-maligned British system, he said, because it would not contribute to a permanent underclass of semiskilled laborers. After a few years, the young women workers would leave their factory jobs to marry, and they would be replaced by other young women who would in their turn work for a few years until they too would be swept away by marriage.[7]

Francis Cabot Lowell died in 1817, but in 1823—when a textile plant was opened on the banks of the Merrimack River, twenty miles from his original factory—the town was given his name.[8] Textile mills proliferated in Lowell and many other towns near rivers or streams that could power the machines. The jobs that were now available to women paid much more than spinners, weavers, laundresses, seamstresses, or domestic servants could earn. Women left home to take the new jobs.

It was the start of the female wage-labor force, which became the largest industrial labor force in America at that time. Young women moved to factory towns, where they lived with other members of the laboring class, away from the strictures of family life. Never before had there been so many females living together, without parents or husbands. Their exodus from domestic life and their prospect of financial independence caused concern that the meaning of "woman" could be turned upside down. "The times are out of joint," a *Boston Courier* reporter lamented. "The women are assuming the prerogatives and employments which, from time immemorial, have been considered the attributes and duties of the other sex." The reporter, with only a little facetiousness, worried that soon men would have to do the work of "seamstresses, milliners, cooks, wet nurses, and chambermaids."[9]

But in the town of Lowell, Francis Cabot Lowell's vision for women workers came to life. Mill agents were sent to villages in large horse-drawn wagons, where they hawked an exhilarating new opportunity to healthy and wholesome girls. Farmers' daughters were especially welcome. According to Harriet Hanson Robinson, who was one of the "mill girls," the agents "collect[ed] them at so much a head, and deliver[ed] them at the factories."[10] The agents had little trouble in filling the wagons. Many a farmer's daughter was delighted to leave her predictable young woman's life on the farm and go off on a brave new adventure.

The stream of young women, hitherto sheltered, who settled in a strange town—out of range of their parents' control and their community's vigilant eye—worried moral reformers. The possibilities for the tragedy of seduction and loss of innocence could be endless. Occasionally the reformers' worries were confirmed by sensationalistic cases, such as that of Sarah Cornell, who worked as a mill girl in Lowell in 1828 and 1829 and there met her seducer, a married Methodist minister, Rev. Ephraim Avery, who eventually impregnated and killed her. Her story became a cautionary tale, and was even committed to verse:

> In times like these, when murderers roam
>   And search around for prey,
> 'Tis a fearful step to leave our home,
>   Lest dangerous men betray.
>
> This lovely girl in youthful pride,
>   From virtue's path did stray,
> A vile seducer for her guide,
>   And by him led away.[11]

But the preponderance of mill girls apparently had happier stories. A young woman at a Lowell mill could make enough money to afford an unaccustomed modicum of independence—enough even to sock some money away at the Lowell Savings Bank, which many did. Lowell mill girls had few expenses. They earned between $2.50 and $6.00 a week, and their room and board in the company-owned boarding-houses was only $1.25 a week. In the early years, the perks of their job included free access to a lending library and lectures by literary celebrities such as Ralph Waldo Emerson, Henry David Thoreau, John Greenleaf Whittier, and Edgar Allan Poe. They could also take lessons in a variety of genteel subjects, such as drawing, dancing, and foreign languages. They organized "Improvement Circles" because they believed that "an urgent need existed for all working women to make an effort to improve their minds," and they met regularly to read each other their poems and essays. They even produced a monthly magazine of their writings, *Lowell Offerings*.[12]

They "bettered themselves," though they never forgot their place on the social scale. They saw themselves as "working girls, wearing coarse aprons suitable to our work," as the memoirist Lucy Larcom, who had been one of them, recalled. But they knew that they were pioneers, and they admired one another. "I regard it as one of the privileges of my youth that I was able to grow up among those active, interesting girls, whose lives were not mere echoes of other lives, but had principle and purpose distinctly their own," Larcom wrote.[13] The sororal atmosphere they created helps explain how these country girls were eventually inspired to organize for workers' rights.

Despite the perks, their labors were heavy. They worked up to fourteen hours a day. Their lungs were assaulted by cotton dust; their eyes were assaulted by smoke from oil lamps; and their ears were assaulted by the thunderous bangs and clangs of the machinery. The job was repetitious and tedious. The matrons who oversaw them in the factory-owned houses where they lived were tyrannical, spying to see who was skipping church on Sundays or posting overbearing decrees such as "The door will be closed at ten o'clock at night, winter and summer, at which time each border will be expected to retire to bed."[14] The curfew was intended to ensure that the young women would be ready for work at the crack of dawn—and that they would avoid the error that felled Sarah Cornell.

At other mills, too, the young women workers, though happy for the unwonted independence their jobs gave them, had reasons to be unhappy. In 1828, at a Dover, New Hampshire, textile factory, the owners issued a series of obnoxious regulations, such as "The bell to call the people to their work will be rung five minutes and tolled five minutes; at the last stroke the entrance will be closed and a fee of 12½ cents exacted of anyone for whom it may be opened." It could take four or five hours of labor to make 12½ cents. The mill girls bonded together and spurred one another to indignation. At a prearranged signal hundreds of them left their looms at the Dover mill and poured out of the factory doors. They carried banners that protested the mill owners' mistreatment of them. They chanted angry slogans, and they fired off gunpowder. It was one of the first labor strikes in America. The newspapers reported it half-admiringly and half-mockingly. "The female operatives of New Hampshire exhibit the Yankee sex in a new and unexpected light," the *National Gazette* declared. "By and by the governor may have to call out the militia to prevent a gynecocracy."[15]

The Lowell mill girls struck in 1834. In the midst of an economic downturn, factory directors had announced that there would be a series of gradual reductions (up to 15 percent) in the girls' wages. The reductions felt like a betrayal. Those workers who wanted a "turn-out" (as strikes were called) prodded their comrades in militant language that was new to woman: "The oppressing hand of avarice would enslave us; and to gain their object they tell us of the pressures of the time," they wrote in a labor magazine.[16] The number of workers in favor of the strike grew. They held meetings to discuss what their strategy should be. They would not strike if they could convince the bosses not to reduce wages. They chose a leader, who went to the directors to ask them to cancel the proposed gradual reductions.

The directors responded by announcing a punitive new decision: The cuts would not be gradual after all, since the mill girls seemed set on griping at every little new reduction. The workers could expect to receive 15 percent less money in their very next pay envelope.

Their leader was summoned back to the company office. The mill girls, guessing she would be dismissed, arranged that some of them would watch from the windows, and if the directors fired her, when she got out into the yard, she would wave her bonnet in the air. She did—and at the signal, the turn-out began. Hundreds of young women swarmed out of the mill buildings and assembled around her. Their numbers soon increased to two thousand.[17]

One mill agent who watched in disgust declared, in the usual terms of accusation against female assertiveness, that real women could not act as these creatures did. It was "an Amizonian [sic] display," he noted. Unnatural females had cast "a spirit of evil omen" upon the mill girls. The newspapers were scandalized too. A reporter for the Boston Transcript wrote that he had been informed that the leader "mounted a stump, and made a flaming Mary Woolstonecroft [sic] speech on the rights of women and the iniquities of the 'monied aristocracy.'" Her speech, the reporter said mockingly, "produced a powerful effect on her auditors, and they determined to 'have their own way, if they die for it.'" He described the young women marching through the town, "to the amusement of a mob of idlers and boys, and we are sorry to add, not altogether to the credit of Yankee girls."[18]

The mill directors, who controlled the town, were not intimidated by the pesky girl strikers. On Sunday, the young women were the subject of scolding sermons in Lowell's churches. On Monday, the directors arranged for a Methodist preacher to meet with them and tell them they should be grateful to have such fine jobs. The directors also let it be known that they were recruiting girls from nearby farms, who would be taking the jobs the strikers would be losing. The mill girls, still novices in the business of demanding their rights, were defeated. Before the first week of the strike was over, they had accepted the 15 percent cut and returned to work.[19]

But they did not forget their grievances. They established the Factory Girls' Association, the first working-women's union in the United States. Twenty-five hundred Lowell workers signed up for membership. Their declaration of purpose was a redefinition of woman. She was now a warrior against injustice, no different from men who fought injustice: "As our fathers resisted unto blood the lordly avarice of the British ministry, so we, their daughters, will never wear the yoke which has been prepared for us," they proclaimed.[20]

The Factory Girls' Association did not succeed in making great changes in the conditions under which they worked. The members knew nothing of the game of unionizing. But they inspired mill girls all over New England to become more militant. In 1848, at a cotton mill near Pittsburgh, women strikers threw eggs at scabs and then descended on the factory and destroyed the machinery. The mill girls eventually even learned a bit about how to maneuver politically. Sarah Bagley, who had been a Lowell mill girl since 1835 and had had only a grammar school education, began leading night classes for other mill girls: her usual topic was social injustice. In 1844 she brought together a group of her coworkers and formed the Female Labor Reform Association. The organization's motto, "Try Again," signified that though their first union had fizzled out, they would never give up trying to force Lowell factory owners to stop exploiting them.[21] They had become women who dared defy male authority.

Under Bagley's firebrand leadership, the members of the Female Labor Reform Association bypassed the mill owners and went straight to the lawmakers. In 1845, thousands of mill girls signed a petition to the Massachusetts Legislature for a ten-hour workday. The legislators assumed that the working-class women would be petrified to speak to an audience of men, and they informed the Female Labor Reform Association that "as the greater part of the petitioners are female, it will be necessary for them to make the defence or we shall be under the necessity of laying [the petition] aside."[22]

Bagley was delighted to break taboos, especially the one against women speaking to male audiences. Showing up at the legislature with a posse of supporters, she testified vehemently: Women workers' rights had been "trampled upon."[23]

However, it did not matter what she and the eight other Female Labor Reform Association members who addressed the legislators said. The men had already decided that they would not interfere in the activities of the mill owners. Anyway, the legislators proclaimed, a law that mandated a ten-hour workday would "close the gate of every mill in the state." The mill girls continued to work fourteen hours a day.[24]

Yet working women had found a collective voice. They had learned that they could speak to the government. They also learned that they could make their displeasure felt if elected officials disappointed them. Though they could not vote themselves, the Female Labor Reform Association members mounted an unprecedented get-out-the-vote campaign against the chairman of the legislative committee that had decided against them, William Schouler. The women lobbied every male worker in the Lowell factories (men made up 20 percent of the Lowell labor force), convincing them to vote against Schouler. That was enough to decide the election. When Schouler lost his seat, the members of the Female Labor Reform Association were not shy about making known their role in his defeat. In *The Voice of Industry*, a weekly labor magazine that Bagley edited, the women proudly "tender[ed] their grateful acknowledgement to the voters of Lowell, for consigning Wm. Schouler to the obscurity he so justly deserves."[25]

The following year Schouler was elected again, and despite the mill girls' repeated attempts to sway the legislature, the workday would not be shortened to ten hours in Massachusetts until 1874, almost thirty years later. But the fact that these young women publicly fought for their rights was an important shift in how working women might perceive themselves. Larcom, the memoirist, represented the new spirit among the young women who left home and went to work. "I felt that I belonged to the world, that there was something for me to do in it," she wrote.[26]

Previously almost all women had belonged to parents or husbands—certainly not to the world. There had not been much for a woman to do in the world, and even by 1870, only 15 percent of American women were working outside the home.[27] However, the women who did cross the threshold pioneered a new way of being. When a woman left home to enter the workforce, she became part of a larger world and could begin to define herself outside of her roles as daughter, wife, and mother.

WOMAN GOES WEST

"I am a worshipper at the shrine of Liberty."
—MARY JANE MEGQUIER, letter, 1849[28]

From the beginning of Americans' westward movement, women were part of the "irresistible army of Anglo-Saxon emigration," as John O'Sullivan, editor of the *United States Magazine and Democratic Review*, phrased it. O'Sullivan declared in 1845 that it was white Americans' "manifest destiny"—decreed by nothing less than "Providence"—to spread out over the continent and claim it for "our yearly multiplying millions."[29] By 1865, when Horace Greeley famously advised young men to "Go West," about a third of the white population, including women and children, already had done so. They had fanned out from the East, moving across the Midwest, Southwest, and far West in search of land and opportunities they could not find where they had been.

Some women, such as Mary Jane Megquier, found extraordinary liberation through the move. In 1849, Megquier and her doctor husband left their three children in the care of relatives in Turner, Maine, and sailed along the Isthmus of Panama, eventually reaching San Francisco. There she re-created herself in ways undreamed of in New England, where women of her class still strove to be domestic and pure exemplars of true womanhood. The Megquiers arrived in the midst of the gold rush. Miners were coming into town with pockets full of nuggets, and as Mary Jane wrote to a relative back in Maine, she intended to "make hay while the sun shines." She opened a boardinghouse for the flush miners and became a savvy businesswoman with an eye toward maximizing profits. She made a fortune. Megquier claimed liberation from the pious part of true womanhood also. In San Francisco, she wrote, there were plenty of churches, but "you can do as you please about attending, it is all the same whether you go to church or play monte." In the brand-new milieu of early San Francisco, Megquier could overturn notions about woman that even she had once accepted as inescapable. She declared herself now "a worshipper at the shrine of liberty."[30]

But for many women who moved across the continent or the Atlantic to unknown and sparsely populated territory, life could be grim. An 1850 report depicted the unrelenting struggle of white women on the western prairies—tough especially for those of the middling classes who were used to the niceties of "civilization." "On the females of this class fall terribly the hardships of frontier life," the author wrote. "In thousands of humble cabins, by forest and prairie, are found pale, intellectual-looking women, broken down with unwonted drudgery." He concluded morbidly, "In silence they struggle on, and one by one they fade from the earth." Those who survived had willed themselves to become a new breed of woman.[31]

The white migrants to the frontier usually brought with them ideas about "man's work" and "woman's work." Husbands "would tame the land with the plow," and wives "would tame it with the spinning wheel." Or if they worked together in the fields, husbands would steer the yoked oxen and wives would follow behind, dropping seeds.[32] But faced with real life out West, such neat divisions of labor could not always be maintained. Spinning-wheel sorts of duties accounted for only part of woman's work.

If a woman lived in a sparsely populated area, where there were no shops such as she might have been used to back home, her work would be as unremitting as it had been for colonial women two hundred years earlier. She would be in charge of the garden, chickens, cows, and all that went on in the kitchen and the rest of the house. She would be doctor and nurse to anyone in the household who was sick or injured. She would make the family's clothes, candles, and medicines. She would also bear and raise seven, eight, nine, or even ten children (essential as future farm help). In addition, if crops had to be brought in and hired hands could not be afforded, she would be out in the fields doing backbreaking labor along with her husband. Any troubles she had adjusting to life as a pioneer would have been compounded if she were stubborn about holding onto notions such as woman's role or womanly delicacy. Those who flourished flouted the old ideals.

In 1831, Rebecca Burlend came from Yorkshire, England, with her husband and five children to the wilderness of Pike County, Illinois. They arrived almost penniless and determined to make their fortune. As Burlend recalled in her 1848 memoir—a tale of success that was intended to encourage the emigration of other ambitious British families—their labors were seldom divided along the lines of men's jobs and women's jobs. She and her husband together made the furniture for their little log cabin and their own candles and soap. Before they had the money to hire help or even purchase a plow and a horse, Burlend and her husband cleared the fields and then sowed acres of "Indian corn" with a hoe. One year, her husband was incapacitated by a freak accident just as the wheat needed to be cut. Worried that it would spoil if it were not taken up right away, Burlend and her nine-year-old son reaped the entire crop, carried it home, and stacked it. She was then seven months pregnant with twins.[33]

The grueling trip westward on overland trails pulled many other women from the confines of womanhood—whether or not they wished to be pulled. Catherine Haun and her new husband left Clinton, Iowa, in 1849 and headed for California, hoping to "'pick up' enough gold to pay our debts," as she later wrote. They traveled in a small party of six men and two women, which required everyone to "lend a 'helping hand.' It was expected of us all—men and women alike." What passed for appropriate gender behavior back in "civilization" had to be forgotten by the small party. Everyone pitched in irrespective of the old roles. They all built campfires, washed dishes, fought the Indians who tried to discourage their invasion, and helped hold back a loaded wagon on a downgrade or lift it over boulders in the path of their mountain climb. Haun seems never to have shirked the unaccustomed duties, yet a hint of worry that "men's work" was making her masculine crept into her account as she recalled that she was happy to get together with other women on the trail for "tatting, knitting, crocheting, exchanging recepes [sic]." It was important, Haun concluded, to "keep us in practice of feminine occupations."[34]

Mothers might be particularly anxious when daughters forgot what was appropriate to womanliness. Mary Ellen Todd recalled that as a young girl in 1852, traveling for months with her family on the Oregon Trail, it sometimes fell to her to steer the oxen that pulled their wagon. Wanting to match the efficiency of the men, she kept trying to crack a big whip over the head of oxen just as they did. Finally, she succeeded. "How my heart bounded a few days later," she recorded, "when I heard father say to mother, 'Do you know that Mary Ellen is beginning to crack the whip?'" But to Mrs. Todd it signified a dangerous impropriety. "I'm afraid it isn't a very ladylike thing for a girl to do," she told her husband. "After this," Mary Ellen Todd wrote, "while I felt a secret joy in being able to have a power that sets things going, there was also some sense of shame in this new accomplishment."[35] She learned that she had to hide her joy in achieving a competence not meant for woman; she had trespassed in men's territory. Nevertheless, she had experienced that joy. And writing years later as an adult, she still had not forgotten what it felt like.

Rebecca Ketcham wrote in her diary in 1853 that she left her home in Ithaca, New York, and got herself to Independence, Missouri, the gathering point for covered wagons heading west. She reported that she paid $150 to join one of the wagon trains, though she did not say why she had left home or why she was traveling alone. Few women braved the overland trails west without a husband, and it took some serious incentive to do it as a feme sole. By the end of the months-long trek in the wilderness, a single woman was a different person from the one she had been at the start of the trip. If she did not realize in the beginning that she had to cast off the ideal of womanly delicacy, she learned it very soon. As Ketcham discovered when she was forced to ride a horse for miles in driving rain, her dress sopping wet and no invitation forthcoming into the shelter of a covered wagon, the chivalry due to a lady back home did not obtain on the trail.

Whatever Ketcham's reasons for leaving Ithaca, they were so grave that she had begged money from friends and family members for the passage west. Her wagon train was led by a stranger who was herding a large flock of sheep to Clatsop Plains, Oregon. She knew no one in Clatsop Plains, an area of wetlands and sand dunes in the middle of nowhere; but that was where the wagon train was going, so that was where she went. She guessed correctly that the new little towns of the West were looking for teachers, and she found a teaching job once she got to Clatsop Plains. But along the way, Ketcham often regretted embarking on the journey. "How little I knew what risk I was running when I started," she told her diary, and she wondered whether it was possible to change her mind and go home.[36]

Yet she persisted through the many months it took to get to Clatsop Plains. Her diary traces how she coped with the trials she faced and how, little by little, her competence grew beyond what she thought a woman could do. During the first weeks, Ketcham was terrified of horses, loathed riding, and shrieked at the sight of rattlesnakes. Gradually she rose to challenges. She was proud, for example, that in navigating a steep pitch down to a river that had to be crossed, "I was not in the least afraid." The first time she had to hold the lines to steer the oxen, she almost overturned the wagon. But in the course of the journey she learned the skill so well that, as she boasted toward the end of the trip, the trail leader told her he "would sooner trust my driving than Phill's," one of the men who often held the lines.[37] It was a tremendous affirmation: she had become adept at a tough skill. She had been challenged as she would never have been back in "civilization." She was no longer the delicate woman she had been months earlier. In order not to go under on the trail, she and many other women discovered that they had to rewrite, at least for the duration, what "woman" meant. Daintiness and delicacy were hindrances. Even if they later found themselves in a position where those attributes were again relevant to their lives, they had learned that they were capable of unwomanly feats.

Some went further in moving the parameters of woman. They lived in the West as men, proving (if only to themselves, in secret) that "woman," so far from being nature's lifelong sentence, was a negotiable concept. They decided to live as men for many different reasons. Some were, in the parlance of late nineteenth-century sexologists, born as "men trapped in women's bodies"—or, in contemporary parlance "transgender." Joe Monahan, raised as a girl by a foster mother in Buffalo, New York, left home in 1868 at the age of fourteen, according to a Buffalo newspaper that announced Monahan's death almost forty years later: "she" had told her foster mother that "she was going away to acquire a fortune in the mining country."[38] But Monahan was also going to anonymity. In the West, where no one knew him as Johanna, he could be Joe.

Monahan had probably heard rumors about the Owyhee mines after news of them began circulating because of an enticing article in the *New York Times*. The southwestern portion of Idaho Territory had "the richest and most valuable silver mines yet known to the western world," the article claimed. Idaho was where the fourteen-year-old headed, to prospect for silver along the ridges of the Owyhee Mountains, near Ruby City. He had no success, but returning to Buffalo was not an option. He next wandered to Oregon and became a cowboy and then a sheepherder. Finally, he went back to Idaho, staked out a homestead claim in Rockville, bought some horses, and ran a modest ranch. Monahan was not more than five feet tall, but despite a bit of speculation that he might be a woman (a census taker in 1880 checked the box that said "male" but penciled above it "doubtful sex"), he was credible enough to most of his neighbors, who did not examine too closely the origin stories of their fellow pioneers. Monahan participated in the civic duties from which women were excluded: he served on juries and even voted in the 1880 election. But he was mostly a loner. It was only at his death, when the undertaker was preparing his body for the funeral, that Monahan's anatomical sex was discovered.[39]

Others who presented themselves as men may have done so because they did not trust gallantry to protect a lone woman in the wilds or because they relished the freedoms and perquisites reserved for men. Mountain Charley, who in 1861 published an autobiography under the name Mrs. E. J. Guerin, lived for thirteen years as a man. Guerin, who had gone by the name Elsa Jane in an earlier life, wrote that even as a child she had felt in herself "a strength of character, a firmness and self-reliance, that amounted to almost masculine force."[40] Strength, firmness, and self-reliance she understood to be antithetical to the idea of woman. Nevertheless, she married, became a conventional housewife, and had two children.

When her husband, a riverboat pilot, was shot and killed in a quarrel, leaving her penniless, she sought work to support herself and her little family. Finding that there were no decent-paying jobs open to women, Guerin put the children in a Sisters of Charity boarding school in St. Louis and, as she declared in her memoir, decided to "dress myself in male attire and seek for a living in this disguise among the avenues which are so religiously closed to my sex." She reveled in the new freedom. It confirmed for her how stifling and unreasonable the limitations imposed on women were. As a man, she wrote, "I could go where I chose, do many things which while innocent in themselves were debarred from association with the female sex."[41]

Among the things she did was to make the arduous journey west several times. The first time was in a party of sixty men on the Overland Trail, which brought her to Feather River in California, where she prospected for gold and became the proprietor of a saloon. Then she returned to St. Louis, donned women's clothes, and spent time with her children. But she grew restless. As a man again, she took the Santa Fe Trail to Colorado, where she mined for gold in Pike's Peak and bought another saloon. On still another trip, she headed a wagon train of fifteen men, twenty mules and horses, and a large herd of cattle that she had bought. When her party was attacked by Indians protesting the whites' presence, she fought not only with a gun but also in hand-to-hand combat with a knife.

However, thirteen years after first donning men's clothes, she married the barkeep in the saloon she owned. "Genderqueer" long before the term was coined, even after her anatomical sex was revealed Guerin continued to wear men's clothes. But she presented herself as a proponent of dress reform, a movement that started in the East soon after the 1848 women's rights convention that Elizabeth Cady Stanton and Lucretia Mott had organized. Dress reform was even more important in the rough-and-tumble West than it was in the East, Guerin insisted, touting "the change from the cumbersome, unhealthy attire of woman to the more convenient, healthful habiliments of a man."[42]

President Abraham Lincoln signed the Homestead Act into law in 1862. It granted 160 acres of public land, mostly west of the Mississippi, to any applicant who was over twenty-one or the head of a household. Immigrants, free Blacks, and even women—if they were spinsters, unwed mothers, widows, or divorcées—were eligible to claim land. Only Indians were excluded. In return for 160 acres, the claimant had to pay a filing fee of $18, live on the land, and "prove it up"—that is, develop it—within five years. The opportunity was unprecedented, especially for single women. In some areas they accounted for 12 percent of the homesteaders; in other areas they made up as much as 22 percent.

The proposal that the Homestead Act be open to women triggered dismay. Arkansas Senator Robert Ward Johnson, a plantation owner and southern gentleman, was not happy that Black people could claim land under the Homestead Act, but he was livid when a fellow senator also supported unmarried women's right to 160 acres: "Young women over the age of twenty-one are to be brought into the wilderness, make a settlement, build a house, and live in it by themselves, unmarried," Johnson declared. "Why Sir, I hope the senator does not wish to encourage that state of things, even if there are those who would accept it. But there are few who would accept it!"[43]

In fact, thousands of single women rushed to "accept it." Though it was no easy task to "prove up" barren land in the wilderness, over 42 percent of the single women who tried succeeded—compared to only 37 percent of the men homesteaders. It was the first time in American history that large numbers of non-Indian women, from the working class as well as the middle class, had the chance to own property in their own name. The federal government's tacit assumption in extending the Homestead Act to single women had been that they would be tempted to move to the "unsettled" territories by the offer of free land, which would serve as their dowries. They would choose their mate among the surfeit of homesteading bachelors, marry and raise families, and populate the land for the United States—and that was the scenario that was played out often among the homesteaders.[44]

But other women took advantage of the bounty of the Homestead Act for reasons that flouted woman's traditional role. Homesteading brought women to uncharted territory, which allowed them to create new rules and start afresh. Away from the prying eyes of their families and established communities, they could break out of the old prisons of propriety. They could escape the predictability of woman's life in the East. They could be experimental and expansive. As Mary Price Jeffords, a female homesteader who settled in Custer County, Nebraska, declared, she could not "see why a girl could not do anything a boy could do"—but to put her convictions into play she had to flee the gender restrictions of the East. E. J. Wilder, a woman who settled in Dakota Territory, wrote that she homesteaded because she "had the great desire and ambition since a child to secure a home [of her own],"[45] but in the established East there were no opportunities for a woman to secure her own home.

Other women went west to homestead because they loathed domesticity or their ambitions were not compatible with woman's life as they had been taught it must be lived. They were spurred on, as Clarissa Griswold, another female homesteader, wrote, through stories of "the thrills experienced, and the fortunes made" by single women who had already succeeded as homesteaders.[46] It was a heady possibility. Men had always been the ones who expanded their prospects through land acquisition. Now women could head west and do the same thing.

The prospects were less bright for those women who were already living in the West—Mexicans and Indians. In 1848, Mexico lost a war with the United States and was forced to cede much of the Southwest to the victor. Laboring-class Hispanic women found their lives contracted when white emigrants to the new territories squeezed out the businesses in which the Hispanic women had been engaged. For instance, in 1850, the census in Santa Fe, New Mexico, still showed Hispanic women making a living in a variety of trades such as "confectioner," "farmer," and "midwife." But they could not compete long against the new residents who came with money to open fancier candy stores or buy larger farms or who held medical degrees in obstetrics. The narrowing of the Hispanic women's sphere was soon evident. In the 1860 and 1870 censuses, almost all of them who were employed were listed as "domestic servant," "seamstress" or "launderess."[47] Clearly, "the thrills experienced, and the fortunes made" by westering white women were not for them.

Upper-class Hispanic women had also been better off before the southwestern regions were absorbed by the United States. In Spanish Mexico, there had been no law of coverture. A married woman retained the sole right to the property she owned before marriage and even to the property she acquired after marriage. Article 8 of the Treaty of Guadalupe Hidalgo specified that that law would be unchanged. However, Article 8 was eroded when U.S. legislators and judges failed to sympathize with the strange Latin notion that a married woman had a right to own property in her own name.[48]

Yet there were wealthy Hispanic women who did manage, in one way or another, to retain their independence. Maria del Carmen Calvillo owned and operated Rancho de las Cabras, a 15,000-acre spread in San Antonio. She had inherited the ranch from her father in 1814, when she was still married. However, soon after taking possession of the property, she shed her husband, directed her multiple hired hands to build a large granary and a sugar mill, and expanded the huge spread by obtaining additional land grants. There was no question about who was in charge at Rancho de las Cabras. After the Treaty of Guadalupe Hidalgo was signed, she petitioned the courts for "return of property lost during the Anglo-American invasion," and she won. Maria del Carmen Calvillo defied all images of woman as dainty, demure, or domestic. She dressed in men's clothes (far more suitable for running a ranch than petticoats), was adept at shooting, and could rope as well as the best of her men. She operated the ranch with its 2,000 head of livestock until 1851, when she was eighty-five years old. There were not many women anywhere in America who enjoyed her remarkable privilege. She and other Hispanic women who were able to hold onto and manage large properties were aspirational models to the Anglo westering women who hoped to remake themselves.[49]

While horizons were expanding for the white woman, for the Native woman, as for the laboring-class Hispanic woman, they were shrinking. President Lincoln had urged passage of the Homestead Act in order that "the wild lands of the country should be distributed so that every man [sic] should have the means and opportunity of benefitting his condition."[50] The convenient fiction was that these "wild lands" were virtually unpopulated. The president may have been sincere in his justification for the Homestead Act, but it was passed for more nefarious reasons as well. It permitted the territories that Native Americans had made their home and hunting grounds—including land that had been created by Congress in 1834 as Indian Territory—to be claimed and tamed by non-Indians.

The Indian woman's stature had been under attack for some time, since the early colonists were baffled by the power that women held in some tribes. But the assault on the Indian woman's power began in earnest with the birth of the new republic, and it spread west with westward expansion in the nineteenth century. The Indian woman's elevated status was seen as an obstacle both to expansion and to the white man's aim to "civilize" the Indians. As George Washington had told the men of the Cherokee Nation in 1796, "Your wives and daughters can soon learn to spin and weave," which would leave room for the men to do the "men's work" as small farmers and ranchers—and so cease to hunt on land that was coveted for white settlement.[51] This became a major goal for the U.S. Office of Indian Affairs, which was established in 1824.

But the Indians continued to resist. In 1839, T. Hartley Crawford, the commissioner of Indian affairs and a proponent of true womanhood for all women, suggested to Congress, "If the [Indian] women are made good and industrious housewives, and taught what befits their condition, their husbands and sons will find comfortable homes and social enjoyments, which, in a state of society, are essential to morality and thrift."[52] The implication was that if their women were refashioned to conform to the ideal of white womanhood, Indian men would stop being savage. The Indian women needed to be convinced, Hartley believed, because they were the key to domestication—that is, to containing Indian men peacefully, or "civilizing" them—just as white women were responsible for making their men more "civilized."

That could only be done if the Indian woman was drastically altered, but the altering took time. In 1854, George W. Manypenny, then commissioner of Indian affairs, reiterated with frustration in his annual report that the Indians of New Mexico and Utah must be "induced to resort to agriculture and kindred pursuits, instead of relying, as they now do, for support upon the uncertain and precarious supplies of the chase, and when that fails upon the more hazardous and injurious practice of theft and plunder" (of the white citizens who were manifesting destiny by claiming the West). But the Indians had an "inveterate determination . . . to resist domestication," the commissioner complained.[53]

The first Europeans that the Indians of the Southwest encountered were the conquistadors. Like tribes in the East, the southwestern Indian tribes had often appointed women to negotiate peace with their adversaries, and they were particularly optimistic about the efficacy of female peace emissaries when they observed that the Spaniards idolized the image of a woman (the Virgin Mary). They learned that they were mistaken in their assumption when the Spaniards raped the Indian women sent as emissaries.[54] Women could not be used as emissaries.

The missionaries tried to control the sexual brutality of the conquistadors, but they were also bent on "instilling" into the Indian women "the modesty, delicacy, and virtue belonging to their sex," as Father Fermin Francisco de Lasuen, a Franciscan missionary, wrote. By the nineteenth century, the seventeenth-century observation by Baron de Lahontan about "woman" among the Indians with whom he lived—that she was "Master of her own Body, and by her Natural Right of Liberty is free to do what she pleases"—would have been puzzling almost anywhere among the Indians. The Apache woman, for instance, was urged to be "modest and chaste," and the sexual "degradation" of an Apache woman came to be considered "much worse than death." She was valued for her femininity: "Not too tall . . . small hands and feet. . . . A plump, full body is best." Her role came to be identical, at least in its ideal, with that of the white "true woman": she must create a comfortable home, make clothing for her family, and teach her daughters what was appropriate to woman's role.[55]

Yet like Calvillo, who defied the limits set for Hispanic woman, some Indian women stretched the boundaries. The most notable boundary stretcher was Lozen, a Chiricahua Apache woman whose name signified "one who steals horses in a raid." From early childhood she refused to be indoctrinated into proper gender behavior. In 1847, when she was seven years old, she insisted on learning to ride like the boys. She played rough boys' games and participated in the arduous physical training that adolescent Apache boys were put through. Marriage, usually arranged by parents when a girl was still in her teens, defined the nineteenth-century Apache woman, but Lozen never married.

The Chiricahua Apaches had been living in New Mexico when white settlements began encroaching on their land. In 1870, the Apaches were forced onto a reservation in Arizona. They rebelled, pillaging and plundering white settlements and battling the U.S. cavalry when it tried to prevent them from returning to New Mexico. Lozen, by now a warrior, a sort of Apache Joan of Arc, went on the warpath with Chiricahua men. From all accounts, she rode, shot, roped, and fought "like a man." A cavalry officer remembered her as "one of the most dexterous horse thieves" in the tribe. Victorio, her brother and the revered leader of the Chiricahua Apaches, described her as his "right hand . . . strong as a man, braver than most, and cunning in strategy." She claimed to have a direct connection with Ussen, the Apaches' highest deity and the creator of life. "Ussen has Power / His Power is Mine," she chanted before battles. Ussen guided her to the enemy when she stretched out her arms, palms raised to the sky where he dwelt, Lozen claimed. That was how she had what seemed to be an uncanny ability to know not only when the U.S. cavalry was planning an attack, but also from which direction they were coming and how close they were. The Chiricahua warriors venerated her.[56]

Lozen died in 1889, just about the time that European sexologists such as Richard von Krafft-Ebing were giving names to females who in childhood played boy's games and refused to be girls, and in adulthood engaged in activities reserved for men and never married. Such females were called "sexual inverts" and "pathological." But the Apaches had not heard of the European sexologists, and they made a space for a female who could not be contained in the boundaries of "woman," especially one who exhibited Lozen's powers. Her tribe dubbed her "Holy Woman."[57]

WOMAN GOES TO THE CIVIL WAR

> "Utterly devoid of fear, and manifesting perfect indifference to shot or shell."
>
> —MARY LIVERMORE, *My Story of the War* (1888)[58]

Though women have seldom been combatants in wars, they have always suffered from war's collateral damage: the loss of loved ones, property, and quietude. But wars have also given women space to step beyond the boundaries that were deemed natural to them and refashion themselves in ways that would have been impossible in peacetime. This was especially true of the Civil War, which provided opportunities for refashioning that would have been inconceivable in the Revolutionary War of the previous century, when women were officially encouraged to do no more for the war effort than boycott tea and sew shirts for soldiers. Because women did as much as they did in the Civil War, women's righters took the opportunity after the war to argue that now America owed women first-class citizenship.

Elizabeth Cady Stanton, Susan B. Anthony, and Matilda Joslyn Gage devoted an entire section of their multivolume *History of Woman Suffrage*, which they began writing in the decade after the Civil War, to reminding the country that "while the nation's life hung in the balance . . . the patriotism of woman shone forth as fervently and spontaneously as that of man." The authors presented rousing depictions of women who labored for the Union: Anna Ella Carroll, an "astute military genius," who, though a southerner and a daughter of a former Governor of Maryland, drew up plans for the War Department that were instrumental in the Union Army's major victory in the Tennessee Campaign; Dorothea Dix, who began as a volunteer hospital nurse and became superintendent of nurses for the entire Union Army; and Clara Barton, who founded the American Red Cross, was called the "Angel of the Battlefield," and daily risked her life on the front lines to tend the wounded and comfort the dying.

History of Woman Suffrage spent pages on "Women as Soldiers." There were hundreds of them, "obliged by army regulations to fight in disguise," and many were compelled to leave the army because their sex was discovered. Stanton told a tale of patriotism so strong in a woman's breast that the frustration of it led to tragedy: When the provost-marshall of the Fourteenth Iowa Regiment suspected a certain soldier was a woman, he ordered an investigation. Knowing she would be found out, "'Charlie' placed the muzzle of her revolver to her head, fired and fell dead on the parade ground. No clue was obtained to her name, home, or family." Stanton followed the story of Charlie with a paean to the many other women soldiers who fought undetected and died on the battlefield. They were buried in national cemeteries, alongside their male comrades in arms, "with headboards marked 'Unknown,'" Stanton concluded in a heart-wrenching argument for why women had the right to full citizenship.[59]

It was true that an estimated 400 Union soldiers and 250 Confederate soldiers were individuals who had been assigned female at birth. Their enlistment as men was made possible because army physical examinations consisted of a doctor asking a recruit to open his hands and then make a fist, bend his elbows and knees, rotate his shoulders, and vouch that he enjoyed general good health. Patriotism had surely been a reason, as Stanton suggested, why many of the soldiers assigned female at birth enlisted to fight in the Civil War, but there were other motives as well. For some, their acceptance into the military was a confirmation of the gender they had always known themselves to be. Others appear to have been genderfluid, even spending part of their lives as wives and mothers (though it is impossible to know whether their cisgender histories can be accounted for by pressures such as those that caused Frank Dubois to return to his life as Mrs. Della Hudson, as discussed in the introduction). The most complete accounts of these soldiers come from two memoirists: Sarah Emma Edmonds, who served in the Union Army as Franklin Thompson, and Loreta Janeta Velazquez, who served in the Confederate Army as Lieutenant Harry T. Buford. Both wrote of having married (Velazquez claimed to have had four marriages), and each gave birth to three children.[60]

But whether Edmonds, Velazquez, and others felt themselves to be men or were women "in disguise," there was no more dramatic escape from the limits of woman's sphere in the mid-nineteenth century than to play an active role in war. Doing so was a radical refusal of all that woman was supposed to be, requiring the most unwomanly tolerance for gore and violence, demanding skills antithetical to womanly delicacy, and offering excitements and high adventure forbidden to nineteenth-century woman.

Regardless of women's true motives, the argument Stanton made about women's patriotic self-sacrifice was bolstered by numerous other firsthand accounts detailing women's heroic exploits in the Civil War, such as Mary Livermore's 1888 memoir *My Story of the War: A Woman's Narrative of Four Years Personal Experience as Nurse in the Union Army*. Livermore's book was not only about herself as a war nurse but also about women who fought on the front lines qua women. She too told dramatic tales of patriotism, including those about Nadine Turchin, the wife of a wounded colonel, who first nursed her husband and then took his place at the head of his regiment, "utterly devoid of fear, and manifesting perfect indifference to shot or shell"; and Bridget Devons, who followed her husband to the field, where she took the place of fallen soldiers, fighting in their stead "with unquailing courage."[61] All such post–Civil War authors were making the case, whether explicitly or implicitly, that justice demanded that women's patriotic service during the war, in which they stepped out of the domestic sphere for the sake of the country, be rewarded by first-class citizenship. The argument did not succeed then, but eventually it would.

The Civil War section of *History of Woman Suffrage* confronted the supposed passivity and timidity of women by presenting them as bold state actors, but its focus on white women of the Union left Black and Confederate women entirely out of the picture. The authors barely mentioned Harriet Tubman, and they missed her story as the first woman in the United States to lead a military operation. In 1849, the twenty-seven-year-old, five-foot-tall Tubman had escaped from slavery in Bucktown, Maryland, and trekked alone—across a hundred miles of swamps, salt marshes, and forests infested with mosquitoes, copperheads, and timber wolves—to freedom in Philadelphia. Using the code name Moses, Tubman returned to Maryland thirteen times as a conductor on the Underground Railroad. In dramatic feats of endurance, she led seventy family members and other enslaved people to freedom along the same path she had taken. The abolitionist John Brown called her "the most of a man."[62] (For once, the "manly" appellation was not meant to shame its subject as unnatural.) During the Civil War, Tubman, by now a celebrity among abolitionists, again went south—this time on a government transport ship, at the behest of Massachusetts governor John Andrews—to work as a nurse with escaped enslaved people in a Union hospital off the coast of South Carolina. She was also to be an intelligence agent, gathering any information that might help assess Confederate strength and positions.

Tubman learned from the fugitives where the Confederates had set torpedoes under water in the low country of rice plantations that bordered the Combahee River. On June 2, 1863, in the hours before dawn, she guided three gunboats for twenty-five miles along the river, avoiding the torpedoes. The gunboats were manned by the Union's Second South Carolina Volunteer Colored Regiment, most of whose members had once been enslaved. That night, they rescued slaves who were hiding in wait for them along the banks of the river. A northern newspaper, the *Wisconsin State Journal*, enthused about the Combahee River raid that the soldiers "dashed into the enemy's country, and struck a bold and effective blow, destroying millions of dollars' worth of commissary stores, cotton, and lordly dwellings and, striking terror to the heart of rebeldom, brought off near 800 slaves and thousands of dollars' worth of property, without losing a man or receiving a scratch! It was a glorious consummation." But as excited as the reporter was about the terror visited on rebeldom, he was even more thrilled about the phenomenon of Tubman, whom he described as "the black woman who led the raid, and under whose inspiration it was originated and conducted," whose "energy and sagacity cannot be exceeded," and who was "head and shoulders" above men who "vaunt their patriotism and boast their philanthropy, swaggering their superiority."[63] It was an unprecedented full-throated encomium for a Black woman in a white newspaper.

The Civil War also forced southern white women to begin to grapple with the rigidity of the boundaries that confined them. Willingly or forced to do so by the circumstances of the war, many of them left the captivity or shelter of their homes to become workers for the Confederacy. Even those who stayed home were forced into unaccustomed independence. The challenges of re-creating themselves in wartime were greater for southern white women than they were for those women of the North who for decades had been venturing out into the public sphere through social movements and the workforce. With most able-bodied men off fighting, southern white women now had to manage their lives and livelihood on their own.[64]

From the beginning of the war, southern white women encouraged one another to see themselves as patriots for the Confederacy, to stop being belles, and to remake themselves as serious citizens. Even those southern white women who were opposed to the war's cause felt the call to cast aside the conventions of ladyhood in order to contribute to the war effort. Martha Low Fort, the genteel wife of a man who had been a Georgia legislator before the war, proclaimed "great dislike for both the buying and selling of negroes" and thanked God after the war that "I have seen slavery abolished." Yet in 1861 she became the president of her city's Soldiers' Relief Society, and she headed a drive to get all white women to roll up their sleeves and make coats and cartridges for the soldiers.[65]

"Every true woman of the South will feel that now is the time to banish entirely the follies and extravagances," a young Tennessee woman wrote in *Southern Monthly*. The southern woman must give up luxuries and comforts and turn herself to "habitual industry" in order to support the war effort, the writer urged: "She must rise above the weakness . . . usually attributed to her sex, she must learn to depend on herself." A young Georgian expressed utter contempt for ladies who ignored the exigencies of the times. She exhorted her "Sisters of the South" to stop frittering their hours away in frivolous pastimes. They must throw into the fire the novels they read as they lounged on the sofa. They must turn their favorite lapdog out of doors. They must convert their pianos into spinning wheels and start helping the war effort. They must be transformed, as she had been. The war made her feel "a new life within me." She was now "ingenious, economical, industrious" and "an Independent Southern woman."[66]

The war also opened new occupations to southern white women. Professional nurses in the South had always before been men, but the war created a critical shortage that was filled by women. In the beginning they were unpaid volunteers. Though it was universally agreed that women had an innate capacity for nursing duties and were therefore indispensable in war, it was not until September 1862, seventeen months into the war, that the Confederate Congress declared that women nurses should be paid. Yet even without pay, as soon as the war started, women volunteered in great numbers. They felt, as the Confederate nurse Kate Cumming wrote, that "the war is certainly ours as well as that of the men. We cannot fight, so we must take care of those who do." Cumming traveled to a hospital in Corinth, Tennessee, with thirty-nine other Mobile, Alabama, ladies who had volunteered to nurse the wounded after the Battle of Shiloh. After Chattanooga fell to the Union Army in 1863, she worked as a nurse in field hospitals all over Georgia, until the South finally surrendered. By then, Cumming had become a professional.[67]

Through the demands of the war, nursing became an occupation for southern white women—until the war was over. Then they were urged to go home again. The first nursing school in the South, the South Carolina Training School for Nurses, did not open until 1883, almost twenty years after the Civil War. And even then, the old resistance to the southern woman's leaving her accepted sphere was so strong that the school was forced to close in 1886 for lack of support.[68]

Even during the war, the South could be intransigent about appropriate behavior for a lady. A woman perceived as stepping out too far, even if it was in service to the Confederacy, made people unhappy. Phoebe Levy Pember, an assimilated Jewish woman from an affluent South Carolina family, was widowed when her husband died of tuberculosis in 1861. She was only thirty-eight years old, and at any other time, Pember might have been absorbed back into the social whirl that she had enjoyed before marriage. Her socialite friends, such as Mary Randolph, wife of a prominent lawyer, would surely have introduced her to eligible suitors who would have been eager to marry a well-to-do young widow. But the Civil War had begun. Randolph's husband, George Wythe Randolph, became the Confederate secretary of war in 1862. Knowing that Pember had nursed her husband for years until his death, and recognizing her "will of steel under a suave refinement," Mary Randolph asked Pember if she would consider accepting a position as a superintendent at Chimborazo, a hospital in Richmond that, with 7,000 beds, was the largest military hospital on either side of the Mason-Dixon line.[69]

Pember was very aware of herself as a southern lady. She was "frightened and nervous" at the prospect of the job, she wrote her sister. She was appalled by the thoughts that her life as a hospital supervisor "would be injurious to the delicacy and refinement of a lady" and that her "nature" would deteriorate and her sensibilities would be "blunted."[70] But the war was inviting women to change. On the other side, Dorothea Dix, the Union's superintendent of army nurses, had already taken the giant leap: she was a woman administrator in charge of thousands of people. Pember accepted the job that she had been offered.

The male doctors and staff members with whom she worked during the war were not charmed. This was "petticoat government," they complained. Hoping to win them over, Pember tried to soften her "will of steel" reputation. She was slow even to question a doctor's competency when she thought he had chosen the wrong course of treatment for a patient. But the men banded together anyway to undermine her authority, even covering up for doctors or male nurses whom Pember suspected of having gone AWOL or being drunk on the job.[71]

She struggled constantly with trying to maintain control without appearing Amazonian. The balancing act was sometimes ludicrous. For example, she had to keep an eye on the hospital's supply of whiskey, which was used to abate patients' pain, since doctors and staff members were pilfering it for their own pleasure (and perhaps also to thumb their masculine noses at a woman boss). The vats of whiskey were stored in her office, but the tipplers found ways to break in. Near the war's end, one would-be thief tried to make off with a thirty-gallon barrel, and when Pember burst in on him, he defied her. She felt she had to show him that she was in charge, yet she could not make matters worse by blatantly disavowing her gender. She pulled out the pistol she kept in her desk drawer and waved it at him, declaring that she might not manage to hit him on the first shot but there were five more bullets in the gun—and "the room is too small for even a woman to miss six times."[72]

Despite Pember's cautious needle threading, her aptitude for her position was affirmed after the South had lost the war and Chimborazo was taken over by federal troops. She was asked to stay on and supervise the care of the wounded from both sides. She did, though the doctors continued to complain that having a woman at the helm wreaked institutional havoc.

Pember's worry that regardless of her competence she must not do anything that would be "injurious to the delicacy and refinement of a lady" was not unique among women who ventured onto new ground. Like Mary Ellen Todd on the Oregon Trail, who would not allow herself the great pleasure of cracking the big whip because it was not "a very ladylike thing for a girl to do," they had anxieties: they must not reject entirely what had been instilled in them about how a woman was supposed to comport herself. Yet ambivalence notwithstanding, they had taken giant steps away from the ideals of *Godey's Lady's Book*. Even the readers of *Godey's*—and, more importantly, their daughters—could not avoid seeing by their example new ways to be a woman.

6.
Woman Goes to College and Enters the Professions

Catharine Beecher, who founded one of the first institutions of advanced education for females, was very clear about what was appropriate to woman: "delicacy of appearance and manners, . . . a shrinking from notoriety and public gaze, a love of dependence and protection." She was equally clear about what was inappropriate, and Frances Wright, a women's rights pioneer and one of the first women in the United States to speak to mixed audiences of men and women, was the epitome of inappropriate. Wright advocated ideas that were shockingly radical: free love, birth control, and the liberalization of divorce laws. "There she stands, with brazen front and brawny arms, attacking the safeguards of all that is venerable and sacred in religion, all that is safe and wise in law, all that is pure and lovely in domestic virtue," Beecher wrote after seeing Wright lecture.[1] Students at Beecher's Hartford Female Seminary would learn to eschew the brazen and brawny. They would learn to assert themselves for the betterment of domestic life.

WOMAN GOES TO COLLEGE

"Under such influences the female character is fast becoming masculine."

—E. A. ANDREWS, commentary on Mary Lyon's proposal for Mount Holyoke Female Seminary, 1837[2]

Like her contemporary Sarah Josepha Hale, Catharine Beecher was a study in contradictions. Both women spent their lives cultivating an influential voice in the public sphere while promulgating the idea that woman's influence should be in the domestic sphere. Beecher claimed that motherhood was woman's most important calling, but she never had children. Her ideas about education for women represented a bold leap forward in the decades before the Civil War, but she veiled its boldness through the claim that education would make women more fit for the responsibilities of running the home. Beecher never married, and she let it be known that she remained faithful to the memory of a fiancé who died when she was twenty-two. But in truth she had gotten engaged reluctantly, at the urging of her father, the prominent Rev. Lyman Beecher, and had complained that her suitor was "lacking in affection" and "unsuited to the kind of social life [she] enjoyed."[3] In 1823, soon after his death, Catharine Beecher discovered her calling.

She used the small inheritance her fiancé had left her to found the Hartford Female Seminary. It was one of the first educational institutions to take young women's education seriously rather than offering them courses in the usual genteel pursuits of ladyhood such as French, drawing, and piano playing. But though Beecher's school was revolutionary, she did not present it in that light. Students were offered subjects such as chemistry and philosophy, which Beecher carefully called "domestic chemistry" and "domestic philosophy." Such a curriculum, she emphasized, would make the young woman better able to navigate the challenges she would eventually face in the kitchen and nursery. She would learn why food spoils and how to prevent it from going bad, for example. She would learn how to teach her sons wisdom and morality and everything else they would need to make them good citizens.[4]

Margaret Fuller, America's first female public intellectual and a contemporary of Beecher, was her antithesis. In 1840, Fuller became editor of the era's premier highbrow magazine, *The Dial*. She was then thirty years old. She was almost forty and already the mother of a one-year-old child when she married. Her husband, the child's father, was a twenty-nine-year-old marquis whom she had met in Rome when she was a foreign correspondent for the *New York Tribune* there. A rara avis—yet a beacon of the possible—Fuller lived life on her own terms and encouraged other women to do the same. Before leaving the United States to work in Europe, she conducted classes—"conversations," she called them—mostly for women, on subjects such as women in Greek mythology and German romanticism. Women flocked to Boston to hear her. They revered her. She had an encyclopedic knowledge, a "captivating address & grace," as one attendee recalled, and startling new ideas about the rights of women and how they had been wronged.[5]

Women—not the simplistic abstract "woman," but rather female individuals—were not all the same, Fuller dared to posit. Women had varying aptitudes and interests, and they should have the right to choose their education or occupation according to what suited them and not be bound by the strictures placed on "woman." "If you ask me what offices [women] may fill, I reply—any," she famously asserted in her 1845 book *Woman in the Nineteenth Century*. "I do not care what case you put; let them be sea captains, if you will. I do not doubt there are women well fitted for such an office." She assured those who continued to cling to the prevailing notion of woman that most women, if they were free to choose, would in fact remain domestic creatures. And that being the case, she argued, there is "no need to clip the wings of any bird that wants to soar and sing, or finds in itself the strength of pinion for a migratory flight unusual to its kind."[6]

Beecher and Fuller represented the two major camps in the nineteenth-century struggle to get women educated. The Beecher camp contended that a woman should be educated for the good of her family, especially to enable her to prepare her sons to make the world better. The Fuller camp argued that a woman should be educated for her own good, especially to enable her to enter any occupation for which she was suited and herself make the world better.

When Emma Hart Willard, the principal of a girl's boarding school, appeared before the New York State Legislature to present a unique plan for woman's higher education, she knew what she must say. It was not what she believed. But as she had complained to a woman friend a few years earlier, there was an "absurd prejudice that, if women's minds were cultivated they would forget their own sphere, and intrude themselves into that of men."[7] Willard trod carefully with the legislature.

In her boarding school, Willard had offered her students serious academic subjects that had generally been kept from girls, such as sciences and the classics. In the female seminary she hoped to open in 1819, she wished to offer an even more advanced curriculum. "The education of females has been too exclusively directed to fit them for displaying to advantage the charms of youth and beauty," Willard told the men of the legislature. But not forgetting the men's probable "absurd prejudice," Willard hastened to assure them that though the pupils at her proposed seminary might study serious subjects such as geology, geography, and trigonometry, her school would be as different from men's colleges as "the female character and duties are from the male."[8]

Willard guaranteed that the young woman who went through her seminary would continue to be a true woman, taught to understand her role. She would even spend her Sundays "in hearing discourses relative to the peculiar duties of [her] sex," which included "submission and obedience" to the man who supported and protected her. Of course, the young woman's education would make her a better mother, too, because wise mothers molded wise sons.[9] Yet as careful as Willard was to reassure the legislators that education would not unwoman her students, the men were not persuaded. They would not charter a female seminary.

Two years later Willard was finally able to persuade the city fathers of Troy, a newly incorporated town near Albany, New York, to grant her land and build the Troy Female Seminary on it. The school opened with ninety students. Each year the seminary accepted many hundreds more, mostly daughters of the wealthy, including the young Elizabeth Cady before her marriage to Henry Stanton.

Willard was often assisted in her school by her sister, Almira Hart Phelps, the youngest of their father's seventeen children. Phelps married twice and had four children, but in her youth she had been tutored by a male relative who taught her the subjects he was being taught at Middlebury College. She was so outstanding in botany and chemistry that she would become the second woman to be admitted to the American Association for the Advancement of Science. But for the students at the Troy Female Seminary, Phelps wrote textbooks in which she was careful not to suggest that the young women in her charge could aim to intrude themselves into men's sphere. In between her rigorous instruction in geometry, for instance, she stopped to remind the women students that they were accumulating knowledge "to make them better daughters, wives and mothers; better qualified for usefulness in every path within the sphere of female exertions." Lest the young woman studying geometry miss the point, Phelps reiterated that she must "discern the boundary between your duties, and those of the other sex." The young woman will never be "called upon to lead armies, to make and execute laws, and to preside over public safety," Phelps emphasized, but she may be called upon "to preside over the domestic circle, to regulate families by your wisdom, and to guide and enlighten the youthful mind."[10]

Most young women at the Troy Female Seminary absorbed the lesson as it was taught. Rebels were rare. But there were others, such as Elizabeth Cady, who took the grain but left the chaff: the future Mrs. Stanton learned geometry from Phelps's textbook but ignored Phelps's commands that woman's "elocution" be "confined to the fireside, and to the domestic circle."[11] Elizabeth Cady went on to found a whole movement that rebelled against the dictum that woman—even educated woman—must stay in her sphere. Yet even those Troy alums who did not challenge what Phelps taught them had already taken steps outside the sphere allotted to woman: they had left home to be educated; and they had learned that their female minds could comprehend geology, geography, and trigonometry, which only men had been supposed capable of understanding. It was a beginning.

Mary Lyon founded Mount Holyoke Female Seminary in 1837 to offer a rigorous education to women like herself, daughters of artisans and farmers—"adult female youth in the common walks of life," she wrote when planning Mount Holyoke. Mount Holyoke students would learn Euclid, human physiology, and astronomy not to be better mothers, wives, and daughters but to go out into the world and teach. And they would not be mere teachers, as those who taught briefly before getting married had been: they would be professionals—"educators of youth," Lyon proclaimed them. She urged her students to bravery, to "be willing to go where no one else will go and do what no one else is willing to do." It was a bold new vision of who a young woman might be. Yet even Lyon felt obliged to pay lip service to convention, agreeing that "God has designed a difference in the situation of the sexes."[12]

Lyon's concept of training young women to become "educators of youth" caught fire far beyond Mount Holyoke. The Cherokee Nation, driven out of the Southeast and forced to relocate in Oklahoma, had established their own elementary and high schools in the new territory. The Cherokee National Council wanted control over the education of their young people, but they also wanted them to learn to function in the white world. In 1851, two leaders of the council visited Mount Holyoke to study its curriculum in preparation for opening the Cherokee Female Seminary to train full- and mixed-blood Cherokee women to educate the children. Since there were no models in Oklahoma of what a women's college should look like, the council ordered the buildings of the Cherokee Female Seminary to be designed to look like those at Mount Holyoke. They also hired Mount Holyoke graduates to be the seminary's principal and teachers and to bring with them Mount Holyoke's curriculum and values. That was both good and bad.[13]

Cherokee Female Seminary students studied Latin, botany, chemistry, and physics. They became teachers and enjoyed more autonomy and respect than Cherokee women had had since the Trail of Tears destroyed much of traditional Cherokee culture. However, the seminary also encouraged in the women students a sad amnesia. They forgot (or perhaps never knew) about the power that women had had among the Cherokee in the past. The Cherokee Female Seminary taught them nothing of the old culture except that it was not refined. As one student wrote in the college journal, *Cherokee Rose Buds*, the campus had "elegant white buildings" instead of "the rudely constructed wigwams of our forefathers." (The Cherokee never lived in wigwams, but the student did not know that since Cherokee history was not taught at the seminary.) In place of crude Cherokee traditions, she wrote—knowing nothing of the dignity of her grandmothers—"Everything around denotes taste, refinement, and progress of civilization among our people."[14]

Women's colleges were also opening all over the South. Some were little more than finishing schools, promising courses in aesthetics, literature, music, hygiene, and the "science of domestic economy." The administrations of these colleges took pains to assure parents that the material their daughters studied would be presented in ways suited to a woman, The Female Collegiate Institute in Virginia, for instance, promised that students would receive "easy lessons" in geometry. Others had more serious curricula, but—unlike Mount Holyoke or the Cherokee Female Seminary—they were not intended to prepare a young woman to go out into the world to teach. The students were daughters of wealthy planters or merchants. The purpose of their education was to boost their refinement and confirm their ladyhood.[15]

Nevertheless, some southern parents did take their daughters' education seriously. Charles Cotton, a merchant in Macon, Georgia, hired tutors to prepare his two daughters to enter the recently founded Georgia

Female Seminary. Cotton wrote his eldest daughter, Eliza, in 1838 that of course she must learn to speak French, a sine qua non of gentility. However, he reminded her, "there are so many branches of education of even more importance which you must first become mistress of." Sixty years earlier John Gregory had advised his daughters that men looked with "a malignant eye" at females of "cultivated understanding," and Alice Shippen had told her daughter that "needlework is the most important branch of female education." But Cotton urged Eliza to be a serious thinker. When her tutor gives her a composition assignment, she must "commence reflecting upon it at once, and let it occupy your thoughts at all times when you are not engaged in other pursuit." She was to do research in books but never plagiarize. When an idea struck her, she was to write it down at once. Before she submitted her composition to her tutor she was to revise it, correct it, and copy it: "By getting in the habit of reflecting, your mind and your recollection will become strengthened, and what now seems to you a task will in a short time become perfectly easy to you."[16]

Cotton's advice was no different from what a father might have given his son who was being prepped for Duke University, where he would become a cultivated gentleman. Eliza was being prepped to be the wife of such a cultivated gentleman. The Georgia Female Seminary, where Cotton sent Eliza, would finish her preparation. The seminary's first president, George Foster Pierce, was an enlightened Methodist minister who had urged the church to involve itself in education lest it grow "bigoted, ignorant, [and] superstitious." As president of the seminary, Pierce professed to despise the old order that taught women it was their "business to feel and not to think, to sew and not to write, to look pretty and talk nonsense." The seminary would teach astronomy, chemistry, and physiology no differently from the way young men were taught such subjects. Pierce's enlightenment, however, went only so far. He emphasized that the primary purpose of giving young southern ladies such a fine education was to make them mothers who would mold their sons into warriors, heroes, patriots and orators.[17]

But whether the course of study was "easy" or rigorous, higher education for woman met with opposition in both the North and the South. An 1831 mock advertisement in North Carolina's *Raleigh Register* for a "Refined Female College" announced courses in "talking idly, & dressing ridiculously" at $2.00 a session, "Backbiting your friends" at $1.00 a session, and "Lacing yourself into the shape of an hourglass" at $0.50 a session. No sooner had Mount Holyoke opened when *The Religious Mag-*

azine and Family Miscellany complained that "in place of all which is most attractive in female manners we see characters expressly formed for acting a *manly* part upon the theatre of life.... Under such influences the female character is fast becoming masculine, and all that is elegant, all that is attractive in woman is sacrificed." The following year, Henry F. Harrington, a newspaper editor, opined on "Female Education" that only "semi-woman . . . mental hermaphrodites" who had a "masculineness [sic] of mind and character" would wish to engage in pursuits outside the sphere where God had set woman.[18]

Wealthy southerners lost their fortunes as a result of the Civil War, and higher education for their daughters went dormant. But in the North, women's colleges proliferated. Hysteria proliferated, too. In 1873, for example, Edward Clarke, a Harvard-trained physician, warned young women that if they engaged in serious study their ovaries and uterus would be unhappy, and they would be punished by a slew of female troubles—"leucorrhoea, amenorrhea, dysmenorrhea, chronic and acute ovaritis, prolapsis utari, hysteria, neuralgia, and the like." Worse yet, they risked becoming unwomanly: they would "drop out of maternal instincts" and develop "an appearance of Amazonian coarseness and force."[19] Clarke had sensed that higher education for women could trigger social upheaval. In that, he was not wrong.

When M. Carey Thomas was fourteen years old, in 1871, she heard Anna Dickinson, a fiery woman's rights agitator, lecture on the girlhood of Joan of Arc. A boy with Joan's talents, Dickinson had said, would have been blessed and encouraged to go forth by his parents. But because Joan was a girl, her parents had silenced her, locked her up, and believed that they had "done their duty." The young Thomas was deeply troubled by the story, as she wrote in her diary: "Oh my how terrible, how *fearfully* unjust that seems. A girl [should] certainly do as she chooses as well as a boy. When I grow up—we'll see what will happen." A month later, she decided what she would make happen. Her "one *aim* & concentrated purpose," she vowed to her diary, would be to show that a woman "*can learn, can reason, can compete* with men in the grand fields of literature & science & conjecture that open before the nineteenth century."[20]

A few universities had started admitting women soon after the Civil War for practical reasons: many of the young men who would have been students had been killed in the war. Cornell University permitted women to enroll in 1870, and Thomas became a student there in 1875. She graduated two years later and applied to a PhD program at Johns

Hopkins University. Her father, a prominent Baltimore physician, was a trustee at Johns Hopkins, but his influence was not limitless. His daughter was told that the university would bend their no-women-allowed rules in her case so she could be tutored by faculty members, but she could not attend classes, and it was doubtful that she could receive a PhD.[21]

Thomas left for Europe, where she studied linguistics at the University of Leipzig. When it became clear that Leipzig would not grant a woman a PhD, she moved on to the University of Zurich, which had started admitting women to its PhD programs in 1875. Thomas became the first woman and first American to receive a doctorate summa cum laude from the University of Zurich. Clarke would surely have considered her a prime example of the dangers of female education: she was zealous in her studies, had no "maternal instincts," and possessed a good dose of the "Amazonian . . . force" that troubled him in women. (She was also an embodiment of a still-unspoken anxiety behind the accusation that such women were "unnatural": her important love relationships were all with other women.)[22]

No sooner had Thomas received her PhD than she learned that a new college for women would be opening in Bryn Mawr, Pennsylvania. Though only twenty-six years old, her academic triumphs, her vast ambition, and her family's stature had given her no paucity of self-confidence. She was also passionate in her belief that a woman of intellectual attainment—not a man—should head a college for women. A woman president could serve as a role model for the woman student. It was a revolutionary notion. She offered herself as Bryn Mawr's first president.[23]

She knew just what she would do as president. It was the antithesis of what Emma Willard had promised: that the students in her charge would learn the "peculiar duties" of their sex. Thomas's students would not even be offered domestic science courses. She would hold them to the highest academic standards. She would offer PhD programs at Bryn Mawr so that American women would not have to go off to the University of Zurich, as she had been forced to do. She would build a college for women unlike any that existed. She would bring in as professors the best women scholars in the world because she believed that only women scholars could assist women students "to tide over the first discouragements" of arduous study in fields that men had claimed for themselves.[24]

Bryn Mawr's Board of Trustees chose as the college's first president James Rhoads, who was thirty years older than Thomas. However, Thomas was given the second most powerful position at Bryn Mawr, dean of the college. And because Rhoads's health was poor, Thomas was soon running Bryn Mawr. When Rhoads announced in 1893 that he was resigning, Thomas put her name forward again. She was strongly opposed by some of the trustees, who did not approve of her ideas and did not think a woman should be a college president. But in 1894, by a vote of seven to five, Bryn Mawr's Board of Trustees chose her to succeed Rhoads.[25]

Throughout her presidency, which lasted until 1922, Thomas fought to encourage women students to pursue careers. "Medical experts" of her day, such as the prominent psychologist G. Stanley Hall, continued to declare in voluminous books and articles that education that did not train a woman "primarily to become a wife and mother" was interfering with "the deepest law of the cosmos." But Thomas plowed ahead. Under her presidency, women students were urged to be pioneers. They were taught that they must go out and change the world and the concept of woman in it. Many of them worked hard to do just that. Between 1889 and 1908, an astonishing 61 percent of Bryn Mawr students went on to graduate study—compared, for example, to 36 percent of Wellesley students. And only 35 percent of Wellesley alums reported having a career, compared to 90 percent of Bryn Mawr alums. "Only our failures marry," Thomas was reported to have said, though she later claimed she had said "Our failures only marry."[26]

Thomas was very much a spiritual descendant of Fuller. Just as Fuller had declared "let them be sea captains, if you will," Thomas believed that if a woman was well-fitted to be even a bridge builder, she had a right to first-class training for it, no matter that she wore a skirt rather than knickerbockers.[27] To the women of the 1840s, when Fuller was writing, sea-captain ambitions in women seemed the stuff of dreams. But forces that were pulling women across their thresholds and into the world—the opening of higher education to them and the growing women's rights movement—made such ambitions less inconceivable.

Sadly, despite all that Thomas did to refashion the meaning of woman and higher education, she shared some of her day's horrific blind spots. She wanted a student body and faculty at Bryn Mawr that was made up of women in her own image: white Protestant daughters of the wealthy. She was racist, admitting that if a Black student applied to Bryn Mawr, she would encourage her to go elsewhere—because, she claimed, many Bryn Mawr students were from southern states and would not welcome a Black classmate. She was also classist: as dean of the college in the 1880s, she fought a proposal to establish scholarships for working-class women, arguing that Bryn Mawr was intended for young women of the upper classes. She was anti-Semitic, too, and opposed to hiring Jewish professors. She blatantly declared that "it is much more satisfactory to have a faculty made up as far as possible of our own good Anglo-Saxon stock."[28]

But she was fiercely feminist, and by 1920, with the imminent ratification of the Nineteenth Amendment, she had come to believe that there should be a women's voting bloc. To bring that about, she decided, women needed to develop solidarity across class lines. She imagined a "deep sex sympathy" among women and suddenly began to speak of "the coming of equal opportunities for [women] manual workers."[29] She decided that working-class women ought to be educated, too. In 1921, shortly before she retired from the presidency, Thomas established the Bryn Mawr Summer School for Women Workers in Industry, which brought dozens of young factory workers to the posh campus for a yearly eight-week program of liberal arts study. Thomas's summer school even challenged her anti-Semitism: less than 3 percent of the U.S. population was Jewish at the time, but 25 percent of the students at the school were Jewish.

Thomas's racism remained an intractable blind spot, as was common among leaders of the early elite colleges for women in the United States. Black women were admitted to a few coeducational institutions such as Cornell, the University of Michigan, and Oberlin College, but prejudice abounded. Mary Church Terrell, an early civil rights leader who graduated from Oberlin in 1884, hinted at the ubiquity of discrimination when she observed in her autobiography, "It would be difficult for a colored girl to go through a white school with fewer unpleasant experiences occasioned by race prejudice than I had." Radcliffe College admitted Black women in 1894, but they had to live in a private, segregated boardinghouse, a policy that continued well into the twentieth century. Barnard College admitted no Black student until 1925, when it accepted Zora Neale Hurston. Vassar College accepted its first Black student in 1940.[30]

EARLY BLACK WOMAN'S COLLEGES

"The elevation of this race depends emphatically upon the education of these women."
—SOPHIA PACKARD, letter to John D. Rockefeller, 1883[31]

Black women after the Civil War fought an uphill battle for education, even within Black communities. In an effort to create lives of stability after slavery, Black publications depicted the Black woman's most sacred duty as the "preparation of her sons for manhood." Echoing white ideals, the publications glorified the Black woman as homemaker—despite economic realities that meant that many Black women were forced out of the house and into the workplace. As the historian Joel Williamson has suggested, after the Civil War "Negro males internalized fully the role of Victorian men," and they strived to make their wives into Victorian women.[32] Few Black women had the luxury to dream of higher education. Those who did had few choices.

In the South, several small institutions were opened soon after the Civil War to train Black teachers for the Jim Crow public schools. Sarah Dickey, a thirty-seven-year-old white spinster and graduate of Mount Holyoke, had taken seriously Lyon's exhortation to her women students that they must "be willing to go where no one else will go and do what no one else is willing to do." In 1875, Dickey arrived in Clinton, Mississippi, with the intention of opening a school for young Black women. Whites would not rent to her once they heard what she wanted to do, and the Ku Klux Klan tried to drive her out of town by taking potshots at her. But Dickey managed to raise $3,000 "from both white and colored citizens," according to an 1875 newspaper report, and she bought a deserted planter's mansion outside of Clinton, where she opened the Mount Hermon Female Seminary. Dickey had dreams of replicating for the Black women students the curriculum she had been taught at Mount Holyoke, but lack of money stood in the way. Instead, students took a one- or two-year program that enabled them to teach Black children in Mississippi's segregated schools.[33]

Spelman College in Atlanta finally fared better. Its Baptist founders, two white women from Massachusetts, opened the Atlanta Baptist Female Seminary in April 1881. Sophia Packard and Harriet Giles intended their school to be a college, but less than a generation after the end of slavery, the eleven young women of their first class were mostly illiterate. They were taught basic reading and writing in the "dank and dark" basement of Friendship Baptist, a Black church where there were not even any desks: to write, the students had to kneel and balance their papers on wooden benches.[34]

Packard and Giles had started the college after traveling around the South on behalf of the Women's American Baptist Home Mission Society, to explore how the society could help former slaves. Before their travels, Packard had served as principal at the Oread Collegiate Institute for young women in Worcester, Massachusetts, where she had showed herself to be "a woman of powerful intellect and strong will, aggressive and energetic, with almost a masculine genius for business and capacity for leadership," as an Oread historian wrote. ("Amazonian," Dr. Edward Clarke might have said of her.) Harriet Giles, Packard's devoted companion, had been a music teacher at Oread. Like many of the women pioneers who did not marry and pursued their work in dyads, they were committed to educating women, and committed to one another as well. As Packard told her diary, Giles's "depths of tenderness and intensity of affection" sustained her.[35] Because what Packard and Giles knew best was higher education for women, they proposed that the Women's American Baptist Home Mission Society could best help the struggling female ex-slaves by establishing an institution of higher learning for them. Their college, the women proposed, would offer courses in algebra, physiology, geometry, Latin, rhetoric, essay writing, and even study of the Constitution of the United States.

That was not what the leaders of the Women's American Baptist Home Mission Society had in mind. There was a great distance between offering former slaves shelter and salvation and offering them a college education. Indeed, the society was dubious about the educability of the Black woman. Packard and Giles tried to make their project more palatable to the society by saying that they would teach the former slaves how to be Christian women. "When we use the term educational we by no means confine ourselves to the knowledge of the sciences and arts but to the soul and body as well," Packard promised. They would be saving the students from immorality, too. The young women were now "prey to the passions of [men of] both races," Packard wrote, but the school would counter bad influences by devoting "the first hour of the morning to the study of God's word."[36]

Packard made clear that the college's purpose would certainly not be to re-create the Black woman in the image of the lady. The students would be trained to work. Some would learn to become teachers of Black children, and Packard and Giles also proposed the creation of an Industrial Department, where instead of rigorous academic training some students could learn trades, such as nursing, printing, dressmaking, laundry work, cooking, and other practical domestic arts.[37] Despite Packard's and Giles's care not to present their project in terms that were too radical, the society's leaders refused to help.

The society even refused to let Packard and Giles appeal to donors through its monthly magazine, *Home Mission*.[38] To raise money, Giles sold her piano for $100. The women received a $100 donation from the First Baptist Church in Medford, Massachusetts, and $15 from the Ladies Society of Everett, Massachusetts. In late 1882, the American Baptist Home Mission Society overrode its women's auxiliary and gave Packard and Giles $17,500 for a down payment on a nine-acre site in Atlanta, which had been used for barracks and drill grounds for federal troops. But that was still not enough to ensure the college's future.

At a Baptist conference in Cleveland, Ohio, it was Packard's and Giles's good fortune to meet the wealthiest Baptist in America, a robber baron who was also a philanthropist: the oil tycoon John D. Rockefeller Sr. Rockefeller was conservative on most social issues, but he was impressed by the women's impassioned fund-raising speech about their ambitious goals. Packard and Giles promised that they would not only educate Black women, they would also Christianize them. "Are you going to stick?" Rockefeller reportedly asked the two women. They assured him that they would. He emptied his pockets into their donation basket and promised much more. When the money was not quickly forthcoming, Packard, who understood what would appeal to a devout Baptist, wrote to remind Rockefeller that her college was saving the souls of Black women who needed "most of all, virtue to be taught them, and that morality is not to be divorced from religion." By saving them, Packard emphasized, the college would be saving all Blacks, because "the elevation of this race depends emphatically upon the education of these women." Rockefeller's wife, Laura Spelman Rockefeller, who came from a family of abolitionists involved with the Underground Railroad, heartily agreed. Eventually the Rockefellers gave the school millions of dollars. It was renamed Spelman College in Laura Spelman Rockefeller's honor.[39]

Humble as some of the early Black women's schools were, or mired as they were in assumptions about the Black woman, they nevertheless gave Black women the first opportunity to claim professional roles, and they forged new models of who a Black woman in the South could aspire to be. Mary McLeod Bethune's parents and fourteen older siblings, who were largely illiterate, had been born into slavery. They worked the family's small farm in Mayesville, South Carolina, where Bethune as a child daily picked 250 pounds of cotton, the family's cash crop. When a Black missionary, Emma Wilson, started a school for Black children at a Presbyterian Church five miles away, Bethune, who had already taught herself to read, was allowed to go. She later won a scholarship to the Scotia Female Seminary, another college for Black women modeled on Mount Holyoke. By 1888, several Black women had joined the previously all-white faculty. Bethune's Black teachers enabled her to conceive of new possibilities.

Despite the bitter times that followed the end of Reconstruction, they seemed to have an agency that was rare for southern Blacks in the 1880s. They made her feel, as she later wrote, "If they could do it I could do it too."[40]

Bethune went on to claim spaces that no Black woman had ever before inhabited. She founded a college for Blacks in Florida and became the first Black woman college president. She was appointed to President Herbert Hoover's White House Conference on Child Health. She became President Franklin D. Roosevelt's director of the Division of Negro Affairs in the National Youth Administration. Bethune parlayed her 1880s education at Scotia into a career as a canny politician who brought into the twentieth century what had never before been conceivable: the idea of Black woman as a powerful political leader.[41]

The expansion in the nineteenth century of education for both Black and white women was one of the greatest galvanizers of change in how woman—particularly women in or aspiring to join the middle class—was viewed and how she viewed herself. In 1821, ninety women were enrolled in the Troy Female Seminary. By 1880, 40,000 women accounted for one-third of the students at American colleges and universities. In 1900, there were over 85,000 women students. Even women who were in the Beecher camp (those who hoped no more from their education than that it would prepare them to navigate smartly the challenges of kitchen, nursery, and wifehood) discovered in the process that a woman could also meet the challenges of serious intellectual pursuit, and that those who did, did not develop leucorrhoea, amenorrhea, or dysmenorrhea. Other college women (those in the Fuller camp) were determined to take what they had learned and make it count for something in the larger world. As one observer wrote, looking back at them appreciatively in 1914, they had ushered in "a troop of departures from the established order of women's lives."[42]

PIONEERING IN THE PROFESSIONS

"The natural and proper timidity and delicacy
which belongs to the female sex evidently unfits it
for many of the occupations of civil life."

—*Bradwell v. Illinois* (1873)[43]

At the start of the nineteenth century, teaching had been mostly a male profession, but by the 1880s, women comprised almost two-thirds of America's teachers. It was an occupation approved even by Beecher, who saw teaching as an extension of mothering. Most college-educated women who wanted to work became teachers. But between 1880 and 1920 the country underwent a huge metamorphosis, which opened other professional possibilities for college-educated women. The population more than doubled, from 50 million in 1880 to 106 million in 1920. Much of that growth was due to immigration. Twenty million people—primarily from Eastern and Southern Europe—left their homes and came to the United States to make a new home. Most settled in urban areas. They were generally poor, illiterate in any language, and did not speak English. More than 10 million rural Americans also moved to urban areas during those years, and the lot of many of them was little better than that of the immigrants. New arrivals crowded big cities and squeezed into wretched dwellings. They provided cheap labor for booming urban factories and construction, where wages were low and working conditions were miserable. They were exploited at every turn.

The poor and their children were in desperate need of social services that offered guidance, advocacy, and practical assistance. Volunteers from church groups, ladies' aid societies, and various reform and betterment organizations had offered some services, but rapid immigration created a colossal need that could not be met by amateurs and charities. College-educated women began offering themselves as professional providers of those services.

It was a plausible offer. Like teaching, the work was akin to mothering. As social workers, public health nurses, factory and housing inspectors, guidance counselors, and social scientists who wrote about why and how social problems had to be addressed, women could take responsibility for the well-being of the new American family. They could concern themselves with reform, just as their mothers and grandmothers had in the women-led reform movements of the 1830s and 1840s—movements that had sprung up out of the conviction that women were morally superior to men, who had been making a mess of the world. Women would step in once again, to do housekeeping on a large scale by cleaning up the new mess of poverty, ignorance, and exploitation. But now they would earn salaries for their efforts.

Those who became professional protectors of and advocates for the poor did not challenge essentialist notions of woman that prevailed in their day. In fact, they appropriated them. Those "woman" characteristics were what America sorely needed now, they said. As the women's rights speaker Anna Howard Shaw proclaimed in an 1891 speech, of course the "mother heart" was intrinsic to woman: "Finding any wrong, any weakness, any pain, any sorrow, anywhere in the world, [woman] reaches out her hand to right the wrong, to heal the pain, to comfort the suffering."[44] Pioneering women professionals seized that notion of "mother heart." They claimed it as the reason why they, natural possessors of the mother heart, were best able to right the terrible new wrongs. They entered public spaces in the new jobs carved out for women.

Despite the "mother heart" rhetoric, people who still thought that a woman had no business crossing the threshold of her home were upset. An anonymous letter written to Jane Addams, a pioneering social worker and settlement house founder, in 1898 expressed their consternation in no uncertain terms:

> I love your sex, but no man can love a woman who takes her place among men as you do.... Of course I can speak very plainly to you, as your highest ambition is to be recognized as capable of doing a man's work. When your maker created you, it was evidently a rush job, as the most important part of the work was overlooked. Here then is your only resource. Did it ever occur to you that while on a tour of inspection, through alleyways, old barns, and such places where low depraved men with criminal records may be found (such a place a virtuous woman would be afraid to go) you might for a small sum induce one of such men to sell you his pecker and balls? It would not be much loss to him and will be your only chance to prove yourself a man."[45]

Such deranged missives aside, in the midst of the overwhelming new needs, many men did seem to acknowledge that women were more suited than they for jobs that involved working with women and children. As a Pennsylvania legislator declared approvingly about woman's new roles, "Women by natural instinct as well as long training have become the housekeepers of the world, so it is only natural that they should in time become municipal housekeepers as well."[46] Workers in a variety of reform endeavors related to "municipal housekeeping" were desperately needed in the late nineteenth century, and college-trained women—by now the third generation of women to receive a higher education—were welcomed into those jobs. Middle-class women on a sizable scale left home to go to work.

Feminist historians in the later twentieth century were sometimes chagrined by nineteenth-century pioneering women professionals who had ostensibly agreed that woman had special characteristics that made her innately different from man. They accused the pioneers of being complicit in making women "municipal housekeepers" instead of demanding that they be permitted into the more prestigious professions that men claimed for themselves. But the feminist historians failed to credit the ways in which the proponents of "municipal housekeeping" were revolutionary. The new jobs that had opened for "municipal housekeepers" gave the middle-class woman of their era more choices than she had ever had before. She no longer had to marry because there were few acceptable ways she could support herself. She could marry later, or not at all if she chose. She could choose to be an actor in a varied world that was outside the confines of domesticity. She could reap the satisfactions of contributing to the larger public welfare. She could even begin to make subversive moves into territories that had been the exclusive purview of men—social science research and public policy making, for instance. Most middle-class women were not yet ready for such choices. But many were.[47]

Hull House, the settlement house established by Jane Addams, was a model for social reform work, and Addams was a model for what women might strive to do and be. She virtually founded a new profession for college-educated women of the late nineteenth century. Addams had graduated from the Rockford Female Seminary in Illinois in 1881 and then had no idea what to do next. She was confined to bed rest for two years for spinal pain; she toyed with the idea of becoming a doctor for a year; she took a grand tour of Europe, as did many affluent Americans, trekking to art museums, opera houses, and lavish hotels; and she fell into a depression. What she needed—what she later said any woman needed after she graduated from college and was at a loss about what to do with her life—was that "some demand be made upon her powers" that would involve "the use of all her faculties," which had been sharpened through her education.[48]

The demand that had always stirred Addams, though she did not know in the beginning how to address it, was to give "succor to the helpless and tenderness to the unfortunate."[49] Her father had been a director of railroad companies and a bank president, but she had been moved as a child by lives different from her own, which she knew about only from novels such as *Oliver Twist*. When Addams took a second trip to Europe with her intimate friend Ellen Gates Starr, the two women gravitated to Whitechapel, the most impoverished district of London, and specifically to Toynbee Hall, the first settlement house in the world. Toynbee Hall's purpose was to bring rich and poor together: Oxford and Cambridge students moved to Whitechapel and set up social services there. It was an epiphany for Addams.

In 1889, together with Starr, Addams leased an old mansion in a once-posh area of Chicago. Hull House, as it was called, had been built in the 1850s by Charles Hull, a real estate magnate. In faded glory, the mansion was now surrounded by tenements and factories where poor immigrants from Southern and Eastern Europe lived and worked. Addams and Starr invited other college-educated women to leave their families, come live at Hull House, and involve themselves in the community. The young women would use the skills they had learned in college to set up a day nursery for working mothers, teach immigrant women about American food, offer literacy and vocational training classes, conduct wellness clinics, establish a free library, and even help shirt makers organize a strike and cloak makers organize a trade union. Hull House expanded, adding—with the help of Mary Rozet Smith, an heiress who became Addams's life partner—a dozen other buildings, including a girls' boardinghouse; the Jane Club, which provided apartments for wage-earning women; and a convalescent cottage for women with tuberculosis.

Much of the labor at Hull House was volunteer in the beginning, and the middle-class women who lived and worked there even paid for their room and board. But as the endeavors grew more sophisticated, women professionals became indispensable. Addams invited in women who had been trained in social-science graduate programs, such as the one at the recently established University of Chicago. They were led by Florence Kelley, who was described in retrospect by Supreme Court Justice Felix Frankfurter as being the individual most responsible for "shaping the social history of the United States during the first thirty years" of the twentieth century. These women used what they had learned in their training to conduct sophisticated research and investigation into social ills. In their hands social science became a tool for social reform. They investigated tenements, and their reports led to the passage of ordinances that addressed unsafe and unsanitary living conditions. They studied problems such as the exploitation of sweatshop workers, and their research led to the passage of the Illinois Factory Act of 1893, which mandated an eight-hour day for women workers all over the state.[50] The women who led the way in social housekeeping also led the way onto larger public stages. Kelley's leadership in the investigations, for instance, earned her a political appointment unprecedented for a woman, as chief factory inspector for all of Illinois.

Addams had figured out what she must do to make her revolutionary ideas palatable to the general public. She avoided emphasizing that she was pulling young middle-class women out of the domestic sphere and creating new professions for them. "A city is in many respects a great business corporation, but in other respects it is enlarged housekeeping," she said. "City housekeeping has failed partly because women, the traditional housekeepers, have not been consulted as to its multiform activities." To run a city well, she argued, required the help of housekeepers who had "a sense of responsibility for the cleanliness and comfort of other people."[51] But those "housekeepers" were soon paid social workers, a profession that college-educated women dominated then and have ever since.

Addams's approach garnered extraordinary support. In 1906, when Theodore Roosevelt, also a social reformer, was serving a second term as U.S. president, he wrote to Addams, thanking her for the "eminent sanity, good-humor, and judgment you always display in pushing matters you have at heart." Roosevelt saw her exactly as she wished to be seen. He contrasted her to the less womanly reformers with whom he had "such awful times." In 1912, though women still could not vote, he chose Addams to second his nomination for president on the Progressive Party ticket. In her womanly guise Addams became the voice of a new national conscience. The work Hull House did, she argued—such as offering child care to working mothers and subsidizing food programs for the poor—was what the government ought to be doing.[52]

Nineteenth-century women who aspired to "men's professions," such as medicine and the law, encountered more outraged resistance than did the municipal housekeepers (the writer of the "pecker and balls" letter notwithstanding). In 1852, when twenty-six-year-old Emily Blackwell walked into a classroom at Chicago's Rush Medical College for the first time, she saw chalked on the board a caricature of a woman in bloomers, and written across it the words "Strong-Minded Woman."[53] Like the epithet "Amazon," the phrase was not intended as a compliment.

Blackwell's older sister Elizabeth had received a medical degree three years earlier from Geneva Medical College in New York, the first American woman to be awarded the degree. But Elizabeth's hard-fought accomplishment had not opened doors to other women medical students. Geneva Medical College declared the experiment of admitting a woman student to be a failure and would accept no more women. It had been long forgotten that healing and midwifery were once women's jobs. Emily Blackwell was turned down by eleven medical schools. When she was finally accepted at Rush Medical College, the administration received such unremitting pressure from the state medical society and such angry complaints from male students that despite her competence she was expelled after a year. Western Reserve University in Ohio finally admitted her and in 1854 awarded her a medical degree.

Emily discovered more barriers. She and Elizabeth decided to start a private practice, but before they could hang out their shingle they had to purchase a house, because no respectable establishment would rent office space to a woman doctor. To make ends meet, they rented out most of the house, slept in the garret, saw their few patients in the parlor, and dined at a cheap basement restaurant in the neighborhood. Emily later quipped that that was the life of female doctors at the time: "They slept in the garret and dined in the cellar."[54] The Blackwells opened the New York Infirmary for Indigent Women and Children in 1857 and the Women's Medical College of the Infirmary in 1868, testing whether it would be more acceptable for women doctors to take care only of women and children.

The Blackwells started their medical college with nine faculty members, six of whom were men because there were still few female doctors. But the male doctors were deemed traitors by the rest of the profession: they were enabling women to come into a professional world that belonged to men. In 1870, two of the male doctors on the faculty were criticized so virulently that they felt compelled to resign. By then Elizabeth had chosen to live in England, leaving Emily to deal with the problems of the hospital and medical school. As she wrote to Elizabeth, the male doctors' connection with the school had "brought them in contact with all the professional dislike & distrust & jealousy" toward medical education for women. Emily nevertheless carried on the work into the 1890s, when major medical schools such as those at Johns Hopkins and Cornell began accepting women. She was assisted by a gynecological surgeon and professor named Elizabeth Cushier, who eventually became her life partner.[55] By the time Blackwell retired, the hospital and medical school had trained hundreds of women doctors and was serving thousands of patients yearly.

Emily Blackwell was indeed a "strong-minded woman," which made it possible for her to defy the persistent taboo against women doctors. She disdained the notion of woman that was still current in her day. She attributed to herself the characteristics that were supposedly men's, as she told her diary when she was twenty-four years old, describing herself as "very persevering and very resolute—and very ambitious," with "a something sprawling in my character and way of doing things." A couple of years later, finally on her way to becoming a doctor, she euphorically hoped that her example might bring about systemic changes in the very idea of woman. She harbored an ambitious fantasy, she confessed to her diary in 1852: "If I might see that I was doing something to raise [women] not in position only but in nature—to inspire them with higher objects—loftier aspirations—to teach them that there is a strength of woman as well as of man."[56]

But to change the meaning of woman was more complicated than she had dreamed as a twenty-six-year-old. She was discouraged when she discovered that even interns at her hospital—who had challenged the idea of woman enough to go to medical school—still had not succeeded in escaping from the troubling attributes of "nature" that Blackwell had hoped to eradicate. She scoffed at many of her students' "ladylike" dispositions and "little womanly airs." How could they become doctors, she vented in a letter to her sister, if they "had no more idea of taking hold of things and working like a man than flying"? "They are utterly disqualified by their nature itself," she grumbled.[57] Yet as the director of a woman's medical college, she persisted in her mission: to alter what had been seen as woman's "nature" and to replace "ladylike" characteristics with competence, forcefulness, and other admirable traits that men claimed for themselves.

Like so many of the nineteenth-century pioneers, Blackwell had no interest in marrying. Rather, she saw herself as married to Cushier, with whom she lived for almost thirty years. It is perhaps not surprising that many of the women who opened the professions to women did not marry and chose to make their home lives with other women. Their partners were often also forging new paths. Heterosexual marriage in the days of imperfect birth control meant numerous children, which was usually not compatible with path breaking. There were certainly men in the second half of the nineteenth century who encouraged their wives to pursue professional ambitions. For example, Judge James Bradwell taught his wife, Myra, law in the 1860s so that she might become the country's first woman lawyer.[58] But there were many more men who could not rise above what most nineteenth-century Americans still believed: that woman's sole sphere was the home. In 1880, twenty-three-year-old M. Carey Thomas wrote to her mother from Zurich, where she had gone to study for a PhD:

> If only it were possible for a woman to select women as well as men for their li[f]e's love . . . all reason for an intellectual woman's marriage w[oul]d be gone. Women understand women better, are more sympathetic, more unselfish, etc. I believe that will be—indeed is already becoming—one of the effects of advanced education for women.[59]

Thomas was right: the term "Boston marriage" was coined in the 1880s to describe just the sort of relationship that was being made possible by "advanced education for women" and the economic independence to which that education could lead. A "Boston marriage" signified an arrangement between two women—usually college-educated women's righters earning their own living or financially independent through inherited money—who lived together in a long-term committed relationship.[60] Women in Boston marriages figured heavily among the pioneers in education and the professions in the late nineteenth and early twentieth centuries.

Some Boston marriages included a sexual relationship between the women, though there was probably no descriptive term for those relationships with which these serious and respectable nineteenth-century middle- and upper-class ladies would have been comfortable.[61] "Lesbian" connoted Baudelairean decadence, or flowers of evil: the original title of Baudelaire's 1857 book of poems, *Les fleurs du mal*, was *Les lesbiennes*. The term "homosexual," coined in the 1860s, put the emphasis on sex, and Boston marriages were more than simply sexual. "Sexual invert," a term that the British sexologist Havelock Ellis used in his 1897 book *Sexual Inversion*, connoted pathology, which was irrelevant to these pioneering women. Many nineteenth-century female couples may simply have lived their relationships without naming them.

Those objecting to women who claimed spaces that had been reserved for men called the women any number of shaming terms such as "strong-minded" and "Amazonian," to suggest they were "unnatural" and to discourage other women from following in their path. But the words were apt. The nineteenth-century pioneers in education and the professions, who expanded the possibilities of women beyond what they had ever been before, were indeed strong-minded, Amazonian women.

By the 1870s it was not unusual for a woman to get a medical degree, and it had finally been agreed that women doctors were suited for specialties such as gynecology and pediatrics. But there were no specialties in the law for which women were peculiarly suited, and law schools remained closed to them. Belva Lockwood, the first woman to plead before the U.S. Supreme Court (the second was Ruth Bader Ginsburg, almost a hundred years later) had been refused admission to the Columbian College of Law because as a woman, she "would be likely to distract the attention of the young men." She had also been refused admission to Georgetown Law School because no woman had ever attended the school before. In 1871, she and fourteen other women were admitted to the National University Law School in Washington, DC, but they were not allowed to go to classes with the men. Even so, the men were still unhappy: the mere presence of females on campus defiled the school, they complained. Thirteen of the women quit. Lockwood and one other student stuck it out.[62]

Even the Supreme Court agreed that women had no business being lawyers. Myra Bradwell had passed the Illinois bar examination after studying under the direction of her husband, but Illinois would not license her as an attorney. She appealed to the Supreme Court. In 1873 the justices voted eight to one to uphold Illinois's prohibition. Justice Joseph Bradley (who was also on the wrong side of history when he voted with the Court's majority to declare unconstitutional the provision in the Civil Rights Act of 1875 that banned racial discrimination in public accommodations) wrote the opinion in *Bradwell v. State of Illinois*. According to the Court, Illinois was justified in not letting Bradwell practice because "civil law, as well as nature herself, has always recognized the respective spheres and destinies of man and woman. Man is, or should be, woman's protector and defender. The natural and proper timidity and delicacy which belongs to the female sex evidently unfits it for many of the occupations of civil life.... The domestic sphere [is] that which properly belongs to the domain and function of womanhood."[63] It was as though all the efforts women had been making to expand the parameters of "woman" had not moved the needle one bit from where it had been at the beginning of the nineteenth century.

Yet the persistence of individual women ultimately did make a difference. Lockwood completed the curriculum at the National University Law School, but then the administration refused to give her the diploma she had earned because no woman had ever before been awarded a diploma from the school. In a peremptory tone that would surely have made Jane Addams blush, Lockwood wrote to President Ulysses Grant, chancellor ex officio of the law school:

> Sir,
>
> You are, or you are not, President of the National University Law School. If you are its President, I desire to say to you that I have passed through the curriculum of study in this school, and am entitled to, and demand, my diploma. If you are not its President, then I ask that you take your name from its papers, and not hold out to the world to be what you are not.

Grant never answered her letter, but a week later she received her diploma in the mail.[64] Lockwood was equally tenacious when her application to the bar of the Supreme Court was turned down because she was a woman. She appealed to Congress. In 1879, she won. Both houses of Congress passed a bill agreeing that any woman with the proper credentials and "good moral character" should be permitted to plead in the Supreme Court. This was front page news in newspapers everywhere. At a loss for how to present Lockwood's unwomanlike persistence and assertiveness, the stories emphasized instead her femininity, reporting that after the Senate decided in her favor, she placed on the desk of each senator who had supported her bouquets and baskets of flowers and noting that her victory "shows what one weak but determined woman can do when she makes up her mind."[65]

In 1898, the theorist and social critic Charlotte Perkins Gilman marveled in her book *Women and Economics* at how the conception of "woman" had evolved in the course of the nineteenth century. The false sentimentality, false delicacy, and false modesty that had characterized the ideal woman in the early years of the century had almost disappeared, Gilman declared. Even women's physical strength and agility had been improving because they moved more in the world; barriers to their education had fallen; and they were now represented in the arts, sciences, trades, and professions. Gilman argued that women had been able to accomplish all they had in a century because "that relic of the patriarchal age, the family as an economic unit," had broken up. Woman was no longer tied full-time to the home: cooking or obtaining food and clothing were no longer the great challenges they had been a hundred years earlier. She was free to go out, make her own money, and be independent.

Gilman admitted that many women now worked outside the home not because it gave them pleasure or they desired economic self-sufficiency, but because they had not yet found a husband to support them. But that reason to work would soon change, she wrote. She gave as evidence "the increasing desire of young girls to be independent, to have a career of their own." Gilman characterized the late-nineteenth-century woman euphorically—"braver, stronger, more healthful and skillful and able and free, more human in all ways." Such a "clearly marked improvement in an entire sex," she concluded, "had never before taken place in the course of one century."[66]

Gilman was premature in her notion that the younger generation of women were ambitious for careers for the sake of self-fulfillment. At the time she made her optimistic prediction, few women could dream of "careers": women's employment was still primarily in grueling occupations such as factory work. Nor had the tyranny of the old conception of woman and the place where God had set her died by the last decades of the nineteenth century. (Supreme Court Justice Bradley's opinion on why a woman should not cross the threshold of her home could easily have been written one or even two centuries earlier.) Yet Gilman was partly right. The nineteenth century had seen brand new ideas of woman. A platform had been built on which even greater changes could take place in the next century.

7.
The Struggle to Transform Woman into Citizen

At 7:00 A.M. on November 5, 1872, Susan B. Anthony, leading a troop of eight other women, descended on a polling place in Rochester, New York, and voted. "Well I have been & gone & done it," she wrote Elizabeth Cady Stanton the minute she got home. Newspapers from New York to Knoxville, Sioux City, and San Francisco—even the *Neodesha Citizen* in Kansas—reported the event. The *Chicago Tribune* scoffed that Anthony and her "Amazonian adjuncts" were getting ready to take the issue of suffrage to the courts. A newspaper in York, Pennsylvania, reported that officials had let Anthony vote because she "was as much entitled to [vote] as any other man."[1] Snide as the newspapers were, women all over the country were informed that some members of their sex were radically demanding rights that men had always reserved for themselves.

Two weeks later, the Rochester marshal arrived at Anthony's home to arrest her for fraudulent voting. She demanded that he put handcuffs on her and walk her through the streets to the jail, so that everyone might see. He refused. He led her, without handcuffs, to the street car. "I am travelling at the expense of the government. This gentleman is escorting me to jail. Ask him for my fare," she announced loudly as she boarded.[2]

In court, Anthony was ordered to pay $500 for bail or await her trial in jail. She refused to pay. She expected the judge to sentence her to jail for an indeterminate period. Then she would tell her lawyer to draw up a writ of habeas corpus, and she would petition the U.S. Supreme Court to hear her case. But without her consent, her lawyer paid the $500 bail. She was outraged. He explained that he "could not see a lady he respected put in jail." Anthony stormed back to the courthouse, demanding to reclaim the bail money and be imprisoned, but to no avail.[3]

RADICALS

"The only chance women have for justice in this country is to violate the law."

—SUSAN B. ANTHONY, quoted in the *Leavenworth Weekly Times*, July 3, 1873[4]

In 1848, the year of the first women's rights convention in Seneca Falls, New York, "woman suffrage" was such a revolutionary proposition—indeed, so oxymoronic a term—that it was even beyond the imagination of many of those set on expanding woman's sphere. Elizabeth Cady Stanton, the first proponent of woman suffrage, had to battle Lucretia Mott, who had been her mentor since they had met in 1840 at the World's Anti-Slavery Convention. Mott was horrified when Stanton, insisting that the vote was "the right through which all other rights could be secured," added a woman suffrage resolution to the 1848 convention's "Declaration of Sentiments." Mott, the co-organizer of the convention, chided, "Why, Lizzie, thee will make us ridiculous," but the resolution remained. Stanton debated long and hard to overcome objections from those at the convention. She was aided by Frederick Douglass—an escaped slave, prominent abolitionist, and advocate for women's rights—who proclaimed, in an eloquent speech seconding the resolution, that the strictures against woman's voting degraded her and robbed government of "one-half of [its] moral and intellectual power."[5] The resolution finally passed, but newspapers mocked it as ludicrous. Some women's rights supporters believed that Stanton had overreached with her notion that women ought to vote, and they withdrew their support.

But Stanton continued to be outrageous in her attack on the reigning notions of woman. In 1861, she managed to appear before the judiciary committee of the New York State Senate to testify on the need to liberalize the divorce laws so that a woman could more easily exit from an unhappy marriage. In 1866, when women still had no say in the polity, she ran for Congress on a ticket of "free speech, free press, free men [sic], and free trade."[6] She received twenty-four votes.

Stanton longed to do more to end the limits imposed on woman, but her own mobility was limited: she had seven children. When the sixth child, Harriot, was five months old, Stanton wrote to Susan B. Anthony, by now a close friend: "Imagine me, day in and day out, watching, bathing, dressing, nursing and promenading the precious contents of a little crib in the corner of my room. I pace up and down in these two chambers of mine like a caged lioness, longing to bring nursing and housekeeping cares to a close." But pessaries and douches were unreliable, and less than three years later she had another child. Yet Stanton was the suffrage movement's most radical thinker and writer. She inspired Anthony's radical thinking and writing—and action, too. "She forged the thunderbolts, and I fired them," Anthony said, looking back on their collaboration after Stanton's death.[7]

Anthony's willingness to take iconoclastic positions had grown exponentially since 1848 when, having been told by her father that women were gathering in Seneca Falls to discuss women's rights, she replied that she thought they "were getting a good deal ahead of the times." Her meeting with Stanton in 1851 radicalized her and led her to redefine what "woman" ought to mean. In an 1857 lecture called "The True Woman," Anthony decried the still-dominant notion that said the true woman must "rest content [to be] the teacher of children, the genial companion of man, the loving mother of sons." Anthony's "true woman" did not belong in the domestic sphere, nor in any one sphere. Her true woman roamed freely. She was her own individual self, did her own individual work, stood or fell by her own individual wisdom and strength, and—like man, Anthony said—was made for her own individual happiness.[8]

"The True Woman" was Anthony's battle cry in her campaign to change the idea of woman. "Cautious, careful people, always casting about to preserve their reputation and social standing, never can bring about reform," Anthony declared in 1860. "Those who are really in earnest must be willing to be anything or nothing in the world's estimation," to "avow their sympathy with despised and persecuted ideas and their advocates, and bear the consequences."[9] She was very much "in earnest" and absolutely willing to "bear the consequences" of the incautious acts she would commit for the sake of women's rights.

In 1868 she and Stanton began publishing *The Revolution*, a radical woman's rights weekly that uncompromisingly demanded on its masthead, "Justice, Not Favors," and "Men, their rights and nothing more. Women, their rights and nothing less." Unencumbered by husband or children, Anthony traveled everywhere, taking trains, boats, wagons, and horse-drawn carriages, to promote woman's rights. Through it all, she was on the lookout for a radical way to make woman's right to vote incontestable. She believed she had found it when she read an article in her local Rochester newspaper reminding male citizens that it was time to register to vote for the 1872 election. Section 1 of the Fourteenth Amendment, adopted three years after the Civil War ended, to protect the rights of former slaves in the stubborn South, stated, "No state shall make or enforce any law which shall abridge the privileges or immunities of citizens of the United States." Women did not count for much in the polity, but they were citizens of the United States. Section 2 of the amendment did specify that only males had the right to vote. However, Section 1 could be construed to mean that state laws against women's voting were prohibited.

On November 1, in one of the first woman-led acts of civil disobedience in America, Anthony steered her troop of suffragist women to the Board of Registry—which was housed in that most masculine of venues, the local barbershop—and announced to the voting inspectors that she and the other women were there to exercise their rights as American citizens: to register to vote. When the inspectors hesitated, she read them Section 1 of the Fourteenth Amendment. "If you refuse us our rights as citizens I will bring charges against you in Criminal Court and I will sue each of you personally for large, exemplary damages," she told the inspectors. They registered the women—which led to Anthony's voting a few days later and to her arrest and aborted hope of carrying the case of woman suffrage all the way to the Supreme Court.[10] Almost half a century would pass before women could do legally what Anthony had dared to do illegally.

Those opposed to woman suffrage attacked radical women such as Anthony by complaining that they "had no right to pretend to represent their sex," because they were not real women. The real woman's life was "crowded with duties that only she could discharge," the opponents wrote. The real woman was busy being a mother and wife and manager of the home. She had no desire to violate her true nature: "The nature of most women is not attracted by the contentious spirit in which political warfare is conducted," opponents argued even into the twentieth century—sounding no different from Thomas Jefferson, when he declared in 1788 that "good American ladies" had no desire to wrinkle their foreheads about politics because their purview was "domestic happiness."[11]

Who were these females who wanted to vote like men? The *New York Herald* asked that question and supplied the answer: they were creatures who wanted to turn the world upside down by consigning men to nursing the babies, washing the dishes, and mending the stockings. They had "so much of the virago in their disposition that nature appears to have made a mistake in their gender." They were "mannish women, like hens that crow." When Antoinette Brown, the first American woman to be ordained as a Protestant minister, spoke at an 1853 suffrage convention, the newspapers described her and her audience as "a gathering of unsexed women, unsexed in mind, all of them publicly propounding the doctrine that they should be allowed to step out of their appropriate sphere to the neglect of those duties which both human and divine law have assigned them." Not even Sojourner Truth—a formerly enslaved woman who, by some accounts, bore thirteen children—escaped gender-shaming. At the 1851 Women's Rights Convention, she had brought her cheering audience to its feet when she recounted her experiences that refuted the reigning concept of woman: no man had ever helped her into a carriage or across the street, she said; she had labored in the fields as hard as any man, and she had the strength for such work as much as any man did. "And ain't I a woman?" was her repeated refrain. The *New York Times* later described Truth with innuendo, saying that she was six feet tall and "lank in the breast," with a "stentorian voice." A Kansas paper, the *Leavenworth Weekly Times*, did not even bother with innuendo: "Sojourner Truth is the name of a man now lecturing in Kansas City," its reporter announced.[12]

Such malicious epithets were often hurled at Anthony, too: She was "a grim old gal with a manly air"; she was an "Amazon of the female army";

she was a "pantaloonatic she-rooster." In 1893, after Anthony spoke at a woman's conference in Kansas, more than a dozen small-town papers carried the text of an answering speech delivered in Topeka by David Overmyer, an attorney and Democratic Party stalwart who was running for governor. Overmyer was liberal in his views: he defended a couple who engaged in a "free love marriage" in 1886, he fought a Kansas alcohol prohibition law all the way to the U.S. Supreme Court in 1891, and he litigated one of the first cases against mandatory school prayer in 1904. But his view of women voting would have resonated with the ideas of Governor John Winthrop. Overmyer savaged Anthony and her followers. Females who wanted to vote, he said, "sneered and scoffed [at] woman's sphere." They encouraged "woman to unsex herself." They wanted to hurl civilization back to the uncivilized days of the frightening Amazon who burned off a breast to be able to shoot an arrow like a man. "Kansas has already a plethora of Amazons," the liberal would-be governor warned. "Let the state once adopt female suffrage and these people would flock to it from the four quarters of the earth."[13]

The intent behind the epithets was not only to shame the suffragists but also to warn other women not to become like them. Anthony, a main target for half a century, finally found a way to defuse the slurs. The woman who was called "manly" was simply the woman who was fully human, Anthony argued in a 1900 essay, "The New Century's Manly Woman." The woman of the new century, she predicted, would escape the prison of "woman." She would be nothing like the "pale, delicate, sentimental woman," the "menial" of her husband, which had been the ideal when Anthony was a girl. The woman of the new century would strive to be "manly"—since men had claimed for "manliness" all the positive virtues of a fully adult human being. A manly woman meant a woman who was an "all-around being," with "body and brain fully developed," Anthony wrote, "educated alongside her brother, equally equipped to fight the battle of life and contribute to society and the commonwealth." Already, Anthony declared, there was a "mighty change in the status of the sex" as more women claimed "manliness." And the change would continue, she predicted, because evolution, progress, modern civilization, and women themselves would see to it.[14]

She was prescient. Future generations would challenge the notion of "woman" not only by expanding the limits of what women could do but also by complicating the idea of gender—as feminists did in the 1970s by elevating androgyny as an ideal, or as some in Gen Z are doing by rejecting altogether the choice of "woman" and "man" and identifying themselves as "gender nonbinary," "genderqueer," or "genderfluid."[15] Anthony's purpose in "The New Century's Manly Woman" had been to take an epithet meant as an insult and turn it into high praise, but she also knew that the "manly woman" was a powerful challenge to the tyranny of gender. She had a radical understanding of the fact that the idea of "woman" had been constructed by social forces that prevented women from being fully human. It could be changed by women who were not intimidated by being called "manly."

THE ANTIS

"Keep mother, wife, and sister in the protected home."
—National Association Opposed to Woman Suffrage, newspaper advertisement, 1911[16]

The movement to enfranchise women did grow in the two decades after the Seneca Falls convention—but not enough so that it could not be easily dismissed when New York State held its Constitutional Convention in 1867–1868. The influential editor of the *New York Tribune*, Horace Greeley, was the chairman of a committee charged with discussing matters of the franchise that affected the state. Greeley had been a social reformer and a crusader for the rights of poor people and Blacks. He had declared in an 1850 editorial, "What Woman imminently needs is a far wider sphere of action, larger opportunities for employment of her faculties, and a juster reward for her labor." However, like the Kansas gubernatorial candidate, the liberal Greeley became a staunch conservative when it came to woman suffrage. He was not pleased when suffragists delivered to his committee petitions with 20,000 signatures favoring votes for women. He had already complained to Anthony about the "ultraradicalism" of women righters and had withdrawn all support for her and her cause. By 1866, he was characterizing suffragists as "unfortunate creatures" who felt powerless in life because they could not get a man. A "true woman," Greeley wrote, does not need a ballot. "She rules the world by a glance of her eye."[17]

As a committee chairman, Greeley tried to couch his antipathy in more reasoned terms. He characterized woman suffrage as "an innovation so revolutionary and sweeping" that it would involve radical and unwelcome transformations in social and domestic life, and it would be "openly at war with a distribution of duties and functions between the sexes." In other words, voting women would violate the long-honored arrangement of separate spheres. Public sentiment did not demand woman suffrage, Greeley said—indeed, it would not accept woman suffrage. He and his all-male committee felt free to ignore the 20,000 signatures.[18]

It was not only men who opposed votes for women: women were among the fiercest anti-suffragists. Stanton had complained in her Seneca Falls address in 1848 that "the most discouraging, the most lamentable aspect our cause wears, is the indifference, indeed, the contempt, with which women themselves regard the movement." When Stanton and other suffragists persisted in promulgating their new ideas, the "contempt" she had worried about became organized. Sarah Josepha Hale, the editor of *Godey's Lady's Book*, urged her readers to circulate anti-suffrage petitions and send them to Congress, "to show that for one woman who desires [the vote], there are fifty who disapprove." Women did not need to vote, women antis argued, because they already had a voice in the polity when fathers or husbands voted with their women's interests in mind. "The male vote does not represent male thought alone; it is the product of both male and female thinking," Gail Hamilton, the author of *Woman's Wrongs*, optimistically contended in 1868. Such resistance to woman suffrage continued all over the country, up to the time the Nineteenth Amendment was ratified, when there were 2 million organized suffragists and, still, half a million organized women antis.[19]

Women antis worried that the vote would cast women into a purgatory of impossible demands: they would have to learn about politics, which was antithetical to a woman's domestic nature. And they would lose what had always been theirs: a man would no longer feel responsible for a woman who was so independent as to have political ideas. "American women would regard the gift of the ballot not as a privilege conferred, but as an act of oppression, forcing them to assume the responsibilities belonging to man, for which they are not, and cannot be, qualified," Catharine Beecher predictably proclaimed in 1872. She had not changed over the previous thirty years. She still cherished the notion of separate spheres. She still saw all women as woman, making little allowance for different aptitudes or desires. The vote would be burdensome to woman, she insisted, because it would distract her from "the distinctive and more important duties of [her] sex."[20] The vote would unwoman her.

In Massachusetts, which had been a center of suffrage activism, the first statewide organization to fight against it—the Massachusetts

Association Opposed to the Further Extension of Suffrage to Women—was founded in 1895. Oblivious or hostile to the millions of women who had by now left home to go to work or college, or even to enter a profession, the organization published essays such as "The True Function of the Normal Woman," in which a "Mrs. Horace A. Davis" declared a woman's true function to be "a wife and mother and home-maker." If a woman was taxed with men's jobs—forced to vote and even hold office—"she would have to think, read, and talk politics" instead of taking care of her true duties, Davis worried: "I am convinced she will have to let something else go, [and] that 'something else' seems to be her home."[21]

Organized anti-suffrage groups proliferated in the new century. In 1911 they joined forces in the National Association Opposed to Woman Suffrage to wage a deadly earnest battle. State chapters sprang up everywhere. Women's natural modesty and purity would be endangered if they mixed in the messiness of politics, the anti-suffragists argued. Financed by liquor interests who feared that woman suffrage would usher in prohibition, they ran full-page ads in local newspapers, appealing to men (the voters) to help them preserve their right to be a woman:

> As women, we do not want the strife, bitterness, falsification and publicity which accompany political campaigns.
>
> We women are not suffering at the hands of our fathers, husbands and brothers because they protect us in our homes.
>
> We have women's greatest right—to be free from the political medley [sic]. We do not want to lose this freedom. . . .
>
> Keep mother, wife, and sister in the protected home. Do not force us into partisan politics.[22]

Even some radical women who themselves had no interest in living in "the protected home" were opposed to women getting the vote. Emma Goldman, a Russian Jewish immigrant, had defied the prejudice against women as political thinkers and became a prominent anarchist philosopher. She was a militant "feminist" (as those who fought for women's rights were just beginning to be called). She courted provocation, demanding not only "the independence of women, her right to support herself, to live for herself," but also "to love whomever she pleases, or as many as she pleases."[23] Her boldness was generations ahead of her times.

Yet Goldman split with feminism in the early twentieth century to attack the suffragists. They were misguided women, "prostrate before a new idol," she wrote in 1910 (though there was nothing "new" about the suffragist struggle: by then, women had been fighting for suffrage for sixty years). Suffragists were fools for thinking that the vote would give a woman "life, happiness, joy, freedom, independence," Goldman mocked. As an anarchist, she considered voting to be a waste of time for anyone: it tricked people into believing they had control over government, while in truth it merely enabled "one set of people to make laws that another set is coerced by force to obey." But for women, voting was worse than a waste of time, Goldman thought. She pointed out that in the states where women had already gotten the vote—Wyoming (1869), Utah (1870), Colorado (1893), and Idaho (1896)—they had achieved nothing. Labor conditions were no better for women in those states than elsewhere. A woman was still a "sex commodity," despite the women's vote. There was still a "Puritanical double standard of morality for men and women." True, Goldman admitted, women were guaranteed equal rights to property in the suffrage states. "But of what avail is that right to the mass of women without property, the thousands of wage workers who live from hand to mouth?" she asked.[24]

In fact, Goldman's antipathy to the suffragists went deeper than her sympathy for workers or her anarchism. She was as much an essentialist as Catharine Beecher was. But while Beecher thought that a woman should not be burdened with the vote because it would cast her out of the sphere in which she naturally belonged, Goldman thought that a woman should not be allowed to vote because she was "a greater danger to liberty wherever she has political power." That was because a woman was inherently narrow, Goldman complained as she turned what had been regarded as a virtue—woman's "natural" modesty—into a vice. "Woman, essentially a purist, is naturally bigoted and relentless in her effort to make others as good as she thinks they ought to be," Goldman groused.[25]

Even worse, she claimed, the women most likely to vote—women of the bourgeois class—harbored views that were particularly narrow. They would vote for the wrong thing. That had already been proven, Goldman said: in Idaho, women voted to punish their "sisters of the street" with anti-prostitution laws; and in Colorado, women helped vote out a fair-minded and liberal governor. Goldman piled on arguments relentlessly. It was not only a woman's nature that made her unfit for the vote; it was nurture, too. "Her lifelong economic parasitism has utterly blurred her conception of the meaning of equality." Women, she said, would never cast their vote in favor of policies to help the laboring class. She accused suffragists of being "idle, parasitic ladies, who squander more in a week than their victims earn in a year."[26] With such virulent opposition from both the right and the left, suffragists had a long war to wage.

MODERATING THE MESSAGE

[The new woman] "is the same old woman, with a few modern improvements."
—ANNA HOWARD SHAW, "The New Man" (c. 1898)[27]

"There is no such thing as a sphere for a sex," Stanton had announced in her 1848 Seneca Falls "Declaration of Sentiments." Women had been tricked by the "perverted application of the Scriptures" to believe that God had set them in their limited little sphere.[28] But it was high time they escaped the lie, Stanton argued, and demanded the space and rights men had reserved for themselves, including the inalienable right to claim a voice in the government to whose laws they were subject. It was a message couched in such radical terms that few nineteenth-century women dared concur, and the movement progressed slowly.

The next generation of suffragists guessed that they needed to moderate the message, to disassociate themselves from the radicalism of their predecessors and suggest somehow that a woman did not have to reject the womanly ideal in order to be a suffragist. They devised an approach very different from that of Stanton and Anthony: women, who knew all about repairing things, would be able to use their know-how to help fix government, they said. A popular chant at suffrage rallies proposed:

> Mother mends my socks and shirts,
> Mother mends my coat,
> Maybe she could mend some laws
> If she had the vote.[29]

What would the woman voter do that the man voter was not doing? She would see to it that government focused on problems of tidying and healing and caring, which had always been woman's area of expertise: "How shall we make our streets clean; how shall we banish contagious and preventable diseases . . . ; how shall little children's lives be spared from avaricious business which contaminates food and drink."[30]

The most prominent proponent of that approach was Anna Howard Shaw, president of the National American Woman Suffrage Association (NAWSA) from 1904 to 1915. In the course of her career, Shaw spoke in every state of the union about why women should be allowed to vote. She reached an estimated 5 million people. She appeared in churches, lecture halls, opera houses, and even revivalist tents in small towns such as Emporia, Kansas, where droves of men and women braved the July afternoon heat and dust to listen to her woman suffrage message. Suffrage speakers, particularly in rural areas, had often encountered hecklers. But Shaw's audiences sat in rapt attention and applauded often and wildly. Though only five feet tall, Shaw was a powerful presence on stage: she was charismatic and quick-witted, and she had a strong, clear voice. She was widely considered the most accomplished woman orator of her day. She was even compared favorably to prominent male orators such as Robert La Follette and William Jennings Bryan.[31]

For thirty years, until her death in 1919, Shaw was also the life partner of Susan B. Anthony's niece, Lucy Anthony, who handled the womanly duties of their household while Shaw was out representing the cause. In her personal life, Shaw was vehement in her refusal to be woman. At an age when most women of her cohort were looking for husbands, Shaw was busy getting a degree in theology and then another degree in medicine. She despised heterosexual marriage, as she wrote to a friend in 1902: "Just think of the men along your street. . . . If a human being or god could conceive of a worse hell than being a wife to any one of them I would like to know what it could be." She claimed that she never failed to include in her nightly prayers: "I thank Thee for all good but for nothing more than that I have been saved from the misery of marriage."[32]

Early in her career the antis tried to discredit Shaw through the usual aspersions that were cast on suffragists. But Shaw figured out how to dodge them for the good of the cause. She had been baited by a pompous young minister who, finding her style mannish, asked her why she wore her hair so short. Shaw retorted: "I will admit frankly that it is a birthmark. I was born with short hair." But flippant as her response was, she confessed in her autobiography that his disapproval served as a catalyst for her.[33] If she appeared to be unwomanly, how could she speak convincingly to and for women? She decided that to advance the suffrage cause, it was vital to appeal to average women, who might worry that the vote would transform them into the unsexed creatures described by the antis. She understood too that she needed to pull in voters—men who, like Horace Greeley, might feel threatened by the suffrage movement's "ultraradicalism."

To reach the holdouts, Shaw changed both her style and the tone of her suffrage message. "No woman in public life can afford to make herself conspicuous by an eccentricity of dress and appearance," she concluded. She would be pragmatic and dissemble for a higher purpose. She let her hair grow long, and despite her decidedly unfeminine sartorial preferences, she appeared always in sedate dresses—even though many suffragists at the time were wearing bloomers and calling for dress reform. "Miss Shaw looked particularly beautiful, [her prematurely] white hair coiled on top of her head," a newspaper reporter gushed in a glowing summary of her appearance in Philadelphia. She succeeded so well in presenting her womanly public persona that reporters who covered her speeches typically raved not only that her arguments were compelling and her diction elegant but also commented that, for example, "she is graceful and well dressed and presents an attractive appearance," and that "she is a woman—a true, lovable woman."[34]

It was for the sake of the cause, too, that Shaw promoted an essentialist notion of woman. "The great defect in our government," she declared in one of her most popular speeches, was that woman was not allowed to participate in it. Woman must be given the vote not because she was like man, but precisely because she was different from him. The social ills that plagued society would be cured if a woman could bring her "mother heart" (which all women had, Shaw said, even if they were not mothers) to the ballot box. Though she was childless, she was quoted in scores of newspapers around the country for her "mother heart" bons mots such as "Call not that man or woman wretched who, whatever ills he or she suffers, has a child to love."[35]

In her lectures, Shaw allayed worries and warmed her audiences with good-natured humor. Women would never want to rid themselves of femininity by invading men's prerogative in dress, Shaw typically assured them. "That is a useless fear," she claimed. She continued comically that even the woman who votes and goes out to work "will always want to look as well as she can, and no human being could look well in men's clothes; so, the new woman will not wear them for that reason if for no other." She followed such levity with serious assurances, such as that the new woman "is the same old woman, with a few modern improvements" and "the new men and the new women will be helpers, each of the other, building up a new home." Having assuaged fears of radical change, she moved to the meat of her message. Just as you cannot "build up homes without men," you cannot "build up the state without women"—and, she slipped in, a woman must be given the right to train for and work in any profession for which she had an aptitude and to "walk down any avenue that would bring her into contact with the larger life of the world." In the mouths of other suffrage speakers that last part would have been seen as disturbing, a radical plot to unwoman woman. But Shaw had lulled her audience with reassurances. "She wins over the hostile," a Sedalia, Missouri, newspaper wrote of her lecture, calling it "common sense from start to finish."[36]

Frances Willard, head of the Woman's Christian Temperance Union (WCTU), also knew how to win over the hostile for the sake of suffrage. The WCTU, with its 200,000 dues-paying members and millions of sympathizers, had taken no official position on suffrage when Willard became its national president in 1879. The members were concerned with getting rid of drunkenness in order to protect the sanctity of the home, and the suffrage movement seemed irrelevant to their goal. Suffrage also seemed unsexing for the women of the WCTU who had no quarrel with traditional notions about woman, such as her natural domesticity. But Willard convinced the members that votes for women ought to be a top priority. Women's enfranchisement was crucial if they wished to protect the home, she argued, because if they had the vote, they could vote for prohibition. They could also vote to get rid of other threats to the sanctity of the home, such as prostitution. They could bring womanly virtues into the public sphere. The vote would be a "Home-Protection Ballot," Willard explained. In 1881, the WCTU officially endorsed woman suffrage.

However, Willard had little investment in the sanctity of the traditional home. She never married, and her own domestic relationships were first with Kate Jackson, a locomotive heiress, and then with Anna Gordon, who became her second in command at the WCTU. In her home, Willard liked to be called Frank. She hated cooking, sewing, and ironing, but she loved carpentry, repaired her own guns, and prided herself on "doing the rougher work" around the house. In public, however, very much like Shaw, Willard performed "woman" for the sake of her cause. She did it phenomenally well, as the *Boston Times-Democrat* attested when it described her ultra-womanly persona as "never abrupt or angular" but always gentle, sympathetic, and kindly—in short, motherly. But as one of her favorite maxims hints, it was a performance calculated to allow her to lead and to avoid the usual aspersions cast on women like her: "Womanliness first—afterwards what you will."[37]

WOMEN OF COLOR IN THE FIGHT FOR THE VOTE

> "The fashion of saying 'I do not care to meddle in politics' is fast disappearing among the colored woman . . . for [she] has learned that politics meddle constantly with her and hers."
>
> —ADELLA HUNT LOGAN, "Colored Women as Voters" (1912)[38]

The first organized movement to change the idea of woman was born at the 1840 World's Anti-Slavery Convention, so it is especially ironic that it was a conflict over former enslaved people that triggered the first internecine battle in the movement for woman suffrage. In 1865, at the end of the Civil War, Stanton—anticipating that the Constitution would be amended to acknowledge the rights of men who had been enslaved—wrote in the *National Anti-Slavery Standard* that the time had come for "universal suffrage." Universal suffrage would include not only formerly enslaved men but also all women, Black and white.[39]

Susan B. Anthony too acknowledged the "inalienable rights of the Negro" while pointing out that extending suffrage only to Black men would mean that still "one half of the people will be in subjection to the other half."[40] The following year, at the Eleventh National Women's Rights Convention, Anthony and Stanton helped form the American Equal Rights Association, whose purpose was to promote the call for universal suffrage. White women were joined by Black women, including the most famous Black poet of the day, Frances Harper, and Sojourner Truth, who had been an icon in the women's movement since her powerful speech at the 1851 Women's Rights Convention.

The new group quickly met with opposition from unexpected places. Stanton had first encountered Wendell Phillips, a Boston Brahmin and prominent reformer, at the 1840 anti-slavery convention, where he had come with his abolitionist wife, Ann Green Phillips. The Phillipses were both incensed when Ann was forbidden to participate in discussions and was sent to the balcony with the other women. Wendell demanded the floor and lectured his fellow convention-goers about the right of the women to be seated with the male delegates. Though he failed to convince his audience, he became a passionate advocate for women and a good friend to Stanton. Twenty-five years later, after the Civil War, Phillips was elected president of the American Anti-Slavery Society, which had decided not to disband until the Black man could vote. Now—to Stanton's shock—Phillips told woman suffragists that they must understand that this was not their time: their campaign for universal suffrage might ruin the Black man's chances for enfranchisement. Phillips reiterated that he was certainly not against woman suffrage, but there should be "one question at a time. This hour belongs to the negro." Stanton shot back at him, "Do you believe the African race is entirely composed of males?"[41]

In an editorial for the *National Anti-Slavery Standard*, Phillips not only ignored her plausible question, but he also doubled down on his position: "We cannot agree that the enfranchisement of women and enfranchisement of the blacks stand on the same ground or are entitled to equal effort at this moment."[42] Phillips's view was affirmed by the Fourteenth Amendment, which was passed in 1868: Section 2 effectively gave all male citizens who had reached the age of twenty-one the right to vote. It totally disregarded all women, white and Black.

Stanton was further upset when her old friend Frederick Douglass—who two decades earlier had so movingly seconded her woman-suffrage resolution at the Seneca Falls convention—also now seemed to believe that "the African race is entirely composed of males." At an American Equal Rights Association debate, Douglass declared angrily, "When women, because they are women, are hunted down through the cities of New York and New Orleans, when they are dragged from their houses and hung upon lamp posts, . . . when they are in danger of having their homes burnt down over their head . . . then they will have an urgency to obtain the ballot equal to our own." Stanton was especially stunned at Douglass's seeming betrayal because Sojourner Truth had sensibly explained earlier in the debate, "There is a great stir about colored men getting their rights, but not a word about the colored woman, and if colored men get their rights, and not colored women get theirs, you see the colored men will be masters over the women, and it will be just as bad as it was before." Despite Truth's plea, many woman suffragists were persuaded by Phillips and Douglass. The organized movement split into two camps: the American Woman Suffrage Association (made up of both men and women and led by Lucy Stone and her husband, Henry Blackwell), which did not mind women ceding to "the [male] Negro's hour," and the National Woman Suffrage Association (made up only of women and led by Stanton and Anthony), which vehemently did.[43]

With battle lines so heatedly drawn, the debate about woman suffrage among Black women became complex. Frances Harper declared at the 1866 National Women's Rights Convention that "justice is not fulfilled so long as woman is unequal before the law," but she was ambivalent about votes for women. "It would not cure all the ills of life," she said, because some white women would simply vote their prejudice or malice, along with racist white men. Harper joined the American Woman Suffrage Association, complaining of Anthony and Stanton that "the white women go all for sex, letting race occupy a minor position." She became the association's only Black speaker, supporting its work toward the passage of the Fifteenth Amendment that would affirm the enfranchisement of Black men. But she also argued in her speeches that Black women needed the vote even more than white women did because they suffered double jeopardy. They were "no longer sold on the auction block," she said in 1873, yet as Black women they were "subjected to the legal authority of ignorant and often degraded men."[44] Long before the term "intersectionality" was coined, Harper understood and was troubled by the ways in which the issue of race complicated the issue of sex.

Mary Church Terrell, almost forty years younger than Harper, was not at all ambivalent about the importance of suffrage for Black women. She too was troubled that Black women were "double-crossed"—as she termed it—by burdens levied on them for both their race and their sex. In her autobiography, *A Colored Woman in a White World*, Terrell wrote that she could not recall a time in her life since she was "a very young girl" and first heard a discussion of woman suffrage when she had not been an ardent woman suffragist. As the Oberlin-educated daughter of the first Black millionaire (a real estate mogul who had been born into slavery) and the stately and gracious wife of Robert Terrell, the first Black municipal judge in Washington, DC, Mary Church Terrell had her own megaphone, particularly among middle-class and upwardly striving Black women. In 1896, she helped unite the Colored Women's League of Washington, DC, and the National Federation of Afro-American Women of Boston into the National Association of Colored Women. Black women's clubs from around the country soon merged with the new organization. As the National Association of Colored Women's first president, Terrell focused the organization not only on uplifting the race—"Lifting as We Climb" was its motto—but also on getting the vote.[45]

When Robert Terrell was courting Mary Church (who was already twenty-seven years old), she confessed that she was very involved in the woman suffrage movement. "Well, you have ruined your chances for getting a husband," he said. He was joking, of course: he was an ardent supporter of woman suffrage. But he knew that many in his community were not. Black women suffragists who promoted their cause were reportedly told that they "ought to be at home taking care of the babies" or they had better stop "trying to take male places in politics." White women who tried to shift the idea of woman had always been targets of such hostility. However, the hostility may have been amplified for Black suffragists by the historical memory of white suffragists' resistance to the enfranchisement of Black men: "woman suffrage" was perceived by some as "a white thing." In any case, Mary Terrell understood, as she wrote, how tough it was to join "the few brave souls who have [the] courage of their convictions and who are willing to fight until victory is wrested from the very jaws of fate."[46]

Terrell was eager to defuse a favorite attack on woman suffrage, which was as virulent in the Black community as in the white—namely, that any woman who demanded rights reserved to men "ought to get into pantaloons immediately" because they were not real women, as Rev. Samuel Cornish had put it in America's first Black newspaper three generations earlier.[47] It was "unnatural for woman to vote," Terrell heard Blacks say often. She turned that attack on its head in "The Justice of Woman Suffrage," her most popular speech: "Whatever is unusual is called unnatural the world over," she wrote, "[but] nothing could be more unnatural than that a good woman should shirk her duty to the State," which the vote would allow her to fulfill. Terrell thus moderated the radical message of woman suffrage, presenting woman's civic participation as an extension of womanly duties.

The message needed as much moderating in the Black community as it did in the white one if the vote was ever to be "wrested from the very jaws of fate." Even women like Pauline Hopkins, a successful Black novelist and journalist writing in 1900 for the "Women's Department" of a new magazine, *The Colored American*, roundly opposed federal enfranchisement for women because, she said, "morally, we should deplore seeing woman fall from her honorable position as wife and mother." But Terrell's argument about a good woman's duty to the state, as well as her own magnetism, had a greater impact. The following year, the editor of *The Colored American Magazine* heard Terrell speak on suffrage. "Her womanly grace and her charming and stately attractiveness [are] not diminished one degree by the position she takes on this vital question," he enthused. "She reasons with strength and argues with force, and the strongest and most determined opponent to woman suffrage must give consideration to her clear cut logic." *The Colored American Magazine* had become a woman-suffrage convert.[48]

By spring 1912, after more than sixty years of struggle, women could vote in only seven U.S. states, but in China, Sun Yat-sen's republicans had just overthrown the Qing dynasty and promised that in the new government women would have voting rights equal to those of men. The news became a great focus of a May 4, 1912, "Votes for Women" parade in New York City. Leading the 10,000 marchers up Fifth Avenue was a contingent of fifty women wearing three-cornered feathered hats, riding astride dark horses, and looking as though they meant business—and leading them was Mabel Ping-Hua Lee, a young Chinese immigrant and Barnard College student. Though news coverage patronizingly described her as "a little Chinese Barnard girl," reporters and suffragists alike marveled at the ostensible victory she represented. As one reporter observed incredulously, the women of China "do not know even the outdoor freedom of the Western world, and yet their men have enfranchised them."[49]

But in fact, the revolutionary movement of the women of China had for several years been an inspiration to Chinese women in America. Their lives in America had been no freer than those they had left behind. Even the women who worked for wages—sewing, washing clothes, or rolling cigars—did so from their homes and had little contact with the world outside. But their lives began to change not only through their American-born daughters, who went to school and brought new ideas home, but also through the Chinese-language newspapers, which told them about remarkable new upheavals in the idea of woman in China and advocated for such upheavals among Chinese women in America.

In 1904, *Chung Sai Yat Po*, the most popular Chinese American newspaper, reprinted a fiercely militant poem by a woman revolutionary in China:

> I want to arouse women with the rising roar.
> With rage and martial spirit, we must unite to set things right.
> Rescuing our sisters out of hell,
> In this we will be brilliant.
> Though we may die in battle, yet will we be elated.[50]

Chung Sai Yat Po's editorials did not call women to "martial spirit," but they did rouse them to change. The editorials abjured the old Chinese proverb "Ignorance is a virtue in a woman" and encouraged "scholastic achievement" for girls. They expressed disgust at the time-honored Chinese traditions of polygamy and foot binding. "How can men treat their wives with such contempt? How can women treat their bodies with such contempt?" a 1907 editorial demanded. So when Sun promised revolutionary changes in China, including a role for women in the polity, Chinese immigrant women in America were inspired. They donated money and jewelry to help fund the revolution across the ocean, and they even "made speeches of fire and patriotism" in long-distance support of Sun. China's revolution became the occasion for Chinese American women to enter the political arena for the first time.[51]

The significance of what seemed to be happening in China was not lost on American suffragists. "White suffragists across the nation seek out Chinese suffragists to learn more about the role of women in the Chinese Revolution," an American newspaper announced. Suffragists shamed politicians by holding up China—which the provinciality of American racism had deemed backward—as the ideal toward which America needed to strive. China had "a government of all the people and not just half the people as we have here," an Oregon suffragist complained. Anna Shaw told the newspapers, "If the Democratic Party wants to catch up with China, they can give women the vote. China has waked up. Will they?" In the "Votes for Women" parade, Shaw, decked out in her academic regalia, marched directly behind Chinese women waving the five-colored flag of the new Republic of China. Shaw carried a banner that announced, "NAWSA Catching Up with China." Other women carried banners proclaiming "Light from China" and "Women Vote in China But Are Classified with Paupers and Criminals in New York."[52]

The history of American Indian women and the woman suffrage movement is not a happy one. Marie Louise Bottineau Baldwin, a Chippewa and one of the first Indian women to graduate from law school, told a newspaper reporter who interviewed her in 1914, "Did you know that Indian women were the first suffragists and that they exercised the right of recall [of chiefs that displeased them]?"[53] The reporter had never heard of Indian women's long-gone political heft: few white people had. But American Indian women like Baldwin who joined the suffragist movement hoped eventually to win agency for women similar to what many of their female ancestors had once had.

Stanton was one of the few who had researched the story of Native women's political power in the past. In an 1891 speech on "The Matriarchate, or Mother-Age," she used that history as a trope—to draw an angry contrast with women's present plight: "Our barbarian [sic] ancestors seem to have had a higher sense of justice to women than American [sic] men in the nineteenth century," she declared. Whether or not organizers of the 1913 suffrage parade in Washington, DC, also knew of the whilom Indian "matriarchate," they used Indian women to make another point: they wanted to show, as they announced in the media, that "the sisterhood of all women, barbarous and civilized [sic], forms the very essence of the suffrage movement."[54]

Despite being anxious to have a visible Native presence marching with them down Pennsylvania Avenue, the parade planners could not transcend their prejudices. They asked Mary Louise Bottineau Baldwin to organize a float of Indian suffragists, but they wished the Indians to be dressed just as white people envisioned "squaws": in braids and buckskin. Baldwin did not organize the float, though it is not known whether this was because she objected to the stereotype or simply did not have the time. She announced that she would march in the parade with her women classmates from the Washington College of Law.[55]

The organizers then invited to a prominent place in the parade a cavalry unit of ten Indian women in Native dress, headed by Princess Dawn Mist, who was billed as the daughter of Chief Three Bears of the Blackfeet Indians of Montana. It was a dramatic image. But "Dawn Mist" was Daisy Norris, who was indeed an Indian and a suffragist but not the princess daughter of any Indian chief. Norris had been an actress who performed the part of Dawn Mist for a promotional campaign called "See America First—Great Northern Railway—National Park Route." Nevertheless, the organizers succeeded to a degree in getting the press to feature "the sisterhood of all women, barbarous and civilized," with Dawn Mist exoticized as "the most beautiful Indian girl in the world" and reporters describing in irrelevant detail the traditional deerskin and beaded moccasins of her contingent, even the horses "caparisoned with elaborate bead work" and the "real Indian saddles."[56]

Such trivializing aside, American Indian women who were suffragists had to make a huge leap of faith. They knew that even if suffragists succeeded in winning the vote, Indian women could not benefit. Until the passage of the Indian Citizenship Act of 1924 (also known as the Snyder Act), which finally declared Indians to be U.S. citizens, not even Indian men could vote if they maintained an affiliation to their Indian nation. Indian women would, ironically, be the last women in America to enjoy the right of franchise.

MILITANTS

"[We have] shirked [our] duty and left it in the hands of older pioneers, whose faces are turned to the past."
—FLORENCE KELLEY, 1906[57]

During the eleven years that Shaw was president of NAWSA, the number of members rose from 17,000 to 183,000, and the number of states where women had full suffrage rose from four to eleven. But in thirty-seven states, women still could not vote. A new generation of suffragists began to question the propitiating tactics of Shaw and her generation. Shaw was deeply disturbed when two passionate and attractive young militants, Alice Paul and Lucy Burns, got a foothold in NAWSA. Paul and Burns had met in a London police station after being arrested at a rowdy suffrage rally in front of Parliament. Their work with the British suffragettes had taught them to be far more militant and unladylike in their approach than Shaw and NAWSA had been. In spirit, they were closer to Stanton and Anthony. But Paul and Burns also knew how to grab headlines with colorful parades, dramatic battles with police, and arrests that led to force-feeding in jail and increased public sympathy for their cause. They captured the imagination of the younger suffragists, who now lamented that "[we have] shirked [our] duty and left it in the hands of older pioneers, whose faces are turned to the past."[58] Young suffragists scoffed at notions of "ladylike" and "womanly" behavior. They were ready to seize public space and demonstrate for their cause, to fight as woman did not know how.

Uncomfortable with militancy but confused about how to react to demands that her organization become livelier, Shaw merely acquiesced to the huge suffragist parade down Pennsylvania Avenue on March 3, 1913. That date was chosen because it was the day before Woodrow Wilson's presidential inauguration. Elaborately staged by Paul and Burns, the parade was the first march on Washington in history. The paraders demanded that the new president urge Congress to amend the Constitution to enfranchise all women citizens. Paul and Burns understood spectacle. At the front of the parade, alone and mounted on a spirited white horse, was Inez Milholland, a young lawyer who was dressed all in white, her face dramatically framed by her long hair—a beautiful twentieth-century Amazon who paid no obeisance to the old idea of woman. As Milholland described the image she wanted to project, she was "the free woman of the future . . . herald[ing] the dawn of a new day of heroic endeavor for womanhood."[59]

But spectacle turned into debacle. Rowdies among the hostile onlookers scrambled over the stout wire ropes that were put up to separate the crowd from the parading women. The rowdies hurled insults at the marchers and tried to grope them or block their way. One newspaper reported that "thousands were laughing and jeering without interference from officers of the law." Uniformed Boy Scouts rushed to the women's aid with poles, prodding and forcing the crowd back from the street. Another newspaper reporter claimed to have observed a "member of the petticoat cavalry strike a hoodlum a stinging blow across the face with her riding crop in reply to a scurrilous remark as she was passing." Policemen were on the hoodlums' side, telling marchers that they ought to be home with their children. One officer informed a marcher that if she were his wife, he would beat her with a broom. Cavalry from a nearby fort were summoned to keep the peace. Had it not been for them, the Associated Press observed, "a heavy toll of life might have been exacted." Paul, an early master of the sound bite, told reporters that "the actions of the police constituted the biggest scandal in the history of the United States government."[60]

However, there was a worse scandal in the parade—a failure of moral courage, for which Paul was responsible. By 1913 there had been Black woman suffrage clubs not only in Washington, DC, and on both coasts but also in states such as Montana, North Dakota, Illinois, Ohio, Wisconsin, Indiana, Oklahoma, Nevada, Arizona, and New Mexico. At the invitation of Paul, Black suffragists arrived in Washington on March 2, ready to march the next day with their suffrage club or with other groups (Black teachers with the teachers' contingent, Black lawyers with the lawyers' contingent, Blacks from Illinois with the Illinois contingent, and so on). Southern white suffragists, horrified by the arrival of Black women, demanded a meeting with Paul. They would not be marching "if negro women are allowed to take part," the southerners told her.[61]

NAWSA's "southern strategy" had been to enlist the aid of southern suffragist women to woo southern male voters and congressmen (virtually all white since the end of Reconstruction) into the woman suffrage camp. Paul panicked. Her "compromise" with the complainers was to inform the Black suffragists that they could only march together, at the back of the parade. Ida Wells-Barnett—the Black journalist well known for her campaign against lynching and the founder of the Alpha Suffrage Club in Chicago—let her outrage be known. As W. E. B. Du Bois reported in *The Crisis*, a Black magazine, "telegrams and protests poured in" objecting to the meanness of Paul's decision. On the day of the parade, Wells-Barnett joined her white suffrage friends in the Illinois contingent. Other Black suffragists followed suit. "Eventually," Du Bois wrote, "the colored women marched according to their State and occupation without let or hindrance."[62] Yet the harm had been done, and resentments rankled on all sides.

This was not Shaw's idea of how to win the vote for women—public race confrontations, unwomanly clashes with hostile crowds, a war with the police, and headlines that announced "Women Pour out Their Wrath." The whole debacle went against the image of womanly reasonableness that she had long cultivated. "We will never win the battle by 'bullyragging,'" she warned. But Paul and Burns wanted more unwomanly drama, like suffragists had provided in England: pickets and skirmishes that would lead to arrests, hunger strikes, and force-feeding. The struggle became a battle for the soul of the movement. "Votes for women can never be obtained by militant methods," Shaw declared after easing the hoydens out of her organization.[63]

But the younger generation of suffragists resonated with the transformation of woman into militant. The suffrage movement was too tame, they believed. Word needed to be gotten out about the urgency of their cause. They set themselves to a task that has always been central to radical activism: how to make headlines. They found a champion in Alva Belmont, who had divorced her philandering first husband, Willie Vanderbilt, settled for many of his millions, and a year later married the equally wealthy Oliver Belmont. She was left one of the richest widows in New York after Oliver died in 1908. It was then that Alva, who had from childhood on "nurtured a deep resentment of male power and privilege," became a staunch suffragist and an outspoken feminist.[64]

Already in her fifties, Belmont was impatient with the "placidity" of old-style suffragists such as Shaw, her contemporary. Belmont much preferred the "lively and picturesque" militancy of the British suffrage radicals, the "suffragettes." The suffragettes were making headlines by direct actions such as attacking young Winston Churchill with a horsewhip on a railway station platform because he had said publicly, "Nothing would induce me to vote for giving women the franchise."[65] Belmont approved of Alice Paul's and Lucy Burns's suffragette style. She not only contributed great sums of money to their militant branch of the suffrage cause, but she also convinced several of her wealthy friends in the Colony Club, New York's first socialite women's club, to shed their notions of upper-class womanly propriety and do likewise.

The militants found another champion in Harriot Stanton Blatch, Elizabeth Cady Stanton's sixth child (the one whose tending had made her mother feel like "a caged lioness"). Blatch was as radical as her mother had been. Under Blatch's leadership the Equality League of Self-Supporting Women, an organization she founded, barraged the public with militant street tactics. "New methods of propaganda," she called her unwomanly approach. Equality League members—elite college-educated women in camaraderie with laboring-class women who wanted the vote in order to push for better working conditions—stood on street-corner soapboxes to shout out their demands. They passed out leaflets, campaigned at factory gates, confronted politicians, and demanded hearings in front of legislative committees. They characterized the members of NAWSA as ladies at a tea party.[66]

Shaw, upset that her approach seemed dated to the younger generation of suffragists, left the presidency of NAWSA in 1915. To her partner Lucy Anthony she explained wistfully, "I realize that my day, except for speaking and 'inspiring' has gone by. And this is all right; I will speak and 'inspire' my best. I might do worse I suppose."[67]

Paul and Burns founded their own organization, called first the Congressional Union for Woman Suffrage and then, starting in 1916, the National Woman's Party. The women of the National Woman's Party would not be ladies at a tea party. They vehemently opposed President Wilson in his bid for a second term, since his first term had not led to woman suffrage at the federal level. They twisted his campaign slogan "He Kept Us out of War" into "He Kept Us out of Suffrage." After Wilson was re-elected, he agreed to meet with leaders of the National Woman's Party who wanted to deliver to him petitions with a half-million signatures demanding a woman suffrage amendment to the Constitution. Wilson advised the contingent that they must do more work to turn public opinion in their favor.

Those were fighting words. A few weeks later, the National Woman's Party staged the first picketing at the gates of the White House, where silent sentinels held banners that demanded to know "How long must women wait for liberty?" In the next months, more than a thousand women picketers showed up to occupy the sidewalk in front of the White House. "America Is Not a Democracy," their banners proclaimed. They captured headlines by getting themselves arrested. And strategically, they did not hesitate to fall back on the image of woman as a delicate creature—the women were shamefully abused by being hauled off in police wagons, mercilessly thrown in jail, unable to sleep in their cold cells because of severe attacks of rheumatism, and "suffering acutely," as newspapers reported in 1918.[68]

The National Woman's Party claimed victory. Their militant tactics, they said, provided the crucial push to make politicians and the public finally understand that women demanded the vote. As a result of the party's dramatic protests, both houses of Congress agreed to establish committees to study the question of woman suffrage. But larger forces were also operating to lead to the culmination of the seventy-year-long battle for women to have first-class citizenship.

WOMAN, TRANSFORMED, WINS THE VOTE

"We have made partners of the women in this war."
—WOODROW WILSON, "Address to the Senate on the
Nineteenth Amendment" (1918)[69]

On April 2, 1917, Wilson announced that the United States could not continue to stay out of the war that was raging in Europe. "The world must be made safe for democracy," he told the country. The saucy reply of the National Woman's Party was a banner slogan: "Democracy should begin at home." In their weekly newspaper, *The Suffragist*, they called the president "Kaiser Wilson" because, like the German Kaiser Wilhelm, he ruled over millions—women—who did not have the right of self-governance.[70]

The new leaders of NAWSA took a very different approach. Two months before war was officially declared, Shaw's successor, Carrie Chapman Catt, saw a chance to bring the seventy-year suffrage struggle to fruition. She let the newspapers know that she was calling a conference of NAWSA leaders in Washington, DC, to discuss "whatever work [suffragists] may do in a national crisis." Two million suffragists were ready to roll up their sleeves and aid their country, Catt declared, and the government must not underestimate women's capacity to be of service in the event of war. "Women must be put to work in munitions factories immediately upon the outbreak of war, thus leaving the men free to go to the front," she proposed.[71] She understood that since 8 million women were already in the workforce, it would not be seen as a fresh violation of the idea of woman to propose that even more women could be working outside the home, to keep the country running for the duration. She also exhorted NAWSA members to lead drives for the Red Cross, War Saving Stamps, and Liberty Loans. She informed Wilson that her organization stood ready, willing, and able to aid the United States in defeating the German aggressor.

Catt had been a pacifist (after the war she organized an annual conference, The Cause and Cure of War). But for her as for Shaw, winning suffrage was the first priority. In her combative manner, Paul charged that NAWSA had taken up war work and abandoned its true goal—getting votes for women.[72] But that was untrue. Catt and NAWSA promoted both, at the same time. Catt was a consummate chess player: she had correctly calculated how one move must lead to the other.

She was right that women would happily roll up their sleeves and get to work in the new occupations that World War I opened to them—jobs that had earlier been unimaginable for woman. They ran the banks, for instance, as tellers, managers of departments, and junior and senior officers. They not only took over the work the men had left behind, but they also "manned" the new jobs created by war. They became munitions and airplane factory workers, locomotive dispatchers, truck drivers, and motor mechanics. They operated drill presses and lathes. They donned overalls and were Rosie the Riveters long before World War II. Black women were also hired to fill many kinds of jobs from which they had been excluded—positions such as stevedores, streetcar conductors, and elevator operators—though not even war halted race discrimination. Black women's salaries were much lower than those of men doing the same job, of course; but they were also lower than the salaries of white women.[73]

Women were enlisted to do emergency agricultural work too. In thirty-three states they saved America's food supply by harvesting crops that men would have harvested had they not been off fighting in Europe. The project was given a quasi-military title, the Women's Land Army, to highlight the seriousness of the job. Women's Land Army recruiting posters featured a whole new concept of woman: behind plows, driving tractors, wielding pitchforks, and almost always in knickerbockers or overalls—garb that had been unthinkable for women just months before.

Posters urged women to "Pitch in and Help." Woman's delicacy, her sphere, and her domestic duties were all irrelevant now. Blatch, who had merged her group with Paul's National Woman's Party and urged more drama in the fight for suffrage, now rejoiced that a turning point had been reached. "American women have begun going over the top," she wrote in 1918. "They are going up the scaling-ladder and out into All Man's Land."[74]

In 1776, John Adams, contemplating the new United States, had concluded that woman should not be given the rights of full citizenship because, among other limitations, she was unfit for "the hardy Enterprises of War." He could not imagine a time when that might change. During the Revolutionary War, women had fought in male guise, and during the Civil War, they had also served as nurses. But in World War I, for the first time, they could officially enlist and be assigned to military jobs that only men had held before. In March 1917, Secretary of the Navy Josephus Daniels, who had long been a supporter of woman suffrage, announced that he saw no reason why the Naval Reserves should not be opened to female yeomen. About 12,000 women enlisted as "Yeomanettes." Frilly feminine clothes were replaced by single-breasted jackets and brimmed hats made of stiff felt. At the start, the women were assigned to clerical work, but the more the Navy needed its men to serve on ships, the more the Yeomanettes' duties expanded. They were given jobs that no woman had ever held before the war, serving as truck drivers, mechanics, and cartographers. They even earned the same pay as men sailors of their rank, because Daniels had actually declared—perhaps for the first time in history—that "a woman who works as well as a man ought to receive the same pay."[75]

Because women were desperately needed in industry, Wilson appointed Mary Van Kleeck—a Smith College graduate who had gotten her start as a New York settlement house advocate for working women—to a specially created position in the Department of Labor, to look out for women's needs. She was not the only woman to have the president's ear and admiration: he also called Shaw back into prominence. Shaw was no longer head of NAWSA, but Wilson considered her one of the sanest and most reliable representatives of American woman. Though Shaw was already seventy years old, the president chose her to head the Women's Section of the Council on National Defense. The position gave her a government-sponsored podium from which to tell the country why woman suffrage was important to the war effort. "Our country needs the army of women at home just as much as the army of men in France," she said over and over in the speeches she gave and the articles she wrote in her new position. She always emphasized that there were 2 million women in the United States who put great energy into the suffrage movement, and just one act of Congress—the signing of a federal woman suffrage amendment—could free those 2 million women to serve the war effort with a singleness of purpose and undivided allegiance.[76]

"Your counsel is good and I shall follow it," Wilson wrote Shaw a month before he announced to Congress his support of such an amendment. "I took the liberty of writing to you because your counsel I have found to be a thing to be depended upon," he explained.[77] To the president, there had been "bad cops" and "good cops" among the organized suffragists. Paul's National Woman's Party and the NAWSA were pursuing the same goal: a woman suffrage amendment to the Constitution. But Paul's hoydenish militants were upsetting to Wilson, a southern gentleman born at the height of American Victorianism. Sympathetic as he was to woman suffrage, he could stretch only so far in reimagining woman. The unwomanly militants pushed him in the direction of suffrage leaders such as Shaw and Catt, whom he had assured of his good will toward their cause and his certainty of their eventual success. That promissory note came due with women's participation in the war.

Wilson acknowledged in a speech to Congress on September 30, 1918, six weeks before the armistice, "This war could not have been fought, if it had not been for the services of the women." He reminded the congressmen that "we have made partners of the women in this war." And he asked, "Shall we admit them only to a partnership of suffering and sacrifice and toil and not to a partnership of privilege and right?" Just as Shaw and Catt had hoped, Wilson urged Congress to pass the Nineteenth Amendment as "a vitally necessary war measure."

Despite Wilson's remarkable acknowledgment, it took Congress nine more months to pass the amendment that recognized woman as a first-class citizen with the right to vote. The seventy-year struggle finally ended on August 1920, when Tennessee became the thirty-sixth state to ratify the amendment.

Shaw died on July 2, 1919, and so never witnessed the final victory. But her major role in winning the vote for women was widely recognized. Catt credited her with making "more converts to the suffrage cause than any other one person." Shaw's obituary in the *New York Sun* depicted her as "perhaps the strongest force for the advancement of women that the age has known." The *New York Times* printed a July 4 eulogy to her, reverently observing, "There passed away on Wednesday a genuine American." The newspaper compared her to Abraham Lincoln; contrasted her "wise guidance in the woman suffrage cause" to "the antics of the mad wing, the so-called militants"; and even suggested that her wisdom was a major factor in bringing about the recent suffrage triumph in Congress. *The Nation*'s obituary called her "the despair of the anti-suffragists, because she was so normal and sane"—and though her mind "was a match for any man's in its cleverness and logic," the obituary writer said, "her feminine charm never left her."[78]

Crystal Eastman, who had been a lecturer for the NAWSA, declared soon after ratification that men were saying, "Thank goodness that everlasting women's fight is over." But women were saying, "Now we can begin." "Begin," Eastman explained, meant begin to overturn whatever was left of the old notions of woman and to break down all the barriers that interfered with women choosing a profession, going into business, and learning and practicing a trade. It meant economic independence and equality. It meant making drastic changes not only to the meaning of woman but also to the meaning of man. "It must be womanly as well as manly to earn your own living, to stand on your own feet," Eastman wrote. "And it must be manly as well as womanly to know how to cook and sew and clean."[79]

It would be a very long time before Eastman's ideal was even contemplated outside of feminist circles. The head start toward "economic independence and equality" that women were given during the war was quickly erased. Men returned from Europe and immediately took back their "men's jobs" as locomotive dispatchers, truck drivers, motor mechanics, stevedores, and streetcar conductors. The Yeomanettes were soon done away with because there was no place in the military for women during peacetime. Of course, a woman did not have to start from scratch after the war to claim her right to get an education or work outside the home, and now she could even vote. But during World War I she had taken two more steps forward. After the war, she took one step back. It would not be the last time that she would be forced to do such a jig.

8.
The "New Woman" and "new women" in a New Century

"We want the four primitive home industries socialized and mechanized," the president of the Feminist Alliance, Henrietta Rodman, announced to the world through the *New York Times* in 1914. Rodman and the other New Women of the Feminist Alliance abhorred the old notion of woman as tied to her insular little domestic sphere. They had well-thought-out plans for cooperative housing that included the hiring of experts who would clean the New Woman's apartment, fix her meals, mend her clothes, and mind her children. Rodman reminded those who might be upset at the idea of a woman's not taking care of her own children, "We have the example of royal families to show us that when proper upbringing of children is the chief end it is done not by mothers, but by trained and competent servants." By pooling money and efforts and hiring competent people to do the "primitive" domestic work, the women who would live in the cooperative apartment houses that were envisioned by the Feminist Alliance would not only be free from drudgery, but they could also work in fulfilling jobs that would contribute to the larger social good.[1]

THE NEW WOMAN

> "We're sick of being specialized to sex. We intend simply to be ourselves, not just our little female selves, but our whole big human selves."
>
> —MARIE JENNEY HOWE, quoted in the *New York Times* (1914)[2]

While Congress and President Woodrow Wilson may have preferred the moderate tactics of Anna Howard Shaw and Carrie Chapman Catt when he dealt with suffragists, it was the image of the militants that helped effect dramatic cultural shifts. The militants' wrath and rhetoric; their confrontations with police and politicians; and their "marching, marching, marching" all gave the lie to the notion of woman as naturally delicate, passive, and domestic. Unsettling as that was for many, it inspired a rethinking of what was natural to woman.

That rethinking was also pushed along in the new century by women's massive migrations from small towns and rural areas everywhere to big American cities, where they entered the workforce in unprecedented numbers. By 1920, women made up almost 30 percent of the U.S. labor force. They were factory workers, domestic workers, waitresses, stenographers, and "typewriters."[3] They were also nurses and doctors, school teachers and professors, and social workers and lawyers—though no matter the job, their salaries were almost always lower than those of men. Employers justified the disparities by claiming that men had families to support but "working girls" (as most women who worked were dismissively called) did not. Nevertheless, new spaces continued to open for women outside the domestic sphere.

College-educated young women were also entering the workforce in escalating numbers. They had "imbibed a new doctrine," one author declared in 1907 in a chapter titled "The Larger Womanhood." They refused to be "buried in the seclusion of home." They sought self-development in place of self-sacrifice, and they sought meaningful work that would take them out into the world. A 1911 article in a New York weekly observed that the so-called home daughter—the unmarried woman who stayed in her parents' home until a suitable man carried her away in marriage—

was fast disappearing. The author quoted an independent young woman who had told her: "I was at a preparatory school for four years and four more in college. Why were time and money expended in my education if I am to settle down to the duties of an unsalaried companion?"[4] The nineteenth-century assurances of the Catharine Beechers and the Emma Willards, who had claimed that a woman would use what she learned at a female seminary to become better in her domesticity, had been in vain. The education of middle- and upper-class young women created longings in them for a larger life and for a degree of self-sufficiency and agency that would have been unimaginable to their foremothers. Those longings helped fashion the "New Woman." She ushered in the zeitgeist. Owing in good part to her, the shift in the meaning of woman in the first decades of the twentieth century was quicker, more deliberate, and more spirited than it had ever been before.

It was far easier to be a New Woman in big cities, so many young women who wanted to live their New Woman ideals gravitated to urban centers. In the relative anonymity of city life, the New Woman could escape the watchful eyes and the old moral authority of her birth family. In a city's diverse population, she might find a community of kindred spirits, both other New Women and the men who (more or less) championed them. In a big city, it seemed, women could be reimagined and remade. They could slough off notions of woman's duty and restraints. Free from small-town disapproving eyes, they could even smoke and drink like a man, as only dissolute women had done before. Even more importantly, in a big city, women were more likely to find a decent job that would allow them to be self-supporting—a sine qua non for the New Woman.

The New Woman was sometimes a wife, but she did not marry for the sake of financial need or in the interest of bourgeois morality, which certainly would have canceled out her New Woman bona fides. As Mary Heaton Vorse, a progressive journalist and fierce New Woman, quipped in 1912, after she married for the second time: "I am trying for nothing so hard in my own personal life as how not to be respectable when married." Many married New Women insisted on being "Lucy Stoners," following the example of the nineteenth-century suffragist who had reinforced the point of her independence by refusing to assume her husband's last name. Vorse compromised: she took her first husband's last name but did not change her name again when she married Joe O'Brien, a New Man— who stayed home with Vorse's three children in 1914 while she went abroad as a journalist to report on a women's international peace conference at The Hague.[5]

The New Woman disdained the True Woman ideal of delicacy and spirituality. She was robust, athletic, and comfortable with her body. For centuries women had been in fear of damaging their reputation if they gave in to sexual desire. Men had used sex against women to keep them in their place. The New Woman met the old injustice head-on. She professed to engage in sex for her own pleasure. She leaped easily into liaisons. She claimed for herself the privilege men had selfishly hogged, the right to participate in "the game of life." She mocked notions of the good woman's "purity" and the delusion that only prostitutes were sexual creatures.[6]

In her 1898 book *Women and Economics*, Charlotte Perkins Gilman had lamented what she called the "sexuo-economic relation"—by which she meant that historically a woman had no choice but to use her sexuality to attract a man to support her. The New Woman could support herself, so she need never be party to the "sexuo-economic relation." If sex was not fun, she had no reason to engage in it. The New Woman was encouraged too by *Love's Coming of Age*, which virtually became her Bible. Written by the English philosopher Edward Carpenter and published in America in 1911, *Love's Coming of Age* propounded a New Morality, an enlightened view of sex. Carpenter spoke directly to the New Woman when he declared that woman would never be man's equal until she was able "to dispose of herself and of her sex perfectly freely."[7]

Indeed, the heterosexual New Woman might be so free and so focused on her sexual pleasure that even the most progressive men, those who claimed to be "feminists" (a term that began to be used in America around 1910), might feel disoriented and threatened by the new paradigm. As the anarchist author Hutchins Hapgood wrote of the discombobulation of his male buddies, "No matter what his advanced ideas were, his deeply complex, instinctive and traditional nature often suffered [from woman's] full assumption of his old privileges" as the sexual aggressor.[8] It was not easy to let go of male prerogatives and become a New Man, even if doing so meant getting a lot more sex.

Nor, in truth, was it easy for some New Women to adapt to the new ideal of sexual liberation. The old ideal had been so entrenched in the middle and upper classes, and New Women were still so new at the game, that sometimes they failed in their attempts to change. Mabel Dodge, the independent free spirit who helped introduce America to modern art through the 1913 Armory Show, agonized over the sexual mores about which the New Woman was supposed to be cavalier. Dodge, who had been born and raised a Victorian, grew up associating sex with "furtiveness and shame." But as a New Woman she had to learn to shed Victorianism and seek in its place the joy of sexual expression. Dodge left her second husband and moved to New York City's Greenwich Village, a center of New Womanhood, where she began an open relationship with the dashing young journalist John Reed. But she could not completely shed the old-fashioned woman's ideas about love. She was profoundly disturbed by Reed's infidelities and demanded constancy from him—and when she did not get it, she took an overdose of veronal. Dodge recovered from her suicide attempt and was ashamed of preferring monogamy, which was counter to the New Woman ethos. She chided herself when she suspected her preference was due to a primitive, selfish, unworthy instinct that must be overcome. However, she could not overcome it. Liberationist ideology resonated with her in theory, but in practice she found that "sexual freedom could be as oppressive as sexual repression."[9]

Despite such complications, the New Women shook the old notions of woman as they had not been shaken before. Perhaps that was why New Women's enemies were legion. Medical experts, ignoring the rampant heterosexual behavior of many New Women, often conflated their feminism with sexual abnormality, just as in earlier eras, pioneers in women's rights battles were accused of being "mannish" and "Amazonian." The European sexologists of the late nineteenth century such as Richard von Krafft-Ebing (author of *Psychopathia Sexualis*) and Havelock Ellis (author of *Sexual Inversion in Women*) had provided new terms for females who did not conform to conventional ideas of woman. Such women were sexually inverted or even perverted. The terms were imported into American medical discourse. In 1900, for example, William Lee Howard declared in the pages of the *New York Medical Journal* that "the female possessed of masculine ideas of independence" and "the female sexual pervert" are simply "different degrees of the same class—degenerates."[10] The imputation was used often in the early twentieth century as a weapon to bludgeon the New Woman.

Even women who benefited greatly from the struggles of "female[s] possessed of masculine ideas of independence" professed to disavow the New Woman. Margaret Deland was a hugely successful writer in her day, one of the first women to be elected to the National Institute of Arts and

Letters and spoken of in the same breath as Mark Twain and Thomas Hardy. Married but childless, Deland admitted that she was seldom "at home making soup": her career kept her busy. She had little time for True Woman values in her own life, but she endorsed them in her writing. In a 1910 *Atlantic Monthly* article titled "The Change in the Feminine Ideal," Deland looked back nostalgically at the previous generations of women who "did not talk about their rights; they fulfilled them—by taking care of their families." Though Deland had gone to college, she declared her ambivalence about the freedoms that higher education gave women. She railed against the generation of educated women who had come out of college "supplementing a certain old-fashioned word, *duty*, by two other words, 'to myself.'" In worshipping at the shrine of self-fulfillment, Deland complained, the New Woman had exchanged the selfless ideals of her mother for shockingly selfish ones: "Never mind other people; make the most of your own life. Never mind marriage; it is an incident; men have proved it so for themselves; it is just the same for women; never mind social laws; do what your temperament dictates." When Deland was not discussing the dangers posed by the New Woman, she was dismissive of her. "One can hardly say 'The New Woman' with any hope of being taken seriously," Deland declared.[11]

It was true that the New Woman was a subject of ridicule and worse. She was hoping to reinvent the meaning of woman for her class, and her ideas and behavior provided an electrifying jolt to custom. Mainstream media reports about the New Woman were hostile, as the changing coverage of the quintessential New Woman, Inez Milholland—the white-gowned beauty on the white steed who led the 1913 suffrage parade in Washington, DC—illustrates. Max Eastman, editor of *The Masses* and one of Milholland's many lovers, left a vivid description of her extraordinary good looks (skin, "crimson and ivory as though it had just been rubbed with snow"; hair, "a deep lustrous brown like Juno's"; eyes, "a deep hue of the jewel called aquamarine, bright mischievous lakes," and so on). People "gasped" at her beauty, Eastman wrote.[12] She attracted attention from newspapers and magazines all over the country. She was America's sweetheart—as long as she behaved.

Milholland had seemed to epitomize woman as the megaphone holders of the early twentieth century wished her to be: gracious and graceful, nurturing, sympathetic even to those far beneath her, and a lady. As the extraordinary daughter of a wealthy family, Milholland caught the public eye. In 1908, when she was a junior at Vassar College, newspapers regularly pronounced her "charming" in their society pages. They praised her "true feminine perception [that] got at the heart of things" when, as junior class president, she organized women students to offer their services to juvenile court in order to help solve school truancy problems. The summer after her junior year, society pages, reporting that she would be spending the summer in Japan, observed that she was "amply endowed with feminine charm" and that "her human sympathies have led her to do much good work among the poor people."[13] But the mainstream press and other megaphone holders did not seem to know what to make of Milholland when it became clear that she was a radical New Woman and a feminist, doing things that a woman was not supposed to do.

When she was still a student at Vassar, Milholland invited Charlotte Perkins Gilman, Harriot Stanton Blatch, and the labor activist Rose Schneiderman to campus to speak on the importance of woman suffrage and the exploitation of women workers. Vassar's president, James Monroe Taylor—who had earlier been delighted by how Milholland enhanced Vassar's image—was horrified. He would not let his college be known as "a hotbed of suffrage and socialism." Despite his position as the president of a woman's college, Taylor—who was also an ordained Baptist minister—was a staunch admirer of the True Woman. He affirmed his college's beliefs in "the home and in the old-fashioned view of marriage and children and the splendid service of society wrought by these quiet and unradical means." Milholland, undaunted by the reaction of the president of her college, organized the feminist event anyway. Unable to use a campus building, she used the Calvary Cemetery, across the street from the campus, and the event became known as the "Graveyard Rally." Only forty students dared attend.[14]

Milholland's New Woman radicalism did not stop with graduation. She applied to law schools that were closed to women: Yale, Harvard, Columbia, Oxford, and Cambridge. She was turned down by them all; admissions officers admitted that was because she was a woman. When she finally got a law degree from New York University in 1912, her first big case was to defend Elizabeth "Rebel Girl" Gurley Flynn—a leader in the Industrial Workers of the World and a future chair of the Communist Party USA—after Flynn had been rowdy in a textile workers' strike and had been arrested. Milholland became a labor activist too, organizing women workers, picketing alongside those on strike, and getting herself sent to jail.

The media had become derisive as soon as it was clear that the lovely debutante had transmogrified into a New Woman. Milholland had played sports at Vassar, and when she announced in 1909 that she was going to England to work with the suffragettes, one newspaper declared sarcastically that "no doubt her record as an athlete will help her in the encounters with London police that are a forgone conclusion." That same year reporters smirked when she was disinvited from a suffrage drive in Washington state: they quoted a woman suffrage leader as saying, "Society spell-binders and Vassar girls are not needed in this state to assist in the battle for the ballot." Articles about a 1912 fund-raising ball for the woman's Political Union provocatively depicted her as "an ardent and militant suffragette" who insulted the men present by choosing as her dance partners for the evening other "ardent women suffragettes." When Milholland declared to an audience that "ten minutes a day is plenty of time to devote to 'keeping house,'" reporters ridiculed her cluelessness about real women "who have no maids who bring their breakfasts to their bedsides and who, incredible as it may seem, have actually to cook things over a kitchen range [and] who have to do all kinds of things for [their] babies, and with their own hands, too."[15]

As a thoroughgoing New Woman, Milholland had been a firm believer in free love and had none of the apparent ambivalence that plagued Mabel Dodge. As Eastman jealously wrote after she had spurned him, Milholland enjoyed a "kaleidoscope succession" of men: millionaires, bounders, opera singers, and laborers. Her freewheeling life had been shocking to the press, and in 1913, reporters seemed to sigh in collective relief when they could announce that "The American Joan of Arc Startles Her Many Admirers by Marrying a Mere Man" and she was "Just Like a Woman after All!" The twenty-seven-year-old Milholland had finally bent to an eternal truth, they said: "Even the mighty and haughty suffragette who led her sisters against the opposition, man, has at last acknowledged her master."[16]

The press did not know that it was Milholland—true to a New Woman ideal—who played the "master's" role: she had proposed to Eugen Boissevain, a Dutch feminist from a family of militant feminists. Nor did the press know that she and her husband had agreed from the start that Milholland would continue to be a New Woman. Despite Boissevain's wealth, she would continue to work as a lawyer; she would continue to be an activist on behalf of laboring women; and she would travel the country and the world, without her husband, to promote woman suffrage. Nor did the reporters who gloated over her "fall" to "her master" know that she refused to wear a wedding ring, which she believed was a "badge of slavery." Nor did they understand that she and Boissevain agreed that they would never stifle one another's sexual freedom: they would take lovers, and they would feel free to tell one another about their adventures—as when Mulholland wrote Boissevain (referring to herself in the third person and by her nickname) about her fling with a man on a ship going to Europe: "Naughty, naughty Nan!—but she adores being naughty. It's the most enticing thing of life."[17]

In 1916, Milholland was on a multicity tour of the West to urge women in the states where they already had suffrage to vote out of office those politicians hostile to a federal suffrage bill. She collapsed as she was speaking on stage in Los Angeles. The *New York Times*, after reporting with little sympathy that she was hospitalized because "her frequent speeches pleading for women's votes proved too much for her throat," apprised readers almost weekly of the terrible progress of her disease. Milholland lingered for ten weeks in a Los Angeles hospital before dying of pernicious anemia. After her death, some newspapers forgave her for being a militant feminist and a New Woman. In their pages she became again the ideal woman. She died "in the bloom of her beautiful womanhood," their reporters wrote, presenting her as heroic in championing the "cause of the poor and the oppressed." Newspapers that remembered her New Woman radicalism forgave it in a dead woman. "We may never have sympathized with some of Mrs. Boissevain's ideas and methods, but we cannot help but sincerely regret the untimely death of so young and beautiful, so brilliant and ardent a woman," a Pennsylvania newspaper granted.[18]

The redefinition of woman that the New Woman was propounding struck a particular chord with some Indian women, such as Zitkala-Sa, a Dakota Sioux who became a prominent Indian leader. Her writing suggests that she knew of the days when the Indian woman was "Master of her own Body, and by her Natural Right of Liberty is free to do what she pleases," as Baron de Lahontan had observed of Algonquin women in the seventeenth century. Zitkala-Sa's graduation speech from a Quaker boarding school in 1895 suggests that she was already a "feminist": "Half of humanity cannot rise while the other half is in subjection," she told her classmates.[19] Though she was ambivalent about the attempt of her white teachers to "take the Indian out of [her]," Zitkala-Sa became her own version of a New Woman. She supported herself as a teacher, professional musician, and author; she claimed a political voice as president of the National Council of American Indians, the first group to lobby Congress for Indian rights; and in New Woman rhetoric she let her lovers know exactly who she was.

"I am too independent. I would not like to obey another—never!," she wrote in 1901 to Carlos Montezuma, a Native American medical doctor who was hoping to woo her. He persisted in his suit, and they were briefly engaged. However, she told him in no uncertain terms that if they married, "I do not mean to give up my literary work." She reiterated to him: "I do not belong to anybody. I do not wish to be!" She made sure he knew that she had no intention of being a housewife. "I know so little about keeping a house in running order that the undertaking is perfectly appalling," she wrote him only months before they were to be wed.[20]

Their relationship was in serious trouble after Montezuma told her he planned to start an Indian rights organization for men. Her response exploded on the page: "Am I not an Indian woman as capable in serious matters and as thoroughly interested in the race—as any one or two of you men put together? Why do you dare leave me out? Why?" The coup de grace to their romance came when he informed her that after they were married he would not be moving to her reservation, where she wanted to immerse herself in the Dakota Sioux culture and be close to her mother. The days when Indian nations were matrilocal were long gone, Montezuma believed. He wanted her to move to Chicago, where he had an established medical practice. Zitkala-Sa broke off their engagement.[21]

That same year she wrote "A Warrior's Daughter," a story that revealed her metaphorical sense of herself. The young Dakota Sioux heroine rides in a war party, astride her father's warhorse and by the side of her lover. He is captured and held prisoner, but she, who has a true warrior's heart, kills his tormentor and frees her lover from the enemy. Then she literally carries him off to safety on her powerful shoulders.[22] The eponymous warrior's daughter (who, like Zitkala-Sa, was a beautiful woman) is the actor in the story and its splendid heroic center. The fantasy recalled the ancient Sioux ideal of woman's strength and spoke to the New Woman ideal of woman power, which was unimaginable to Zitkala-Sa's modern Indian lover.

The hostility and puzzlement with which the New Woman had to contend was only one of the trials she faced as she tried to radically redefine woman. She had moved light-years away from the generations that had gone before her, and she discovered that the process of inventing new ways of being a woman was laden with highs and lows. There was the excitement of breaking paths, but there were also the difficulties of making choices women had never before had to make. There were the joys of inhabiting physical places and moral spaces from which women had been strictly barred, but there was also the despair when idealistic expectations met dull reality. To be a New Woman was not for the faint of heart. Most women in the first decades of the twentieth century did not dare to be New Women. They stayed close to the path their mothers and grandmothers had trod, yet the New Woman opened new pathways to walk for the old woman's daughters and granddaughters.

BLACK WOMEN AS "NEW WOMEN"

> "The position of woman in a society determines the vital elements of its regeneration and progress."
> —ANNA J. COOPER, *A Voice from the South by a Black Woman of the South* (1892)[23]

Among educated, middle-class Black women in urban areas such as Washington, DC, the New Woman had a counterpart in the "New Negro Woman." But if she declared, as the white New Woman did, that "I intend simply to be myself, not just my little female self, but my whole big human self," she was bound to endure all the disdain the white New Woman suffered and more—because she violated her community's understanding that "race trumps gender."[24] To most Black women, only a few decades removed from slavery, the New Woman's rebellion against female delicacy, sexual modesty, and the monotony of life in the domestic sphere had little meaning anyway. Enslaved women had never been permitted delicacy, modesty, or their own domestic sphere. Their daughters and granddaughters were not encumbered with the True Woman legacy that was so stifling to the New Woman. Most Black women had other things to worry about, like survival.

Black women leaders who were working toward racial uplift considered the Black woman's pursuit of her independence trivial and even counterproductive. Fanny Barrier Williams, a prominent clubwoman, advised women that the race would achieve uplift when the Black man could give his woman precisely what the New Woman had decided to relinquish. "Every colored man who succeeds in business brings his wife and daughter a little nearer to that sphere of chivalry and protection in which every white woman finds shelter and vindication against hateful presumption," Williams wrote in 1904, expressing a yearning for an idealized past that Black women had never gotten to live. "A beautiful home built by a man is a tribute not only to his own wife and family but is also a tribute to womanhood everywhere," she said.[25]

Though few Black women would have described themselves as a "New Woman," cultural shifts in the early twentieth century did turn some of them into "new women." Anna Julia Cooper, a Black public intellectual of the era, helped draw the distinction between the two. Cooper had been born to an enslaved woman in 1858 and had been an overachiever from the start. She taught mathematics as a pupil-instructor at Saint Augustine's Normal School and Collegiate Institute in Raleigh, North Carolina, when she was ten years old. She fought to be excused from the easier "Ladies' Course" designed for female students and took the "Gentlemen's Course" at Oberlin College, where she loved to challenge the idea of womanly propriety. Each member of her graduating class was to give a five-minute speech. As Cooper recalled with satisfaction, she discomfited Oberlin's faculty by delivering hers, on "Strongholds of Reason," "mannishly, not pretending to read an essay as a lady properly should."[26]

Cooper married when she was twenty-one, but she was widowed two years later and never remarried. She fulfilled her "womanly duties" by raising two foster children (supporting them on her salary as an educator) and, at the age of fifty-seven, assuming the guardianship of her stepbrother's five grandchildren. In the 1920s, when she was already in her sixties, she went to Paris, where she earned a PhD in history from the Sorbonne. She published voluminously, lectured widely, and was a mainstay of clubs such as the Colored Woman's League and the National Association of Colored Women.

Cooper has been considered a pioneering Black feminist. Some historians have even called her the "mother of Black feminism." She was unequivocally a defender of the Black woman, even castigating Black men who "seem thoroughly abreast of the times on almost every other subject" but who "drop back into sixteenth-century logic" on the subject of women. Yet Cooper's feminism, always sensitive to the issues of race, was different from the feminism of the white New Woman who was her contemporary. Cooper addressed Black women of the middle class and those who were upwardly striving, showing them why they needed to reject what she saw as the New Woman's triviality and narrowness. White women's righters were engaged in "blue stocking debate" and "aristocratic pink tea," Cooper said. She accused them of being "oblivious to any other race or class who have been crushed under the iron heel of Anglo Saxon power." She promoted higher education for Black women, but its purpose, she argued, was not selfish self-fulfillment. As a teacher, homemaker, and mother, the "earnest, well-trained [Black] Christian young woman" would be a vital element in the regeneration of the race. That was the Black woman's crucial job, Cooper believed, as well as the Black woman's greatest contribution to her society: to attend selflessly to the needs of her people and fix what had been "impoverished and debased" by centuries of slavery.[27]

Cooper was also a suffragist, but again not in the mold of the New Woman: she demanded the vote on the principle of equal rights. Cooper's arguments for woman suffrage were much like Anna Howard Shaw's, with her essentialist notions about woman's universal "mother heart." Women should be allowed to vote, Shaw had said, because they naturally seek ways to mend society's ills. Cooper believed that woman must have a voice in the polity not by virtue of the fact that she was entitled to full citizenship but because she "needed to bring a heart power into this money-getting, dollar-worshipping civilization."[28]

Nor did Cooper promote New Woman ideas about the personal value of work. Most Black women worked because they had no choice, as she knew, and not because they were seeking meaningful occupation or rebelling against being "buried in the seclusion of home." She pointed out that 57 percent of Black households were supported by "female heads," and she argued that since women were forced into the "struggle for bread," they ought to have "fair play." But ideally, she believed, the Black woman would not have to concern herself with that struggle. The Black woman would be able to fulfill her most vital role, which was to uplift the race, as a homemaker who brought to her family "plain living and homely virtues." Black women had neither time nor space, Cooper reiterated, for what she saw as New Woman frivolity.[29]

However, it was not only responsibilities to family and community that kept many Black women from being New Women or New Negro Women. A white New Woman encountered hostility because she challenged entrenched notions of who she was supposed to be as a woman. A New Negro Woman had to challenge not only notions of who she was supposed to be as a woman but also notions of who she could be as a Black person in a white world. Opportunities in new occupations and the professions had been expanding for white middle-class women since the late nineteenth century, but that was hardly true for Black women. By 1920, more than 70 percent of Black women worked outside the home, but most of them were domestic servants, washerwomen, or agricultural workers.[30] Though there had been a handful of Black professional women even as early as the nineteenth century, their struggles were amplified far beyond those of white women in the professions.

Charlotte E. Ray, daughter of a prominent pastor of the Bethesda Congregational Church in New York City, was the first Black woman graduate of Howard University Law School and the first woman admitted to the bar in the District of Columbia. She planned to practice corporate law, an area in which she had excelled as a student. But white companies would not hire her because she was Black, and Black companies would not hire her because she was a woman. Ray took what clients she could get, whatever their case or assets. She represented Martha Gadley, a poor and illiterate Black woman who sought a divorce from her alcoholic husband because he threatened to break her neck, nailed up their front door to keep her out of the house, and threw her clothes out the window. In 1875, Ray succeeded in bringing *Gadley v. Gadley* to the Supreme Court of the District of Columbia. She was the first woman of any color to plead before that body. But there is no evidence that she ever pled corporate law cases. She gave up after a few years and moved to Brooklyn, where she joined her two sisters and became a teacher of Black children. Unsurprisingly, few Black women followed her into the legal profession. According to the U.S. Census of 1910—conducted twenty-five years after Ray argued the Gadley case in the Supreme Court of the District of Columbia—there were only two practicing Black women lawyers in the entire country.[31]

There were more Black women doctors by 1910 (over 300). But they too continued to face huge struggles. For instance, Virginia Alexander, who had worked her way through the Women's Medical College of Pennsylvania as a waitress and maid, was granted a medical degree in 1925, but no local hospital would accept a Black woman intern. The director at the Philadelphia General Hospital told her outright that he would not give her an internship even if she "stood first in a thousand applicants." Alexander was forced to uproot herself from Philadelphia, which had always been her home, and resettle in Missouri, where she could intern at the Kansas City Colored Hospital. She was almost denied an internship there, too—not because she was Black, of course, but because she was a woman. Alexander returned to Philadelphia in 1927 and founded in her own home a maternity hospital for poor Black women, called the Aspiranto Health Home.[32] Again unsurprisingly, there was no immediate flood of Black women following her into medicine.

In the 1910s, during the first years of the Great Northward Migration from the rural South to big cities in the East and West, the Black population grew by 66 percent in New York City, 148 percent in Chicago, 308 percent in Cleveland, 500 percent in Philadelphia, and 611 percent in Detroit. Hopes for decent employment were raised during World War I. But jobs in factories, offices, and stores were mostly closed to Black women—even those like Addie Hunter, who had graduated from Massachusetts's prestigious Cambridge Latin and High School. In 1916, when Hunter was refused a civil service job for which she was eminently qualified, she used all her savings to sue. She lost. She was "out of pocket, out of courage," as she complained in *The Crisis*. Hunter warned other educated Black women that "the way things stand at present, it is useless to have the requirements. Color—the reason nobody will give, the reason nobody is required to give—will always be in the way." The few stores that did hire Black women drew strict lines, such as the Chicago clothing store where Black women were maids (and ate lunch in the basement) while white women were salesgirls (and ate lunch in the first-floor lunchroom). Most Black women who had to work settled for domestic service jobs. But strangely, the Black press seemed to worry anyway about the possibility that Black women might become New Women. The *Pittsburgh Courier*, for instance, was critical of Black "career girls" who were "evading motherhood" and "refusing to lay aside their selfish and false pleasures for the sake of the race."[33]

Yet Black women saw other images in the media that served to create aspirations for change. Race films (movies made for Black audiences using Black actors) introduced viewers to new women. One of the most popular of the race films, Oscar Micheaux's *Within Our Gates* (1920), presents Sylvia Landry, a Black woman who has not only moral strength but also agency. Described in an opening title card as "typical of the intelligent Negro of our time," Sylvia is a middle-class career woman and teacher—with a social conscience right out of the pages of Anna Cooper. "It is my duty and the duty of each member of our race to destroy ignorance and superstition," Sylvia proclaims, and she raises money to rescue a poor Black school that is about to close for lack of funds. She is a suffragist, too, battling an ignorant white woman who is appalled that Black women might vote. Sylvia is a "new woman" (though not a "New Woman") whose great reward for her merit is marriage in the denouement to a handsome Black doctor who, of course, shares her ideas of obligation to the community.

Though the New Woman was not a staple in race films, she was in Hollywood studio films, which also had wide distribution in urban Black neighborhood theaters. Silent film serials, such as *The Perils of Pauline* and *The Exploits of Elaine*, featured the actress Pearl White in spunky New Woman athleticism, regularly defying old images of woman. As Pauline or Elaine, Pearl White flew airplanes, raced cars, leaped from great heights, toted guns, and even engaged in fisticuffs. The New Woman was also portrayed in popular films such as the "war readiness" movie *Patria*, made in 1916 and starring a short-haired Irene Castle, who plays the owner of the great Channing Munitions Works. Castle wears a military uniform and drills her employees, all of whom are men, in marching, shooting, and flag waving. In the extravagant fantasy of the film, her dashing second in command, also in uniform, defers to her in awe and admiration. Even women who lived in communities where such images were disdained could not escape knowing that in the larger world the image of woman, whether real or fantasized, was undergoing huge transformation. Though that image was mostly of white women, it could be fodder for dreams by any woman with twenty cents to spend on a movie.[34]

Changing laws also potentially had an effect on all women, regardless of race and of whether or not they were feminists. By the 1890s, Married Women's Property Acts (laws for which women's righters had agitated since the first women's rights convention in Seneca Falls, New York) had been passed in all the states. The laws gave a married woman independent rights: she now had jurisdiction over her own wages, over property that she inherited or accumulated on her own, and over any business that she conducted in her own name. For women who were struggling daily to put food on the table for their families, such laws had little practical effect. But they could be hugely important for some women in the Black community—"new women" who, inspired by revolutionary images of woman in the larger culture, had gone through doors that might have opened just a crack in their own communities and had recast themselves.

Sarah Breedlove, born in Delta, Louisiana, to former slaves, had been married when she was fourteen years old and widowed by the time she was twenty. She married a second time but left that husband in 1903 because he drank and was a serial cheater. She was raising her young daughter by herself, working as a washerwoman to support the two of them, until she found a better job with the Poro Company. That business was owned by Annie Malone, a Black woman who was fast becoming a millionaire. Breedlove went door-to-door in Black neighborhoods, selling Malone's hair care products. But in 1904 Breedlove attended the St. Louis World's Fair, at whose "Colored Pavilion and Exhibition" she heard speakers from the National Association of Colored Women, the uplift organization founded by Mary Church Terrell, in which Anna Cooper also played a big role. The speakers talked about race betterment. Breedlove was inspired to better herself further by starting her own business.

Breedlove had had serious hair loss because for years, when she was a laundress, she washed her hair in a basin that contained traces of the lye she used for her customers' laundry. Her hair was restored after she applied herbal medications she had ordered from Africa. She then decided to start her own door-to-door business, selling her own hair-growth products.

In 1906 Breedlove moved to Denver, where she married Charles Joseph Walker, an advertising salesman. "Madam C. J. Walker" became her professional name. It sounded distinguished, she thought, and the "Madam" sounded French, which signified glamour. Again going door-to-door in Black neighborhoods she peddled her wares: not just Madam C. J. Walker's Wonderful Hair Grower but also Madam C. J. Walker's Vegetable Shampoo; Madam C. J. Walker's Glossine (to "beautify and soften" Black hair); and an assortment of cosmetics concocted for use by Black women, all of which prominently bore the name Madam C. J. Walker. She began traveling around the country to sell her line. Her reputation and business grew. She hired agents who would peddle her products in cities and towns she could not get to herself. If her wares had been targeted primarily at men instead of women, she might not have been so easily accepted as an authority. But she was a woman speaking mostly to women.

With business skills that she seemed to come by naturally, she established a laboratory to develop more cosmetic and hair products and then a factory to manufacture her expanding line. She moved her operations to Indianapolis, where there was a large and well-established Black community and connections to eight different railroad lines, which would make it easy to ship Madam C. J. Walker products anywhere in the country. She was soon the head of a multimillion-dollar empire. She traveled everywhere, giving lectures and demonstrations on the Madam C. J. Walker methods of beautification. She also took to heart the motto of the National Association of Colored Women, "Lifting as We Climb." In Pittsburgh she opened a college to train beauticians—hair culturalists, she called them—who would learn the art and science of beauty culture as well as marketing skills. They would become experts in running a multidimensional beauty care facility, using the Madam C. J. Walker line of hair care and cosmetic products exclusively.

Walker's husband understood advertising and had helped her promote her products in newspapers and magazines, but she outstripped him in ambition. As she complained after she shed him, "When we began to make $10 a day, he thought that was enough, thought I ought to be satisfied. But I was convinced that my hair preparation would fill a long-felt want. And when we found it impossible to agree, due to his narrowness of vision, I embarked on business for myself." She put her twenty-one-year-old daughter A'Lelia, who had just graduated from Knoxville College in Tennessee, in charge of the mail order business. As one of Madam Walker's biographers quipped, "She hungered for economic empowerment more than she hungered for a husband."[35] In 1912, when she discovered that her husband was having an affair with another woman, she divorced him on the grounds of adultery. Under the Indiana Married Woman's Property Act, Madam C. J. Walker's businesses were hers alone.

She opened more beauty colleges—in Indianapolis, New York City, and Chicago. She encouraged young Black women from the South to take her courses, at a cut rate, and then "go back to their homes and be independent business women." She also hired tens of thousands of agents, Black women who might otherwise have been making a meager living as washerwomen or cleaning ladies. Carefully groomed and wearing white blouses and black skirts, they carried black briefcases stuffed not only with order forms for Madam C. J. Walker's moneymaking products but also with pamphlets of instruction about "hygiene and the value of good personal appearance."[36]

Walker's phenomenal success had its basis in talent, but it could not have begun to happen without the external developments that affected her life. There was the Black migration to cities from tiny towns like Delta, Louisiana; there were models of women who had already made it big, such as Annie Malone with her Poro Hair Products; there were new ideas of who a woman might be that infiltrated the Black community through groups like the National Association of Colored Women or newspaper stories (negative as some were) about "career girls" or movie fantasies; and there was the Indiana Married Woman's Property Act, which gave Madam Walker and not her husband control of the empire she had created.

"The Most Wonderful Business Woman in the World," Black newspapers such as the *Kansas City Sun* called Walker. In fewer than fifteen years she had gone "from the washtub to a million-dollar fortune." She was the richest self-made woman, Black or white, in America. Her story was "a fairy tale," upon which the Black woman might dream.[37]

WORKING-CLASS WOMEN FIND THEIR VOICE

"Ah, then I had fire in my mouth."
—CLARA LEMLICH, looking back on the 1909 garment workers' strike[38]

The college-educated New Woman wanted to work for the sake of independence and self-fulfillment. Women of the laboring class had to work because they needed the money. In America's expanding industries they were exploited, just as their nineteenth-century mill girl counterparts had been. Like the mill girls, they banded together in unions to fight against horrific working conditions—but unlike the mill girls, they often succeeded. Their fight and victories changed them. They would not have recognized themselves in the concept of the "New Woman," but they too became "new women."

The International Ladies Garment Workers Union had been around since 1900, formed to fight the sweatshop conditions under which workers in the booming garment industry labored. When young women—mostly poor immigrant Jews who had recently arrived in America from Eastern European shtetlach—began working in the garment factories in large numbers, it seemed to union leaders that the women were undermining their efforts. Bosses fired men and hired women to replace them because they could pay women much less—a young woman did not have a family to support, the bosses said. The union leaders made no effort to recruit women workers, claiming that a woman worked only until she married. She was "satisfied to take home a couple of dollars to buy a feather for [her] hat." She lacked the will, motivation, and inner strength to engage in any struggle with the factory owners.[39]

But the conditions women workers had to put up with were brutal. In some factories they worked eleven hours a day, seven days a week. "If you don't come in on Sunday, don't come in on Monday," signs in both

English and Yiddish notified them as they rode the elevator to and from their factory's floor. They were fined for being late, and they were pushed to speed up and produce more. They were charged for any damage they did to a garment, barely allowed bathroom breaks, and cursed at by the foremen "even worse than the Negro slaves were in the south," they complained.[40] Factory owners used an economic downturn in 1908–1909 as an excuse to cut the workers' wages, which had been at starvation level to begin with.

On September 15, 1909, the women workers at the Leiserson Company and the Triangle Shirtwaist Factory walked out on strike. They were aided by the New York branch of the Women's Trade Union League (WTUL), an organization made up of wealthy college-educated New Women who—in the spirit of Jane Addams and her volunteers at Hull House—had committed themselves to helping women workers. The WTUL pledged to put up bail money for strikers who were arrested and even to help them buy groceries and pay their rent. The media also came to the aid of the women strikers. The same newspapers that loathed New Women who had no regard for womanliness were captivated by the working-class "girl" strikers who, after all, were beneath the rules for middle- or upper-class womanly propriety. "Arrest Strikers for Being Assaulted," one front-page headline announced ironically, condemning the New York police officers who had stood by and watched striking "girls" being beaten up by the factory owners' hired thugs and then had arrested not the thugs but the strikers. "Rowdies Attack and Seriously Injure Girls," another front-page headline announced.[41] Reporters focused especially on one pretty young garment worker, Clara Lemlich, who had been beaten by strikebreakers. The press made her the face of the struggle.

The WTUL in New York City organized a mass meeting on November 22, 1909, at Cooper Union's Great Hall to address whether there should be a major strike against all the big garment factories. All of the 2,000 seats were filled, most of them by women workers. For two hours the audience was addressed by representatives of groups such as the International Ladies Garment Workers Union and the all-male American Federation of Labor. They droned on and on in English and Yiddish about the tyranny of the bosses, the oppression of the laborer, the importance of workers' unions, and how crucial it was to do "due deliberation" before making a decision to strike. Lemlich—well known to the workers since the news had spread that the rowdies had beaten her unconscious, broken her ribs, and sent her to the hospital—did what a working-class woman had seldom done before. She walked up to the stage, demanded to be recognized, and ended the endless deliberations by shouting in Yiddish: "I am a working girl, one of those striking against intolerable conditions. I am tired of listening to speakers who talk in general terms. What we are here for is to decide whether we shall or shall not strike. I offer a resolution that a general strike be declared—now!" Those who were there remembered that the crowd leaped to its feet, yelling "Second!" The women waved their handkerchiefs, and the men who were there threw their hats into the air.[42] It was the beginning of the biggest labor strike to that time, with Lemlich as its poster girl. It came to be called the Uprising of the 20,000, though some newspapers put the number of strikers at 40,000.

The newspapers made Lemlich into a gutsy girl hero. They described her as "little Clara Lemlich . . . a small, dark, quick-eyed girl, absolutely unafraid," and "a pretty eastsider of nineteen years." In fact, Lemlich was twenty-three at the time of the Cooper Union meeting. She was not simply a girl who had suddenly popped up from the audience after growing impatient with boring speeches, though that story too made good press. She was a seasoned labor activist and a firebrand. She had already been arrested and charged with disorderly conduct for distributing leaflets that urged a factory boycott. She stood on soapboxes regularly on the Lower East Side. "Ah, then I had fire in my mouth," she later recalled of her impassioned street-corner orations in the heart of the garment industry. But even years later the image persisted of her as "a wisp of a girl, still in her teens."[43] It was a new image of the underclass woman that could touch Americans: a young immigrant girl—working not because she wanted a career, but because if she did not work she would starve—and so brave that she risked her life to fight the injustices perpetrated against her by fat-cat bosses. Joan of Arc, newspapers often called Lemlich without irony.

The image of the working girl struggling to survive was much more palatable to the general public than that of the New Woman. Yet many working girls were new sorts of women. Most of them would probably have liked to have the luxury of staying home instead of punching a time clock day in and day out, but they had no choice. Their lives allowed them to have no illusions about female delicacy or male chivalry. They became "industrial feminists," banding together to fight for their rights as women workers. As Rose Schneiderman—another Jewish immigrant from Eastern Europe, a capmaker who became a feminist leader—phrased it, "We are learning that as we must work the same as our brothers and sweethearts, it behooves us to organize the same as they for higher wages and better conditions." Many of these wage-earning women became suffragists too. In 1911, Leonora O'Reilly, a labor organizer and former seamstress who was a daughter of Irish immigrants, joined Lemlich and Schneiderman to form the Wage-Earners' League for Woman Suffrage. "Why are you paid less than a man?" one of their flyers challenged the woman worker. "Why are your hours so long? Because you are a woman and have no vote. Votes make the law," the flyer explained. "Women who want better conditions must vote."[44]

The strike and picketing of the Uprising of 20,000 lasted fourteen weeks, throughout the bitter cold of New York's late autumn and winter. In the first month, the police, on the side of the factory owners and oblivious to chivalry, arrested 723 striking women. But the general public continued to view the strikers not as women who had stepped from propriety but as helpless immigrant girls suffering gross injustice. Ministers gave sermons supporting them, and the press continued to defend them.[45]

Members of the WTUL were faithful to their promise to help the strikers, but the strike was also liberating for these elite women. It was an occasion for long-desired nose thumbing at the expectations of behavior imposed on women of their class. Anne Morgan's father, the multimillionaire J. P. Morgan, had asked her when she was a girl what she intended to be when she grew up, and she had answered, "Something better than a rich fool anyway." Alva Belmont, who had been the wife of two of the richest men in New York and was also a WTUL member, had seen herself as a "born rebel," resenting always the "degrading position of women." Now they found themselves deeply stirred by the strikers, whose women's lives had been lived on a plane so different from theirs and who were willing to picket in snowstorms, endure humiliating arrests and imprisonment, deal with verbal and physical abuse, and even attack a deputy sheriff and knock him down with a blackjack—as happened in a January 1910 riot when the "girls" were getting impatient with the bosses' recalcitrance. The women workers did not always know what to make of these upper-class women who involved themselves in workers' problems. With some irony, they called their rich allies the "mink coat brigade." But the wealthy WTUL women marched at the strikers' side, got arrested along with them, and even formed a committee of "watchers," socialites who pledged to testify against police abuse of the picketers.[46]

Anne Morgan invited a group of young strikers to tell their stories to 150 of her friends who were members of the exclusive Colony Club. When the workers were done, hats were passed around the room. The socialites emptied their considerable purses to establish a strikers' fund. Alva Belmont rented the New York Hippodrome with its seating capacity of over 5,000—at that time the world's largest theater—for a rally to raise more money. When several strikers were arrested, Belmont put up her mansion as bond for their bail. Sympathy for the strikers spread, and more upper-class women rushed to help the workers. Newspapers reported that Helen Taft, a New Woman and the daughter of the president of the United States, took a train from Bryn Mawr College where she was a student to attend a meeting in New York in support of the strikers.[47]

These New Women were spiritual daughters of the women of the mid-nineteenth-century moral reform and temperance movements. Like their spiritual mothers, they were inspired to action by the troubles of the underclass. But unlike their spiritual mothers—who wanted to lift up women who had fallen to prostitution or been victimized by alcohol—the hope of the elite women, fostered by the progressive idealism of the era, was to empower working-class women. These New Women were social-justice feminists. The affluent members of the WTUL saw themselves not as protectors but as allies ready to hand over the power in the organization to those for whom it had been started.[48] In the beginning, most of the WTUL's executive board was made up of college-educated women, but the goal—which was eventually achieved—was to have working women who were trade unionists take over the leadership.[49]

It was a unique partnership whose effect went beyond the primary aim of winning rights for the worker. The women workers and their elite allies overturned the idea of woman as it related to the class of each group. The workers challenged the bosses, sticking up for themselves and in doing so sloughing off vestiges of passivity and subservience that had long been inculcated in poor women. Affluent women walked the picket lines, jeered at the scabs, got arrested with the workers, and in doing so defied the rules for women in their class.

By February 1910, most of the factory owners understood that they had lost the war of public opinion, and they conceded to many of the strikers' demands. The workweek would be reduced to fifty-two hours; workers would get four paid legal holidays; money would no longer be deducted from a worker's pay envelope because she did not punch the clock the minute she was supposed to; and the worker's right to bargain for wages would be recognized. The women could feel that they returned to work as victors.[50] Almost immediately, the Uprising of 20,000 inspired women workers to strike in Philadelphia; Chicago; Cleveland; Kalamazoo, Michigan; and even Muscatine, Iowa.[51] A new image of working-class woman was born.

The working women of the early twentieth century who rose up and struck for better pay and better treatment had probably not known about their predecessors in the 1830s and 1840s, the mill girls who had also gone on strike because of bad working conditions. The twentieth-century women strikers had newer sources of inspiration. Lower Eastside Yiddish-language newspapers such as *Vorwerts* (Forward) and *Fraye Arbiter Shtime* (Free voice of labor) were devoted to working-class struggles, and radical political meetings were held in halls big and small all over the Lower East Side. While immigrant men were seldom feminists, they did not prevent women from reading or going to meetings. The women, roused by what they learned, became militant in demanding workers' rights, and the financial and moral support they got from social-justice feminists, their New Woman allies, allowed them to hold out in their demands.

Heady as the experiences of being a New Woman may have been, some of the pioneers eventually backslid. It was surely scary to try to forge brand-new meanings for women when, as Margaret Deland suggested, most of America still preferred the older meanings. The retreat from proud New Womanhood by some women such as Ida Tarbell speaks to entrenched psychological forces that created painful ambivalences when a woman rejected the role she had been taught she should want. Tarbell was considered the leading investigative journalist of the twentieth century.[52] Her expose of John D. Rockefeller's corrupt business methods, which began as a series of articles for *McClure's Magazine* in 1902, is credited with having led not only to the breakup of his oil monopoly but also to important federal acts to regulate commerce. In 1911, Tarbell wrote *The Tariff in Our Times*, a book so respected that President Wilson invited her to be on his Tariff Commission. The administration of President Warren Harding also recognized her importance by appointing her to presidential committees. Her talents—and the times that permitted a few women to push through doors that had been cracked open—made her a celebrity. She became one of the most sought-after journalists and public speakers in America. She was so well paid that she had the wherewithal to support numerous members of her extended family.

Tarbell had started out as a feminist before the term was even coined: she was a girl who loved science and hated woman's work, such as sewing, cooking, and taking care of children.[53] As a young writer in 1887, Tarbell was infuriated by a magazine article that derided the notion of woman as inventor. She wrote an answering article, pointing out, with unambivalent female chauvinism, that though women had limited opportunities for education, they had still managed to register almost 2,000 patents with the U.S. Patent Office. "There is no branch of industry in which woman has operated and not left proof of her mechanical skill," Tarbell declared, enumerating examples of devices patented by women: the first submarine telescope, a steam generator, locomotive wheels, a machine for drilling gun stocks. Women's accomplishments were all the more remarkable, Tarbell wrote in the same article, because girls were dissuaded from "preferring a hammer to a doll" or "making kites instead of patchwork." She was thinking back on her own childhood, when she had bemoaned how girls like her were discouraged by "hearing herself called unmaidenly if she showed a talent for a carpenter's bench rather than a piano."[54]

But in 1909, when she was fifty-two years old, Tarbell—who never married and never had children—began a phase that would continue for the rest of her career: writing articles, books, and even fiction about woman's true nature, which could be fulfilled only in the roles of wife and mother. In her major anti-feminist book, *The Business of Being a Woman* (1912), Tarbell claimed (in a strange denial of her own experiences as she had recalled them) that ineluctable female nature emerged in early childhood, when little girls demonstrated their natural preference for pretty frocks and dolls. Disavowing the facts of her own life, Tarbell proclaimed that the "central fact of a woman's life, nature's reason for her," was "to bear and to rear, to feel the dependence of man and child—the necessity for this—to know that upon them depend the health, the character, the happiness, the future of certain human beings."[55]

One can only imagine the inner conflicts and misery that led Tarbell to diminish the meaning of her life and attack the feminism that had inspired her. She was in her fifties when she became an anti-feminist: Did she regret that she had never had a fulfilling love relationship or that she had missed the chance to have children? Or had she decided that she was an odd anomaly, a proverbial exception that proved the rule—that no other women in America had achieved what she had because a woman really was fitted only for the domestic sphere? Or had an old childhood wound suddenly ripped opened to ooze resentments? Tarbell recalled in her autobiography that when she was a girl two leading suffragists, Frances Willard and Mary Livermore, had come to visit her suffragist mother. The vulnerability of the child Tarbell peeks through in the raw self-pity with which she related the story. Neither of the suffragists, she wrote, "touched me, saw me. Of this neglect I was acutely conscious." She added, with a resentment surprisingly fresh forty years after the experience, "The men we entertained did notice me, talked to me as a person—not merely as a possible member of a society they were promoting."[56]

Whatever triggered her sudden convictions, Tarbell pronounced the feminist movement to be irresponsible and predicted that its irresponsibility would have dire consequences for the family and society. The only way women could compete in the world of men, she opined, was by crippling their nature and becoming repellent. In *The Business of Being a Woman* she wrote of girls in the early days of the women's movement who had been misled to do just that: they "prayed on their knees that they might escape the frightful isolation of marriage; might be free to 'live' and to 'work,' to 'know' and to 'do.' What it was really all about they never knew until it was too late."[57] That had been her own story, as she revealed in her autobiography. It was she as a fourteen-year-old girl who had "pray[ed] to God on my knees to keep me from marriage." After a lifetime of successes, Tarbell angrily attributed her girlhood prayer to having been misled by "the strident femini[st] cry that was in the air at the moment."[58] Feminists of Tarbell's generation were, of course, disgusted with her. Jane Addams spoke for them all (though her language was probably more subdued than that of Alice Paul or Lucy Burns might have been). "There is some limitation to Ida Tarbell's mind," Addams remarked.[59]

But Tarbell's repudiation of her life—or the strange disconnect between what she wrote and how she lived—stands as evidence of how emotionally exhausting it must have been for a woman to be a pioneer in a man's world. It also exposes the tenuousness of the shift from True Woman to New Woman, and it foreshadows the astonishing resurrection of true-woman values that emerge repeatedly during or after stressful times, such as during the Depression and the years right after World War II.

9.
"It's Sex o'Clock in America"

The popular press began working overtime to introduce America to Sigmund Freud's most colorful views about sex. Articles that touched on Freudian theories, simplified for the masses, began appearing even in magazines for housewives. "The libido wants, wants, wants. . . . If it gets its yearning it is as contented as a nursing infant. If it does not, beware! It will never be stopped except with satisfactions," a male writer for *Good Housekeeping* explained to the ladies in 1915. By the 1920s, newspapers throughout the country were sprinkling Freudian declarations liberally into advice columns and general interest articles. The *New York Tribune* told readers that "the latent motivation fundamental to all human beings . . . is the sex impulse." "Nervous disorders result from suppressed desires," the *Tampa Tribune* informed its audience. "Sex puzzles have the key that will unlock great areas of untracked land," the *Dayton Daily News* announced. "The libido is active from the time of conception," Eau Claire's *Leader-Telegram* stated.[1]

SEX RADICALS VS. THE PURITY OF WOMAN

"The idea that women in any great number would resort to promiscuity is absurd."

—WILLIAM MARION REEDY, *St. Louis Mirror* (1913)[2]

The notion that nature had given the woman no autonomous sex drive survived into the twentieth century. Woman was sexual only to do her duty in the conjugal bed or if, in her natural innocence, she had been seduced by some cad. But that idea of woman had been coming under public attack, along with the notion that she had no interest in wrinkling her forehead about politics. By the 1870s, a small but proud "sex radical" movement had emerged.

Victoria Woodhull—thirty-three years old in 1870, a former actress and mesmerist, and a rising star in the radical wing of the woman suffragist movement—led the charge. Woodhull announced that year that she was running for president of the United States.[3] She would be the candidate of a new Equal Rights Party. As a woman, she could not even vote, of course, and the minimum age for the office was thirty-five. In addition, she named Frederick Douglass as her vice-presidential running mate but never informed him of his selection. Clearly, she had little illusion that she could win the presidency. But she wanted to get her message out to the public. She was running on a platform of woman suffrage, divorce reform, and "free love."

It was the latter that created the most outrage, as she knew it would. That same year Woodhull and her sister, Tennessee Claflin, had started publishing *Woodhull and Claflin's Weekly*, for which they wrote incendiary articles openly advocating free love, declaring in one of the first issues that "the time is approaching when public sentiment would grant women the right to hold relations with those to whom their hearts may be inclined without marriage." In an era that claimed to cherish the notion that the woman who did have an autonomous interest in sex was not only immoral but also unnatural, the response was predictable. Woodhull's "shameless" defense of free love was evidence that the entire women's rights movement was a threat to womanhood, her attackers said. Women were warned that before they foolishly became suffragists, they had better look into the awful things that suffragists were supporting. Her ideas were "the disordered vaporing of a bad woman."[4]

Thomas Nast, the most famous political cartoonist of his day, depicted her advocacy of free love in a *Harper's Weekly* cartoon that he titled "Get thee behind me, (Mrs.) Satan." In the foreground of the cartoon was Woodhull, sporting Luciferian wings and horns and holding a sign that read "Be Saved by Free Love," and in the background was a woman weighed down with two children, a drunken husband riding her back. In the caption, the virtuous woman says to Woodhull, "I'd rather travel the hardest path of matrimony than follow your footsteps."[5]

Undaunted by insults and enjoying her succès de scandale, Woodhull delivered cheeky speeches on "the principles of social freedom." In Manhattan's Steinway Hall, a few months before the presidential election, 3,000 people came to hear her declare her "inalienable, constitutional, and natural right to love whom I may, to love for as long or as short a period as I can; to change that love every day if I please." She was distracted by neither the cheers nor the "perfect tempest of hisses" that followed her statements. Lest anyone try to "defend" her by claiming she was not really talking about sex, Woodhull stated emphatically, "I trust that I am fully understood, for I mean that and nothing less." Susan B. Anthony, who had initially been enchanted by Woodhull's glamour and boldness, was finally horrified and broke with her. Just before the November election, Woodhull and Claflin were arrested and charged with publishing "obscenity" in their *Weekly*—including an exposé of sexual hypocrisy that focused on Rev. Henry Ward Beecher and his affair with a parishioner. The charges against the *Weekly* triggered a scandalized Congress to pass the first U.S. sex censorship law: the 1873 Act for the Suppression of Trade in, and Circulation of, Obscene Literature and Articles of Immoral Use, commonly known as the Comstock Act.[6]

But sex radicals would not be silenced. In magazines such as *Lucifer, The Light Bearer, Age of Freedom,* and *Good Time Coming* they promoted free love, contraception, and a woman's right to be sexual on any terms she chose. They published explicit articles about sex experiences, from childhood to adulthood. Fully 40 percent of the readers appear to have been women—from small towns and rural areas as well as big cities, judging by the correspondence the editors received—and many of them shared their own stories about sexual desire.[7] But the Comstock Act made the publications virtually criminal. Even subscribing to them entailed some risk, so circulation of most of the sex-radical magazines was small. However, *Woodhull and Claflin's Weekly*, which also included articles on spiritualism, socialism, and suffrage, attracted as many as 20,000 readers.

Under the Comstock Act most male editors of the sex-radical magazines were sooner or later arrested and landed in jail. Women editors were often beneath the law, perhaps because the authorities preferred (if they had a choice) not to believe that a middle-class white woman might willingly be a sex enthusiast. One of the most long-lived of the magazines—*The Word*, published by Ezra and Angela Heywood from 1872 to 1893—was a case in point. Ezra was arrested five times for graphic articles that appeared in *The Word*, which were often written not by him but by Angela. "There are times," Angela declared in "The Ethics of Touch," when every woman "wants man's fingers to pass through every two hairs on Mt. Venus." In response to that piece, the chief inspector of the U.S. Post Office Department ordered a raid on the office of *The Word* during which Ezra, but not Angela, was arrested.[8]

"Sex Nomenclature—Plain English," published in *The Word* in 1887, was particularly shocking to the censors. In that article, Angela argued that it was hypocritical and unfair that men used whatever words they pleased in private discourse to describe female sex organs, while woman, the subject of those words, was never allowed to use equivalent words. It would go a long way toward ending hypocrisy and equalizing male-female relationships, Angela contended, if both women and men could use good Anglo-Saxon words in public, such as "cock," "cunt," and "fuck." The authorities simply refused to acknowledge that a woman of their class was capable of having so foul a mouth. Ezra was again arrested.[9]

The first survey of American women and sex was begun in 1892, the same year Ezra was arrested for a fifth time. Thus, it is probably not surprising that the survey was not published during the lifetime of the researcher, Clelia Duel Mosher, a physician. Mosher questioned women about subjects such as their desire for intercourse, how often they had orgasms, and what they thought was the purpose of sexual relations. The sample for her survey, which she conducted between 1892 and 1920, was small—only forty-five women—and the respondents were all of the same socioeconomic class: they were elite white women, mostly wives of professors at the University of Wisconsin or Stanford University. Nevertheless, the results give interesting insights into women born in the Victorian era and imbued with the idea that sex was something husbands desired and wives acquiesced to as a marital duty.

A few of Mosher's subjects were indeed faithful to that expectation. "The ideal would be to have no intercourse except for reproduction," one respondent said. Another stated that without the aim of pregnancy, marital sex was nothing but "legalized prostitution." However, most of the respondents gave the lie to the Victorian notion of a proper woman's lack of sexual appetite. The women reported that they did not simply do their duty in the conjugal bed; rather, they desired sexual intercourse. One commented that sex "is a very beautiful thing. I'm glad that God gave it to us." Several described experiencing ecstasy. Intercourse "sweeps you out of everything that is every day," one woman wrote. Another described orgasm as bringing "a sense of absolute physical harmony." Many agreed that sex was "a necessity."[10]

That Dr. Mosher believed their venereal enthusiasms would have been considered shocking is attested to by her secretiveness about her survey. She continued working on it over a period of twenty-eight years; but though she regularly published her other research—on posture, menstruation, intestinal stasis, gallstones, the importance of drinking more water—this study she buried among her papers. (It did not see the light of day until a Stanford University professor, Carl Degler, discovered it in the Stanford archives thirty-three years after her death.)[11]

Mosher worried perhaps about people like William Marion Reedy, a prominent newspaper editor, who coined the catchphrase "sex o'clock in America" in 1913 to describe what he feared had become a new obsession. Reedy was radical on most social issues, but he was as disturbed as any straitlaced conservative that sex was suddenly a pervasive topic everywhere, including in the theater and literature and on the silver screen. He opined that the purity of woman was being maligned. Born in the mid-nineteenth century (in the same cohort as most of Mosher's subjects), Reedy could not transcend the notions that his class and generation professed to believe about sex: to wit, that a woman was by nature passionless. She could be led astray, but not by her own sexual drive. He penned a heated defense of woman against the allegation that she was complicit in the striking of "sex o'clock." "The idea that women in any great number would resort to promiscuity is absurd," he declared.[12]

Refusing to believe in woman's innate sexual drive, Reedy was oblivious to whatever contradicted old theories about woman's natural "modesty" and "purity." He was a great admirer of his fellow radical, Emma Goldman, deeming her "about eight thousand years ahead of her age." Yet he ignored her ecstatic statements about the "depth and glory of sex experience" and her promotion of free love.[13] Like the Victorian he was, Reedy preferred to think, as he said in his "sex o'clock" essay, that woman's passion is mostly a pretense.

But by the second decade of the twentieth century, the discussion of woman's passion and even the possibility of her willing "promiscuity" was everywhere. Agreeing with William Reedy, a writer for the literary magazine *Current Opinion* lamented that "a wave of sex hysteria seems to have invaded this country. Our former reticence on matters of sex is giving way to a frankness that would even startle Paris."[14] Suddenly, more ink was being spent on the subject of women and sex than ever before: out-of-control daughters, unfaithful wives, so-called white slavery, and prostitution.

New Women and sex radicals were joined in their defiance of old notions about woman and her sexuality by young immigrant women from Europe, farmers' daughters from rural America, and Black women from the South—all of whom were pouring into big cities looking for work and creating sexual upheavals.

SEX, THE WORKING GIRL, AND HER RESCUERS

> "Why, yeh poor kid! Ain't yeh got a bit o' sense? Don't yeh know there ain't no feller goin' t' spend coin on yeh fer nothin'?"
> —CLARA E. LAUGHLIN, *The Work-a-Day Girl* (1913)[15]

Most wage-earning women in the urban working class were young and unmarried. Almost 40 percent were on their own, away from the watchful eyes of family members. But even those living under parental roofs spent little time at home. They worked long hours, and because living arrangements for the big-city poor were cramped, they would likely spend their little bit of leisure in amusements outside the home.[16] Millions of young women were essentially on their own for the better part of each day. Never before had so many of them been so free of close scrutiny. The mores about woman's behavior they had learned from their parents or church were tested by the mores they were learning at work and at new kinds of recreation.

The situation created an unprecedented degree of moral panic. More than a billion pages of government and social agency reports were published between 1900 and 1920 by those who were determined to stamp out activities that they considered dangerous to the working-class woman and the social order.[17] Much of the anxiety was over the real or imagined growth of white slavery. However, there was also worry about the threat of a general loosening of morals among working girls, who were in fact creating daring new ways of expressing woman's sexuality.

All of this led to an interesting paradox. The middle- and upper-class college-educated women who staffed settlement houses and government social agencies were often New Women who had fought for their own right to be as sexual as they pleased. But ironically, they saw the working girl as being in peril, helpless before sexual lures. They stepped in, believing that they were intruding for the working girl's own good.[18] They could not recognize in working-class women their own feminist struggle for sexual agency. If a working girl was sexual, it was because she was seduced, financially desperate, or deluded by her enchantment with pretty things and urban diversions. She had to be rescued from sex. It was dangerous to her as well as to society if, in her ignorance, she got pregnant out of wedlock. Seldom did the college-educated women entertain the possibility that the working girl knew what she was doing, chose freely to have sex, and was claiming her right to erotic pleasure, just as the New Women did.

Attempts to suppress the working girl's bold behavior usually failed. A huge population of young women employed as factory workers, department store clerks, hotel maids, and waitresses had been created in big cities. The women were forming communities that fostered new kinds of public amusement and play, as well as new ideas about women and their sexuality. Dance halls became a favorite leisure-time hangout of working girls whose jobs kept them confined for ten hours a day or more. On the dance floor their bodies were free. Exuberant or sensual dances became the rage, including the shimmy, which involved wild shaking of breasts and hips; slow rags; the bunny hug; and the grizzly bear, also called "tough dancing," in which a woman put her arms around a man's neck, he put his hands on her hips, and their cheeks and bodies touched.[19] To some observers the dances seemed to simulate sex acts.

The reformers, not trusting men to keep their sex urge in check, fretted that ignorant working-class girls were being taken advantage of. "The dance hall, as we have permitted it to exist, [is] practically unregulated," the journalist and militant suffragist Rheta Childe Dorr bewailed. Dorr was a passionate defender of the New Woman, whose aim, she said, was "to belong to the human race, not the ladies' aid society of the human race." But she panicked at the situation of the working girls, who in her mind were decidedly not New Women—not educated, middle-class, and capable of looking out for themselves. The dance hall, Dorr wrote, "is a straight chute down which, every year, thousands of girls descend to the way of the prodigal." Other reformers even held the dance hall responsible for the abduction into white slavery of 50,000 foolish, pleasure-seeking young women every year: "There are very few girls who visit the public dance hall who do not in the end come to grief. The act of dancing excites sexual feeling, and no girl who wishes to retain her virtue should visit these public traps of sin," explained E. Norine Law, the author of *The Shame of a Great Nation*, in 1909.[20]

Reformers also worried about the newly visible sexuality of working-class "female inverts." In small towns or rural areas, inverts (who might be called "queer" in contemporary terminology) generally had no community; they were isolated. Many gravitated to urban areas to find work, but they were also drawn because in big cities they could live in both anonymity and community. Where no one knew them, they could create semipublic spaces, such as "resorts"—dance halls located in slum areas like New York's Bowery, where "masculine-looking women in male evening dress" cavorted with feminine-looking partners in gowns. They had to hide their unconventional sexuality from the hostile world outside, but in their resorts they were free to affirm it with one another.[21]

In women's "homosexual" relationships there were obviously no male seducers for reformers to worry about. But even reformers who were lesbian were alarmed by the sexuality of the working-class invert. The reformers were certain that the lower-class female sexual invert was out of control and obsessed with sex. What she did was hazardous to her physical well-being. Ruth Fuller Field, a New Woman, wrote a pseudonymous memoir in which she discussed frankly a happy lesbian sexual relationship she had had in the early twentieth century with "Juno." But Field also recalled going "slumming" to invert "resorts" where, she claimed, she was appalled. She made sharp distinctions between the wholesome and transcendent lesbian sex she and Juno enjoyed and the decadent carryings-on of their working-class counterparts:

> Our lives were on a much higher plain than those of the real inverts. While we did indulge in our sexual intercourse, that was never the thought uppermost in our minds. That was but an outlet for emotions which too long had been pent up in both our lives for the good of our health. We found ourselves more fit for good work after having been thus relieved. But we had seen evidence of overindulgence on the part of some of those with whom we came in contact, in the loss of vitality and weakened health, ending in consumption.[22]

Field's assumptions are curious because in depicting her own lesbian love, she defied the pathologizing of same-sex relations that was widespread when she wrote her autobiography. Yet her ideas about the morbidity of sex between women not of her class were straight out of books by nineteenth-century sexologists such as Richard von Krafft-Ebing, who considered all homosexual relations to be sick.[23] Like heterosexual women reformers who saw the sexuality of straight working girls as different from and more perilous than their own, reformers who were lesbian panicked about the unrestrained sexuality of working-class female queers.

According to reformers, even the work site was sexually risky to a working-class young woman. In her 1912 study *The Girl Employed in Hotels and Restaurants*, the woman's rights activist and moral reformer Louise DeKoven Bowen concluded that the physical hardships of the work "are nothing compared to the moral dangers to which [the girls] are exposed." She claimed to have learned in her investigations that "very few of these originally honest [that is, virginal] girls come safely through the dangers to which they are constantly exposed." Unwilling to dwell on the possibilities of working girls' autonomous sexual appetites, Bowen explained their "fall" in other ways. The work was boring and lonely, she wrote, and the girls were seduced by men who promised to take them out for amusements and give them respite. Many of the workers were immigrant girls, alone and with no one to look after them. They were "ignorant of our standards." They were not aware of the seriousness of a moral lapse.[24]

Progressive women reformers' fight for a decent minimum wage for the working girl was triggered by fears of her susceptibility to seduction. The feminist journalist Clara Laughlin, for instance, was horrified at learning of the sexual bargain young women were supposedly taught to accept if they wanted a little bit of pleasure after their hard day's work. In her 1913 book *The Work-a-Day Girl*, Laughlin presented Katie, a sixteen-year-old Chicago department store clerk who earned $3.50 a week and had to turn over all but $1.00 of it to her family. The other female clerks seemed to enjoy good times with young men, but the men Katie went out with dropped her after a couple of dates. Laughlin reported, in language that tried to emulate working-class dialect, that Katie was let in on the secret of dating success by Myrtle, a coworker: "Why, yeh poor kid! Ain't yeh got a bit o'sense? Don't yeh know there ain't no feller goin' t' spend coin on yeh fer nothin'?"[25]

"The next time a fellow took [Katie] out and gave her a swell time, then asked her to go to a hotel, she went," Laughlin grimly declared.[26]

Along with many of those who wrote reports on vice and on the economic dilemmas of female wage earners, Laughlin preferred to see working girls as having naturally innocent hearts. Sounding very much like moral reformers of the 1840s, these authors presented the young working woman as childishly eager for little pleasures and susceptible to male lusts. She was in danger of becoming, in the vernacular of the day, a "charity girl"—one who let herself be seduced not for money but for the treat of a nice dinner and an evening on the town. The reformers generally refused to consider that a working girl might enjoy sex without having been first coarsened by a debaucher. If they found a young woman who admitted to enjoying sex, they presented her as an anomaly. "In one case reported, the girl said, 'What's the harm?,'" a 1910 study admitted, as though the girl were a lone oddity.[27] Not many young working women would have been likely to expose themselves to the judgments of the moralists by admitting that their sexual desires matched those of the men who took them to dinner and a movie.

The panic about lower-class woman's autonomous sexuality was not peculiar to white reformers. When waves of poor Black women from the South began migrating to northern cities in the late nineteenth and early twentieth centuries, the North's Black bourgeoisie had worries like those of their white counterparts who panicked over the influx of poor immigrant girls from Europe. Poor Black girls were being seduced into violating sexual mores, and middle-class Black women who were committed to uplift and "respectability" hoped to teach them to resist seducers and be chaste. One of the most prominent of the would-be teachers was Victoria Earle Matthews. Born into slavery at the start of the Civil War, Matthews "uplifted" herself, beginning with books in her employer's library when she was a maid. She became a writer and prominent clubwoman. In 1898 she was a keynote speaker at the annual Hampton Negro Conference, which was devoted to "developing the best traits of the Negro." In her speech, Matthews castigated the Black middle class for failing to "watch over and protect" the young southern Black women who had come north to the big cities, where they were ensnared by dangers that were "so overwhelming in their power to subjugate and destroy, that no woman's daughter is safe away from home."[28]

Distressed about the seduction and ruination of young Black women, Matthews founded the White Rose Home for Working-Class Negro Girls. Her staff members went out to the piers to meet the steamers arriving from the South. They promised to take young Black women who got off the boats to a shelter for "Negro girls" where they would receive lodging, food, and training for a job. Matthews's anxiety about the "girls" is reflected in the name she chose for her shelter: she called it White Rose, she said, so that "the girls will think of the meaning—purity, goodness, and virtue—and strive to live up to the name."[29]

Like their white counterparts, middle-class Black women reformers took particular aim at dance halls. In such dens of iniquity, "to the tune of St. Louis voodoo blues, half-naked Negro girls dance shameless dances with men in Spanish costumes," the reformer Jane Edna Hunter lamented. She deemed the dance-hall atmosphere to be "one of unrestrained animality." Hunter, a professional nurse and a member of the Black elite in Cleveland, Ohio, was distressed about the expression of sexuality in dance halls because it "tumbled gutterward" the progress that "the Negro had made toward the state of good citizenship."[30]

Hunter's moral panic was a function of her desire to show that the Black woman was no different in sexual modesty and purity from the respectable white woman. To quash the menace that working-class Black women's sexuality posed to racial progress, Hunter founded the Working Girls Home Association. Like White Rose, it offered shelter and rescue to those who had come from the South. Hunter believed that she could keep young Black women from succumbing to the lure of prostitution by training them to earn an honorable living as domestic servants.

A young Black woman who took her sexual pleasures was in trouble if she was subjected to reformers such as Matthews and Hunter or, even worse, to the law—as happened often, even to those who had done nothing criminal. Early twentieth-century reformatory case files reveal that working-class Black girls could be incarcerated merely for being considered "wayward," as was sixteen-year-old Mattie, an inmate at the New York State Reformatory for Women at Bedford Hills. She had been pregnant twice and was unmarried. Though there were no bastardy laws in early twentieth-century New York, her sexual history was enough to warrant a three-year sentence. Her case file illustrates how confusing it must have been for a young woman who liked sex to come into contact with reformers who believed that she was not supposed to, and who saw it as their duty to drill her in purity, goodness, and virtue. When Mattie's caseworker at the reformatory pried into her sex life, demanding to know about her first experiences, Mattie's answers revealed her struggle: should she proudly proclaim her sexual agency, or should she say what she knew a young woman was supposed to say? She stated alternately about her first sex experience: "I went wrong with Herman Hawkins. . . . I liked doing it. . . . He forced me. . . . I knew better. . . . I wanted it."[31] "I went wrong," "I knew better," and "he forced me" was what she needed to say if she wanted her freedom back.

HOW AMERICA CAME TO UNDERSTAND THAT WOMAN IS A SEXUAL BEING

"The truth—bold, naked, sensational."
—Newspaper ad for *Flaming Youth* (1923)[32]

The clock struck a loud "sex o'clock" not in 1913, as William Reedy had written, but in the next decade. In the post–World War I climate, whatever vestiges remained of notions about woman as innately passionless seemed antediluvian, as did much else that had been accepted for centuries as sacred truth. Hundreds of thousands of Americans had been killed or wounded during the war, and many came home suffering from shell shock. Worldwide, war casualties numbered in the tens of millions. World War I had caused an unprecedented sacrifice of human life, for reasons that were hard for most people to fathom. For the first time on a massive scale, despondent young Americans questioned the wisdom of authority that had led the country so far astray. Cynical, angry, and rebellious, they felt justified in throwing out old rules and making their own or in operating by no rules at all. Women chimed into the discussion with voices louder than ever, emboldened by their victory in the struggle to win the vote. In a climate so ripe for social upheaval, potent forces came together and seemed to give the coup de grace to old notions about women and sex.

A 1923 article titled "The Changing Morality of Women" presented the apparent transformation in sweeping terms. "For the first time in the history of man, girls from well-bred respectable middle-class families broke through those invisible claims of custom and asserted their right to a nonchalant, self-sustaining life of their own with a cigarette after every meal and a lover in the evening," the writer Alyse Gregory declared. Her blunt assertion made a few who still hoped to turn "sex o'clock" back to a tamer time bristle in denial. Gregory's article was answered in a following issue of the same magazine by a PTA leader who indignantly reminded readers that "New York is not America" and that even in New York, "the vast majority of our girls and women are clean-minded and self-respecting"—though there may be "a few who prefer to live on a very inferior moral plane." The *Social Hygiene Bulletin*, devoted to stamping out vice and venereal disease, also joined the debate triggered by Gregory's article, speculating that in America's small towns, young women from bourgeois homes were probably "still living lives of impeccable chastity." But even the *Social Hygiene* author had to admit that in recent years there had been a significant change in moral strictures, and that it was "unlikely that the Western World will ever again ask of women that strictness of behavior which was never demanded of men."[33]

It was hard to ignore the fact that even bourgeois women had become more overtly and autonomously sexual. In the first decades of the twentieth century, the moral panic of reformers had been triggered by young women who were beneath them on the social scale and whose sexuality, the reformers believed, had to be controlled. But in the 1920s, middle-class young women also seemed out of control. Pioneering feminists of the older generation, such as Charlotte Perkins Gilman, were unhappy about it. Gilman called the new sexual behavior the "physical indecencies of our misguided young people." To feminists like her, it was particularly upsetting because the young woman of the 1920s seemed to think of nothing but bodily pleasures instead of fighting for serious issues such as women's rights to political power and better jobs.[34]

But there was no turning "sex o'clock" back. Even a young woman in a small town living in a bourgeois home could no longer be as sheltered from all things sexual as she presumably once had been. As long as there were newspapers, magazines, and—most of all—movies in her life, she did not have to reside in New York in order to learn the new ways.

The silent films of the 1920s were not silent on the subject of sex. They played an outsize role in disseminating new ideas about woman's right to proclaim her sexuality with unabashed zeal. A survey of movie house owners revealed that many of them believed that "audiences were larger when 'sex pictures' were being shown," and they were willing to oblige with films such as *Flaming Youth*, billed as "a startling exposé of the women of today." Ads for this 1923 film, which had great box office success, promised that it would portray "neckers, petters, white kisses, red kisses, pleasure-mad daughters and sensation-seeking mothers. . . . The truth—bold, naked, sensational."[35] If a young woman in the South or the Midwest had not already known of the new morality, films like *Flaming Youth* would teach her.

And even if she was not allowed to go to racy movies, she could read about them in the newspapers. Readers of the *Daily Times* in Davenport, Iowa, for example, were informed that *Flaming Youth* "paints a true picture of the age in which we are now living" and depicts the modern girl "who takes her fun where she can find it." Those who read the *Weekly Iberville South News* in Plaquemine, Louisiana, were told that *Flaming Youth* was "amazingly frank" about the "ever-growing abandonment of conventions on the part of the younger generations." Though reviews sometimes moralized about "the price pleasure lovers pay for their fun," they also proclaimed, even in the same sentence, that the movie was "daring, flaming, overflowing." It was virtually impossible to hold back the zeitgeist almost anywhere in America. Young women far from big cities were learning, if they did not already know it, that their peers were having "overflowing" fun as "neckers [and] petters."[36]

Even young women in immigrant communities of color were learning about the new mores. Most Mexican immigrants in the United States had come from small towns and villages. There, when a young woman was brought into contact with members of the opposite sex, she was chaperoned by an older female relative. It was understood that if she transgressed sexually she ruined not only her own life, but also the entire family's standing in their small community. Immigrant families tried to replicate chaperonage in the barrios of the United States. But by the 1920s, it did not work so well. The onslaught of popular culture was overwhelming.

Young women in the barrios of Los Angeles, for instance, went to movie matinees, read popular magazines, and mixed with white students at school. They learned that modern American girls were not saddled with chaperones, and they came to resent the old tradition. They sneaked away from the barrio to go dancing at the Cinderella Ballroom at Fifth and Hill Streets in downtown Los Angeles, or they took the street car to Long Beach, where they met boys at the Nu-Pike Amusement Park. Young Mexican American women often quit school after the eighth grade and went to work at a factory or in a service job to help support the family. Though a dutiful daughter might hand over most of her salary to her parents, her much-needed contribution could earn her a stronger voice in the family—which she might use to refuse to be supervised in her free time.[37]

Even Spanish-language magazines and newspapers helped Americanize and sexualize the young woman. The magazine *Hispano-America*, for instance, included slick Max Factor ads showing Mexican girls, lips glossy red and eyes mascaraed, looking like Hollywood starlets. *La Opinion*, a Los Angeles newspaper for the immigrant community, featured articles such as "How Do You Kiss?," which informed young women that "kissing was not an art but a science" and proceeded to make them osculating cognoscenti.[38]

The immigrant community in San Francisco's insulated Chinatown also had a hard time keeping its American-born girls sequestered. In their families and immediate community, Chinese American females were subject to traditional ideas about sex segregation. But they too went to movies and read magazines, and at school they were thrown together with boys. They heard the jazz music their classmates listened to; they saw the sexy dances their classmates danced; and they learned to do likewise, if only surreptitiously.[39] It was inevitable that the American-born daughters of immigrants, exposed to American culture from so many different directions, should initiate a shift in their community's notion of woman and sexuality.

But even slight changes worried the keepers of custom. For instance, in 1924, after a flood and famine devastated a province of China from which some Chinatown families had emigrated, a group of girls planned to raise money for the victims. They would do it, they decided, through a "jazz dance." These young women were hardly wild nonconformists intent on flouting sexual mores, but the local newspaper could not hide its discomposure about "American dancing by Chinese girls"—wearing high heels yet! "To those who know the customs of old China," the reporter wrote, "this undertaking by the flappers of Chinatown is a remarkable event in the annals of convention smashing."[40] It was a vast exaggeration to think of these young women as flappers, but the reporter had understood correctly that their acting outside "the customs of old China" created a crack that would inevitably widen.

Automobile ownership also cranked the clock to "sex." In a car, a young woman and her date could escape her parents' scrutiny. The couple could have almost as much privacy as if they were in a hotel room. The advice columnist Dorothy Dix had recognized the disturbing potential of the automobile as a sex site as early as 1913, when only about 1 million Americans owned cars. Dix dubbed the automobile "the devil's wagon."[41] By 1919, 7.5 million Americans owned cars, and Dix's fear seemed to have been realized. In cities and towns everywhere, there were "lovers' lanes" to which couples drove and where they parked, petted, and even had intercourse. "I call my car Mayflower because so many girls have come across in it" was a common boast by young men.

The clock was cranked too when Freud's name became as well known as the names of movie stars. Freud had visited America only once, in 1909, when he lectured on psychoanalysis at Clark University in Worcester, Massachusetts. Civilization, Freud told his audience of laypeople and physicians, interfered with natural drives and demanded too much repression of the libido. "We ought not go so far as to fully neglect the original part of our animal nature," he said. Emma Goldman, sitting in the front row with her lover, Ben Reitman, recognized in Freud's words an affirmation of her own provocative ideas about woman's sexuality and free love. She proclaimed him "a giant among pygmies."[42]

New Women generally loved Freud. They refashioned his theories to support their own ideas of sexual liberation, though to do that they had to ignore his phallocentric Victorian notions about woman's sexuality. They focused instead on what he said about the deleterious effects of libido repression.[43] It seemed to the New Women that Freud had imbued with medical prestige their own challenge to the idea that woman had no sex desire of her own.

But by far the greatest driver of woman's new claim to sex was "birth control," a term coined by its pioneering proponent, Margaret Sanger. In the early twentieth century, Sanger had been an obstetric nurse among immigrant women on the Lower East Side of New York. There, witnessing tragic effects of unwanted pregnancies—starving children, physically and emotionally depleted mothers, and fatal self-induced abortions—she committed herself to teaching women how to avoid getting pregnant. In 1910, when she and her husband became denizens of bohemian Greenwich Village, she met Goldman, who radicalized her further. Goldman had attended a Malthusian conference in Paris about contraception, and she became a fierce advocate of a woman's right to prevent pregnancy. It was imperative for family planning, she thought, and it was crucial for a woman's freedom as a sexual being.[44]

Inspired by Goldman, in 1914 Sanger began publishing a newsmagazine called *The Woman Rebel*, which focused on women's rights in general and birth control in particular. The publication's title indicated Sanger's solemn commitment to struggling against the status quo, but in case anyone missed her radical meaning, on the masthead was the logo "No Gods, No Masters." Contrary to centuries of opinion in America, a woman has the right to do as she wishes with her body, Sanger wrote defiantly in *The Woman Rebel*—including the right to have sexual intercourse without the fear of getting pregnant: "Her body belongs to herself alone."[45] Sanger ultimately reshaped sex: it was thanks in good part to her that intercourse stopped being as chancy as Russian roulette for a woman, married or not, who did not wish to be pregnant.

Sanger was able to publish only eight issues of *The Woman Rebel* before the newsmagazine was deemed to be "lewd, filthy, vile and indecent" under the Comstock Act, which in addition to forbidding sex talk in print also prohibited any discussion of birth control, including the dissemination of information about it through the mail.[46] Copies of the publication were confiscated by the U.S. Post Office, and Sanger was indicted by a federal jury. Threatened with a long prison sentence and a $5,000 fine, she left her three children and her husband in New York, disguised her identity, and fled to England by ship with forged papers.

But she was undaunted in her commitment to the cause. On the ship, Sanger cabled her assistants to tell them to arrange the immediate distribution of 100,000 copies of a pamphlet she had written called *Family Limitation*. The pamphlet gave precise instructions to women about using pessaries, sponges, plugs, or suppositories before they had sex and using douches or hot drinks spiked with quinine to "expel the semen from the uterus" after they had sex. "Don't be over sentimental," Sanger firmly advised her women readers. "The inevitable fact is that unless you prevent the male sperm from entering the womb, you are going to become pregnant."[47]

She had intended to stay out of the United States indefinitely, but she learned that there was immense protest against her indictment. Government authorities were being inundated by letters from all over America, "educating" them about the need for safe birth control. Respected doctors and clergymen were giving lectures and writing articles in her defense. Sanger returned to stand trial.[48] She was acquitted of publishing obscenity by a federal judge who realized that popular opinion was overwhelmingly in her favor.

Almost immediately after her acquittal, Sanger opened America's first birth control center, the Brownsville Clinic in Brooklyn, from which she intended to dispense pamphlets dealing with female sexuality and contraception. She knew, of course, that such a clinic was illegal, but she distributed 5,000 handbills in English, Yiddish, and Italian in the most congested neighborhoods of Brownsville, announcing the clinic's imminent opening. If anyone missed the announcement, they heard about the clinic a few days later, when the *Brooklyn Daily Eagle* ran a front-page article on it, even giving its address and broadcasting the news that "Clinic Opened Here for Birth Control; Challenges Police."[49]

Three days later, a woman "large of build and hard of countenance," as Sanger described her, came into the clinic and said she wanted to buy a copy of *What Every Girl Should Know,* a pamphlet written by Sanger that depicted the "sexual impulse" in graphic detail for the education of adolescent females. The clinic charged ten cents for pamphlets, but the woman insisted on giving Sanger's assistant two dollars for it. Sanger guessed that something was up. The woman, an undercover vice squad police matron, returned the next day with a male officer to make an arrest. When Sanger refused to walk to the police station with them, they summoned a paddy wagon. Sanger was dragged into it, screaming at the police matron, "You dirty thing. You are not a woman, you are a dog." Newspapermen were there with cameras. The story made front-page headlines.[50]

At her trial in January 1917, Sanger sat in the court holding a big bouquet of hothouse red roses, a gift from affluent supporters who sat behind her, next to scores of working women who were also grateful to her for helping them avoid unwanted pregnancies. Sanger's lawyers argued that a woman had a right to copulate without conception and that the legislature had no right to forbid the sale of "articles necessary to the free enjoyment of such a right."[51]

The judge who wrote the damning opinion on Sanger's case was especially angry that she had not even bothered to plead what might have been acceptable—that her work was on behalf of married women whose health would not permit them to have more children. Instead, the judge said, Sanger was promoting an unmarried woman's right to have sex without consequences. The legislature had an overriding right to make laws "on matters in aid of public morals," he proclaimed, and those women "lacking in moral stamina" had to be "deterred from fornication by fear of detection through pregnancy."[52] Sanger was given a choice of paying a fine or spending thirty days in the workhouse. She chose the workhouse, knowing that that sentence would make the more dramatic statement about the injustice of the law. Sanger spent much of her free time in the workhouse giving birth control advice to the other inmates.

She remained undeterred. After her release, she announced to the newspaper reporters who flocked around her, "I feel ready to begin work again." And she did just that. In her writing and lectures she became more militant than ever. "The most far-reaching development in modern times is the revolt of woman against sex servitude," she proclaimed in her 1920 book, *Woman and the New Race*. To have the power to control whether sex will lead to pregnancy enabled a woman to break out of the chains that "bound her to her lot as a brood animal for the masculine civilizations of the world." With birth control, Sanger wrote, a woman could create "a new sex morality." She could "develop her love nature separate and independent of her maternal nature."[53] It was a battle cry that demanded the recognition of woman's right to be as sexual as she desired and her freedom from consequences she did not desire.

Though Sanger was arrested several more times, it was clear by the early 1920s that she was winning the battle to enable woman to separate sex from maternity. Wealthy feminists and male philanthropists such as John D. Rockefeller put money into funding "a glorious 'chain' of clinics," as Sanger had envisioned. By the mid-1920s, 90 percent of middle-class women thought that birth control devices should be made available to married women, and over 60 percent believed that they should be made available to unmarried women. Furthermore, 71 percent believed that women should have legal access to abortion. Middle-class married women were clearly practicing birth control. It had not been unusual for their mothers and grandmothers in the nineteenth century to have had more than six children, but in the 1920s, middle-class women were having an average of two children. Before the decade was over, the birth rate in the United States had dropped by 20 percent. Sanger became a hero in big cities and small towns all over America.[54]

WOMAN IN THE FLAPPER AGE

The playful flapper here we see,
The fairest of the fair.
She's not what grandma used to be—
You might say, au contraire.

—DOROTHY PARKER, "The Flapper" (1922)[55]

Dorothy Parker was right. The flapper was the antithesis of everything that her grandmother's generation claimed a proper woman should be. A woman's hair was her crowning glory? The flapper cut hers to a boy's bob. A woman laced her waist up in a tight corset, announcing her fecundity by exaggerated hips and breasts? The flapper declared that "the corset is as dead as the dodo's grandfather," and she prided herself on her boyish figure. A woman kept her limbs covered in public? The flapper wore sleeveless dresses and skirts that skimmed her knees. A woman's major goal was to be a superlative homemaker? The flapper's major goal was to have a fine time. A woman left the streets to men and prostitutes? The flapper claimed the streets and any other public place she damn pleased.[56]

She did other things that only prostitutes had done in earlier generations. She could outswear any sailor if she chose. She made up her face: scarlet lips, Kewpie-doll rouged cheeks, mascaraed lashes, and arched eyebrows that were plucked and penciled. Prohibition had shut down the saloons, but that did not stop her from drinking: she was a habitué of speakeasies and nightclubs, where she shared the hip flask of her "sheik" (as the flapper's boyfriend was called). She danced madcap sexy dances as only working-class girls had dared do only a few years earlier. "Young women from the best of society are allowing their baser natures to dominate in the ballroom," a Northwestern University student lamented in 1922. The flapper smoked, too. A 1925 *Life* magazine cover depicted both her penchant for the weed and her alienation from family life: bare-legged, berouged, and becloched, she stands holding a long cigarette holder, lighting up a cigarette, huge puffs of smoke over her head. Beside her the caption read, "She left home under a cloud."[57]

The flapper was neither a do-gooder nor a reformer. Unlike the New Women who worried about working-class girls living on their own and going out with men, the flapper romanticized and emulated working-class freedoms. She particularly enjoyed the freedom to date, which working-class women in the big cities had virtually invented. Courting, the social ritual that formerly had paired middle-class men and women, presupposed seriousness: its distinct purpose was to give a couple the opportunity to discover whether they wished to marry one another. Dating was a far more casual affair. The term had been coined in 1896 newspaper columns in the *Chicago Record* about working-class life in Chicago: the writer George Ade told of a young clerk complaining to a shopgirl who had lost interest in him, "I suppose the other boy's fillin' all my dates." Ade also told of a working-class girl who was so popular with the boys that "her Date Book had to be kept on the double entry system."[58] Dating meant that a woman could be seeing any number of men who would take her out for a good time. Like working-class girls before them, flappers dated.

Flappers were largely middle class and white. Though in Mexican and Chinese immigrant communities a young woman who committed even the slightest infraction of traditional behavior was deemed a flapper, there were few actual flappers among them. Middle-class Blacks, still as concerned with uplift and respectability as Anna Julia Cooper and Victoria Earle Matthews had been a generation or two earlier, also looked askance at the flapper phenomenon. In 1922, the leading Black newspaper, the *Chicago Defender*, described flappers as mostly white girls who used coarse and vulgar language and danced suggestively to jazz, their dress "more noticeable for what it displays of the body than what it hides." The writer of this article admitted that there were perhaps "a few rattle-brained 'flappers' among black girls," but he insisted that most young Black women did not throw virtue to the wind. In fact, he boasted, "Today the colored girl is the most modestly dressed member of the female sex on our streets." On the front page of the same issue of the newspaper, a brief piece titled "Not a Flapper Mother" demonstrated emphatically the virtues most important to the race: Evelena Burton—a sharp moral contrast to the "rattle-brained 'flappers'"—had seventeen children; two of them were already in college, and the other fifteen would be following in their footsteps. Fecundity and racial uplift: those should be the goals of young Black women, the *Chicago Defender* implied.[59]

One of the newspaper's criticisms of the flapper (that she "danced suggestively to jazz") elides the obvious: the Black roots of the flapper's dances and music. The Charleston, the shimmy, the Black Bottom, jazz, and the blues were all born in Black communities. Not many Black women were flappers, but flappers adored Black culture. They were particularly fascinated by working-class Black sexuality, which they imagined to be primitive, uninhibited, and subversive. In a kind of sexual colonialism, or what has been called a "sex-race marketplace," flappers and their sheiks went "slumming" in ghetto nightclubs such as those in Harlem, which they saw as a "synonym for naughtiness" and a "jungle of jazz."[60] Blues songs, with lyrics that would have horrified Anthony Comstock, enthralled flappers. The blues seemed to give women permission to be as sexual as they pleased. "My man rocks me, with one steady roll," Trixie Smith—a Black middle-class college graduate who broke away from respectability to sing the blues—belted out in 1922:

There's no slippin' when he wants take hold.
I looked at the clock, and the clock struck six
I said, Daddy, y'know I like those tricks
Cause he was rockin' me, with one steady roll.[61]

For the white woman, the blues were deliciously errant. For the Black woman, they were a brazen defiance of the Black bourgeoisie's obsession with her duty toward race uplift and motherhood. The blues even seemed to mock those demands: "Mama" in blues songs was a woman who craved sexual satisfaction from her "Daddy." She might suffer because she had a no-good Daddy, but she could give as good as she got. In "Mama's Gone, Goodbye," written in 1924 by Clara Smith, a popular blues singer from South Carolina, Mama is red hot. She kicks out a disappointing Daddy and, with no sentimentality, announces that she is ready for his replacement:

> I'm going to get me a Daddy to treat me right
> One who will come home and sleep every night.
> There's a fire in my range, bakes nice and brown
> All I need is some good Daddy turn my damper down. . . .
> Fare thee well, Mama's gone, goodbye.[62]

The blues could be about all manner of sexual desire, even desire that was hardly acknowledged in the white world, such as lesbian desire. According to Katharine Bement Davis, a prominent sociologist who in 1929 published *Factors in the Sex Life of Twenty-Two Hundred Women*, women were having sex with other women in astonishing numbers in the 1920s: fully a quarter of her sample, which was made up mostly of middle-class white women, admitted to having had same-sex sexual relationships.[63] Despite its apparent ubiquity, however, lesbian sex was still the love that dared not speak its name publicly in most of white America. But in blues lyrics, homosexual women ("bull daggers" or "bull dykes" in the Black parlance of the 1920s) could find out-loud affirmation of themselves as sexual beings.

Gertrude "Ma" Rainey, who was bisexual, sang straight blues such as "Down in the Basement," in which she proclaimed, "I want something lowdown, Daddy, want it nice and slow." But Rainey also violated the Comstock Act with lesbian lyrics, such as in "Southern Blues": "I went to the Gypsy next door. / She say you can get a man anywhere you go. / Let me be your rag doll." In Rainey's best-known lesbian blues, "Prove It on Me Blues," she defiantly announced that she goes out with women "'cause I don't like no men," that she wears "a collar and a tie," and that, as she teases, "They say I do it, ain't nobody caught me, / They sure got to prove it on me." Another one of the prominent blues singers of the 1920s and

1930s, Lucille Bogan, also performed both straight and gay blues. In "Coffee Grindin' Blues," for instance, Bogan sings "Going to keep it for my Daddy, ain't going to give nobody none,/ I ain't ever loved it this a-way before." But in "B.D. Woman's Blues," she celebrates bull dykes who "got a head like a sweet angel and they walk/ just like a natural man," who "drink up plenty whiskey, and they sure will strut their stuff," and who "need no men." Only among Greenwich Village bohemians were lesbians acknowledged as openly, even in the Roaring Twenties.[64]

If the Black bourgeoisie worried that Black flappers might bring down the "Negro race," the white bourgeoisie, still invested in bygone notions of woman, worried that flappers would bring down the entire human race. "Flapperism" was blamed when coeds showed up on college campuses wearing bobbed hair, makeup, and sleeveless dresses. Objections to higher education for women suddenly echoed those in 1870, when Belva Lockwood was refused admission to a college on the ground that her "mere presence would be likely to distract the attention of young men." Flappers were making it hard for male students to control themselves, administrators complained. The dean of the Graduate School at the University of Southern California reproached coeds for the "pernicious near-cult" of "Flapperolatry [that] challenged young men to exceed all the speed limits of immodesty." Coeds' mothers were blamed along with the alleged flappers. The mothers were "neglectful to an extreme degree of the modesty and virtuous grace of their daughters which, after all, are the virtues which true men love and admire," the president of a North Dakota college protested in a 1922 jeremiad (which could have been written two hundred years earlier) against coed flappers. Fathers also blamed mothers. A retired farmer from Michigan—whose two daughters had become too modern when the family moved to Chicago—shot his wife and then killed himself. According to a newspaper report, the grieving daughters said that their father had been furious with their mother for failing to exercise more control over them: the parents had quarreled over the daughters' "flapper conduct."[65]

But flapperism ended before the 1920s did. "Now we can say farewell to the flapper," a *New York Times* fashion-page writer declared with ostensible relief in January 1929. "Her day over, she goes on her way, and her successor is visible evidence of a change in feminine type." Long graceful skirts were back. The bob was obsolete: the debutante, the *Times* announced, was wearing her hair parted and gathered into a knot at the back of her head. An article in *Ladies' Home Journal* titled "The Return to Feminine Charm" agreed that breasts and hips were in again.[66] The flapper was absolutely passé.

Yet it was not just the vagaries of fashion that sounded the death knell to the unprecedented freedom among young middle-class white women that the flapper represented. Ten months after the *New York Times*'s farewell to the flapper, the prosperity that had helped birth the tenor of her times came to a halt. The stock market crashed, and the decade-long Depression began. The mood of the 1920s, triggered by rebellion against the clueless elders who had gotten the country into the devastating World War, gave way to worry about paying the rent in the devastating Depression.

So what remained of woman's move—flapper or not—to claim her sexual pleasure? By 1933, national income dropped to more than half of what it had been in the 1920s, and car ownership dipped—which may have put a crimp in petting possibilities. It was harder, especially for young people still living with their families, to find privacy. Notions of sexual morality also tightened with the tightening of people's belts. Cardinal William O'Connell, the archbishop of Boston, begged "all good women, Catholic and non-Catholic," to eschew the "modern pagan ideas" about illicit sexuality that "shattered the ideal [that] women's first and principal place is in the home." Emily Post, the maven of social manners since the first edition of her etiquette book had appeared in 1922, added a section to the revised edition of 1937 about what happens when young women are not chaste. She sermonized that "petting and cuddling have the same cheapening effect as that produced on merchandise which has through constant handling become faded and rumpled, smudged or frayed, and thrown out on the bargain counter in a marked-down lot." Other 1930s advice gurus agreed.[67]

The Depression did muffle the striking of sex o'clock, but there could be no turning the clock all the way back. The sociologists Robert Lynd and Helen Lynd, whose 1937 study *Middletown in Transition* focused on Muncie, Indiana, discovered a range of sexual behaviors in this small midwestern city. Some behavior was Victorian, but some was very much like that of 1920s big-city flappers and sheiks—which, the Lynds suggested, young people in Muncie had learned through the movies. The Lynds interviewed Muncie residents who claimed that even high school students were sexually sophisticated. "They know everything and do everything—openly. And they aren't ashamed to talk about it," the Lynds were told. But they found in the local newspapers advice-to-the-lovelorn columns instructing the young that, for example, "a girl should never kiss a boy unless they are engaged." And at a high school they discovered a "preachers' kids club" whose members pledged not to "smoke, drink, chew, and neck." As the Lynds concluded, in the 1930s sexual behavior and attitudes had become much more diverse than they were before the Roaring Twenties, even in Muncie.[68]

The clock was also not turned all the way back because those who "know everything and do everything" were no longer inevitably worried about unwanted pregnancy. Contraception became increasingly available during the Depression. In 1936, a federal court struck down prohibitions on the sale and distribution of birth control devices. In 1937, the American Medical Association even recommended that contraception be taught in medical schools and that doctors prescribe contraceptives when requested by a patient. Married couples who knew their family could not afford another mouth to feed may have been the most frequent users of birth control during the Depression, but unmarried women could avail themselves of contraceptives, too. By 1938, there were over four hundred companies in the United States that manufactured them, and it became far easier to get birth control devices. Men could buy condoms in vending machines in many public restrooms, should they need them spontaneously, when out on a date. But the most popular form of contraception, accounting for 85 percent of all contraceptive sales, were those that women had control of: over-the-counter vaginal jellies, suppositories, and antiseptic douches, which they could even get without a doctor's prescription.[69]

A woman who claimed the right to be sexual in the 1930s no longer had to play Russian roulette if she had sex with a man. The judge who ruled against Sanger in 1917 because he believed that women must be "deterred from fornication by fear of detection through pregnancy" had essentially lost the battle.

1660: Mary Dyer being led to the gallows, where she was hanged "like a flag for others to take example by," remembered in a nineteenth-century woodcut.

1774: A satirical cartoon of the Edenton, North Carolina, Ladies Patriotic Guild, which pledged to boycott British tea.

1832: The murder of Sarah Cornell (*far left*), a mill girl seduced and impregnated by Rev. Ephraim Avery (*center*, being rowed away by demons), became a cautionary tale for young women who left the shelter of home.

c. 1863: Assigned female at birth, "Loreta Janeta Velazquez" served in the Confederate Army as "Lieutenant Harry T. Buford."

1872: Cartoonist Thomas Nast's commentary on presidential candidate Victoria Woodhull, who ran on a "free love" platform.

1876: "The Resolutes," a Vassar College ball team.

1901: Temperance women like Carrie Nation wielded hatchets to smash saloons—from the 1840s until liquor was outlawed.

1863: Harriet Tubman, rescuer of hundreds of enslaved people and called a "Black she-Moses," was described by the *Wisconsin State Journal* as "head and shoulders" above the men who were "swaggering their superiority."

1902: Anna Julia Cooper: "[Women] needed to bring a heart power into this money-getting, dollar-worshipping civilization."

1909: Anti-suffrage postcard: the topsy-turvy world that would be created if women could vote.

1898: Zitkala-Sa, Dakota Sioux activist: "Am I not an Indian woman as capable in serious matters and as thoroughly interested in the race—as any one or two of you men put together?"

1911: Madam C. J. Walker behind the wheel of her Ford Torpedo roadster. The Black press deemed Walker "The Most Wonderful Business Woman in the World."

1925: The Flapper: "She's not what grandma used to be—
You might say, au contraire."

1943: Mary McLeod Bethune and Eleanor Roosevelt at the opening of a residence hall for "Negro government girls." Bethune pushed at the reigning notions of Black womanhood.

1943: Interned at a war relocation camp, learning to teletype. Paradoxically, young women "were pretty free to do whatever they wanted because there was no real family control."

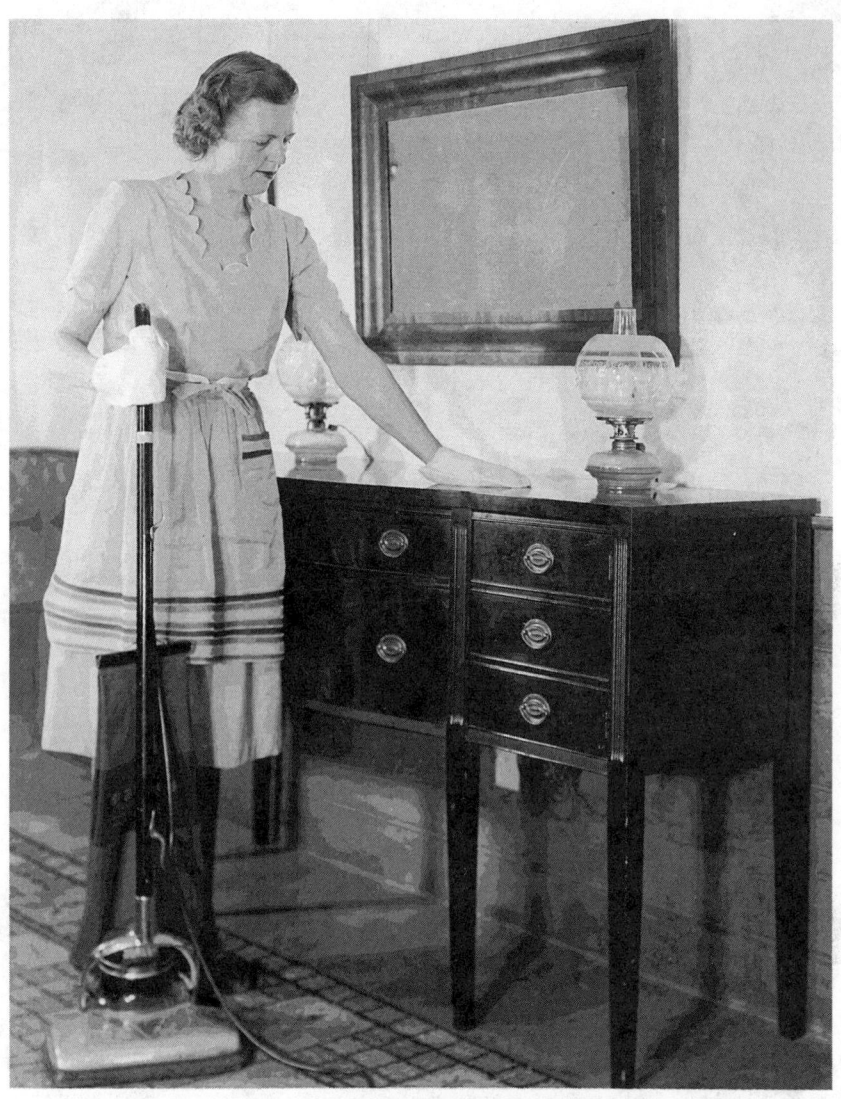

1950s: Housewives were advised by the Department of Agriculture's Home Demonstration Activities division that using mitts to dust as you vacuum "eliminates travel time."

1950: Roller derby players were encouraged to declare, "I want what I think every girl wants—my husband to be happy in his work, my own home, raise a family, and live a normal, everyday life."

c. 1965: Dolores Huerta, cofounder of the United Farm Workers: "We have a lot of machismo here, and I'm not going to take it anymore."

WANTED BY THE FBI

INTERSTATE FLIGHT - MURDER, KIDNAPING
ANGELA YVONNE DAVIS

FBI No. 867,615 G

Photograph taken 1969   Photograph taken 1970

Alias: "Tamu"

Age:	26, born January 26, 1944, Birmingham, Alabama		
Height:	5'8"	**Eyes:**	Brown
Weight:	145 pounds	**Complexion:**	Light brown
Build:	Slender	**Race:**	Negro
Hair:	Black	**Nationality:**	American
Occupation:	Teacher		
Scars and Marks:	Small scars on both knees		

Fingerprint Classification: 4 M 5 Ua 6
                                               I 17 U

CAUTION

ANGELA DAVIS IS WANTED ON KIDNAPING AND MURDER CHARGES GROWING OUT OF AN ABDUCTION AND SHOOTING IN MARIN COUNTY, CALIFORNIA, ON AUGUST 7, 1970. SHE ALLEGEDLY HAS PURCHASED SEVERAL GUNS IN THE PAST. CONSIDER POSSIBLY ARMED AND DANGEROUS.

A Federal warrant was issued on August 15, 1970, at San Francisco, California, charging Davis with unlawful interstate flight to avoid prosecution for murder and kidnaping (Title 18, U. S. Code, Section 1073).

IF YOU HAVE ANY INFORMATION CONCERNING THIS PERSON, PLEASE NOTIFY ME OR CONTACT YOUR LOCAL FBI OFFICE. TELEPHONE NUMBERS AND ADDRESSES OF ALL FBI OFFICES LISTED ON BACK.

DIRECTOR
FEDERAL BUREAU OF INVESTIGATION
UNITED STATES DEPARTMENT OF JUSTICE
WASHINGTON, D. C. 20535
TELEPHONE, NATIONAL 8-7117

Entered NCIC
Wanted Flyer 457
August 18, 1970

1970: When the FBI's 10 Most Wanted list began in 1950, it was inconceivable that women could be "dangerous" enough to warrant inclusion. In 1970, the list included four women.

2017: The day after Donald Trump's inauguration, 4 million women gathered in cities across America for the largest single-day protest in U.S. history.

10.

Woman on a Seesaw

•

THE DEPRESSION AND WORLD WAR II

It was an emotional reaction born of the desire to counter the social destabilization: to return to a time when life was more predictable, when woman honored her domestic sphere. The journalist Norman Cousins—who would become editor in chief of the *Saturday Review*, a magazine with almost 700,000 readers—proposed a sweeping plan that would at once end the Depression and restore woman to the place where God had set her, erasing generations' worth of unwise permutations. "There are approximately ten million people out of work in the United States today," Cousins wrote. "There are also ten million or more women, married or single, who are job holders. Simply fire the women, who shouldn't be working anyway, and hire the men. Presto! No unemployment. No relief rolls. No Depression."[1]

WOMAN IN THE DEPRESSION

"We are the result of an education that taught 'career.' We have not learned to take satisfaction in work well done at home."

—KATHERINE GAUSS JACKSON,
"Must Married Women Work?" (1935)[2]

A year into the Depression, two women psychologists published a widely read book on the modern young woman, based on what they claimed to have learned by questioning 252 "girls" in their late teens and early twenties. The psychologists announced that the girls thought their predecessors misguided. They no longer believed that work brings women a "new freedom" or that having a career is the way to happiness. Girls were no longer interested in "feminine independence." They were seeing "the loneliness of older unmarried friends," and they did not want "the rewards from a material success that must be accomplished at the expense of love." The psychologists (themselves beneficiaries of the New Woman's struggles) did not grapple with practical reasons that helped explain why young women might be giving up on careers, such as the fact that husbands continued to expect even working wives to take sole responsibility for the cooking, the cleaning, and the kids.[3] Nor did the psychologists acknowledge that young women witnessed the Depression cutting into women's career opportunities, or that they bore the brunt of a widespread social campaign to push woman back to "the place where God had set her."

Magazines were barraging readers with articles by women who were proudly renouncing their careers and hurrying home. "You May Have My Job," one writer, an erstwhile feminist, declared in an essay about how a career made women "narrow, hard, efficiency bitten"—and even worse, made them forget the most important thing: that a woman's children "are her immortality." "Must Married Women Work?" another career woman asked in the pages of *Scribner's*. The answer was a resounding "No!" The author criticized First Lady Eleanor Roosevelt (ER) for telling a gathering of headmistresses and seniors from private girls' schools that it was "worthwhile to work." "We are the result of an education that taught 'career.' We have not learned to take satisfaction in work well done at *home*," the author complained. The jobs that most women hold, she argued, "aren't of the slightest importance in comparison to what they might be contributing to the lives of their children." "Should Wives Work?," a male writer for *American Mercury* asked. "No!" was his short answer, too:

"We would all be happier if we could return to the philosophy of my grandmother's day [when a woman] took it for granted that she must content herself with the best lot provided by her husband."[4]

The married woman worker was especially damned in public opinion. A 1936 poll in *Fortune* magazine asked, "Do you believe that married women should have a full-time job outside the home?" Only 15 percent of the respondents answered with an unqualified "yes."[5] In the rush to send married women home it was seldom mentioned that many of them worked because their husband's salary was insufficient to support the family, or that he could not find a job and the wife was the family's sole support.

It was in fact easier for working-class women to find employment during the Depression than it was for working-class men. Women were cheaper to hire. In the garment industry, for instance, semiskilled women workers received on average $13.02 a week, while semiskilled men workers earned an average of $24.75. The discrepancy had always been justified by the false notion that men could not work for wages that were fine for women, because men—but not women—had families to support. But in the Depression employers were forced to cut back on workers who earned higher salaries. Labor segregation by gender thus had an upside for women. Throughout the 1930s, the unemployment rate for them was lower than it was for men of their class.[6]

Educated women did not fare so well: the gains they had been making were reversed during the Depression. At the start of the 1920s women accounted for 3.4 percent of all dentists, but in 1930 their share was 1.9 percent. Similarly, in 1920 they had accounted for 5.2 percent of all chemists and 3.9 percent of all draftsmen, but in 1930 their shares were only 3.0 percent and 1.9 percent, respectively.[7] The psychological destabilization that the Depression triggered created a zeitgeist that made people yearn to turn the clock back to a simpler time, when sex roles were stable and predictable—a time before career women or professional women existed. Women's colleges that had trained their students away from their old roles became prime whipping girls.

Of course, only a tiny fraction of American women had graduated from women's colleges, but nonetheless they were blamed for many of the social ills that seemed to threaten America. The birthrate had fallen below the replacement rate for the first time in U.S. history.[8] It had actually begun to decline when contraception became widely available in the 1920s, and a series of court victories during the 1930s made birth control devices even more readily available. This meant that couples who could not afford to have numerous children during the Depression were able to choose not to have them. Nevertheless, it was women's colleges that were often blamed for the dramatic dip in the number of births because, it was said, the colleges had educated women to want fancy careers, which they chose over motherhood.

Women's colleges were also blamed for the decline in marriage. In 1935, there were 30 percent more single women than there had been in 1929, largely because fewer couples could afford to marry and set up their own household. But again, those opposed to higher education for women contended that female college graduates refused to marry because they had been made to believe that they were intellectually superior to mere men or had been taught to prefer economic independence to a normal life with a husband; or higher education had given them "a fanatical pride in and a contempt for anything less magnificent than a life of acute mentality, sterilizing their bodies from normal activities," as Willis J. Ballinger, who had taught briefly at Smith College, scoffed in a 1932 article. Ballinger issued a dire warning to parents not to send their daughters to the "spinster factories," as he dubbed women's colleges.[9]

Ballinger also had a solution for the general miseducation of women: revive the curriculum of 150 years earlier. Young women should learn to be pleasing and attractive rather than intellectually prideful. They should be instructed in the social graces, etiquette, and interior decorating. They should learn ballroom dancing, good posture, and how to play a musical instrument. They should have thorough training in child psychology. "I would make homemaking the last word in intelligence," the professor concluded in all seriousness, confident that America shared his conviction that "spinster factories" ought to be converted to finishing schools that prepared a young woman to get married and to be supported by a man instead of taking the jobs that men needed.[10]

The woman who was president of Mount Holyoke College from 1901 to 1937 suffered a direct blow from the new zeitgeist. In the course of her thirty-six years at the college, Mary Woolley had transformed an indifferent little women's college into one of the best schools for women in the country. Thirty-eight years old when she became president, Woolley announced her intentions in her inaugural speech. A Mount Holyoke education, she believed, should create a woman who—no different from an educated man—knew how to accumulate facts, apply knowledge, and "develop the power of controlling circumstances rather than being controlled by them." Woolley had vowed that Mount Holyoke under her leadership would train its students not only to be "grounded in reality but well-versed in ideals"—most particularly in the ideal of public service "among all sorts and conditions of people."[11] It was a daring aspiration, worthy of the ardent New Woman of the early twentieth century, and it inspired Mount Holyoke students.

From the start of her presidency to the 1920s, when more than 90 percent of American women were married, about half of Mount Holyoke graduates, New Women, chose careers over husbands. Most went into public service.[12] To people such as Ballinger who preferred the old womanhood, or who worried about so-called race suicide among white women, that was not a happy statistic. Woolley was unmarried and partnered with Jeannette Marks, a Mount Holyoke English professor. All this would eventually be used as ammunition against woman's leadership in higher education.

Woolley had had a sterling reputation. In 1931, *Good Housekeeping* named her one of America's twelve greatest women.[13] President Herbert Hoover had even appointed her to be the first woman to represent America at a major convention about international diplomacy. She was widely recognized throughout the country not only for her work in revolutionizing Mount Holyoke but also as president of the American Association of University Women, vice president of the American Civil Liberties Union, and a national leader in multiple reform causes. Though in 1931 she was already two years past the usual retirement age of sixty-five, she decided to continue as Mount Holyoke's president until 1937, which would be the college's one hundredth anniversary.

Mount Holyoke had been led by women since its founding by Mary Lyon in 1837. But a hundred years later, as the Depression dragged on and popular sentiment now overwhelmingly agreed, as Cousins wrote, that "women . . . shouldn't be working anyway," a woman president of a woman's college came to be seen by Mount Holyoke's trustees as an unhealthy throwback. Over Woolley's protests and those of the faculty and older alumnae, including Secretary of Labor Frances Perkins, the trustees chose as Woolley's successor an undistinguished academic, Roswell Ham, who had been unable to get promoted to full professor at Yale University.

The press appeared delighted by the termination of petticoat rule. The *Boston Globe* proclaimed on its front page that "Mr. Ham's big durable he-man personality and solid scholarship [sic]" would be "a fine tonic for the spinster management of Mount Holyoke." *Newsweek* thought Mary Woolley a poor sport for protesting the choice of Ham as her successor and opined that a male president was desperately needed to get Mount Holyoke "out of its feminine rut." Woolley's fears about a setback for women were well-founded. Mount Holyoke students no longer had the role model of a woman at the helm. President Ham even squelched new hires of women professors. "There are too many older women at the college," he believed. "Any new appointment should go to a younger man."[14] Women were seldom being hired at coeducational colleges, and now, at the height of the Depression, an aspiring woman professor had one less job possibility.

ELEANOR ROOSEVELT AND TAKING WOMEN SERIOUSLY

"The fact is that generally women are not taken very seriously."
—ELEANOR ROOSEVELT, "Women Must Learn to Play the Game as Men Do" (1928)[15]

It is a great paradox that at a time when career women were being sent home in droves, a few managed to acquire more serious clout than any women had ever had before in U.S. history. Their success was due to having friends in the highest places—particularly ER, who helped them to positions in which they could influence the president of the United States. She and they became a main conduit to bring social-justice feminism into the political mainstream. What the country desperately needed in the midst of the Depression, these women believed, was a national policy of what Anna Howard Shaw, half a century earlier, had called "mother heart" values. Those values became the essence of the New Deal.[16]

ER had learned to be a fiery advocate for social justice when she was sent to a British finishing school for daughters of the wealthy. There the fifteen-year-old fell under the spell of the school's charismatic headmistress, Marie Souvestre—who, like Jane Addams, believed that women had a special role as moral housekeepers and that women of privilege had a particular role as "champion of the underdog." In 1902, ER, then eighteen, returned to America, had a lavish social debut at the Waldorf-Astoria, and then promptly threw herself into doing what Souvestre had taught her. She began by working as a volunteer teacher of poor immigrant children at the Rivington Street Settlement House in Manhattan. Despite her passion for social betterment, however, she was apolitical. Politics had little attraction for her because, she believed, it was rough and dirty business, man's domain. Joseph Lash, her close friend and biographer, even depicted the young Eleanor as being "an anti-suffragette, and vigorously so."[17]

In 1905, she married a distant cousin, Franklin Delano Roosevelt (FDR). Between 1906 and 1916 she bore him six children. In 1920, FDR was picked as the vice-presidential running mate of Ohio's governor, James M. Cox. ER—not only the vice-presidential candidate's wife but also the favorite niece of Theodore Roosevelt, who had given the bride away at her marriage to FDR—was featured often in media human-interest stories about the Democratic vice-presidential candidate. Cox lost the election and disappeared from history. However, ER—with her entrancing pedigree, ladylike voice, charismatic demeanor, and majestic height (at almost six feet tall, she towered above most women and many men)—became a public figure. She changed her mind about women voting, even stretching the truth in declaring to reporters, "I have always been for woman suffrage and regard it as much a duty for women to vote as for men to."[18] She worked with progressive groups such as the Women's Trade Union League (WTUL) (even picketing with them) and the National Consumers League, through which she campaigned for laws that would ensure the safety of products for consumers and minimum wages and maximum hours for laborers. She became vice president of the New York State Women's Division of the Democratic Party.

In 1924, ER was invited by the Democratic National Committee to chair a woman's group that was asked to make recommendations to the party's platform committee. It was a pivotal experience for her. The recommendations her group hoped to make were for social-welfare legislation such as equal pay and a maximum workweek of forty-eight hours for women, as well as the ratification of a child-labor amendment to the U.S. Constitution. She and the members of her group asked to present their recommendations in person to the all-male Resolutions Committee, which had the ultimate say about what planks would make up the party's platform. Thinking that they had a firm appointment to appear before the committee, the women sat patiently outside the locked door of the meeting room. They waited until dawn. The door never opened. The men decided in a vote of twenty-two to eighteen that they had no need to hear the women's proposals.[19] The experience was mortifying and infuriating. Clearly the women's input meant nothing to the men in power.

Yet because the Democrats wanted the women's vote, the final Democratic Party platform gave lip service to women's political participation (lazily echoing Woodrow Wilson): "We welcome the women of the nation to their rightful place by the side of men in the control of the government whose burdens they have always shared." The platform also included tepid and vague language about the protection of children, as well as "necessary safeguards against exhausting, debilitating employment conditions for women."[20] It fell maddeningly short of the specifics ER and her committee had hoped for. She decided—in a complete about-face from her former idea that politics was too dirty for women—that, as she titled a 1928 article for *Redbook* magazine, "Women Must Learn to Play the Game as Men Do." Women would never have real political influence unless they upended the prevailing idea of "woman." They must stop being ladylike, the future First Lady wrote.

To begin to have a voice, ER said, women must first "organize as women" and must create a women's voting bloc. Then they must accept and back women "political bosses," similar to the "bosses" of Tammany Hall—the executive committee of New York City's Democratic Party, which had controlled the city's politics for over a hundred years. As a lifelong New Yorker, ER had witnessed the canny political maneuvers of Tammany Hall. Its bosses were strongmen with devoted supporters, and they got things done for their constituents. The women "bosses" ER envisioned would be as tough as the men. They would empower women and fight for their causes. They would know the tricks of "bartering and dickering in the hard game of politics" just as the men did, ER declared.[21]

But women had not even mastered the first step yet: how to band together in exercising the hard-won privilege of the vote. In 1920, 43 percent of eligible women voted in the presidential election: not a great showing, but a respectable one for novices. In 1924, the number of women voters dropped dramatically, as though the novelty had worn off: only 35 percent of eligible women voters were interested enough in who would be their president and who would represent them in Congress to get themselves to the polls. Women showed up in greater numbers in November 1928 to support Hoover because he promised to keep Prohibition safe.[22] But because on most issues there was no women's voting bloc, politicians ceased to fear the women's vote. Women even lost what little ground they had had in getting elected to public office. In 1929, there had been 149 women in state legislatures across the country, but their numbers steadily dropped throughout the 1930s. Women continued to fare poorly on the federal level, too. At any time during the 1930s, in the House and Senate combined they could be counted on the fingers of two hands—with one or two fingers left over.

In 1932, FDR was elected president. ER became a first lady unlike any of her social-hostess predecessors. At the height of the push to return woman to the domestic sphere, when the timing was clearly terrible for women's pursuit of a public voice, ER managed the impossible: she got women into positions of real power, where they accomplished the large-scale housekeeping reforms for which she and the social-justice feminists had long hoped. Of course, as the wife of the president of the United States, she could not openly declare, as she had in her 1928 article for *Redbook*, that if women wanted power they had to play the game of politics like tough men. She found more subtle ways to push women forward.

One of her first acts—only days after her husband took office—came about through the urging of her intimate friend Lorena Hickok, the country's most prominent woman journalist. Hickok suggested that ER hold weekly press conferences at which only women reporters would be allowed. Through them the first lady could speak directly to the women of America. Because women reporters had been much more likely than their male colleagues to be fired in Depression cutbacks, ER won their gratitude when she created a role for them that made them fire-proof: their briefings with the first lady permitted them alone to write human-interest stories that revealed to women readers the quotidian life of the first family. But ER also had in mind a much more serious role for the women reporters. "You are the interpreters to the women of the country as to what goes on politically in the legislative national life," she told them, charging them with the huge task of finally making the average American woman politically savvy. To that end, in the next twelve years ER held 348 weekly meetings with the women reporters, the final one only hours before FDR's death.[23]

But most remarkable was ER's ability to maneuver women into positions of unprecedented power, to place the shrewdest and toughest of them in key governmental spots. She had come to understand that the ballot box would not get women into leadership roles. As she would write, the age-old prejudice against them had still not abated.[24] They were seldom elected to high offices. But they could be appointed. ER made that happen. Women were given crucial roles in the Roosevelt administration, some in administrative positions so elevated that they required Senate confirmation. They not only had more clout than American women had ever had before, but they had more than they would have again for many decades. They designed and administered programs that became central to the tenets of the New Deal—tenets such as ER and her social-justice feminist friends had been passionate about since the early twentieth century.

To make it all happen, ER teamed up with Molly Dewson, a close friend and head of the Women's Division of the Democratic National Committee. Dewson was a perfect image of the tough-woman wheeler-dealer that ER had envisioned in her 1928 article. After graduating from Wellesley in 1897, Dewson cut her teeth in corrections, as superintendent of parole for reform-school girls. Her no-nonsense manner, buxom solid figure, and sensible shoes inspired Jim Farley, chairman of the Democratic Party, to dub her "The General." As one biographer described her, she was "America's first female boss." Together, ER and Dewson were instrumental in handpicking eligible women and getting them placed in positions where no woman had ever been before: secretary of labor, assistant secretary of labor, director of the mint, assistant secretary of the Treasury, member of the Social Security Board, on the U.S. Circuit Court of Appeals, and on the U.S. Customs Court—over a hundred federal appointments. When Dewson wanted the president's ear about an issue or a candidate, ER would invite her to dinner at the White House and place her next to FDR, and as Dewson recalled, "the matter was settled before we finished our soup."[25]

ER's and Dewson's major coup was the placement of Frances Perkins, with whom they had worked in social-justice groups such as the WTUL. Perkins, as she later recalled, recognized in ER "a woman's woman" who took women seriously. ER took Perkins seriously enough to envision her as the first female cabinet member in America's history, and that goal was achieved when FDR appointed Perkins secretary of labor. Perkins had been preparing for the position her whole adult life—beginning with her student days at Woolley's Mount Holyoke College, where she learned about sweatshops and child labor, and her early Chicago days, when she volunteered at Addams's Hull House, believing that she had a responsibility to "do something about unnecessary hazards to life, unnecessary poverty." Perkins and her "Ladies Brain Trust"—a cognomen coined by the syndicated columnist Drew Pearson to describe the women who worked with her—shaped the Social Security Act of 1935.[26]

ER resolutely championed Black women leaders, too, even as she was cognizant of nasty prejudice in her own backyard. Whenever her friend

Mary McLeod Bethune was invited to the White House for lunch, ER made sure to wait at the door until she saw Bethune. Then she hurried down the walkway to greet her and walked arm and arm with her into the presidential residence. She thus staved off disrespectful looks from racist White House guards, many of whom were southerners. Perhaps she also hoped to teach by modeling.[27]

Bethune, like ER, was a feminist, a polar opposite to the mother of seventeen who was held up as a shining example of Black womanhood by the *Chicago Defender*. Bethune had only one child, and after nine years of marriage she had separated from her husband and never remarried. But as one of the most revered figures of her generation, she created another image of who the Black woman could be. She was remarkably outspoken. "The work of men is heralded and adored, while that of women is given last place or entirely overlooked," she complained in a keynote speech at a Black women's conference. She told her hearers, "We must go to the front and take our rightful place; fight our battle and claim our victories!"[28]

Bethune certainly went "to the front" herself as a civil rights leader, a fierce spokeswoman in Ida B. Wells's anti-lynching campaign, head of Bethune-Cookman College in Florida, president of the National Association of Colored Women, and founder of the National Council of Negro Women, which brought together all the major Black women's organizations. ER could credibly encourage FDR to invite Bethune to Washington in 1936, where she would take a unique job in large-scale social housekeeping: Bethune was appointed head of "Negro Affairs" in the National Youth Administration, the first federal position created for a Black woman in the history of the country. She promoted the advancement of almost 300,000 young Black men and women, directing federal money to Black schools and colleges and funding vocational training and employment programs to place Black youth in jobs. She was able to get more Black social workers hired by the National Youth Authority, too, arguing that Black youths were best served by Black professionals.[29] The lone woman among several dozen Black advisors in FDR's administration, Bethune pushed at the reigning notions of Black womanhood. She led her male colleagues, organizing a "Black Cabinet" or "Black Brain Trust," as it was sometimes dubbed. In their meetings, held in her Washington, DC, apartment, they plotted ways to force regional administrators of the New Deal (who often brought their race prejudice with them to their jobs) to give Blacks a fairer deal.

In the 1930s, women like Bethune, Dewson, and Perkins could not have been elected to positions of power such as they enjoyed as FDR appointees. However, the country sorely needed what they were able to do in guiding and defending key New Deal policies: minimum wage and maximum hours legislation, unemployment insurance and old-age pensions, worker safety laws, and child labor laws.[30] The core ideals that they had learned through their work in settlement houses and in organizations such as the National Consumers League and the WTUL were exactly the same social-housekeeping values they helped bring into the federal government.

ER's role in pushing forward these women who made critical contributions to the New Deal was detested by those who wished that women (especially the first lady) would go back to earlier times. A Republican campaign button, popular during the 1940 campaign, succinctly groused about the influence of the president's wife. It said, "And we don't want Eleanor either."

THE FORGOTTEN WOMAN

"The uncounted thousands of jobless, homeless women."
—GERALDINE SARTAIN AND EVELYN SEELEY,
"The Forgotten Woman" (1932)[31]

In a 1932 campaign address, FDR promised his radio listeners that if elected he would come to the aid of "the forgotten man at the bottom of the economic pyramid." Much of his presidency was about fulfilling that promise. But ER believed that there was a forgotten woman, too, who was having "the hardest time of all." Because the forgotten woman at the bottom of the economic heap was excluded from various New Deal programs, ER was determined to "get something done" for her as well.[32]

In 1933, as part of FDR's New Deal, the Civilian Conservation Corps (CCC) was established. A work relief program for single, destitute young men who could not find a job, CCC participants were called "Roosevelt's Tree Army." They were sent to rural areas, where they could use their muscles to protect and develop public lands. They planted trees, built dams, and fought wildfires, and in return they were housed, fed, clothed, and given small salaries. City boys learned to appreciate nature and open spaces. Eventually 3 million young men benefited from the CCC. It was considered one of the most successful of the New Deal programs.

In the same year that the men's CCC was established, ER proposed an equivalent program for women. Participants in the women's program, like those in the men's program, were to be single, young, destitute, and unemployed. The plan was that CCC women would work in less muscle-dependent conservation jobs, such as cultivating forest nurseries, and they would be taught employable skills, like toy making, that they could use when they left the program. Young women rushed to apply, but the selection process was made so stringent (in an attempt to sabotage the program, some speculated) that only a handful were accepted for the first camp.[33] Eventually ninety camps were established around the country, and 8,000 young women worked in them.

The men's CCC was seen as crucial, not only providing work for young men but also helping them find themselves, but the women's CCC was the butt of trivializing jokes. A newspaper cartoon depicted a sign in the forest that announced "She, She, She Camp" and showed beside it an ogling young man who tells his friend, "Say! We shoulda joined up with this outfit instead of th' C.C.C." The women's CCC also came under more serious attack by people who objected to the use of public funds to "induce innumerable girls to take vacations in the woods" when they should have been in their home.[34] Never mind that some of them had no home to be in.

The National Youth Administration, which was put in charge of the women's CCC, tried to appeal to the public's sympathy for the impoverished young women who were in desperate need of help. The purpose of the women's camps was "the restoration of health to bodies weakened by malnutrition," Hilda Worthington Smith, chair of the National Youth Administration's committee on camps, told the press. The camps would help America's young women by "rebuilding self-confidence undermined by the fruitless search for work," Smith emphasized.[35] Her reassurances did not work. A woman belonged in the home, not frolicking in the woods, the program's detractors would not stop insisting. The men's CCC continued, with great public approbation, until 1942. The "She, She, She" was disbanded in 1937.

But little sympathy as there seemed to be for any idea of woman other than one that would return her to a disappeared past, for thousands of women the Depression was oddly liberating. They were poor and footloose, and they found a fresh way to snub conventions about how a woman ought to live. They became hoboes, taking to the road, hitching lifts from truck drivers, riding the rails, and tromping the highways. Perhaps ER had hoped to come to their rescue, too, when she proposed a women's CCC. But many of the women hoboes would have said that they did not need rescuing. They were all ages, from newbie sixteen-year-old reform-school runaways to fifty-year-olds who had racked up years of perfecting the tricks of hoboing, such as the art of "mooching" to survive.[36] In the anomie of the Depression, a space had opened for them to break free and venture into the wide world just as men had long done.

Some set out on their own or with a male companion. Others traveled in groups or in lesbian couples. Many flouted the still-sacred rules of woman's attire, wearing overalls, army breeches, boy's jackets, and caps pulled low over the forehead. Those who traveled alone tried to make their voices husky and walk with a man's stride. Some dressed in male garb because it was easier to hop on a moving train in pants than in a dress; others hoped that if they presented themselves as men, they would be in less danger of rape, which always loomed as a threat in boxcars and hobo encampments. As one woman hobo, who did not try to pass as a man and had been raped several times, told the social scientist who interviewed her, "Men on the road never have a woman, and when there is a woman they always come around every time. It ain't the looks of me but it's just because I'm a woman."[37]

Still other hoboes dressed in male garb not for convenience or to avoid rape but because they were "men trapped in women's bodies," as the sexologists described "inverts" long before terms such as "transmen" or "genderqueer" were coined. For them, the anonymity of peripatetic hobo life was liberating. They could express who they were more easily than they could back home, whether home was a small town where conventional opinion made them outcasts or a big city where ordinances against "masquerading" or cross-dressing" made them outlaws. The odds of meeting others like them, even of forming little bands, were also much better for the invert who went hoboing than for the one who tried to live in a straight community.[38]

FDR's relief administrator, Harry Hopkins, estimated that there were 6,800 women hoboes wandering the country; other estimates placed the number at twice that. Social workers blamed the unemployment crisis for the proliferation of women hoboes. And it was true that some women became hoboes after losing a job or being unable to find one at a time when 17 percent of white women and more than 43 percent of Black women were out of work. It was a lot cheaper to live riding the rails than to pay rooming-house rent. But there had been depressions in the 1870s and the 1890s, too, and women had been less likely to be hoboes at those times.[39] It was the loosening of social controls on woman, which had become increasingly slack beginning at the start of the century, that explains why many more women dared to be hoboes in the 1930s.

Women often became hoboes not because they could not find a job, but because they loathed the settled life of domesticity. Wanderlust was domesticity's antithesis. Other women hit the road after quitting jobs that paid starvation wages. Hobo life, they claimed, was better and healthier than life in a factory: they were not cooped up, breathing unwholesome factory air or struggling with the headaches of monotonous toil. Mostly, like male hoboes, the women craved adventure, the freedom of anonymity that hoboing gave them, and the feeling of independence. As one woman hobo said, she loved the "sense of power" she got from "making a go of life on the road."[40] To be a female hobo was the ultimate challenge to the restrictions placed on woman.

WOMAN AND WORK IN WORLD WAR II

"The more women at work, the sooner we'll win."

—Poster (c. 1943)[41]

The United States entered World War II on December 7, 1941. Almost immediately, women were urged out of the home that they had so recently been urged into. They were needed to help in America's war effort, as they had already proven they could do during World War I. During the Depression, they had had to apologize for working, but now their work was a patriotic act. They had to go to work to save the country. Even women who had never before held a job outside the home were begged, in a national campaign by the War Manpower [sic] Commission, to get one. In case women's patriotism alone would not be strong enough to make them leave the domestic sphere to which they had so recently been relegated, the National War Labor Board's General Order No. 16 mandated that if a woman performed work for the war effort that was the same as the work a man did, she was to get the same pay that he got. This was unprecedented. Women rode the "up" of the seesaw happily. The number of women workers increased by 43 percent. Before the war was over, more than one-third of America's women, both single and married, were bringing home pay envelopes.[42]

The war even brought about remarkable changes in appropriate dress for women. In the mid-nineteenth century, when bloomers were introduced by dress reformers, the style was so lampooned that it never quite caught on. In 1934, when Greta Garbo dared to wear trousers in public, it was shocking news: "GARBO IN PANTS!" one headline blared, and the accompanying story reported, "Innocent bystanders gasped in amazement to see . . . Greta Garbo striding swiftly along Hollywood Boulevard dressed in men's clothes." A 1937 Associated Press article, "Dietrich Defends Use of Pants to Hide Legs," quoted a defensive Marlene Dietrich explaining, "I just happen to like trousers. They save a lot of trouble." But few women who were not insouciant film stars or female hoboes took up the style. When they did, they were as heckled as the bloomer wearers had been. The men of Battle Creek, Michigan, issued a proclamation that made national news: "Women have been wearing the pants in the house too long. Now they've started wearing them on the street. We formally protest." The men planned to stage a parade in which each male marcher would wear a skirt and carry a banner vowing to dress in skirts permanently if women did not give up pants.[43]

But during the war, what had recently been ridiculed became an emblem of woman's patriotism. Many jobs in the defense industry demanded that women wear pants. A skirt might get caught in the machinery; and the daintiness of dresses was out of place in the shipyards and steel mills and on the assembly lines where women made tanks, planes, jeeps, bullets, and bombs. Government posters, distributed all over the country, displayed woman's new fashion and touted her new role. "COME ON WOMEN OF [name of the city], LET'S HELP GET THIS WAR OVER . . . IN A WAR JOB!" one poster pleaded above a photo of a smiling young woman with goggles lifted to her head and holding a welder's torch. The American woman was now depicted in most posters wearing jeans or overalls, holding decidedly unfeminine pieces of equipment such as a wrench or a rivet gun, and with her tresses well hidden under a bandana. "We Can Do It!," she exclaims in a cartoon-speech bubble on one of the most popular posters of 1942, where she is flexing her muscled bicep.[44] Womanly delicacy was passé. Female frailty was out.

The most famous illustration of the woman defense worker was drawn by Norman Rockwell for the cover of the May 29, 1943, *Saturday Evening Post*. Rockwell aimed to capture in his drawing the popular 1942 song, played incessantly over the airwaves, about Rosie the Riveter and her commitment to the cause:

All the day long, whether rain or shine,
She's part of the assembly line.
She's making history, working for victory,
Rosie, brrrrrrrr, the riveter.[45]

In Rockwell's illustration the riveter is identified by the letters R-O-S-I-E printed large on her working-man's lunch pail. She is decked out in very unladylike baggy denim overalls and holds a huge rivet gun on her lap. Her face and astonishingly brawny arms are smudged with dirt. Her penny-loafered foot treads on a copy of *Mein Kampf.* The woman defense worker is shown as a heroic Amazon. The bit of lipstick she is wearing is the lone nod to her gender.

Some "Rosies," though, had anxieties about giving up the signifiers of womanliness that had been instilled in them since girlhood. "No matter how dirty the work was," they said, even if they were required to wear pants, it was important to them that they also wear perfume and makeup while riveting or welding—not to attract men, but to remind themselves of their "femininity despite the harsh surroundings."[46] For other women workers, war-work garb had pushed open the doors of the fashion prison that gender had created. Now they could decide how far out they wanted to wander. "Slacks to work in, play in, live in," Sears, Roebuck offered in a 1940s catalogue ad illustrated by models wearing twill, flannel, and herringbone weave pants—together with "man-tailored" shirts. But regardless of whether some "Rosies" desired to put mascara on their eyelashes before they walked out of the house in their overalls, the ubiquitous image of women in pants had a lasting impact. Daughters had seen their mothers wearing pants. Pants were no longer a forbidden garment for women. The next generation would popularize the pantsuit. In the generations after, pants for women would be as common as dresses.

Though Rosie the Riveter was always depicted as being white, in reality she was all colors. For some women of color who worked in the defense industry, this was their first venture out of the domestic sphere. Their new status as wage earners, making good pay, had the potential to change their ideas of who they were or could be. Even those from traditional families could come to feel that because they were contributing to the household they had a right to demand more of a voice in the home. They even counted for more in the community. Some had to struggle with guilt as they challenged tradition and seized a modicum of independence, but to the extent that they succeeded they were dismantling their culture's construction of woman.[47]

Many Latinas had had to find work even during the Depression. They usually earned a pittance, both because they were women and because they were Latina. Those working in federally sponsored sewing rooms, for instance, made thirty-six cents an hour, while unskilled male laborers were making fifty cents an hour. When the state director of employment in Arizona was challenged about the pay difference, he claimed it was justified because the women were only doing "light work." In addition, they were sewing for the needy, including their families, who were getting the clothes "absolutely free of charge." And on top of that, if women's wages were raised to fifty cents, they would have "no incentive to accept private employment at a wage below this figure." (Why his worry about "incentive" did not also apply to men, he did not say.) Gender and race had intersected to keep Latinas in their place in the 1930s, regardless of the skills they had: Mexican American girls who were in high school during the Depression took courses in typing and shorthand, but that generally did them no good when they sought work. Skin color determined who got a job. As one typing teacher purportedly told her young student, "Who's going to hire you? You're so dark." Only 2.6 percent of Mexican American working women had jobs in clerical occupations at the Depression's height.[48]

During the war, however, Mexican American women became welders, crane operators, assemblers, and railroad section workers. They received time-and-a-half pay for double shifts and overtime. Bertha Morales went to work as a riveter despite her husband's "hit[ting] the roof because he was one of those men who didn't believe in the wife ever working." She had married at fifteen and had considered herself "just a mother of four kids, that's all." But the job brought her into a new world, where for the first time she made friends with white women, wore pants and low-heeled comfortable shoes ("even in the house I always used to wear high heels"), and felt unaccustomed mastery in learning a skill that had been foreign to her. Margarita Salazar had been the operator of a beauty parlor, but she became a riveter after seeing billboard ads in her East Los Angeles barrio and reading in *La Opinion* that women were being hired in the defense industry and were getting paid what to her was a fortune. Salazar took a job in an aircraft plant because "you were doing something for your country—and at the same time making money." She believed the job to have been transformative: earning good wages, being socially valued for her efforts as a worker outside the home, and feeling for the first time that "a woman had a brain just as much as a man" and could "produce just as well as anyone else."[49]

Chinese American women had the farthest to travel in fashioning for themselves new concepts of woman. The Chinese Exclusion Act of 1882 meant not only that no new immigrants could come into the United States from China and that no Chinese immigrants who were already here would be eligible to become naturalized citizens—it also meant that if an American-born woman married a Chinese immigrant man, she lost her citizenship.[50] At a time when almost all women in the United States were no longer governed by coverture laws, Chinese American women were still in potential danger of being victimized by a virtual resurrection of such laws aimed at them. Finally, in 1943, because China was America's ally in the war against Japan, the Exclusion Act was repealed. American-born women who had married Chinese immigrants could then apply for naturalization and become American citizens again, just as they had been before they married.

The law had confirmed to the community how little independent standing Chinese American women had. Economically, too, they had almost no independence. Those of the working class were usually housewives or helped out in a modest family business such as a neighborhood restaurant, or they worked in one of Chinatown's small garment shops that doubled as the living space of the owner. They seldom crossed the boundaries of Chinatown.

But during the war, they were hired as welders and riveters at wages four times greater than what they had usually earned before the war. They were even sought after for defense jobs that required particular dexterity, such as making delicate aircraft instruments—supposedly because they were thought to be, as the stereotype went, "for centuries patient with their embroidery needles and skillful with their paint brushes."[51]

Daughters of the Chinese American middle-class sometimes went to college, but anti-Chinese prejudice had meant that graduates were seldom hired by whites to fill middle-class women's jobs such as teacher, nurse, social worker, or even secretary. Before the war, a Chinese American woman with a college degree who wanted to work outside of Chinatown could expect to be an elevator operator, waitress, or maid, but the growing labor shortage during the war was a turning point. In 1942, when Jade Snow Wong graduated Phi Beta Kappa from Mills College (a leading West Coast women's college), she was told by the school's placement officer not to bother applying for jobs outside of Chinatown because "racial prejudice on the Pacific Coast will be a great handicap to you." However, the next year, the defense industry in the San Francisco Bay Area began hiring regardless of race. Wong started as a secretary at a Marin County shipyard, but when her supervisor discovered her skills, she was soon doing shipyard-sponsored research on preventing absenteeism and the efficacy of vitamins in warding off workers' colds.[52]

Prejudice did not magically disappear, of course. Chinese American women were seldom promoted to supervisory positions in the defense industry because companies assumed that white workers would not follow their orders. Nevertheless, many Chinese American women hopped a bus or rode a ferry every day that took them outside their insulated communities. They worked with people of all races. They even spent some of their free time and money at Hollywood-made movies. When the war was over, many became housewives and settled in Chinatown forever, but others left the community and its traditional notions of woman. They went to work in jobs like those the Mills College placement officer had once told Jade Snow Wong that women of her race would never get.[53]

Japanese American women endured the worst home-front injustices during the war. Along with their families, they were removed from their homes on the West Coast and sent to "War Relocation Camps." Yet paradoxically, incarceration broadened the narrow parameters of the young Japanese American woman's life. Traditional parental discipline that the Issei generation had firmly exercised over their Nisei daughters deteriorated in the camps. Sue Kunitomi was interned soon after her high school graduation in 1942 at Manzanar, a California relocation camp in the middle of nowhere. She recalled that in the camps the young "were pretty free to do whatever they wanted because there was no real family control."[54] It meant that Japanese American girls were more at liberty than they had ever been to reinscribe what "woman" might mean.

Before the internment, Kunitomi had worked with her widowed mother in a small family grocery store on the border of Little Tokyo in Los Angeles, where they seldom saw anyone who was not part of the Japanese American community. Kunitomi had no thought of going to college because when she was in the eighth grade her father had told her that college was pointless for a Japanese woman.[55] His wife, Kunitomi's mother, had been a picture bride.

During the war years, Kunitomi's life expanded. In the camp she worked as a reporter for the *Manzanar Free Press*. As soon as she could request inland resettlement, she went alone to the Midwest and found a job; there, her best friend was a Black woman. After the war, she resisted returning to live with her mother because she feared that her mother would "restrict" her activities. A few years later, Kunitomi married a white man, telling her mother, in words that would have been unthinkable for the picture-bride generation, "It's my life and I'm going to marry whomever I choose to marry and you cannot tell me what to do."[56] She also finally went to college.

None of that challenge to her parents' cultural concept of woman would have been possible, Kunitomi recognized, without the dislocation brought on by the war. The traditions that had kept women firmly rooted in their culture's notion of woman were hard to maintain in relocation camps. While the emotional toll of their uprooting during the war is impossible to discount, this young Japanese American woman exited the relocation camp with far more freedom than she had had when she entered it.

During the Depression, Black women had fared even worse than Latinas. They were seldom hired in offices or factories except as "janitresses." In the South, if they could get a job at all, they were most often agricultural workers; in the North they were domestic workers. But almost half of all Black women workers in the North had been unemployed in the 1930s, because many households that could once afford domestic help had to cut back on spending. At a low point, in 1931, Black women were two and a half times as likely to be unable to find work as white women.[57]

By early 1941, before the United States joined the Allies in World War II, jobs had already begun proliferating in industries that manufactured military materiel. But Black workers were being turned away at the hiring gate. To address the discrimination, in June 1941, at the urging of Mary McLeod Bethune and other Black leaders, FDR signed Executive Order 8802, which said, "It is the policy of the United States to encourage full participation in the national defense program by all citizens of the United States regardless of race, creed, color, or national origin." FDR also created the Fair Employment Practices Commission, which was charged with enforcing the executive order in all factories and businesses that had government contracts. But the commission's budget was minuscule, and the executive order was seldom honored. If Black people were hired at all in the defense industry, it was usually to sweep the floors. When civil rights groups such as the National Negro Congress protested to factory owners, they were baldly informed, as a personnel officer of the aircraft manufacturer Consolidated-Vultee put it, "It is not the policy of this company to employ people other than the Caucasian race."[58]

Only toward the end of 1942, when there were not enough "Caucasians" to fill the industry's ballooning vacancies, were Blacks hired in larger numbers. Black women were able to get on-site training and move into skilled and semiskilled jobs in steel mills, foundries, aircraft plants, and shipyards and even into government-service jobs, such as postal workers—where their numbers quadrupled. But the outrages of race prejudice continued. At the U.S. Rubber Plant in Detroit, over 2,000 white women workers walked off the job, demanding toilet facilities that were separate from those used by Black women workers. A Black woman welder, who had graduated from a three-month-long government training course, was fired from her job at a shipyard only weeks after she was hired because white women workers complained to their union that they would not work with any Black person, regardless of her credentials. The Fair Employment Practices Commission (FEPC) could do nothing: as Black leaders complained, it was "as toothless as a month-old baby."[59]

Finally, in 1943, the FEPC was placed under the War Manpower Commission and given a larger operating budget to enforce Executive Order 8802. The War Manpower Commission grandly assured Blacks in publications such as the National Urban League's magazine *Opportunity* that now hiring for war work would be done "the American way" because "the fighters on the Solomons do not ask the creed or color of the men and women who make their guns." Black women workers began to have somewhat better experiences, but discrimination persisted. The National Urban League complained that Black women were still being turned away by hiring bosses who would tell them "We have our percentage of Negroes" or "We have not yet installed separated toilet facilities." As one historian has observed, "Whatever the hierarchy of preference [in wartime hiring] Black women would always be found at the bottom." Nevertheless, the war did open new opportunities for many Black women. Tina Hill had worked for years in domestic service until she got a job at Lockheed Aircraft in Los Angeles. As she wryly commented, "Hitler was the one who got us out of the white folks' kitchen." Six hundred thousand Black women found work in the wartime labor force.[60]

The war had a unique effect on Native American women. Over 20 percent of them left reservations to work in the defense industry or enlist in the military. Indian women were particularly encouraged by the government to participate in the war effort—not only because their labor was needed, but also because it would bring them closer to leaving their Indian ways, which had not stopped being a white obsession. From the start of the war, Indian females were courted by the defense industry. Training programs were set up in government Indian schools. At the Chilocco Indian School in Newkirk, Oklahoma, girls could take a nine-week course on working with aircraft sheet metal. At the Sherman Institute in Riverside, California, they could be trained in acetylene welding. Indian girls were learning to be riveters, machinists, truck drivers, and munitions inspectors.[61]

Their new role was widely touted in clumsy newspaper stories. The *Los Angeles Times* announced, "Indian Women Harness Old Talents to New War Jobs," describing the women as "adept at many skills usually reserved for men" and, more condescendingly, as "turning from the making of Indian bead work to inspecting ammunitions." "Indians on Warpath: More Than 50,000 Redskins under Arms" and "Indians All Out to Scalp the Axis," other newspapers announced in articles about Indian men in the military and Indian women aiding the national defense by driving trucks, repairing heavy automotive equipment, and working in defense factories. The accounts sometimes betrayed a renewed anxiety about the Indian woman's gender behavior but found reassurance in her learning to emulate the white woman's mythic femininity: "A touch of rouge, a fashionable hairdo, and modern clothes ease [the Indian woman's] assimilation into the community of workers," one white newspaper reported.[62]

The putative transformation of the Indian woman was good news in many quarters. The Office of Indian Affairs had always hoped to detribalize Native Americans. White "betterment" groups had long sought ways to integrate them into American society. The Indian woman's participation in the war effort was applauded as a step in that direction, as Bertha Eckert, secretary for Indian work at the National YWCA, told the *New York Times*. Indian women's "speeded-up living in industrial war centers [could] be a principal chapter in the story of the vanishing reservation," Eckert said hopefully. War work would end the Indian woman's "isolation from normal American life." It would assimilate her.[63]

For the Indian women who resisted war work and remained on the reservations, the opposite of assimilation was happening. In the absence of the men who had gone overseas to fight, Indian women again took over the responsibilities that in many tribes had once belonged to women. They virtually turned back the clock to the time before George

Washington urged that Indian men farm and tend livestock rather than hunt on lands that whites wished to settle; and that Indian women take up "woman's work" such as spinning and weaving. During World War II, it again became the Indian woman's responsibility to plant and harvest and tend the animals. The white media was confounded to learn of their "strange" husbandry customs. When they tended sheep, for instance, "each squaw wears at least a dozen flaring skirts," which she takes off one by one to wrap around any "chilled newborn lamb" she encounters, newspapers widely reported in amusement.[64]

Indian women who remained on the reservation during the war also assumed an active role in tribal affairs. After a long hiatus, they again began to serve on tribal councils. They even assumed positions such as judge for the tribe.[65] With the war's end, however, the push and pull on Native Americans to give up traditional life and become urban began again. Before the war, only 8 percent of American Indians were living in cities. After the war, the government encouraged a Great Migration of Native Americans by offering urban job-training programs. By the next generation, almost half of the Indian population had moved to metropolitan areas. There the Indian woman's special status was again lost.

WOMAN AND THE MILITARY

"American women are not losing their femininity
by training in the Waacs!"

—Congresswoman Frances Bolton (R-Ohio) to the League
of Republican Women (1943)[66]

More than a quarter-million women served in the U.S. military during World War II. They were in the WAC (Women's Army Corps—called the Women's Army Auxiliary Corps [WAAC] until "Auxiliary" was dropped in 1943), the WAVES (Women Accepted for Volunteer Emergency Service), SPAR (the Coast Guard Women's Reserve), and the Marine Corps Women's Reserve. Another 76,000 women were Army and Navy nurses. The notion of woman in any military role other than nurse triggered worries that she would transmogrify into an Amazon. A bill for the creation of the Women's Auxiliary Army Corps was first introduced by Massachusetts Representative Edith Rogers in 1941. It languished until 1942 and then was met with some hysteria in congressional hearings. If women went off to the military, Michigan representative Clare Eugene Hoffman demanded of Rogers, "Who will then maintain the home fires? Who will then do the cooking, the washing, the mending, the humble, homey tasks to which every woman has devoted herself; who will rear and nurture the children?" A writer for *Commonweal* echoed Hoffman, complaining of "the perilous stress today . . . upon woman's function." The WAAC, he wrote, was a conspiracy, "an opening wedge" in the effort to remove women from the home.[67]

But womanpower was sorely needed. Those in charge of explaining woman's military service to the public made clear that her primary role in the military was to take over the jobs of men who had been military stenographers, typists, and switchboard operators, so that the men could go off to combat. Oveta Culp Hobby, director of the WAAC, emphasized that military women were performing only the duties they were particularly fitted for—the same jobs they already held in civilian life. Cognizant of the worry about Amazons, Hobby determined that all members of the WAAC must wear skirts rather than slacks, so that they would not look masculine. Even the *New York Times* cooperated in allaying the public's fears by quoting reassuring military officials and members of Congress about the woman soldier's womanliness: "Says Waacs Retain Femininity," a 1943 headline announced. "Says Wacs Will Be Fine Wives," a 1944 headline declared. Lieutenant Mary Cady conducted a poll of 1,025 women soldiers and found, according to the *New York Times* in 1945, "Wac's Femininity Is Increased by Service." And lest the public fret that military women might have illusions about making a career of the service, Cady emphasized that most of the members of the WAC surveyed had agreed that "nothing could send them back to their own homes and kitchens so fast as life in the Army."[68]

Despite such assurances, worry was rife about the changes wrought by the war. The proposal that women be enlisted to serve as pilots sparked the greatest controversy. Jacqueline Cochran, a pilot whose fame and dashing vied with those of Amelia Earhart, was also a beauty whose glamour and influence were enhanced by her marriage to Floyd Odlum, one of the world's richest men. Cochran had been ferrying American planes across the Atlantic for the Royal Air Force since the beginning of the war in Europe. She proposed, first to ER and then to General Henry Arnold of the Army Air Forces, that America could also use women pilots in noncombatant roles. The women would test aircraft, train men to fly, ferry cargo, and deliver planes to where they were needed. The male pilots who had had those duties would thus be freed to fight in the war. Despite

Cochran's bona fides, the Civil Aeronautics Administration (CAA) resisted the proposal with fury. Women were "psychologically not fitted to be pilots," the CAA argued. ER responded personally to the CAA's criticism in her syndicated "My Day" column. "We are in a war and we need to fight it with every weapon possible. Women pilots," she wrote, "are a weapon waiting to be used."[69]

Finally, in 1943, the Women Airforce Service Pilots (WASP) was established. Thirty-three thousand women—many of whom already had aviator licenses—applied. About a thousand were accepted. But the controversy did not stop. Though the WASPs did the duties Cochran had proposed, they were refused military status. The CAA, under whose jurisdiction they fell, decreed that they must be grounded from one day before menstruation until two days after menstruation—because menstruation, the CAA opined, increased a woman's chances of fainting and made her accident-prone and less dependable.[70]

In the last year of the war, after the WASPs had flown over 50 million miles and in every type of aircraft, Henry Arnold, as commanding general of the Army Air Forces, supported militarizing them. The CAA continued to be vociferously opposed, now arguing that there were plenty of male personnel who could take over the ferrying jobs the women had been doing. Congress sided with the CAA. A congressional report expressed outrage at the idea of women flying for the United States. The report trivialized who they were and reduced them to mere woman. The recruitment of "teen-aged schoolgirls, stenographers, clerks, beauticians, housewives and factory workers to pilot the military planes of this Government is as startling as it is invalid," the report stated. It concluded that the WASP program was "unnecessary and undesirable" and "should be immediately and sharply curtailed."[71] The WASP was disbanded in December 1944.

In 1942, at one of ER's weekly meetings with women reporters, one of them asked her, "How can you get girls back into the kitchen after the war?" Since ER believed that many "girls" did not belong in the kitchen, it was a tricky question to answer. She attempted to give a nuanced reply:

> You should try now to get them to do things that are needed now. Many of those girls will get married when the war is over. Those who are very good and really like their work will probably stay in work of some kind. So that I doubt very much if you could plan

> now. I would rather try to plan now to keep them out of the kitchens after war.[72]

ER was prescient: it would be a great challenge to "keep [women] out of the kitchens after the war." But she underestimated the panic that had already been occasioned by women's release from old notions of woman.

FDR's secretary of the interior, Harold L. Ickes, better understood the ubiquitous fears about gender upheaval that the exigencies of the war had unleashed. In 1943, Ickes wrote a seemingly lighthearted essay for the *Saturday Evening Post* on the serious subject of how woman was being "trained to do things that would make her grandfather turn over in his grave if he could see her do them." Women had become mechanics, technicians, and competitors in areas that men had claimed for themselves, believing that only they had the "brains and brawn" to do them, Ickes said. He warned that women had proven men wrong. "When this war is over," he admonished men, "the going will be a lot tougher, because [men] will have to compete with women whose eyes have been opened to their greatest economic potential."[73]

Lighthearted as Ickes's tone was, his essay reflected real worries that woman's wartime activities would alter her beyond recognition. Margaret Mead reported at the war's end that a young American soldier was asked, as his outfit was approaching Berlin, about what he and his buddies were thinking in their state of victory. "Well, mostly we've been wondering whether it's true that women are smoking pipes at home," was his answer.[74]

Ickes was right that woman had proven during the war that she had "brains and brawn." But how could she hope to keep using her "brains and brawn" and also allay the fears of the returning soldiers that the war had unwomaned her? To both compete with men and yet be reassuringly feminine for them was impossible for women unaccustomed to such a balancing act. They would have to choose. Most had barely adjusted to the new way of being a woman that the war had created. They were tired out by unaccustomed labors. They were emotionally exhausted by war worries. And then they were dismissed from jobs where they were no longer needed and bombarded by pundits who told them where they were needed. The choice may have seemed clear. It may even have seemed that it was made freely.

11.
Sending Her Back to the Place Where God Had Set Her

•

WOMAN IN THE 1950s

In February 1947, Christian Dior, on his way to becoming a top fashion designer on two continents, rolled out his first women's fashion collection. He called it the New Look. It reimagined woman—or rather, it imagined her right back to where she once had been. It evoked the style of the late nineteenth-century Gibson Girl: long, flowing skirts; padded hips and busts; tiny hourglass waists; and ruffled necklines. Dior, who announced that he was "fed up with Amazons," intended the New Look to bring back the womanly woman and put to rest the fear that World War II had turned women into pipe-smoking quasi-men.[1] For the remainder of the 1940s the New Look was a leading fashion style in America. It was enhanced in the 1950s by the crinoline petticoat, worn often in multiples: a style that took woman back even further in time, to the mid-nineteenth century, when ladies wore hoopskirts. The look became an emblem of the era.

WHY DID SHE RETREAT?

"[The womanly woman] graciously concedes the top-rung jobs to men."
—LAURA BERGQUIST, "A New Look at the American Woman" (1956)[2]

Women of the 1950s were a strange contrast to their mothers, the women of the 1920s who had torn up the playbook for women and written a new one. Fashion? Insouciant young women after World War I donned straight-waist dresses that made their figure look like that of their adolescent brother, and skirts that had never in the history of the United States been so abbreviated. Social daring? They had the audacity to demand their right to have, as Alyse Gregory put it in 1923, "a cigarette after every meal and a lover in the evening."[3] In the years after World War II, however, their daughters dusted off a much older playbook for woman. Not only did their dresses hark back to earlier times, but their ideals often seemed to do so as well.

Perhaps the two postwar generations of women were so different from one another because the midcentury woman had lived through not only a war but also a dozen years of the Depression before the war; and after the war she had to deal with a new threat, from the Soviets—who, propagandists said, would not rest until they turned America communist. For most of her life she had witnessed exhausting national turmoil. It made sense that she would be susceptible to whatever harked back to an era of safer, steadier times.[4]

The pressure on her to do so was undergirded by a tribe of experts. They spoke to the yearning for authority and surety after years of upheaval followed by political uncertainty. Experts—particularly those who opined on health and happiness—were listened to as reverently as if they preached from a pulpit. Almost all of them agreed that woman's place was in the home, tending full-time to the needs of her family: not because God had set her there, of course (they were scientists, not theologians), but because it was normal woman's essence to want to nurture her loved ones and not be distracted from her natural duties.

Even those mental health professionals who had once believed in the benefits of woman's broader self-fulfillment seemed to change their minds in the 1950s. The pioneering marriage counselor Emily Hartshorne Mudd had started out in the 1920s as a firebrand advocate for sexual equality. Though the dissemination of birth control information was still illegal in Philadelphia, Mudd had volunteered as a nurse in the city's first birth control clinic, risking arrest because she thought that the ability to control pregnancy was vital to women who wanted a career. She had supported the right of even unmarried women to have access to contraception. Later, when colleges began preparing women for marriage and motherhood rather than a profession, Mudd objected because she knew that there was no reason why a woman could not have both: she was married and had four children.[5]

She had even written that men must learn to adapt to the modern woman, to accept that she was not like women in other eras. The modern woman had been winning greater economic independence and greater sexual freedom, and during World War II she had even proven herself a contributor to the world's work, Mudd argued in 1946. Obviously, marriage could no longer be the same as it had been when a woman did not venture beyond the threshold of her home.[6] However, Mudd's convictions, overwhelmed by the dominant climate of the 1950s, suffered a sea change.

She had always granted that some women freely opted to be housewives. However, she had fiercely championed not only women who chose to combine marriage and a career, but also women for whom marriage was incompatible with their devotion to a great cause. She gave as examples of such venerable women Susan B. Anthony, Florence Nightingale, M. Carey Thomas, and Jane Addams. But her view of woman and woman's place could not survive the midcentury. Her 1955 article for the popular *Reader's Digest* was titled "Woman's Finest Role." Writing as one of the most widely respected marriage counselors in the country, Mudd declared, "In these modern days, there are many women who feel their finest contribution can be made through marriage, motherhood, and identification with their husband's creative activities." She offered not a word about the choices made by women like herself and the venerable Anthony. Instead, she bolstered her argument about "Woman's Finest Role" by quoting a "modern and prominent" woman who stated that "to be a successful wife is a career in itself . . . the most completely rewarding of all careers."[7]

Yet despite the temper of the times, many women, whether married or single, could not afford to play "woman's finest role" full-time. They had learned during World War II that they could earn money, and financial exigencies made it desirable for them to keep doing so. Though at the war's end they had been fired from their jobs, in the booming economy of the 1950s they found "women's jobs" such as secretary, office clerk, bank teller, salesgirl, telephone operator, and cashier.

But the days of good wages for women had disappeared with the armistice. Indeed, women's low salaries in the 1950s served as almost a cultural corrective. The blues singer Lead Belly seemed to capture the resentment that women's high wages during wartime had elicited, as well as schadenfreude and relief that the social order had been righted. The singer complains in "National Defense Blues" that he had a "little woman" who made "so much dough" working in the defense industry that "her check was big as mine," and she "got to the place, she did not love me no more." But now "that Defense be gone, that woman done lose her home." He concludes with satisfaction, "Well, all right, then."[8] The uppity woman worker of the war years was getting her comeuppance in the postwar years. Personal life could get back to normal.

But the number of working women, low wages notwithstanding, swelled steadily throughout the decade. The only demographic group of women whose employment numbers did not grow in the 1950s were those between the ages of twenty-five and thirty-four; they were busy having babies. Dior's ultrafeminine fashions—emphasizing spacious hips and large breasts, subliminal evocations of childbearing and baby nursing—resonated with the renewed ideal of the fertile woman. Many American women cooperated fully, making up through a baby boom for women's relative infertility in the preceding quarter-century. In the 1950s, they gave birth to about 4 million babies annually.[9] Childbearing years were maximized: women typically got married at age twenty, which was seven years younger than women's median marriage age at the start of the century.

Early marriage gave the American woman plenty of time to bear many children but not much time for higher education, that privilege for which some women had fought so hard for more than a century. By 1920, women accounted for almost half of all college students, while in the 1950s their share was about 30 percent. As a writer for *Harper's* observed, "A girl who gets as far as junior year in college without having acquired a man is thought to be in grave danger of becoming an old maid."[10] A term coined in the 1950s summed up the supposed purpose of college for a woman: she was there to get an "MRS degree."

Mary Woolley's worst fears when Roswell Ham was appointed to replace her as president of Mount Holyoke came to pass. Presidents of women's colleges—almost all men—were now telling students that the purpose of their education was not to train them for a profession but to make them better wives and mothers. In his 1950 book *Educating Our Daughters*, Lynn White Jr., the president of Mills College, quoted a young mother whose complaint pinpointed what had been wrong with woman's higher education. "I have come to realize that I was educated to be a successful man," she said, "and now I must learn by myself how to be a successful woman." White was determined that Mills students would never have such a pitiable problem. "The curriculum for female students should prepare women to foster the intellectual and emotional life of her family and community," White wrote, sounding very much like Catharine Beecher a hundred years earlier.[11]

After years of hard times and Cold War insecurities, the shift to early marriage, prolific motherhood, and domesticity was billed as a return to normalcy. It was a return that elided a good bit of the previous century's struggles to redefine woman. Even personal ambition was now abnormal in a woman. As *Look* declared in 1956, the womanly woman "graciously concedes the top-rung jobs to men."[12] Why would she not? Her real job, after all, was not one for which she earned a salary.

To be sure, culture is never monolithic, yet in all manner of public discourse women were squeezed to fit the mold. Remarkably, this was so even in the 1950s Black civil rights movement. The story of Rosa Parks—riding home on a bus from her job at a Montgomery, Alabama, department store, ordered by the bus driver to give up her seat to a white man—triggered the 1955 Montgomery Bus Boycott, which finally brought national attention to the movement. The sympathetic media made Parks into an icon, but always within the parameters of womanliness. She was usually identified as a seamstress, the banal racism she experienced deemed to be especially shocking because she was a defenseless woman, weary after a long day's work at a grueling job. It was seldom acknowledged that Parks had been a civil rights activist since 1943, when she became a member of the Montgomery NAACP, or that she held office in the NAACP (she was the secretary, of course). Nor was her toughness acknowledged in the media. Parks wrote in her autobiography almost a half-century later: "People always say that I didn't give up my seat because I was tired, but that isn't true. I was not tired physically. . . . No, the only tired I was, was tired of giving in."[13] Such blatant anger and political consciousness in a woman would have been far less sympathetic in the 1950s than was the media's version of Parks.

Parks was apparently disappointed when the Montgomery Improvement Association, formed by the city's Black male leaders to conduct the bus boycott, elected as its head not her, the forty-two-year-old woman who had started it all, but a twenty-six-year-old man, a young pastor who was new to civil rights work and fairly new to Montgomery: Martin Luther King Jr. At the first rally of the association, where King spoke, Parks offered to speak too. She was told, "You have had enough and you have said enough, and you don't have to speak." "So I didn't," Parks wrote in her autobiography.[14] But she clearly enjoyed speaking and, unwomanly as it was, enjoyed the limelight. Sponsored by the NAACP, she traveled around the country lecturing about her experience, which had triggered the boycott that brought the Black civil rights movement out of the shadows and onto nightly TV.

Some in the Black press hinted that Parks had expected to play a role beyond that of icon, and that she was angry that a woman was not permitted to do that. A 1957 article titled "Why Mrs. Parks Left Ala." in a major Black newspaper, the *Pittsburgh Courier*, observed that it was the bus boycott that made Martin Luther King Jr. "rise to the prominence of a national leader." The article also announced that Parks and her husband and mother had just moved to Detroit to live "among virtual strangers." The reporter hypothesized that the move was because of "a certain bitterness of experiences that may have sprung from her becoming lost, so to speak, in the shuffle of events." The reporter included among that "shuffle" the fact that "Mrs. Parks was seldom mentioned as the real and true leader of the struggle. Others more learned—not to take a thing from Dr. King—were ushered into the leadership and hogged the show."[15] "Bitter" as Parks's experiences may have been, however, she could not protest too loudly. Black women, like white women, were expected to "graciously concede the top-rung jobs to men."

Ella Baker, one of the most effective and dynamic of the early Black civil rights activists, was also "lost . . . in the shuffle of events." Baker's activism began in 1930 when she worked with the Young Negroes' Cooperative League, an economic empowerment group. She joined the NAACP in 1940, and during the war she was named its national director of branches. In 1955 she organized the first NAACP protests against de facto school segregation in New York. In 1957 she moved to Atlanta and helped found the Southern Christian Leadership Conference (SCLC). She coordinated the SCLC's first statewide project and acted as its first unofficial director. She had reason to expect that she would be named its official director, but that was an unrealistic expectation for a woman in the 1950s. When the organization's board was ready to hire an official head, it would not choose a fifty-four-year-old woman. The board hired instead the now twenty-eight-year-old Martin Luther King Jr., fresh from Montgomery. Though Baker remained with the SCLC for three more years, she clashed often with King. She mocked that he "wore silk suits and spoke with a silver tongue," and she was angry because she believed that his ego was overwhelming and he encouraged adulation. Looking back on her experiences in the 1950s, Baker later complained that Black women—even those who devoted their whole lives to the civil rights movement—had to "take a back seat."[16]

In all American communities in the 1950s, retrogressive opinions about women dominated. While a few midcentury women may have found spaces where they could claim the legacies that had been won by their foremothers, they were outnumbered by far. This was so for several reasons. The spiritual heirs to the "antis" of the nineteenth century who had begged to "keep mother, wife, and sister in the protected home" colluded with men weary of the Depression and war and panicked by the Red Scare in bringing back the old concept of woman.[17] Other women, lacking historical memory, were carried along because "what is" seemed to be "what has always been." Still other women gave only lip service, pretending to go along because it was too tough not to. A few discovered ways to resist, but there was usually a price to be paid for their defiance.

WOMAN AS HAPPY HOMEMAKER, AGAIN

"The satisfaction she might receive from an outside job is not so important, after all."

—BENJAMIN SPOCK, *Baby and Child Care* (1957)[18]

The production of labor-saving devices from gas stoves to washing machines and vacuum cleaners, for sale at increasingly affordable prices, meant that in many homes cooking and cleaning could not possibly be a full-time job. Nevertheless, woman's full-time presence in the home became as glorified as it had been when Cotton Mather declared in 1692 that a "vertuous" woman spent her days spinning and weaving for the sake of her family. The 1914 proposal put forth by Henrietta Rodman and her Feminist Alliance—to provide collective housing in which child-care experts would mind the children while mothers worked at fulfilling occupations—would have been tantamount in the years following World War II to a proposal for child abuse. Benjamin Spock, a medical doctor and leading expert on baby and child care, suggested as much in his book, which became the mother's Bible and ultimately sold 50 million copies worldwide. Spock did recognize that in some families a mother had no choice but to go to work, but even so, he warned, by being absent from the home, she risked having her children "grow up neglected and maladjusted."[19] How could a mother who went out to work not feel guilty?

Her guilt was compounded if she worked not because she had to but for selfish self-fulfillment. In 1953, Violet Weingarten, who had been a journalist for fifteen years, finally could not bear it, as she wrote in "Case History of an Ex-Working Mother." Though her two young daughters were in school most of the day, when she worked she felt culpable if one of them sucked her thumb or the other had a cough or was not learning to read quickly enough. Weingarten acknowledged that as a working mother she used to come home and spend more uninterrupted time playing with her children than she did when she was at home all day but busy cooking or recovering from her busyness. She recognized that when she worked "it used to take me ten minutes to plan a week's meals," which a "warm-hearted" housekeeper would cook each day. However, tasks expand according to the time allotted for them: "Now it takes me a half hour to decide what to have for dinner." She even theorized that working mothers inspired respect in children as stay-at-home mothers did not. Nevertheless, she quit her job because "I was tired of feeling guilty." Staying home, she concluded, "just seemed to make more sense."[20]

The old view that home was woman's proper place had never really died. It had only been subdued by the strength of the convictions of some women. They were the ones who had led the charge to win the vote for all women, even the antis. They had made it seem normal for women to be educated, go out to work, and claim the right to personal fulfillment. But the revolutionary changes they wrought were fragile. The competing idea of true womanhood, which had not been erased from historical memory, was easily brought back in a country that felt itself to have been turned upside down.

There seemed to be a wide consensus about how to turn it right-side up again. A returning soldier who had risked his life for the country needed a job more than a woman did. Women needed to make up for the decade and a half when they were hardly having babies. Social stabilization depended on going back to the old ways, when men were men and women were women—or, as Talcott Parsons, an influential midcentury sociologist, phrased it in a scholarly book about nuclear-family dynamics, there needed to be "differentiation" and "complementarity" between men and women, not sameness. Men needed to accept manly responsibilities, to be breadwinners and power figures; and women needed to balance men by accepting womanly responsibilities, to be nurturers and providers of emotional support. Deviation from those roles disadvantaged their children, Parsons said.[21]

Best sellers such as *Modern Woman: The Lost Sex* (1947) helped disseminate such ideas to a general public anxious for stabilizing, authoritative voices. The oddly paired authors of *Modern Woman*—Ferdinand Lundberg, a gadfly journalist previously famous for books that assailed the rich; and Marynia Farnham, one of the few women psychiatrists in the country—wrote that the modern woman had lost her balance because she had strayed from the traditional home to take on men's roles. She was miserable because she had tried to escape her biology, which was inescapable. The modern woman had even endangered civilization, which depended on her fulfilling her only important duties: to be bearer and rearer of children and keeper of the home. She had been misguided by feminism, which was "at its core a deep illness" brought on by penis envy that led the woman to reject her natural role and wish to be a man. Among the remedies that Lundberg and Farnham suggested for the disasters that feminists had caused was the barring of all "spinsters" from teaching children, because spinsters were "emotionally incompetent" and must not serve as role models. Only married women should be permitted to teach. (The authors did not say who would watch the married woman's offspring while she taught.)[22]

As was appropriate for a book about how women had gone astray by trying to rival men, the cover of *Modern Woman* listed Lundberg's name before that of Farnham, though she was by far the more credentialed of the two. But Dr. Farnham did not step back from celebrity after the book's publication. To promote *Modern Woman* she flew around the country, at a time when commercial air travel was still rare, lecturing everywhere but especially to women's groups. Billed as a "famed author," she appeared on early television programs and granted numerous newspaper interviews. "If you're born a woman you can't be happy as long as you're not being a woman," she declared. She even starred in a newsreel about the dangers to society posed by women who worked. The reel is set in her psychiatric clinic. Dr. Farnham wears a white lab coat and expounds her convictions to a woman reporter who attentively takes down her every word, while

Farnham's deferential nurse flits about. "Abandoning their feminine role has made women unhappy because it has made them frustrated," Dr. Farnham dictates, looking very Amazonian indeed. "It has made children unhappy because they do not have maternal love, and it has made their husbands unhappy because they do not have real women as partners."[23]

Modern Woman remains interesting for the peripheral insights it gives into Farnham, a curious case study of painful ambivalence over the meaning of woman that invites the drawing of a direct line from Catharine Beecher and Ida Tarbell to Farnham and beyond. In newspaper interviews Farnham recalled that she had been a girl in the early twentieth century with outsize dreams, wanting to be "some kind of world-shaking glamour figure" and settling finally on a goal that pioneering feminists had made attainable: to become a medical doctor. As Marynia Foot, she had been an undergraduate at Bryn Mawr during the presidency of M. Carey Thomas, who had aspired to instill in the college's students her own burning ambition for a professional career. Marynia was an enthusiastic acolyte. Though she would later describe women like Thomas as "deviant" and unfeminine, she became one of Thomas's highest achievers.[24]

After graduating from Bryn Mawr in 1921, Farnham attended medical school at the University of Minnesota and then did postgraduate work at Harvard University before going on to study psychiatry in London and Vienna. She became a psychiatrist at a time when there were fewer than twenty women psychiatrists in the entire United States.[25] While still a medical student, she married and gave birth to a son. That marriage had ended by the early 1930s, and she married again and had a daughter. Though her second husband, Charles Nison, died in 1945, when Farnham was only forty-five years old, she never remarried in the remaining thirty-four years of her life.

Two years after Nison's death, with her ten-year-old daughter in elementary school, Farnham—by then busy on the staff of the New York State Psychiatric Institute and also conducting a private practice—published *Modern Woman*, in which she advised women to do as she said and not as she did.

Despite her considerable success, Farnham was tormented. At some point she had the rare insight with reference to herself to recognize that women, just as much as men, are "conditioned by forces that have been at work in our lives from our earliest years. Each of us has some deep need to be who we are." But most of the time she saw modern woman, including herself, not as following a "deep need to be who we are" but as having been deceived by "crusaders for women's rights [who] have led women not into the promised land but smack into a mountain of frustration." Farnham had been "nurtured on talk of the promised land," she told another reporter, but she had "found it none too promising," she added bitterly. She presented herself in the interview as "a victim of the psychoses she analyzes in her book"—that is, a victim of the early twentieth-century feminists who had urged women into careers and independence.[26]

But if Farnham was a victim, it was of her internalized cultural conflicts, which were (to use language she often used in relation to the women of whom she disapproved) a source of "severe neurosis." She had grown up in Red Wing, Minnesota (population, 8,000), where the most elaborate building was the Minnesota State Reform School for boys and girls. But she had dreamed big and had had fantasies of becoming "some kind of world-shaking glamour figure." She spent her life in efforts to reify her "world-shaking" dreams. However, in Red Wing, "woman" and "housewife" were generally one and the same thing, and despite her ambitions, she internalized the notion that only deviant women, or those misguided by them, wanted more. Her inner conflicts, the challenges of being a professional woman in unsympathetic times, the "loneliness" of her job as a psychiatrist, to which she admitted in a rare interview in which she talked about her personal life—all that together made her an unhappy woman.[27]

Farnham never ceased being ambitious or stopped competing with men, and she never gave up her career and went home. But her book, which became iconic in the midcentury, helped confirm the idea that that was what women must do. It did not convince her daughter—who, taking advantage in the late 1960s of a resurgent feminist movement, changed her name to Linda Charlton and became a reporter for the Washington bureau of the *New York Times*.[28]

A Gallup poll conducted in 1957, however, found that 80 percent of Americans agreed that a woman who chose not to marry was sick, neurotic, or immoral. Mental health experts were joined by the media in creating this near-unanimity of opinion, and in raising the anxieties of young women who were not married. A Sunday insert titled *Family Weekly Magazine*, which appeared in newspapers all over the country, included full-page illustrated articles such as "Men Dislike Women Who . . . ," with advice on how a woman makes herself marriage material. For example, "If you want your boyfriend to be gallant give him a chance—don't be a lady Amazon and rush through doors before he can open them for you." The *Ladies' Home Journal* ran a four-month series titled "How to Be Marriageable" by the psychologist Clifford R. Adams, which focused on Marcia, a schoolteacher who at the ripe age of twenty-nine had still not succeeded in finding a husband. The installments followed her month by month, through desperate steps: she moves from a small town to Los Angeles, where her odds of finding an eligible man are much improved; she takes a course in marriage readiness at the American Institute of Family Relations, founded by Paul Popenoe, America's most famous marriage counselor; and finally, in the last installment of the series, she achieves the grand prize of a marriage proposal.[29]

The *Ladies' Home Journal* also featured a monthly column by Adams titled "Making Marriage Work," whose purpose was to advise the young woman reader on how she must behave once she wins her prize. "When a woman becomes a wife, she undertakes an entirely new role. Since her principal occupation will be running the house, in a sense marriage is a change of jobs," Adams wrote, recommending that the young wife must please her new "boss" by indulging his whims, helping him relax, and sharing his burdens.[30]

Television became another source of coaching for women (and men and children) on how a woman ought to behave. Family sitcoms introduced America over and over again to virtually the same family—always white, nuclear, wholesome, and middle class. *Father Knows Best, The Adventures of Ozzie and Harriet, Leave It to Beaver,* and *The Donna Reed Show*—in all of them the wife and mother and the husband and father display what Talcott Parsons deemed necessary for the happy, well-functioning couple: differentiation and complementarity. The sitcom wife and mother (often clad in an apron, the emblem of her femininity and domesticity) may occasionally be ditzy, but most often she is a fount of womanly wisdom. The husband and father (often wearing a suit and tie, as befits his responsible middle-class profession) is repeatedly seen returning from a hard day at the office to the bosom of his family ("Honey, I'm home!"). He may sometimes make silly mistakes—these are after all situation *comedies*—but he remains the unquestioned chief executive of the household and never loses the adulation of his wife, who does indeed indulge his whims, help him relax, and share his burdens.[31]

CONTROLLING THE REBELS

"Coya, Come Home!"

—*New York Times* headline mocking the election defeat of
Congresswoman Coya Knutson, (1958)[32]

Of course, there were competing voices. Even television offered up a few surprising counterimages to the sitcoms' perfect housewife—most remarkably, the rough and tough women of *Roller Derby*. Through much of the 1950s, live matches were beamed weekly into America's living rooms by the major networks. Millions watched. Reportedly 70 percent of the viewers were female, attracted perhaps by the bracingly bold image of woman as polar opposite to what she was supposed to be. *Roller Derby* players went by names such as "Toughie" (Midge Brashun) and "Big Red" (Annie Jensen). Daintiness was a disqualifier. "Little Iodine" (Loretta Behrens), who played throughout the 1950s, had prided herself as a girl on her pugnacious tomboy persona. She auditioned for *Roller Derby* when she was seventeen years old because she was enchanted with how the players were "knockin' the shit out of each other." *Roller Derby* women were not only decidedly unfeminine as they elbowed and shoved each other out of the way to lap the opposition on a banked track; they were also breathtakingly skilled in a rough contact sport, which only men were supposed to play. Even the impressive earnings of the top stars in women's *Roller Derby* challenged the prevailing idea of woman: they made as much as $12,000 a year, at a time when the average annual family income was $3,300.[33]

However, publicity agents for *Roller Derby* made sure to convey that the women skaters were just normal girls after all, who had husbands and "usually prefer the home and fireside when the evening is done." In the interviews that *Roller Derby* women gave to the press, language such as "knockin' the shit out of each other" was prohibited. They were to be as ladylike as if they had stepped out of the pages of *Woman's Day Magazine* or *Ladies' Home Journal*. "I want what I think every girl wants—my husband to be happy in his work, my own home, raise a family, and live a normal, everyday life. When you come right down to it, there really isn't much else that matters," Gloria Mack of the Philadelphia Panthers told an interviewer. To promote the skaters' feminine image, *Roller Derby* producers staged beauty pageants, pressing the skaters to compete for the title of "The Prettiest Girl in Roller Derby." Newspaper photographers posed players as though they were pinup models. Articles gushed about their charms. "Queen of queens," the press dubbed Monta Jean Payne of the Jersey Jolters: "she has green eyes, red hair, and a pug nose."[34]

The *Roller Derby* skaters were proof that there was a bit of space in the 1950s for women whose lives ran counter to the reigning image of woman—but also that they had to moderate their message. Audiences loved their on-track roughhousing: shoving, occasional hair pulling, jiu-jitsu acrobatics (usually staged for audience delectation). But paradoxically, *Roller Derby* women were required to present their real off-track selves as being as conventionally feminine as the wholesome young daughters of *Father Knows Best* or *The Donna Reed Show*.

Some women rebels would not or could not moderate their message. Whether or not they committed crimes, their mien and manner were condemned not only by public opinion but also by the law. Pachucas—young, tough, and colorfully rebellious Mexican American gang girls—were outcasts even in their own community. Pachucas were usually the daughters of immigrants who had come to the United States from villages in Mexico, looking for ways to make a decent living. In cities such as Los Angeles, El Paso, and Tucson, the immigrants settled into a very different world from what they had known. To many of them, it was especially troubling that their unmarried daughters could no longer be watched by chaperones, as girls had been when they ventured out in their villages. Their U.S.-born daughters had a different set of worries. They did not feel completely Mexican, nor did they feel completely American. They had to steer between two cultures that were not wholly theirs and to fashion for themselves what "woman" could mean to them.

Those who became pachucas were extreme in breaking away from their parents' mores about how a woman behaves. Together with pachuco boys, they created their own subculture in gangs (or "clubs," as they were often called). In the 1940s and 1950s, the media presented these girls and boys as outlaws, regardless of whether they had broken any laws. Their demeanor alone was enough to make them suspect, and their exploits were reported in details meant to shock and disturb. Pachuca girls defied not only the Anglo world but also people in their Mexican American communities who strove for middle-class respectability. Rosa Linda Fregoso—who grew up in southern Texas and went to Catholic school, where girls were taught to be well-behaved and modest—recalled being warned by her mother to keep away from pachucas. Her mother called them "cheap, street-roaming girls." They knew about sex and were as crude and dangerous as the pachuco boys. The Spanish-language newspaper

La Opinion agreed. Pachucas, the paper opined, were disgraceful for drawing attention to themselves, for street fighting, and for dragging their feet as they walked.[35]

At a time when women's and girls' place was in the home, pachucas would not let themselves be confined. They paraded down the boulevards in rude packs at hours when girls were supposed to be sleeping under their fathers' roofs, they smoked cigarettes and went to dance halls, and they were assumed to be promiscuous. When flowing skirts of modest length were the mainstream fashion, they wore their skirts short and tight. They also wore see-through nylon blouses or tight sweaters that emphasized their breasts. They shaved the thin part of their eyebrows and reshaped them with strokes drawn in Maybelline pencil that pointed upward, like fierce wings. They wore black eyeliner and heavy, dark-red lipstick that overlapped their lips to make their mouths look fuller. They styled their hair to be big by ratting it, and rumor had it that in their high pompadours they hid razor blades with which to slash their rivals or anyone else they disliked. Newspapers compared pachucas to "gun molls of other days" and speculated that they carried their pachuco boyfriend's weapons to rumbles.[36]

The pachucas' rebellious demeanor was accentuated by homemade tattoos, such as drawings of a tiny dagger or a radiant cross between the thumb and index finger or on the forehead. The tattoo, created by puncturing the skin with a blade and inserting ink into the cut, was one more visible sign of pachuca toughness. The pachuca had no interest in emulating the ideal woman of either her parents or of Anglos. She spoke a raunchy Spanglish patois, a "snarl" language that was angry, cynical, and filled with expletives. Sensationalistic media accounts said that she outdid the pachuco in her penchant for violence.[37]

Pacuchas paid for their rebellion. Not only were they shunned by more traditional Mexican Americans such as Fregoso's mother and shamed by community megaphones such as *La Opinion*; they were also scrutinized by the watchful eye of the law, and they were criminalized. The police—their suspicions often triggered by racism as much as by pachuca and pachuco misdeeds—might pick them up for "violating curfew," even if they were standing in front of their own homes. The most recalcitrant (or unlucky) of the pachucas were sent to girls' reform schools, where Mexican Americans made up a disproportionate number of the adolescent inmates.[38]

Actual lawbreaking was not a requirement for being sentenced to reform school. Many pachucas were committed as "social delinquents" or "incorrigibles" for having violated midcentury tenets of a woman's proper behavior. They were also incarcerated for sex-related "crimes," sometimes even if they were the victims. In some instances they were given harsher sentences than those pachuco boys received for comparable violations or were given indeterminate sentences, which could amount to incarceration at penal institutions such as the Ventura School for Girls until they were twenty-one.[39]

School truancy, being "well-acquainted with sex or liquor," or merely "refusing to obey parents or guardian," could get them sent to a maximum-security girls' reform school such as Los Guilucos, which was in an isolated mountainous area of Northern California. The pachuca who arrived at Los Guilucos with a high pompadour and a short skirt would be forced to change her style immediately. Those entering Los Guilucos were deloused on arrival (whether or not they showed signs of having lice), and their heads were swathed in towels for three days. All newbies at Los Guilucos were isolated for an entire week, "pending results of a thorough medical examination" that looked for pregnancy and diseases but also had the effect of frightening a tough girl and breaking her down. They were given a battery of psychological tests to determine why their conduct deviated so badly from how a young woman was supposed to comport herself. The resources of the state were put into reeducating the pachuca, taking the rebel out of her.[40]

The efforts often failed because they required pachucas to reject the only way of being that seemed viable to them. They had formed their community to navigate between two cultures that were not comfortably theirs. Because they could never be village women any more than they could be Donna Reed, they tried to fashion a new way. But they could not escape punishment for their rejection of the acceptable ways of being a woman.

In a zeitgeist that apprised women that the true woman "graciously concedes the top-rung jobs to men," the combination of woman and political power seemed oxymoronic. Throughout the 1950s, women accounted for only about 3 percent of those elected to Congress. As women with some modicum of political power, they were anomalies, and they had to soft-pedal what was anomalous about them. They had to convey that they were leaders by virtue of their abilities, yet leadership attributes had always been considered to be masculine. So they also had to convey that those abilities had not unsexed them and caused them to wander too far from what woman should be. Women in politics could not survive without maneuvering between two hugely contradictory images: they had to present themselves as being tough in their job but no different from the woman next door in their personal lives. Their challenge was not so different from that faced by the women on *Roller Derby*.

Because women in politics were so rare, they lived in a fishbowl. But the media did not know quite what to do with them. News articles about women politicians sometimes read like fashion-show reports. For instance, in 1957, when Florence Dwyer (a Republican from New Jersey) and Kathryn Granahan (a Democrat from Pennsylvania) took their oaths of office as members of Congress, the Associated Press coverage included not one word about where they stood politically. Instead, readers were informed that "Mrs. Dwyer wore a black dress with a square cut neck," while "Mrs. Granahan wore a beige wool." Readers only learned about Elizabeth Kee (a Democrat from West Virginia who had been elected for a fourth term) that at the inauguration she "took time out to put on some powder and again to add lipstick."[41] Such trivializing coverage seemed so normal—and normalizing—that no congresswoman ever pointed out that nobody had cared what congressmen Sam Rayburn or John Dingell wore when they were sworn in.

If a woman in politics fell short in her womanly bona fides, the media could be merciless and even capsize her career, as Representative Coya Knutson discovered. Knutson first became interested in politics in 1942. She was a twenty-nine-year-old schoolteacher and the wife of the proprietor of a tiny hotel and restaurant in Oklee, Minnesota, when she heard Eleanor Roosevelt speaking on the radio, telling her audience that the nation needed wise men and women to run for political office. Years earlier, Knutson had been admitted to the Juilliard School as a singer and had dreamed of having a big career. She gave it up after the humiliation of being gonged out of *Major Bowes' Original Amateur Hour* after singing only four bars of *O Sole Mio*. But after hearing Eleanor Roosevelt's speech, Knutson was filled again with purpose. She claimed ever after that the speech had made her feel "as if the sun burnt into me that day." Though she had no examples of woman as a political being in her immediate environment, she felt she had the encouragement of the first lady.[42] Knutson set out to achieve her goal by getting a New Deal job as a field representative with a government agency that had been established to serve farm families. She was soon appointed to her county's welfare board.

When the Democratic Farm Labor Party was established in her area, she joined it, and a few years later she was elected its chair. She was spirited and outspoken. Her robust voice and charismatic presence had been polished in her days at Juilliard, and she had no trouble making the farmers notice her. She understood their problems, too, having been born on a farm and having worked at every part of farm life since childhood, as she claimed. In 1950 she ran for the state legislature. In the old family car, she drove herself all over the county, campaigning in fields and barns and not hesitating to grab a cow's udder and start milking beside a farmer as she told him why he ought to vote for her. She campaigned at county fairs, too. Her stump speeches, about the importance of fighting agribusiness conglomerates and how the government must help the family farm, were supplemented by her singing and accordion playing.

Minnesota newspapers were more discombobulated by a woman running for office than the farmers who met her seemed to be. The Minneapolis *Star Tribune* reported that Knutson had carefully mulled over going into politics and "more important [sic], she talked it over with her husband." (The fact that Andy Knutson was an alcoholic and a wife beater too was outside the purview of the article.) When Coya Knutson won her race and became one of only two women elected to the Minnesota House of Representatives, the *Star Tribune* reporter, grasping for familiar ground, wrote that "Mrs. Knutson" would not be going to St. Paul until the legislature convened on January 2—because she would be staying "at home in Oklee, cooking for Christmas."[43]

Knutson did a yeoman's job in the state legislature, fighting not only for bills that would help the small farmer, but also for those that had been important to her as a teacher, such as increases in state aid to education. She fought for women's issues, too, including health care for expectant mothers who could not afford it and legislation to ban the media from publishing the names of rape victims (the latter was the first bill she sponsored in the Minnesota House). She was easily reelected in 1952, receiving the highest number of votes that her district had ever given to a candidate.[44] This sparked her ambition to run for Congress in 1954, even though only 11 of the 435 members of the House of Representatives were women.

Knutson financed her bid with $5,000 she raised by selling property she had inherited from her father. She campaigned among the farmers again, as well as in all the towns in the Ninth Congressional District. She delivered as many as a dozen stump speeches a day. To draw crowds, she plastered her car with "Elect Coya" posters, attached a loudspeaker to its roof, and, as "I Love to Go A-Wandering" blared, drove the car down the main streets of every town in her district.[45] And she won, becoming the first woman ever elected to Congress from Minnesota. She had beaten a six-term Republican incumbent who had been beloved by agribusiness. It was an astounding feat.

But the media, still at a loss as to how to present a woman as a formidable politician, fell back on the usual approach when covering Knutson. After she racked up another first, becoming the first woman appointed to the powerful House Committee on Agriculture, the Minnesota papers focused not on her achievement but on her femininity. An article titled "How Coya Stormed the Capitol" was accompanied by a photograph of her in her kitchen at home, decked out in an apron, and pouring coffee for her husband and adopted teenage son. "Her eyes—blue as the skies of Norway where her parents were born—were dancing," the writer effused. Knutson was complicit in such journalistic pap. She understood how jarring the image of a woman with power was in 1950s America, and she presented herself to the reporter not with the gravitas of her office but rather as disarmingly feminine. "She talks much, she gestures much, and her candid words flow without guile or pre-calculation of their effect," was the writer's assessment.[46]

Knutson was, in fact, politically shrewd and astute. She knew very well how to maneuver in Washington and push through remarkably progressive legislation, including the creation of a federal student loan program, which became Title II of the National Defense Education Bill; a food-stamp program that would make use of farm surpluses; free milk for all primary school children; and a federally supported school lunch program. But she also worked hard at cultivating an attractive and very womanly image. She shed many pounds along with the farmwoman demeanor of her Minnesota days, traded her sensible flat-heeled shoes in for pretty high heels, wore feminine costume jewelry, and even dyed her hair blonde. When she won a second term, it seemed that she had perfected a rare art: high politicking while woman.

But her political enemies eventually brought her down with charges that she was not woman enough. Her relationship with her husband, who had remained in Oklee, had deteriorated further. She seldom went home after he, in a drunken rage, blackened her eyes, forcing her to wear dark glasses on her return to Washington. Yet her political effectiveness was at a high, and in 1958 she announced her intention to seek a third term. That was when she received a letter signed by her husband, though he later claimed it was not written by him:[47]

> Coya, I want you to tell the people of the 9th District this Sunday that you are through with politics. That you want to go home and make a home for your husband and son. As your husband I compel you to do this. I'm tired of being torn apart from my family. . . . I love you, honey. Come back to our happy home.[48]

The letter even hinted that Coya, who was now forty-five years old, was having an affair with her campaign manager, the twenty-nine-year-old Bill Kjeldahl, who had gone with her to Washington to be her administrative assistant. The allegation was disseminated to the major media, where Knutson was depicted not as a serious congresswoman but as a floozy. *Time*, saying not a word about her political work, presented her as a noir villainess right out of *The Postman Always Rings Twice*. Describing her, like Lana Turner's Cora Smith, as a "blond, comely wife . . . slimmed down and modishly coifed," the article reported that Coya's husband had asked her to fire "her handsome executive assistant. . . . But Coya Knutson would have none of that. Kjeldahl would stay, she cried. Her life was her own, and she aimed to live it a long, long way from Andy's Kitchen."[49]

She was mocked all over America, with headlines jeering, "Coya, Come Home." She lost her bid for a third term in Congress to Republican Odin Langen, whose campaign slogan "A Big Man for a Big Job" reminded voters that woman's job was in the home, not the House. After her defeat, the *New York Times* smugly announced that Coya Knutson would indeed be coming home: "Voters and Husband Agree That It's the Place for Congresswoman." Her women colleagues in Congress rallied behind her, but women who were deeply invested in the reigning midcentury ideal of woman were furious with her. "You are a typical American career woman. You are a disgrace to womanhood," a New Jersey woman wrote. It would take more than forty years—and a new century—before another woman from Minnesota would be elected to the U.S. House of Representatives.[50]

Knutson's story stood as a cautionary tale. There was space all right in the 1950s to step outside the narrowest strictures on women that the zeitgeist tried to impose. A woman could run for high political office and be elected, she could play a rough professional sport, and she could reject some of the most stifling customs of her parent culture. But she had to moderate her departures from convention by hiding the extent of her rebellion and professing to be not so different from other women after all. If, like pachucas, she refused or did not know how to hide, or if she was accused by a disgruntled husband of neglecting her most important duties, she paid a steep price.

WHAT OUGHT TO BE AND WHAT WAS IN WOMAN'S SEX LIFE

> "Our civilization has become so preoccupied with sex that it now oozes from all pores of American life."
> —PITIRIM A. SOROKIN, *The American Sex Revolution* (1956)[51]

The demarcations between the "good girl" and the "bad girl" in the 1950s seemed to hark back to the prudery of the Victorian era. Again, great value was placed on the "pure" young woman who "saved" her virginity to give to her husband on her wedding night. Again, religious and social authorities decried all sex outside of wedlock and warned young women that illicit sexual pleasure invariably led to suffering. As Howard Whitman, a popular television commentator on mental health, social problems, and sex education, phrased it: "Sex freedom has simply sunk unhappy individuals deeper into the mire."[52]

Yet despite the ubiquitous exhortations to girls to remain virginal until marriage, contradictory messages were everywhere. Pitirim Sorokin, the ultraconservative founder of Harvard University's Sociology Department, observed with disapproval in 1956 that the country had "become so preoccupied with sex that it oozes from all pores of American life." There was truth to his jeremiad. Rock 'n' roll (the term itself was Black slang for *sex*) originated in Black communities but captivated teenage girls of all races in the midcentury. Rock 'n' roll's explicitly sexual lyrics defied the morality of prudes. "Good golly, Miss Molly, sure like to ball. / When you're rocking and a rolling can't hear your mama call," Little Richard sang, knowing that his teenage listeners were more "hep" than to think that "ball" meant dancing. "There'll be fifteen minutes of kissin'/ Then you'll holler 'Please don't stop.'/There'll be fifteen minutes of teasin'/ Fifteen minutes of squeezin'/ And fifteen minutes of blowin' my top," the Dominoes promised girl listeners in lyrics that moved from foreplay to orgasm.[53] Elvis Presley, the white southern boy who was dubbed "King of Rock 'n' Roll," adapted Black style, enhancing it with pelvic gyrations that looked like sexual thrusting—which brought his mostly white audience of adolescent girls to lip-biting and bosom-clutching emulations of orgasmic frenzy.

A new print industry that presented women as unashamedly sexual also emerged in the postwar years. The 1953 inaugural issue of *Playboy* featured a nude photo of Marilyn Monroe, who was on her way to becoming Hollywood's top starlet. The photo was a huge hit that guaranteed the magazine's success. Every subsequent issue featured a new voluptuous nude as the centerfold. *Playboy*'s circulation soon topped 1 million. Inspired by *Playboy*, girlie magazines with titles such as *King, Ace, Don Juan,* and *Duke* (the latter aimed at Black male readers and featuring Black pinup models) proliferated. The titles were intended to liberate pasha-like fantasies in men. Some of the pinup models saw their work as liberating for themselves, too. They were defying the fear a 1950s woman was supposed to have of being thought sexually immodest. "Being in the nude isn't a disgrace. . . . In the Garden of Eden, God was probably naked as a jaybird too," Bettie Page, one of the most famous of the 1950s pinup models, quipped insouciantly as she flaunted the dictates about woman's sexual propriety.[54]

The magazines were sold on newsstands and in cigar stores everywhere, their covers displaying curvaceous young women with only their pubes concealed (to avoid charges of pornography). The images presented women as sexual, without reference to conjugal confines—and to many, that was pornographic enough. Even mainstream liberals such as Congresswoman Kathryn Granahan were upset. Nothing less than "the American home is the target of [the girlie magazines'] pornographic attack," she complained. Estes Kefauver, another liberal Democrat and a leading member of the U.S. Senate, convened a special senate committee to investigate. "Smut Held Cause of Delinquency," one newspaper announced in 1955. Kefauver vowed that his committee would propose federal action to "stiffen penalties" for affronts to decency.[55] But the girlie magazines continued to proliferate and flourish throughout the 1950s, the photographers and models always being careful to avoid imputations of "pornography" by flirtatiously using a drape, a beach ball, or an umbrella to hide the pubic area.

During the same years, newsstands and even drugstores began selling a new genre of paperback originals that also came under investigation by congressional committees. Their covers announced their content in lurid language such as "Half-angel, half-devil, loved by many men, Katie was wildly UNTAMED." The cover pictures were equally lurid. *Untamed*, for instance, presented an exotic redhead, breasts popping out of her blouse, eyes closed in ecstasy, and swooning in a man's embrace. Lesbian subjects were particularly popular in these books, which often had sensationalistic titles such as *The Evil Friendship*, *A Twilight Affair*, and *Forbidden*. The latter's cover was typical, showing two attractive, half-undressed young women, above the caption, "The gripping story of Hilda, whose twisted desires led her to the brink of degradation."[56]

To escape censorship, these paperbacks always included so-called redeeming social value—which generally amounted to a denouement of a few pages that portrayed the sexually transgressive woman character either repenting or suffering moral retribution, such as miserable loneliness or a violent death. It was "filth on the newsstands," the popular novelist Margaret Culkin Banning complained in a *Reader's Digest* article, which garnered her an invitation to Washington to be a key witness in the hearings of a House of Representatives select committee on pornography.[57] Such hearings notwithstanding, like girlie magazines, paperbacks portraying over-the-top bad girls continued to be published. Though the writers always had to take a perfunctory axe to the unrepentant sinner by the last page, the books nevertheless reinforced the idea that women were much more interested in nonconjugal sex than they had been taught to believe they ought to be.

In real life, that interest seemed to be substantiated by the number of "illegitimate" births, which skyrocketed in the 1950s, increasing 36 percent between 1951 and 1957. Forty percent of unwed mothers were teenagers. They did not have an easy time of it among the moralists who dominated the era. Though an unmarried pregnant woman could no longer be brought to court on bastardy charges or publicly whipped, as her counterpart had been in colonial days, her pregnancy nevertheless was proof that she had snubbed the ideals of female sexual purity, and she was widely stigmatized. The stigma was sometimes less severe in working-class Black communities, where babies born outside of marriage might be brought into an extended family. However, in middle-class Black communities as well as in white communities an unmarried pregnant woman was, as the phrase went, "in trouble."[58]

To escape the stigma of being pregnant out of wedlock, before a young woman began to show her state, she might be whisked away by her distressed parents to an "unwed mother" refuge. There were many of them in the 1950s, such as the Florence Crittenton "maternity homes." Founded in 1882 by the wealthy businessman Charles Crittenton (named after his daughter, who died at the age of four of scarlet fever), they were intended to aid women who were deemed lost and fallen. In the 1950s, the young woman sent to a Florence Crittenton home would be taught that though she had lapsed from grace, her error could be repaired by her repentance as she awaited the birth of the baby.[59] She would also be pressured to give her baby up for adoption at its birth. It was unfair to the child to make it go through life with the terrible stigma of illegitimacy, she would be told. With a flat belly and no baby, the young woman could then return to her community from "a long visit to her favorite aunt and uncle in another city," with hardly anyone the wiser.

Even if she were not "caught" by pregnancy, a young woman had reason to worry about "ruining her reputation" by being known as "easy" if she let a boy "go too far" (all terms that were current in the 1950s). Yet as Sorokin put it, sex "oozed from all pores of American life." Movies and movie magazines, for instance, featured big-breasted stars in décolleté dresses—Americans Marilyn Monroe, Jayne Mansfield, Kim Novak, and Jane Russell, and European imports such as Sophia Loren, Anita Ekberg, and Brigitte Bardot—"oozing" sex appeal. "Sexy" became synonymous with female attractiveness, for which young women, hoping to attract young men, strived. But paradoxically, it was a young woman's responsibility to fight off the sexual arousal that "sexiness" had on young men.

The pressure on the young woman of the 1950s was not much different from what it had been in 1810, when Rev. Joseph Buckminster charged women with guarding and fortifying society's morals. In the 1950s, too, women were charged with making young men control themselves. But the responsibility of the virtuous young woman in 1810 was surely much less confusing than it became in the 1950s, with sex "oozing" from everywhere. A 1950s girl learned that it was normal for a man to want sex, yet it was incumbent upon her to stop him from having it with her unless he married her. Failure to stop him meant the loss of her reputation, but a boost to his. In the nineteenth century a seducer was condemned as a cad; in the 1950s he was admired as a cocksman. The 1950s girl learned too that the loss of her virginity could even end her hope for a happy future, because though men were free to have as many sex partners as they craved (all bad girls), they would not marry "damaged goods."[60]

Alfred Kinsey's *Sexual Behavior in the Human Female,* which was published in 1953, should have put an end to the confusion. It should have blasted through sexual hypocrisy. Kinsey and his team reported the results of in-depth interviews with 5,940 women. The researchers found that 40 percent of the women admitted to having engaged in petting before the age of fifteen; 62 percent had masturbated; and 48 percent admitted to having had premarital sex, and 77 percent of those women said that they were not sorry they had done so. By age forty, more than 25 percent of married women had had sex with someone other than their husband. Kinsey also found that twentieth-century women had gotten more sexual than their predecessors. Premarital petting, he wrote, "had become more widely spread among those who were born after 1900. . . . Its incidence has steadily increased down to the present day."[61] That is, young women were more likely to pet in the repressed 1950s than they were in the naughty Roaring Twenties.

Perhaps the most disquieting claim Kinsey made was that 19 percent of the women that his team interviewed admitted to having had homosexual experiences, and 6 percent claimed to be predominantly homosexual. That is, huge numbers of American women had engaged in lesbian acts. Those figures challenged midcentury psychiatrists' insistence that lesbianism was a rare and psychically debilitating disease that required medical intervention. The figures also blasted the wisdom of 1950s sex manuals that presented woman's sexuality as naturally dormant until awakened by her husband.[62] Obviously, there was no husband in lesbian sex—clear proof that women could be sexually autonomous. *Sexual Behavior in the Human Female* was a shocker.

Commentators shrieked that Kinsey had "dropped an atomic bomb designed to destroy what is left of sex morality in the United States" and that *Sexual Behavior in the Human Female* "will cause revolts in homes, churches, schools." The same week the book was published, Congress deliberated on whether to order the U.S. Post Office to refuse to mail it on the grounds that it was obscene. A few months later, Congress discussed whether to investigate Kinsey's financial backing. The psychiatrist Edmund Bergler, together with the gynecologist William S. Kroger, accused Kinsey of not knowing what he was talking about: he was not a medical doctor, did not understand female anatomy, and had been duped by neurotic and exhibitionistic women. Healthy, normal women, the doctors wrote, would have responded to Kinsey's request to discuss their sex lives by telling him, "Mind your own business!"[63]

In fact, Kinsey's published sample was skewed. Not only did it exclude all women of color, but it was biased toward highly educated, religiously liberal, middle-class women. Seventy-one percent of his respondents had attended college, though only 13 percent of the women in the general population had. Only 4 percent of his respondents had left school by the eighth grade, but 43 percent of the women in the general population had had no more than an eighth-grade education. Only 12 percent of his respondents were Catholic, compared to 33 percent of the women in the general population.[64] It was true that Kinsey's book did not present a good snapshot of the general female population. Nevertheless, it demonstrated that for a sizable number of women, what the loudest voices said ought to be was not necessarily what was.

Kinsey's book did not quiet those loudest voices, but by the start of the 1960s, their decibel level diminished as the social insecurities that had reawakened the old ideals of woman lessened. For the baby boomers of the immediate postwar period and the 1950s who were growing up in relative prosperity and peace, the Depression might as well have been ancient history, and World War II was something their fathers were engaged in before they were born. The Cold War was far from over, but McCarthy-type hysteria about the communist threat became subdued. Dior's New Look, which had revived the fashion of the nineteenth century, became a very old look. The "vertuous" woman who tended to her home, the hypocritical elevation of sexual purity that distinguished good women from bad women (and kept the good woman cowed lest she be mistaken for a bad woman), woman's "differentiation" and "complementarity" in relation to man, her duty to "graciously concede" worldly success to him and indulge his whims at home—all those notions were on their way to becoming quaint again. At the start of the new decade, the Food and Drug Administration approved the Pill, which would promise woman unprecedented sexual freedom: it coincided with a rethinking of the role woman had been occupying since the soldiers came home.

12.

A New "New Woman" Emerges
(Carrying Baggage)

•

THE 1960s

In 1962, shortly after she was named "chairman" of President John F. Kennedy's Commission on the Status of Women, the venerable Eleanor Roosevelt told America on her National Educational Television program *Prospects of Mankind*, "Children whose mothers work come home from school with far fewer emotional problems than those whose mothers stay at home and worry about them." This created an uproar. Even wives of Kennedy's cabinet members weighed in. Margaret McNamara, wife of the secretary of defense, told reporters that National Educational Television should be "aimed at creating in mothers more enthusiasm and pride in their job" rather than promoting views about women such as Roosevelt's. Jane Freeman, wife of the secretary of agriculture, concurred. What was really needed on National Educational Television, she said, was "education for mothers on the development of their children." Lee Udall, wife of the secretary of the interior, was the most exercised. "I was very much offended because no one said what's best for the child," she complained. "[Mothers] should be encouraged to stay at home and encouraged to understand parenthood and its creative best and lend their talents to child rearing and homemaking."[1]

THE SEXUALLY LIBERATED WOMAN

"Nice, single girls *do* have affairs."
—HELEN GURLEY BROWN, *Sex and the Single Girl* (1962)[2]

Mary Quant, the anti-Dior of women's fashions, was a British designer who described her clothes as "a tool to compete in life outside the home." If Christian Dior clicked with postwar women's desire to return to an idyllic past, Mary Quant resonated with a new generation of women who wanted to vault from the prison of domesticity into the world. Quant's most famous creation, the miniskirt, went on sale in 1965. It was intended to be a symbol of social and sexual liberation. It was short, Quant declared, to enable a woman to "move, run, catch a bus, dance." It was unapologetically sexy because the 1960s had moved light-years away from the recent past. Thanks in good part to the Pill, Quant said, women were less timorous about their sexuality and much more in charge than women had ever been before.[3]

The miniskirt traveled quickly across the Atlantic. It was featured in *Seventeen*, sold by major retailers such as J. C. Penney, and became the rage among young women all over America. Retailers reported that it made up half of their skirt sales. The new fashion, profoundly challenging to the notion that the woman was by nature a creature of modesty, caused an uproar in many places. In Indianapolis, Indiana, one employment agency announced that "if a girl shows up in a miniskirt, we may not tell her why, but we don't usually ask her to come back." Lester Maddox, Georgia's segregationist governor, wanted to segregate the miniskirt, too. He declared with horror that he had seen skirts so short that he thought they were blouses. If a woman wished to work in the state capitol, Maddox stated, she had better be wearing her skirt down to her knees.[4] But despite the consternation, a new breed of feisty young woman was reveling in a fashion that sassed the 1950s revival of Victorianism and proclaimed that this generation would be doing things differently.

The Pill did put women "much more in charge," as Quant phrased it, at least of their own bodies. Though various contraceptive devices had been widely available for decades, they could be messy, they squelched spontaneity, and—most disturbing of all—they were unreliable. The Pill had none of those drawbacks, which made it all the more controversial. In 1960, when the Pill was approved by the Food and Drug Administration, it was illegal in thirty states. That changed in 1965 with the U.S. Supreme Court's decision in *Griswold v. Connecticut*, which ushered in a new day by declaring a ban on the Pill to be an unconstitutional violation of the right to privacy. Heterosexual women all over America, whether married or not, could now, with total confidence, separate having sex from the possibility of getting pregnant. Traditional moralists despaired, just as they did over the miniskirt. Modesty and chastity, imperatives for their ideal of woman, were now both under threat.

In hearings held by a U.S. Senate subcommittee on family planning, experts decried the deleterious social effects of the Pill. Rev. Dexter L. Hanley of Georgetown University's Law School testified that the Pill would threaten the "preservation of public morality," which women had always guarded by keeping in check men's natural impulse toward promiscuity.[5] In the past, a woman knew that if she gave in to sexual desire, she risked the shame of "illegitimate" pregnancy. But the Pill removed that risk. Now women could match men in unbridled lust and never have to worry about paying the old price.

Magazines for the masses such as *Reader's Digest* agonized that the Pill would literally destroy civilization by destroying the morality of young women. The Nobel Prize–winning novelist Pearl Buck wrote in an emotional article on "The Pill and the Teen-Age Girl" that the Pill threatened to upend the values girls must learn, such as controlled and regulated living and self-discipline. "Everyone knows what The Pill is. It is a small object. Yet its potential effect upon our society may be even more devastating than the nuclear bomb," Buck lamented melodramatically. Even relatively liberal publications such as *U.S. News and World Report* worried that the Pill had the potential to be "a license for promiscuity" and to lead to "sexual anarchy." In a 1966 feature, "The Pill: How It Is Affecting U.S. Morals, Family Life," the magazine worried that young females were already being ruined: college girls everywhere were talking about the Pill, many were using it, and "it was turning up in high schools too." The article lamented that the Pill was even leading to scandalous doings among married women. In California there was "wife-swapping," and in the suburbs of Long Island wives were earning pin money as prostitutes.[6] Women could now do those things with unfortunate impunity. Such hysteria reflected the fear that women would be unwomaned, transformed into libertines (in imitation of many a man), oblivious to all distinctions between the sexes.

In 1961, triggered perhaps by worry over the Food and Drug Administration's approval of the Pill in the preceding year, the *Ladies' Home Journal* published an article that asked, "Is the Double Standard out of Date?" The author's answer to her own question was an unconditional "No!" Women were not like men, she declared. Sex for sheer pleasure was fine for men, but for women—who, after all, were designed to have babies—it was simply frustrating. So if a woman was confronted by a man who "insists," the author advised, she had two choices: "She can marry him, or she can say 'No!'"[7]

The article caught the attention of Helen Gurley Brown, a thirty-nine-year-old ad copywriter. Brown, who had married for the first time only a couple of years earlier, after a wildly satisfying bachelorette-hood, thought the article was a pack of silly lies. It led her to write a response, which became *Sex and the Single Girl*. Maybe in Philadelphia, where the *Ladies' Home Journal* was published, a girl had only two choices, Brown quipped in her book, but "in Los Angeles, where I live, there is something else a girl can say and frequently does when a man 'insists.' And that is 'yes.'"[8]

It was what many women, all over the country, were ready to hear. *Sex and the Single Girl* sold 2 million copies in the first three weeks after its publication. The book celebrated the unmarried woman who was "irresistibly, irrepressibly, confidently, enviably single." The "old maid"—an outcast, her hideous or pathetic image a cautionary tale aimed at girls even in the children's card game Old Maid—became, in Brown's rendition, the new glamour girl, footloose and joyously sexual. Brown even dared to say that marriage was no big deal in a woman's life. "You may marry or you may not. In today's world [where a woman can support herself] that is no longer the big question for women," she wrote, warning young women not to "glom on" to a man as an easy escape but instead to "reach, stretch, learn, grow, face dragons . . . make a living."[9]

Sex and the Single Girl also blasted through the hypocrisy of the double standard. It set women free, erotically at least, informing them that they had as much right to sexual pleasure as men did. And at a time when sexual relations were still widely referred to as "the marriage act,"[10] the book told the single girl that she did not have to wait to be married to claim her sexual pleasure. She could even be the one to initiate a sexual encounter, if she wished. Brown torpedoed the distinction between "good girl" and "bad girl." She encouraged the woman to be equal to the man—a hunter in free pursuit of her erotic bliss.

However, bold as Brown's message was, she could not divest herself entirely of the baggage she had inherited. Her tips to the single girl about how to make a man like her would have satisfied even Governor John Winthrop. "Never interrupt a man when he is telling you a story," she advised the single girl. Appear to be "hanging on his every word. . . . It was good in your grandmother's day, and it's still a powerhouse!" Since the way to a man's heart is through his stomach, the single girl must also do what women had always been called upon to do, Brown advised: *"Feed him! . . .* Show him how talented you are [in the kitchen]." *Sex and the Single Girl* even included recipes for "fabulous little dinners"—including stuffed lobster tails or lobster brochette with devil sauce, champagned peach, and chocolate soufflé (never mind the required labor-intensive hours in the kitchen or the dent in the working girl's wages).[11]

Brown also took for granted inequities that continued to keep women in their place. For instance, her enthusiasm for affairs with married men is disturbing not just for the obvious reasons but also for what it does not challenge about the plight of the working woman. A "visiting married man on an expense account is the greatest date since Diamond Jim Brady," Brown effused. "He will take you to the best restaurants, the best nightclubs, order the best champagne." Her single girl in 1962 is reminiscent of Katie, the sixteen-year-old department-store clerk who in 1913 had to rely on men to take her out for a "swell time" because she earned only $3.50 a week.[12] Apparently not much had changed half a century later. Women's wages were still so low that if they wanted a "swell time" they still needed a man, even a married one, to provide it.

Yet as rearward as such advice was, Brown's overall message to the masses of women—that an unmarried woman should not be ashamed of desiring sexual freedom—was groundbreaking. The nineteenth-century sex radicals and the New Women of the early twentieth century had also advocated for sexual freedom, but there were no multitudes of women in America who were ready for it then. In the 1960s, there were. Some feminist historians have credited Brown with being "the first spokeswoman of the revolution."[13] She was certainly the first to whom millions of women listened when she told them they had a right to what men had always claimed as their prerogative: sex for sheer pleasure, absolutely irrespective of marital status.

THE (VERY GRADUAL) RISE OF THE SECOND WAVE OF FEMINISM

"Widening the choices for women beyond their doorstep does not necessarily imply neglect of their education for responsibility in the home."

—President's Commission on the Status of Women (1963)[14]

The affluent women of the early twentieth century who joined forces with working-class women in organizations such as the Women's Trade Union League had heirs such as Esther Peterson, who became one of the few women to hold high office in the Kennedy administration. Peterson had grown up in an upper-middle-class Mormon family in Provo, Utah, and had been a dyed-in-the-wool Republican until she married a solid Roosevelt Democrat. In the 1930s, she had been teaching at Boston's Winsor School for daughters of the wealthy, but at her husband's urging she began volunteering in a YWCA program for girls who worked in the garment industry. She visited their homes in the slums, saw the sweated-labor conditions under which they worked, and joined them in a strike after their low wages were made even lower. Like the earlier generation of elite women who were moved to fight by the side of working-class women, Peterson decided that she would "throw my lot in with the labor movement." But unlike many of her elite predecessors, she disdained feminists—women who wanted to ignore what she saw as the essential differences between women and men. Feminism, she scoffed, was "an antiquated, more-than-slightly ridiculous notion." Moreover, Peterson believed, to ignore the essential differences between the sexes would be perilous for the woman worker.[15]

Peterson not only helped women workers organize and joined them in sit-down strikes, but she also led them in singing fervid union songs. Her devotion to their cause garnered her a position as assistant director of the Amalgamated Clothing Workers of America and then (with her four children cared for by her supportive husband and a devoted housekeeper) as a legislative lobbyist in Washington, where she educated members of Congress on issues such as minimum wage laws. In 1947, Peterson targeted a newly elected young congressman from Boston, John Fitzgerald Kennedy, who was, as she later recalled, very receptive to learning from her about the plight of the woman worker.[16] By the time Kennedy became a senator and chair of the Senate Labor Committee, he and Peterson were old friends. He trusted her to educate him about workers' needs. She trusted him to do right by the worker.

When Kennedy ran for president in 1960, Peterson organized a group called Labor Women for Kennedy and helped him land the labor vote.[17] He called her soon after the election. "What do you want?" he asked. He offered her a position at the United Nations, but she wanted instead to head the Women's Bureau of the Department of Labor.

The Women's Bureau had been established in 1920 to watch over the rights of working women. Peterson's predecessor, Alice Leopold, had focused on the problems of women in the professions. Peterson shifted the bureau's focus completely away from them and to the "millions of women who had to work in low-wage occupations."[18] After a few months, Peterson's title was cranked up to assistant secretary of labor for labor standards. She was sure of the president's ear on all issues related to women and work.

Peterson was hostile to the few feminists who were still pushing for the Equal Rights Amendment (ERA), which had been drafted in 1923 by Alice Paul and her National Woman's Party. The ERA, which declared that equality of rights could not be denied or abridged on the basis of sex, was a radical rejection of any legal difference between "woman" and "man." Year after year, a few feminist diehards had continued to push Congress to hold hearings on it. The ERA finally reached the floor of the Senate in 1946 in a brief euphoric move to thank women for their war work, but it was defeated by a vote of thirty-eight to thirty-five. It failed to even reach the floor of the House.[19] The failure of the ERA had been due not to conservatives who feared doing away with distinctions between women and men. That opposition would come later. It was organized labor that had opposed the amendment since it was first introduced. The unions had fought long and hard for legislation that protected the woman worker—laws based on her putative inferior strength vis-à-vis men, as well as on her biological and social role as a mother. To opponents of the ERA, its passage would mean that a working woman could be forced to lift a hundred pounds, refused maternity leave no matter how near delivery she was, or be compelled to work overtime or on swing shifts even if she had toddlers that had to be picked up from nursery school at 5:15 P.M. sharp. But to the ERA's proponents, its passage would mean that a woman could not be denied a job, a raise, or a promotion simply because she was a woman.

By the 1950s, the National Woman's Party was all but defunct, made up almost entirely of elderly white businesswomen and a smattering of lawyers and other professionals, representing a minuscule fraction of America's women. When Kennedy was in Congress, the National Woman's Party repeatedly asked him to endorse the ERA, and during his campaign for president he did. But he complained, according to Peterson, that he "had trouble always with these women's groups that keep swarming the Hill with demands for equality." Peterson told Kennedy that she too "didn't like the feminists' equal rights approach." She said that she wanted to "come up with some more constructive answer to this question of equality."[20] She proposed that he establish the President's Commission on the Status of Women.

In December 1961 Kennedy signed Executive Order 10980, establishing the commission. Its charge, at Peterson's suggestion, was to develop "recommendations [to] enable women to continue their role as wives and mothers while making a maximum contribution to the world around them." Kennedy also gave Peterson control over the commission's makeup. She selected people, as she confessed, "who would vote along the lines that I thought the commission should go." The one ERA sympathizer appointed to the commission—Marguerite Rawalt, the first woman president of the Federal Bar Association—was shut up in no uncertain terms by other commission members, such as John Macy (head of the Civil Service Commission), who told Rawalt that it was time she stopped "rid[ing] the equal rights amendment horse."[21]

Peterson invited Eleanor Roosevelt to be the commission's "chairman." As Peterson knew, she had opposed the ERA when she was member of the Women's Trade Union League because she had worried that it was too sweeping and that working women would lose protections if it became law. However, Roosevelt was also a feminist, and it was only a few months after becoming chair of the commission that she caused an uproar among Washington stay-at-home wives when she announced on her National Educational Television program that "children whose mothers work come home from school with far fewer emotional problems than those whose mothers stay at home and worry about them." But Roosevelt died just five months after that declaration, and Peterson, who had made herself vice chair of the commission, took over its leadership.

In speaking of what Roosevelt would have wanted had she been able to see the commission through to the end, Peterson put an emphasis where Roosevelt had not intended. Roosevelt, Peterson said, "was very concerned that we hold on to family life. She kept saying that the work we were doing would strengthen family life. . . . If we solved some of the unemployment and low pay problems women would be happier and they'd strengthen family life."[22]

Peterson's "interpretation" of the sentiments she attributed to Roosevelt may not have accurately reflected the latter's ideas. However, they did reflect the ideas of the majority of the commission's participants, who still endorsed the old version of woman that had been resurrected after World War II. Daniel Patrick Moynihan, the Department of Labor's liaison to the commission, objected to "the widespread notion that women can and *ought* to work." Moynihan said that he would prefer "to see a country and an economy in which men made enough money that their women can stay home and raise their families." The chair of the commission's Committee on Social Insurance and Taxes, Senator Maurine Neuberger, agreed: women should not be working at all. She averred that women preferred to stay at home, "to rear their children, to entertain the husband's boss, to have a nice home, and to work in some volunteer committee activity." (She had served in the Oregon House of Representatives before winning a special election to complete her deceased husband's term in the U.S. Senate. She then ran for an additional term as senator and served for six more years.)[23]

The report the commission issued in October 1963 was careful to assure Americans that it was not asking for a revolution in the concept of woman. But it did propose that women be protected from arbitrary sex discrimination, that hiring practices be reformed to give women more opportunities, and that state laws not make distinctions between men and women that were not reasonable in the light of modern women's multiple activities. It even recommended that the states pass laws mandating that if women worked in the same jobs as men, they should be paid the same wages (though women were seldom hired to work in the same jobs as men). The salient points made by the commission was that woman's most important role was as wife and mother, and that any public policy must take that fact into account.[24]

Tame as the commission's report was, it nevertheless caused great consternation among critics who believed that it thrust woman out of her natural place. For instance, the president of Chatham College, a women's college in Pittsburgh, wrote in his *New York Times* review of the published report that the commission had done America a big disservice in its "startling denial of the right of woman to be female."²⁵

Not a lot came of the work that had occupied the commission for almost two years. Most members of the commission had been irreconcilably torn between two ideas: huge numbers of American women left their home every day to participate in the work world, so the laws ought to be just to them; but, as Kennedy had reiterated in 1962, "woman's primary responsibility is in the home." The plan had been that the ex officio representatives from the various governmental departments, such as Macy of the Civil Service Commission and Moynihan of the Department of Labor, would weave the pertinent recommendations into their departments' programs. But as Peterson recognized years later, "we weren't successful in that as we should have been. It was," she said, "kind of a flop."²⁶

Alice Paul's ERA had long seemed moribund, but she had not given up. She was now almost eighty years old, and the awakening of a civil rights movement in the 1950s had given her hope that a feminist movement might yet reawaken. She also took hope from a strange bedfellow: Congressman Howard W. Smith from Virginia, leader of the hard-shell southern Democrats and chair of the powerful House Rules Committee. Smith had actually been endorsing the ERA since 1945, not out of southern chivalry for the ladies but because he was opposed to protective legislation for them. Smith believed that Virginia textile mill owners, reliable big donors to his campaigns, had a right to demand that the women they employed not take so many bathroom breaks and that they work overtime when needed by their bosses.²⁷ But whatever Smith's reasons for supporting the ERA, Paul saw him as a useful ally.

In 1963, a civil rights act that would outlaw segregation as well as employment discrimination against minorities came before the House Rules Committee. As chair of the committee since 1954, Smith had managed to postpone or water down more progressive legislation than any congressman of the twentieth century. Finally, though, he could do no more to delay the act from coming to the House floor. Paul saw this piece of legislation as her main chance. Title VII of the act banned discrimination on the basis of "race, color, religion, and national origin." Paul asked Smith to add the word "sex."²⁸ Smith agreed—though it will never be known for certain whether he did so because he thought it was a good joke, because he believed it would scuttle the proposed legislation, or because he thought Black men should not be given more rights than white women.

If Smith genuinely wished his proposed addition to be adopted, his introduction of it, which ridiculed the notion of women's "rights," was odd. He read a letter by a lady constituent who complained that according to the 1960 census there were 2,661,000 more women than men in the United States and asked him "what course our Government might pursue to protect our spinster friends in their 'right' to a nice husband and family?" The hilarity among the congressmen that followed was surpassed only when the sponsor of the original bill, Emanuel Celler, a liberal Democrat from New York, took the floor. Celler, who had been a long-time opponent of the ERA, declared that the inclusion of "sex" in the Civil Rights Act was unnecessary because women had enough power already. For instance, he said, with his wife of fifty years he always got the last words: "Yes, dear."[29]

There were twelve women in the House in 1964. They were not amused by Smith's and Celler's heavy-handed attempts at wit. Katharine St. George, a Republican from New York, grew emotional. "Why should women be denied equality of opportunity? Why should women be denied equal pay for equal work?" she demanded. "That is all we are asking. We are entitled to this little crumb of equality!" Martha Griffiths, a Democrat from Michigan, told her chortling colleagues, "If there had been any necessity to have pointed out that women were a second-class sex, the laughter would have proved it."[30]

Griffiths, guessing that members of Congress who might support the amendment, for whatever reason, would be reluctant to announce their support in a roll-call vote, moved that a ballot vote be taken. She and Celler were appointed to collect and count the ballots. The House approved the inclusion of "sex" by a vote of 168 to 133. According to an interview with Griffiths years later, most of the yes votes were cast by conservative southerners or Republicans.[31] Feminists again had interesting bedfellows.

In the Senate, Minority Leader Everett Dirksen, a Republican from Illinois, would have preferred to leave the word "sex" out of the legislation. Margaret Chase Smith, a Republican from Maine and one of only two women senators, dissuaded him. Dirksen jocularly announced that he had agreed to vote yes on the inclusion of "sex" "in order to avoid the wrath of the women."[32] Clearly, politicians in both parties could not conceive of woman's equality as a serious issue.

Regardless, the Civil Rights Act, with its ban on employment discrimination based on "race, color, religion, sex and national origin," passed the Senate by a vote of 73–27 and was signed into law by President Lyndon Johnson on July 2, 1964. Joke or no joke, it provided the legal underpinning for unprecedented changes in who a woman could be. Yet legal underpinning notwithstanding, many a tough battle would have to be waged before substantive changes were made.

The Equal Employment Opportunity Commission (EEOC) was created in 1965 to enforce the Civil Rights Act. Very soon, more than one-third of the complaints it received were being lodged by women. But the EEOC brushed off most of them. The commision's executive director, Herman Edelsberg, believed that the addition of "sex" to Title VII of the Civil Rights Act was, as he stated, a "fluke," "conceived out of wedlock"—a bastardization of the act's true intent.[33]

The majority of the commissioners of the EEOC agreed with him. They looked for reasons to drag their feet on women's complaints, and they found one. A clause in Title VII stated that certain jobs could be classified under Bona Fide Occupational Qualifications. Airline stewardesses, for instance, could be required to be shapely, single, and under the age of thirty-two. Griffiths again rose to do battle on the floor of the House; she wanted to know what the airlines' requirements for the job of stewardess had to do with a stewardess's duties. When airline executives tried to defend their policies, the irrepressible Griffiths asked, "What are you running, an airline or a whorehouse?"[34]

Griffiths had been a lawyer in the 1940s, when only about 2 percent of all U.S. lawyers were women, and when she had been elected to the House of Representatives in 1954 there were only ten other congresswomen. She had bulldog tenacity and was determined to hold the EEOC accountable. In 1966, she again raised objections in the House about the EEOC's misdeeds. The commission was still displaying "a wholly negative attitude toward the sex provisions of Title VII," she complained. It was examining ridiculous issues: whether Title VII required Playboy clubs to hire male bunnies and whether the refusal to hire a man as a "house mother" for a college sorority house violated the law. The EEOC was ignoring the real problems of sex discrimination. For example, it ruled that help-wanted ads could be separated by gender, though it had prohibited ads from being separated into "white" and "colored." "Why was it legal then to separate help-wanted ads into 'men' and 'women'?" Griffiths asked. "This is legal schizophrenia," she argued. "It has no basis in the law or in ethics, and is in my judgment intellectually dishonest."[35] But it would take a lot more than one congresswoman's righteous anger to make the EEOC do something about gender inequities.

THE WOMEN'S MOVEMENT, REBORN

> "Women can no longer ignore the voice from within that says, 'I want something more than my husband and my children and my home.'"
>
> —BETTY FRIEDAN, *The Feminine Mystique* (1963)[36]

The Feminine Mystique was published one year after *Sex and the Single Girl*. It too sold millions of copies to women hungry for a revolutionary message. Betty Friedan's focus was very different from that of Helen Gurley Brown, but both books urged women to reject boundaries imposed on woman. Friedan addressed *The Feminine Mystique* primarily to women like herself: white, middle-class, suburban, and married. She was inspired to write the book, she said, after doing a survey of 200 women who were Smith College graduates, as was she. Most were living the life to which women had been urged since the end of World War II. It was the life that psychologists, psychiatrists, social scientists, women's magazines, the media, and advertising had all promised would truly fulfill a woman, but Friedan's respondents were miserable. She set about figuring out why that was so.

She puzzled over the paradox. The hard-fought victories that the pioneers of the late nineteenth and early twentieth centuries had won for women had not disappeared completely. Women could still venture beyond the domestic threshold. They could go to college and graduate school and work in a profession. The pioneers had broken down legal, political, and economic barriers. Women could still do all the things the pioneers had made possible—but they were urged not to want to. They were taught that only "unfeminine, unhappy women" wanted careers and political rights and that the truly feminine, healthy woman wanted no more than to be a good wife and mother. "The spirited New Woman had been replaced by the Happy Housewife," Friedan declared.[37] Yet the Happy Housewife was not happy.

Friedan argued that women needed more but had learned to bury that need "as deeply as the Victorian woman buried sex." They were aided in the burying by doctors who handed out tranquilizers such as Librium as blithely as if they were handing out jelly beans. Women's repression of their needs, Friedan wrote, led to "the problem that has no name": a discontent, a feeling of worthlessness. Friedan's passionate purpose was to rouse women to cease to "accept a half-life, instead of a share in the whole of human destiny."[38] For many American women, the chord she struck resounded deeply. Its reverberations helped create a second wave of the feminist movement.

By 1966 *The Feminine Mystique* had sold 3 million copies, and Friedan had become recognized as a leading voice in the renewed feminist struggle. The EEOC's refusal to protect women became her first target. Friedan approached the only two commissioners who were sympathetic to women's issues, Aileen Hernandez and Richard Graham, about how to make the EEOC do its job. They suggested that women's groups needed to be putting relentless pressure on the EEOC. But what women's groups were prepared to do that?

After Kennedy had established the President's Commission on the Status of Women, forty-eight states adopted their own commissions on the status of women. Some basic headway had been made in individual states. Alabama and South Carolina finally permitted women to serve on juries. Massachusetts prohibited sex specification in advertisements for civil service jobs. Pennsylvania rescinded a prohibition on women's working overtime. Several states passed fair employment practices acts, essentially reiterating Title VII's prohibition of employment discrimination on the basis of sex. Each year, representatives from the various state commissions met at an annual conference in Washington, DC, to discuss what their states had accomplished. Friedan was always present.

In 1966, at the third annual conference, she invited several key women to her room at the Washington Hilton Hotel to discuss Hernandez's and Graham's suggestion that women's groups needed to be pressuring the EEOC to do its job. Among those who came was Pauli Murray, who had been on the President's Commission on the Status of Women and in 1965 had been the first Black woman to receive a law degree from Yale University. Murray had also been one of several prominent Black women who were instrumental in organizing the 1963 March on Washington that featured Martin Luther King Jr. She had thought it "bitterly humiliating" that the male leaders had limited the women to "secondary, ornamental, or honoree roles" at the march, that the only woman invited to speak as part of the official program was the widow of the recently assassinated Medgar Evers, and that no woman was permitted to attend the Oval Office meeting with Kennedy after the march. "Jane Crow," Murray called sex discrimination.[39] "What we need," she purportedly said at the meeting in Friedan's hotel room, "is an NAACP for women."

The NAACP had been the driving force behind *Brown v. the Board of Education* in 1954, and it had played a pivotal role in the passage of the 1964 Civil Rights Act and the 1965 Voting Rights Act. Friedan understood: an NAACP for women was exactly what feminists needed—a large, highly respected organization that could tackle big issues that affected women and win.

The next day, the conference held a closing luncheon. Friedan sat with some of the women who had been present at the meeting in her room, and on a paper napkin she jotted down notes on their ideas for the proposed organization. It would have a national presence. It would put pressure on the EEOC and lobby Congress. It would also have grassroots groups everywhere, to exert pressure locally. It would finish the unfinished revolution for woman's equality—now. Friedan jotted down her idea for its name, too: NOW, the National Organization for Women.

Four months later, NOW held its first organizing conference. Betty Friedan was voted president. Aileen Hernandez, who would resign as an EEOC commissioner, became executive vice president. Richard Graham, who had not been reappointed as a commissioner and had left the EEOC soon after the June conference, was voted vice president. (Friedan had called NOW the "National Organization *for* Women" rather than "National Organization *of* Women" because she thought male participation would be important in lending credibility to the group.) NOW's statement of purpose declared that the time had come to move beyond discussions of the "special nature of women which has raged in America in recent years" and instead to fight "the conditions that now prevent women from enjoying the equality of opportunity and freedom of choice which is their right as individual Americans, and as human beings."[40] It was a rallying cry that had not been widely heard in America for half a century.

NOW would work to make its presence felt, on all levels: it would agitate locally and hire lawyers to work nationally. NOW's first direct-action grassroots picket, in August 1967, was an attack on the *New York Times*'s sex-segregated help-wanted ads. The protestors, dressed in suffrage-era costumes to emphasize the point that they were fighting an unfinished battle, carried signs such as "WOMEN CAN THINK AS WELL AS TYPE." They picketed the *Times* for months, upping the emotion decibels with signs that announced, "THE NEW YORK TIMES IS A SEX OFFENDER!"[41] As NOW chapters formed in other cities, their members too picketed local offending newspapers that ran sex-segregated help-wanted ads. They also targeted EEOC field offices across the country, protesting the commission's refusal to acknowledge how sex-segregated ads harmed working women.

NOW lawyers petitioned the EEOC to hold public hearings on the ads and filed a lawsuit against the EEOC. The ad policy was now finally being scrutinized. As Hernandez and Graham had predicted, the EEOC could not stand up to the scrutiny. On August 5, 1968, the commission reversed its former stance and agreed that the ads were in direct violation of Title VII of the Civil Rights Act.

NOW continued acting as a watchdog, to make sure that newspapers complied. When the *Pittsburgh Press* refused to stop running sex-segregated ads and claimed that it was an infringement of First Amendment rights to prohibit a newspaper from printing what it liked, NOW's objections went all the way to the U.S. Supreme Court. There the majority concluded that the *Pittsburgh Press* had no legitimate reason to publish separate help-wanted ads for men and women.[42] It was a colossal victory, for which NOW could and did claim credit.

The termination of sex-segregated help-wanted ads announced the theoretical end of the notion that only certain jobs were suitable for woman. It would be a while before practice would catch up to theory. Women entered the workforce in increasingly great numbers throughout the 1960s, at a time when jobs for clerical workers were proliferating. Stenographer and filing clerk remained women's occupations. Professional women were still at the lower end of the professions in terms of prestige and salary. They were schoolteachers, nurses, and social workers but seldom doctors or administrators. They were stewardesses but almost never pilots, bookkeepers but almost never certified public accountants, legal secretaries but seldom lawyers. A woman with a degree and all A's from Bennington or Wellesley College might be hired by *Time* as a researcher, but almost never as a news writer. Women workers across the board earned on average fifty-nine cents to every dollar that men earned. Politically, women lost even more ground. Through much of the 1960s, the number of women elected to the U.S. Congress hovered between eleven and fourteen. "Millions of American husbands are opposed to their wives getting into politics," the *Boston Globe* announced in the early 1960s in an article that demonstrated, as its title suggested, that "It's Still a Man's World."[43] That did not change much by the end of the decade.

Friedan had a grand vision to remake the "man's world" into a world more equitable for woman—or, more specifically, for women like her:

middle-class, college-educated, and straight. She was distraught when detractors of the movement began to do what had always been done to keep the woman rooted to her place. In other eras, women's righters were traduced as "Amazons" and "manly women." By the 1960s, those terms were obsolete. "Lesbian" was the word used to scare women away from the new women's movement: all feminists were condemned as man-haters who were opposed to marriage and childbearing because they were lesbian. Friedan panicked that the imputation would drive out the women she was most concerned with, those who "wanted equality but also wanted to keep on loving their husbands and children."[44]

There were in fact many lesbians in NOW, among both the leaders and the grassroots activists. Friedan claimed to believe that "everyone has a right to sexual privacy" and that she did not mind lesbians as long as they stayed in the closet. But when some feminists actually began embracing the term "lesbian" and claiming it as their own, Friedan was outraged. They were a "lavender menace," she complained. They were "warping the issue of women's rights." Murray, NOW's cofounder, shared Friedan's outrage, even though Murray believed that she herself had "inverted sexual instincts." Murray, a product of the repressive midcentury that taught her to view her sexuality as a private matter (and shameful), complied with Friedan's wish that NOW members who were not heterosexual keep mum about it. When other lesbians in NOW refused to hide who they were, Murray was as incensed as Friedan was. "Most women relate to men," Murray scolded, and "a lesbian take-over would be comparable to the tail wagging the dog."[45]

If Murray and Friedan had cared to think about it, they might have guessed that from the very beginning of the movement's first wave, women who made their emotional and sexual lives with other women had been in its forefront. It made sense that because those women had no husband to support them and they had to support themselves, they would be on the front line in battles for decent wages, higher education, and entrance into the professions. Because no man represented them at the poll, they would also be on the front line in the struggle for the vote, which would enable a woman to represent herself. In those more reticent times, of course such women did not discuss their private lives; in the 1960s, their counterparts defied reticence. Lesbians in NOW chapters everywhere began exiting the closet.

Friedan hoped that at least she might fill the leadership positions in NOW with "normal" women. She was thrilled when Ti-Grace Atkinson, a blonde southern belle, was willing to serve on the national board and in 1967 to become the first president of the New York chapter. Atkinson projected precisely the right image. She was attractive, feminine-looking, and a real lady who only wanted women to have, as Friedan wrote, "more in life than peanut butter sandwiches with the kids [and] throwing powder into the washing machine." Friedan was disillusioned when Atkinson turned out to be a flaming radical. Atkinson published broadsides such as "Vaginal Orgasm as a Mass Hysterical Survival Response." She wanted to make abortion a central issue in NOW. She defended lesbians. (Eventually she would coin the aphorism "feminism is the theory; lesbianism is the practice.") The conflict between Atkinson and Friedan became heated. Atkinson resigned her position as president in October 1968.[46]

She was succeeded by Ivy Bottini, a married woman with two daughters. Bottini was lively and charismatic, and she looked like the housewife next door, like a woman of Middle America. Friedan was again thrilled. Here was a poster woman for NOW—this was who the woman of the new women's movement was.

But very early in Bottini's presidency it became apparent that she too was a radical. She gave air to the most taboo of subjects by organizing a NOW forum titled "Is Lesbianism a Feminist Issue?" Worse, she then came out as a lesbian. Not only did Friedan make sure that Bottini would not be reelected, but she organized a purge of all the out lesbians in New York NOW. Closeted lesbians in NOW supported Friedan because they feared they would be outed if the lesbian issue were openly discussed.[47]

But Friedan's lesbophobia was not shared by NOW leaders around the country. They defied the founder by confronting head-on the age-old ploy of discrediting women who pushed at the parameters imposed on woman. In 1971, NOW held a conference in Los Angeles whose purpose was to hammer out the organization's national policies. When Friedan heard that a resolution would be presented on the "lesbian issue," she told a *Los Angeles Times* reporter, "Oh, God, I hope it doesn't become anything big. Now that the movement has become a major force in social and political change, enemies have managed to infiltrate, weaken and try to destroy it." The resolution presented to the delegates affirmed every woman's "right to define and express her own sexuality." It expressed regret that though lesbians had been in the forefront of fighting for women's rights, they were treated "as the step-sisters of the movement . . . expected to hide in the upstairs closet when company comes." It acknowledged that "lesbian-baiting" had been a tactic to "bring women to heel," and it avowed that fighting against the oppression of lesbians was "a legitimate concern of feminism." Ninety percent of the 1,000-plus delegates voted aye.[48]

WOMAN AND WOMEN OF COLOR

> "If the white groups do not realize that they are, in fact, fighting capitalism and racism, we do not have common bonds."
> —FRANCES M. BEAL, "Double Jeopardy" (1969)[49]

Middle-class white feminists of the 1960s could trace their lineage back to the women's righters of the mid-nineteenth century, who had been inspired by the abolitionist movement to realize that just as enslaved people needed freeing, so did white women. A hundred years later it was the Black civil rights movement that had reawakened in white women the impulse to fight for their own rights. Conversely, for many Black and Latina women in the 1960s, though their feminism had been triggered by sexism in racial-justice movements, it was mainstream feminism that gave them a language to use in their fight, even as they focused their battles differently.[50] Yet despite the cross-fertilization between the feminism of women of color and that of white women, the movements were sharply divided.

There had been several women of color among the founding members and officers of NOW: the Puerto Rican businesswoman Inez Casiano; the Mexican American lawyer Graciela Olivarez; and Black women such as Aileen Hernandez, Pauli Murray, Florynce Kennedy (a lawyer), and Congresswoman Shirley Chisholm (a Democrat from New York). Hernandez had succeeded Friedan as national president. Yet few other women of color joined the organization. Even Murray, who had been central to NOW's founding, distanced herself after attending NOW's second national conference. "I saw no Catholic sisters, no women of ethnic minorities other than about five Negro women, and obviously no women who represent the poor," she complained.[51]

Few women of color found a home in NOW because their biggest challenges were very different from those of typical NOW members. For most Black women, economic realities meant that they had always had to work, even if they were married: they had seldom been placed on a pedestal that they needed to jump off of. "Happy Housewife" propaganda had never been aimed at them. "Gender equality" was not the same issue for them as it was for whites, because Black women were already, as Eleanor Holmes Norton observed, "roughly equal" to Black men—just as they had been in the days of slavery, when their gender had not saved them from abuse.[52]

In fact, as Assistant Secretary of Labor Daniel Patrick Moynihan saw it, Black women were more than equal: they were their family's matriarchs, which was not a good thing. As Moynihan declared in his infamous 1965 report, *The Negro Family: The Case for National Action*, it was Black matriarchy that was the "fundamental problem" of Black people and at the root of Black inequality. The Black matriarchy was seriously out of line with the rest of American society, Moynihan said, and it must end because it "impose[d] a crushing burden on the Negro male."[53] Moynihan, a liberal whose study was in support of President Johnson's War on Poverty, was seriously misguided in his simplistic assessments. But he was right that the woman in Black working-class society was very different from his own ideal of woman, which had been based on a 1950s notion of the white middle-class housewife. Never mind that many of those white middle-class housewives were trying very hard by 1965 to escape precisely what Moynihan was idealizing.

Whether or not Black women held power in their families, they were permitted little acknowledged power in their community as it fought for civil rights. For some, this was a source of frustration as they continued their work in the struggle. Ella Baker, who had been passed over when the Southern Christian Leadership Conference was ready to hire an official head in 1957, went on to form another crucial Black civil rights group in 1960, after she quit the conference. Baker brought together college students who were part of the lunch-counter sit-ins and exhorted them that now they must struggle for something "much bigger than a hamburger or even a giant-sized Coke." She organized them into the Student Nonviolent Coordinating Committee (SNCC), which played a major role in the Freedom Riders and Black voter registration drives in the South. Yet despite her crucial role in the fight for Black civil rights, dating all the way back to 1930, Baker expected that she would be virtually lost to history. As she told the historian Gerda Lerner, it had been "sort of second nature" to Black women not to push themselves into the limelight, regardless of what they had accomplished. Yet acquiescence to "second nature" brought bitterness. Baker wistfully confessed to Lerner in 1970, a period of heightened feminist consciousness, that some young activists had been telling her "if I had not been a woman, I would have been well-known in certain places, and perhaps held certain kinds of positions."[54]

Ironically, the SNCC, which Baker had started, was so dismissive of women that eventually its female members grew angry. They had been as active as the men in keeping the organization running, yet only the men were allowed to be visible leaders, the women complained—and in 1964 they began to question the justice of what had long been taken for granted. Ruby Smith Robinson, a SNCC staffer, had dropped out of Spelman College to participate in pickets and sit-ins. She had been beaten, had shed blood for civil rights, had been arrested, and had even served time on a chain gang for her work in the movement. But despite her sacrifices and those of other women activists, in SNCC, Robinson complained, woman's chief role was as office lackey. In the spring of 1964, Robinson led women staffers in a feminist sit-in. They did not speak, they did not type letters, they did not answer the phones. They "sat-in," as Robinson had done in race protests. It was a dramatic statement. Yet after a while, unhappy about disrupting the work of SNCC, the women capitulated. The strike changed nothing.[55]

That November, at a SNCC retreat in Waveland, Mississippi, two white women staffers, Mary King and Casey Hayden (who had been reading Simone de Beauvoir's *The Second Sex*), submitted an anonymous position paper to the SNCC leadership. They had not signed their names, they wrote, because they feared they would be ridiculed. The paper was another litany of complaints about the way the men of SNCC treated the women. No matter how "competent, qualified and experienced" a woman was, the paper charged, she was assigned to "female" jobs—"typing, desk work, telephone work, filing, library work, cooking." If a woman was allowed even a bit of a leadership role, she was "required to defer to men for a final decision." The authors accused SNCC men, Black and white, of condescension and paternalism. They compared the men's sexism to the racism they had joined the organization to fight. "Assumptions of male supremacy are as widespread and deep-rooted and very much as crippling to the woman as assumptions of white supremacy are to the Negro," the women wrote. But like the strike six months earlier, the position paper changed nothing. As the writers recalled, it "caused hardly a ripple."[56]

Except that the evening after the paper was submitted at the retreat, Stokely Carmichael, a leader in SNCC, famously remarked (jokingly, according to some accounts), "What is the position of woman in SNCC? Prone."[57]

Robinson, who led the 1964 office protest, was elected executive secretary of SNCC in 1966. This was the highest rank a woman had ever held in the organization. But it made some SNCC staffers uncomfortable to be "bossed" by a woman. "Big Mama," they called her hostilely.[58] Carmichael, elected chairman of SNCC in the same year, refocused the organization, declaring it would henceforth be devoted to Black nationalism. Carmichael coined the phrase "Black Power," disinvited the organization's white members, and made an alliance with the newly formed and supermasculinist Black Panthers. Women feared that they would have even less of a voice.

Frances Beal had witnessed it all. Beal was a feisty young woman—Black, Native American, and Russian Jewish—who had quit the NAACP in disgust because the leadership opposed pickets and sit-ins. In SNCC she helped establish a Black Women's Liberation Committee, though she was careful to say that the group rejected the term "feminist." "Feminist," the committee agreed, meant "women who put female first." "Feminist" elided the issues of race and class, which were equally important to Black women. But Beal was bothered by the new influence in SNCC of the militantly macho Panthers, whose spokesman, Eldridge Cleaver, told women students in a 1968 speech at Stanford University that their big role in the revolution was to exercise "pussy power." "You're talking about liberation and freedom half the night on the racial side, and all of a sudden men are going to turn around and start talking about putting you in your place," Beal groused about SNCC's growing machismo. When she complained to SNCC men, she was called a "dyke" and accused of "dividing the movement."[59]

In her 1969 pamphlet *Double Jeopardy: To Be Black and Female*, Beal emphasized again that Black women's liberation was different from the white women's liberation movement. Of course, Black women were enraged by their derogation even among Black men, but the Black women's movement, Beal wrote, was also concerned with the problems of "our husbands, fathers, brothers, and sons [who] have been emasculated, lynched, and brutalized." For that she laid the blame on capitalism and other white social forces that misled Black women into accepting lies that tore them asunder from their men—such as "Black men are shiftless and lazy, otherwise they would get a job and support their families as they ought to."[60] Beal's pamphlet navigated difficult territory, exhorting Black women to defy "pussy power" ideas without sacrificing class and race coalitions.

But Beal's group ultimately broke from SNCC over its machismo and in 1970 became the Black Women's Alliance. It soon morphed again, forming coalitions with other women of color—Puerto Rican, Mexican American, Asian American, and Native American—in a Third World Women's Alliance. The Third World Women's Alliance called their newspaper *Triple Jeopardy,* declaring in its pages that they were Socialists, devoted to fighting their "oppression as workers, as third world people, and as women." Long before 1989, when Kimberlé Crenshaw coined the term "intersectionality," Beal and the Third World Women's Alliance were concerned with the intersections of discriminations: "woman" had no meaning separate from race and class, they said. That became the major tenet of their movement.[61]

The Third World Women's Alliance was an urban phenomenon: Latina women outside of cities had fewer outlets to question their cultures' traditional ideas of woman. But in California, where men and women from Mexico comprised the majority of farm workers, it was a fight for higher wages that encouraged Chicana women to stretch boundaries. Jessie Lopez de la Cruz, a farmworker and the first Chicana to organize field workers, had been taught by her immigrant parents that "the woman just walked behind her husband and kept quiet, no matter what the husband does."[62] But even as a child, she had worked alongside men. By the time she was thirteen she was lifting twelve-foot sacks of cotton that weighed over 100 pounds. She was barely five feet tall, but she was compact and sturdy, and she prided herself on matching the farmworker men in the money they earned. Even after she married and bore six children, she continued working because farmworkers could not survive on the man's wages alone and needed all family members to bring in money.

De la Cruz had never heard feminist rhetoric before—her reading had consisted of *True Romance* magazine—but she heard it from Cesar Chavez, who came to organize in the fields where she hoed beets. Chavez was urging women workers to help unionize along with the men. If they could go out to the field to work, they could certainly go to union meetings, Chavez said when he visited her and her husband in their home. For de la Cruz it was an epiphany. On her kitchen wall she had hung a poster of Emiliano Zapata and the Zapatistas, who had defied Mexican landowners and demanded economic justice. Chavez had inspired her to think that women too should be part of the struggle for economic justice.

But when she tried to organize the men with whom she worked, she had to battle what she called "the old customs of Mexico." The men informed her that they believed in unionizing, but they were "not taking orders from women." She turned to organizing the women instead, telling them that times had changed, that "it's way past the time when our husbands could say, 'You have to do as I say.'" She led them in strikes, getting them to swell the picket lines, and brought little armies of them to invade offending farms. They brandished "Huelga!" flags, their only weapon, and they scared off scabs. De la Cruz never managed to get many men to join the offensives she organized, but in 1968—perhaps in an indication of the changes wrought from the beginning of the decade to its later years—she was selected to run the hiring hall of the United Farm Workers (UFW), where both men and women went to find their next union job.[63]

The UFW had been founded in 1962 by Cesar Chavez and Dolores Huerta. It was Huerta who had convinced Chavez that women must join in the fight to unionize farmworkers. Huerta, a middle-class college graduate, had been a young teacher when she became aware of the problems of working-class Chicanos whose poverty she saw in her students: they were coming to school hungry. She began volunteering in the community, doing "woman's work" by registering voters for the Community Service Organization—a Mexican American rights group in Stockton, California, whose executive director was Chavez. By the time Huerta began working with Chavez, she had already given birth to seven children (she would eventually have four more), but that did not slow her down.

Huerta was disarming: petite and pretty, with intense dark eyes and long black hair, she was dazzling in her passion and eloquence. She challenged the notions of woman in her community with a vengeance. Her boldness upset Father Thomas McCullough, a priest who had started a local group called the Agricultural Workers Association. He told her in no uncertain terms that organizing "was no place for a woman." That did not slow her down, either. She rose to a paid position as political director of the Community Service Organization, and she became a savvy lobbyist with a flair for the dramatic. She brought hundreds of poor Latinas to Sacramento, where they camped outside legislative offices until politicians agreed to sponsor public assistance reforms that would help Mexican American families. With Chavez she dreamed up the idea of a farmworkers union. Together they began organizing in the San Joaquin Valley, the richest agribusiness area in the country. Huerta took the northern half of the valley and Chavez took the southern.[64]

They agreed, when they formed the union, that she would be vice president and Chavez would be president. She coined the union's motto, "*Sí, Se Puede*" (Yes, we can). In 1966, together with Chavez, Huerta led farmworkers on a 340-mile march from Delano to Sacramento to call attention to their strike against grape growers who had refused to recognize the union. She was the union's chief negotiator, too, and was responsible for its first significant success: a collective bargaining contract with Schenley wineries, a company that had been dependent on the grapes that San Joaquin Valley workers picked. As the Federal Bureau of Investigation (FBI) acknowledged in its file on her, Huerta became one of the best-known faces of the union. A 1965 FBI report on subversive activity described her (with a bit of grudging admiration) as the "driving force on the picket lines" who "daily inspires the pickets and their cause." She was a reincarnation of Emma Goldman. "Don't be a marshmallow. Walk the street with us into history!" Huerta yelled at farmworkers who were reluctant to join the pickets.[65]

Despite her successes, there were men in the union who refused to work with her. It was unwritten policy that even when strikers congregated in the mornings to go out on strike, it was always men who led them. "We have a lot of machismo here, and I'm not going to take it anymore," Huerta shot back at farmworkers' male chauvinism. The only woman on the union's executive committee, she kept a running tally of how many times during each meeting the men made remarks offensive to women—and she reported the number to them at the meeting's end.[66]

Huerta traveled throughout the country to encourage grape boycotts until growers yielded. Those who might have been relieved to see a little Hispanic woman walk into the negotiating room learned that their stereotypes did not apply, as one bewildered grower remarked: "Dolores Huerta is crazy. She's a violent woman, where women, especially Mexican women, are usually peaceful and pleasant." Huerta defied all notions of woman, despite having eleven children. She admitted to hating the limits of wifedom: cleaning the house and doing her hair were not for her, she said. She often left her children to be taken care of by union members or friends. "My life is the union, every minute of it," she told the *Chicago Tribune* on a trip to the Midwest to encourage grape boycotts.[67]

When Chavez died in 1993, Huerta was his heir apparent. She was, after all, the cofounder of the UFW. But despite that fact, despite her having served the union with single-minded devotion for thirty years, and despite her triumphs in winning higher wages and safer conditions for the farmworkers, the UFW's board members could not bring themselves to select a woman to replace Chavez. Instead they chose Arturo Rodriguez, Chavez's son-in-law, as the UFW's second president. It would take another quarter-century before a woman would become president of the UFW.

Urban Latinas, inspired by women such as de la Cruz and Huerta, also tried to push beyond the notions of woman that their community honored. In 1966, Chicana students in East Los Angeles became members of Young Citizens for Community Action. The staid moniker and subdued approach of the group was short-lived. As happened in SNCC, the imagination of the men in the group was captured by the supermasculine militancy of the Black Panthers. Young Citizens for Community Action soon morphed into the Brown Berets. The women joined the men in declaring themselves to be Chicano nationalists. They donned bush jackets and other paramilitary apparel. They drilled and marched in Chicano protests against the war in Vietnam, chanting "Brown Is Beautiful!" alongside the men and demanding "Chicano Power!" Brown Beret groups were soon established in twenty-eight cities around the West and the Midwest.

But despite their military look, Brown Beret women were usually assigned to "women's jobs" in the organization—writing letters, answering phones, cooking for Brown Beret parties and cleaning up, and typing articles for the Brown Beret newspaper *La Causa* about the men's exploits and achievements. The successes of Huerta notwithstanding, Chicano cultural nationalism was tied up with the notion that men led, and if woman stepped outside her traditional domestic role it should be only to assist the men.

Yet many of the Chicanas in Brown Berets had already broken loose from tradition. They were college students or they were supporting themselves in white-collar jobs or as teachers or nurses. Some even drove cars. They wanted to do serious work and help build community institutions. They saw themselves as revolutionaries, not as wives or girlfriends or as helpers of the revolutionaries. In Los Angeles, the conflict came to a head over space. Brown Beret women were permitted to open the East Los

Angeles Free Clinic in a small building on Whittier Boulevard. The clinic was their brainchild and purview. They chose as its director Gloria Arellanes, a no-nonsense, self-described "big mouth" and big woman who was five feet eight inches tall and weighed almost 300 pounds. Arellanes got licensed nurses and doctors, most of them white, to work as volunteers. She got local hospitals to donate pharmaceuticals and testing supplies. The young and poor of the barrio, who did not trust establishment doctors or could not afford to go to them, flocked to the clinic. At its peak, the clinic was serving over a hundred patients a night.[68]

However, Brown Beret men on the antiwar Chicano Moratorium Committee began to hold meetings at the clinic. They not only appropriated the women's space, but they also brought their guns with them. Even Arellanes, daunting as she may have been, could not control them. She and the other Chicana clinic volunteers worried that the police might raid the place and that what they had lovingly built would be destroyed. When they could not convince the men to meet elsewhere, Arellanes and the other women resigned from the organization en masse, complaining: "We have been treated as nothings, and not as Revolutionary sisters. We have found that the Brown Beret men have oppressed us more than the pig system has."[69]

They formed their own organization, for women only. "Chicanas, find yourself!" they wrote in a flyer they distributed in the barrio. "Do you have a part in the Movement? Are you satisfied? Are your ideas suppressed? Come and CREATE your ideas! Help CREATE Las Adelitas de Aztlan!" The name they chose for the group honored a Mexican *soldadera*, the legendary woman soldier named Adelita, who fought beside men in the 1910–1920 Mexican Revolution. The Adelitas were careful to distinguish themselves from the women's liberation movement—which, they claimed, was narrowly focused on the rights of the individual woman. But Brown Beret men accused them anyway of copying white women and betraying the Chicano cause. *Vendidas* (sellouts), the men called them, as well as *malinches* (traitors to the race), *agringada* (whitewashed), and (worst of all) "women's libbers."[70]

The Adelitas replied to the insults that yes, they wanted women's rights: they wanted the Chicana to step beyond the threshold of her home and take her place as an equal with man in society. But they also wanted better housing, health care, jobs, and education for the entire Chicano community. They were not joining white "women's libbers," they emphasized. They just wanted to be given credit as "Revolutionary sisters."

But they remained a lonely minority among Chicana women. In 1969, the year before the Adelitas founders resigned from the Brown Berets, a Chicano youth conference was held in Denver, Colorado. The Chicanas who attended the only workshop on women delivered a one-sentence report at the plenary session: "It was the consensus of the group that the Chicana woman does not want to be liberated."[71] There was no elaboration.

Nevertheless, the sentiments that the Adelitas were the first to voice among Chicanas spread. The new Chicana activists echoed the Adelitas in distinguishing themselves from mainstream feminists. As one Chicana feminist phrased it, the white women's liberation movement "has rejected the traditional family, [but] for us, the family has been a source of unity and our major defense against oppression." Yet Chicana feminists also demanded what tradition had denied them, a presence outside the family and a public voice. Their desire for a voice, they said, had little to do with self-fulfillment; rather, it grew out of their desire to serve their Raza. Enriqueta Vasquez, who wrote for the Chicano newspaper *El Grito del Norte*, summed up their stance in pronouncing herself to be *"Chicana primera,"* but also proclaiming that Chicanas now "realize that they must begin to develop and function as complete human beings." La Raza would not be liberated until its women were liberated, she wrote.[72]

However, Latinas were still torn. At the National Raza Women's Conference held in Houston, Texas, in May 1971, a group of Chicana students from the University of California, Los Angeles and California State University, Los Angeles—members of Movimiento Estudiatil Chicano de Aztlan (MEChA)—staged a planned walkout, protesting that a conference devoted to women's issues alone was "divisive . . . separating Chicanas from Chicanos." Those who stayed were careful to acknowledge that Chicanas suffered not just from sexism but also from racism and classism. Yet they also held firm in demanding a lot of what the mainstream feminist movement demanded: woman's control over her own body through free legal abortions and access to birth control, twenty-four-hour childcare centers, and an end to the sweeping patriarchal powers of institutions such as the Catholic church. They did not call for the abolition of the traditional family, as many white feminists were doing. However, they declared, "Chicana motherhood should not preclude educational, political, social, and economic advancement." They reenvisioned the Chicana woman. Though she would maintain her old role as wife and mother, she would also have a presence far beyond the threshold of her home.[73]

Women had come into the 1960s carrying the baggage of the past, and the question of whether, how, or how much to divest often led to internecine conflicts. But the trend to defy essentialist ideas of woman was gaining momentum. Two women's demonstrations in Washington, DC— one in the early years of the 1960s, the other in the later years—are emblematic of the trajectory. In 1962, Women Strike for Peace marched on Washington against war, against nuclear testing, and in defense of women's right as mothers to influence the government. They were heirs of the nineteenth-century reformers who believed that society needed the moral voice of woman qua woman, with her special claims.

Despite their womanliness, the House Un-American Activities Committee, suspecting that the women were communists, subpoenaed the leaders to testify. A crowd of Women Strike for Peace members showed up in support of the leaders. They brought their children with them and even nursed their babies in the hearing room. The women who were interrogated and the women there to cheer them on were so disarming in their womanliness that one newspaper announced "Peace March Gals Make Red Hunters Look Silly."[74] In 1962, in the context of the feminine mystique, Women Strike for Peace seemed as bold as the Female Moral Reform Society of the preceding century, whose members also protested man's wrongheadedness with their womanliness.

In 1968, thousands of women again descended on the Capitol, this time to protest U.S. involvement in the war in Vietnam. The members of Women Strike for Peace once again claimed womanliness as their main credential. Many were clad in mourner's black because, they announced, as mothers they were in sympathy with all the American mothers who had lost sons in the Vietnam War.[75] But by now the women of Women Strike for Peace seemed to be from another era. A group that had formed a few months before the march, New York Radical Women, was no less antiwar than the women of the older group, but they hated the mother rhetoric and banners with such slogans as "War Is Bad for Our Children," which were the hallmark of Women Strike for Peace. War was bad for everyone, the New York Radical Women argued, and the sentimentality of Women Strike for Peace was downright counterrevolutionary.

The radicals showed up at the march carrying a dummy that they labeled "Corpse of Nurturing Femininity." They distributed flyers that announced, "You are joyfully invited to the burial of WEEPING WOMANHOOD who passed with a sigh to her Great Reward this Year of Our Lord 1968, after 3000 years of bolstering the egos of the war makers and aiding the cause of war." The radical women remonstrated with the members of Women Strike for Peace, urging them not to approach lawmakers in the old feminine guise of the tearful woman—who, the radicals argued, was "synonymous with powerlessness."[76] Their challenges ushered in a new generation of revolutionary women who would reject essentialist ideas that woman was "by nature" tender or selfless, or indeed that woman was anything "by nature."

13.
Radical Women and the Radical Woman

Radical women of the 1970s demanded transformations that would be revolutionary, earthshaking, and shocking. Those who were feminists jeered at the tameness of National Organization for Women (NOW)–type feminism. They called for bold confrontations with the enemy. Did men dub women who were too aggressive "bitches"? Well, women must assume their bitch identity with gusto, "The Bitch Manifesto" proclaimed in 1970. After all, what is a "bitch"? A bitch is "aggressive, assertive, domineering, overbearing, strong-minded, spiteful, hostile, direct, blunt, candid, competitive." A bitch disdains "femininity" because it is ineffectual. A bitch claims her right to androgyny. She refuses to live vicariously through a man. She demands a life of her own. A bitch embraces all the dynamic qualities that men have always hoarded for themselves while they reduced females to "woman." "A bitch"—not a "woman"—is who all women must aspire to be. "A bitch," the author of "The Bitch Manifesto" wrote with scatological élan, "takes shit from no one."[1]

RADICAL WOMEN

"A woman needs a man like a fish needs a bicycle."
—IRINA DUNN (1970)[2]

Radical women were the bad cops. Their well-publicized call to demolish everything that signified "woman" moved the locus of the center: what had once seemed to be outrageous feminist demands no longer seemed so far out. An equal rights amendment to the Constitution? A federal law that said female athletes in high school and college must be given the same opportunities that male athletes enjoyed? Legalized abortion? All came to be considered eminently reasonable in comparison to declarations that men were entirely disposable and proposals for mechanical wombs.

Radical women who had cut their teeth on the New Left were disgusted when they complained to New Left men about the oppressions visited on women and found the men to be as unenlightened as the most buttoned-down bougie. Anne Koedt and Shulamith Firestone had spent much of the 1960s earning "impeccable revolutionary credentials."[3] But like women in the Black and Chicano movements, they resented their brethren who believed that the role of women in the movement was—literally and figuratively—to make the coffee. Koedt and Firestone left the New Left men behind. In 1969, they cofounded New York Radical Feminists.

They became heretics to the New Left because they argued that "woman's oppressor" was obviously not capitalism alone. Women were being oppressed in noncapitalist countries too: look at Russia, China, and Cuba, they said. Even the revered Che Guevara had written ecstatically in *Guerilla Warfare*, his handbook for revolutionaries, that his own guerrilla movement had enjoyed having women along in the mountains because they could cook and serve the food. "Woman's oppressor is man!" radical feminists declared.[4]

They prided themselves on busting icons of all sorts. In "The Myth of the Vaginal Orgasm," a 1970 essay that was passed eagerly from hand to hand among feminists, Koedt took on the Freudians who had disseminated falsehoods in claiming that mature female sexuality depended on a woman's ability to attain orgasm through heterosexual vaginal intercourse. If a woman failed at the task, Freudians claimed, it was because she was frigid and neurotic. Koedt argued that that very idea was outrageously male-centered. Women knew that the clitoris and not the vagina was the primary organ of sexual pleasure. And clitoral pleasure was attainable homosexually or through masturbation just as easily—no, even more easily—than through heterosexual intercourse.[5] As a popular witticism proclaimed, even for sex "a woman needs a man like a fish needs a bicycle." It became a logo on radical feminists' T-shirts and a proclamation on posters that they hung above their beds.

By 1970, it was clear that the general public's interest was piqued by the colorful extremes of radical feminists. The media obliged. One newspaper predicted that the 1970s would bring "a far-reaching feminine [sic] revolution," which would "be to this new decade what the black revolution and youth rebellion were to the 1960s." As the *New York Times* observed, "almost every major publisher either has a feminist under contract or wishes he did." Shulamith Firestone, a twenty-five-year-old who had been supporting herself by nude modeling, waitressing, and painting portraits on sidewalks, spent a few months writing an intensely passionate screed that landed her a contract with the mainstream publisher William Morrow. Firestone declared in *The Dialectic of Sex: The Case for a Feminist Revolution* that the end goal of feminism must be to "crack through the most basic structures of our society." All distinctions of sex had to be abolished—particularly "woman's bondage to motherhood," the burdens on women of child bearing and child rearing. Only when that bondage came to an end would a woman regain ownership of herself and her body. And unless that happened, women would always be powerless.[6]

Indeed, Firestone called for the complete demolition of the nuclear family. In its place there would be collectives where children would be communally raised. The idea was not entirely new. Firestone echoed Henrietta Rodman and the New Women of the Feminist Alliance of 1914, who believed that women must be free of the prison of child rearing. But Firestone was more forceful in her rhetoric than Rodman could have dared to be in her day. Firestone went much further, too, suggesting *Brave New World*–type solutions to parturition, such as mechanical wombs that would liberate women from the job of reproduction.[7]

Firestone's publisher was right to bet on a yearning that many women felt in 1970 for drastic ideas to yank them free of what had been most sacred to womanhood. The book was promoted that season as Morrow's "major nonfiction release."[8] It became a best seller.

Kate Millett, the author of another 1970 feminist classic, *Sexual Politics*, had been head of the education committee of NOW but had left to join a livelier group—Koedt and Firestone's New York Radical Feminists. Millett's book, a reworking of her Columbia University PhD dissertation, was published by Doubleday, which gambled that a book (even one rife with footnotes) by a spirited and angry woman with impressive credentials could, in the climate of the day, have a vast readership. *Sexual Politics* was advertised in mainstream newspapers across the country as being by a "radical feminist"—clearly a selling point. Doubleday's gamble paid off. The book sold 10,000 copies in the first weeks and became a best seller when *Time* put a portrait of Millett on the cover of its August 31, 1970, issue.

Sexual Politics was a scathing (and entertaining) critique of woman-hating in the work of D. H. Lawrence, Henry Miller, and Norman Mailer, canonized writers who had been revered as sexual liberators. Millett argued that those venerated authors, whose novels pretended to celebrate sexuality, celebrated instead men's power over woman. She reduced the canonized writers to crass puerility. She showed that with adolescent fervor, Miller distinguished women by their sex parts: "that big, bushy thing," "that rose-bush," "huge teats." She called Mailer "a prisoner of the virility cult" and postulated that it was his "secret terror" of and fascination with homosexuality that drove him to "heterosexual posturing." To make her arguments, Millett peppered her analysis with graphic descriptions of sex from the novels. About a "liberating" love scene in Lawrence's *Lady Chatterley's Lover*, for instance, Millett sneered: "The phallus is all. Connie is 'cunt,' the thing acted upon, gratefully accepting the will of her master."[9]

"The Mao Tse-Tung of Women's Liberation," *Time* christened Millett. "The Karl Marx of the Women's Liberation Movement," the *Miami Herald* crowned her. One reviewer speculated with an apparent straight face that *Sexual Politics* "may rank in literary history some day with *Das Kapital* and *Mein Kampf*." Millet was soon being described not only as the movement's "principal theoretician" but as its "high priestess." She had long prided herself on her modest lifestyle as a bohemian leftist. Now major mainstream media attention led to the great commercial success of *Sexual Politics* and made her, as she noted with chagrin, "shamefully, painfully rich."[10]

The mainstream media had created a star, but not without ambivalence. *Sexual Politics*'s wildly radical potential to cause women to rebel against the "politics" of heterosexual sex, in which man comes out as mighty and woman comes out as demeaned, was newsworthy. But it was also troubling. The book compounded dangers in its effect on men. As one reviewer confessed, "it grabs the male ego where it hurts, [and] one can only squirm uncomfortably." Another reviewer, Irving Howe, a leading cultural critic of the day, was brutal in defending the male ego against Millett's book. *Sexual Politics*, he wrote in *Harper's*, was "a farrago of blunders, distortions, vulgarities, and plain nonsense."[11]

Millett, painfully shy and neurotically insecure, had been overwhelmed when her work was lionized. She was deflated when it was trashed. And then the trashing got personal. Millett had presented herself in media interviews as the wife of a Japanese sculptor, Fumio Yoshimura. She did not tell the media that she had married Yoshimura, a good friend, to keep him from being deported. But it was well known among feminists in New York that Millett had lesbian relationships, and when her fame reached its pinnacle, she was outed by a radical lesbian in one of her audiences who demanded that Millett tell the truth about herself. She did. Word spread beyond the audience. To the media, the flustered Millett admitted to being "bisexual," thinking perhaps that the term was less damning than "lesbian."

What had been happening—from the seventeenth century, when a female who did not act womanly was vilified by being called "Amazon," "manly," and "unnatural," to the twentieth century, when she was vilified by being called "lesbian" and "dyke"—happened again. *Time*, which had sent Millett into the stratosphere of stardom in August 1970 by its cover article about her, ran another article in December 1970 titled "Women's Lib: A Second Look." It said that Millett's admission had "contributed to the growing skepticism" about women's liberation and would discredit the entire movement. *Time* quoted at length from Howe's brutal takedown (written before Millett was outed), which referred to her as "a female impersonator." Aha, the *Time* reporter now wrote: Howe had "sensed her sexual ambiguity." The reporter dug up all the leading critics who had attacked Millett and feminism. "Can feminists think?" they had asked. "Do they know anything about biology? What about their maturity? Their morality? Their sexuality?" It was Betty Friedan's worst nightmare come true. The women's movement was being discredited by a "lavender menace."[12]

But for the first time, women circled the wagons to fight the lavender herring. Prominent feminists issued a statement deploring *Time*'s attack on Millett, which they called "sexual McCarthyism." Gloria Steinem (who would soon launch *Ms.*, the premier feminist magazine), along with

Susan Brownmiller (who was working on her classic book *Against Our Will: Men, Women and Rape*), Florynce Kennedy, Ti-Grace Atkinson, and over two dozen other leading lights in the movement, stood behind Millett at a press conference held at the Washington Square Methodist Church in Greenwich Village. They wore lavender armbands, inspired by the Danes who during World War II had worn yellow Star of David armbands to express their refusal to give the Danish Jews up to the Nazis. (Friedan was reported to have been invited to join the press conference and given a lavender armband, which she was said to have thrown on the ground and stomped on.)[13]

Millett sat on the dais, at a table banked with a dozen media microphones, surrounded by her supporters. "The time when you could call a woman a lesbian and expect her to drop dead is over," Millett read from a statement she had prepared along with six other leaders who called themselves "feminists and lesbians." They were defanging the timeworn tactic of intimidation. Yes, there were lesbians in the feminist movement, Millett read, and yes, the movement supported lesbians—because women and homosexuals were "struggling toward a common goal, a society free from defining and categorizing people by virtue of gender and/or sexual preference."[14]

Radical feminists not only continued to circle the wagons to fight the lavender herring. Many also came to embrace a lesbian identity themselves: it was the next logical step in their radical feminism, they argued. Atkinson, the Southern belle who had been the first president of New York NOW and had metamorphosed into a flaming revolutionary, observed in her 1973 essay "Lesbianism and Feminism" that when she and other NOW members had picketed the *New York Times* in 1968 to demand that the newspaper put an end to help-wanted ads by sex, they had been taunted by onlookers who called them "lesbians." Atkinson claimed to have been puzzled, asking herself what the connection was between lesbianism and the demand that women not be relegated to jobs as telephone operators or stenographers. "Whenever the enemy keeps lobbing bombs into some area you consider unrelated to your defense, it's worth investigating," Atkinson decided. She concluded that not only was use of the term "lesbian" intended to scare those who were fighting to expand who a woman might be, but that women who were lesbians truly were in the forefront of the fight. In fact, a heterosexual feminist made as little sense as a World War II French soldier who was "serving in the French army from 9 to 5, then trotting 'home' to Germany for supper and overnight."[15]

Among radical feminists, the lesbian came to be seen as the true resistance fighter.

Small consciousness-raising groups, devoted to discussing how sexual politics affected women's lives, popped up in feminist circles everywhere. A raised consciousness led to an overwhelming conclusion: men were able to dominate women because women had been socialized to let them do so. If "the personal is political," as a popular feminist essay proclaimed, a feminist had to rethink her relations with men. For many radical feminists, rethinking led to the conclusion that intimacy with other women matched their convictions better than heterosexuality did. Even women who were not attracted to other women sexually called themselves "political lesbians." A 1984 comic novel looked back on the 1970s to capture the mood that pervaded radical feminist circles. "One day half the women's movement came out as lesbians," Sarah Schulman wrote. "It was like we were all sitting around and the ice cream truck came, and all of a sudden I looked around and everyone ran out for ice cream."[16]

But many radical feminists who chose to become lesbians were entirely serious about their choice. Rita Mae Brown, a magnetic dark-haired beauty and the author of *Rubyfruit Jungle* (1973), the best-selling lesbian novel since the lugubrious *Well of Loneliness*, became a pied piper of a lesbian-feminist movement. Brown founded Radicalesbians, whose manifesto, "The Woman-Identified Woman," declared: "The lesbian is the rage of all women condensed to a point of explosion." Radicalesbians made "lesbian" virtually synonymous with "feminist," presenting the lesbian as a woman who "acts in accordance with her inner compulsion to be a more complete and free human being than her society ... cares to allow her." Nineteenth-century sexologists had claimed that lesbians suffered from congenital inversion—that is, they were born with their malady. Radical feminists claimed that the sexologists were wrong: any woman could choose to be a lesbian, and for anyone deeply concerned about sexual politics, lesbianism was the only logical choice. Brown declared of her own choice: "I became a lesbian because the culture I live in is violently anti-woman. How could I, a woman, participate in a culture that denies my humanity? How can any woman in touch with herself participate in this culture? To give a man support and love before giving it to a woman is to support that culture, that power system."[17]

It was a remarkable leap from a decade or two earlier, when lesbians were depicted by "mental health" gurus such as Albert Ellis as being "not merely neurotics [but] actually borderline or outright psychotics" because they had failed to make a heterosexual adjustment.[18] Among radical feminists, love between women was the manifestation of mental health, and female heterosexuality was tantamount to masochism. Lesbian feminists even reclaimed the scare words: they called themselves dykes, and they gave their magazines titles such as *Amazon* and *Dyke*. They disassociated themselves from the word "woman," which they said signified a history of the female's subservience to man. They were "womyn" (after the Greek root "gyn"), "womben" (referring to "womb"), or "wommin" or any other variation that avoided the "man" root.

In 1973, a group of Black feminist friends met often in the apartment of a founding member of NOW, the lawyer Florynce Kennedy. She was a vibrant personality, partial to cowboy hats and wont to respond to fools by raising her middle finger defiantly in the air. She was notorious for her quick tongue: "If men could get pregnant abortion would be a sacrament," she said in campaigning for *Roe v. Wade*. "There are very few jobs that actually require a penis or a vagina. All other jobs should be open to anybody," she said in protesting segregated help-wanted ads. Now Kennedy cajoled her friends into starting a national organization that would address the concerns of Black women, since neither NOW nor radical feminist groups were doing it sufficiently.[19]

Margaret Sloan, the first Black editor at *Ms.*, and Eleanor Holmes Norton, New York City's human rights commissioner, were convinced to take charge. They called a press conference announcing the start of the National Black Feminist Organization. Following on the headlines-grabbing Black Power movement and radical feminism, their announcement was hot news. The Associated Press and United Press International sent the story out to papers all over the country. To Sloan's and Norton's surprise, they were inundated with over 200 phone calls from Black feminists everywhere, ready to start chapters in their own towns.[20]

The National Black Feminist Organization issued an angry "Statement of Purpose" in which they argued that Black women were being deprived, by white women and Black men, of their own redefinition of woman. The women's liberation movement, they wrote, "has been characterized as the exclusive property of so-called white middle-class women, and any black women involved in this movement have been seen [by Black activists] as selling out, dividing the race, and an assortment of nonsensical epithets" (such as "lesbian," "dyke," and "bull dagger"). The organization's statement decried the "cruel suffering" of "living the phenomenon of being black and female, in a country that is *both* racist and sexist." They blasted white culture's depiction of Black women as "grinning Beulahs, castrating Sapphires, and pancake-box Jemimas," and they reminded the Black liberation movement that "there cannot be liberation for half the race." Finally, they pledged to "develop a politics that was anti-racist, unlike those of white women, and antisexist, unlike those of black and white men." Margaret Sloan, who became the organization's chair, was a lesbian, but unlike radical feminists, neither she nor the organization had an interest in making a political issue of it. The National Black Feminist Organization's statement said nothing of the "cruel suffering" imposed on Black women who dared call themselves lesbians.[21]

But some Black women were also becoming radicalized in their feminism. Among the members of the Boston chapter of the National Black Feminist Organization were several stars, including Audre Lorde (who in 1974 won the National Book Award for her poetry), Gloria Hull, Barbara Smith, and Chirlane McCray (later the wife of Mayor Bill DeBlasio and thus first lady of New York City). All were openly lesbian and far more radical than the leaders of the stiffly respectable National Black Feminist Organization. In 1974 they broke away and formed their own group, in which the lesbian part of their identity could be as prominent as the other parts. They called themselves the Combahee River Collective to commemorate the 1863 raid in which Harriet Tubman rescued scores of enslaved people on the bank of the Combahee River in South Carolina.

In their April 1977 "Combahee River Collective Statement" the women identified themselves as feminists and lesbians—and, in an important corrective to the notion that those categories signified white women, as Black. They made a clean break with white lesbian feminists, whose interest in Black problems seemed to the Combahee women to be phony or insulting. Lorraine Bethel, a graduate of Yale University and a Combahee member, summed up the group's exasperation in her poem "What Chou Mean We, White Girl? Or The Cullud Lesbian Feminist Declaration of Independence (Dedicated to the Proposition that All Women Are Not Equal, i.e., Identical/ly Oppressed":

> I am so tired of talking to others
> translating my life to the deaf, the blind
> the "I really want to know what your life is like without giving
>   up any of my privileges to live it" white women
> the "I want to live my white life with Third World women's
>   style and keep my skin class privileges" dykes.[22]

The Combahee River Collective distinguished itself from both white groups and other Black groups. The members made clear that though they were fighting on behalf of women, they had no intention of dropping out of the fight on behalf of their race. But, as they emphasized, "we struggle together with Black men against racism, while we also struggle with Black men about sexism." In this they were not different from the Black Women's Alliance that Frances Beal had started a few years earlier. They talked about the complexity of their battles, declaring that "the major systems of oppression are interlocking." They were Black and women and feminists and lesbians and—though they were middle class by virtue of their education—they identified with the working class. They were the first to use the phrase "identity politics," and they pledged to fight not just for Black women and lesbians but on all fronts—against racial, sexual, heterosexual, and class oppression—neglecting no part of their multiple identities.[23]

Chicana lesbians too, aware of their "intersectionality," found white women's organizations irrelevant or worse. The pioneering Chicana theorist Gloria Anzaldúa—who suffered, just as white feminists often did, from what she called "the onus" to marry and have children or be made to feel like a failed woman—wrote about why it was nevertheless impossible to make common cause with white feminists. They either ignored the needs of women of color, tried to talk for women of color ("a rape of our tongue"), or (worst of all) acted like they bore the "white women's burden." Anzaldúa compared white feminists' noxious ignorance about women of color to that of the monkey in a Sufi story who, "seeing a fish in the water[,] rushes to rescue it from drowning by carrying it up into the branches of a tree." Who women of color were or wanted to be was for women of color alone to decide, without the butting in of monkeys, Anzaldúa declared.[24]

However, that position elided complexities—as she acknowledged by calling into question simplistic essentialist ideas about "the woman of color." Anzaldúa, who grew up in a little Texas town bordering Mexico, positioned herself to see, literally and figuratively, borderlands, borderland conflicts, and the battles of multiple identities—complexities that went even beyond intersectionality. If her identity is brown, what will she do with the history of her German grandmother, who has fair skin and blue eyes and "coils of once blond hair"? If she pledges allegiance to her Chicano world, what will she do with her allegiance to the "Third World," which includes her Black and Asian friends? If her allegiance is to women and lesbians, what about her allegiance to a socialist revolution, the New Age, magic, and the occult? If she wants to live in the working-class world, how can she also live in the literary world? Anzaldúa concluded finally that "I belong to myself and not to any one people."[25] Her implicit questions complicated the idea of feminist identity politics: If one has conflicting identities, how is it possible to choose an "identity" from which to practice identity politics?

Internal conflicts arose even over the term "feminist," which became controversial for women of color. "Feminist" was associated in the media and everywhere else with a white woman's movement. The Black writer Alice Walker, whose 1982 novel *The Color Purple* had just won both the Pulitzer Prize and the National Book Award, coined a new term in 1983 that she claimed was more consonant with Black culture: "womanist." A Black mother might tell her daughter, "you acting womanish" if the girl's behavior was willful, audacious, outrageous, or beyond what is appropriate for a young female, Walker wrote. "Womanist" derived from "womanish." A "womanist" too is willful, audacious, and outrageous: she refuses to act the way she is supposed to. A "womanist" is different from white feminists because she is committed to "an entire people, male *and* female," Walker declared—while elaborating that a womanist "loves other women, sexually and/or nonsexually. Appreciates and prefers women's culture . . . and women's strength." In fact, Walker conceded, a womanist actually is a feminist, but she is a feminist of color—deep color, as in "Womanist is to feminist as purple is to lavender."[26]

OUTLAWS

> "We are not picketing in front of bra factories now. . . . This is not a self-indulgent bullshit women's movement. . . . Bullets are not going to stop us. Threats are not going to stop us. We are living behind enemy lines."
> —BERNARDINE DOHRN (1969)[27]

Radical feminists who declared men to be power-obsessed even in lovemaking—or dreamed up science-fiction alternatives to childbearing, or held bra-burning protests and funerals for "Weeping Womanhood"—regarded feminists who simply wanted equal pay or sovereignty over their own bodies as naïve in their failure to understand the deeper roots of the injustices they suffered. But radical feminists were "out-radicalized" by ultraradical women who regarded them as merely self-indulgent.

The ultraradicals claimed to be fighting not only for women's issues but also against racism and imperialism. They embraced an outlaw identity, even putting their own lives (and the lives of others) on the line in armed struggle.[28]

The ultraradicals challenged every essentialist aspect of the notion of woman, but most pointedly the one that attributed tenderness to her. Intrinsic to woman was that she was—as a writer in 1836 described her—"the gentler sex whose sympathies are always more soothing than man's." Anomalies—ungentle women—did appear from time to time, such as Bonnie Parker, who went on a violent crime spree with Clyde Barrow during the 1930s. But their rarity proved the rule. Even into the 1950s, "the gentler sex" was a descriptor of woman. When the epithet was used ironically, it was usually because a female had accomplished some feat such as swimming the rough waters of the Catalina Channel.[29]

In 1950, when the Federal Bureau of Investigation (FBI) began publishing its list of America's "most wanted" fugitives from the law, it was practically inconceivable that women could be violent enough to warrant appearance on the list. For its first eighteen years, the list was all male. In 1968, Ruth Eisemann-Schier had the dubious distinction of being the first woman to land on the list. She had assisted the man she loved in a bizarre kidnapping. In 1969, Marie Arrington appeared on the list after escaping from prison. She had been convicted of killing the public defender's stenographer because the public defender had failed to win acquittal for Arrington's son and daughter, who were convicted of robbery and forgery.

In 1970, four women—all in their twenties, college-educated, and from middle-class families—appeared on the list: not for crimes committed as girlfriends or as mothers gone berserk, but as instigators and perpetrators of violence in the name of political convictions. Post-office walls all over America displayed their black-and-white photos: four young women, looking like studious college students or pouty sorority girls. All were part of the ultraradical left.

The four women emerged in an era when middle-class college students and professors, who often skewed left, encouraged one another in passionate politics. They felt deeply about the multiple injustices perpetrated by America—the senseless waste of life in war (this time in Vietnam), racism, classism, and the many facets of sexism. This was not the first time that women in America had been deeply disturbed by all those injustices and had worked to ameliorate them. But now, for the first time, some young women made their political convictions felt through violence involving guns and bombs. The idea of woman as "the gentler sex" would have been laughable to them if they had ever heard of the epithet. A Students for a Democratic Society pamphlet titled *Women Rise Up* explained, "We're women fighters and we're part of a Revolutionary Army that's gonna take this country away from the few and give it back to all the people including women. We need women fighting to win this battle, and we can't let women remain slaves under capitalism." They were soldiers in a war against the various sins of what they called "Amerikkka." Their uniform—jeans and a denim work shirt, worn by both genders in the unisex styles that were popular on college campuses—helped obliterate vestiges of femininity.[30] If an excess of anger in ultraradical young men boiled over into violence, why would it not do the same in ultraradical young women?

Three of the women on the FBI's list were identified as belonging to the Weathermen, a far-left revolutionary youth movement whose members were pledged not only to the destruction of U.S. imperialism and the achievement of a classless world but also to the rising of women.[31] All three had started out as traditional nice girls who would have fit seamlessly into an earlier ideal of woman. Katherine Ann Power had received a scholarship to Brandeis University after winning a national Betty Crocker Homemaker Award. Her roommate at Brandeis, Susan Saxe, had grown up in a conventional upper-middle-class Jewish family. She had been a Girl Scout and an honor student since elementary school. But the 1970s was a transforming time for many bright students, and Power and Saxe were transformed: by the unpopular war in Vietnam, the campus climate that lent itself to dramatic action in protest of anything establishment, and the radical feminist movement that told women they had a right to express their fury. Saxe and Power became organizers of classroom walkouts for the National Student Strike Force after four students were killed by National Guardsmen in an antiwar protest on May 4, 1970, at Kent State University. It seemed that the war had been brought home to America.

Through the National Student Strike Force, Saxe and Power had met Stanley Bond, who was at Brandeis in a special program for ex-offenders out on parole. Believing that the war would never be stopped without revolutionary action, the two young women teamed up with Bond and two other former convicts, and on the evening of September 23, 1970, they broke into a National Guard Armory in Newburyport, Massachusetts. There they "liberated" rifles, blasting caps, 400 rounds of ammunition, walkie-talkies, and a green duffel bag on which was printed "COMPANY A 101st ENGINEER BATTALION." They intended to donate everything to the Black Panthers, whose "armed struggle against police power" they encouraged. A few days later they robbed the State Street Bank and Trust Company in Boston of $23,000. They hoped to use the money for antiwar protests. In the course of the bank heist, one of the former convicts shot and killed a police officer. Under the law, the two women were as culpable as if they had themselves pulled the trigger. They landed on the FBI's list when they became fugitives, hiding out for a time on radical feminist communes in Connecticut and Kentucky.[32]

The third woman, Bernardine Dohrn, had been a high-school cheerleader in the 1950s. She too was transformed in the new zeitgeist. Rather than get married to a Whitefish Bay High School quarterback, she went to college and then to law school at the University of Chicago, from which she graduated in 1967. At the height of opposition to the war in Vietnam, Dohrn became the counsel for Chicago's draft resisters and a leader in Students for a Democratic Society. Her movie-star good looks made her legendary on the left. "The she-goddess of the revolution," she was called by her admirers, though the only nod she gave to her femininity was through the miniskirts and sexy thigh-high boots of Italian leather that she wore.[33]

Dohrn's militancy grew with her growing opposition to what she saw as American imperialism, racism, and a host of other crimes. She broke from Students for a Democratic Society and was soon the most prominent member of the Weathermen. J. Edgar Hoover, the head of the FBI, testified in a report to Congress that Dohrn had "declar[ed] a state of war against the United States and was calling for revolutionaries and youth to join in the revolution." Hoover named her "La Pasionaria of the Lunatic Left," a reference to Dolores Ibarruri, a communist who fought in the Spanish Civil War and roused men as well as women to battle with the declaration that "it is better to die than to live in [a] fascist hell."[34]

Dohrn's battle was with everyone who, she imagined, contributed to America's fascist hell, including all who lived bougie lives (such as she had lived in her parents' home). Violence became a value. She scoffed at the notion of peaceful protests. "Guerrilla strategy" and "street fighting," she believed, would damage the "ruling class." It was good, she announced, that the Weathermen were seen as "being crazy motherfuckers and scaring the shit out of honky America." Of the murders by Charles Manson's followers of Sharon Tate (who was then eight months pregnant), four of her friends, and a bougie married couple, Dohrn reportedly announced, "Dig it, first they killed those pigs, then they ate dinner in the same room with them, then they even shoved a fork into a victim's stomach. Wild!"[35]

Her anger was triggered by men's treatment of women, too, though she loathed the NOW variety of feminism that cared only about women doing better in capitalism. She loathed the radical feminists as well, because they wasted their time burning bras. Dohrn wanted the ultraradical movement to tap into the "incredible fury" that lay just beneath the surface in most women, she said. She wanted to turn woman's anger into force: to hell with equal pay; women needed to destroy—by any means necessary—the very nature of American society that produced patriarchy and all other oppressions.[36]

Dohrn was a key figure in the Days of Rage, four days of rioting during which Chicago's central business district was turned into a war zone, with protestors breaking every window in sight to "bring the Vietnam war home" to America. The plan was for a woman's brigade, a "Women's Liberation Army," to descend like Furies on the Armed Forces Induction Center and tear it apart. The women congregated in Grant Park, ready for battle. Their heads were covered by helmets. They wore jeans, leather jackets, and heavy gloves. They carried three-feet-long clubs, iron pipes, and Viet Cong flags. They chanted allegiance to North Vietnam's nationalist revolutionary leader, Ho Chi Minh. Dohrn reminded them of the difference between the "self-indulgent shit" of radical feminist organizations that thought bra burning was a big deal, and the earth-shattering purpose of the troops that stood before her. She called for an armed struggle.[37]

The Chicago police were waiting for the Women's Liberation Army at the induction center. But the police were overwhelmed, for a while at least. The women attacked them with clubs, chemical spray, and teeth. Five policemen were injured. Finally, a dozen women, including Dohrn, were arrested.[38] In other eras, when militant women had engaged in protest, as Alice Paul and members of her Women's Party did in 1917, violence was sometimes visited on them, but they did not initiate it. Militant as Paul and her followers might have been in 1917, they were still tied to the idea that violent fisticuffs was what men did. That notion had lost its currency in the 1970s.

Dohrn was given a court date. But a few days after the Women's Liberation Army riot, five Weathermen—three women and two men—were building pipe bombs in the basement of a townhouse in New York's Greenwich Village. An explosion leveled the building, and three of the Weathermen were killed. The two surviving women, Kathy Boudin and Cathlyn Wilkerson, were helped to safety by the police and then escaped. Dohrn went underground, knowing that when it was discovered that the Weathermen had been making explosives, she would be implicated. In July 1970, she was indicted in absentia by a federal grand jury. The FBI accused her of conspiring to form a nationwide revolutionary network to bomb and kill. She stayed underground until 1980.[39]

Angela Davis was the only woman on the FBI's most-wanted list of 1970 who was not white. Davis, a Black militant, had been born to middle-class parents in Birmingham, Alabama, where she had been a Girl Scout. In 1959, when she was fifteen, she left Alabama for New York: she had received a scholarship that was intended to help bright Black southern children escape segregation. Elisabeth Irwin High School, in the heart of Greenwich Village, was nicknamed the Little Red School House because it was housed in a red brick building and mostly because its curriculum was ultraprogressive. It was there, in the midst of the McCarthy era, that the adolescent Davis first studied Marxism. As an undergraduate at Brandeis University a few years later, her work with Herbert Marcuse, a leading political theorist of Marxism, confirmed her commitment to communism. She followed Marcuse to the University of California, San Diego, where she was awarded a master's degree in 1969. Davis was then hired as a lecturer in the Philosophy Department of the University of California, Los Angeles (UCLA), which was just beginning to expand the number of women faculty members in disciplines other than nursing, social work, and women's physical education.[40]

The year before Davis was hired by UCLA, she had joined the Communist Party. Campuses in the University of California system had a written policy, dating back to 1949, against hiring communists. The regents of the University of California were doubly discomfited when they discovered that Davis was also associated with the Black Panther Party. They ordered her terminated.

UCLA's Academic Senate had never before been called upon to comment on the case of a woman professor (there had been few women on the faculty). But firmly on the side of academic freedom, the senators supported Davis's retention and communicated that to the regents. A short while later, Davis made a fiery speech on the steps of the Los Angeles City Hall at a rally to protest the arrest of several Black Panthers. There was "a national conspiracy of genocide to murder every Black in the land," Davis told the crowd.[41] The regents attacked again, insisting that the Philosophy Department fire her.

Like Bernardine Dohrn, Davis was brilliant, fierce, and photogenic, and her image captured the public's imagination. The story of her struggle with the regents, enhanced by her iconic image—her trademark Afro bordering her attractive young face like a halo—transformed her into a national symbol and a cause célèbre practically overnight. In her drama with the regents, she was the hero and they the villains. America's youth relished her colorful passion. Here was the new militant Black woman.

It was as a result of her new fame that Davis decided to lend her name to her Communist Party cell's campaign to defend three Black prisoners who were accused of murdering a guard at Soledad State Prison. Already in the sights of the FBI for her Communist Party membership and her speeches, Davis ended up on the agency's most-wanted list when Jonathan Jackson, the seventeen-year-old brother of one of the accused prisoners, George Jackson, used a gun registered in her name in a botched attempt to free the so-called Soledad Brothers. Jonathan Jackson had burst into a courtroom and kidnapped several people, including the judge, who was killed by a bullet from Davis's gun during a shoot-out with the police. Davis knew that under the law she would be held responsible for "supplying" the gun. She fled across the country.

The FBI found her two months later at a Howard Johnson's hotel in New York City. She had worn a wig of straight hair, but the ubiquitous photos of her—showing her tall, slim build and light skin—made her easy to spot. FBI agents arrested Davis and deposited her at the New York Women's House of Detention, a big brick building in Greenwich Village that was not far from the high school where she had been a student only a decade earlier. It took no time at all for word to get out that Davis had been imprisoned. Large crowds gathered on the street in front of the jail, straining for a glimpse of her and chanting "Free Angela Davis!" ("Free all political prisoners!" they could hear Davis chanting back.) A National United Committee to Free Angela Davis and a nationwide movement emerged, the first movement whose purpose was to defend an individual political woman. In her honor John Lennon wrote "Angela," a song in which he depicted Davis as a martyr, a prophet, and a "people teacher" whose words reach far to change the world.[42]

Davis was extradited to California to stand trial. When she walked into the Marin County courtroom, accompanied by police officers, she was greeted by thunderous applause, which she answered with a glowing smile and a raised fist. Liberal newspapers, both Black and white, gushed adoration. Progressives dubbed her a "heroine of the black revolution."[43] Leading Russian scientists and literary figures petitioned President Richard Nixon for clemency on her behalf. *Time* named her its woman of the year.

Not many women had been elevated to high status among the militants of the Black revolution. The shift was remarkable, even to Davis. She had complained a few years earlier, when she worked with the Student Nonviolent Coordinating Committee, that the men told women who hoped to take an active role in the organization to stop their "matriarchal coup d'état" because it was "aiding and abetting the enemy who wanted to see Black men weak and unable to hold their own." In 1967, when she joined the Black Panthers, the men were even more determined to let the women know where they belonged. Davis was informed that leadership was "a man's job" and that a Black woman's role was only to "inspire her man and educate his children."[44] She was troubled not only by the men's refusal to let her use her talents but also by their failure to understand the depth of her commitment—not to "her man" and "his children" but to the cause.

Shortly after Davis was found not guilty of the murder and conspiracy charges against her, she told a filmmaker who was producing a documentary about her life, "I have given my life to the struggle. My life belongs to the struggle. If I have to lose my life in the struggle, well, then, that's the way it will have to be."[45] The other three women on the FBI's most-wanted list had also committed themselves totally to a political cause and were willing to sacrifice their lives for the love of something abstract and outside the bonds of family. They all accepted with insouciance the possibility of a violent and fatal outcome, and they had no reluctance about trafficking in guns and explosives and creating mayhem for the sake of their cause. They inhabited a distant universe from the one that had defined woman's essential qualities and dubbed her "the gentler sex."

Ironically, despite the radicals' disdain for the bougie mainstream feminist movement, they contributed to its success, making moderate feminists into the proverbial good cops whose demands seemed, by contrast, no longer bizarre. NOW's legal campaign for girls to be given a fair share of their school's athletic budget, for example, would have been considered far more immoderate if radical feminists had not been fiercely agitating to dismantle the patriarchy altogether. The far left, as it often does, had moved the center.

As a result of NOW's legal maneuvers, an Equal Opportunity in Education Act was brought to the floor of Congress. The act proposed that educational programs and activities that received funds from the federal government be prohibited from discriminating against females. The passage of the act's Title IX would mean that females had to be treated just as males were in college admissions and faculty recruitment. It would mean that from elementary school through college, they had to be given the same opportunities that males had for athletic scholarships, coaching, and space in school gyms. It would fully recognize a female's right to aspire to be as Amazonian as she pleased. It would endorse her invasion of what had been unquestionably male space. The outraged National Collegiate Athletic Association, devoted to gridiron football and other supermasculine sports, mocked the notion of female athletes. The assistant executive director of the National Collegiate Athletic Association told the press, "Many coaches spent years building nationally respected programs, and now 10 or 12 girls want to get into the gym. They can't even shoot or dribble."[46] But in June 1972, after passing both houses of Congress, Title IX became law.

Other claims that had long been rejected as outré—a woman's right to sovereignty over her own body, for instance—no longer seemed excessive in the new climate. In 1971, a Florida court had found twenty-three-year-old Shirley Ann Wheeler guilty of having terminated a pregnancy through an illegal abortion. She had been threatened with a twenty-year prison sentence, but she was finally sentenced to two years on probation—with conditions that turned back the clock to another century. She must not stay out at night, go to bars, live alone or with another woman, or associate with people of harmful character or bad reputation. And she must put herself under the jurisdiction of a man: she must either marry the man with whom she was living, who had impregnated her; or she must return to North Carolina and submit herself to the guardianship of her older brother. Her sentence affirmed that under the law a woman's sovereignty over herself was still illusive: in 1971, a court could still forbid a woman free access to the world, send her home, and place her under male supervision.

The National Association for the Repeal of Abortion Laws had been founded in 1969 by feminist leaders, including Friedan; other abortion rights organizations soon followed. The "pro-choice" women made Shirley Ann Wheeler a "martyr for abortion reform," as the *San Francisco Examiner* called her. She became a catalyst, too. A week after Wheeler was sentenced, the Women's National Abortion Action Coalition designated October 21, 1971, "Shirley Wheeler Day." Press conferences were held in San Francisco, Chicago, Philadelphia, and New York protesting her treatment. Women marched in front of the White House carrying "Defend Shirley Wheeler" signs. They rallied in San Francisco and Washington and raised money for an appeal. The following year the Florida Supreme Court reversed her conviction.[47]

By the time *Roe v. Wade* reached the U.S. Supreme Court, the social climate on the subject of abortion had been transformed. The Court was dominated by Republicans in 1973: two of the justices had been appointed by President Dwight Eisenhower and four by President Nixon. Yet the vote that gave women the legal right to abortion was 7–2, with all but one of the Republican-appointed justices siding with two Democrat-appointed ones.[48] The majority opinion was written by a Republican-appointed justice, Harry Blackmun, who declared that a woman's right to choose abortion was protected by the Fourteenth Amendment's guarantee of the right to privacy.

THE RADICAL WOMAN: A BACKLASH

"Let's not permit this tiny minority to degrade the role that most women prefer."

—PHYLLIS SCHLAFLY, "What's Wrong with Equal Rights for Women?" (1972)[49]

The *Roe v. Wade* decision was particularly distressing to women on the right who were radically invested in traditional ideas of woman as nurturing mother. "Pro-family conservatives" they now called themselves, and they organized with as much vigor as had their predecessors who argued more than half a century earlier that women wanted to be kept in the "protected home" and not forced to go to the voting polls. Pro-family conservative women opened "crisis pregnancy centers" (sometimes masquerading as abortion providers) where they showed already distraught pregnant women videos that demonstrated that life begins at conception, and they offered support to those who promised not to have an abortion.[50] They took for themselves the emotionally charged appellation "pro-life," and they staged "rescue" operations in front of actual abortion clinics, screaming "Don't let them kill your baby!" at any woman about to go through the door. They held demonstrations at which they carried aloft giant color photos of aborted fetuses, and they staged dramatic candlelight memorials that culminated in the blowing out of candles to signify that abortion meant taking an innocent life. They made their voices heard politically, too, pressuring members of Congress to chip away at abortion rights through legislation such as the 1976 Hyde Amendment, which denied indigent women the help of Medicaid if they needed to terminate a pregnancy.

But though women on the right did yeoman's work in fighting *Roe v. Wade*, they fell short of killing it. Their attack on the Equal Rights Amendment (ERA) was much more successful. The amendment had been introduced in Congress, yet again, in 1970. For years it had languished in the House Judiciary Committee, which was chaired for more than two decades by Emanuel Celler, the Democratic congressman from Brooklyn who had so adamantly opposed the addition of "sex" to the 1964 Civil Rights Act. Celler was hostile to the ERA, too. "What would become of traditional family relationships?" he asked. "Would fathers rank equally with mothers in child custody cases?" Martha Griffiths, the Democratic congresswoman from Michigan, butted heads with him once again. This time she managed to force the ERA out of his committee through a discharge petition—a rare and difficult maneuver that required the signatures of an absolute majority of Congress. Griffiths's success seemed a clear indication that the ERA's time had indeed come—and that Celler was clueless about the cultural shifts all around him. "Neither the National Woman's Party nor the delightful, delectable, and dedicated gentlewoman from Michigan can change nature," Celler had jested patronizingly about the wrongheadedness of the ERA and Griffiths's tireless attempts to get the proposed amendment onto the House floor.[51] But on October 12, 1971, the House of Representatives held a roll-call vote on the ERA. It passed 354 to 24.

The ERA had languished for years in the Senate, too. When it came up again in the early 1970s, Sam Ervin, a southern Democrat from North

Carolina, tried to lead a charge against it. Like Celler, the seventy-four-year-old Ervin could not appreciate that a new day had come. If the ERA passed, he declared, women would be drafted, homosexual marriage would become legal, separate restrooms for males and females would become illegal, and the distinction between men and women would entirely disappear. But Ervin got little traction. His fellow legislators found his fears far-fetched, and his worry about the disappearance of sex distinctions seemed as outdated as the buggy. In the midst of the Senate hearings on the ERA, Minority Leader Hugh Scott (a Republican from Pennsylvania) had written to President Nixon to ask his opinion. Even the politically conservative president was not oblivious to the zeitgeist. Nixon responded that he believed in equal rights for women and that a Constitutional amendment was absolutely "warrant[ed] to achieve that goal."[52] Scott shared the message with his colleagues. On March 22, 1972, the ERA came to a vote in the Senate. It passed 84 to 8. Now it had only to be ratified by thirty-eight states.

Celler was then the most senior member of Congress. Voters had kept him in office for fifty years, and he was considered "the uncrowned king" of his district, the Flatbush section of Brooklyn. That June, the eighty-four-year-old Celler was challenged for his seat by a short, slight, Harvard-trained woman lawyer, Elizabeth Holtzman. Thirty years old, Holtzman was young enough to be Celler's granddaughter. Her pretensions seemed laughable to him, "an attempt to topple the Washington Monument with a toothpick." But in her campaign, Holtzman made certain that women voters were informed about Celler's "high-handed opposition to the women's equal rights amendment." She beat him in the primary and went on to win 66 percent of the vote in the general election.[53] In liberal districts, it was clearly perilous by 1972 to ridicule women's desire for equality. Among right-wing women, however, it was a different story—as would very soon become clear.

Though Ervin and Celler lost on the issue of the ERA, they had managed to wrest from their fellow members of Congress what seemed like a hollow concession: the House and the Senate agreed to set an arbitrary time limit of seven years for ratification of the amendment. But quick ratification had seemed certain. Less than two hours after the Senate passed the ERA on March 22, 1972, both houses of the Hawaii legislature ratified it. The next day, it was ratified by New Hampshire and Delaware, and the day after that by Iowa and Idaho. Before the spring was over, nineteen states had ratified it. Other states were not so quick, but by March 22,

1973, only a year after the House and Senate passed the amendment, thirty states had already ratified it. The amendment needed ratification by three-fourths of the states, so there were only eight left to go. "The ERA will be part of the Constitution long before the year is out," Griffiths exulted.[54] She was too optimistic: the ERA did not become part of the Constitution by the end of 1973. But the deadline for ratification was still a comfortable six years away. What could go wrong?

Unsurprisingly, the ERA had been opposed by radical right groups such as the Daughters of the American Revolution, who were pledged to "God, Home and Country," and the John Birch Society, which had declared war on "feminoids" because they were as dangerous as communists. But furious as the right wing was about the ERA, it could make little dent in the amendment's public approval. A 1974 Gallup Poll showed that almost 75 percent of Americans supported the ERA.[55] That began to change when a fifty-year-old midwestern "housewife" (as she called herself) figured out how to bring together and mobilize tens of thousands of grassroots women of the radical right who were personally invested in keeping alive the old concepts of woman. What they had sorely needed was a leader who could organize their fight, and Phyllis Schlafly stepped into the role with zest.

Schlafly was in all things an overachiever. She far surpassed the women of her cohort who, during the baby boom era, bore an average of three children: Schlafly bore six. She boasted that she breast-fed them all and taught every one of them to read before they started school.[56] Schlafly had also graduated Phi Beta Kappa from Washington University and had gone on to earn a master's degree in government from Radcliffe College. In 1952, when housewives were reading Benjamin Spock's *Baby and Child Care* and baking angel food cakes, Schlafly ran, unsuccessfully, for the U.S. Congress. (Her husband, a corporate lawyer, had indulged her by hiring helpers to care for the children.) She later went to law school and got a doctorate of jurisprudence in constitutional law. But curiously, like the long line of overachieving women before her—from Catharine Beecher to Marynia Farnham—Schlafly led an all-out war aimed at women who fought for the right to do the things she did.

Schlafly first came to fame in 1964 when she wrote *A Choice Not an Echo*, a book promoting the presidential candidacy of a conservative U.S. senator from Arizona, Barry Goldwater. The book sold 3 million copies and helped Goldwater win the Republican nomination ("I would remind you that extremism in the defense of liberty is no vice," he proclaimed in his acceptance speech at the 1964 Republican Convention).[57] Goldwater lost the race spectacularly, garnering only about 38 percent of the vote. It was also a loss for Schlafly, who had imagined herself a kingmaker. But her ambition was still intact, and three years later she ran for the presidency of the National Federation of Republican Women. She lost her race as overwhelmingly as Goldwater had lost his. In 1970 she ran for the second time for a seat in the U.S. Congress, and she lost again. Her string of defeats did not stop her drive toward the limelight. In 1972, after the Senate voted to approve the ERA, Schlafly found her path.

Perfectly coiffed and ramrod straight, looking like a well-off 1950s housewife, she called her campaign STOP (Stop Taking Our Privileges) ERA and attracted an army of radical-right women followers. Through her newsletter, the *Phyllis Schlafly Report*, she kept them excited and alarmed. She told them that the ERA had been imposed on them by "a tiny minority cramming its views down the throat of the majority . . . a noisy claque of women's lib agitators who rammed the ERA through Congress, intimidating the men to vote for it." She spread fear, warning women who were committed to hanging onto woman's traditional spaces that they would be cast out of them, that the ERA would even wipe out their husbands' financial obligations to them and their children. She roused her readers by demanding, "What about the rights of the woman who doesn't want to compete with men on an equal basis? Does she have the right to be a woman? . . . the right not to take a job?" "Why should we lower ourselves to 'equal rights' when we already have the status of special privilege?" "WOMEN'S LIBBERS DO NOT SPEAK FOR US," she proclaimed in capital letters.[58]

She was tireless in her attacks. The ERA would mean that women would have to use the same public toilets as men used. It would mean that homosexuality would become legal and homosexuals could teach in public schools. She appeared on *Issues and Answers*, an ABC Sunday news program, where she debated Congresswoman Pat Schroeder, a Democrat from Colorado who had cosponsored the ERA. If the amendment were ratified, Schlafly declared (knowing exactly how best to upset women who just wanted "the right to be a woman"), "Congress will be constitutionally required to draft women on the same basis as men"—the weaker sex would be forced into combat and women would have to serve on warships alongside men.[59]

Schlafly was right that feminists had mobilized and pressured legislators to pass the ERA. Now she focused on mobilizing radical anti-feminists to pressure legislators to rescind it. The legislatures of Nebraska and Tennessee had ratified the amendment soon after Congress passed it. But through the efforts of the radical women of STOP ERA, in 1973 Nebraska withdrew its ratification. Tennessee withdrew its in 1974. Only three states ratified the ERA in 1974. The next year, Schlafly founded the Eagle Forum, a "pro-family" organization devoted to guaranteeing that America honors the full-time housewife. Under Schlafly's guidance, Eagle Forum's 50,000 members became foot soldiers—garbed in knee-length dresses, of course, and with their tresses neatly coiffed—in the STOP ERA battle. They inundated legislators with letters and telegrams that said they liked the old meaning of woman and did not want it changed.

Only one state ratified the ERA in 1975. Several states debated whether to join Nebraska and Tennessee in rescinding. By 1979, three more had done so. The ratification deadline approached, and a tug-of-war was on. When it looked as though the legislature in Illinois might ratify the amendment, Schlafly organized her STOP-ERA Eagles to bring the lawmakers homemade turkey sandwiches and fresh-baked cookies, accompanied by a note intended to flatter male egos: "From the bread makers to the bread winners." Illinois did not ratify the ERA. Wherever and whenever lawmakers were asked to consider ratification, the Eagles went into the kitchen to bake.[60]

By the time the new deadline rolled around, not a single additional state had ratified. The ERA was dead. It was a major victory for women of the radical right, a recognition that "woman" had not breathed her last. A jubilant Schlafly threw an "ERA Going Away" party, which was cosponsored by Jerry Falwell's far-right Moral Majority. To the media, Schlafly announced plans to "fold" STOP ERA into her Eagle Forum, where the groups would join forces in the "crusade for strong families."[61]

In 1977, *Time* had been astute in calling Phyllis Schlafly a "chief philosopher" of the "pro-family forces." She continued to fight to keep woman "safe in the protected home" for almost forty more years. In her old age Schlafly had again hoped to be a kingmaker, just as she had when she wrote *A Choice Not an Echo* and helped Goldwater win the 1964 Republican nomination for president. On September 6, 2016, the day after Schlafly's death at the age of ninety-two and two months before the next presidential election, her twenty-sixth book, *The Conservative Case for Trump*, was published. In it she said of the future president of the United States that "anyone who meets him today will meet an old-fashioned man" who is "grounded" in one of his greatest priorities, family.[62]

In July 1978, when it had seemed clear that the ERA was not going to be ratified by the requisite thirty-eight states before the deadline in the following year, NOW organized a march on Washington. A hundred thousand ERA supporters demanded an extension. Congress bowed to the pressure and set a new deadline for ratification: 1982. However, in 1980 Ronald Reagan became the presidential nominee of the Republican party. Support for the ERA, which had been a plank on the party's platform in 1976, was removed from its 1980 platform. No longer enjoying Republican support, the ERA's second death was a foregone conclusion.

Women on the radical right knew that they had a friend in the highest of places when Reagan became president, and he did not fail them. He was so strongly opposed to *Roe v. Wade* that in 1983 he even took time out from running the country to write a book (the first president ever to have done so while in office) in which he presented abortion as "infanticide." In his dramatically titled *Abortion and the Conscience of the Nation*, Reagan argued that *Roe v. Wade* must be reversed. "Make no mistake, abortion-on-demand is not a right granted by the constitution," he declared, contradicting from his high office the Supreme Court's decision ten years earlier. Though *Roe v. Wade* was not overturned during Reagan's eight years in office, his reactionary positions on most women's rights issues set the tone for the era. The 1980s ushered in a "backlash," as the author Susan Faludi has characterized it, against the feminist victories of the preceding years.[63]

Women on the radical right would be justified in gloating about their triumphs not only over their radical counterparts on the left, but also over moderate feminists whose struggles for legal rights and the moral right to choose careers over domesticity were now seen as a fad on the way out. The liberal media was oddly complicit in the drive to turn the clock back to the 1950s. The *New York Times* blared smug headlines throughout the 1980s, such as "Many Young Women Now Say They'd Pick Family over Career," "Putting a Career on Hold," and "Professional Women Do Go Home Again." In 1986, the *Atlantic* invited George Gilder—who worried in his 1973 best seller *Sexual Suicide* that the rising tide of feminism would threaten marriage and family—to write about "Women in the Work Force." Though it seemed that women were blurring traditional sex roles in the workforce, Gilder said, it was really not so. Yes, it was true that in 1960 women accounted for only 9 percent of bankers and financial managers and in 1984 they accounted for 39 percent; yes, it was true that the number of female butchers in packinghouses had risen by more than one-third and that 80 percent of new bartending jobs were going to women. Nevertheless, gender disparity in the workplace continued, Gilder pointed out with some relief. And that, he wrote, probably had "less to do with discrimination than with women making the choice to stay at home."[64]

Warnings to women who had not made such a choice were suddenly everywhere. A 1985 study by a Harvard sociologist and a Yale economist found that if a college-educated white woman had not married by the time she was twenty-five years old, she had only a 50 percent chance of ever marrying. In a major cover story, Newsweek put career women on dire notice. "Many women who seem to have it all—good looks and good jobs, advanced degrees and high salaries—will never have a mate." If a woman over forty was still unmarried, the Newsweek reporter warned, it was statistically more likely that she would be killed by a terrorist than that she would find a husband.[65]

Despite such hysteria about the disasters befalling women who crossed their domestic thresholds and went to work, their percentage in the labor force continued to rise: from 43 percent of all American women in 1970 to 58 percent in 1990. The ratio of their salaries to those of men rose too, from 63 percent in 1979 to over 70 percent in 1990. Women also continued to outnumber men in college enrollment, a trend that had started in the 1970s and would continue into the next century. In the most prestigious professions, women's progress was especially impressive. For instance, there were fewer women medical doctors in 1960 (about 5 percent of the profession) than there had been in 1900; by 1970 the share had risen to about 13 percent, and by 1990 it was almost 40 percent.[66] Despite the best efforts of women on the radical right, the 1950's woman had not been widely resurrected. The increase in the number of women working outside the home, the salary gains that affected working women at all levels, and the reopening of elite professions to women all happened because feminists succeeded in stretching the boundaries of woman.

But though the lives of broad swaths of women had been permanently changed by the feminists' struggles to expand the parameters, few women in the 1980s were willing to call themselves feminists. The term had become "a dirty word," according to a 1982 New York Times article that quoted several women who feared to be "smeared" by it personally as well as professionally. "For the guy next door that would mean I'm a lesbian," one woman told the reporter. "I'm afraid the lesbian connotation would affect my credibility with many of the people I want to reach."[67]

Feminist groups of all stripes had trouble attracting a new generation. The National Black Feminist Organization, the Combahee River Collective, New York Radical Feminists, and Radicalesbians all disbanded. NOW membership decreased sharply. *Ms.* lost subscribers, and the staff discussed shutting down. The new generation, though it had greatly profited by the struggles of both radical and moderate feminists, was decidedly postfeminist.

14.
How Sex Spawned a New "Woman"

•

THE 1990s

B*ust* began in 1993 as a do-it-yourself underground photocopied "zine" for "riot grrrls"—an alternative movement of young women in the punk rock scene. The zine was dedicated to encouraging the riot grrrl to "remember your own fierce inner girl" and to "helping you stay that way." Riot grrrl fierceness included confronting sex head-on, not being intimidated by it as woman was supposed to be. *Bust*'s readership mushroomed and took in a larger swath of third-wave feminists. It became a glossy magazine, featuring articles such as "Me and My Cunt," "Talking Dick with Cynthia," and "What Kind of Slut Are You?" In the pages of *Bust*, absolute sexual freedom was a road to women's empowerment, a crucial frontier that third-wave feminists were avidly breaching. As *Bust* cheekily vowed on behalf of its readers: "In our quest for sexual satisfaction we shall leave no sex toy unturned and no sexual avenue unexplored. Women are trying their hands (and other body parts) at everything from phone sex to cybersex, solo sex to group sex, heterosex to homosex. Lusty feminists of the Third Wave, we're more than ready to drag race down sexual roads less travelled. Ladies, start your engines!"[1]

THE SEXY POSTFEMINIST AND THE (STRAW-WOMEN) FEMINIST PRUDES

> "Leaving sex to the feminists is like letting your dog vacation at the taxidermist's."
> —CAMILLE PAGLIA, "Perspective Needed" (1991)[2]

There had never been a monolithic attitude toward sex among feminists, but postfeminists invented one for them, setting up straw women to draw a contrast between their own sexually liberated generation and the prudes who preceded them. For instance, the social critic Camille Paglia smartly mocked second-wave feminists as being not only hopelessly out of touch with eroticism but also neurotically repressed. Paglia's 1990 book *Sexual Personae: Art and Decadence from Nefertiti to Emily Dickinson* had started as her PhD dissertation at Yale University. Her pronouncements, aimed to tweak the feminist nose on various subjects, vied with one another for outlandishness. "If civilization had been left in female hands, we would still be living in grass huts," she declared. "Male urination really is a kind of accomplishment, an arc of transcendence. A woman merely waters the ground she stands on," she wrote.[3] With her book's title, Paglia was signifying her response to Kate Millett's book of the preceding generation, which had been a sacred text of feminism: *Sexual Personae* was *Sexual Politics*'s polar opposite.

Overlooking the historical detail that in the early twentieth century it was feminists of the first wave, the New Women, who fought hardest for the right of women to claim their sexuality, Paglia presented feminism as priggish and fatuous. Feminists had set themselves against nature and had not a clue, Paglia argued, that sex was necessarily chthonic, dark, and born of violent impulses. Because feminists were oblivious to the real forces of life, she suggested, they were at best irrelevant.

Sexual Personae was an academic study and had its greatest audience among intellectuals, but Paglia's brand of postfeminism was soon commercialized. In Katie Roiphe's *The Morning After: Sex, Fear, and Feminism on Campus* (1993), Paglia recognized a popularizing heir to her ideas, and with mama-bear ferocity she defended *The Morning After* against "shallow, dishonest feminist book reviewers."[4] Paradoxically, Roiphe's birth mama, Anne Roiphe, was a writer who in 1970 had published *Up the Sandbox*, a feminist novel whose protagonist was a frustrated, college-educated housewife right out of the pages of *The Feminine Mystique*. The younger Roiphe, born five years after Friedan's book was published, had moved far beyond the cri de coeur of *The Feminine Mystique* and her mother's novel.

Twenty-five years old when her own book came out, and looking like a pretty teenager with long, curly hair, Katie Roiphe had super-smart bona fides as a doctoral student in literature at Princeton University. In *The Morning After*, she complained about the older generation of feminists who were inhibiting young women's sexual freedom, trying to convince them there was a big bad wolf under every bed and a rapist behind every consensual sexual encounter. She accused feminists of encouraging young women to claim date rape when the real problem was usually regret over bad sex to which they had been too passive to say no. Roiphe named names: the dangerous prudes of the 1980s who were poisoning young women's minds such as Catharine MacKinnon and Andrea Dworkin, who had campaigned for laws that would punish men's sexual misbehaviors as civil-rights violations against women.[5] Feminists in *The Morning After* were simply hysterical anti-sex neo-Puritans.

To the media, it was an irresistible story: a sassy young woman scoffing at the outdated sour feminism of the older generation, liberating herself to be as unfearful about sex as men were. The *New York Times Magazine* made Roiphe a star overnight, announcing on its cover that "Rape Hype Betrays Feminism" and featuring in its pages a 4,700-word excerpt from *The Morning After*. The *New York Times Magazine* did for Roiphe's postfeminist book in 1992 what *Time* had done for Millett's feminist book a generation earlier. *The Morning After* was soon featured in glossies such as *Playboy* and *Mirabella*, which played up Roiphe's idea that man-hating feminists had led young women astray by exaggerating the incidence of rape (and particularly date rape). Indeed, Roiphe argued, feminists were making young women needlessly fearful about sex by setting up rape crises centers, chattering about a rape epidemic, and staging foolish "Take Back the Night" marches. Feminists had neither a sense of humor nor a sense of proportion. They were silly to feel threatened by everything and to see insults everywhere—even in appreciative ogles from a boss or innocent sexual jokes.[6]

But Paglia's and Roiphe's straw-woman representations of a monolithic feminism willfully elided "sex-positive feminists," who had had a voice in the movement almost from the start. Sex-positive feminists had always argued that women's escape from the straitjacket of woman depended on their freeing themselves from the sexual double standard in which men could do as they pleased and women had to be fearful. In 1973, NOW sponsored a Women's Sexuality Conference, at which women talked about their own sexual liberation, presented workshops about sex practices such as S&M, and ended the conference with a "sexual fantasy" costume party. Feminists opened woman-centered sex shops, beginning with Eve's Garden in New York in 1974 and Good Vibrations in San Francisco in 1975, where they sold erotica and sex toys such as dildoes, vibrators, cock-ring sets, anal beads, and bondage kits for beginners—all for women's delectation. Anything goes, as long as it is the woman who gets to say what is done to her body, sex-positive feminists proclaimed. In 1982, academic feminists organized a conference at Barnard College, "Toward a Politics of Sexuality," which was essentially a response to the radical feminists who were opposed to pornography or S&M. The position of most of the conference participants was that sexual liberation was the sine qua non of women's liberation, that women could not be free if they felt threatened or terrified by sex, and that a revival of social purity politics like that promulgated by the nineteenth-century moral reformers was a "limited and limiting vision for women." Women must claim their sexual agency and their right enjoy any sexual act that gave them pleasure, the participants agreed.[7]

But postfeminists reveled in assailing all second-wave feminists as enemies of sex: squelchers of woman's sexual freedom, victimizers of men and their natural sex drives, and perpetrators of the melodrama of sexual-harassment allegations—which, postfeminists said, feminists had created out of their prudish imaginations. That was the image that stuck and turned young women further away from second-wave feminism.

However, just when feminism as a movement seemed to be breathing its last, a spectacle centered directly on the subject of sex spawned a whole new generation of feminists. It was an issue of unwanted sexual attention that revived feminism at the start of the 1990s. But before the decade was over, feminists of the third wave would also be breaking new ground as sexual liberators.

ANITA HILL ON TRIAL

"If what you say this man said to you occurred, why in God's name would you ever speak to a man like that the rest of your life?"
—ALAN K. SIMPSON, "Nomination of Judge Clarence Thomas to Be Associate Justice of the Supreme Court of the United States" (1991)[8]

Senate deliberations on Supreme Court nominees had been televised since 1986, but the Senate Judiciary Committee hearings that were beamed into America's living rooms from October 11 to October 13, 1991, were unique. For three days, viewers witnessed painful interrogations and testimonies, often startlingly graphic, about whether a nominee to the Supreme Court had been a sexual harasser. The hearings became theater, a multithemed drama about woman's vulnerability in the workplace; about whether a woman can be believed when she says she has been abused; about race and gender—or rather, about race versus gender in a hierarchy of allegiance. The conclusions of the Senate committee would resonate for decades, beyond its decision about President George H. W. Bush's nominee to the Supreme Court.

Anita Hill, the youngest of thirteen children in a strict Baptist family, grew up on a hardscrabble farm in rural Oklahoma. Few of her high-school classmates had considered college an option, but Hill went to Oklahoma State University, and after graduating she was accepted at the law schools of both Harvard and Yale Universities. She chose Yale, where she was one of only eleven Black students (nine of them were women) in a class of 165. The other students, Hill discovered, had come from institutions such as Princeton, Stanford, and Brown Universities, not from an "aggie college" like Oklahoma State. Hill identified with the Black custodians, she said, "much more easily than I did with my [white] professors."[9]

When she graduated from law school in 1980, she was twenty-four years old. Though she had not gone to law school to become a corporate lawyer, she took a job in Washington, DC, at Wald, Harkrader and Ross, a corporate-law firm, to pay off her college debts. She had been at the firm for a year when a former Yale classmate introduced her to Clarence Thomas, who had just been appointed by President Ronald Reagan to be assistant secretary of education for the Office of Civil Rights. Thomas spoke to Hill about Black solidarity and his desire to hire as his "personal assistant" someone Black whom he "could trust in civil rights matters."

Hill was relieved to leave corporate law and take a position—her official title was "attorney advisor"—where she might make a difference in matters she cared about.[10]

A few months later, Thomas asked her out on a date. Hill replied that she thought it "ill-advised" to have a social relationship with someone who was supervising her work. Thomas was persistent. As Hill later testified, he would insist that they go to lunch to "talk about work," but instead he would talk graphically about pornographic videos he had seen that showed group sex, women having sex with animals, rape scenes, women with gigantic breasts, and the porn star Long Dong Silver, whose erect penis was reputedly eighteen inches long. When Hill tried to change the topic to education issues, Thomas would talk about his own sexual prowess, the pleasure he had given women through oral sex, and the size of his sex organs. It seemed to her that he enjoyed seeing her discomfort. But eventually he gave up. He stopped insisting they have lunch together, and Hill heard no more sex talk from him.

When Thomas was appointed to head the Equal Employment Opportunity Commission (EEOC) the following year and offered to take Hill with him, she accepted. She later testified that she had agreed to go with Thomas to the EEOC because Reagan was threatening to abolish the Department of Education, and she feared she would be unemployed if she did not make the move. And she trusted that Thomas's harassment of her was finished. And she had gone to law school to get just the kind of civil rights job that Thomas was offering her at the EEOC. "I wanted to do the work," she reflected. "I did not want to let that kind of behavior control my choices."[11]

After a few months in the new office, however, Thomas's old behavior began again. The irony was not lost on Hill that as head of the EEOC, Thomas was supposed to be overseeing the protection of women employees against sexual harassment all over the country. The stress put her in the hospital for five days with acute stomach pain. Shortly after she was released, she resigned from her job and returned to Oklahoma, where she became a teacher at Oral Roberts University, an evangelical Christian institution.[12]

In the 1960s, during his undergraduate days at the College of the Holy Cross, Clarence Thomas was an admirer of the Black Panthers and called himself a radical; but by the time he graduated from Yale Law School, he had drifted rightward. When President Reagan appointed him to head the EEOC in 1982, Thomas was already widely known in Washington to be a staunch Black conservative, against busing, affirmative action, and abortion. In 1990 President Bush, on the lookout for reliable conservatives for the judiciary, nominated him to be on the U.S. Court of Appeals. Thomas had been a judge for only a year when Bush tapped him again, this time to replace Thurgood Marshall, the first Black justice on the Supreme Court, who had announced that he was retiring because of poor health.

It was protocol that the background of Supreme Court nominees be investigated. During the first week of September 1991, staffers of the Senate Judiciary Committee (whose duty it was to make recommendations to the full Senate on Supreme Court nominees) contacted Hill because she had worked with Thomas. Hill was now a professor at the University of Oklahoma's School of Law, the first Black to receive tenure there. She had hoped the past was long behind her. But with some reluctance, she told the staffers what she had experienced and signed a detailed affidavit.

On September 10, Thomas's hearings in front of the Senate Judiciary Committee began. Senator Joe Biden, the committee's chair, purportedly had made a promise in the Senate gym to Senator John Danforth, Thomas's chief supporter. "Let's get my guy in," Danforth had said, and Biden had promised that the hearings would be "quick and fast." But Thomas's answers were often so noncommittal that Democratic senator Howard Heflin complained to a querying reporter that it was hard to tell whether Thomas was "a closet liberal, a conservative, or an opportunist." Despite such criticism, as the reporter who sat through all four days of the hearings concluded, the Democrats "were squeamish about examining a black candidate closely."[13] Thomas never took a clear position on *Roe v. Wade*, for instance, and the committee did not press him on the matter—though four years earlier the committee, also led by Biden, had sent Robert Bork's nomination to the Senate floor with an unfavorable vote of 9 to 5, in good part because Bork opposed *Roe v. Wade*.

Halfway through the Thomas hearings, the committee heard of Hill's allegations. Biden and the committee's ranking Republican member, Strom Thurmond, asked the Federal Bureau of Investigation (FBI) to investigate further—to "spot inconsistencies" in her story, Hill later wrote.[14]

On September 26, the White House reviewed the FBI report and concluded simply that the allegations were unfounded. The committee's response to the report was mixed: some members took it seriously, but others did not. Biden called for a vote on whether to support Thomas's nomination. The committee of eight Democrats and six Republicans was deadlocked, 7–7, when Democratic senator Dennis DeConcini (who later began his questioning of Hill by saying that his mother had been sexually harassed by an employer when she was twenty-two) voted with the Republicans. On September 27, the committee agreed to send the nomination on to the full Senate without a recommendation. The vote to forward had been 13–1. Democratic senator Paul Simon voiced the lone objection.

An anonymous member of the committee (Simon?) then leaked Hill's signed affidavit to Nina Totenberg of National Public Radio. On October 6, 1991, several million people were listening to NPR's *Weekend Edition* when Totenberg described details of Hill's affidavit and interviewed her and Simon. Biden was briefly interviewed, too. "I believe there are certain things that are not at issue at all, and that is [Clarence Thomas's] character," he told Totenberg, adding, puzzlingly, "This is about what he believes, not about who he is."[15]

An unprecedented drama ensued. There were twenty-eight women in the House of Representatives—making up less than 6 percent of the members but still an all-time high. Almost all of them had been incensed by what they heard on Totenberg's radio report. The next day many congresswomen got up on the House floor to voice displeasure that the Senate would be voting without giving Hill a chance to tell her story. Seven Democratic women decided on more direct action. Patricia Schroeder led the charge of women marching from the floor of the House to the Senate. But before they marched, Schroeder told her press secretary to call all the media in DC and say that the congresswomen were descending on the senators to demand that Hill be allowed to testify. By the time the women got to the Senate, more than two dozen journalists were waiting to snap their photo and hear their story.

The members of the Senate's Democratic Caucus were sequestered in the Lyndon B. Johnson Room, having lunch. The congresswomen knocked on the closed door, which was opened by the assistant to Senator George Mitchell, the majority leader. They were told that they could not come in because they were not senators. The phones in the room began to ring as members of the media sought a comment from the senators on the congresswomen's protest. Barbara Mikulski, the lone Democratic woman senator, told Mitchell, "You don't get that this is really going to be big. You need to meet with the women."

"Did you see all those cameras out there?" Congresswoman Barbara Boxer pointedly asked Mitchell when he came out to see the congresswomen.

Mitchell and Biden agreed that Hill could testify before any further action would be taken on Thomas's nomination.[16]

On October 11, Hill sat alone at a small table, a microphone before her, in the Caucus Room of the Russell Senate Office Building. Her elderly parents and a half-dozen of her siblings were behind her, and the august Judiciary Committee was in front of her—a long row of fourteen white male senators, most of them dressed in dark gray suits.[17] The Democrats purportedly treated Thomas gingerly because they were sensitive to the issue of race, as the reporter who covered Thomas's first hearing suggested; but the Republicans in their grilling of Hill had no such sensitivity to the issue of gender. Arlen Specter was chosen to interrogate Hill for the Republicans. Her accusations made no sense, Specter declared. If Thomas "had been so disgusting to you, had victimized you with sexual harassment and had violated the Civil Rights Act," why had Hill continued to work for him, Specter demanded, though Hill had already answered that question in her written statement to the committee.

Biden had announced a limit on the number of people who would be allowed to testify, but Specter got around the limit on witnesses by reading aloud from hostile affidavits. Hill kept working for Thomas, one affidavit said, because she was dishonest and conniving: "She wanted to derive whatever advantage she could from a cordial professional relationship with him." Another affidavit that Specter read to the committee (and the millions of television viewers) was from a man who claimed to be acquainted with both Thomas and Hill: he knew that Hill had been "disappointed and frustrated" that Thomas "did not show any sexual interest in her."

Senator Ted Kennedy tried to stop Specter from reading testimonies by people who had not been sworn in and could not be cross-examined, but Specter continued. Another affidavit writer claimed that Hill had had fantasies that he was sexually interested in her. "Miss Hill's fantasies," Specter read, "were an indication of the fact that she was having a problem being rejected by men she was attracted to." The affidavits gave the conservative media explanations of why Hill had made charges against Thomas: it was because she was "a little bit nutty and a little bit slutty." The *American Spectator* announced in a cover story that Hill had a "fatal attraction" to Thomas—a reference to the 1987 horror film *Fatal At-*

traction in which a woman goes murderously berserk when she is spurned by her married lover.[18]

Republican senators Orrin Hatch and Alan Simpson looked for other ways to discredit Hill's testimony. She had testified earlier that one day at the EEOC, Thomas had picked up a can of soda and asked, "Who has put pubic hair on my Coke?" Hatch whipped out a copy of the 1973 novel *The Exorcist* and read a passage in which a character says that there appeared to be "an alien pubic hair floating in my gin." That was where Hill had found the outrageous line she attributed to Thomas, Hatch declared.

Simpson made use of the updated version of the "Amazon," "manly," and "unnatural woman" aspersions to discredit Hill. Women in Oklahoma, he told the committee, had been "sending me things" related to Hill's "proclivities." He was hinting that Hill had made accusations against Thomas simply because she was a homosexual. A tabloid reporter, hot on the trail of Simpson's suggestion, called the owner of a lesbian bar in Oklahoma City to ask whether Hill was a habitué of the establishment.[19]

Since both Hill and Thomas were Black, the issue was in no way about race, but Thomas managed to make race the issue in his angry defense of himself:

> This is a circus. It is a national disgrace. And from my standpoint, as a black American, as far as I am concerned, it is a high-tech lynching for uppity blacks who in any way deign to think for themselves, to do for themselves, to have different ideas, and it is a message that, unless you kowtow to an old order, this is what will happen to you. You will be lynched, destroyed, caricatured by a committee of the U.S. Senate, rather than hung from a tree.[20]

Thomas's speech dexterously turned the focus away from himself as a sexual harasser and to himself as an embodiment of the horrific history of American Blacks who had been victimized by white violence. He was being tortured, lynched, only because he was an independent Black man.

His complaint about race was far more compelling to the majority of the Senate (whose membership then was all white and 98 percent male) than the complaint of a woman, no matter her race, about her vulnerability in the workplace. The senators could not be oblivious to the heavy burden placed on Black men by prejudice. (But in case they were, Danforth reminded his fellow senators that "this poor guy has been tortured enough."[21]) It stirred them to feel shame and guilt. But they had not been forced to contemplate in any depth the burden placed on women by sexual harassment. And even had everything happened as Hill claimed, the senators may have reasoned, how damaging could some words possibly be to a woman—especially one who had been able to go on with her career and become a tenured university professor?

On October 15, the full Senate, dominated by Democrats, deliberated on Thomas's confirmation. The vote was 52–48, with two Republicans voting no and eleven Democrats voting yes.[22] Thomas began serving on the Supreme Court on October 23. (When Justice Anthony Kennedy retired twenty-seven years later, in 2018, Thomas became the most senior justice on the Court.) His confirmation was a painful message to the women's movement that despite all its efforts and triumphs since the 1960s, some things remained as they had always been: men could abuse women with impunity, and women still had to suffer in silence or be shamed.

Yet Senator Ted Kennedy, in his assessment of the meaning of the hearings, was hopeful that Hill's ordeal had forced awareness of woman's vulnerability in the work world. "I do not think that this country is ever going to look at sexual harassment the same tomorrow as it has in the past," Kennedy said.[23] He was at least partly right. The hearings did not stop all men bosses from making sexual advances to the women who worked under them, but the hearings did make manifest to the millions of American women who were watching that the Senate was a boys' club whose members had little regard for woman. The image of an embattled Hill attacked by an army of powerful men stirred so many women to join the struggle for change that the next year, 1992, came to be called the "Year of the Woman."

Record-breaking numbers of women ran for political office. More women than ever were elected to state legislatures. (In the state of Washington, women made up a whopping 40 percent of the legislature as a result of the 1992 election.) More were elected to executive offices, too, becoming attorneys general, lieutenant governors, and state treasurers. Emily's List, a national organization founded in 1985 to raise money for women political candidates, grew from 3,500 to 24,000 members in less than a year after the Hill–Thomas hearings and quadrupled the donations it received.[24] In federal races, twenty-four new women were elected to the House, bringing the number of congresswomen to forty-seven. Four more women were elected to the Senate, including the first Black woman,

Carol Moseley Braun. A year later Kay Bailey Hutchinson won a special election, bringing the total number of women senators to seven. When Ruth Bader Ginsburg was nominated to the Supreme Court in 1993, the Senate Judiciary Committee, still smarting from the flak it received over the Hill–Thomas debacle, approved her by a vote of 18–0. She was confirmed in the Senate by a vote of 96–3 and became the second woman on the Court, joining Sandra Day O'Connor, who had been the lone woman justice since 1981.

Without the disturbing optics of the Hill–Thomas hearings—an all-male Senate committee passing judgment on a woman forced to defend herself as though she were the perpetrator of a crime rather than its victim—would there have been such a sudden and tremendous groundswell to make women's voices heard? It is doubtful. The story of Hill, the Rosa Parks of sexual harassment, even triggered a third wave of feminism.

Rebecca Walker was twenty-one years old when she watched the televised hearings. Her mother, Alice Walker, author of the feminist novel *The Color Purple* (1982), had been a leader among Black feminists (or "womanists," her preferred term). But the younger Walker, like other post-feminists of her generation, had had little interest in her mother's cause. She had caricatured what she saw as its fanatical dictates: "You had to live in poverty, hate pornography, and must always be devoted to the uplift of your gender."[25] But Hill's ordeal made her reconsider.

In an article published in *Ms.* in January 1992, Rebecca Walker wrote of the Hill–Thomas hearings as an epiphany. To her, the hearings were not simply about determining whether Thomas had harassed Hill. Rather, they put all women's credibility on trial. And they raised important questions: "Can a woman's experience undermine a man's career? Can a woman's voice, a woman's sense of self-worth and injustice, challenge a structure predicated on the subjugation of our gender?" With Thomas's confirmation, Walker believed, those questions had been answered with a loud "No." "Men were assured of the inviolability of their penis/power," she complained. "Women were admonished to keep their experiences to themselves."

And as if the lesson Walker had learned through the treatment of Hill was not enough, she wrote, her fury was exacerbated by another epiphany a week after the hearings: an experience on a train—three men behind her outdoing one another with boasts of their sex conquests ("Man, I fucked that bitch all night, and then I never called her again"). Walker exhorted her women readers to understand as she now did that the feminist fight was not over. Men had always used sex to affirm their power over woman and keep her in subjugation. Now women must feel outrage and turn that outrage into power: "Do not vote for them unless they work for us. Do not have sex with them, do not break bread with them, do not nurture them if they don't prioritize our freedom to control our bodies and our lives." She announced that she herself was no longer a "postfeminist." Her feminism, however, was different from that of her mother's generation: "I am the Third Wave," Rebecca Walker proclaimed.[26]

SEX IN THE THIRD WAVE

"Economic parity is less threatening to the system than sexual equality."

—NANCY FRIDAY, *Women on Top* (1991)[27]

Feminists of the third wave recognized that their second-wave mothers had done the heavy lifting that gave the daughters freedoms that had been inconceivable two generations earlier. But the daughters, steeped in theories of intersectionality and postmodernism, also rejected many ideas of second-wave feminism. They had particular trouble with the idea of "woman" as a collective term. As twenty-three-year-old JeeYuen Lee put it, "These days, whenever someone says the word 'women' to me, my mind goes blank. What 'women'? What is this 'women' you're talking about? Does that mean me? Does that mean my mother, my roommates, the white woman next door, the checkout clerk at the supermarket, my aunts in Korea, half the world's population?" Because there was no such thing as universal womanhood, they argued, it was foolish or disingenuous to strive for unity of thought and behavior, as the older generation had putatively tried to do by assuming that all feminists were "sisters" and alike.[28]

Nevertheless, third-wave feminists were unified in their outrage over Hill's story of unwelcome sexual attention because they recognized that regardless of their differences, all women—reduced to "woman"—were potential prey. Third-wave feminists looked back at the long history of women's cooperation with men's notions about female sexuality, and for them that history elucidated how woman had been confined to her place. Sex had been a major mechanism of control over woman's body and her life. Men had used sex as a weapon of intimidation through rape and social ostracism. The idea of the "good" woman and the "bad" woman (fashioned out of men's insecurities about paternity) had even limited how far a woman might venture beyond the threshold of her home before she suffered stigma.

But men were not solely to blame for this weaponizing of sex: women had internalized men's ideas and agreed—even against the evidence of their own feelings—that nature made men sexually aggressive and (good) women sexually passive. Female moral reform societies had made distinctions between moral women like their members and "fallen women," who needed uplift and rescuing. Young women had accepted the idea that a man would always want to see how far he could get with a girl, and her job would always be to hold him off until marriage. Girls had agonized over lost virginity and lost reputations. Women had long been complicit in accepting the sex rules men made. Women of the third wave would no longer be.[29]

The third wave had emerged out of a sex issue: feminist anger over the treatment of Hill. However, many third wavers soon developed ideas related to a very different sex issue: their right to be more boldly, aggressively, and diversely sexual than women had ever been before. The third wavers challenged the sex rules, and they did it with a vengeance.

Even their desires, whether expressed or fantasized, purportedly became different from those of the previous generation. In 1973, Nancy Friday had published *My Secret Garden*, a best-selling compilation of women's sexual fantasies. Eighteen years later she published *Women on Top: How Real Life Has Changed Women's Sexual Fantasies*. The latter title reflected the metamorphoses that had come about in the intervening years. In her introduction to *Women on Top*, Friday compared the differences she had found in compiling her two books. The voices of the women who shared their fantasies with her for *My Secret Garden*, she wrote, were "tentative and filled with guilt, not for having done anything but simply for daring to admit the inadmissible: that they had erotic thoughts that sexually aroused them." But the years that followed had brought light-years of change. In *Women on Top*, the voices of those who shared their fantasies "sound like a new race of women," Friday remarked with astonishment.[30]

To illustrate, she observed that both generations of women had had rape fantasies. But that was where the similarity ended: "Today's woman is just as likely to flip the scenario into one in which she overpowers and rapes the man." In the 1970s, Friday exclaimed, "this sort of thing just didn't happen." Through their fantasies, the *Women on Top* informants declared themselves to be new sexual beings. They desired control in the sex act; they were determined to "experience the fullest sexual release";

and—most shocking of all—their sexual fantasies were suffused with anger. Friday recalled of the women of *My Secret Garden* that in their generation, "nice women didn't express anger. They choked on it and turned whatever anger they had against themselves." But the new generation of women had liberated themselves, at least in their fantasies, to feel things their mothers would not let themselves feel. Even those young women who had few real sexual experiences, Friday wrote, aspired to "free their sexuality from the iron rules that have always been clamped on untamed feminine eroticism."[31]

The new yearning that Friday recorded helps explain the tremendous popularity of the television series *Sex and the City*. The series was based on a best-selling 1997 book by Candace Bushnell in which she brought together her 1994–1996 essays from the *New York Observer* about a circle of women friends, all in their thirties or early forties—unmarried, smart, attractive, and drawing impressive salaries in their high-powered jobs. They do not have to think twice about spending $400 on a pair of Manolo Blahnik strappy sandals, or about having sex with any man they please. Nor do they have to think about whose pleasure is most important in the sex act: it is not, as had been long taken for granted, the man's. "By the time you get to your mid-thirties and are not married, you think, why should I settle?" one of the women, Charlotte, observes after announcing that she turned down a second date with a "beautifully eligible" man because "his unmentionable" was too small. "Index finger," she sighs—a telling counterpoint to the man overheard by Rebecca Walker on the train ("Man, I fucked that bitch all night, and then I never called her again)."[32]

The television series *Sex and the City*, which aired for six seasons beginning in 1998, was not the first to deal with sex and the independent professional woman. Viewers of the *Mary Tyler Moore Show*, which appeared on network television from 1970 to 1977, had been made to understand that Mary Richards, an unmarried thirty-something television news producer, slept with her boyfriends. There were not-so-oblique references to the birth control pills she was careful to take, and there were episodes such as the one in which she left for a date in the evening wearing a dress with a distinct pattern and was shown returning home the next morning wearing the same unmistakable dress. Sex was not often a topic of discussion on the show, but the message was clear that Mary was sexually active.[33]

Beginning in 1988, another network television series, *Murphy Brown*, featured a woman in her forties—like Mary Richards, unmarried, professionally employed in the media industry, and completely independent. In an unprecedented episode, Brown not only announced she was pregnant (she had had a fling with her former husband), but she would be raising the baby alone. The episode triggered a culture skirmish. Vice President Dan Quayle, recognizing its significance as a marker of changing times, famously despaired in a speech to San Francisco's Commonwealth Club that *Murphy Brown* was mocking the nuclear family by dismissing the importance of a father in a child's life and calling a woman's bearing and rearing of a child by herself "just another 'lifestyle choice.'"[34] From the perspective of an ultraconservative like Quayle, the presentation of woman's sexuality and "lifestyle choice" on programs such as the *Mary Tyler Moore Show* and *Murphy Brown* were indeed cataclysmic. But they were tame compared to what followed in the 1990s.

The four leading characters of the *Sex and the City* show—a writer, a lawyer, a public relations executive, and an art dealer—divide their nonworking hours mostly between the pursuit of sex (in which the woman is usually the subject and not the object, the ogler and not the ogled) and meeting each other in womanly camaraderie, chatting over a meal both about the sex they just had or will have or want to have and about their defiance of the expectations that society tries to impose on woman. Nothing sexual is taboo in their talk. Female ejaculation, foot fetishes, phone sex, cybersex, anal sex, fuck buddies, cunnilingus, sex toys, S&M, filming one's sex acts, and having sex while watching films of other people's sex acts—the subjects are endless. The repartee too is often sexual. "Threesomes are huge right now. They're the blowjob of the nineties," Samantha (the public relations executive) informs Charlotte (the art dealer) in the first season. "What was the blowjob of the eighties?" Charlotte asks. "Anal sex," Samantha tells her. In a later episode, Samantha announces, "I'm a trisexual. I'll try anything." Like the other main characters, she cherishes her right to claim her sexuality in any form she wishes, including lesbian sex, of course, and she soon has a fling with a Brazilian woman artist.[35]

The characters of *Sex and the City* do not usually call themselves feminist, though Miranda (the lawyer) is often given feminist lines about, for instance, the importance of woman's economic independence, and the other characters tacitly agree with such feminist observations. It was after all the women's movement that had made their lives possible. They embody the major cultural shift started by Helen Gurley Brown in the 1960s and taken for granted by the 1990s: the unmarried woman in her thirties or forties is no longer a pathetic spinster. In her embodiment as a career woman, she is proud, gutsy, financially independent, and as sexually driven as only men had been permitted to be in the past. In fact, to the women of *Sex and the City* the right to untrammeled sexual pleasure is as sacred as the right to vote had been to first-wave feminists and the right to abortion had been to second-wave feminists.

Sex and the City has had its share of feminist detractors. The characters' focus on sex has caused some feminist critics to misread them as apolitical and even anti-feminist. One critic declared that "*Sex and the City* is to feminism as sugar is to dental care," and another lamented that the popularity of *Sex and the City* was proof of "the death of feminism." To be sure, important feminist issues were elided in *Sex and the City*. The glass ceiling, for instance, certainly impacted women like the main characters: they did well financially and in terms of job prestige, but most of the men they met did even better. *Sex and the City* did not acknowledge sufficiently that some battles may have been won, but the war was far from over. Even among the women fans of *Sex and the City*, only 20 percent said that their sex lives were as liberated as those of the characters.[36] For the other 80 percent, sexual liberation was still largely the stuff of fantasy.

Yet the big claim that the series embodied, that women had a right to break free of sexual boundaries, was not trivial. The *Sex and the City* women flouted the age-old sex boundaries that had scared woman into staying in her place. Their erotic aggressiveness, which vitiated the weaponizing of sex to intimidate women, grabbed hold of the American psyche: *Sex and the City* became the highest-rated cable comedy show in America. It won seven Emmy awards and eight Golden Globe awards and was included by *Time* in its list of the 100 best TV shows of "All-TIME." *Sex and the City* was acknowledged by a *Time* cover, too, on August 28, 2000—a photo of the four stars looking stunningly sexy and very much in charge.[37] The series may have reflected fantasy, but it resonated with a broad swath of women. While only a small minority of American women were as liberated as the four characters, for many others the freedom of the women in *Sex and the City* was aspirational and inspirational.

RIOT GRRRLS

"Those slut rocker bitches walking down the street."
—BIKINI KILL, "White Boy" (1993)[38]

Young radical women such as riot grrrls were conducting their own sort of sex revolution in the 1990s. The riot grrrl movement was part of the anti-establishment punk subculture that had emerged out of punk rock twenty years earlier. Punk women in the 1970s—like bohemian, beatnik, and hippie women in previous years—had joined the underground subculture because they were arty or nonconformist or loathed bourgeois conventionality. But male chauvinism and male bonding flourished even in "alternative" groups, where women were allowed no louder a voice than they had in the bourgeois world. Punk in particular represented high testosterone. Patti Smith, one of the few women stars in early punk rock, made it in the 1970s by laying a convincing claim to high testosterone. "Female. Feel male," she had written of herself and her inner "boy rythums [sic]." On stage, music reviewers said, Smith was "a little Brando, a little Blackboard Jungle." She was a "macho woman." There had been little space for other representations of women in punk. Men were punk's center. Women were the girlfriends, the camp followers who were there mostly for the men's sexual pleasure.[39]

But in the 1990s, for women whose punk identity was filtered through third-wave feminism, the old setup was untenable. Women punk musicians of the 1990s led a new movement that challenged the testosterone-laden punk scene. They created a subculture that reimagined punk women and, in the process, slashed at the limits of sexual expression for all young women. They were mostly young, white, and from middle-class backgrounds, but they envisioned a utopian unity among all "girls," as they emphatically called themselves (no "boy rythums" for them). Through a new girl culture, they planned to fight the evils perpetrated on females by unregenerate men.

Other revolutionary movements for women had been spawned in major metropolitan areas, but this one started in Olympia—the sedate state capital of Washington, sixty miles from hip Seattle—with a do-it-yourself women's punk zine, *Jigsaw,* and a women's punk rock band, Bikini Kill. In 1991, Tobi Vail (the publisher of *Jigsaw* and Bikini Kill's drummer) wrote a feminist fantasy of what "girl power" would look like:

> Can you picture it—gangs of girls . . . all across america [*sic*], breaking through boundaries of race and class and sexual identity, girls who are so strong together that they don't listen to people who tell them that they are stupid or they don't mean anything because they don't really exist—girls so strong together that no one dares to fuck with them when they are walking down the street—GIRL SOLDIERS![40]

Vail's fantasy was reified in Bikini Kill and the other women's punk rock bands—Bratmobile, Heavens to Betsy, Excuse 17, and Team Dresch—that were suddenly emerging in Washington and soon wherever young women had a garage in which to practice.

Kathleen Hanna was a student at Evergreen State College in Olympia when she became Bikini Kill's lead singer and the writer of most of the band's songs. Hanna had learned second-wave feminism in the 1970s through her mother, a not-happy housewife who read *The Feminine Mystique* and subscribed to *Ms.* As a nine-year-old, Hanna cut pictures out of *Ms.* and pasted them on posters that she lettered with personal rallying cries such as "GIRLS CAN DO ANYTHING." When Gloria Steinem and Bella Abzug came to town for a joint appearance in 1977, Hanna and her mother were in the audience. It was the first time the nine-year-old had ever been in a crowd of fervently cheering women. It made her "want to do it forever." But Hanna was a young women in the 1980s, when "feminism" had become a bad word and hip women were "postfeminist." The reductive image that impinged on her consciousness was that all feminists "have hairy legs and are anti-sex."[41] When the third wave came along, though, it caught her. She became a "new feminist," empowered to claim for women the punk boldness and bravura that men had always monopolized for themselves.

A central theme for the women punk-rock performers and their audiences was that they were strong together and so tough that no man would dare to mess with them. The audiences for Bikini Kill and other women's punk-rock groups were masses of wildly cheering women, like the audience that had enchanted Hanna as a nine-year-old. The mosh pit—where male punk fans had always body-slammed and rammed one another in Dionysian violence and eroticized frenzy—became woman space in girl punk concerts. "Girls to the front!" Hanna would holler at performances, demanding a protected spot where women could rock it out without being knocked over or assaulted by testosterone gone wild.

But Hanna's call for "girls to the front" was not only an invitation to young women to enjoy the Dionysian freedom that punk men had always claimed for themselves. "Girls to the front!" was also a revolutionary statement about girl power.[42]

Bikini Kill moved its base to Washington, DC, in 1991. Not long before the group arrived, a Black rookie policewoman in the inner-city ward of Mount Pleasant had shot a Salvadoran man in the chest. Allegedly, he was drunk and had lunged at her with a knife after a Cinco de Mayo street party. Three nights of riots led by young Hispanic males followed, dominating the news cycle. The riots made an impression on the Bikini Kill women. With rare exceptions, such as the Women's Liberation Army's mini-riot at the Armed Forces Induction Center, rioting had always been a super-macho expression of anger. Women had been all but invisible in riots. Now the women punk musicians decided to appropriate rioting. But instead of participating in a riot with looting and burning, they and their music and zines would be the riot. "Riot grrrls," they named themselves. Though they were women in their twenties, they agreed that by calling themselves "grrrls" they were reclaiming a word that had been associated with female powerlessness. The media got it. As the *San Francisco Examiner* explained in a 1992 article on the rapid spread of the riot grrrl movement, "That's girl with an angry grrrrowl."[43]

Local newspapers all over the country—finding the image of defiant young grrrls talking sex and feminism irresistible—broadcast the ubiquity of the movement and abetted its growth. It was as though Vail's fantasy of "GIRL SOLDIERS" had already come true. "Groups of Riot Grrrls are quickly assembling all over the nation," North Carolina's *Daily Tar Heel* announced in 1992, reporting that riot grrrls were "meeting in nightclubs, in laundromats, in frilly pink bedrooms with stuffed animals on the bed."[44]

The first issue of *Riot Grrrl* zine, in 1991, complained of "the general lack of girl power in society as a whole." "GIRL POWER!" became the logo on the cover of subsequent issues. It also became the rallying cry of a movement.[45] "Girl power" had been oxymoronic in the past. Girls demanding power was a gender-bending notion, the antithesis of a social tyranny that turned docile "girl" into docile "woman." The most vulnerable of females, mere girls, were claiming power, insisting on a share in what men had considered their exclusive birthright.

Riot grrrls even tried to alter power's semiotics by giving new meaning to the symbol of crotch clutching, which had become iconic in the

1980s, beginning with a feminine-looking Michael Jackson in his music video *Bad* (1987), signaling to a bunch of toughs that he had cojones by grabbing his crotch. In her music video *Express Yourself* (1989), Madonna, exchanging her slinky green gown for a man's suit, had also claimed cojones by grabbing her crotch to signal that she was as virile as the men surrounding her. In "Resist Psychic Death" (1992), Kathleen Hanna, belting out that she would "resist with every inch and every breath" the forces that tried to tell her what to think and how to be, also clutched her crotch. Like Jackson's and Madonna's crotch grab, the gesture was meant to jolt the audience. But far from claiming that a woman can have "balls," it communicated that Hanna was signaling that the vulva (her essentialist synecdoche for woman) was the source of her power to resist.[46]

Despite that essentialism, riot grrrls tore away the facade of a characteristic that had continued to be thought natural to woman: her tenderness. Riot grrrls were unmitigatedly tough, as even the various monikers of their bands suggested. Bikini Kill, one of the first bands, took its name from a B movie in which bikini-clad females, determined to remake the world into a matriarchy of peace and love, kill the evil men in their way. Other grrrl bands announced their fury at wrong-doing men by giving themselves names such as Cutthroats, Seven Year Bitch, Gore Gore Girls, and Cold Cold Hearts. They even threatened that women's anger at male abuse could boil over into homicide: "My revenge is death / 'cuz you deserve the best, / And I'm not turned on by your masculinity. / Dead men don't rape," the Seattle group 7 Year Bitch sang.[47]

Riot grrrls saw themselves as a corrective to Madonna's "Material Girl"—who, in her 1985 song, offered her glamorous favors to "the boy with the cold hard cash." Riot grrrls not only disdained materialism and living off of men, they also sneered at glamour. One group even called itself The Frumpies. Insouciant frumpiness was grrrls' preferred style, featuring pointy cat-eye glasses; plastic baby barrettes; vintage baby-doll dresses with round collars and puff sleeves, worn with combat boots or sneakers and bobby socks; grrrl punk hairdos of shaved heads or hacked-off hair; and "whore-like" incandescent red lipstick that was purposely jarring. Riot grrrls dressed any damn way they pleased. They rejected what a woman was supposed to look like. They also rejected what a man was supposed to look like. Riot grrrls in Washington, DC, chalked graffiti all over the city announcing "REAL BOYZ WEAR PINK." They delighted in challenging the sacrosanct signifiers of gender. At a Riot Grrrl Extravaganza in Olympia, the cover charge was two dollars for women and three dollars for men, but if a man showed up in drag he could get a dollar discount.[48]

On stage and in life, riot grrrls used their bodies as billboards. On their exposed midriffs, they scrawled the words "slut" and "whore" with lipstick or magic markers, to confront the hypocrisy that penalized women (but never men) for having multiple sex partners. Or they scrawled "rape" or "incest" on their torsos or arms—not only to shame men for their sexual misdeeds, but also in the conviction that exposing such abuses instead of locking them up inside made women stronger. (It was a revolutionary notion that would catch fire in the next millennium through social media as the Me Too movement.) They wore T-shirts proclaiming, "I've had 21 abortions." They jeered at men's claim that women were "asking for it" by the way they dressed or acted, and they depicted themselves as "those slut rocker bitches walking down the street." Riot grrrl singers sometimes appeared on stage bare-breasted—not for allure but to assert the right that men claimed for themselves, to uncover their chest whenever they liked.[49] They confronted and affronted.

In their music and in the do-it-yourself zines they wrote, typed, photocopied, stapled together, and passed out to friends and at concerts, they claimed grrrls' right to verboten words. It was a way of wresting power from men who had used those words to intimidate woman. It was an assertion of grrrl toughness, a rejection of the notion of womanly fragility and vulnerability. Women had understood the power of that tactic before. In "Sex-Nomenclature" (1887), Angela Heywood had claimed woman's right to say sex words like "cunt" and "cock," just as men did. In "The Bitch Manifesto" (1970), Jo Freeman had reclaimed "bitch" to mean a woman who "takes shit from no one." But the reach of riot grrrls went much further than that of Heywood or Freeman. Mainstream magazines were intrigued by the flamboyantly rebellious grrrls who would say forbidden things: "SLUT. Yeah, I'm a slut. My body belongs to me. I'm not your property," *Newsweek* quoted a riot grrrl's outrageous trash talk, spreading the word about riot grrrls' defiance, as well as the whole riot grrrl phenomenon, to 20 million weekly readers.[50] When riot grrrls claimed words that had been forbidden to woman, their well-reported new vocabulary went a long way toward shifting what a woman might say in public.

"Bitch"—meaning what "The Bitch Manifesto" twenty years earlier had said it ought to mean—became a favorite riot grrrl self-descriptor. "Bitch Theme," a song from the album *Pottymouth* by Bratmobile, is made up of two lines, "You're such a bitch," and the flattered response,

"Do you really think so?" The bitch in Bikini Kill's "Lil' Red Riding Bitch" reverses the victimized girl image, declaring, "Here are my ruby red lips / Ready to suck you dry." [51]

With particular relish, riot grrrls claimed the right to say "fuck," using the word both as an uncensored description of a sex act and as an expletive. In Bratmobile's "Juswanna," the would-be male seducer declares "I love you so much I can't see you . . . I juswanna fuck you," and he is told by the woman, "I hate you so much fuckin' fuck you . . . I'm not your fuckin' living dead." In Bikini Kill's "Don't Need You," the singer shouts: "Don't need your atti-fuckin-tude boy / Don't need your dick to fuck." In another Bikini Kill song, "This Is Not a Test," a detractor snarls at a grrrl, "You're fucked!" She responds with confidence, "I'm nahhhht!" The Frumpies warn in their song "Fuck Yr. Frumpies" that they are "ballbreakers," they are "the evil bitch no one can slay."[52]

Riot grrrls took it as an objective: they would tear away all facades of womanly propriety. They would not be intimidated by sex or anything else. They would be aggressively sexual because a woman who feared sex, was sexually reticent, or valued sexual modesty handed back to men the power they had had over women in the midcentury and earlier. A woman had a right to flaunt her sexuality any damn way she wanted, riot grrrls insisted. When Hanna was low on money, she danced in a strip club. Sex work was not exploitative, Hanna believed, as long as the woman was in charge of what she did. Having to work as a low-paid, harried waitress—now, that would have been exploitative.[53]

But riot grrrls also warned women away from being complicit in their own sexual victimization. For example, in the chillingly titled "Broken Teeth" by the grrrl punk band Cold Cold Hearts, a woman sees a tough guy walking down the street, thinks "That's the kind of asshole I'd like to meet," and asks herself "How many ways can I be a fuckin' bore doormat?"[54] Grrrl power meant rejecting such victimization while claiming the same freedom to have and talk sex that men had always claimed for themselves. Any sort of sex expression was fine in riot grrrl culture—as long as a woman chose it freely, and it did not turn her into "a fuckin' bore doormat."

Women's new assertive sexuality was as basic to third-wave feminism and riot grrrl culture as it was to the fantasy world of *Sex and the City*. More insistently and more vociferously than in any previous generation in America, women were declaring themselves totally liberated from the tyrannical myths of woman that had depicted her as sexually passive and "passionless." They were free of the cultural bugaboos that had shamed women as "nymphomaniacs" and "bad girls" if they violated those myths. Women were now pronouncing themselves entitled to the sex privileges men had always hoarded exclusively for themselves. For masses of women, in mainstream as well as underground culture, their relationship to sex seemed to undergo a sea change in the 1990s.

But in reality, sex freedom was more complicated than was acknowledged in their assertions or aspirations. Despite the bravado of "Grrrl Power!" boasts, men were still the ones with the real power. They were still the most likely to make the decisions about whether an Anita Hill could keep her job and what sexual impositions she had to tolerate in order to do so. Despite fantasies of an army of "GIRL SOLDIERS," men were still physically stronger than women. Threats of rape or "broken teeth" had not gone away. The sex-positive milieu encouraged by social phenomena such as *Sex and the City* and *Bust* gave woman the freedom to say "yes" and even "let's." But was she equally free to say "no" if she were harassed? Would "no" stop her harasser? Would she be believed if she told on him? Could women really claim sex equality with men as long as men were almost always keepers of the gates of employment, able to overwhelm women with superior strength, and more credible in their denials than women were in their accusations? Women may have changed their relationship to sex in the 1990s, but their daughters in the next century still had basic sex battles to fight.

15.
"Woman" in a New Millennium

October 12, 2020: A half-century earlier, she might have been taken for some powerful man's executive secretary—dressed in a fuchsia-pink frock and pale-pink high-heeled shoes, with pearls around her neck and her blonde hair styled shoulder length, her voice girlishly high. As she appeared before the Senate Judiciary Committee, Amy Coney Barrett, the forty-eight-year-old nominee to fill the U.S. Supreme Court seat of the recently deceased Justice Ruth Bader Ginsburg, was a sharp contrast to women of other eras whose work placed them in the public eye. A century earlier, for instance, Sarah Josephine Baker, a health director for the city of New York, had felt obliged to print her name on official stationery as "Dr. S. J. Baker" so that the Health Department could, as she later recalled, "disguise the presence of a woman in a responsible executive post." Baker had worn "man-tailored suits," shirtwaists, stiff collars, and four-in-hand ties because, she said, "I badly needed protective coloring . . . [so that] when a masculine colleague of mine looked around the office in a rather critical state of mind, no feminine furbelows would catch his eye and give him an excuse to become irritated by the presence of a woman where, according to him, a woman had no right to be."[1]

Clearly, in 2020 Amy Coney Barrett did not feel the need to hide her feminine appearance or what was most conspicuously feminine about her life. In her Rose Garden speech accepting her nomination to the Supreme Court, Barrett highlighted her attention to traditional woman's duties: "While I am a judge, I am better known back home as a room parent, car-pool driver, and birthday party planner." In her twelve-minute opening statement to the Senate Judiciary Committee, Barrett also talked a lot about her husband and children. She described each one in loving detail, including the girl and boy whom she and her husband had adopted from Haiti and her youngest child, who has Down syndrome. The six oldest children sat behind her, in full view of the senators.[2]

"WOMAN" REBORN

"I don't want to conquer the world. I don't want that kind of life."
"The Opt-Out Revolution" (2003)[3]

American women entered the twenty-first century less tied to the limits of womanhood than ever before. Unwanted pregnancy could be a dilemma of the past. Among heterosexual women, 98 percent had at some point used birth control, most often the reliable Pill. And if contraception failed, as it did for about a million women a year, *Roe v. Wade* was still the law of the land. Higher education—from Ivy League universities and professional schools to community colleges—was now wide open to women. Asian American women, like white women, were outstripping men in earning degrees. The numbers of Latinas and Black women in college were growing exponentially.[4]

Careers from which women had once been excluded now embraced them. By 2000 almost half the law students and half the medical students were women. They occupied 40 percent of the seats in dental schools. Fifty percent of the undergraduate business majors were women, and after graduation they were being recruited by the top firms. They would soon become the majority of veterinarians. Eighty-six percent of corporations had at least one woman on their board. By 2001, about one-third of the states had had women governors, and there were sixty-two women in the U.S. House of Representatives and thirteen in the Senate. Working- and middle-class women by and large still clustered in the sorts of jobs to which their great-grandmothers had been limited—office and service work, as well as teaching and nursing—but some of them found jobs in construction, on police forces, or as firefighters.[5] The twentieth-century women's movements truly had transformed who women could be.

But there were rumbles of discontent, just as there had been in the 1980s when newspaper headlines announced "Many Young Women Now Say They'd Pick Family over Career" and "Professional Women Do Go Home Again." As the new millennium approached, books began appearing such as *Surrendering to Motherhood* by Iris Krasnow, a former journalist with United Press International who realized she could not "have it all"—fulfilling work and a full personal life—and gave up her glamorous globe-trotting job to be a stay-at-home mom with her four boys, all of whom were under the age of seven. National polls seemed to confirm that many women really did yearn to give up their complicated new lives and turn the clock back to a simpler time. In 1997, the same year that *Surrendering to Motherhood* was published, a poll conducted by the Kaiser Family Foundation, Harvard University, and the *Washington Post* asked, "Considering everything, do you think it would be better or worse for the country if men and women went back to the traditional roles they had in the 1950s?" Fully 42 percent of the women respondents said a return to roles of the 1950s would be "better"; only 35 percent thought it would be "worse." Another national poll conducted in 1997, by the Families and Work Institute, found that 50 percent of married working women agreed that it was "much better for everyone involved if the man earns the money and the woman takes care of the home and the children."[6]

The proportion of working women with children had risen steadily after World War II, from 17 percent immediately after the war to 77 percent in 1997. But the long upward trend suddenly came to an end and soon was reversed. By 2005 there was a two-percentage-point drop in the share of working women who were mothers of school-age children. In addition, women with preschool children were 6 percent less likely to work than their counterparts had been just eight years earlier: 5.6 million women with children did not cross their threshold to go to work in 2005, which was 1.2 million more stay-at-home mothers than there had been in 1995. Even women who had devoted years to climbing the career ladder were going home. The cultural historian Linda Hirshman tracked down women whose society-page wedding announcements in 1996 indicated that they had had professional jobs. By 2004, 90 percent of them had become mothers and only 15 percent of the mothers were still working full-time; the rest worked part-time or had given up their careers entirely.[7]

Were millennial women retreating from a life outside the home because they had lost the passion of their mothers' generation to blast through the limits that had been imposed on "woman"? Was a woman's retreat from the spaces that men had historically claimed for themselves inevitable once she acknowledged biology and became a mother? Was the work world intrinsically hostile to women's special needs, or were husbands to blame for not lightening their wives' duties at home? Or was the hope to "have it all" an unrealistic ambition that had lived only in the hearts of hard-bitten feminists?

The news media were again depicting feminism to be as antiquated as tie-dyed T-shirts. For instance, there was a 2003 news story of a women's book club made up of eight women who had all gotten their BA degrees from Princeton University and gone on to get law degrees at Harvard or Columbia University. They had worked for high-prestige companies. They were in line to make partner. Then they married men with equally high-prestige jobs, had children, and quit their jobs. They had decided that life on the fast track was unappealing. As one of them concluded—all her hard work to get Ivy League degrees notwithstanding—"I don't want to be famous. I don't want to conquer the world. I don't want that kind of life." Women were essentially different from men, the women agreed. Relationships were what was important to women. They don't rule the world because they don't want to. The former lawyers even insisted that women have "different brains" from men, which causes women to "inevitably make different choices." Career feminists had tried to bury the truth about woman, but these Princeton alumnae were unearthing them, as one of the women proclaimed: they were not ashamed of "swinging to a place where we enjoy, and can admit we enjoy, the stereotypical role of female/mother/caregiver. I think we were born with those feelings."[8]

For twentieth-century women who had fought ardently against the feminine mystique and had managed to tear down so many of the limits on what women could do, the tales of how lightly a new generation was taking their hard-won victories were disturbing. But opt-out women resented the fact that, as they saw it, they had been brainwashed by those feminists into thinking they wanted things they now concluded they did not really want. Lauren Burns, a Columbia University–trained psychologist, complained that the feminists had incessantly filled her head "throughout my childhood and my years of education" with ill-conceived ambitions. Burns had become a clinical supervisor for developmentally disabled children, and just before she began a maternity leave, she was given a "huge promotion in title and compensation." She had been certain that she would go back to her profession after her baby was born. Everything seemed to be falling into place to permit that: the infant had been accepted into a "coveted" child-care program. Her husband had a flexible work schedule, which made him able to share household responsibilities. Her clinic's generous maternity leave plan would allow her to work from home and resume work-site duties gradually. What twentieth-century feminists had fought for was now in Burns's grasp.

However, she concluded in an essay about her joy in saying goodbye to her career and literally dancing about the house with her first child and then two more babies: "Many others were skilled, knowledgeable, and compassionate enough to step into my shoes. But no one could know like I did when my baby was hungry."[9]

A nostalgia for the way things were, before the women's revolution succeeded in turning things topsy-turvy, crept into even sophisticated media. In "To Hell with All That" (2004), Caitlin Flanagan, a writer for the *New Yorker* and the *Atlantic*, recalled her idyllic 1960s childhood—when her mother kept on a kitchen counter a copy of Benjamin Spock's *Baby and Child Care* and one of *The Settlement House Cookbook*, when "God was in his heaven and a rump roast was in the oven." But, as Flanagan's essay's title hints, the feminist bug bit her mother in 1973 and made her suddenly exclaim, "to hell" with housewifery and full-time mothering. She took a job. Flanagan's explanation for her mother's cavalier rejection of her domestic duties was that feminism just happened to be the mode of the time: had her mother lived in another time, Flanagan dismissively speculated, she might have "read *Middlemarch* or taken up watercolor."

While her mother's job did cheer her up, Flanagan reported, it traumatized the adolescent Caitlin, who loathed afternoons alone in an empty house and felt abandoned. As an adult, reading the crumbling pages of her mother's edition of Spock's book—in which the doctor declared that children of working mothers "grow up neglected and maladjusted"—Flanagan pronounced Spock's words to be "politically radical, morally compelling, and honest."[10]

When Flanagan's own children were born, she chose to stay home with them, certain that they gained by her constant presence "an immersion into the most powerful force on earth: mother love." Flanagan was supported in her convictions by a spate of new expert books such as *Maternal Desire* by Daphne de Marneffe, a female clinical psychologist who was critical of women who devalued a "natural instinct" that she described as woman's "embodied, aching desire to be with [her] children."[11]

Young college women too were reprising the feminine mystique, even before they graduated—unabashedly deciding, as their grandmothers had, that their purpose in going to college was to get an MRS degree. Despite rigorous academic study intended to prepare them to step onto the world stage, they planned to settle into the domestic roles that had been thought fitting for woman long before the advent of feminism. "Many Women at Elite Colleges Set Career Path to Motherhood," a 2005 *New York Times* headline announced. The journalist who wrote the article had interviewed 138 women college students and claimed that 60 percent of them told her they would "happily play a traditional female role, with motherhood their main commitment." Cynthia Liu, a nineteen-year-old who had gotten into Yale University because of her high SAT scores, 4.0 grade-point average, trophies in speech tournaments, polished musicianship, and so on, was quoted as saying: "My mother always told me you can't be the best career woman and the best mother. You have to choose one over the other." She would choose to be the best mother. Liu's roommate at Yale, Angie Ku, claimed to be ambitious only for a conventional domestic life. She retorted to anticipated criticism from feminists that she, unlike them, accepted "things how they are. I don't mind the status quo. I don't see why I have to go against it."[12]

Such reports emboldened those who believed that the demands of the feminist movement had been wrongheaded to begin with. Just days after the publication of the *New York Times* article, Richard Posner, an eminent jurist and University of Chicago law professor, argued that, indeed, most women did not want the prizes for which the feminists had fought. He pointed out that, for instance, a decade or so after getting their fancy degrees from Harvard Business School, merely 38 percent of the women graduates were still working full-time. Posner knew why this was so. Just as in 1776 John Adams had declared women unsuited for dealing with "the great business of life" and pronounced them "fittest for domestic cares," so in 2005 Posner observed that "women on average have a greater taste and aptitude for taking care of children, and indeed for non-market activities, than men do." This sex differentiation was a problem, Posner wrote, only when women pretended it did not exist and demanded unqualified entry into men's spaces, taking up "a significant percentage of places" in the best professional schools where only a very limited number of students could be admitted.

Since it was dubious that a woman would work long in the profession for which an elite school prepared her, Posner argued, her education was wasted, and her admission "in effect kept a man who would be productive in [that] profession from achieving." Advanced education for women was, in the long run, a misuse of resources, he wrote. It did not make them better mothers—and anyway, most of them were in school for no more weighty reason than to satisfy their intellectual curiosity or to look for a husband. The logical conclusion was that professional schools must admit fewer women.[13]

The millennial women who triggered what was being called the "opt-out revolution"—who had been educated for a profession and chose to immerse themselves in domesticity instead—were upper-middle-class. The paucity of good professional day care was not the problem for them: they could easily have afforded the best. But they shared Burns's belief that not even the best nanny "could know like I did when my baby was hungry." The media were fascinated with their stories as a retort to feminism. Leslie Stahl announced on the television newsmagazine 60 *Minutes* that to be stay-at-home mothers they had elected to "give up money, success and big futures." Close to 10 million viewers watched as Stahl introduced Sheilah O'Donnel, who had been earning half-a-million dollars a year as a top sales representative for Oracle, the multinational computer technology corporation. O'Donnel was captured in an opening shot, smiling and pushing a baby stroller, a happy housewife now.[14]

The media focus on affluent wives who opted out helped revive 1950s-style domesticity among the less affluent, too. Middle- and lower-middle-class women were quitting work and going home to be full-time mothers.

Unlike upper-middle-class professionals, many of them had had to struggle to find affordable day care, which could make work outside the home problematic. But for some to be able to opt out became something of a status symbol: it was proof that one had a husband who was making good wages. Even if it meant that their families would have to "sell cars and houses, eat beans and rice, and count every penny," women were going home. Motherhood was again transformed into a cult of "mommies" as obsessive as it had been in the days of June Cleaver. Women who had not had the heart to withdraw entirely from the careers for which they had trained cut back at least, sometimes with guilty ambivalence about working even part-time. As Leslie Steiner, a Harvard graduate with an MBA from the Wharton School of Business, explained somewhat defensively in the introduction to her edited volume *Mommy Wars*, she now worked several hours a week, but if she had to work at a job that required too much of her time she would not work at all, because of course her children's "psychological well-being and the joy I get from being the emotional linchpin of their lives mean more to me."[15]

The new mommy mystique left out critical masses of women, including those who could not afford to stay home and those who refused to surrender the spaces for which the women's movement had fought in the previous century. Working-class and single mothers of all races, who were not sure of even having beans and rice if they stopped working, did not have the luxury of opting out. Lesbians of all races did not opt out either. Like their nineteenth-century predecessors who were in same-sex relationships, lesbians kept working because they had no man to support them and because their job made their independence possible. Nor was opting out a fashion among most Black women who had been trained for careers. Richard Posner may have been right that only a fraction of the women who earned MBAs were still working ten years later, but that was not true of Black women MBAs, who continued working at a rate closer to that of white male MBAs. Lonnae O'Neal Parker, a Black journalist, suggested in her 2005 book *I'm Every Woman* that this was so because Black women had always had a different relationship to work than most white women had. "I was in college before I realized some women considered working to be an option," Parker wrote. The need to earn a living that had been imposed on Black working-class women was communicated to their educated daughters, even as the daughters moved into the middle class. Parker was twenty-four years old and working for the *Washington Post* when she learned from a white female colleague that some mothers felt guilty about working. That was "something I had never heard in all the conversations with all the Black women I had ever known."[16]

Interviews with a group of women in the affluent Black community of Mitchellville, Maryland, confirm her point. The women were lawyers, technology experts, corporate managers, and entrepreneurs, and they were dismissive of the opt-out revolution. As one woman put it, Black women "don't generally have the time or luxury for the guilt . . . that some white mothers engage in." Black women might wrestle with the same worries and longings, but they felt a responsibility to build security for their families. Even among those Black women with college degrees who had children under eighteen at home, 84 percent were working.[17]

Yet Black women were not universally immune to the opt-out trend. Only fifteen miles from Mitchellville, in Prince George's County, in 1997—the year that the Families and Work Institute poll found that 50 percent of married working women agreed that it was "much better for everyone involved if the man earns the money and the woman takes care of the home and the children"—some middle-class Black women also agreed. Four of them, including Cheli English-Figaro, a Columbia Law School graduate and stay-at-home mom, started Mocha Moms, an organization dedicated to "mothers of color for whom parenting is a priority." Mocha Moms were largely college-educated Black women who, like their class counterparts among white women, were fervent devotees of the mommy mystique. There were soon a hundred Mocha Moms chapters and thousands of members around the country, though as one Mocha Mom complained, other Black women had so little understanding of her decision to give up her career that they thought "I'm on crack for being at home."[18]

TWENTY-FIRST-CENTURY WOMAN LEAVES HOME

> "The risk of divorce reduces by about half when a wife earns half the income and a husband does half the housework."
>
> —SHERYL SANDBERG, *Lean In* (2013)[19]

The opt-out revolution and the mommy mystique were short-lived. In 2008–2009, a recession hit that was dubbed a "mancession" because men, from construction workers to Wall Street money managers, suffered 82 percent of the job losses. Women who had been trained for traditional woman's professions—teaching or nursing, for example—had less trouble finding employment than their laid-off husbands did. Many women, even those with young children, became their family's main wage earner. By 2011, the number of women in the U.S. labor force reached an all-time high. Though many had gone back to work because they had to, they continued working even when the mancession was over. By 2013, upper-middle-class women who had dropped out of the workforce were clamoring to return. Now the news media were blaring headlines such as "The Opt-Out Generation Wants Back In." Sheilah O'Donnel, the woman who had given up an annual salary of half-a-million dollars, had by now been through a messy divorce. She was very ready to opt in again. But she had been out of the job market for almost a decade, she was approaching middle-age, and the economic landscape had changed. O'Donnel finally found a midlevel sales job, at a fraction of her former salary.[20]

The opt-out fervor had been explained in essentialist terms (woman's inherent "aching desire" to be near her young), and many women who opted out had certainly longed to be full-time mommies. Yet the choice to quit a job for which a woman had worked hard to qualify or that gave her a sense of independence was complicated by other factors, too. By the 1980s, the majority of women with children under eighteen had been crossing the threshold of their homes every morning to go to work. Women had changed. But most men had not. When women crossed back in the evening they went to work again, putting in a "second shift," doing "woman's work" that men would not deign to do because, tautologically, it was "woman's work." The sociologist Arlie Hochschild, author of *The Second Shift* (1989), interviewed dozens of couples of all classes who lived in the progressive San Francisco Bay Area. As she discovered, a husband might "help" his wife with household duties—but they were her duties, woman's duties, and he was just lending a hand. Hochschild found that even husbands who professed to believe in egalitarian marriages weaseled out of second-shift duties. Typically, the wife came home from her outside job to do the cleaning, cooking, shopping, and most of the child care. The husband took care of the car and walked the dog.[21]

With the start of the new millennium, little had changed. Women were still doing 80 percent of the housework and two-thirds of the child care, in addition to the jobs most of them held outside the home. The legal scholar Joan Williams declared in 2000 that that was so because gender had remained "unbending." True, women were seen as serious participants in the workforce. True, there were few jobs from which they were barred. True, even the best professional schools were open to them. But at home, it was sex roles as usual. Women now had the right to work as hard as men did at jobs outside the home, but men did not work as hard as women did at jobs inside the home. "Every woman knows her pediatrician's telephone number, but I have yet to meet a man who does," the author Susan Cheever quipped.[22]

Though most husbands remained recalcitrant, some employers, hoping to be responsive to women's special needs, began offering flextime, part-time schedules, job sharing, paid maternity leaves, and "phasing back" programs. *Working Mother* published an annual list of "100 Best Companies" for career women. Companies that did not have such special options for women employees did not make the list. But a woman who took advantage of those options often would be deemed to be on the "mommy track." The "mommy trap," Betty Friedan called it, referring to the fact that career women who chose to have children were forced to pay a permanent price in professional advancement.[23] Needless to say, there was no such thing as a "daddy track."

However, just as the idea of "woman" mutates, so can the idea of "man" mutate. That happened in surprising ways as the twenty-first century progressed. The Bureau of Labor Statistics found in 2019 that on most days, 71 percent of men were now doing household chores: cooking, cleaning, lawn care, and household management. Among white men the average amount of housework time spent per day was one hour and forty-five minutes. Black, Latino, and Asian men spent somewhat less time than white men—but in all demographics, though men gave less time to housework than did women, they were doing much more of it than in the days when they mostly took care of the car and walked the dog. The metamorphosis was due in part to rapidly changing ideas about appropriate gender behavior. In 2006, 38 percent of men believed that it was woman's job to "tend the home." In 2016, only 27 percent believed that. A Pew Research poll found that among Gen X respondents (those born between 1965 and 1980), 36 percent of men called themselves "very masculine" and 32 percent of women called themselves "very feminine." But among millennials, only 24 percent of men considered themselves "very masculine" and only 19 percent of women considered themselves "very feminine." Many millennial men had ceased to identify with the brand of masculinity that their fathers and grandfathers had favored.[24]

The shifts in gender notions were reflected in women's view of their right to work, too. As the opt-out revolution faded, working women—from Walmart greeters to corporate executives—became litigious when their employers assumed that they were on the mommy track. The women began suing over comments such as "Don't you feel bad leaving your kids at home? Don't you miss them?" Articles told working women that "Yes, Being 'Mommy Tracked' Is a Real Thing—But You Don't Have to Put Up with It," and advised them how to fight back against their company's assumption that all women subscribed to the mommy mystique. A former vice president at Goldman Sachs who was fired after being mommy tracked sued the company for millions, complaining that "it's clear that Goldman Sachs views working mothers as second-class citizens who should be at home with their children." Women lawyers at the high-powered San Francisco law firm Morrison and Foerster filed a $100 million class-action suit because when they returned from maternity leave they were "mommy tracked" and not promoted with the rest of their associate class.[25]

One indication of the new thinking about women and work was the popular success of Sheryl Sandberg's 2013 book *Lean In: Women, Work, and the Will to Lead,* which spent more than a year on the *New York Times* best-seller list (including twelve weeks in the number one spot) and sold over 4 million copies. Sandberg, the chief operating officer and second in command at Facebook, exhorted women to stop internalizing the messages that said it was wrong for women to be outspoken, aggressive, and more powerful than men. If women wanted career success, they must stop pulling back and "lean in." They could indeed "have it all" (Sandberg was making $25 million per year), if that was what they wanted. But, Sandberg emphasized, they could not have it all without cooperation from their spouses. "As more women lean into their careers, more men need to lean into their families," she wrote, striking a note that many women were now ready to hear. Sandberg never downplayed the hard parts of having children plus a high-powered career or the inevitable painful conflicts. But she told stories of how she had done it. After a difficult first pregnancy her husband, the chief executive officer of SurveyMonkey, became the baby's primary caregiver—bringing the infant to her for feedings, getting up with him in the middle of the night when he was fretful, and changing his diapers. When their two children were old enough for school, she and her husband sat down "at the beginning of every week

[to] figure out which one of us will drive our children to school that day," she wrote. "If one of us is scheduled to be away, the other almost always arranges to be home."[26]

The point was crucial to her argument: if a woman planned to "lean in" at work, she needed to—as a chapter title said—"Make Your Partner a Real Partner" at home. That, Sandberg promised, was the formula not only for professional success but also for personal success. "The risk of divorce reduces by about half when a wife earns half the income and a husband does half the housework," she declared, and she documented the fact.[27]

Sandberg recognized that not every woman longed to rise to the top in her field. She voiced respect for women who wanted to be stay-at-home mothers and for those who thought that they would work for a while and then start a family. But she encouraged those who anticipated opting out to lean into their job for as long as they had it. "Don't leave before you leave," she wrote, and she admonished them to keep their options open. (That would have been excellent advice for women like Sheilah O'Donnel a few years earlier.) Her most insistent message to women was that they must cast aside the voices in their head that told them that leadership was only for men. After three waves of women's movements, the essence of her advice was not wildly radical.

Yet it was received by many as though it were. Her critics agreed with Anne-Marie Slaughter, a working mother who had been a Princeton University dean and the first woman director of policy planning at the State Department. Slaughter observed in "Why Women Still Can't Have It All," a cover article in the *Atlantic*, that "having a family is a career barrier for women in a way that it is not for men," and though some women have figured out how to have it all, "the success of the few cannot be the answer to the problems of the many." Sandberg's vision for women was making them "downright scared to death," her critics complained. "Leaning in is killing women," a female therapist and career coach wrote in *Forbes*. "What about the children?" Caitlin Flanagan demanded in a *Time* review of Sandberg's book.[28] Sure, Sandberg could bring her baby to work because she was the chief operating officer, but most mothers could not do so, nor could they find worry-free child care. Maybe Sandberg's husband was willing to be the baby's primary caregiver, but most husbands were not. Sandberg was ignoring the stubborn realities and placing an impossible burden on the individual by telling women they just had to work harder.

No less a luminary than Michelle Obama took a potshot at Sandberg and the lean-in movement. The former first lady told a sold-out audience of 19,000, who had come to Brooklyn's Barclay Center to hear her talk about her new autobiography, "That whole 'So you can have it all.' Nope, not all at the same time. That's a lie. And it's not always enough to lean in, because that shit doesn't work all the time." (Obama was no doubt being empathetic with less fortunate women, but she was not being autobiographical. While her own children were young, she did indeed lean in, rising to be a vice president at the University of Chicago Hospitals and earning almost twice the salary her husband made as a U.S. senator.[29])

Yet despite vehement detractors, Sandberg's advice to women to "lean in"—to go for what they wanted and block out the social messaging that kept a woman in her place, to find a partner who was really a partner—touched a nerve with many women who considered *Lean In* to be a powerful manifesto that encouraged them to strive for success. Senator Amy Klobuchar suggested in a 2018 interview that Sandberg's lean-in lessons even helped explain why the number of women in the U.S. Senate kept growing: there had been only fourteen in 2005, but there were twenty-two in 2018. (In 2020 there were twenty-five.) The women senators leaned in enough so that by 2018 they were chairs and ranking members of the Senate's Budget, Agriculture, Appropriations, Environment, and Health Committees, as Klobuchar noted—and she was the ranking member of the Rules Committee. Klobuchar credited "lean in" with making "real, substantive changes. It's not just about getting there. It's about having real impact *while* you're there." She pointed out that the women senators altered Senate culture in ways that would once have been inconceivable, such as pushing through a rule change that made it possible for senators who were mothers to bring their babies onto the Senate floor.[30]

WAR ON MAN'S ANCIENT TACIT PRIVILEGE

"Whatever we wear,
Wherever we go,
Yes means yes, and no means no."
—Chant at a Me Too rally (2017) [31]

Women who were enslaved or were domestic servants had always been at the mercy sexually of men who had power over them. When other women began stepping beyond their threshold and going out to work, they too became more vulnerable—as the reformer Louise DeKoven Bowen lamented in 1912. The physical hardships of work, she had written, "are nothing compared to the moral dangers to which [working women] are exposed." Though Bowen's language became dated, the problem of unwanted sexual advances at work persisted. In 1976, *Redbook* announced in an article titled "What Men Do to Women on the Job: A Shocking Look at Sexual Harassment" that 90 percent of the women who responded to the magazine's survey claimed they had been sexually harassed at work. Only 25 percent of them said they believed that their harasser would be asked to stop if they reported him to a supervisor. In a *New York Times/CBS News* poll taken in 1991, at the time of the Clarence Thomas confirmation hearings, 40 percent of women claimed to have been "the object of sexual advances, propositions, or unwanted sexual discussions" from men at work who had power over their advancement. More than half of the men surveyed in the poll acknowledged that they had said or done something at work that a woman could construe as sexual harassment. Yet despite the numbers that indicated how rife sexual harassment was in the workplace, the same poll showed that only about 20 percent of Americans believed Anita Hill's testimony against Thomas. Forty-seven percent said they thought she was lying. The rest did not know what to think.[32]

The reluctance to believe women and girls who accused men of unwanted sexual moves had long had "scientific" backing. Even the founder of psychoanalysis deemed female patients delusional and hysterical if they reported that they had been sexually abused by a male relative. With Sigmund Freud's imprimatur, subsequent "experts" viewed women's claims of sexual abuse with great skepticism. Dr. Charles Mapes advised his fellow physicians in 1906 that women's accusations of sexual assault should be taken *"cum grano salis"* because the accusations were often based on illusion or worse. Mapes offered as his example of worse an observation from a legal expert: "Not only innocent men but those who have been actually seduced have 'danced at the rope's end' on account of the woman's swearing away the life of the man in order to shield her priceless reputation." Gurney Williams, a forensic medicine specialist, opined in a respected clinical journal in 1913 that so-called rape victims lie as easily as morphine fiends, and that the truth is told about once in thirteen cases. Williams did not say how he arrived at that number, but he did say that if a female really did not want sex all she had to do was cross her knees. The psychiatrist F. R. Bronson wrote in a 1919 article titled "False

Accusations of Rape" that females who make accusations of sexual abuse were frequently acting out of vengeance or hysteria.[33] It was a consensus among medical men that women who cried "rape" or "abuse" were not to be believed.

The legacy of disbelief lived on. Because women had to worry that they would be accused of imagining or lying, it is not surprising that only 10 percent of those who said in the 1991 poll that they were sexually harassed at work had filed a complaint. No matter that women had finally attained rights and even approached equality in some areas, sexual harassment was a reminder of the inherent vulnerability of woman: she could be mastered by man physically or through his position of economic dominance over her. For the abused woman, harassment could erase even the memory of the progress that women had made: it could transform her into a creature as helpless and diminished as woman had been long before the progress had been achieved.

In the months leading up to the 2012 election, the subject of sexual abuse became a surprising focus. First, Todd Akin, a Republican congressman from Missouri who was running for the U.S. Senate against the Democratic incumbent Claire McCaskill, uttered an inanity. Akin was asked in an interview on St. Louis television whether he thought abortion was justified in the case of rape. "If it's a legitimate rape [sic]," Akin answered, a woman would not need an abortion because she would not get pregnant. In a legitimate rape, he explained, "the female body has ways to try to shut the whole thing down." Then Richard Mourdock, a Tea Party candidate from Indiana who defeated Senator Richard Lugar, a six-term incumbent, in his state's Republican primary, managed to outrage his female constituency. Just a couple of weeks before the general election, Mourdock said in a debate against his Democratic opponent that he opposed abortion because even a pregnancy caused by rape was "something God intended." Women's groups let their displeasure be known. Washington, DC, feminists even sent a message directly to Congress by lighting up the Capitol with projected bright-green light that spelled out in huge letters "RAPE IS RAPE."[34] Akin lost by a landslide. Mourdock, who had been the front-runner before the debate, lost too. Both were defeated largely by infuriated women voters.

Democrats were more savvy on the subject. The Obama administration, gearing up for a reelection bid, understood the power of the women's vote and went after it by, for example, issuing new guidelines in 2011 to prevent sexual assault on college campuses. Vice President Joe Biden announced the new guidelines in no uncertain terms: "No means no if you're drunk or sober, or in a dorm room or on the street, even if you said yes, and changed your mind. No means no." The administration's sensitivity to women paid off. In the 2012 election Obama received 55 percent of the women's vote. His Republican opponent, Mitt Romney (who had endorsed Mourdock the day before he declared that pregnancy caused by rape was "something God intended") received 43 percent of the women's vote. Among unmarried women, Obama enjoyed a thirty-point margin over Romney.[35]

Acknowledging that women's support had cemented his win, Obama established in his second term a presidential Task Force to Protect Students from Sexual Assault, to which he assigned the attorney general and three cabinet members. The Department of Education made public a list of fifty-five universities that were under investigation because they had mishandled sexual assault cases. Senators Claire McCaskill and Kirsten Gillibrand introduced a bill to fine such universities.

Women students felt encouraged to come forward as they had not before, though they could still be suspected of lying "as easily as a morphine fiend," as Gurney Williams had put it a hundred years earlier. In 2013, Emma Sulkowicz, a junior at Columbia, complained to the university administration that she had been raped at the start of her sophomore year by a fellow student, Paul Nungesser, who had forcibly sodomized her. For several weeks before the unwanted act she had had a consensual sexual relationship with Nungesser—who, in his defense, produced emails showing that Sulkowicz had at various times agreed to sexual encounters with him. Despite the 1994 prohibition on introducing an accuser's sexual history, and despite Vice President Biden's explanation of the 2011 federal guidelines as "No means no," the university, as well as the New York City Police Department and the district attorney, sided with the accused.

Sulkowicz was tenacious. The feeling that she had been violated by the forced sodomy had not left her. She was majoring in performance art, and she made her anger public in her senior project: "Mattress Performance: Carry That Weight." Throughout her entire senior year, she appeared on campus dragging a fifty-pound mattress. She became the poster girl for a burgeoning movement against campus sexual assault. Sulkowicz was featured on the cover of *New York*—a pretty coed in a pink summer blouse, balancing a huge blue mattress, with the words "A Very Different Kind of Sexual Revolution on Campus" blazoned across the middle of the magazine's cover. For *Time*, Sulkowicz wrote an op-ed titled "My Rapist Is Still on Campus." Major newspapers around the country such as the *Chicago Tribune* sent their photographers to capture images of Sulkowicz and her blue mattress. Kirsten Gillibrand invited her to attend President Obama's State of the Union address.[36]

However, Nungesser sued Columbia for permitting Sulkowicz to receive course credit for a stunt that damaged his reputation. The District Court dismissed his claim, but Columbia, having already judged that Nungesser was not guilty of rape, settled with him for an undisclosed amount, doubly affirming his "innocence" and Sulkowicz's culpability.[37]

The "different kind of sexual revolution on campus" was not the first war waged on "sexual harassment"—a term that had been coined by feminists in consciousness-raising sessions in the 1970s. In 1979, Catharine MacKinnon (whose work had so troubled Katie Roiphe in *The Morning After*) published *Sexual Harassment of Working Women*, a groundbreaking book in which MacKinnon argued that sexual harassment reinforced woman's inferior role in the work world, and therefore harassment was in effect "sex discrimination in employment."[38] MacKinnon was able to test her assertion when she became co-counsel in a Supreme Court case, *Meritor Savings Bank v. Vinson*.

Mechelle Vinson was a young Black woman who had gone to work as a bank teller in 1974, when she was eighteen years old. Over the next four years she had sex forty or fifty times with the bank's vice president, her immediate supervisor. He had told her that if she refused, "Just like I hired you, I'll fire you." "It was just like, you're an animal, you're nothing, and I'm going to show you you're nothing," Vinson recalled of her coercer. The Supreme Court heard the case in 1986, and in an astounding vote of 9–0 upheld a lower court's decision in favor of Vinson. William Rehnquist, the most conservative member of the Court, wrote the majority opinion, which said, "Without question, when a supervisor sexually harasses a subordinate because of the subordinate's sex, the supervisor discriminates on the basis of sex"—a violation of Title VII of the 1964 Civil Rights Act. Inspired by the decision of the Court, thousands of women in the following years sued their employers for sexual harassment.[39] But as the 1991 *New York Times*/CBS News poll suggested, millions of women did not.

However, women's old reticence in discussing sex abuse—because of fear that they would not be believed, shame left over from the days of womanly modesty, and self-blame ("What did I do to deserve that?")—virtually vanished in the new millennium. Through social media, women began sharing with a hundred, a thousand, a million other women what had once been mortifying secrets. It was a riot grrrls' dream come true. It gave birth to an astonishing fourth wave of the women's movement. Though the term "feminism" had become moribund again in the first decade of the twenty-first century, by 2020, there were more women in America than ever who said that the word "'feminist' describes them very well": 75 percent of Democratic women and 42 percent of Republican women agreed with that statement.[40] The light thrown on the ubiquity of sex abuse had led to a massive feminist resurgence.

The "fourth wave arguably began in 2014, when President Obama's senior advisor, Valerie Jarrett, explained to the public the need for a White House Task Force to Protect Students from Sexual Assault. Jarrett said that "1 in 5 women experienced rape or attempted rape in their lifetimes." A predictable backlash to her announcement came quickly. Caroline Kitchens of the American Enterprise Institute, a right-wing think tank, penned an op-ed for *Time* in which she ridiculed the task force. It perpetrated the idea that "there was a rape culture in America," Kitchens wrote, complaining that though this was a lie, it would "poison the minds of young women and lead to hostile environments for innocent young men."[41]

Zerlina Maxwell, a Black feminist who had already achieved fame as one of fifty top political tweeters in the country, had been raped by her roommate's boyfriend while a college student. Maxwell believed that she had experienced firsthand the "rape culture in America." In response to Kitchens's piece, Maxwell started #RapeCultureIsWhen on Twitter and invited women to tell what they knew about rape culture. Almost immediately, her tweet began trending nationally. The massive response to #RapeCultureIsWhen revealed that now there were legions of women, brought into being by social media, who were determined to hold men accountable for what they had been able to perpetrate in the past with near impunity.[42]

The evolution of the Bill Cosby story became a dramatic example of the change. Cosby, long called "America's Dad" for his role as the warm and wise Dr. Huxtable on *The Cosby Show*, had been accused in 2005 by thirteen women in eight states of drugging and raping them. Cosby settled with the women out of court, and his lawyers were able to keep the *National Enquirer*, a tabloid, from writing about the story. A year later, *People*, which had the second highest readership of all American magazines (well over 90 million), ran a long piece about the accusations, replete with graphic sex details. But no one seemed to notice.[43] Cosby continued to be honored and to rack up awards, such as the prestigious Mark Twain Prize for American Humor, which he received in 2009.

It was social media that would spark the change in his fate. In 2014, a reporter from *Philadelphia* magazine had gone to the Trocadero nightclub to film the comedian Hannibal Buress. In the course of his stand-up routine, Buress joked, "Google 'Bill Cosby rape.' It's not funny. That shit has more results than Hannibal Buress." The reporter uploaded the clip to PhillyMag.com.[44] BuzzFeed and Gawker disseminated it further. It was soon all over Facebook and Twitter. It went viral.

Forty-six more women came forward to accuse Cosby of sexual assault. Thirty-five of them agreed to be interviewed by *New York* magazine. In an article titled "'I'm No Longer Afraid': 35 Women Tell Their Stories about Being Assaulted by Bill Cosby, and the Culture That Wouldn't Listen," each woman was explicit about how Cosby had sexually abused her, and her photo appeared alongside her story.[45] Whatever shame women had felt in talking about rape was gone: the days of the deep, dark secret were at an end. And now people were paying attention, too. The John F. Kennedy Center, which administers the Mark Twain Prize, rescinded Cosby's award. A jury found Cosby's accusers credible, and he was sentenced to three to ten years in state prison.

Perhaps the single most unifying cause of the fourth wave of a feminist movement was the exposure of Donald Trump, caught on tape bragging: "I don't even wait. When you're a star, they let you do it. . . . Grab 'em by the pussy. You can do anything." On January 21, 2017, the day after Trump's presidential inauguration, an estimated 4 million women, easily alerted by social media, gathered for women's marches in cities big and small across America. It was the largest single-day protest in U.S. history. The marchers had come to vent their anger at the defeat of the woman who was finally supposed to crack the glass ceiling of the presidency and at the threats they anticipated to reproductive rights, paid family leave, a livable minimum wage. But the biggest reason they had come was made manifest by the visual image of the crowds: seas of pink pussy hats everywhere, a defiant jeer at a man who thought himself entitled to gross sexual harassment and who had just been sworn in as president of the United States. The women marched again in 2018, their anger not abated and Trump still a symbol of men's abuse of women. Some marchers carried an effigy of his testicles that they had decorated with a pouf of orange hair. Some carried signs that sputtered with their rage at him, such as "FUCK YOU, YOU FUCKING FUCK."[46] By then an organized movement had emerged to fight sexual harassment.

"Me Too" had first surfaced twenty years earlier, not as a movement but as an idea. In 1997, Tarana Burke, a Black community activist, had been told by a thirteen-year-old girl that she had been sexually abused by her mother's boyfriend. The twenty-four-year-old Burke wanted to let the girl know that she also had been abused when she was a child. She wanted to say "me too." But she said nothing, and she became deeply upset with herself that she had failed to speak up. Ten years later, Burke—by then the head of Just Be, a nonprofit she had formed to work with girls of color—started a group around the words she wished she had said to the thirteen-year-old girl: "Me Too." Just Be encouraged abused girls to speak up instead of hanging their heads in quiet shame, for the sake of their own healing and to let others know that they were not alone. But the vast proliferation of social media had not yet kicked in. Outside of the New York and Philadelphia communities where Just Be operated, Burke's "Me Too" catchphrase had little fanfare or exposure.[47]

Another ten years later, in 2017, the internet and social media made "#MeToo" an international movement. After the allegations against Cosby hit the headlines, actresses began telling their own stories of sexual abuse by powerful men in the entertainment industry. In 2017, when the allegations broke against Harvey Weinstein, a mega-influential movie producer, the actress Alyssa Milano, who had not heard of Burke's "Me Too" efforts, tweeted to her followers urging them to reply "me too" if they had also been sexually harassed or abused, thinking that it would be liberating for women to share what they had kept bottled up. Almost immediately she got tens of thousands of "Me Too" responses. They spread to Facebook, where 12 million "Me Too" posts worldwide were racked up in less than twenty-four hours. Inspired by the dramatic stories of sexual harassment in the entertainment industry, in November of that year the Alianza Nacional de Campesinas, an organization of 700,000 women who work in agricultural fields and packing sheds or who are from farmworker families came forward to complain that "countless farmworker women throughout the country suffer in silence because of the widespread sexual harassment and assault they face at work." They inspired women in the entertainment industry to start Time's Up, which in its first few months raised $22 million for legal suits against powerful harassers.[48]

In the early twentieth century, respected doctors had gotten away with claiming in prestigious medical journals that a woman could avert rape if she would only cross her knees, and victims had kept their lips sealed lest shame be heaped on them. At the other end of the century, second-wave feminists revealed their secrets in consciousness-raising groups and third-wave feminists flaunted secrets by creating punk rock lyrics that shamed the perpetrator; in the next century, a feminist tried to shame a perpetrator by carrying a mattress around campus as performance art. But most of America could and did brush aside the women's complaints—as even the 2005 exposé of Bill Cosby in *People* showed. Most people, perhaps not knowing anyone personally who admitted to having been abused, had virtually no reaction to stories of abuse. By 2020, however, 82 percent of American women were identifying "sexual harassment" as the greatest "obstacle to women having equal rights with men."[49] Twitter, Facebook, Instagram, YouTube, Reddit, TikTok, and Snapchat all made possible the mounting of huge campaigns against sexual harassment that would have been inconceivable in earlier years. The millions of women's voices—complaining, exposing, and demanding justice through the megaphone of social media—meant that nothing could stuff back into the closet the new knowledge of the ubiquity of sexual abuse. It remains to be seen whether the risk of public exposure through the modern pillory and stocks will end for good men's ancient tacit privilege that worked to keep woman in her place.

A FIVE-PART TALE OF WOMAN IN THE PUBLIC SPHERE

> "Sometimes the reason 'women's rights' feels so tenuous is because the question 'which women?' is as central as it is overlooked."
> —MELISSA GIRA GRANT, "The Elite Sisterhood of Amy Coney Barrett" (2020)[50]

Hillary Clinton I

In 1980, Bill Clinton lost his bid for a second term as Arkansas's governor. Among the voters' dissatisfactions that turned them against him was their conviction that the wife of a governor should not be using her maiden name. So when Bill decided in 1982 to run for governor once again, his wife, Hillary Rodham, promised to use the name "Hillary Rodham Clinton" because, as she told him, keeping her maiden name "wasn't worth offending the people who cared about it."[51] "Strong-minded women" were still not popular in Arkansas.

During the 1992 Democratic presidential primaries, Hillary had trouble again. It started when Bill was accused by his rival, Jerry Brown, of taking advantage of his position as governor to funnel public money to his wife's law firm. Hillary, asked by the press whether she and Bill could not have found a way to avoid the appearance of conflict, answered defensively, "I suppose I could have stayed home, baked cookies and had teas, but what I decided instead was to fulfill my profession, which I entered before my husband was in public life." Stay-at-home wives exploded: they accused her so vehemently of trivializing them that Bill's worried campaign managers asked her to make herself scarce for a while on the campaign trail.[52]

When Bill chose Al Gore as his running mate, journalists who covered stories about political wives were delighted. At last they had a traditional one on whom they could focus: "Democrats found a way to balance the presidential ticket by adding Tipper Gore," a syndicated reporter announced at least half seriously. Tipper fulfilled what was still in some circles a popular ideal of woman as domestic angel, no matter that the majority of women now worked outside the home. The media that supported Bill Clinton speculated with relief that Tipper Gore could "take on the Republicans in family value issues in a way that Governor Clinton's career wife cannot." Hillary was depicted as "an ambitious lawyer . . . very career oriented and very competitive." That was not a compliment. In contrast to Hillary, the "bossy, humorless Valkyrie with a briefcase," as detractors called her, Tipper made few forays outside of her wifely role. Those she did make—such as writing a book about how mothers could steer their children away from violent and sexually explicit rock lyrics and videos—only burnished her family-values credentials.[53]

Much of America was not ready for a first lady who was a Yale Law School graduate and a partner in a high-powered law firm, and who had been included by the *National Law Journal* on its 1988 and 1989 lists of America's most powerful lawyers. She was unfavorably compared during her husband's campaign to Barbara Bush, the current first lady, who had never in her life worked for pay and who liked to say that "nobody ever died regretting time not spent on a job, only time lost with family." Mrs. Bush was "universally revered," "the most popular person in the country." "She seems to glory in being the wife of a prominent man," one reporter wrote effusively, pointedly contrasting her to Hillary—who "fights being identified as 'wife of.'"[54]

To patch up the potential harm she might have done to her husband's campaign by "trivializing" women who were homemakers, and to show herself not so hostile after all to woman-type activities, Hillary agreed in July 1992, four months before the presidential election, to a *Family Circle* publicity scheme, participating with Barbara Bush in a "Great Political Cookie War." Both women would present their own cookie recipe, and readers would select the winner by voting via postcard.[55] As demeaning as Hillary may have felt the whole thing was, it was part of her continuing effort not to "offend the people who cared about [such things]."

Sarah Palin

By the new millennium, the woman political figure was no longer a rarity. Still, her detractors often aimed their attacks not on her politics but on her as a woman. In 2008, the governor of Alaska, Sarah Palin—who had five children ranging in ages from eighteen years to five months—was chosen by John McCain, the Republican presidential candidate, to be his running mate. The NBC anchor Amy Robach pointed out in a segment called "The Mommy Wars" that Palin's youngest child had Down syndrome and that her seventeen-year-old unmarried daughter was pregnant. "If Sarah Palin becomes vice president, will she be short changing her kids," Robach worried, "or will she be short changing the country?" John Roberts, a CNN correspondent, worried, too. "Children with Down syndrome require an awful lot of attention," he announced on CNN's *Newsroom*, and since the role of vice president "would take up a lot of [Palin's] time, it raises the issue of how much time she will have to dedicate to her newborn child." "It's the Mommy Wars: Special Campaign Edition," Jodi Kantor and Rachel Swarns announced in the *New York Times*, reporting that Palin's baby had been born that April and Palin had gone back to work three days later, and quoting horrified Americans who made pronouncements such as, "You can juggle a BlackBerry and a breast pump in a lot of jobs, but not in the vice presidency."[56]

But in a remarkable reversal, the most conservative of conservatives now read from the liberals' old script. On his Fox News program *The O'Reilly Factor*, the ultra-right commentator Bill O'Reilly mocked the left-wing media on the subject of Palin's nomination. The media was "dominated by pinheads who don't know any of the regular folks," O'Reilly complained, "who just hang around with each other and spit out this stuff like, 'how can this little woman have the audacity to run for vice president?'"[57]

The reversal of positions was all the more astonishing in the light of a Pew Research Center poll taken in the early summer of 2008, shortly before McCain named his running mate. Only 20 percent of Republicans said that they would be "very likely to support a candidate for Congress if she was the mother of small children." A third of Democrats said that they would be "very likely" to support such a candidate. But a few months later, after McCain had chosen Palin, conservatives suddenly dropped their prejudice against a woman candidate with small children. That, of course, was because Palin was absolutely in line with all the issues conservatives held dear. She was a staunch opponent of abortion even in cases of rape or incest. She was a strong proponent of the death penalty, the Second Amendment, and the Defense of Marriage Act. Contrary to the poll taken only months before, Republicans had no trouble accepting the fact that Palin had five children, or even that the child with Down syndrome was only five months old and would surely require special care. They acknowledged the complicated facts of her family, however—by declaring that they were "thrilled to see so prominent a display of pro-life commitment."[58]

Conservatives also praised Palin for characteristics they had once adamantly reserved for men: her "toughness," "executive decision capabilities," and "leadership." Though her political experience had been limited to elected office in Wasilla, population 9,000, and twenty-one months as Alaska's governor, 84 percent of Republicans had faith that Palin was "qualified to serve as president if it becomes necessary."[59] Thanks to the preceding forty years of a women's movement, by 2008 conservatives too had apparently become acclimated to the idea of woman in politics. No more "Coya, come home." If the woman was a reliable advocate of Republican values, it turned out that even her small children were no longer a problem.

Carly Fiorina and Hillary Clinton II

Despite the right's ostensible shift on woman's suitability for political office, in the 2016 presidential race Donald Trump targeted his female rivals for woman's vulnerabilities. His crude attack on Carly Fiorina, the only female in the 2016 Republican primary debates, would have been inconceivable had Fiorina been a man. "Look at that face," Trump taunted. "Would anyone vote for that? Can you imagine that, the face of our next president? . . . I mean, she's a woman, and I'm not s'posedta say bad things, but really folks, come on. Are we serious?" Trump's boorish evaluation of a credible presidential contender's deficits in the looks department was reported, as though it were worth giving space to, on CNN and CBS and in the *Huffington Post, USA Today, Rolling Stone*—everywhere.[60]

Nor would Trump have used on a man his ploy to discombobulate Hillary Clinton, the Democratic nominee, during their second presidential debate. Trump left his podium and loomed in the dark behind Clinton as she spoke, as though he were a stalker ready to pounce. It was atavistic. It was an age-old meme of man menacing woman. The political commentator Nicolle Wallace remarked, "If a man did that to me on the street, I'd call 911."[61]

Clinton felt the menace of it, of course, but she chose to react as a presidential candidate rather than as a woman, "to stay focused, to keep my composure," she later said. It was the wrong response. Clinton had already been criticized for seeming too strong and too unflappable—qualities that were important in a presidential candidate but were still widely regarded as unnatural in a woman. She had already been advised that if she wanted to be perceived as more "likable," "to win people's trust and generate enthusiasm," she had to show her womanly character.[62] But what real woman would ignore a stalker? Yet if Clinton had reacted in a way that was more "womanlike"—had shown that Trump's coarse attempt to intimidate her had distressed her or made her feel vulnerable—that would have been the wrong response too, because a presidential candidate cannot seem distressed or vulnerable. In fact, there was no right response that a female who was a candidate for president of the United States could have made to Trump's primeval lurking that was intended to rattle her as a woman.

Vice President Joe Biden, speaking on *Face the Nation* before the 2016 election, pinpointed Clinton's dilemma. There still existed a "double standard," as he characterized it, that made it impossible for a female candidate to strike the right note in emotional situations. Biden, who had just lost his son, reflected that when he wept people said of him, "Well, he's just a good decent father." But if Clinton were to cry about something, Biden observed, "You'd have a chorus of 'She's playing the woman card here.'"[63]

Amy Coney Barrett

When Barrett was confirmed by the Republican-dominated Senate and became a Supreme Court justice on October 27, 2020, it was a painful day for liberal feminists. They had revered Barrett's predecessor on the Court since 1971—when, as a young lawyer, Ruth Bader Ginsburg won a monumental victory by arguing before the Court that the Equal Protection Clause of the Fourteenth Amendment protected women from sex discrimination.

In the Rose Garden ceremony at which President Trump had announced Barrett's nomination, she paid homage to Ginsburg, who "not only broke glass ceilings [but] smashed them." It was an ostensibly bold feminist declaration. However, liberal feminists did not mistake Barrett for one of them. Those who believed that *Roe v. Wade* was the sine qua non of women's right to self-determination knew they had good reason to worry. In 2006, Barrett's was one of the signatures on a "Right to Life" newspaper ad that baldly declared, "It's time to put an end to the barbaric legacy of *Roe v. Wade* and restore laws that protect the lives of unborn children."[64]

Liberal feminists were upset too, as they had been with Sheryl Sandberg, that Barrett's personal story gave the wrong idea about what women could realistically accomplish without programs such as government-sponsored child care. After all, most men were still not like Jesse Barrett, about whom his wife bragged in her nomination acceptance speech:

> At the start of our marriage, I imagined that we would run our household as partners. As it has turned out, Jesse does far more than his share of the work. To my chagrin, I learned at dinner recently that my children consider him to be the better cook. For 21 years, Jesse has asked me every single morning what he can do for me that day.[65]

It was a statement that could have been ripped from the pages of *Lean In*.

Liberal feminists such as Lydia Kiesling complained in *Harper's Bazaar* that most women, unlike Barrett, did not have an aunt who could provide in-home child care for sixteen years or a flexible workplace that would allow them to take a baby to their office and keep a box of toys there for the child. Most women were still hampered, Kiesling wrote, because there was still "no guaranteed paid leave, very little public childcare or preschool," and no national health insurance.[66] Other liberal feminists, incredulous and angry at what they called the "gaslighting" being perpetrated on women by Barrett's story, switched places with the right in their attack on her again, as they had done when Palin was the vice-presidential nominee.

The right also switched places with liberal feminists yet again. Senators who wanted Barrett on the Supreme Court were suddenly sounding like the suffragist Anna Howard Shaw, who had argued in the nineteenth century that woman's special knowledge fitted her for a much-needed voice in the public sphere. Right-wing politicians gushed throughout the first day of Barrett's 2020 confirmation hearings that she was, as Thom Tillis, a Republican senator from North Carolina, said, "an inspiration to millions of young women in this country." Her motherhood made her wise, Chuck Grassley, a Republican senator from Iowa, said in defending her against the left's allegations that she would get rid of the Affordable Care Act: "As a mother of seven, Judge Barrett clearly understands the importance of health care." Michael Crapo, a Republican senator from Idaho, observing that Barrett "would be the first mother of school-aged children to serve on the Supreme Court," found her prolific motherhood to be proof that her antiabortion bona fides were impeccable. It made her, Crapo offered, "the ideal candidate to fill the current vacancy."[67]

Only a couple of years earlier, in 2018, when Barrett's name had been floated as a possible replacement for Justice Anthony Kennedy, the telvangelist Pat Robertson had groused about her on the Christian Broadcasting Network, "What does she have, six or seven children? That's going to be tough, to be a judge and take care of all those kids, won't it?" But Robertson had not been keeping up with the shifts even on the right regarding the idea of woman. Conservative women, who not so long ago might have been members of Phyllis Schlafly's Eagle Forum that honored the full-time housewife, now saw Barrett as a new kind of icon. Of course, they were hoping that as a Supreme Court justice she would be the crucial vote to overturn *Roe v. Wade*; but their delight in the prospect of her becoming one of the most powerful people in the country went beyond that issue. To them she was "proof" that, as a Catholic mother of ten who was a lawyer declared, "it's possible for a woman to rise to the top of her profession while having many children." Right-wing women were holding up Barrett as evidence that, as they said, "women are strong enough to walk and chew gum at the same time."[68] The right's thinking about woman and "the place where God had set her" had undergone an astounding transformation.

Just as surprising: worrisome as Barrett's conservative history was to liberal feminists, it was possible to find, as the journalist Ruth Marcus put it, a "micro-thin silver lining" in Barrett's judicial elevation. Without downplaying fears about the future of *Roe v. Wade*, Marcus wrote that Barrett's candidacy "sends an important signal to women—and men, for that matter—who may deeply disagree with the judge's philosophy but cannot help but come away with the message from her selection: It's possible to manage family and career, however imperfectly and stressfully. Success at work does not require giving up the chance to have children, not if you want them."[69]

At the least, Barrett's story suggested to women such as those who had started the opt-out movement—who had quit practicing law or medicine or who, like O'Donnel, had given up corporate success to be supported by a husband who later divorced her—that it might be possible after all to keep a career and be a mother too.

Kamala Harris

As the 2020 Democratic vice-presidential candidate, Kamala Harris was also targeted for vulnerabilities that male candidates did not have to worry about. Predictably, Donald Trump, remembering how Clinton had successfully been tarred as "unlikable," leveled the same charge at Harris. "Totally unlikable," he called her, and "a monster," conjuring up images of the she-monsters of mythology and horror films.[70]

Harris was victimized on social media, too, by crass sexual depictions reserved for women. A Facebook post that blasted across the internet despite its falsehood was viewed on Twitter alone over 600,000 times; conservative radio commentator Rush Limbaugh also spread the word to his 15 million listeners: Willie Brown, an influential California politician, the post had said, "launched [Harris's] career because she was having sex with him. The idea that she is an 'independent' woman who worked her way up the political ladder because she worked hard is baloney. She slept her way into powerful jobs."[71]

In Harris's case, however, such attacks had little effect. She remained an asset to the Democratic ticket because she succeeded in cultivating credible counterimages. Clearly, she was an "independent woman," she did "work hard," and her obvious brilliance obviated her having to "sleep her way" anywhere. Yet Harris realized it was also vital to emphasize her womanly attributes, which made her "masculine" accomplishments broadly palatable. It was a winning formula: "Family is everything to me," Harris said in her acceptance speech at the Democratic National Convention. She talked of how she "cannot wait for America to get to know" her husband and two stepchildren. She enumerated in loving detail the motherly tasks she did for her family—cooking dinner every Sunday, cheering in the bleachers at a swim meet, setting up a college dorm room. She even mentioned helping her goddaughter prepare for a school debate and building Legos with her godson. "I've had a lot of titles over my career," Harris said, reminding her audience of her professional competence, but then stressing what was calculated to warm their hearts: "Momala will always be the one that means the most."[72] Harris had learned well from Clinton's struggle what a woman candidate had to do to "win people's trust and generate enthusiasm": she had to be "likable" as a woman.

Women on the right who were ecstatic over Barrett's elevation to the Supreme Court had also found a new formula. They had long left behind Schlafly's promotion of "a woman's right not to take a job." They too were among the 72 percent of women with children who worked outside the home. Many of them, as they announced, had been "reforming" and "reclaiming" the term "feminism" for themselves. Amy Coney Barrett personified what they stood for and emboldened them. They came charging out of the closet, battling women on the left for the parameters of feminism's definition. Feminism did not mean the right to abort or have government-sponsored child care, they argued. In fact, the left's feminism was "antiwoman" because it denied that a woman could choose "both a big family and a big career," they declared in the pages of right-wing journals such as *The Federalist*.[73]

Spurred on, with Barrett as their new icon, feminists on the right declared themselves tired of being mocked, tired of the depictions of them as "baking cookies while connected to a machine that's popping out babies." They vowed to make their own feminist voices heard.[74] Though woman's biological role as the bearer of children remained fundamental to them, they had made a decided shift in their other basic beliefs about woman. Schlafly's question, "Why should we lower ourselves to 'equal rights' when we already have the status of special privilege?"—a status due woman as the "weaker vessel"—no longer made sense.

Epilogue

•

THE END OF "WOMAN"?

On January 13, 2021, the forty-fifth president of the United States—the man who had bragged before his election that because he was a celebrity, women whom he had just met let him grab them by the genitalia—was impeached for the second time, for inciting a mob to insurrection. The following month, nine impeachment managers from the House of Representatives presented the case against him to the Senate. One of the impeachment managers was Stacey Plaskett, a fifty-four-year-old Black woman, who had grown up in a housing project in Brooklyn and was the mother of five children. Plaskett had also been an attorney specializing in public finance law, a prosecutor in the Bronx district attorney's office, counsel to the House's Ethics Committee, and senior counsel in the Department of Justice. In 2015, she had been elected to the House as a delegate from the Virgin Islands. Plaskett's prosecutorial skills were stunning as she made the argument that Trump had violated his oath to support and defend the Constitution of the United States. She "stole the show," some in the media declared. Her eloquence as an orator was remarkable to reporters. What she wore was remarkable to them too—but this was different from 1957, when newspapers reported that a congresswoman from New Jersey "wore a black dress with a square cut neck" and a congresswoman from Pennsylvania "wore a beige wool." Plaskett wore a blue cape dress: Superman blue. Someone photoshopped a Superman insignia onto Plaskett's chest in a picture of her in her caped dress. The photo went viral and became a meme on social media: Plaskett as a "superhero," "defending our democracy."[1]

•

THE MINISTERS AND MAGISTRATES in colonial New England had declared of woman that she was "helpful in the propagating of mankind," that she "yielded Subjection to [her husband] as her Head," and that she had no desire to be "a rash wrambler abroad."[2] Though often contested, those formulations of the idea of woman—notwithstanding some modifications here and there—kept a tyrannical hold in America for four hundred years. They popped up, briefly at least, even at the start of the new millennium, when "opt-out" women agreed that it was natural to let men head the family as breadwinners and that happiness for a woman was giving up her "rash wrambling abroad" and staying home to take care of the babies.

Opt-out fever broke by the second decade of the new millennium. Was that the end, once and for all, of woman's retreat back to the home? Virtually everywhere in the United States, women had now moved into what had been man's world. Did their unprecedented movement (and its infinite visibility through social media) signify that finally the old notions of woman had died? Was anything left of those ideas that had been so tenacious for centuries?

Woman must not "wrinkle her forehead" about politics?[3] Nancy Pelosi became Speaker of the House of Representatives in 2007, was elected House Minority Leader in 2011 when the Democrats lost their majority, and became Speaker again in 2019, when the Democrats regained their majority. In 2021 there were 123 women in the House of Representatives. Women accounted for almost a quarter of the U.S. Senate. They were the governors of ten states and territories. They were one-third of the justices on the Supreme Court. A woman was sworn in as vice president of the United States.

Woman exhibits a natural "modesty of feeling and manner" about sexual matters?[4] The rap singer Cardi B became well-known in 2016 with her mixtape *Gangsta Bitch Music.* Its cover featured a photo of Cardi B enjoying, simultaneously, a Corona Beer and cunnilingus, a muscular tattooed back and a head of black hair visible between her bare legs. In 2020 her hip-hop single "WAP" (an acronym for "wet ass pussy"), for which she teamed up with the rap singer Megan Thee Stallion, was the number one hit of Billboard's "Hot 100" list. "WAP" celebrates women's sexuality in graphically detailed lyrics. It is pointedly not about women as objects of male desire, but about women as subjects of their own desires; not about women pleasing men sexually, but about women demanding sexual pleasure. No "modesty in feeling and manner" here. "In the food chain, I'm the one that eat ya," the women declare.[5]

The *New York Times* got it: "Cardi B and Megan Thee Stallion Take Control," a headline announced. Women critics pronounced "WAP" "a personal, thorough and incredibly detailed account of what (women's) sexual pleasure looks and feels like." "WAP" was "the epitome of female empowerment," they enthused; its focus on "women's satisfaction in the bedroom" was "healthy" and "sex positive." In the first twenty-four hours after its release, the video of "WAP" had 26 million views on YouTube; it was subsequently streamed over 300 million times. *Billboard* magazine named "WAP" "front and center" among the best rap songs of the year and crowned its creator, Cardi B, "Woman of the Year." *Bloomberg* named her number one in its Pop Star Power Rankings.[6]

Woman's "gentle and unassuming tenderness" makes her a stranger to violence?[7] The most prominent woman on the far right since the death of Phyllis Schlafly was Marjorie Taylor Greene (a Republican from Georgia), who vowed in her 2020 congressional campaign that she would bring "my faith and my family values to Washington." Schlafly and Greene were of one mind on most issues, but their differences in style mark their respective generations: Schlafly with her stiffly coiffed 1950s hairdo and ladylike dresses; Greene with lank hair, garbed in jeans and short-sleeved shirts that show off biceps that prove her fitness-trainer credentials—a very millennial image of how women, even those on the far right, could now look. Schlafly, like Greene, had been a staunch supporter of the Second Amendment. But Schlafly would no doubt have paled at Greene's twenty-first-century Facebook image. In one photo, Greene, stony-faced, wearing dark glasses, and looking like an assassin, caresses a long gun. It is pointed in the direction of photos of Alexandria Octavio-Cortez, Ilhan Omar, and Rashida Tlaib, three of the congresswomen who have been called "the Squad." They look terrified. "Squad's Worst Nightmare," the caption threatens.[8]

Nor would Schlafly have sassed her generation's gender notions as saucily as Greene did in her "likes" of Facebook posts that drooled over bloodshed: "a bullet to the head" as a good way to remove Pelosi from her role as Speaker of the House, and a yearning to hang "H [Hillary Clinton] and O [Barak Obama]." To a reign-of-terror proposal that such traitors "suffer death," Greene responded with chilling deliberation, "Stage is being set. Players are being put in place. We must be patient. This must be done perfectly." A month after taking her seat in Congress, Greene concocted a quintessential rejection of woman's "gentle and unassuming tenderness." Hoping to become the face of Second Amendment rights, she announced that she was raffling off two AR-15s—military-style semi-automatic rifles like the one used by Omar Mateen when he killed fifty people at an Orlando, Florida, gay bar; by Adam Lanza when he killed twenty-six people, including twenty children, at Sandy Hook Elementary School in Newtown, Connecticut; and by James Holmes when he killed twelve people and wounded fifty-eight in a darkened movie theater in Aurora, Colorado. The AR-15, Greene said, was "in the crosshairs of gun grabbers all across America," but she promised that its banning "won't happen on my watch." The ad for her gun giveaway included a photo of Greene in a military-style jacket, looking very ungentle and untender and cradling in her arms an AR-15, her finger on its trigger.[9]

Woman is *"pale, delicate, sentimental"*?[10] In 2019, just before Megan Rapinoe left for France and the Women's World Cup soccer competition, she dyed her hair a vibrant purple-pink. Rapinoe would have stood out even without the colorful hair. She had been playing soccer since 1991, when she was six years old and was placed on an under-eight all-boys soccer team—which she soon "dominated." In 2019, Rapinoe, a midfielder and cocaptain, led the U.S. Women's National Team to victory. She was awarded the Golden Boot as the tournament's top scorer. After Rapinoe had won two goals against France in a quarter-final match, she raised her arms in victory—"like Russell Crowe in *The Gladiator*," one journalist wrote. Rapinoe claimed that her triumphant pose was meant to suggest that she was owning her victory, enjoying her success by standing tall—

and also that she was speaking for women, "No caveat, no apology. Arms out wide. Claim your space."[11]

By the final game of the competition, many of the 20,000 fans in the stadium had dyed their hair vibrant purple-pink to match Rapinoe's. They were chanting "Equal pay!," too, because one of Rapinoe's many sociopolitical battles had been to fight the disparity in prize money between the men's teams, which collectively were awarded $38 million, and the women's teams, which were awarded $4 million. LGBTQ rights was another of Rapinoe's battles after she came out as gay in 2012. The centuries-old fear of aggressive women being dismissed as "Amazonian," "manly," "unnatural," or "dykes" is now history, Rapinoe told the press. She added, only half joking: "You can't win a championship without gays on your team, it's pretty much never been done before, ever. Science right there."[12]

At a celebration party after a ticker-tape parade up lower Broadway's Canyon of Heroes, Rapinoe was interviewed as she clutched her trophy in one hand and a bottle of Veuve Cliquot in the other. A little tipsy, she looked right into the camera and shouted: "I deserve this! I deserve this! Everything!" But it was not simple egotism, as the journalist Jenna Amatulli understood: it was "women owning their victories and praising themselves."[13] It was the antithesis of "pale, delicate, sentimental" woman.

Yet despite huge metamorphoses in the idea of woman, old concepts can still be tenacious. They pop up just when matters seem settled—or rather, when gender distinctions seem more challenged than ever, and when women seem to have evolved so far from what "woman" meant in the past that a return is inconceivable.

A most basic case in point: on the morning of February 25, 2021, Kimberly Boyd, a senior vice president and general manager at Hasbro, one of the largest makers of toys for children, announced that Hasbro would cease to make gender distinctions in marketing its best-selling Mr. Potato Head. The toy had been developed for children in the two- to three-year-old set in 1952 and included a felt mustache and plastic pipe. In 1953 Mrs. Potato Head was introduced, replete with mid-twentieth-century paraphernalia that signified "woman" such as plastic lipstick-red lips and hair bows. Boyd remarked to the media that "culture has evolved" and "the way the brand currently exists—with the Mr. and Mrs.—is limiting when it comes to both gender and family structure." Her company believed that the decision to market gender-neutral Potato Heads was in tune with the zeitgeist. After all, in 2020, 19 million children in the United

States—25 percent of all U.S. children—were living in single-parent families, without either a Mr. or a Mrs. Hundreds of thousands more children were living with two parents of the same sex. Also, a burgeoning number of people were saying they were neither a Mr. nor a Mrs. (nor a Miss or a Ms.)—as the dictionary-makers at Merriam-Webster acknowledged in 2019 by naming "they" the "Word of the Year." But the outcry over the prospect of ungendered potatoes was swift—a proverbial teapot tempest. Hasbro, fearing it had miscalculated in dismissing the fondness for proper-woman and proper-man potatoes, reversed itself only hours later. The passionate protests about gender-neutral Potato Heads came largely from conservative moms, distraught over Hasbro's initial announcement and provoked by right-wing pundits such as Glenn Beck, who lamented, "It's the end of an era. It's the end of freedom in America!" and Mark Dice, who declared, "It's time for Republican states to secede."[14]

Yet despite conservative yearning to conserve the tidy gender distinctions of an older era, Hasbro's original decision to put Mr. and Mrs. Potato Head to rest was, in fact, tuned in to Generation Z—those born from 1997 onward, who will be the next generation of parents. For Generation Z, gender as a category is infinitely more complex than what the proponents of Mr. and Mrs. Potato Head were willing to recognize. Facebook, becoming fully aware in 2013 that not all users considered themselves either a man or a woman, added fifty-six gender options, including "pangender," "gender questioning," "gender variant," "transmasculine," "transfeminine," and even "agender" and "neither." In 2016, the dating app Tinder announced to its tens of millions of users around the world that it was introducing multiple gender choices: those looking for romantic partners could click on "man," "woman," or "more" (which led to about forty autofill suggestions, from "androgyne" to the Native American concept of "two spirit"). Over half of the members of Generation Z say that traditional gender roles are outdated and that rather than woman and man there is in reality a whole spectrum of identities—thus, the notion of binary genders is obsolete. Terms such as "gender nonbinary," "gender nonconforming," "genderfluid," and "genderqueer" have proliferated to accommodate the now-acknowledged spectrum. In 2021, a Gallup poll found that almost 2 percent of those in Generation Z consider themselves transgender.[15]

Gender and even sex have, of course, always been more complex than simply "woman" or man, as the Native American tribes recognized in honoring individuals born with the anatomy of one sex who said that they belonged to the other sex. However, there has also been a long history in America of brutal outrage at those who did not conform: the seventeenth-century sailor who was stripped naked to the waist to reveal "her" breasts and made to run a gauntlet of whips, for instance; the eighteenth-century would-be soldier who, upon being discovered to have "teats of a plump young girl," was paraded through the town while a military drum beat "the whores march"; and Frank Dubois in the nineteenth century, who was forced under fear of imprisonment to return to "her" role as wife and mother. It was not until the new millennium that the firm tie between anatomical sex and gender was frayed as a critical mass of the population began to honor gender complexities.[16]

Even among individuals who consider themselves transgender, the concept of gender is complex and varied. One psychiatrist, Olivia Dunning (a pseudonym), suggests that the gender spectrum can be envisioned on a scale similar to the 0–6 scale that Alfred Kinsey devised to describe the spectrum of sexualities (with 0 being exclusively heterosexual and 6 being exclusively homosexual). If there were a similar scale to mark gender (with 0 being totally man and 6 being totally woman), Dunning, a transwoman, sees herself as a 6. A beautiful woman who looks much younger than her fifty-one years, she speaks in her head-voice range and lives "stealth": few people are aware that she was "assigned male at birth." That has been particularly important to her in her professional capacity because, she explains, "I did not want my transition to be part of my patients' treatment." Dunning understands her gender in essentialist terms, believing that "the average transwoman's brain looks more like that of a woman than [that] of a man." She had lived unhappily for several years as a gay man, but homosexual sex acts were frustrating to her because it was vaginal intercourse she desired. Yet even before she became sexual, she understood herself to be a woman in essentialist terms. Being a woman means to her "realizing that my strength lies in quietness rather than in aggressively asserting myself. It means being a nurturer. It means having more empathy than men generally have."[17] It is a definition of woman that even the early nineteenth-century "True Woman" would have approved.

Other transgender people reject essentialism completely, and they conceptualize gender in ways that might have been entirely perplexing to early generations. A person assigned female at birth, for instance, may identify as a transman while rejecting the usual markers of masculinity, and his sexual relationships may be only with men. Conversely, as one gender scholar points out, a growing number of transwomen identify as butch lesbians. That is, they reject the sex they were assigned at birth, but their gender identity (butch, masculine) and choice of sex partners (women) are like those of cisgender males (men whose gender identity corresponds to the sex they were assigned at birth). Some transwomen butches problematize gender further by priding themselves on skills that had been associated with femininity, such as sewing and embroidery. Tobi Hill-Meyer, a butch lesbian transwoman, quips that trans butch lesbians say, "I'm really looking forward to growing breasts so I can bind them"—just as "lesbians" who wanted to "pass as men" had to do in the days before it was possible to transition.[18] What is clear is that today one can choose whether or not to call oneself a woman. What is more complicated is the meaning that the term "woman" has to those who use it to describe themselves.

Yet, as far as many members of Generation Z have come toward obliterating the old-fashioned ties between sex and gender, the Potato Head protest is only one among several reminders that the traditional woman may not have breathed her last. Notwithstanding the millennium's recognition of the complexities of gender or the distance women have traveled, could old notions of woman ever reemerge in full force? Is it conceivable that political, economic, or environmental forces could again reduce most women to traditional "woman"? Could she again be tied to the domestic sphere where childbearing and child rearing would be her great and sacred duty? Are such possibilities only in the realm of speculative fictions, handmaid's tales?

Since the 1970s, scientists in the area of reproductive medicine have been observing a significant decline in men's sperm count. By 2021 there had been a 59-percent drop in the average sperm count from what it had been in 1973, which has triggered concern about the effects of the increasing "economic and societal burden of male infertility." Scientists speculate that the declining sperm count is caused not only by the modern lifestyle that is often sedentary and promotes obesity, but also by the increase of endocrine-disrupting chemicals in the environment, such as phthalates—used widely in plastics and products such as detergents, shampoos, and food packaging. Because the continuing decline in sperm count seems to be a problem primarily of the Western world, some scientists have worried that the fertility rate "among white people [has fallen] below the levels where the population can be sustained." That worry has been dismissed by others as merely a "doomsday theory embraced by the far right" in their paranoia about an imminent "Great Replacement," in which white populations will be replaced by people of color if change is not effected immediately. But aside from heated political speculations, leading reproductive epidemiologists such as Shanna Swan have argued credibly that if the curve on sperm count is projected forward, by 2045 "the median man would have essentially no sperm."[19]

If that is true, it does not take much of a dystopian imagination to envision widespread social panic within a few generations. What might be the result of such panic—legally and socially approved polygamy, so that males who are not "median men" could inseminate multiple women? The rebirth of "woman," whose chief duty would lie in being "helpful in the propagating of mankind," as Rev. John Cotton Jr. put it in 1694?[20] Apocalyptic terror that would pressure women to have seven or eight children, as American women did in 1800, or ten or twelve children, as many of them did in 1700?

Less speculative snags in the evolution out of "woman" also emerged as a side effect of the COVID-19 pandemic. In December 2019, a month before the first cases were reported in the United States, more women than men were working for pay. Incredible as it seemed, women made up 50.04 percent of the workforce. Their salaries were not yet equal to those of men, but in many areas—particularly in jobs requiring higher education—they were closing in on the gap, earning 92 percent of what their male counterparts made. The women's fall was swift. By the end of 2020, there were over 5 million fewer women in the workforce than there had been a year earlier, and the number of wage-earning women had dropped to what it had been in the late-1980s.[21] It was a "she-cession."

The she-cession was hard on women workers in all socioeconomic categories. Working-class Latinas and Black women, who made up a disproportionate number of employees in the hospitality and leisure industries, lost their positions when the pandemic forced those industries to shed over 8 million jobs between February and April 2020. Women who worked in retail or had other employment that relied on face-to-face interaction also found themselves without a job. Women whose work allowed them to telecommute were better off, but not if they had children at home. With day care centers and schools closed, mothers had to juggle their working hours in front of the computer with doing the job of a teacher's aide for their school-age children struggling with "remote learning," or they had to keep their younger children as entertained and mentally enriched as they would have been at KinderCare. Though many fathers who worked from home did spend more time on child care and household chores than they had in the past, the preponderance of the tasks fell to mothers. For some women, the double shift proved too much. According to a U.S. Census Bureau report half a year into the pandemic, about a third of working women ages 25–44 quit their jobs because of child-care demands.[22]

The pandemic forced a recognition of how tenuous the expansion of women's lives beyond the bounds of domesticity might be. For instance, most licensed child-care providers had to close during the pandemic. Many of them worried that they could not survive financially and that a prolonged closure would mean that they had to shut their doors permanently. By April 2020 it was estimated that half the child-care slots in the United States—almost 4.5 million—would disappear as a result of child-care providers having gone out of business.[23] What would that mean for women's trajectory away from "woman"? Women can move out into the world only if they are childless or if their young children can be watched over. But if millions of child-care slots would indeed be wiped out, millions of women would be again relegated to the domestic sphere. It would take a long time before they would be able to leave the confines of domesticity in numbers comparable to those in December 2019, when they were as likely as men were to be crossing the threshold of their home to earn money.

Nevertheless, indications abound of women's liberation from the prison of "woman." For instance, historically no institution was more implicated in defining woman than marriage. In the governing culture in America, "woman" and "wife" were practically synonymous. Marriage not only defined a woman, it also confined her. Yet the woman who did not marry was pitiable. She had reason to bewail—as Rebecca Dickinson did in the eighteenth century—that everyone "hissed and wagged their heads at me by reason of my Solotary life." In the new millennium, the dominance of marriage has virtually disappeared. Marriage has ceased to be an inevitable definer and confiner. Indeed, over 40 percent of women (and 47 percent of Black women) have never been married. There are more women without husbands in the United States than there are women with husbands. Of women ages 18–44, 59 percent are cohabiting or have cohabited with a partner who is not their husband.[24]

Women can now determine how and with whom they live because what Charlotte Perkins Gilman in 1898 called the "sexuo-economic relation" has been largely broken.[25] Women can earn their own living and no longer need a man to give them economic support. They have been freed in other crucial ways, too. They can have sex outside of marriage without disgrace, for instance. Bastardy laws are no longer imaginable, the shame of "illegitimacy" is history, and women can have children outside of marriage if they wish—or they can be certain never to have children at all if they wish to be childless. They can choose to live alone, make their life with another woman, or change their gender altogether. All the social stigma that controlled the unmarried female and forced her into the role of "woman" have essentially vanished.

Have women moved so far from the confines of "woman" that never again can the tyranny of old notions reemerge—as they did, for instance, in the 1950s, after the upheavals of the Depression and World War II? It remains to be seen whether "woman" will always be the default concept that takes hold in times of duress, or whether ideas of "woman" have now mutated so completely that there will never be a long return to the prison of gender.

NOTES

INTRODUCTION

1. William Glasser was a psychiatrist at the Ventura School for Girls from 1956 to 1967. Sue Reilly, "Dr. Glasser without Failure," in *The Reality Therapy Reader: A Survey of the Work of William Glasser*, ed. Alexander Bassin et al. (New York: Harper and Row, 1976), p. 26; "Studio Youngsters Are Guests at Ventura School for Girls," *Ventura County Star–Free Press* (CA), April 8, 1957, p. 11; Patricia Gallagher, "Santa Rosa Valley Women's Club Has Spring Luncheon in Camarillo, Hears Principal Tell of Rehabilitation at Ventura School for Girls," *Press-Courier* (Oxnard, CA), March 6, 1959, p. 6; "Air of Hope Marks Girls' Institution," *Los Angeles Times*, June 30, 1955, pp. 1, 30; "New Ventura Girls School under Construction," *Ventura County Star–Free Press* (CA), October 24, 1960, p. 11.
2. Roger Williams, "George Fox Digg'd Out of His Burrowes, or an Offer of Disputation," in *The Complete Writings of Roger Williams*, vol. 5, ed. Rev. J. Lewis Diman (Boston: John Foster, 1676), p. 361; Letter, Thomas Jefferson to Anne Willing Bingham, May 11, 1788, in *The Papers of Thomas Jefferson*, vol. 13, ed. Julian P. Boyd (Princeton, NJ: Princeton University Press, 1956), p. 151; Thomas R. Dew, "Dissertation on the Characteristic Differences between the Sexes," *Southern Literary Messenger*, 1 (May 1835), pp. 493–512.
3. Angela Davis, "Reflections on the Black Woman's Role in the Community of Slaves," *Massachusetts Review*, 13/1–2 (Spring 1972), pp. 81–100; George Washington, "Talk to the Cherokee Nation," August 29, 1796, in *The Writings of George Washington from the Original Manuscript Sources*, vol. 35, ed. John C. Fitzpatrick (Washington, DC: U.S. Government Printing Office, 1940), p. 194; T. Hartley Crawford, November 25, 1839, in *Report of the Commissioner of Indian Affairs*, 26th Congress, 1st session, *United States Congressional Serial Set*, vol. 363 (Washington, DC: Gales and Seaton, 1839), p. 344.
4. "Hens" in Richard Saunders [Benjamin Franklin], *Poor Richard, 1734: An Almanack for the Year of Christ 1734*, https://founders.archives.gov/documents/Franklin/01-01-02-0107; Amelia Bloomer, "To the Patrons of the Lily," *The Lily*, January 1, 1849, p. 1; "Just Treatment of Licentious Men. Addressed to Christian Mothers, Wives, Sisters, and Daughters," *Friend of Virtue* (January 1838), p. 4; Clinton Rogers Woodruff, introduction to Mary Beard, *Women's Work in Municipalities* (New York: D. Appleton and Company, 1915), p. x.

5. Michigan Association Opposed to Woman Suffrage, "An Appeal to Men," newspaper ad, April 1913, quoted in Carrie Chapman Catt and Nettie Rogers Shuler, *Woman Suffrage and Politics: The Inner Story of the Suffrage Movement* (New York: Charles Scribner's Sons, 1923), p. 275. Catt accused liquor interests of paying for the ad, but it was signed by women who were officers of the anti–woman suffrage association; Phyllis Schlafly, "What's Wrong with 'Equal Rights' for Women?," *The Phyllis Schlafly Report*, February 1972, https://www.phyllisschlafly.com/family/whats-wrong-with-equal-rights-for-women-february-1972/; Schlafly, "The Fraud Called the Equal Rights Amendment," *The Phyllis Schlafly Report*, May 1972, https://www.phyllisschlafly.com/constitution/the-fraud-called-the-equal-rights-amendment-may-1972/; and Schlafly, "The Right to Be a Woman," *The Phyllis Schlafly Report*, November 1972, https://www.phyllisschlafly.com/constitution/the-right-to-be-a-woman/.
6. "Many Young Women Now Say They'd Pick Family over Career," *New York Times*, December 28, 1980; Brenda Lane Richardson, "Professional Women Do Go Home Again," *New York Times*, April 20, 1988; Lisa Belkin, "The Opt-Out Revolution," *New York Times*, October 26, 2003.
7. Letter, John Adams to James Sullivan, May 26, 1776, in *Papers of John Adams*, vol. 4, ed. Robert J. Taylor et al. (Cambridge, MA: Belknap Press of Harvard University Press, 1980), pp. 208–210; President Woodrow Wilson, "Address to the Senate on the Nineteenth Amendment," September 30, 1918, the American Presidency Project, https://www.presidency.ucsb.edu/documents/address-the-senate-the-nineteenth-amendment.
8. "Half-naked" quoted in Hazel V. Carby, "Policing the Black Woman's Body in an Urban Context," *Critical Inquiry*, 18/4 (Summer 1992), p. 745; E. Norine Law, *The Shame of a Great Nation: The Story of the "White Slave Trade"* (Harrisburg, PA: United Evangelical Publishing House, 1909), pp. 192–193. See also Kathy Peiss's discussion of working-class white women in *Cheap Amusements: Working Women and Leisure in Turn-of-the-Century New York* (Philadelphia: Temple University Press, 1986).
9. William Lee Howard, "Effeminate Men and Masculine Women," *New York Medical Journal*, May 5, 1900, pp. 686–687.
10. Simone de Beauvoir, *The Second Sex*, trans. Constance Borde and Sheila Malovany-Chevallier (1949; rpt., New York: Vintage, 2011), p. 152; Judith Butler, "Sex and Gender in Simone de Beauvoir's *Second Sex*," *Yale French Studies*, 72 (1986), p. 35. Butler developed these ideas further in her classic work *Gender Trouble* (New York: Routledge, 1990); Monique Wittig, "One Is Not Born a Woman" (1981), in *The Straight Mind and Other Essays* (Boston: Beacon Press, 1991), p. 25; Carolyn G. Heilbrun, *Toward a Recognition of Androgyny* (New York: Norton, 1982), p. x; Maurice Godelier quoted in Joan W. Scott, "Gender: A Useful Category of Historical Analysis," *American Historical Review*, 91/5 (December 1986), p. 1069.
11. "Frank Dubois a Woman," *New York Times*, November 2, 1883, p. 1; "Woman Married to Woman," *Boston Weekly Globe*, November 6, 1883, p. 5.
12. "The Waupun Mystery," *Atlanta Constitution*, December 6, 1883, p. 1; "Frank Dubois—Concluded," *Detroit Free Press*, December 4, 1883, p. 3. Gertie Fuller

did not have to divorce Frank Dubois when she married again—according to a newspaper report, "to a man this time" ("Gertie's Two Weddings," *News and Citizen* [Morrisville, VT], October 23, 1884, p. 4). See also the discussion of "female husbands" such as Frank Dubois in Emily Skidmore, *True Sex: The Lives of Trans Men at the Turn of the Twentieth Century* (New York: New York University Press, 2017); Jen Manion, *Female Husbands: A Trans History* (New York: Cambridge University Press, 2020; and Lillian Faderman, *Surpassing the Love of Men: Romantic Friendship and Love between Women from the Renaissance to the Present* (New York: William Morrow, 1981), part 1A, chapter 4.

13. Merriam-Webster, "Merriam-Webster's Words of the Year: 2019," https://www.merriam-webster.com/words-at-play/word-of-the-year-2019-they; "Dictionary.com Names 'Existential' 2019 Word of the Year," *PR Newswire*, December 2, 2019, https://www.prnewswire.com/news-releases/dictionarycom-names-existential-2019-word-of-the-year-300965892.html; Pew Research Center, Survey of Teens Aged 13–17, conducted September 17–November 25, 2018, published January 14, 2019, https://www.pewresearch.org/social-trends/wp-content/uploads/sites/3/2019/02/Pew-Research-Center_Teens-report-topline_final.pdf; Kim Parker, Nikki Graf, and Ruth Igielnik, "Generation Z Looks a Lot Like Millennials on Key Social Issues," https://www.pewresearch.org/social-trends/2019/01/17/generation-z-looks-a-lot-like-millennials-on-key-social-and-political-issues/.

1.

WOMAN IN SEVENTEENTH-CENTURY AMERICA

1. Letter, Roger Williams to John Winthrop, July 10, 1637, in *Papers of the Winthrop Family*, vol. 3 (Boston: Massachusetts Historical Society, Digital Edition), https://www.masshist.org/publications/winthrop/index.php/view/PWF03d351.
2. John Winthrop, *Winthrop's Journal*, vol. 2, ed. James Kendall Hosmer (New York: Charles Scribner's Sons, 1908), p. 225.
3. Winthrop, *Winthrop's Journal*, 2:225.
4. Letter, Margaret Winthrop to John Winthrop, 1628, quoted in Robert C. Winthrop, *Life and Letters of John Winthrop* (Boston: Ticknor and Fields, 1864), p. 247; John Winthrop, "Speech to the General Court of Massachusetts, July 3, 1645," in *The History of New England from 1630 to 1649*, vol. 2, ed. James Savage (Boston: Little, Brown, 1853), p. 279, https://quod.lib.umich.edu/m/moa/AFJ7387.0001.001?rgn=main;view=fulltext.
5. Rev. John Cotton Jr., *A Meet Help, or, A Wedding Sermon Preached at New-Castle in New-England, June 19, 1694* (Boston: B. Green and J. Allen, 1699), pp. 21, 23.
6. Richard Greenham, *The Workes of the Reuerend and Faithfull Seruant of Jesus Christ M. Richard Greenham*, ed. H[enry] H[olland] (London: Thomas Snodham and Thomas Creede, 1612), p. 742. Diane Willen has suggested that under English Puritanism, wealthy Puritan widows served as benefactors and protectors of the clergy; and even Puritan women who were not wealthy widows could find ways to integrate public and private spheres by taking an active interest in the fate of Puritans on the Continent and events in Parliament as they affected Puritans

("Godly Women in Early Modern England: Puritanism and Gender," *Journal of Ecclesiastical History*, 43/4 [October 1992], pp. 561–580).

7. Lonna M. Malmsheimer, "Daughters of Zion: New England Roots of American Feminism," *New England Quarterly*, 50/3 (September 1977), pp. 484–504; Ruth H. Bloch, *Gender and Morality in Anglo-American Culture, 1650–1800* (Berkeley: University of California Press, 2003).
8. Letter, Roger Williams to John Winthrop, July 11, 1637, in *Papers of the Winthrop Family* (Boston: Massachusetts Historical Society, Digital Edition), https://www.masshist.org/publications/winthrop/index.php/view/PWF03d352; Letter, Roger Williams to John Winthrop, July 31, 1637, in *Papers of the Winthrop Family* (Boston: Massachusetts Historical Society, Digital Edition), https://www.masshist.org/publications/winthrop/index.php/view/PWF03d359. See also John M. Barry, *Roger Williams and the Creation of the American Soul: Church, State, and the Birth of Liberty* (New York: Penguin, 2012).
9. "Holy spirit" quoted in Alan E. Johnson, *The First American Founder: Roger Williams and Freedom of Conscience* (Pittsburgh: Philosophia Publications, 2015), p. 44; Roger Williams, *George Fox Digg'd Out of His Burrowes, or an Offer of Disputation*, vol. 5, ed. Rev. J. Lewis Diman, in *The Complete Writings of Roger Williams* (Boston: John Foster, 1676), pp. 360–361, 19.
10. On colonial women's limited exercise of power, see Mary Beth Norton, *Founding Mothers & Fathers: Gendered Power and the Forming of American Society* (New York: Knopf, 1996).
11. Letter, "To My Dear Children," in Anne Bradstreet, *The Works of Anne Bradstreet*, ed. Jeannine Hensley (Cambridge, MA: Harvard University Press, 1967), p. 241.
12. Quoted in Kathrynn Seidler Engberg, *The Right to Write: The Literary Politics of Anne Bradstreet and Phillis Wheatley* (Lanham, MD: University Press of America, 2010), pp. 1–2.
13. Thomas Parker, *The Copy of a Letter Written by Mr. Thomas Parker . . . to His Sister, Mrs. Elizabeth Avery* (London: John Downame, 1649), Early English Books Online Text Creation Partnership, https://quod.lib.umich.edu/e/eebo2/A91430.0001.001?view=toc).
14. John Winthrop, "A Short Story of the Rise, Reign, and Ruine of the Antinomians, Familists, & Libertines," in *The Antinomian Controversy, 1636–1638: A Documentary History*, ed. Donald D. Hall, 2nd ed. (Durham, NC: Duke University Press, 1990), p. 263.
15. Hugh Peter, *A Dying Father's Legacy to an Onely Child, Or Mr. Hugh Peter's Advice to His Daughter* (London: E. Calvert, 1660), p. 27. Peter had returned to England in 1641. In 1660, when Charles II assumed the throne, Peter was implicated in the move to execute Charles I. He wrote his "legacy" to his daughter in the Tower of London and was executed as a regicide soon after completing it; Laurel Thatcher Ulrich, "Vertuous Women Found: New England Ministerial Literature, 1668–1735," *America Quarterly*, 28/1 (Spring 1976), p. 33; Charles Francis Adams, *Three Episodes of Massachusetts History*, vol. 1 (Boston: Houghton, Mifflin, 1808), p. 629; Lyle Koehler, "The Case of the American Jezebels: Anne

Hutchinson and Female Agitation during the Years of the Antinomian Turmoil, 1636–1640," *William and Mary Quarterly,* 31/1 (January 1974), pp. 55–78; Eve LaPlante, *American Jezebel: The Uncommon Life of Anne Hutchinson, the Woman Who Defied the Puritans* (New York: HarperCollins, 2004), pp. 200, 119.

16. Winthrop, "A Short Story of the Rise, Reign, and Ruine of the Antinomians," pp. 312, 314.
17. "Delivered" quoted in Winthrop, *Winthrop's Journal,* 1:277; Letter, William Bradford to John Winthrop, April 11, 1638, in *Papers of the Winthrop Family* (Boston: Massachusetts Historical Society), https://www.masshist.org/database/viewer.php?item_id=1708&mode=dual&img_step=1.
18. Cotton Mather, *Magnalia Christi Americana: Or the Ecclesiastical History of New England from Its First Planting in the Year 1620 unto the Year of Our Lord 1698* (London: Thomas Parkhurst, 1702), book 7, pp. 18–19.
19. *Records of the Governor and Company of the Massachusetts Bay in New England,* ed. Nathaniel Shurtleff (Boston: W. White, 1853–1854), pp. 224, 328.
20. Winthrop, *Winthrop's Journal,* 1:285–286; Ednah D. Cheney, "The Women of Boston," in *The Memorial History of Boston, 1630–1880,* vol. 4, ed. Justin Winsor (Boston: Ticknor and Company, 1886), p. 335; Shurtleff, *Records of the Governor and Company of the Massachusetts Bay in New England,* pp. 232, 265; Koehler, "The Case of the American Jezebels," p. 70.
21. Gerard Croese, quoted in Horatio Rogers, *Mary Dyer of Rhode Island: The Quaker Martyr That Was Hanged on Boston Common, June 1, 1660* (Providence, RI: Preston and Rounds, 1896), p. 30.
22. Rogers, *Mary Dyer of Rhode Island,* p. 32.
23. Winthrop, *Winthrop's Journal,* 1:266.
24. Winthrop, "A Short Story," pp. 280–281.
25. Winthrop, *Winthrop's Journal,* 1: 266–268.
26. "Notes Relating to America: 1660," in *Calendar of State Papers,* Colonial Series, ed. William Noel Sainsbury, J. W. Fortescue, Cecil Headlam, and Arthur Percival Newton (London: Public Records Office, 1860), p. 532. Vane had returned to England. He had been a Cromwell supporter and was charged during the Restoration with high treason. He was beheaded in 1662.
27. Rogers, *Mary Dyer of Rhode Island,* p. 56.
28. "William Dyer's Petition to Governor Endicott for Mercy to His Wife," appendix 3, in Rogers, *Mary Dyer of Rhode Island,* pp. 94–95.
29. Quoted in Rogers, *Mary Dyer of Rhode Island,* p. 66. In more recent times, scholars have interpreted Dyer's resistance to Puritan patriarchy as one of the first instances of protofeminism in America.
30. See, for example, Anne G. Myles, "From Monster to Martyr: Re-Presenting Mary Dyer," *Early American Literature,* 36/1 (2001), pp. 1–30.
31. *Records and Files of the Quarterly Courts of Essex County,* vol. 1, ed. George Francis Dow (Salem, MA: Essex Institute, 1911), p. 44. See also the case of Thomasine or Thomas Hall, who was raised as a girl in England and became an indentured servant in Virginia in 1627/1628. Rumored to have lain with another maid, Hall was declared by the court after physical examinations to be both man and

woman—or what has more recently been called "intersex": in Norton, *Founding Mothers and Fathers*, pp. 184–188.
32. Winthrop, *Winthrop's Journal*, 2:344–345. In 1647, Alse Young of Windsor, Connecticut, became the first woman in America to be hanged as a witch. See George Lincoln Burr, ed., *Narratives of the Witchcraft Cases* (New York: Charles Scribner's Sons, 1914), p. 408.
33. Carol F. Karlsen, *The Devil in the Shape of a Woman: Witchcraft in Colonial New England* (New York: W. W. Norton, 1987); Emerson W. Baker, *A Storm of Witchcraft: The Salem Trials and the American Experience* (New York: Oxford University Press, 2014); Lyle Koehler, *A Search for Power: The "Weaker Sex" in Seventeenth-Century New England* (Urbana: University of Illinois Press, 1980), p. 206.
34. Koehler, *A Search for Power*, pp. 207, 206.
35. Koehler, *A Search for Power*, p. 206.
36. For a discussion of Hibbins's "verbal style" that was considered inappropriate to seventeenth-century woman, see Jane Kamensky, *Governing the Tongue: The Politics of Speech in Early New England* (New York: Oxford University Press, 1998), pp. 81–90.
37. Quoted in Joseph Barlow Felt, *Annals of Salem*, vol. 2 (Boston: James Munroe and Company, 1849), p. 459.
38. Benjamin Tompson, *New Englands Crisis: Or, A Brief Narrative of New-Englands Lamentable Estate at Present* (Boston: John Foster, 1676), p. 30.
39. Koehler, *A Search for Power*, pp. 339, 364.
40. Bernard Bailyn, *The New England Merchants in the Seventeenth Century* (Cambridge, MA: Harvard University Press, 1955), pp. 139–140.
41. Alice Morse Earle, *Costume of Colonial Times* (New York: Charles Scribner's Sons, 1894).
42. Increase Mather, *An Earnest Exhortation to the Inhabitants of New-England* (Boston: John Foster, 1676), p. 9.
43. Michael A. Seidel, "Poulain de la Barre's *The Woman as Good as the Man*," *Journal of the History of Ideas*, 35/3 (July–September 1974), pp. 499–508; James Norris, *Haec et Hic* . . . (London, 1683); anon., *The Wonders of the Female World* . . . (London: J. H. for Thomas Malthus, 1683).
44. Cotton Mather, *Ornaments for the Daughters of Zion* . . . (1692; rpt., Oxford: University of Oxford Text Archive, 2005), p. 9. Mather had already turned his attention to witches in *Memorable Providences, Relating to Witchcrafts and Possessions* (Boston: Joseph Brunning, 1689).
45. Mather, *Ornaments for the Daughters of Zion*, p. 10.
46. Cotton Mather, *The Wonders of the Invisible World. Being an Account of the Tryals of Several Witches Lately Executed in New-England* (1692; rpt., London: John Russell Smith, 1862), pp. 33, 134. See also John Putnam Demos, *Entertaining Satan: Witchcraft and the Culture of Early New England* (New York: Oxford University Press, 1982), p. 19; Paul Boyer and Stephen Nissenbaum, eds., *The Salem Witchcraft Papers*, 3 vols. (New York: Da Capo Press, 1977), 2:357.

47. "Testimony of Thomas Bradbury," in Boyer and Nissenbaum, *The Salem Witchcraft Papers*, 1:117–118.
48. Baron de Lahontan, *Nouveaux voyages dans l'Amerique* (1703), quoted in Richard White, *The Middle Ground: Indians, Empires, and Republics in the Great Lakes Region, 1650–1815* (1981; rpt., Cambridge: Cambridge University Press, 2010), p. 63.
49. Alexander Longe, "A Small Postscript on the ways and maners of the Nashon of Indians called Charikees [sic]," rpt. in *Southern Indian Studies*, 21 (October 1969), p. 8. Longe traded in Cherokee country in the early eighteenth century. His observations about female dominance among the Cherokee are corroborated by a later trader, James Adair, who wrote in 1775 that "the Cheerake [sic] . . . have been a considerable while under petticoat government" (*The History of the American Indians* [London: Edward and Charles Dilly, 1775], p. 232). See also John P. Brown, *Old Frontiers: The Story of the Cherokee Indians from the Earliest Times to the Date of Their Removal to the West, 1838* (Kingsport, TN: Southern Publishers, 1938); Marion E. Gridley, *American Indian Women* (New York: Hawthorn Books, 1974).
50. "The Examination of Sarah Ahhaton, Indian squaw wife unto William Ahhaton of Packemit alias Punquapauge taken the 24th of October 1668 Before Daniel Gookin," in Louise A. Breen, *Daniel Gookin, the Praying Indians, and King Philip's War: A Short History in Documents* (New York: Routledge, 2020), pp. 134–135; Shurtleff, *Records of the Governor and Company of the Massachusetts Bay*, p. 408. See also Joyce M. Clements, "Sarah and the Puritans: Feminist Contributions to New England Historical Archaeology," *Archaeologies*, 7/1 (April 2011), pp. 97–120.
51. John Demos, *The Tried and the True: Native America Women Confronting Colonization* (New York: Oxford University Press, 1998), p. 67; Charles Hudson, *The Southeastern Indians* (Knoxville: University of Tennessee Press, 1976), p. 269; C. C. Trowbridge, *Shawnee Traditions*, ed. Vernon Kinietz and Erminie W. Voegelin (Ann Arbor: University of Michigan, 1939); Baron de Lahontan, *Nouveaux voyages dans l'Amerique*, quoted in White, *The Middle Ground*, p. 63.
52. There is less documented evidence of gender diversity among Indians of the Northeast than among those in other parts of America. Megan K. Willison uses funerary artifacts to show that New England berdaches were accepted within their communities: "Two-Spirits or Changing Gender Roles? An Investigation of Mortuary Remains in Southern New England," in "Gender in Seventeenth-Century Southern New England," MA thesis, University of Connecticut, 2016. Eighteenth-century Spanish missionaries and explorers in the American West left a sizable record of their outrage at unconventional gender behavior. For example, Father Pedro Font wrote of the "nefarious practices" of the Indians of Northern California: "Among the women I saw men dressed like women, with whom they go about regularly, never joining the men": in Herbert E. Bolton, ed. and trans., *Font's Complete Diary: A Chronicle of the Founding of San Francisco* (Berkeley: University of California Press, 1931), p. 105. And Captain Pedro Fages wrote with horror that the Chumash Indians of Southern California "sinn[ed]

against nature": see Herbert Ingram Priestly, ed. and trans., *A Historical, Political, and Natural Description of California by Pedro Fages* (1937; rpt., Ramona, CA: Balena Press, 1972), p. 33. The anthropologist Alfred L. Kroeber speculated that the widespread historical acceptance of transvestism (that is, what came to be called transgenderism) in Native America as well as in northern Asia "suggests that the institution is a single historic growth" ("Psychosis or Social Sanction," *Character and Personality*, 8/3 [1940], p. 210). See also Joseph François Lafitau, *Customs of the American Indians Compared with the Customs of Primitive Times*, ed. and trans. William N. Fenton and Elizabeth Moore (Toronto: Champlain Society, 1974), pp. 52, 603–608; Sabine Lang, *Men as Women, Women as Men: Changing Gender in Native American Cultures*, trans. John L. Vantine (1990; rpt., Austin: University of Texas Press, 1998); Evelyn Blackwood, "Sexuality and Gender in Certain Native American Tribes: The Case of Cross-Gender Females," *Signs*, 10/1 (Autumn 1974), 27–42; Walter Lee Williams, *The Spirit and the Flesh: Sexual Diversity in American Indian Culture* (Boston: Beacon Press, 1992); Will Roscoe, *Changing Ones: Third and Fourth Genders in Native North America* (New York: St. Martin's Press, 1998).

53. Koehler, *A Search for Power*, p. 122.
54. Gretchen L. Green, "Gender and the Longhouse: Iroquois Women in a Changing Culture," in *Women and Freedom in Early America*, ed. Larry D. Eldridge (New York: New York University Press, 1997), pp. 7–25.
55. Lafitau, *Customs of the American Indians*, pp. 295, 336–337; Renee Jabobs, "The Iroquois Great Law of Peace and the United States Constitution: How the Founding Fathers Ignored the Clan Mothers," *American Indian Law Review*, 16/2 (1991), 497–531.
56. Cadwallader Colden, *The History of the Five Indian Nations Depending on the Province of New-York in America* (New York: William Bradford, 1727).
57. Red Jacket, *The Collected Speeches of Sagoyewatha, or Red Jacket*, ed. Granville Ganer (Syracuse, NY: Syracuse University Press, 2006), pp. 19–21.
58. Margaret Brent, *Proceedings and Acts of the General Assembly, Maryland, January 1637/8–September 1664*, vol. 1 (Baltimore: Maryland Historical Society, 1965), p. 215.
59. Cf. Mary Beth Norton, *Separated by Their Sex: Women in Public and Private in the Colonial Atlantic World* (Ithaca, NY: Cornell University Press, 2011). Norton suggests that the notion of rigid gendered divisions between the public (male) and private (female) did not exist from settlement to 1670 for women of high social status.
60. Quoted in James Davie Butler, "British Convicts Shipped to American Colonies," *American Historical Review*, 2/1 (October 1896), p. 18. See also Mimi Abramowitz, *Regulating the Lives of Women: Social Welfare Policy from Colonial Times to the Present* (New York: Routledge, 2017), p. 36.
61. Quoted in Marcia Zug, "Lonely Colonist Seeks Wife: The Forgotten History of America's First Mail-Order Brides," *Duke Journal of Gender Law and Policy*, 20/1 (Fall 2012), p. 85. In 1620, the proprietors of Virginia sent ninety young women to the colony, whom planters could purchase as brides in exchange for 120 pounds of leaf tobacco to defray the cost of their transportation. See Catherine Clinton,

The Plantation Mistress: Woman's World in the Old South (New York: Pantheon Books, 1982), p. 3.

62. William Waller Hening, ed., *The Statutes at Large: Being a Collection of All the Laws of Virginia from the First Session of the Legislature in the Year 1619*, vol. 2 (New York: Bartow, 1823), pp. 114–115.
63. Christopher Tomlins, *Freedom Bound: Law, Labor, and Civic Identity in Colonizing English America, 1580–1865* (Cambridge: Cambridge University Press, 2010), p. 302; Lois Green Carr and Lorena S. Walsh, "The Planter's Wife: The Experience of White Women in Seventeenth-Century Maryland," *William and Mary Quarterly*, 34/4 (1977), 542–571.
64. Zug, "Lonely Colonist Seeks Wife," p. 95; Parke Rouse Jr., "James Blair of Virginia," *Historical Magazine of the Protestant Episcopal Church*, 43/2 (June 1974), p. 189.
65. Linda Grant DePauw, *Founding Mothers: Women in America in the Revolutionary Era* (Boston: Houghton Mifflin, 1975), p. 27. See also Stephanie E. Jones-Rogers, *They Were Her Property: White Women as Slave Owners in the American South* (New Haven, CT: Yale University Press, 2019), chapter 6, "That Oman Took Delight in Sellin' Slaves," regarding eighteenth- and nineteenth-century white women who engaged in slave trading.
66. Dorothy A. Mays, *Women in Early America: Struggle, Survival, and Freedom in a New World* (Santa Barbara, CA: ABC-CLIO, 2004), p. 58.
67. Brent, *Proceedings and Acts of the General Assembly*, p. 215.
68. Julia Cherry Spruill, "Mistress Margaret Brent, Spinster," *Maryland Historical Magazine*, 29 (December 1934), pp. 259–268; W. B. Chilton, "The Will of Margaret Brent," *Virginia Magazine of History and Biography*, 16/1 (July 1908), p. 98.
69. George Fox, "The Woman Learning in Silence, or the Mystery of the Woman's Subjection to Her Husband," in *Gospel Truth Demonstrated* (1706; rpt., Philadelphia: Marcus T. C. Gould, 1821), p. 109. Quoted in Samuel Macpherson Janney, *The Life of William Penn: With Selections from His Correspondence and Autobiography*, 4th ed. (Philadelphia: Friends' Book Association, 1876), p. 384. See also Mary Maples Dunn, "Saints and Sisters: Congregational and Quaker Women in the Early Colonial Period," *American Quarterly*, 30 (1978), pp. 582–601.
70. It is disappointing that even these Quaker women were not free of the narrow moralisms of their day. For instance, they gave shelter and medical care to an unmarried woman whose breasts became infected after she bore a child, but once the woman was cured they cast her out. See Jean R. Soderlund, "Women's Authority in Pennsylvania and New Jersey Quaker Meetings," *William and Mary Quarterly*, 44/4 (October 1987), p. 738; Amanda E. Herbert, "Companions in Preaching and Suffering: Itinerant Female Quakers in the Seventeenth- and Eighteenth-Century British Atlantic World," *Early American Studies*, 9/1 (Winter 2011), p. 86. See also Phyllis Mack, *Visionary Women: Ecstatic Prophecy in Seventeenth-Century England* (Berkeley: University of California Press, 1992).
71. Quoted in J. William Frost, *The Quaker Family in Colonial America* (New York: St. Martin's Press, 1973), p. 176. See also Margaret Hope Bacon, *Mothers of Feminism: The Story of Quaker Women in America* (San Francisco: Harper and Row,

1986), pp. 55–57; Karin A. Wulf, *Not All Wives: Women of Colonial Philadelphia* (Philadelphia: University of Pennsylvania Press, 2005), p. 60.
72. Linda Biemer, "Criminal Law and Women in New Amsterdam and Early New York," *Selected Rensselaerswijck Seminar Papers*, p. 75, https://www.newnetherlandinstitute.org/files/2413/5067/3661/3.1.pdf; Simon Schama, "Wives and Wantons: Versions of Womanhood in Seventeenth-Century Dutch Art," *Oxford Art Journal*, 3 (April 1980), p. 6.
73. Thomas A. Foster, ed., *Women in Early America* (New York: New York University Press, 2015); Carole Chandler Waldrup, *Colonial Women: Twenty-Three Europeans Who Helped Build a Nation* (Jefferson, NC: McFarland, 1999); Jean Zimmerman, *The Women of the House: How a Colonial She-Merchant Built a Mansion, a Fortune, and a Dynasty* (New York: Harcourt, 2006).
74. Zimmerman, *The Women of the House*, pp. 115, 118.

2.
WOMAN, LADY, AND NOT A WOMAN IN THE EIGHTEENTH CENTURY

1. Letters, Benjamin Franklin to Polly Stevenson, May 1, 1760, July 11, 1760, and August 10, 1761, in *My Dear Girl: The Correspondence of Benjamin Franklin with Polly Stevenson, Georgiana, and Catherine Shipley*, ed. James Madison Stifler (New York: George H. Doran, 1927), pp. 24, 28–29, 46; H. W. Brands, *The First American: The Life and Times of Benjamin Franklin* (New York: Random House, 2002); Walter Isaacson, *Benjamin Franklin: An American Life* (New York: Simon and Schuster, 2004).
2. "Animadversions on the Affectation of Ill-Suited Characters of the Female Sex," *American Magazine and Historical Chronicle*, 2 (July 1745), p. 304. This article was reprinted from the *London Magazine and Monthly Chronologer* (September 1737), pp. 504–505, where it appeared under the title "Female Coxcombs."
3. Alice Lounsberry, *Sir William Phips: Treasure Fisherman and Governor of Massachusetts Bay Colony* (New York: Charles Scribner's Sons, 1941), pp. 261–274. Sewall's January 14, 1697, apology appears in Richard Francis, *Judge Sewall's Apology: The Salem Witch Trial and the Forming of An American Conscience* (New York: HarperCollins, 2005), pp. 181–182. For the jurors' apology, see "The Apology of the Salem Jury, 1697," in *The Penguin Book of Witches*, ed. Katherine Howe (New York: Penguin, 2014), pp. 197–198.
4. John Winthrop, "Speech to the General Court of Massachusetts, July 3, 1645," in *The History of New England from 1630 to 1649*, vol. 2, ed. James Savage (Boston: Little, Brown, 1853), p. 279, https://quod.lib.umich.edu/m/moa/AFJ7387.0001.001?rgn=main;view=fulltext; Benjamin Wadsworth, "Duties of Husbands and Wives," *The Well-Ordered Family: Or, Relative Duties . . .* (Boston: B. Green, 1712).
5. "Your Most Obedient Humble Servant, Kitchen Stuff," *New-England Courant*, May 18, 1724. Under the pseudonym Silence Dogood, Franklin wrote a series of comic pieces for the paper, including one in which he ridicules hoop petticoats

(Silence Dogood, "To the Author of the New-England Courant," *New-England Courant*, June 11, 1722, Founders Online, https://founders.archives.gov/documents/Franklin/01-01-02-0013), as did "Your Most Obedient Humble Servant, Kitchen Stuff."

6. "Animadversions on the Affectation of Ill-Suited Characters of the Female Sex," pp. 304–305.
7. *Reflections on Courtship and Marriage: In Two Letters to a Friend* (Philadelphia: B. Franklin, 1746), p. 31.
8. Richard Saunders [Benjamin Franklin], *Poor Richard, 1734: An Almanack for the Year of Christ 1734* (Philadelphia: B. Franklin, 1734); "Animadversions on the Affectation of Ill-Suited Characters of the Female Sex," p. 304.
9. "Natural right of liberty" in Baron de Lahontan, *Nouveaux Voyages dans l'Amerique* (1703), quoted in Richard White, *The Middle Ground: Indians, Empires, and Republics in the Great Lakes Region, 1650–1815* (1981; rpt., Cambridge: Cambridge University Press, 2010), p. 63; Le Petit quoted in John Reed Swanton, *Indian Tribes of the Lower Mississippi Valley* . . . (Washington, DC: Government Printing Office, 1911), p. 102.
10. Quoted in Swanton, *Indian Tribes*, p. 103.
11. Emily Clark, "The Ursulines: New Perspectives on 275 Years in New Orleans," *Historic New Orleans Collection Quarterly*, 20/3 (Summer 2002), pp. 2–5.
12. Marie-Madeleine Hachard and Gabriel Gravier, eds., *Relation du voyages des dames religieuses Ursulines de Rouen à la Nouvelle-Orléans* (1760; rpt., Paris: Maisonneuve, 1872), p. 91. French Jesuits had been trying to convert North American Indians to Catholicism since the seventeenth century. For example, for the complex conversion of Kateri Tekakwitha, a Mohawk woman, see Oliva Espin, *Women, Sainthood, and Power: A Feminist Psychology of Cultural Constructions* (Lanham, MD: Lexington Books, 2020), pp. 153–171; Allan Greer, *Mohawk Saint: Catherine Tekakwitha and the Jesuits* (New York: Oxford University Press, 2005).
13. James Adair, *The History of the American Indians, Particularly Those Nations Adjoining the Mississippi, East and West Florida, Georgia, South and North Carolina, and the Virginias* (London: Edward and Charles Dilly, 1775), pp. 145–146.
14. Quoted in Laura E. Donaldson, "'But We Are Your Mothers, You Are Our Sons': Gender, Sovereignty and the Nation in Early Cherokee Women's Writing," in *Indigenous Women and Feminism: Politics, Activism, Culture*, ed. Cheryl Suzack (Vancouver: University of British Columbia Press, 2010), p. 43.
15. George Washington, "Talk of the President of United States to the Beloved Men of the Cherokee Nation," August 29, 1796, George Washington Papers, series 4, General Correspondence, Library of Congress, https://www.loc.gov/item/mgw440234/. Even in the late eighteenth century, women among the Cherokee still enjoyed an elevated position. For example, in 1787, a Cherokee woman leader declared in a letter to Benjamin Franklin that she had urged her people to keep peace with the new nation, and she had filled the peace pipes for her warriors. She sent Franklin the same tobacco that she had used in the peace pipes, telling him to distribute it among members of the U.S. Congress in order to unite the Cherokee and the white man in peace. She reminded Franklin of women's

right to lead: "Woman is the mother of all," and so men "ought to mind what a woman says." See Theda Perdue, "Cherokee Women and the Trail of Tears," in *The American Indian: Past and Present*, ed. Roger L. Nichols, 4th ed. (New York: McGraw-Hill, 1992), p. 152.

16. Thomas Jefferson, "November 3, 1802, Address to Brother Handsome Lake," Presidential Speeches, University of Virginia, Miller Center, https://millercenter.org/the-presidency/presidential-speeches/november-3-1802-address-brother-handsome-lake. See also the discussion of the refashioning of Iroquois women in J. N. B. Hewitt, "Status of Women in Iroquois Polity before 1784," in *Annual Report for the Year Ending 30 June 1932* (Washington, DC: Smithsonian Institution, 1933), pp. 475–488; Marilyn Holly, "Handsome Lake's Teachings: The Shift from Female to Male Agriculture in Iroquois Culture," *Agriculture and Human Values*, 7 (1990), pp. 80–94.

17. Handsome Lake, "The Code of Handsome Lake," ed. Arthur C. Parker, *Education Department Bulletin* (University of the State of New York, Albany), 530 (November 1, 1912), pp. 31–32.

18. Handsome Lake, "The Code of Handsome Lake," pp. 28, 46. Matthew Dennis discusses the influence of Handsome Lake and the Iroquois witch hunts in *Seneca Possessed: Indians, Witchcraft and Power in the Early American Republic* (Philadelphia: University of Pennsylvania Press, 2010).

19. *Nancy Shippen, Her Journal Book: The International Romance of a Young Lady of Fashion of Colonial Philadelphia with Letters: to Her and About Her*, ed. Ethel Ames (Philadelphia: J. B. Lippincott, 1935), p. 40.

20. Howard Zinn shows that in Boston, for example, in 1687 the top 5 percent of the population owned 25 percent of the wealth, but in 1770, the top 1 percent owed 44 percent of the wealth. In postrevolutionary America, Zinn observes, the division between rich and poor became even more pronounced (*A People's History of the United States* [1980; rpt., New York: HarperPerennial, 2015], pp. 49, 96).

21. Kate Chopin, *The Awakening* (1899), rpt. in *The Awakening and Selected Stories of Kate Chopin* (New York: Simon and Schuster, 2009), p. 20. Catherine Clinton has shown that on the large plantations of the South, even ladies were expected to participate in a variety of household tasks, such as butchering hogs and making sausages (*The Planation Mistress: Woman's World in the Old South* [New York: Pantheon Books, 1982], pp. 20–26). But ladies who lived in towns or cities were generally free of arduous duties. By the nineteenth century, as Gerda Lerner has observed (referring to Thorstein Veblen's 1899 *The Theory of the Leisure Class*), among the upper classes and those who hoped to emulate them, idleness became a status symbol ("The Lady and the Mill Girl: Changes in the Status of Women in the Age of Jackson," *American Studies*, 10 [Spring 1969], pp. 5–15).

22. Quoted in Tilar J. Mazzeo, *Eliza Hamilton: The Extraordinary Life and Times of the Wife of Alexander Hamilton* (New York: Gallery Books, 2018), p. 20. John Quincy Adams described Jefferson's ostensible contradictions as "pliability of principle and temper" (*Memoirs of John Quincy Adams, Comprising Portions of His Diary from 1795 to 1848*, ed. Charles Francis Adams, vol. 8 [Philadelphia: J. B. Lippincott, 1876], p. 272).

23. Quoted in Ames, *Nancy Shippen, Her Journal Book*, p. 40.
24. Robert Morris to Mary Morris, November 15, 1787; Mary Morris to Robert Morris, March 29, 1789; Robert Morris to Mary Morris, November 28, 1787, box 3; and Robert Morris to Mary Morris, May 13, 1789, box 4, Robert Morris Collection, Huntington Library, San Marino, CA (hereafter Robert Morris Collection).
25. Robert Morris to Maria Morris, October 9, 1798, box 6, Robert Morris Collection.
26. John Gregory, *A Father's Legacy to His Daughters* (1761; rpt., Philadelphia: John Dunlap, 1775), p. 15.
27. *The Diary of Hannah Callender Sansom*, ed. Susan E. Klepp and Karin Wulf (Ithaca, NY: Cornell University Press, 2009), p. 86; Linda Grant DePauw, *Founding Mothers: Women in America in the Revolutionary Era* (Boston: Houghton Mifflin, 1975), p. 58.
28. Thomas Jefferson to Anne Willing Bingham, May 11, 1788, in *The Papers of Thomas Jefferson*, ed. Julian P. Boyd, vol. 13 (Princeton, NJ: Princeton University Press, 1956), p. 151. Bingham most certainly did "wrinkle [her forehead] with politics." She was even the one who suggested to Jefferson that to prevent the tyranny of the majority, a Bill of Rights that honored the individual was necessary.
29. *Diary of Anna Green Winslow, A Boston Schoolgirl of 1771*, ed. Alice Morse Earle (Boston: Houghton Mifflin, 1894); "Martin Foy, Dancing Master, Just Arrived from Europe," newspaper advertisement, *Pennsylvania Chronicle*, April 20, 1767.
30. "Female Influence: Being the Substance of an Oration Delivered at the Annual Commencement of Columbia College, May 6, 1795," *New-York Magazine; or, Literary Repository*, 6/5 (May 1795), pp. 303–304; "ungovernable" and "What is my" quoted in Ames, *Nancy Shippen, Her Journal Book*, pp. 116, 233.
31. Quoted in Ames, *Nancy Shippen, Her Journal Book*, pp. 267–268.
32. Quoted in Ames, *Nancy Shippen, Her Journal Book*, pp. 221–222.
33. "A Charleston Vendue in 1812" (rpt., *Sacramento Daily Union*, January 23, 1869).
34. As Margaret Fuller observed with regard to slaves, "women are on a par with men. Each is a work-tool, an article of property, no more!" (*Woman in the Nineteenth Century* [New York: Greeley and McElrath, 1845], p. 51). Or, as Angela Davis phrased it, among slaves, "the Black woman was forced into equality with the Black man. . . . She shared in the deformed equality of equal oppression" ("Reflections on the Black Woman's Role in the Community of Slaves," *The Black Scholar* [December 1971], p. 6).
35. Deborah Gray White, *Ar'n't I a Woman? Female Slaves in the Plantation South* (New York: W. W. Norton, 1999), 92–93.
36. "Old Elizabeth," in *Six Women's Slave Narratives*, ed. William L. Andrews (New York: Oxford University Press, 1989), p. 44.
37. *Women and Slavery in America: A Documentary History*, ed. Catherine M. Lewis and J. Richard Lewis (Fayetteville: University of Arkansas Press, 2011), p. xvii; Jacqueline Jones, "Race, Sex, and Self-Evident Truths: The Status of Slave Women during the American Revolution," in *Women in the Age of the American Revolution*, ed. Ronald Hoffman and Peter J. Albert (Charlottesville: University Press of Virginia, 1989), pp. 293–337; *Slave Testimony: Two Centuries of Letters, Speeches,*

Interviews and Autobiographies, ed. John W. Blassingame (Baton Rouge: Louisiana State University Press, 1977), pp. 380, 372.

38. White, *Ar'n't I a Woman?*, p. 201; John Brickell, "The Present State of North Carolina" (1737), in *The North Carolina Experience: An Interpretive History*, ed. Lindley S. Butler and Alan D. Watson (Chapel Hill: University of North Carolina Press, 2010); "A Charleston Vendue in 1812."

39. Daniel C. Littlefield, *Rice and Slaves: Ethnicity and the Slave Trade in Colonial South Carolina* (Baton Rouge: Louisiana State University Press, 1981), pp. 69, 204; Dorothy Schneider and Carl J. Schneider, *Slavery in America* (New York: Infobase Publishing, 2007), p. 52.

40. Elkanah Watson, *Men and Times of the Revolution; or Memoirs of Elkanah Watson, Including His Journals of Travels in Europe and America, from 1777 to 1842* (New York: Dana and Company, 1856); Davis, "Reflections on the Black Woman's Role in the Community of Slaves."

41. Jane Kamensky, "The Colonial Mosaic, 1600–1760," in *No Small Courage: A History of Women in the United States*, ed. Nancy F. Cott (New York: Oxford University Press, 2004), p. 95.

42. Thavolia Glymph, *Out of the House of Bondage: The Transformation of the Plantation Household* (New York: Cambridge University Press, 2008), p. 26; Stephanie E. Jones-Rogers, *They Were Her Property: White Women as Slave Owners in the American South* (New Haven, CT: Yale University Press, 2019), 106–108, 149.

43. Brenda E. Stevenson, *Life in Black and White: Family and Community in the Slave South* (New York: Oxford University Press, 1996), p. 194; Chesnut quoted in Gerda Lerner, *The Majority Finds Its Past: Placing Women in History* (Chapel Hill: University of North Carolina Press, 2005), p. 74.

44. Harriet Jacobs, *Incidents in the Life of a Slave Girl* (1861; rpt., New York: Dover Publications, 2001), p. 45; Louisa Picquet and Rev. H[iram] Mattison, *The Octoroon: A Tale of Southern Slave Life* (New York: Mattison, 1861); Reginald H. Pitts, "Louisa Picquet, c. 1829–1896," *Legacy*, 24/2 (2007), pp. 294–305. See also Brenda E. Stevenson, "'What's Love Got to Do with It?' Concubinage and Enslaved Women and Girls in the Antebellum South," in *Sexuality and Slavery: Reclaiming Intimate Histories in the Americas*, ed. Daina Ramey Berry and Leslie M. Harris (Athens: University of Georgia Press, 2018), pp. 145–158.

45. *Portrait of a Patriot: The Major Political and Legal Papers of Josiah Quincy, Jr.*, vol. 3, ed. Daniel R. Coquillette and Neil Longley York (Boston: Colonial Society of Massachusetts, 2008), p. 105; White, *Ar'n't I a Woman?*, chapter 1.

46. Jacobs, *Incidents in the Life of a Slave Girl*, p. 46.

47. Martha Hodes, *White Women, Black Men: Illicit Sex in the Nineteenth-Century South* (New Haven, CT: Yale University Press, 1997), pp. 25–26; Randall Kennedy, *Interracial Intimacies: Sex, Marriage, Identity, and Adoption* (New York: Pantheon, 2003), pp. 61–62; Hodes, *White Women, Black Men*, pp. 69–76. Relationships between slave-owning men and enslaved women that seem to have gone beyond sexual gratification on the part of the slave owner have been well documented. Thomas Jefferson's relationship with Sally Hemings is the best known. For other examples, see the relationship between James Henry Ham-

mond, the governor of South Carolina, and Sally Johnson in Drew Gilpin Faust, *James Henry Hammond and the Old South: A Design for Mastery* (Baton Rouge: Louisiana State University Press, 1985), pp. 86–88, 315–320; and the relationship between Ralph Quarles, a military hero of the Revolutionary War, and Lucy Langston in William Cheek and Aimee Lee Cheek, *John Mercer Langston and the Fight for Freedom* (Champaign-Urbana: University of Illinois Press, 1989). John Mercer Langston, one of the four children of Quarles and Lucy Langston, became the founding dean of the Howard University School of Law and represented Virginia in the U.S. Congress.

48. In *Milcah Martha Moore's Book: A Commonplace Book from Revolutionary America*, ed. Catherine La Courreye Blecki and Karin A. Wulf (University Park: Pennsylvania State University Press, 1997), p. 12.
49. Catherine M. Scholten, "On the Importance of the Obstetrick Art: Changing Customs of Childbirth in America, 1760–1825," *William and Mary Quarterly*, 34/3 (July 1977), pp. 426–445.
50. Quoted in DePauw, *Founding Mothers*, p. 151. See also Judith A. Ridner, "To Have a Sufficient Maintenance: Women and the Economics of Freedom in Frontier Pennsylvania, 1750–1800," in *Women and Freedom in Early America*, ed. Larry Eldridge (New York: New York University Press, 1997), pp. 167–190; and Johanna Miller Lewis, "Women and Economic Freedom in the North Carolina Backcountry," in Eldridge, *Women and Freedom in Early America*, pp. 191–208.
51. Quoted in Daniel White Shells and Reuben Field Wells, *A History of Hatfield, Massachusetts, in Three Parts* (Springfield, MA: F. C. H. Gibbons, 1910), pp. 206–207.
52. Marla R. Miller, "'My Part Alone': The World of Rebecca Dickinson, 1787–1802," *New England Quarterly*, 71/3 (September 1998), pp. 341–377.
53. Letter, Abigail Adams to John Adams, December 23, 1782, Adams Family Papers, Massachusetts Historical Society, http://www.masshist.org/digitaladams/archive/doc?id=L17821223aa.
54. Quoted in *The Diary of Hannah Callender Sansom*, ed. Susan E. Klepp and Karin Wulf (Ithaca, NY: Cornell University Press, 2009), pp. 61, 132, 192, 213; Susan E. Klepp, *Revolutionary Conceptions: Woman, Fertility, and Family Limitation in America, 1760–1820* (Chapel Hill: University of North Carolina Press, 2009), p. 125.
55. Havelock Ellis, "Sexual Inversion in Women" (1897), rpt. in *Studies in the Psychology of Sex*, vol. 1 (New York: Random House, 1942), pp. 195–264; Havelock Ellis, *Man and Woman: A Study of Human Secondary Sexual Characters* (1894; rpt., London: A. and C. Black, 1930).
56. Catherine A. Brekus, *Strangers and Pilgrims: Female Preaching in America, 1740–1845* (Chapel Hill: University of North Carolina Press, 1998), p. 87. John H. Martin, "Jemima Wilkinson: Celibacy and the Communal Life," *Crooked Lake Review* (Fall 2005), https://www.crookedlakereview.com/books/saints_sinners/martin5.html. See also Herbert A. Wisbey Jr., *Pioneer Prophetess: Jemima Wilkinson, the Publick Universal Friend* (Ithaca, NY: Cornell University Press, 1964).
57. Martin, "Jemima Wilkinson."

58. Duke de la Rouchefoucauld-Liancourt, *Travels through the United States of North America* (London: R. Phillips, 1799), pp. 112–113. "Lesbian" was not a term commonly used in early America, though in the seventeenth century in the New Haven Colony, sex between women was punishable by the death penalty, as was sex between men. See Louis Crompton, "Homosexuals and the Death Penalty in Colonial America," *Journal of Homosexuality*, 1/3 (February 1976), pp. 277, 280.
59. The Shakers, who also believed in celibacy and were established in America at about the same time as the Universal Friends, fared slightly better: small Shaker communities survived into the nineteenth and twentieth centuries. In the twenty-first century only one very small Shaker community remains, at Sabbathday Lake, in Maine.
60. Karin A. Wulf, *Not All Wives: Women of Colonial Philadelphia* (Philadelphia: University of Pennsylvania Press, 2005), p. 60.
61. Wulf, *Not All Wives*, pp. 62.
62. Quoted in Susan Stabile, *Memory's Daughters: The Material Culture of Remembrance in Eighteenth-Century America* (Ithaca, NY: Cornell University Press, 2004), p. 10.
63. Susanna Wright, "To Eliza. Norris at Fairhill," in *American Poetry: The Seventeenth and Eighteenth Centuries*, ed. David S. Shields (New York: Library of America, 2007), p. 377.
64. Logan quoted in Stabile, *Memory's Daughters*, p. 35, Hudson quoted in Wulf, *Not All Wives*, p. 66.
65. Griffitts quoted in Blecki and Wulf, *Milcah Martha Moore's Book*, p. 78; William J. Scheick, *Authority and Female Authorship in Colonial America* (Lexington: University of Kentucky Press, 1998), pp. 13–14; Thomas Parker, *The Copy of a Letter Written by Mr. Thomas Parker . . . to His Sister, Miss Elizabeth Avery* (London: John Downame, 1649), Early English Books Online Text Creation Partnership, https://quod.lib.umich.edu/e/eebo2/A91430.0001.001?view=toc.
66. Griffitts's poem was published anonymously in the *Pennsylvania Chronicle*, December 1769. It appeared with an attribution to Griffitts in *Milcah Martha Moore's Book*, p. 172.
67. Griffitts quoted in Blecki and Wulf, *Milcah Martha Moore's Book*, p. 12; "To Sophronia. In answer to some Lines she directed to be wrote on my Fan. 1769." Blecki and Wulf, *Milcah Martha Moore's Book*, pp. 173–174.

3.
DAUGHTERS OF LIBERTY

1. Letter, Abigail Grant to Azariah Grant, August 19, 1776, in *The Huntington Letters in the Possession of Julia Chester Wells*, ed. W. D. McCracken (1897; rpt., New York: Appleton Press, 1905), pp. 174–175.
2. *Letters of Eliza Wilkinson, during the Invasion and Possession of Charleston, S.C., by the British in the Revolutionary War*, ed. Caroline Gilman (New York: Samuel Colman, 1839), p. 17.

3. Thomas Paine, *Common Sense: Addressed to the Inhabitants of America* (Philadelphia: R. Bell, 1776), p. 7; Letter, John Adams to James Sullivan, May 26, 1776, in *Papers of John Adams*, vol. 4, ed. Robert J. Taylor et al. (Cambridge, MA: Belknap Press of Harvard University Press, 1980), p. 208.
4. Letter, Sarah Livingston Jay to John Jay, October 25, 1794, in *Selected Letters of John Jay and Sarah Livingston Jay*, ed. Landa M. Freeman et al. (Jefferson, NC: McFarland, 2010), pp. 235–237; *The Selected Papers of John Jay, 1785–1788*, vol. 4, ed. Elizabeth M. Nuxoll (Charlottesville: University of Virginia Press, 2015), p. 196; Diego de Gardoqui quoted in Cokie Roberts, *Founding Mothers: The Women Who Raised Our Nation* (New York: HarperCollins, 2004), p. 165. "Weakness" quoted in Mary Beth Norton, *Liberty's Daughters: The Revolutionary Experience of American Women, 1750–1800* (Boston: Little, Brown, 1980), p. 117.
5. Letter, Abigail Adams to Mercy Otis Warren, c. February 3, 1775, Founders Online, https://founders.archives.gov/documents/Adams/04-01-02-0122; *The Adams Papers: Adams Family Correspondence*, ed. L. H. Butterfield and Marc Friedlaender, vol. 3 (Cambridge, MA: Belknap Press of Harvard University Press, 1973), pp. 157–158.
6. Gilman, *Letters of Eliza Wilkinson*, pp. 16, 17.
7. Gilman, *Letters of Eliza Wilkinson*, pp. 60–61.
8. Linda K. Kerber, "'History Can Do It No Justice': Women and the Reinterpretation of the American Revolution," in *Women in the Age of the American Revolution*, ed. Ronald Hoffman and Peter J. Albert (Charlottesville: University Press of Virginia, 1989), p. 22; New Jersey woman quoted in Mrs. [Elizabeth Fries] Ellet, *Domestic History of the American Revolution* (New York: Baker and Scribner, 1850), p. 70.
9. McDougal quoted in Holly A. Mayer, *Belonging to the Army: Camp Followers and Community during the American Revolution* (Columbia: University of South Carolina Press, 1996), p. 111. The British army had camp followers in America as well. Three thousand women were sent from Liverpool to serve as prostitutes to the British soldiers stationed in New York City: see Christine Stansell, *City of Women: Sex and Class in New York, 1789–1860* (Champaign: University of Illinois Press, 1987), p. 5; Charles Royster, *A Revolutionary People at War: The Continental Army and American Character, 1775–1783* (Chapel Hill: University of North Carolina Press, 1980), p. 205.
10. William Barton, November 17, 1778, quoted in Robert Fridlington, "A Diversion in Newark: A Letter from the New Jersey Continental Line, 1778," *New Jersey History*, 105 (Spring/Summer 1987), pp. 77–78.
11. It has been estimated that during the Civil War, 400 individuals who had been assigned female at birth served as soldiers. See George Washington Adams, *Doctors in Blue: The Medical History of the Union Army in the Civil War* (1952; rpt., Baton Rouge: Louisiana State University Press, 1996), p. 13. See the discussion of Deborah Sampson/Robert Shurtleff in Lillian Faderman, *Surpassing the Love of Men: Romantic Friendship and Love between Women from the Renaissance to the Present* (New York: William Morrow, 1981), pp. 58–60. Revere quoted in Emily J. Teipe, "Will the Real Molly Pitcher Please Stand Up?," *Prologue*, 31/2 (Summer

1999), https://www.archives.gov/publications/prologue/1999/summer/pitcher.html; see also Linda Grant De Pauw, "Women in Combat: The Revolutionary War Experience," *Armed Forces and Society*, 7/2 (Winter 1981), pp. 209–226. De Pauw also discusses Margaret Corbin, who served openly in the army as a "transvestite."

12. *Margaret Hill Morris, Her Journal*, ed. John W. Jackson (Philadelphia: G. S. MacManus, 1949), pp. 39, 44.
13. Jackson, *Margaret Hill Morris*, pp. 47, 59, 61.
14. A very few women were given a brief public forum during the war years, including Hannah Griffitts (whose poem "The Female Patriots" is discussed in chapter 2) and the former slave Phillis Wheatley, both of whom published war poems in the *Pennsylvania Chronicle*. Wheatley's "His Excellency General Washington" appeared in *Pennsylvania Magazine*, April 30, 1776; William Tennent III, "To the Ladies of South Carolina," *South Carolina Gazette and Country Journal*, August 2, 1774, p. 1.
15. "The Female Patriots," in *Milcah Martha Moore's Book: A Commonplace Book from Revolutionary America*, ed. Catherine La Courreye Blecki and Karin A. Wulf (University Park: Pennsylvania State University Press, 1997), p. 172; "Edenton Ladies Agreement, October 27, 1774," in "Political Women in the American Revolution," Alexander Street, https://documents.alexanderstreet.com/d/100407 6968.
16. *Providence Gazette*, March 12, 1766, quoted in Laurel Thatcher Ulrich, "'Daughters of Liberty': Religious Women in Revolutionary New England," in Hoffman and Albert, *Women in the Age of the American Revolution*, p. 215.
17. Tennent, "To the Ladies of South Carolina"; Carol Berkin, *Revolutionary Mothers: Women in the Struggle for American Independence* (New York: Knopf, 2005), pp. 20–21; Norton, *Liberty's Daughters*, pp. 157–158.
18. Quoted in Alfred F. Young, "The Women of Boston: 'Persons of Consequence' in the Making of the American Revolution, 1765–1776," in *Women and Politics in the Age of the Democratic Revolution*, ed. Harriet B. Applewhite and Darline G. Levy (Ann Arbor: University of Michigan Press, 1993), p. 203.
19. *Providence Gazette*, March 12, 1766, quoted in Ulrich, "'Daughters of Liberty,'" p. 215; Connecticut woman quoted in Kate Dickinson Sweetser, "The American Girl: 1719–1919," *Daughters of the American Revolution Magazine*, 53/9 (1919), p. 522; New York woman quoted in Paul S. Boyer et al., *The Enduring Vision: A History of the American People*, vol. 1 (Belmont, CA: Wadsworth, 2010), p. 139.
20. By an American Woman [Esther de Berdt Reed], "The Sentiments of an American Woman," June 10, 1780, folder 3, portfolio 146, Printed Ephemera Collection, Library of Congress, Washington, DC.
21. Letter, Esther de Berdt Reed to George Washington, July 31, 1780, in *Life and Correspondence of Joseph Reed: Military Secretary of Washington*, vol. 2, ed. William Bradford Reed (Philadelphia: Lindsay and Blakiston, 1847), p. 264.
22. Letter, George Washington to Mrs. Francis, Mrs. Hillegas, Mrs. Clarkson, Mrs. Bache, and Mrs. Blair, February 13, 1781, in *The Writings of George Washington: Being His Correspondence, Addresses, Messages, and Other Papers, Official*

and Private, Selected and Published from the Original Manuscripts, vol. 7, part 2, ed. Jared Sparks (New York: Harper and Brothers, 1847), pp. 408–409.

23. Letter, John Adams to James Sullivan, May 26, 1776, in Taylor et al., *Papers of John Adams*, 4:208.
24. Nancy Cott, *The Bonds of Womanhood: Woman's Sphere in New England, 1780–1835* (New Haven, CT: Yale University Press, 1977), pp. 187–188.
25. Quoted in Catherine Johnson Adams, "What I Did Is Who I Am: African American Women and Resistance to Slavery in Colonial and Revolutionary New England," PhD diss., University of Illinois at Urbana-Champaign, 2004, p. 157.
26. "Regarding Dunmore's Proclamation," *Virginia Gazette*, November 25, 1775, and December 2, 1775; Benjamin Quarles, "Lord Dunmore as Liberator," *William and Mary Quarterly*, 15/4 (October 1958), pp. 494–507; Sally R. Frey, "Between Slavery and Freedom: Virginia Blacks in the American Revolution," *Journal of Southern History*, 49/3 (August 1983), pp. 375–398; enslaved girl: Jill Lepore, *These Truths: A History of the United States* (New York: W. W. Norton, 2019), p. 100.
27. Alan L. Olmstead and Paul W. Rhode, "Slave Productivity in Cotton Production by Gender, Age, and Scale," March 2010, https://economics.yale.edu/sites/default/files/files/Workshops-Seminars/Economic-History/rhode-032910.pdf.
28. Deborah L. Newman, "Black Women in the Era of the American Revolution," *Journal of Negro History*, 61/3 (1976), pp. 276–289.
29. Jarena Lee, *Religious Experience and Journal of Mrs. Jarena Lee, Giving an Account of Her Call to Preach the Gospel* (Philadelphia: printed and published for the author, 1849), http://www.umilta.net/jarena.html. An earlier version of this book appeared as Jarena Lee, *The Life and Religious Experience of Jarena Lee, a Colored Lady, Giving an Account of her Call to Preach the Gospel* (Philadelphia: Printed and published for the Author, 1836).
30. Lee, *Religious Experience and Journal*.
31. Lee, *Religious Expereince and Journal*; "begging" quoted in Frederick Knight, "The Many Names for Jarena Lee," *Pennsylvania Magazine of History and Biography*, 141/1 (January 2017), p. 63.
32. Abigail back home: Woody Holton, *Abigail Adams: A Life* (New York: Simon and Schuster, 2010), pp. 127, 133; Letter, Abigail Adams to John Adams, March 31, 1776, in *The Book of Abigail and John: Selected Letters of the Adams Family, 1762–1784*, ed. L. H. Butterfield et al. (Boston: Northeastern University Press, 2002), p. 121.
33. Letter, John Adams to Abigail Adams, April 14, 1776, in Butterfield et al., *The Book of Abigail and John*, p. 123.
34. Letter, John Adams to James Sullivan, May 26, 1776, in Taylor et al., *Papers of John Adams*, 4:208–210. There has been a long debate among women's history scholars about whether the American Revolution advanced women's freedom. For example, Joan Hoff Wilson argues in "The Illusion of Change: Women and the Revolution," in *The American Revolution: Explorations in the History of Radicalism*, ed. Alfred F. Young (DeKalb: Northern Illinois University Press, 1976), pp. 383–446, that in terms of economics, the law, and politics, the revolution had no significant role in changing women's lives. Mary Beth Norton in

Liberty's Daughters suggests that the revolution did make women think differently about their personal life and matters, such as whether to stay in an unhappy marriage. In *Women of the Republic: Intellect and Ideology in Revolutionary America* (Chapel Hill: University of North Carolina Press, 1980), Linda Kerber suggests that women's importance in the semipublic sphere faded after the war. Historians generally agree, however, that the war resulted in more educational opportunities for women.

35. Mercy Warren, *History of the Rise, Progress and Termination of the American Revolution*, vol. 1 (Boston: Manning and Loring, 1805), p. viii; Warren quoted in Nancy Rubin Stuart, *The Muse of the Revolution: The Secret Pen of Mercy Otis Warren and the Founding of a Nation* (Boston: Beacon Press, 2009), p. 91.
36. Stuart, *The Muse of the Revolution*, p. xi; Alice Brown, *Mercy Warren* (New York: Charles Scribner's Sons, 1896), p. 240; Erick Trickey, "The Woman Whose Words Enflamed the American Revolution," *Smithsonian*, June 20, 2017, https://www.smithsonianmag.com/history/woman-whose-words-inflamed-american-revolution-180963765/.
37. Quoted in Rosemarie Zagarri, *Revolutionary Backlash: Women and Politics in the Early American Republic* (Philadelphia: University of Pennsylvania Press, 2007), pp. 34–35.
38. Quoted in Richard J. Werther, "Grace Galloway—Abandoned Loyalist Wife," *Journal of the American Revolution*, March 12, 2018, https://allthingsliberty.com/2018/03/grace-galloway-abandoned-loyalist-wife/#_edn14.
39. Letter, Grace Galloway to Joseph Galloway, May 15, 1779; and letter, Grace Galloway to Elizabeth Galloway, May 15, 1779, Joseph Galloway Collection, Huntington Library, San Marino, CA.
40. "Diary of Grace Growden Galloway Kept at Philadelphia from June 17, 1778 to July 1st, 1778," ed. Raymond C. Werner, *The Pennsylvania Magazine of History and Biography*, 55/1 (1931), p. 45.
41. Benjamin Rush, *Thoughts upon Female Education Accommodated to the Present State of Society, Manners, and Government* (1787; rpt., Philadelphia: Thomas and Samuel F. Bradford, 1798), pp. 77–78.
42. Letter, Eliza Southgate to Mamma, January 23, 1797; letter, Eliza Southgate to Mother, September 30, 1797; letter, Eliza Southgate to Moses Porter, May 1801; and letter, Eliza Southgate to her parents, February 7, 1800, in *Letters of Eliza Southgate: Mrs. Walter Bowne*, Library of Congress, https://www.loc.gov/resource/lhbtn.34525/?st=gallery&c=160. Selected letters were published in Eliza Southgate Bowne, *A Girl's Life Eighty Years Ago: Selections from the Letters of Eliza Southgate Bowne*, ed. Clarence Cook (New York: Charles Scribner's Sons, 1887).
43. Eliza Southgate to Moses Porter, June 1, 1801, in *Letters of Eliza Southgate*.
44. "Animadversions on the Affectation of Ill-Suited Characters of the Female Sex," *American Magazine and Historical Chronicle*, 2 (July 1745), pp. 304–305. This article was reprinted from *The London Magazine and Monthly Chronologer* (September 1737), pp. 504–505, where its title was "Female Coxcombs." Alphonzo, "An Address to the Ladies," *American Magazine*, 1 (March 1788), p. 246; Gardiner quoted in Linda Kerber, "Daughters of Columbia: Educating Women for the Re-

public, 1787–1805, in *The Hofstadter Aegis: A Memorial*, ed. Stanley Elkins and Eric McKitrick (New York: Knopf, 1974), p. 49.
45. "To a Lady, Who Expressed the Desire of Seeing an University Established for Women," *American Museum, or Universal Magazine*, 11, appendix 1 (June 1792), p. 3.
46. "Peculiar," in Rush, *Thoughts upon Female Education*, pp. 78–79. Linda K. Kerber coined the useful term "Republican Motherhood" to encompass arguments such as Rush's about the reason to educate women: see *Women of the Republic: Intellect and Ideology in Revolutionary America* (Chapel Hill: University of North Carolina Press, 1980).
47. Rush, *Thoughts upon Female Education*, pp. 92, 84; *Letters of Benjamin Rush: 1762–1792*, vol. 1, ed. Lyman Henry Butterfield (Princeton, NJ: Princeton University Press, 1951), p. 617. Mather wrote, "In every Lawful thing, she submits her Will and Sense to [her husband]": *Ornaments for the Daughters of Zion: Or The Character and Happiness of a Vertuous Woman* (1692; rpt., London, T. Parkhurst, 1694), p. 10.
48. William Woodbridge, "Female Education in the Last Century," *American Annals of Education*, 1/11 (November 1831), p. 526. Woodbridge signed his essay "Senex"—that is, he was looking back on the pioneering work of his youth with the gravitas of the elderly.
49. John Cosens Ogden, "An Address Delivered at the Opening of Portsmouth Academy, on Easter Monday, A.D. 1791," in *The Female Guide, or Thoughts on the Education of That Sex: Accommodated to the State of Society, Manners, and Government in the United States* (Concord, NH: George Hough, 1793), p. 26.
50. "Shame in Connecticut," *Vermont Chronicle* (Bellows Falls), July 12, 1833, p. 3.
51. Miriam R. Small and Edwin W. Small, "Prudence Crandall: Champion of Negro Education," *New England Quarterly*, 17/4 (December 1944), pp. 506–529; Donald E. Williams, *Prudence Crandall's Legacy: The Fight for Equality in the 1830s, Dred Scott, and Brown v. Board of Education* (Middletown, CT: Wesleyan University Press, 2014), chapter 3.
52. "Hasty," quoted in Sheila L. Skemp, *First Lady of Letters: Judith Sargent Murray and the Struggle for Female Independence* (Philadelphia: University of Pennsylvania Press, 2009), p. 35; Constantia [Judith Sargent Stevens], "Desultory Thoughts upon the Utility of Encouraging a Degree of Self-Complacency, Especially in Female Bosoms," *Gentleman and Lady's Town and Country Magazine* (October 1784), https://pages.uoregon.edu/mjdennis/courses/history_456_murray1.htm.
53. Judith Sargent Stevens, "On the Equality of the Sexes" (1779), first published in two parts by Constantia in *Massachusetts Magazine*, 2 [March 1790], pp. 132–135, and [April 1790], National Humanities Center, http://nationalhumanitiescenter.org/pds/livingrev/equality/text5/sargent.pdf.
54. Stevens, "On the Equality of the Sexes."
55. [Judith Sargent Murray], "The Gleaner Contemplates the Future Prospects of Women in This 'Enlightened Age,'" in *The Gleaner: A Miscellaneous Production* (Boston: J. Thomas and E. T. Andrews, 1798), p. 189.
56. [Murray], "The Gleaner," p. 189.

4.
WOMAN ENTERS THE PUBLIC SPHERE

1. "Female Influence: Being the Substance of an Oration at the Annual Commencement of Columbia College, May 6, 1795," *New-York Magazine, or Literary Repository*, 6/5 (May 1795), p. 303.
2. "Female Influence," p. 303.
3. *Sermons by the Late Rev. Joseph S. Buckminster, with a Memoir of His Life and Character*, 2nd ed. (Boston: Wells and Lilly, 1815), p. 328. On the growing middle class among free Blacks in Philadelphia during the 1820s and 1830s, see "On the Present State and Condition among Free People of Color in the City of Philadelphia and Adjoining Districts . . . ," Pennsylvania Society for Promoting the Abolition of Slavery, January 5, 1838, Library of Congress, E185. 93. P41 P38. The report lists the variety of positions held by free Blacks, including primarily jobs such as laundress, cook, tailor, porter, and butcher but also jobs such as dentist, physician, midwife, preacher, and teacher.
4. Mary Ann B. Brown, *An Address on Moral Reform, Delivered before the Worcester Female Moral Reform Society, October 22, 1839* (Worcester, MA: T. W. & J. Butterfield, 1839), pp. 14–16.
5. "Just Treatment of Licentious Men. Addressed to Christian Mothers, Wives, Sisters, and Daughters," *Friend of Virtue* (January 1838), pp. 2–4.
6. Mary Still, "Daughters of Bethel," in "An Appeal to the Females of the A.M.E. Church" (1857), *in Pamphlets of Protest: An Anthology of Early African-American Protest Literature, 1790–1860*, ed. Richard Newman, Patrick Rael, and Phillip Lapsansky (New York: Routledge, 2000), pp. 257, 261.
7. Classic discussions of this solidarity are in Carroll Smith-Rosenberg, "The Female World of Love and Ritual: Relations between Women in Nineteenth-Century America," *Signs: Journal of Women in Culture and Society*, 1/1 (Autumn 1975), pp. 1–29; Nancy F. Cott, *The Bonds of Womanhood: Woman's Sphere in New England, 1780–1835* (New Haven, CT: Yale University Press, 1977). This solidarity also existed among a small elite class of free women of color in the north. See Jean Fagan Yellin and John C. Van Horne, eds., *The Abolitionist Sisterhood: Women's Political Culture in Antebellum America* (Ithaca, NY: Cornell University Press, 1994); Shirley J. Yee, *Black Women Abolitionists: A Study in Activism, 1828–1860* (Knoxville: University of Tennessee Press, 1992).
8. Beriah Green, quoted in Daniel Wright, *The First of Causes to Our Sex: The Female Moral Reform Movement in the Antebellum Northeast: 1834–1848* (New York: Routledge, 2006), p. 115.
9. "Paths of virtue" quoted in Clare A. Lyons, *Sex among the Rabble: An Intimate History of Gender and Power in the Age of Revolution, Philadelphia, 1730–1830* (Chapel Hill: University of North Carolina Press, 2006), p. 325. "No work" quoted in Marilynn Wood Hill, *Their Sisters' Keepers: Prostitution in New York City, 1830–1870* (Berkeley: University of California Press, 1993), p. 64.
10. Lyons, *Sex among the Rabble*, pp. 325–331.

11. "Do you suppose" in *Advocate of Moral Reform* (August 1835), quoted in Nicolette Severson, "'Devils Would Blush to Look': Brothel Visits of the New York Moral Reform Society, 1835 and 1836," *Journal of the History of Sexuality*, 23/2 (May 2014), p. 242.
12. "Public harlots" in John Robert McDowall, *Magdalen Facts*, 1 (January 1832), p. 63; *The Trial of the Rev. John Robert McDowall, by the Third Presbytery of New York, in February, March, and April, 1836, in the Session Room of the Bleeker Street Presbyterian Church* (New York: [n.p.], 1836); Alexander Moudrov, "The Man Who Counted All Prostitutes in New York City: John R. McDowall and the Scandal of the Magdalen Report," *European Journal of American Studies* (Summer 2018), https://www.researchgate.net/publication/326513537_The_Man_Who_Counted_All_Prostitutes_in_New_York_City_John_R_McDowall_and_the_Scandal_of_the_Magdalen_Report/fulltext/5b51e4d6aca27217ffa793bb/The-Man-Who-Counted-All-Prostitutes-in-New-York-City-John-R-McDowall-and-the-Scandal-of-the-Magdalen-Report.pdf. See also Mary P. Ryan, *Women in Public: Between Banners and Ballots, 1825–1880* (Baltimore, MD: Johns Hopkins University Press, 1992), pp. 98–99.
13. "Devils would blush to look": see Severson, "'Devils Would Blush to Look.'" Wright estimates that female moral reform societies had over 45,000 members in the 1830s and 1840s (*The First of Causes to Our Sex*, p. 2); Green quoted in Wright, *The First of Causes to Our Sex*, p. 115.
14. Catherine M. Rokicky, "Lydia Finney and Evangelical Womanhood," *Ohio History Journal*, 103 (Summer–Autumn 1994), pp. 170–189.
15. *The Constitution and Circular of the New York Female Moral Reform Society* (New York: J. N. Bolles, 1834), p. 3.
16. See Nancy Cott, "Passionlessness: An Interpretation of Victorian Sexual Ideology, 1790–1850," *Signs: Journal of Women in Culture and Society*, 4/2 (Winter 1978), pp. 19–36; New York Female Moral Reform Society, "First Annual Report," May 1835, https://digital.library.pitt.edu/islandora/object/pitt:31735054851674.
17. *Advocate of Moral Reform* (January–February 1835), pp. 6–7, quoted in Severson, "'Devils Would Blush to Look'"; "First Annual Report of the AFMR Society," *Advocate of Moral Reform* (June 1, 1840), p. 82; "Extracts from a Lecture on the Subject of Moral Reform," *Advocate of Moral Reform* (July 16, 1838), p. 5.
18. Carroll Smith-Rosenberg suggests that the shaming of men that was central to the moral reform movement had its basis in "the frustration, anger, and a compensatory sense of superior righteousness" that women felt at having been confined to their sphere and excluded from all the rights and privileges men claimed for themselves ("Beauty, the Beast, and the Militant Woman: A Case Study in Sex Roles and Social Stress in Jacksonian America," *American Quarterly*, 23/4 [October 1971], pp. 562–584).
19. "Report of the Zion's Church (Colored) F.M.R. Society," *Advocate of Moral Reform* (May 1, 1837), pp. 255–256; *Advocate of Moral Reform* (June 1, 1838), p. 86.
20. "Extracts from Report of the Visiting Committee," *Advocate of Moral Reform* (July 1, 1837), p. 284.

21. "Lowest haunts" in "Moral Reform," *Friends' Review: A Religious, Literary, and Miscellaneous Journal* 2/16 (January 6, 1849), p. 248; Rebecca Singer Collins's diary, July 21, 1845, and March 2, 1847, Rebecca Singer Collins Papers, HC MC 1196, folder 2, box 1, Quaker and Special Collections, Haverford College Library, Haverford, PA.
22. Iowa law quoted in Clement Knox, *Seduction: A History from the Enlightenment to the Present* (New York: Pegasus, 2020), p. 257; "Just Treatment of Licentious Men. Addressed to Christian Mothers, Wives, Sisters and Daughters," *Friends of Virtue* (January 1838), pp. 2–4.
23. Amelia Bloomer, "To the Patrons of the Lily," *The Lily*, 1/1 (January 1, 1849), p. 1.
24. Alcohol consumption in the United States in the 1830s: W. J. Rorabaugh, "Alcohol in America," *OAH [Organization of American Historians] Magazine of History*, 6/2 (Fall 1991), pp. 17–19; in 2019: "Alcohol Consumption per Capita from All Beverages in the U.S. Midwest Region from 1977 to 2019," Statista, https://www.statista.com/statistics/442864/per-capita-alcohol-consumption-of-all-beverages-in-the-us-midwest-region/.
25. Mrs. [Eliza] Steele, "An Appeal to the Ladies of America in Favor of Temperance," *Olive Plant and Ladies' Temperance Advocate*, 1/1 (July 1841), p. 1.
26. *The Diary and Life of Emily Hawley Gillespie, 1858–1888*, ed. Judy Nolte Lensink (Iowa City: University of Iowa Press, 1989), p. 71.
27. Rev. Lorenzo D. Johnson, *Martha Washingtonianism, or a History of the Ladies' Temperance Benevolent Societies* (New York: Saxton and Miles, 1843), pp. 41–42; Bloomer, "To the Patrons of the Lily."
28. For *The Lily*'s increasing boldness, see, for example, Amelia Bloomer, "Woman's Rights," *The Lily*, 1/10 (October 7, 1849), p. 186, in which Bloomer declares, "A woman is entitled to the same rights as a man." Woman suffers, Bloomer argues, because she has no voice in the law that makes the sale of alcohol legal. *The Pearl: A Ladies' Weekly Literary Gazette*, 1/45 (April 10, 1847), pp. 358, 356.
29. "Temperance Meeting," *The Liberator*, April 20, 1833, p. 63.
30. "Liquid fire" and "Female Societies" in "Minutes and Proceedings of the Third Annual Convention for the Improvement of the Free People of Color," Philadelphia, June 3–13, 1833 (New York: Published by Order of the Convention, 1833), pp. 18–19, https://omeka.coloredconventions.org/items/show/275.
31. For discussions about Black assimilationism during this period, see Donald Yacovone, "The Transformation of the Black Temperance Movement, 1827–1854: An Interpretation," *Journal of the Early Republic*, 8/3 (Autumn, 1988), pp. 281–297; Jane H. Pease and William H. Pease, *They Who Would Be Free: Blacks Search for Freedom, 1830–1861* (1974; rpt., Champaign: University of Illinois Press, 1990), pp. 124–125; Anne M. Boylan, "Benevolence and Antislavery Activism among African American Women in New York and Boston, 1820–1840," in *The Abolitionist Sisterhood: Women's Political Culture in Antebellum America*, ed. Jean Fagan Yellin and John C. Van Horne (Ithaca, NY: Cornell University Press, 1994), pp. 130–132. The term "politics of respectability" was coined by Evelyn Brooks Higginbotham in reference to upwardly striving Black women's promotion of temperance, sexual purity, and other middle-class values such as thrift, cleanli-

ness, and good manners (*Righteous Discontent: The Women's Movement in the Black Baptist Church, 1880–1920* [Cambridge, MA: Harvard University Press, 1994]); Frances Ellen Watkins Harper, *Trial and Triumph* (1888), https://www.troyspier.com/OER/texts/Trial%20and%20Triumph%20-%20Frances%20Ellen%20Watkins%20Harper.pdf; Frances Ellen Watkins Harper, "Enlightened Motherhood," in *A Brighter Day Coming: A Frances Ellen Watkins Harper Reader*, ed. Frances Smith Foster (New York: Feminist Press, 1993), p. 292.

32. Long before the Spanish conquest, Indians in the Southwest, both women and men, had used fermented corn or pulque made of agave plants in religious ceremonies, but drunkenness outside of those ceremonies was considered a disgrace. See Jack O. Waddell, "The Use of Intoxicating Beverages among the Native Peoples of the Aboriginal Greater Southwest," in *Drinking Behavior among Southwest Indians: An Anthropological Perspective*, ed. Jack O. Waddell and Michael W. Everett (Tucson: University of Arizona Press, 1980), pp. 1–34; Roberta Estes, "Treaty between North Carolina and King Hagler of the Catawba Indians," Native Heritage Project, January 30, 2013, https://nativeheritageproject.com/2013/01/30/treaty-between-north-carolina-and-the-king-hagler-of-the-catawba-indians/.

33. Quoted in Peter C. Mancall, "Men, Women, and Alcohol in Indian Villages in the Great Lakes Region in the Early Republic," *Journal of the Early Republic*, 15/3 (Fall 1995), p. 436.

34. Abraham Luckenbach's diaries, February 13, 1805, September 15, 1805, and January 25, 1806, in *Voices from the Delaware Big House Ceremony*, ed. Robert Steven Grumet (Norman: University of Oklahoma Press, 2001), pp. 43, 47.

35. Johnson, *Martha Washingtonianism*, p. 22; Ruth M. Alexander, "'We Are Engaged as a Band of Sisters': Class and Domesticity in the Washingtonian Temperance Movement, 1840–1850," *Journal of American History*, 75/3 (December 1988), pp. 763–785.

36. Johnson, *Martha Washingtonianism*, pp. 29, 31.

37. Steele, "An Appeal to the Ladies of America," p. 1.

38. Virginia Allen, "First Annual Report, Harper Union No. 11, Daughters of Temperance," *The Pearl: A Ladies' Weekly Literary Gazette*, 1/18 (October 3, 1846), p. 141. See also Alexander, "'We Are Engaged as a Band of Sisters,'" pp. 780–781, and Ian Tyrell, *Sobering Up: From Temperance to Prohibition in Antebellum America, 1800–1860* (Westport, CT: Greenwood Press, 1979), chapter 7. The Marthas did continue to oversee the progress of the male inebriate who, without their watchful eyes, might relapse into intemperance and again be unable to fulfill his role as financial supporter of woman and child.

39. Jed Dannenbaum, "The Origins of Temperance Activism and Militancy among American Women," *Journal of Social History*, 15/2 (Winter 1981), pp. 235–252; Lori D. Ginzberg, "'Moral Suasion Is Moral Balderdash': Women, Politics, and Social Activism in the 1850s," *Journal of American History*, 73/3 (December 1986), pp. 601–622; Amelia Bloomer, "Work First for Power, Then Temperance," *The Lily*, 3/11 (November 1851), p. 86.

40. Bloomer, "Work First for Power."

41. Reflecting on her 1848 views at a women's convention in 1888, Anthony added, "I wasn't ready to vote, didn't want to vote" (quoted in National Woman Suffrage Association, *Report of the International Council of Women* [Washington, DC: Rufus H. Carby, 1888], p. 327); Ida Husted Harper, *The Life and Work of Susan B. Anthony*, vol. 1 (Indianapolis, IN: Bowen-Merrill, 1899), p. 65.
42. Mayor and Hewitt quoted in "World Temperance Convention," *New York Times*, May 13, 1853; "the call for this meeting" in Harper, *The Life and Work of Susan B. Anthony*, p. 89.
43. Quoted in Harper, *The Life and Work of Susan B. Anthony*, p. 90. "Bloomers," the first pant-like garment for American women, were named after Amelia Bloomer.
44. Alex. Hunter, "The Winchester Riots," *The Anti-Slavery Bugle*, June 10, 1854; John Woodburn, letter to the editor (in which the writer recalls witnessing the riots when he was a boy), *Holton Recorder* (Kansas), April 27, 1916.
45. Quoted in *History of the Town of Rockport: As Comprised in the Centennial Address of Lemuel Gott, M.D . . .* (Rockport, MA: Rockport Review Office, 1888), p. 113.
46. "Intoxicating liquors" quoted in *History of the Town of Rockport*, p. 114. See also "Women's Raids Stirred Town: Equipped with Hatchets, They Marched through Rockport to Destroy Liquor 70 Years Ago, Old Resident Recalls," *Boston Daily Globe*, July 11, 1926; Eleanor C. Parsons, *Hannah and the Hatchet Gang: Rockport Revolt against Rum* (Canaan, NH: Phoenix Publishing, 1975); Marshall W. S. Swan, *Town on Sandy Bay: A History of Rockport, MA* (Canaan, NH: Phoenix Publishing, 1980).
47. Johnson, *Martha Washingtonianism*, p. 41.
48. Angelina Grimké in "Ladies Department, Letters to Catharine Beecher," *The Liberator*, October 13, 1837, p. 167.
49. William Lloyd Garrison, "Female Anti-Slavery Society," *The Liberator*, July 14, 1832, p. 110.
50. Mary A. Battis, president of the Female Anti-Slavery Society of Salem, letter to the editor, *The Liberator*, November 17, 1832, p. 3; "The Constitution of the Female Anti-Slavery Society of Salem, Formed February, 22, 1832," *The Liberator*, November 17, 1832, p. 3. In 1834 the organization, renamed the Salem Female Anti-Slavery Society, was expanded to include white women. The new society's constitution called directly for the immediate abolition of slavery. See "Salem Female Anti-Slavery Society," Records, Congregational Library and Archives, Boston, MA, https://www.congregationallibrary.org/POCFindingAid/antislavery-and-abolitionist-materials. See also Julie Roy Jeffrey, *The Great Silent Army of Abolitionism: Ordinary Women in the Anti-Slavery Movement* (Chapel Hill: University of North Carolina Press, 1998).
51. Forten quoted in Carolyn Williams, "Fighting against Race Prejudice and Promoting Women's Rights in Antebellum America," in Yellin and Van Horne, *The Abolitionist Sisterhood*, pp. 166–167. See also Ira V. Brown, "Am I Not a Woman and a Sister?," *Pennsylvania History: A Journal of Mid-Atlantic Studies*, 50/1 (Janu-

ary 1983), pp. 1–19; Stacey M. Robertson, *Hearts Beating for Liberty: Women Abolitionists in the Old Northwest* (Chapel Hill: University of North Carolina Press, 2014), p. 13.

52. L[ydia] Maria Child, *Letters from New-York* (New York: Charles S. Francis, 1843); Lydia Maria Child, *An Appeal in Favor of That Class of Americans Called Africans* (Boston: Allen and Ticknor, 1833), p. 19; Mary Ann B. Brown, "An Address on Moral Reform, Delivered before the Worcester Female Moral Reform Society, October 22, 1839" (Worcester, MA: T. W. and J. Butterfield, 1839), p. 4.

53. Speech of J. Miller McKim (a recollection of the 1833 convention) in *Proceedings of the American Anti-Slavery Society at Its Third Decade, Held in the City of Philadelphia, Dec. 3d and 4th, 1863* (New York: American Anti-Slavery Society, 1864), p. 36.

54. Speech of Lucretia Mott in *Proceedings of the American Anti-Slavery Society at Its Third Decade*, pp. 42–43.

55. Black female literary societies and Black female abolitionists are discussed in Shirley J. Yee, *Black Women Abolitionists: A Study in Activism, 1820–1860* (Knoxville: University of Tennessee Press, 1992), pp. 62–63; Wilma King, *The Essence of Liberty: Free Black Women during the Slave Era* (Columbia: University of Missouri Press, 2006), chapter 2; Julie Winch, "'You Have Talents—Only Cultivate Them': Philadelphia's Black Female Literary Societies and Abolitionist Crusade," in Yellin and Van Horne, *The Abolitionist Sisterhood*, pp. 101–118; Emma Jones Lapsansky, "The World the Agitators Made: The Counterculture of Agitation in Urban Philadelphia," in Yellin and Van Horne, *The Abolitionist Sisterhood*, pp. 91–99; "Contitution of the Afric-American Female Intelligence Society of Boston," https://www.blackpast.org/african-american-history/constitution-afric-american-female-intelligence-society-boston-1832/; Boylan, "Benevolence and Antislavery Activism," p. 130; Sarah Mapps Douglass, "Address," *The Liberator*, July 21, 1832, p. 114.

56. Yee, *Black Women Abolitionists*, pp. 55–56, 115; Ira V. Brown, "Cradle of Feminism: The Philadelphia Female Anti-Slavery Society, 1833–1840," *Pennsylvania Magazine of History and Biography*, 102/2 (April 1978), pp. 143–166; Cornish quoted in Jacqueline Bacon, *Freedom's Journal: The First African American Newspaper* (Lanham, MD: Lexington Books, 2007), p. 142.

57. Quoted in Darlene Clark Hine and Kathleen Thomas, *A Shining Thread of Hope: The History of Black Women in America* (New York: Broadway Books, 1999), p. 112.

58. Marilyn Richardson, *Maria W. Stewart, America's First Black Woman Political Writer: Essays and Speeches* (Bloomington: Indiana University Press, 1987), p. 8.

59. Announcement for "Meditations from the Pen of Mrs. Maria W. Stewart," *The Liberator*, March 17, 1832, p. 3; "An Address Delivered before the Afric-American Female Intelligence Society . . . ," *The Liberator*, April 28, 1832, p. 2; announcement of the lecture "The Disadvantages Which the Free People of Color Labor Under in the New England States," *The Liberator*, September 15, 1832, p. 3; text of "The Disadvantages Which the Free People of Color Labor Under in the New

England States," *The Liberator*, November 17, 1832, p. 3. Several historians have suggested that Stewart's Franklin Hall address was the first instance of a Black woman speaking to a "promiscuous audience," but see chapter 3 for a discussion of Jarena Lee, who preached to mixed audiences earlier in the nineteenth century.
60. James Boswell, *Boswell's Life of Johnson* (1791; rpt., Charleston, SC, 2010), p. 44.
61. "An Address [on African Rights and Liberty] Delivered at the African Masonic Hall, Boston, February 27, 1833," *The Liberator*, April 27, 1833.
62. Samuel Cornish, "Female Temper," *Freedom's Journal*, 1/6 (April 20, 1827); "rotten tomatoes" in Yee, *Black Women Abolitionists*, p. 115; "Farewell Address to Her Friends in the City of Boston, September 21, 1833," in *Meditations from the Pen of Mrs. Maria W. Stewart Presented to the First African Baptist Church and Society of Boston, Mass.* (1835; rpt., Washington, DC: Enterprise Publishing Company, 1879), pp. 74–82.
63. Sarah Grimké, *Letters on the Equality of the Sexes and the Condition of Women, Addressed to Mary S. Parker, President of the Boston Female Anti-Slavery Society* (Boston: Isaac Knapp, 1838), p. 46.
64. Angelina Grimké, *Appeal to the Christian Women of the South* (New York: American Anti-Slavery Society, 1836).
65. Gerda Lerner, *The Majority Finds Its Past: Placing Women in History* (1979; rpt., Chapel Hill: University of North Carolina Press, 2005), p. 97; letter, Angelina Grimké to Theodore Weld, March 8, 1837, in *A Documentary History of Religion in America*, 4th ed. edited by Edwin S. Gaustad et al. (Grand Rapids, MI: Eerdmans, 2018), pp. 227–228.
66. "Pastoral Letter," reprinted in *The Liberator*, August 11, 1837, p. 1. The Grimkés were also attacked for their public appearances by Catharine Beecher, an educator of girls, who wrote that women must concern themselves with being mothers and educators of children and young females and leave the fight over abolition to men: Catharine E. Beecher, *Essay on Slavery and Abolitionism with Reference to the Duty of American Females* (Philadelphia: Henry Perkins, 1837), addressed specifically to "Miss A.D. Grimké."
67. Angelina Grimké, "Ladies Department, Letters to Catharine Beecher," *The Liberator*, October 13, 1837, p. 167; Sarah Grimké, "Woman Subject Only to God," in *Letters on the Equality of the Sexes*, pp. 10–11.
68. Phyllis Cole, "Fuller's Lawsuit and Feminist History," in *Margaret Fuller and Her Circles*, ed. Brigitte Bailey et al. (Lebanon: University of New Hampshire Press, 2013), pp. 11–31.
69. Elizabeth Cady Stanton, *Eighty Years and More (1815–1897): Reminiscences of Elizabeth Cady Stanton* (New York: European Publishing Company, 1898), pp. 25, 31–32; Elisabeth Griffith, *In Her Own Right: The Life of Elizabeth Cady Stanton* (New York: Oxford University Press, 1984); Lois W. Banner, *Elizabeth Cady Stanton: A Radical for Woman's Rights* (Boston: Little, Brown, 1980).
Lori D. Ginzberg points out that Stanton adopted the language of Grimké's 1837 speech in her 1848 Seneca Falls Resolution 8 (*Elizabeth Cady Stanton: An American Life* [New York: Hill and Wang, 2009], p. 59).

70. Stanton, *Eighty Years and More*, p. 80.
71. Stanton, *Eighty Years and More*, p. 79.
72. Stanton, *Eighty Years and More*, p. 83.

5.
NINETEENTH-CENTURY WOMAN LEAVES HOME

1. [Thomas R. Dew], "Dissertation on the Characteristic Differences between the Sexes," *Southern Literary Messenger* (May 1835), p. 495.
2. Lucy Larcom, *A New England Girlhood, Outlined from Memory* (Boston: Houghton, Mifflin, 1889), p. 193.
3. See the discussion of white southern women and slavery in chapter 2. Letter, Charles H. Thiot to Anna Charlton, March 9, 1849, folder 5, box 1, Thiot Family Papers, Stuart A. Rose Manuscript, Archives, and Rare Book Library, Emory University, Atlanta, GA (emphasis in the original).
4. "The Angel in the House" (1854) was the title of a popular poem about woman's role by the Victorian writer Coventry Patmore. Patricia Okker suggests that Hale's ideas about woman were adjusted to meet the expectations of the mass of her women readers. Hale began her career with Enlightenment views of woman, declaring in 1828 (before she became editor of *Godey's Lady's Book*) that "there is no sex in talents, in genius" (*Our Sister Editors: Sarah J. Hale and the Tradition of Nineteenth-Century American Women Editors* [Athens: University of Georgia Press, 2008], p. 58). But as editor she adopted the Victorian views of woman that her publication's readers expected, declaring in 1857 that "the proposition, 'Genius has no sex,' is preposterous" (p. 58). The fact that Hale had not entirely abandoned her Enlightenment views is evidenced by her championing in the pages of *Godey's Lady's Book* women's higher education and the opening of Vassar College; Sarah Josepha Hale, "Editors' Table," *Godey's Lady's Book*, 42 (January 1851), p. 65.
5. Hale, "Editors' Table," p. 65.
6. "True womanhood": see Barbara Welter's classical essay "The Cult of True Womanhood, 1820–1860," *American Quarterly*, 18 (1966), 151–174.
7. Chaim M. Rosenberg, *The Life and Times of Francis Cabot Lowell, 1775–1817* (Lanham, MD: Lexington Books, 2010), pp. 179, 250.
8. Lowell became a city in 1836.
9. Quoted in Helen L. Sumner, *Report on the Condition of Woman and Child Wage-Earners in the United States: History of Women in Industry in the United States*, vol. 9 (Washington, DC: Government Printing Office, 1910), p. 14.
10. Harriet H[anson] Robinson, *Early Factory Labor in New England, Massachusetts Bureau of Statistics of Labor, 14th Annual Report* (Boston: Wright and Potter, 1883), p. 380. Robinson came to Lowell because her mother ran a boardinghouse there (Harriet H[anson] Robinson, *Loom and Spindle; or Life among the Early Mill Girls* [New York: Thomas Y. Crowell, 1898]).
11. "Lines Written on the Death of Sarah M. Cornell," 1833, Fall River Historical Society, https://lizzieborden.org/collections/ephemera/sarah-maria-cornell-broad

side/. Cornell had been working at a mill in Fall River when she was killed in 1832. Her death was deemed by the court to be a suicide, despite strong evidence that she had been murdered. See "The Trial at Large of the Rev. Ephraim K. Avery for the Wilfull Murder of Sarah Maria Cornell, December 20, 1832, at Tiverton in the County of Newport, Rhode Island," Supreme Judicial Court of Rhode Island, http://lawcollections.library.cornell.edu/trial/catalog/sat:kf01. Another mill girl, Berengera Caswell (known as Mary Bean), who died from an abortion, also became the focus of moralists who preached about the dangers of being a factory girl. See Miss J. A. B. of Manchester, "Mary Bean: The Factory Girl, a Domestic Story, Illustrative of the Trials and Temptations of Factory Life, Founded in Recent Events" (Boston: Hotchkiss and Company, 1850).

12. Charles Dickens, who was very critical of the treatment of labor in British factories, visited Lowell in 1842 and confirmed glowing reports of the mill girls' working and living conditions. He observed that their wages were abundant enough that 978 of the women workers had savings in the Lowell Savings Bank. See Charles Dickens, *American Notes for General Circulation* (New York: D. Appleton, 1868), pp. 30–32; Lucy Larcom, *A New England Girlhood, Outlined from Memory* (Boston: Houghton, Mifflin, 1889), p. 182; Robinson, *Loom and Spindle*, pp. 17, 46, 100; Doug Stewart, "Proud to Be a Mill Girl," *American Heritage*, 62/1 (Spring 2012), https://www.americanheritage.com/proud-be-mill-girl.

13. Larcom, *A New England Girlhood*, p. 196.

14. Quoted in Barbara Mayer Wertheimer, *We Were There: The Story of Working Women in America* (New York: Pantheon Books, 1977), chapter 5.

15. Quoted in *Report on Condition of Woman and Child Wage-Earners in the United States: History of Women in Trade Unions*, vol. 10, ed. Charles P. Neill et al. (Washington, DC: Government Printing Office, 1911), p. 23.

16. "The Turn Out at Lowell," *The Man*, February 22, 1834, p. 11.

17. Neill et al., *Report on Condition of Woman and Child Wage-Earners*, pp. 27–28.

18. Mill agent quoted in Philip Dray, *There Is Power in a Union: The Epic Story of Labor in America* (New York: Doubleday, 2010), p. 30; "Mounted a stump" in *Boston Evening Transcript*, February 17, 1834, quoted in Caitlin Leary, "Gold Watches and Old Maids: *The Lowell Offerings*' Role in the Emerging Social Consciousness of 19th Century Factory Girls, 1840–1845," *Atlantic Review of Journalism*, 10/1 (2012), pp. 34–35.

19. Wertheimer, *We Were There*, p. 69.

20. Quoted in Neill et al., *Report on Condition of Woman and Child Wage-Earners*, p. 30.

21. Mary P. Ryan, *Womanhood in America: From Colonial Times to the Present*, 3rd ed. (New York: Franklin Watts, 1983), p. 123; Juliet [pseud.], "A Leaf from My Sketch Book," *Voice of Industry*, 1/42 (April 3, 1846), p. 2.

22. Quoted in David R. Roediger and Philip S. Foner, *Our Own Time: A History of American Labor and the Working Day* (Westport, CT: Greenwood Press, 1989), p. 56.

23. "Remarks of Miss Bagley," *Voice of Industry*, June 5, 1845, p. 2.

24. Quoted in J. Q. A. Thayer, *Review of the Report of the Special Committee by the Legislature of the Commonwealth of Massachusetts, on the Petition Relating to Hours of Labor* (Boston: J. N. Bang, 1845), p. 30.
25. "On the Defeat of William Schouler," *Voice of Industry*, November 28, 1845, http://industrialrevolution.org/petition-and-legislature.html.
26. Thomas Dublin, "Women, Work, and Protest in the Early Lowell Mills," *Labor History*, 16/1 (1975), pp. 113–114; Larcom, *A New England Girlhood*, p. 193.
27. S. J. Kleinberg, *Women in the United States, 1830–1945* (New York: Palgrave, 1999), table 5.1.
28. Letter, Mary Jane Megquier to Milton Benjamin, November 11, 1849, in *Apron Full of Gold: Letters of Mary Jane Megquier from San Francisco, 1849–1856*, ed. Polly Welts Kaufman (Albuquerque: University of New Mexico Press, 1994), p. 43.
29. [John O'Sullivan], "Annexation," *United States Magazine and Democratic Review*, 17 (July 1845), pp. 5–6, 9–10. Linda S. Hudson, in her controversial book *Mistress of Manifest Destiny: A Biography of Jane McManus Storm Cazneau, 1807–1878* (Austin: Texas State Historical Association, 2001), has suggested that it was Cazneau, a pioneering journalist and the first woman war correspondent, who wrote the "manifest destiny" essay for the magazine that O'Sullivan edited.
30. Letter, Megquier to Benjamin, November 11, 1849, p. 43.
31. T. C. C., "Western Prairies," *American Whig Review*, 11 (May 1850), p. 526. Twelve years later, women's lot on the prairies was no easier. An 1862 report by the commissioner of agriculture observed that the farmer's wife was reduced to "a laboring drudge." She usually "works harder [and] endures more, than any other on the place," including her husband and the hired help. See W. W. Hall, "The Health of Farmers' Families," in *The Report of the Commissioner of Agriculture for the Year 1862* (Washington, DC: Government Printing Office, 1863), pp. 462–463.
32. "Tame the land" in Adrienne Caughfield, *True Women and Westward Expansion* (College Station: Texas A&M University Press, 2005), p. 10. Elliott West depicts westering women of all classes as desiring to hold onto woman's "traditional roles and responsibilities," which they had learned in the East: establishing a home, giving it "some semblance of refinement," and taking a major role in their children's education and moral training ("Women of the Rocky Mountain West," in *A Taste of the West: Essays in Honor of Robert G. Athearn*, ed. Duane A. Smith (Boulder, CO: Pruett Publishing Company, 1983, pp. 151, 155); see also John Mack Faragher, *Women and Men on the Overland Trail* (New Haven, CT: Yale University Press, 1979), chapter 2.
33. [Rebecca Burlend as told to Edward Burlend], *A True Picture of Emigration, or Fourteen Years in the Interior of North America* (London: G. Berger, 1848), pp. 20, 49.
34. Quoted in Lillian Schlissel, *Women's Diaries of the Westward Journey* (New York: Schocken Books, 1982), pp. 166–167, 180.
35. Quoted in Linda Peavy and Ursula Smith, *Pioneer Women: The Lives of Women on the Frontier* (Norman: University of Oklahoma Press, 1998), p. 44.

36. Rebecca Ketcham, "From Ithaca to Clatsop Plains: Miss Ketcham's Journal of Travel," part II, ed. Leo M. Kaiser and Priscilla Knuth, *Oregon Historical Quarterly*, 62/4 (December 1961), p. 340.
37. Ketcham, "From Ithaca to Clatsop Plains," p. 391.
38. "Joe Monohan [sic] Was Known Here. Miss Katherine Walter of Seventh Street Was Her Foster Mother," *Buffalo Evening News*, January 12, 1904.
39. "The Owyhee Mines," *New York Times*, October 1, 1865, p. 4. Twentieth-century accounts of Monahan generally presented him as a heterosexual woman who passed as a man for safety in the Wild West. See, for example, James D. Horan, *Desperate Women* (New York: G. P. Putnam's Sons, 1952), pp. 305–310; Maggie Greenwald, dir., *The Ballad of Little Jo* (New York: Fine Line Features, 1993). More recent accounts understand Monahan to have been a transman. See, for example, Peter Boag, *Re-Dressing America's Frontier Past* (Berkeley: University of California Press, 2011), pp. 95–104.
40. Mrs. E[lsa]. J[ane]. Guerin, *The Autobiography of Mountain Charley, or The Adventures of Mrs. E. J. Guerin Who Was Thirteen Years in Male Attire* (Dubuque, IA: published for the author, 1861), p. 12.
41. Guerin, *The Autobiography of Mountain Charley*, pp. 15, 17–18.
42. Guerin, *The Autobiography of Mountain Charley*, p. 18. Though bloomers were introduced in the mid-nineteenth century, women on the westward trails generally wore long, full dresses with full sleeves. See Maria Barbara McMartin, "Dress of the Oregon Trail Emigrants: 1843–1855," MS thesis, Iowa State University, Ames, 1977, pp. 31–35.
43. Quoted in Tonia M. Compton, "Challenging Imperial Expectations: Black and White Female Homesteaders in Kansas," *Great Plains Quarterly*, 33/1 (Winter 2013), p. 53.
44. Sheryll Patterson-Black, "Women Homesteaders on the Great Plains Frontier," *Frontiers*, 1/2 (Spring 1976), pp. 77–88; H. Elaine Lundgren, *Land in Her Own Name: Women as Homesteaders in North Dakota* (Fargo: North Dakota Institute for Regional Studies, 1991); Sarah Carter, *Montana Women Homesteaders: A Field of One's Own* (Helena, MT: Farcountry Press, 2009). The Homestead Act was in effect from 1862 to 1934.
45. Mary Price Jeffords quoted in Emerson R. Purcell, *Pioneer Stories of Custer County, Nebraska* (Broken Bow, NE: Custer County Chief, 1936), p. 74; Wilder quoted in Susan A. Hallgarth, "Women Settlers on the Frontier: Unwed, Unreluctant, Unrepentant," *Women's Studies Quarterly*, 17/3–4 (Fall–Winter, 1989), pp. 23–34.
46. Quoted in Hallgarth, "Women Settlers on the Frontier," p. 25.
47. Deena J. Gonzalez, "The Widowed Women of Santa Fe: Assessments on the Lives of an Unmarried Population, 1850–80," in *Latina Issues: Fragments of Historia(ella)*, ed. Antoinette Sedillo-Lopez (New York: Garland Publishing, 1995), p. 73; Maria Linda Apodaca, "The Chicana Woman: An Historical Materialist Perspective," *Latin American Perspectives*, 4/1–2 (January 1977), pp. 70–89.
48. Gloria Ricci Lothrop, "Rancheras on the Land: Women and Property Rights in Hispanic California," *Southern California Quarterly*, 76/1 (Spring 1994), pp. 102–142.

49. Nora E. Rios McMillan, "Maria Del Carmen Calvillo: How an Independent Spirit Emerged," *Journal of South Texas*, 13/2 (Fall 2000), pp. 175–182; Evelyn M. Carrington, ed., *Women in Early Texas* (Austin: Texas State Historical Society, 1994).
50. Abraham Lincoln, "Speech to Germans at Cincinnati, Ohio, February 12, 1861," *Commercial and Daily Gazette* (Cincinnati), February 13, 1861, rpt. in *The Collected Works of Abraham Lincoln*, vol. 4, ed. Roy P. Basler (Rockville, MD: Wildside Press, 2008), p. 203.
51. George Washington, "Talk to the Cherokee Nation," August 9, 1796, in *The Writings of George Washington from the Original Manuscript Sources*, ed. John C. Fitzpatrick, vol. 35 (Washington, DC: Government Printing Office, 1940), p. 194.
52. T. Hartley Crawford, November 25, 1839, in *Report of the Commissioner of Indian Affairs*, 26th Congress, 1st session, *United States Congressional Serial Set*, vol. 363 (Washington, DC: Gales and Seaton, 1839), p. 344.
53. George W. Manypenny, *Annual Report of the Commission of Indian Affairs for 1854* (Washington, DC: Office of the Commissioner of Indian Affairs), pp. 14, 22.
54. Juliana Barr, *Peace Came in the Form of a Woman: Indians and Spaniards in the Texas Borderlands* (Chapel Hill: University of North Carolina Press, 2007).
55. Lasuen quoted in Antonia I. Castaneda, "Sexual Violence in the Politics and Policies of Conquest: Amerindian Women and the Spanish Conquest of Alta California," in *Building with Our Hands: New Directions in Chicana Studies*, ed. Adela de la Torre and Beatriz M. Pesquera (Berkeley: University of California Press, 1993), p. 29; Baron de Lahontan, *Nouveaux voyages dans l'Amerique* (1703), quoted in Richard White, *The Middle Ground: Indians, Empires, and Republics in the Great Lakes Region, 1650–1815* (1981; rpt., Cambridge: Cambridge University Press, 2010), p. 63; Morris E. Opler, *An Apache Life-Way: The Economic, Social, and Religious Institutions of the Chiricahua Indians* (Chicago: University of Chicago Press, 1941). For discussions of similar transformations in other Indian nations, see John Demos, "The Tried and the True: Native American Women Confronting Colonization," in *No Small Courage: A History of Women in the United States*, ed. Nancy F. Cott (New York: Oxford University Press, 2000); Mary E. Young, "Women, Civilization, and the Indian Question," in *Clio Was a Woman: Studies in the History of American Women*, ed. Mabel E. Deutrich and Virginia C. Purdy (Washington, DC: Howard University Press, 1980), pp. 98–110.
56. "Dexterous": quoted in Sherry Robinson, *Apache Voices: Their Stories of Survival as Told to Eve Ball* (Albuquerque: University of New Mexico Press, 2003) p. 11; "Strong as a man": quoted in Laura Jane Moore, "Lozen: An Apache Woman Warrior," in *Sifters: Native American Women's Lives*, ed. Theda Perdue (New York: Oxford University Press, 2001), p. 93. "Ussen has power": quoted in Eve Ball, *In the Days of Victorio: Recollections of a Warm Springs Apache* (1970; rpt., Tucson: University of Arizona Press, 2015), p. 87. In more contemporary times, Lozen might have been described by terms such as "transgender" and "nonbinary."
57. Eve Ball, *Indeh: An Apache Odyssey* (1980; rpt., Norman: University of Oklahoma Press, 1988), p. 104.

58. Mary Livermore, *My Story of the War: A Woman's Narrative of Four Years Personal Experience as Nurse in the Union Army* (Hartford, CT: A. D. Worthington, 1888), pp. 115–116.
59. Elizabeth Cady Stanton, Susan B. Anthony, and Matilda Gage, *History of Woman Suffrage*, vol. 2 (Rochester, NY: Charles Mann, 1882), p. 19.
60. DeAnne Blanton, "Women Soldiers of the Civil War," *Prologue*, 25/1 (Spring 1993), https://www.archives.gov/publications/prologue/1993/spring/women-in-the-civil-war-2.html; Bonnie Tsui, *She Went to the Field: Women Soldiers of the Civil War* (Helena, MT: TwoDot, 2006); George Washington Adams, *Doctors in Blue: The Medical History of the Union Army in the Civil War* (1952; rpt., Baton Rouge: Louisiana State University Press, 1996), p. 13; Sarah Emma Edmonds, *Nurse and Spy in the Union Army: Comprising the Adventures and Experiences of a Woman in Hospitals, Camps, and Battlefields* (Hartford, CT: W. S. Williams, 1865); Loreta Janeta Velazquez, *A Woman in Battle: A Narrative of the Exploits, Adventures, and Travels of Madame Loreta Janeta Velazquez* (Richmond, VA: Dustin, Gilman, and Company, 1876).
61. Livermore, *My Story of the War*, pp. 115–116. Other notable women's Civil War memoirs include Ferdinand L. Sarmiento, *Life of Pauline Cushman, the Celebrated Union Spy and Scout* ["Carefully Prepared from Her Notes and Memoranda"] (Philadelphia: John E. Potter, 1865), about an actress who was almost executed for spying on the Confederacy for the Union; and Susie King Taylor, *Reminiscences of My Life in Camp with the 33d United States Colored Troops* (Boston: self-published, 1902) by a former slave who headed a nursing corps for a Black regiment.
62. Stanton and coauthors mention Tubman briefly, together with others who "took part in the discussions" at a suffrage meeting (*History of Woman Suffrage*, vol. 1, p. 276). Catherine Clinton describes Tubman after the Civil War as "a grand old lady on the suffrage circuit," where she was a "spell-binding raconteur" (*Harriet Tubman: The Road to Freedom* [New York: Little, Brown, 2005], p. 191); "Most of a man" quoted in Kate Clifford Larson, *Bound for the Promised Land: Harriet Tubman: Portrait of an American Heroine* (New York: One World, 2004), p. 168.
63. "Fernandina," *Wisconsin State Journal* (Madison), June 20, 1863, p. 2. Tubman, who was illiterate, did not write an autobiography, but she told her story to the abolitionist Sarah H. Bradford, who published both *Scenes in the Life of Harriet Tubman* in 1869 and an expanded version in 1886 (reprinted as *Harriet Tubman: The Moses of Her People* [Gloucester, MA: Peter Smith, 1981]). For Tubman's account of the Combahee River raid, see pp. 98–103.
64. See Drew Gilpin Faust, "Altars of Sacrifice: Confederate Women and the Narratives of War," *Journal of American History*, 76/4 (March 1990), pp. 1200–1228; LeeAnn Whites, "The Civil War as a Crisis in Gender," in *Divided Houses: Gender and the Civil War*, ed. Catherine Clinton and Nina Silber (New York: Oxford University Press, 1992), pp. 3–21.
65. *Memoirs of the Fort and Fannin Families*, ed. Kate Haynes Fort (Chattanooga, TN: MacGowan and Cook, 1903), pp. 36, 39.

66. Leila W., "Woman a Patriot," *Southern Monthly*, 1/2 (October 1861), p. 114; G. E. F., "A Word to the Women of Georgia," *Chronicle and Sentinel*, reprinted as "A True Southern Woman!," *Southern Cultivator* [Augusta, Georgia], 19/6 (June 1861), p. 175.
67. Libra R. Hilde, *Worth a Dozen Men: Women and Nursing in the Civil War South* (Charlottesville: University of Virginia Press, 2012); Kate Cumming, *A Journal of Hospital Life in the Confederate Army of Tennessee: From the Battle of Shiloh to the End of the War* (Louisville, KY: John P. Morton and Company, 1866), p. 28.
68. Heather G. Campbell, "A Note on the First Nursing School in Texas and Its Role in the Nineteenth-Century American Experience," *Houston Review*, 19/1 (1997), p. 54. The first nursing school in Texas did not open until 1890.
69. T[homas] C[ooper] DeLeon, *Belles, Beaux, and Brains of the 60s* (New York: G. W. Dillingham, 1909), p. 385.
70. Phoebe Yates [Levy] Pember, *A Southern Woman's Story* (New York: G. W. Carleton, 1879), pp. 14–15.
71. Jane E. Schultz, "The Inhospitable Hospital: Gender and Professionalism in Civil War Medicine," *Signs*, 17/2 (Winter 1992), p. 377.
72. Pember, *A Southern Woman's Story*, p. 183.

6.

WOMAN GOES TO COLLEGE AND ENTERS THE PROFESSIONS

1. Catharine E. Beecher, *Letters on the Difficulties of Religion* [addressed to her father, Rev. Lyman Beecher] (Hartford, CT: Belknap and Hamersley, 1836), pp. 22–23. Beecher was not alone in her dismay over Wright, whose lectures on several occasions led to mini-riots and even the threat of lynching: See, e.g., "Mrs. Frances Wright," *York Gazette* (Pennsylvania), August 26, 1836, p. 3; and "Fanny Wright in New York," *Baltimore Sun*, October 18, 1838, p. 2.
2. E. A. Andrews, commentary on Mary Lyon's "General View of the Principles and Designs of Mount Holyoke Female Seminary," *The Religious Magazine and Family Miscellany* (April 1837), p. 186.
3. Quoted in Kathryn Kish Sklar, *Catharine Beecher: A Study in American Domesticity* (New Haven, CT: Yale University Press, 1973), p. 34.
4. Catharine E. Beecher, *A Treatise on Domestic Economy for the Use of Young Ladies at Home and at School* (1841; rpt., New York: Harper and Bros., 1856). Beecher did acknowledge that women were suited for a variety of municipal housekeeping jobs: "There are several [jobs] in which woman can perform the duties as well [as] or better than men, especially in the care of schools, jails, and all public institutions of benevolence" (*Woman's Profession as Mother and Educator: With Views in Opposition to Female Suffrage* [New York: Maclean, Gibson 1872], p. 192). See also Charlotte E. Biester, "Catharine Beecher's Views of Home Economics," *History of Education Journal*, 3/3 (Spring 1952), pp. 88–91.
5. Quoted in Nancy Craig Simmons, "Margaret Fuller's Boston Conversations: The 1839–1840 Series," *Studies in the American Renaissance* (1994), p. 203.

6. Margaret Fuller, *Woman in the Nineteenth Century* (New York: Greeley and McElrath, 1845), pp. 159–160.
7. Emma Willard, 1815 letter to Mrs. Skinner, quoted in John Lord, *The Life of Emma Willard* (Carlisle, MA: Applewood Books, 1873), pp. 38–39.
8. Emma Willard, "An Address to the Public, Particularly to the Members of the Legislature of New York, Proposing a Plan for Improving Female Education" (1819), reprinted in Lord, *The Life of Emma Willard*, pp. 65, 56. Anne Firor Scott attributes less manipulative intent to Willard's address to the legislature, suggesting that Willard actually was a combination of a "prime exemplar of true womanhood" and a "thorough-going feminist" ("'The Ever-Widening Circle': The Diffusion of Feminist Values from the Troy Female Seminary, 1822–1872," *History of Education Quarterly*, 19/1 [Spring 1979], p. 5.).
9. Willard, "An Address to the Public," p. 65,
10. Almira H[art] Lincoln Phelps, *Lectures to Young Ladies, Comprising Outlines and Applications of the Different Branches of Female Education, for the Use of Female Schools, and Private Libraries* (Boston: Carter, Hendee and Company, 1833), p. 247.
11. Phelps, *Lectures to Young Ladies*, pp. 86–87.
12. "Adult female youth" in letter, Mary Lyon to Miss White, February 26, 1834, series A, subseries 3, Mary Lyon Collection, Mount Holyoke College, South Hadley, MA (hereafter Mary Lyon Collection); "Course of Study and Instruction" (Mount Holyoke Catalogue, 1837–1838), reprinted in Beth Bradford Gilchrist, *The Life of Mary Lyon* (Boston: Houghton Mifflin, 1910), appendix; Mary Lyon, "General View of the Principles and Designs of Mount Holyoke Female Seminary," reel 2, Mary Lyon Collection; "be willing" quoted in Sarah D. Locke Stow, *History of Mount Holyoke Female Seminary, South Hadley, Mass. during its First Half Century, 1837–1887* (Springfield, MA: Springfield Printing Company, 1887), pp. 306, 46.
13. Devon Abbott [Mihesuah], "'Commendable Progress': Acculturation at the Cherokee Female Seminary," *American Indian Quarterly*, 11/3 (Summer 1987), p. 197.
14. "Elegant white buildings" quoted in Abbott, "'Commendable Progress.'" See also Theda Perdue, *Cherokee Women: Gender and Culture Change, 1700–1835* (Lincoln: University of Nebraska Press, 1999).
15. "Science of domestic economy" in Christie Ann Farnham, *The Education of the Southern Belle: Higher Education and Student Socialization in the Antebellum South* (New York: New York University Press, 1994), p. 15; "easy lessons" in William Shepard, "Buckingham Female Collegiate Institute," part 1, *William and Mary Quarterly*, 20/2 (April 1940), p. 176; Amy Thompson McCandless, introduction to *Higher Education of Women in the South: An Annotated Bibliography*, compiled by Margaret Dittemore and Susan Tucker (New Orleans: Tulane University Press, 1992).
16. Letter, Charles Cotton to Eliza Watson Cotton, August 29, 1838, Cotton Family Papers (MSS 279), box 1, folder 1, Stuart A. Rose Manuscript, Archives and Rare Book Library, Emory University, Atlanta, GA (hereafter Cotton Family papers); John Gregory, *A Father's Legacy to His Daughters* (1761; rpt., Philadelphia: Rice

and Company, 1775), p. 15; Alice Shippen quoted in *Nancy Shippen, Her Journal Book: The International Romance of a Young Lady of Fashion of Colonial Philadelphia with Letters: To Her and About Her*, ed. Ethel Ames (Philadelphia: J. B. Lippincott, 1935), p. 40; "Branches of education" in letter, Charles Cotton to Eliza Watson Cotton, August 29, 1838, Cotton Family Papers.

17. George Foster Pierce, "Why Women Should Be Well Educated" (delivered at the commencement exercise of the Madison Female College in Madison, Georgia, July 10, 1856), in *Bishop Pierce's Sermons and Addresses, with a Few Special Discourses by Dr. Pierce* (Nashville, TN: Southern Methodist Publishing House, 1886), pp. 94, 106; George G. Smith, *The Life and Times of George Foster Pierce, D.D., LL.D.* (Sparta, GA: Hancock Publishing, 1888).

18. Goslin Bluff [pseud.], "Refined Female College," *Raleigh Register*, June 16, 1831, reprinted in Charles Lee Coon, *North Carolina Schools and Academies, 1790–1840: A Documentary History* (Raleigh, NC: Edwards and Broughton, 1915), p. 562; Andrews, commentary, p. 186; Henry F. Harrington, "Female Education," *Ladies' Companion*, 9 (October 1838), p. 295.

19. Edward H. Clarke, *Sex in Education; or, A Fair Chance for Girls* (Boston: James R. Osgood, 1873), pp. 23, 93.

20. M. Carey Thomas, diary, January 6 and February 26, 1871, M. Carey Thomas Papers, microfilm edition, reel 1, Bryn Mawr College Archives, Bryn Mawr, PA (hereafter Thomas Papers).

21. The only American institution then open to women PhD candidates was Boston University, which had awarded the degree in 1877 to twenty-four-year-old Helen Magill.

22. I discuss Thomas's intimate relationships with women in Lillian Faderman, *To Believe in Women: What Lesbians Have Done for America—A History* (Boston: Houghton Mifflin, 1999), pp. 197–216.

23. Letter, M. Carey Thomas to Dr. James B. Rhoads, August 14, 1883, Thomas Papers, reel 31.

24. M. Carey Thomas, "Present Tendencies in Women's College and University Education," address delivered at the quarter-centennial meeting of the Association of Collegiate Alumnae, November 6, 1907, reprinted in *Educational Review* (January 1908), p. 83.

25. In her 1893 correspondence with Mary Garrett, Thomas discusses at length what was leaked to her by trustees who supported her presidency about the opposition to her from other trustees. See Thomas Papers, reel 17. It did not hurt Thomas's cause when Mary Garrett (her life partner), heiress to one-third of the entire Baltimore and Ohio Railroad, promised the trustees that "whenever Miss M. Carey Thomas should become President of your College, I will pay into her hands the sum of ten thousand dollars yearly [about $300,000 in today's money] so long as I live and she remains President" (quoted in Edith Finch, *Carey Thomas of Bryn Mawr* [New York: Harper and Brothers, 1947], p. 209). In 1894 this was no trifling sum for academic enrichment programs that would serve Bryn Mawr's 283 students. Enrollment continued to be well under 500 until Garrett's death in 1915 ("Comparative Table of Numbers of Graduate and Undergraduate Students from

1885 to 1918," in *Bryn Mawr College Annual Report of the President, 1917–18*, https://repository.brynmawr.edu/cgi/viewcontent.cgi?article=1004&context=bmc_annualreports. Garrett was an ardent proponent of women's rights who believed, as she wrote Thomas, that woman was "chained," and as a college president Thomas would have a power that had been virtually unheard of in a female: she would be able to help "unchain" woman, to change her into someone she had never been before (Letter, Mary Garrett to M. Carey Thomas, August 30, 1892, Thomas Papers, reel 43).

26. G. Stanley Hall, "The Ideal School as Based on Child Study," *The Forum*, 32 (September 1901), p. 35, and *Adolescence: Its Psychology and Its Relations to Physiology, Anthropology, Sociology, Sex, Crime, Religion and Education*, vol. 2 (New York: Appleton, 1904), p. 60; Roberta Frankfort, *Collegiate Women: Domesticity and Career in Turn-of-the-Century America* (New York: New York University Press, 1977), pp. 75–78; "Only our failures marry": quoted in Helen Lefkowitz Horowitz, *The Power and Passion of M. Carey Thomas* (New York: Knopf, 1994), p. 385.

27. M. Carey Thomas, "Should the Higher Education of Women Be Different from That of Men?," in *Proceedings of the Fourteenth Annual Convention of the Association of Colleges and Preparatory Schools of the Middle States and Maryland, 1900* (Albany: University of the State of New York Press, 1901), pp. 10–19.

28. Racist in Horowitz, *The Power and Passion of M. Carey Thomas*, pp. 342–343; upper classes in Hilda Worthington Smith, *Women Workers of the Bryn Mawr Summer School* (New York: Affiliated Schools for Women Workers, 1929), p. 4; "It is much more" quoted in Horowitz, *The Power and Passion of M. Carey Thomas*, pp. 340–341.

29. Solidarity in John Thomas McGuire, "Maintaining the Vitality of a Social Movement: Social Justice Feminism, Class Conflict, and the Bryn Mawr Summer School for Women Workers," *Pennsylvania History: A Journal of Mid-Atlantic Studies*, 76/4 (Autumn 2009), pp. 393–421; "deep sex sympathy" in Smith, *Women Workers of the Bryn Mawr Summer School*, pp. 256–257.

30. Stephanie Y. Evans, *Black Women in the Ivory Tower, 1850–1954: An Intellectual History* (Gainesville: University Press of Florida, 2008), pp. 22–25; Joan Maria Johnson, *Southern Women at the Seven Sister Colleges: Feminist Values and Social Activism, 1875–1915* (Athens: University of Georgia Press, 2010), p. 100; Mary Church Terrell, *A Colored Woman in a White World* (1940; rpt., New York: G. K. Hall, 1996), p. 99. Oberlin began admitting Black women students to a "Ladies Literary Course of Study" as early as 1848; Francine Rusan Wilson, "'All of the Glory . . . Faded . . . Quickly': Sadie T. M. Alexander and Black Professional Women," in *Sister Circle: Black Women and Work*, ed. Sharon Harley and the Black Women and Work Collective (New Brunswick, NJ: Rutgers University Press, 2002), p. 173; Linda M. Perkins, "The Racial Integration of the Seven Sister Colleges," *Journal of Blacks in Higher Education*, 19 (Spring 1998), pp. 104–108.

31. Letter, Sophia Packard to John D. Rockefeller, December 29, 1883, quoted in Margaret A. Lowe, *Looking Good: College Women and Body Image, 1875–1930* (Baltimore, MD: Johns Hopkins University Press, 2003), p. 60.

32. Linda M. Perkins, "The Education of Black Women in the Nineteenth Century," in *Women's Higher Education in America*, ed. John Mack Faragher and Florence Howe (New York: Norton, 1988), p. 76; Joel Williamson, *New People: Miscegenation and Mulattos in the United States* (New York: Free Press, 1980), p. 91.

33. "Acknowledgements: Mt. Hermon Female Seminary," *Weekly Mississippi Pilot* (Jackson), May 1, 1875; Helen Griffith, *Dauntless in Mississippi: The Life of Sarah A. Dickey, 1838–1904* (South Hadley, MA: Dinosaur Press, 1966).

34. Letter, Harriet E. Giles to Dr. Mason, November 12, 1881, box 1, correspondence, Harriet E. Giles Collection, Spelman College Archives, Atlanta, GA (hereafter Giles Collection).

35. "Woman of powerful intellect": in Martha Burt Wright and Anne M. Bancroft, *History of the Oread Collegiate Institute, Worcester, Mass. (1849–1881): With Biographical Sketches* (New Haven, CT: Tuttle, Morehouse and Taylor, 1905), p. 127. Coincidentally, Laura Spelman had been a student at Oread before she married John D. Rockefeller Sr. in 1864; "depths of tenderness" in Sophia Packard, January 4, 1859, 1859 journal, box 1, Sophia Packard Collection, Spelman College Archives (hereafter Packard Collection).

36. Packard and Giles initially shared the society leaders' prejudices. "Poor creatures—how ignorant and uncouth they are," Giles wrote in shock about her prospective students: Harriet E. Giles, September 20, 1882, 1882 journal, box 1, Giles Collection; "When we use the term educational": letter, Sophia Packard to the Board of the Women's American Baptist Home Missionary Society, April 23, 1881, folder 2, box 1, Packard Collection; "Prey to the passions": letter, Sophia Packard to Mrs. F. L. Hesseltine, May 22, 1881, folder 3, box 1, Packard Collection. Packard and Giles really did work to "Christianize" the young women in their charge. As their letters and diaries attest, it truly was as important to them as teaching their students arts and sciences. For Harriet Giles's tally of conversions among the students, see, for example, her journal entries for November 24, 1883; March 13, 1884; December 31, 1884; January 27, 1887; and March 7, 1887, box 1, Giles Collection.

37. Johnetta Cross Brazzell, "Bricks without Straw: Missionary-Sponsored Black Higher Education in the Post-Emancipation Era," *Journal of Higher Education*, 63/1 (January–February 1992), p. 36; Harry G. Lefever, "The Early Origins of Spelman College," *Journal of Blacks in Higher Education*, 47 (Spring 2005), pp. 60–63.

38. Letter, Sophia Packard to Mrs. F. L. Hesseltine, September 19, 1881, folder 6, box 1, Packard Collection.

39. "Are you going to stick?": quoted in Ron Chernow, *Titan: The Life of John D. Rockefeller, Sr.* (New York: Vintage Books, 1998), p. 240; Packard letter to Rockefeller, December 29, 1883, quoted in Lowe, *Looking Good*, p. 60. Though Packard and Giles were careful not to seem to be radically redefining the Black woman and who she might become, Spelman's later alums did redefine her. They included leaders in the arts, public policy, and politics such as Alice Walker, Marian Wright Edelman, and Stacey Abrams.

40. Quoted in Audrey Thomas McCluskey, *A Forgotten Sisterhood: Pioneering Black Women Educators and Activists in the Jim Crow South* (Lanham, MD: Rowman and Littlefield, 2014), p. 126.
41. Joyce A. Hanson details Bethune's life as the creator of both educational and political institutions "that assured the continuation of African American women's political power" (*Mary McLeod Bethune and Black Women's Political Activism* [Columbia: University of Missouri Press, 2003], p. 207).
42. "Edna Kenton Says Feminism Will Give . . . Women Greater Scope," *The Delineator* (Boston), 85 (July 1914), p. 17. By 1940 there were more than 600,000 women students enrolled in colleges. In 1979 the number of women students in postsecondary institutions began to exceed the number of men students. In the forty years that followed, the differential continued to increase. In 2019 there were over 11.0 million women enrolled in U.S. postsecondary institutions, far outnumbering the 8.6 million men students. See *Digest of Education Statistics*, National Center for Education Statistics, table 303.10, https://nces.ed.gov/programs/digest/d18/tables/dt18_303.10.asp; Richard Fry, "U.S. Women Near Milestone in the College-Educated Labor Force," Pew Research Center, June 20, 2019, https://www.pewresearch.org/fact-tank/2019/06/20/u-s-women-near-milestone-in-the-college-educated-labor-force/.
43. Bradwell v. Illinois, 83 U.S. (16 Wall.), 130 (1873), p. 141.
44. "Mother heart": Anna Howard Shaw, *The Story of a Pioneer* (New York: Harper and Brothers, 1915), p. 124; "finding any wrong": Anna Howard Shaw, "God's Women," in *Transactions of the National Council of Women of the United States*, ed. Rachel Foster Avery (Philadelphia: Lippincott, 1891), p. 249, and Anna Howard Shaw, "The Great Defect in Our Government," reprinted in Wilmer A. Linkugel, "The Speeches of Anna Howard Shaw," Ph.D diss., University of Wisconsin, 1960, vol. 2, p. 175.
45. Letter, "A Voter" to Jane Addams, January 17, 1898, reel 113.3, Jane Addams Papers, Peace Collection, Swarthmore College Library, Swarthmore, PA (herafter Addams Papers).
46. Robyn Muncy, "Gender and Professionalization in the Origins of the U.S. Welfare State: The Careers of Sophonisba Breckinridge and Edith Abbott, 1890–1935," *Journal of Policy History*, 2/3 (July, 1990), pp. 290–315; "Women by natural instinct": Clinton Rogers Woodruff, introduction to Mary Beard, *Women's Work in Municipalities* (New York: D. Appleton and Company, 1915), https://www.gutenberg.org/files/59678/59678-h/59678-h.htm.
47. For later twentieth-century criticisms of "municipal housekeeping" see, for example, Jill Conway, "Women Reformers and American Culture, 1870–1930," *Journal of Social History*, 5/2 (Winter 1971–1972), pp. 164–177. The number of U.S. women engaged in professional pursuits went from 91,963 in 1870 to 724,176 in 1910. Most of those women were teachers and trained nurses, but women were solidly represented among social workers, physicians, college teachers, and even college presidents. By 1920, about one-fourth of all U.S. women were gainfully employed, a share that rose to one-third in New England and the Mid-Atlantic states. See Joseph A. Hill, *Women in Gainful Occupations, 1870 to 1920: A Study of the Trend*

of Recent Changes in the Numbers, Occupational Distribution, and Family Relationship of Women Reported in the Census as Following a Gainful Occupation (Washington, DC: U.S. Government Printing Office, 1929), pp. 42–43.

48. Jane Addams, *Democracy and Social Ethics* (New York: Macmillan, 1902), p. 86.
49. Addams, *Democracy and Social Ethics*, p. 89.
50. On professionalization at Hull House see Muncy, "Gender and Professionalization"; "Shaping the social history" quoted in Kathryn Kish Sklar, "Hull House in the 1890s: A Community of Women Reformers," *Signs*, 10/4 (Summer 1985), p. 658. Kelley had arrived at Hull House in need of its services, a fugitive from an abusive marriage. Under Addams's influence she became a dispenser of aid for the needy rather than a recipient. See Ellen DuBois's discussion of Kelley in *Suffrage: Women's Long Battle for the Vote* (New York: Simon and Schuster, 2020), pp. 155–164. The Illinois Factory Act of 1893 was repealed by the Illinois Supreme Court the following year under pressure from a statewide association of manufacturers, but the fact that it had been in effect—however briefly—encouraged labor groups to fight even harder for the eight-hour workday.
51. Quoted in W. I. Thomas, "Woman and the Occupations," *American Magazine*, 68 (September 1909), p. 467.
52. Letter, Theodore Roosevelt to Jane Addams, January 24, 1906, reel 113.4, Addams Papers. I discuss Addams at greater length in Faderman, *To Believe in Women*, chapter 7. See also Jane Addams, *Twenty Years at Hull-House* (1910; rpt., New York: Macmillan, 1963), pp. 310–313.
53. Emily Blackwell, journal, October 1852, reel 3, Blackwell Family Papers, Schlesinger Library, Radcliffe Institute for Advanced Study, Cambridge, MA (hereafter Blackwell Family Papers).
54. Quoted in Alice Stone Blackwell, "An Early Woman Physician," *Woman's Journal* (October 6, 1906), p. 158.
55. Letter, Emily Blackwell to Elizabeth Blackwell, June 15–24, 1870, folder 164, box 11, Blackwell Family Papers; I discuss the relationship between Blackwell and Cushier and their work together more extensively in Faderman, *To Believe in Women*, chapter 15.
56. "Very perservering" in Emily Blackwell, journal, August 20, 1850, reel 3, Blackwell Family Papers; "If I might see" in Emily Blackwell, journal, January 6, 1852, reel 3, Blackwell Family Papers.
57. Emily Blackwell to Elizabeth Blackwell, October 1858, folder 163, box 11, Blackwell Family Papers.
58. George W. Gale, "Myra Bradwell: The First Woman Lawyer," *American Bar Association Journal*, 39/12 (December 1953), pp. 1080–1083, 1120–1121.
59. Letter, M. Carey Thomas to Mary Whitall Thomas, November 21, 1880, reel 31, Thomas Papers.
60. The term may have been inspired by Henry James's 1886 novel *The Bostonians*, which had been serialized in *The Century Magazine* in 1885–1886. I discuss Boston marriages at length in Lillian Faderman, *Surpassing the Love of Men: Romantic Friendship and Love between Women from the Renaissance to the Present* (New York: William Morrow, 1981), part 2, chapter 4.

61. See, for example, my discussion of the sexual relationship between Carrie Chapman Catt and Mollie Hay in Faderman, *To Believe in Women*. Catt, away on suffrage business, wrote Hay on Hay's fifty-fourth birthday, "I'm sorry I couldn't give you 69 kisses, one for each year" (p. 71).
62. Jill Norgren, *Belva Lockwood: The Woman Who Would Be President* (New York: New York University Press, 2007).
63. Bradwell v. Illinois, p. 141.
64. Belva Lockwood, "My Efforts to Become a Lawyer," *Lippincott's Monthly Magazine* (February 1888), pp. 215–229.
65. "Woman's Right to Practice in the U.S. Supreme Court," *Evening Star* (Washington, DC), February 8, 1879, p. 1; "A Woman's Victory at Work," *Sioux City Journal* (Iowa), February 18, 1879, p. 1.
66. Charlotte Perkins Gilman, *Women and Economics: A Study of the Economic Relation between Men and Women as a Factor in Social Evolution* (Boston: Small, Maynard and Company, 1898), chapter 8.

7.

THE STRUGGLE TO TRANSFORM WOMAN INTO CITIZEN

1. Anthony to Stanton in *The Selected Papers of Elizabeth Cady Stanton and Susan B. Anthony*, vol. 2, ed. Ann D. Gordon (New Brunswick, NJ: Rutgers University Press, 2003), pp. 525–526; *Chicago Tribune*, November 7, 1872, p. 4; "Female Suffrage," *York Daily* (Pennsylvania), November 6, 1872, p. 4.
2. Quoted in Alma Lutz, *Susan B. Anthony: Rebel, Crusader, Humanitarian* (Boston: Beacon Press, 1959), p. 201.
3. Quoted in Ida Husted Harper, *The Life and Work of Susan B. Anthony*, vol. 1 (Indianapolis, IN: Bowen-Merrill, 1899), p. 433.
4. Susan B. Anthony, quoted in Matilda Joslyn Gage, letter to the editor, "Susan B. Anthony's Case," *Leavenworth Weekly Times* (Kansas), July 3, 1873, p. 1.
5. "Why, Lizzie" quoted in Theodore Stanton and Harriot Stanton Blatch, eds., *Elizabeth Cady Stanton as Revealed in Her Letters, Diary, and Reminiscences* (New York: Harper and Brothers, 1932), p. 146; "One-half" quoted in Sally G. McMillen, *Seneca Falls and the Origins of the Women's Rights Movement* (New York: Oxford University Press, 2008), pp. 93–94.
6. "Address of Elizabeth Cady Stanton on the Divorce Bill before the Judiciary Committee of the New York Senate," February 8, 1861 (Albany, NY: Weed, Parsons and Company, 1861); "Free speech": https://www.loc.gov/resource/mss41210.mss41210-003_00094_00095/?sp=2.
7. "Imagine me": Letter, Elizabeth Cady Stanton to Susan B. Anthony, June 10, 1856, in *The Selected Papers of Elizabeth Cady Stanton and Susan B. Anthony*, vol. 1, ed. Ann D. Gordon (New Brunswick, NJ: Rutgers University Press, 2003), p. 103. "She forged": obituary for Elizabeth Cady Stanton, *New York Times*, October 27, 1902. Stanton had made a similar assertion about their relationship in

Elizabeth Cady Stanton, Susan B. Anthony, and Matilda Gage, *History of Woman Suffrage*, vol. 1 (Rochester, NY: Charles Mann, 1881), p. 458.
8. "Were getting" quoted in National Woman Suffrage Association, *Report of the International Council of Women* (Washington, DC: Rufus H. Carby, 1888), p. 327; "The True Woman" (1857), https://iiif.lib.harvard.edu/manifests/view/drs:43831912$1i.
9. "The True Woman."
10. In the spring of 1871, seventy women—including three Black women, Mary Ann Shadd Cary, Amanda Wall, and Mary Anderson—tried to vote in Washington, DC, but their efforts received far less attention than Anthony's civil disobedience because Anthony was already well known to the press. The cases of two of the would-be Washington voters are in *Sara J. Spencer vs. The Board of Registration, and Sarah E. Webster vs. The Judges of Election*, ed. James O[gilvie] Clephane (1871; rpt., Farmington Hills, MI: Gale Group, 2012). The Black would-be voters are discussed in Martha S. Jones, *Vanguard: How Black Women Broke Barriers, Won the Vote, and Insisted on Equality for All* (New York: Basic Books, 2020), pp. 118–119. On October 15, 1872, Virginia Minor tried to register to vote in St. Louis. Her case reached the Supreme Court in May 1873. The justices declared in *Minor v. Happersett* (March 1875) that the Fourteenth Amendment did not give women the right to vote. "If you refuse" quoted in Rayne L. Hammond, "Trial and Tribulation: The Story of *United States v. Anthony*," *Buffalo Law Review*, 48/3 (2000), p. 1005. Anthony's case, tried in the Northern District of the Circuit Court of New York, is *United States v. Anthony*, June 18, 1873.
11. *Anti-Suffrage Essays by Massachusetts Women*, ed. Ernest Bernbaum (Boston: The Forum Publications of Boston, 1916), pp. xi–xiii; Thomas Jefferson to Anne Willing Bingham, May 11, 1788, in *The Papers of Thomas Jefferson*, vol. 13, ed. Julian P. Boyd (Princeton, NJ: Princeton University Press, 1956), p. 151.
12. "Mannish women": "The Woman's Rights Convention—The Last Act of the Drama," *New York Herald*, September 12, 1852; "A gathering of unsexed women": *New York Herald*, September 9, 1853, quoted in Carrie Chapman Catt and Nettie Rogers Shuler, *Woman Suffrage and Politics: The Inner Story of the Suffrage Movement* (New York: Scribner's, 1923), p. 27. Sojourner Truth's speech was delivered in Akron, Ohio, in 1851. Truth was not literate. Various versions of the speech were written down by others or remembered long after the fact. The best known is Frances D. Gage's version, published twelve years after the convention, in the *National Anti-Slavery Standard*. Scholars have speculated that the heavy "Negro dialect" Gage used in her "transcript" was not faithful to Truth's actual speech. See Corona Brezina, *Sojourner Truth's "Ain't I a Woman?" Speech* (New York: Rosen, 2005); "Lank in the breast": "The Spirit Moveth Sojourner Truth," *New York Times*, June 2, 1855; "A man now lecturing": *Leavenworth Weekly Times* (Kansas), January 25, 1872, p. 3.
13. "Grim old gal" quoted in Harper, *The Life and Work of Susan B. Anthony*, 1:397; "Amazon": "An Astounding Development," *Chicago Tribune*, August 24, 1874, p. 4; "Pantaloonatic": *Weekly Caucasian* (Lexington, MO), January 14, 1871, p. 2;

Overmyer cases discussed in Charles J. Reid Jr., "The Devil Comes to Kansas: A Story of Free Love, Sexual Privacy, and the Law," *Michigan Journal of Gender and Law*, 19/1 (2012), pp. 71–148; David Overmyer, "Woman's Suffrage," *Westphalia Times* (Kansas), November 16, 1893, p. 1.

14. Susan B. Anthony, "The New Century's Manly Woman," *Leslie's Weekly*, March 3, 1900, p. 170.
15. See, for example, Carolyn Heilbrun, *Toward a Recognition of Androgyny* (New York: Alfred A. Knopf, 1973); Micah Rajunov and A. Scott Duane, eds., *Nonbinary: Memoirs of Gender and Identity* (New York: Columbia University Press, 2019).
16. Newspaper ad, 1911, signed "National Association Opposed to Woman Suffrage."
17. During the Civil War there was a hiatus in suffrage activism. "What woman imminently needs": Horace Greeley, "Women's Rights and Duties: Remarks," *New York Tribune*, November 2, 1850, p. 6; "ultraradicalism" in Alma Lutz, *Susan B. Anthony: Rebel, Crusader, Humanitarian* (Boston: Beacon Press, 1959), p. 70. Women's righters had been getting aggressive in various areas, demanding that women be granted rights of citizenship that were no different from men's rights, and even demanding that divorce laws be loosened so that a woman could leave an unhappy marriage. Horace Greeley, "A Cry from the Females," *New York Tribune* (1866), quoted in Harper, *The Life and Work of Susan B. Anthony*, 1:267.
18. Horace Greeley, June 25, 1867, in *Proceedings and Debates of the Constitutional Convention of the State of New York Held in 1867 and 1868*, vol. 1, ed. Edward F. Underhill (Albany, NY: Weed, Parsons, and Company, 1868), pp. 178–179. Greeley's concern about woman's sphere also seems to be contradicted by his earlier relationship with Margaret Fuller. In the 1840s he hired her as the *New York Tribune*'s first woman literary editor and then made her the first woman foreign correspondent.
19. "The most discouraging": Elizabeth Cady Stanton, "Address Delivered at Seneca Falls," July 19, 1848, in *The Elizabeth Cady Stanton–Susan B. Anthony Reader: Correspondence, Writings, Speeches*, ed. Ellen Carol DuBois (Boston: Northeastern University Press, 1992), p. 33; "to show that": Sarah Josepha Hale, "Woman Suffrage," *Godey's Lady's Book and Magazine*, 82/491 (May 1871), p. 476; Gail Hamilton, *Woman's Wrongs: A Counter-Irritant* (Boston: Ticknor and Fields, 1868), p. 102; Joe C. Miller, "Never a Fight of Woman against Man: What Textbooks Don't Say about Women's Suffrage," *History Teacher*, 48/3 (May 2015), p. 440.
20. Catharine Beecher, *Woman's Profession as Mother and Educator, with Views in Opposition to Woman Suffrage* (New York: Maclean Gibson and Company, 1872), p. 7.
21. Mrs. Horace A. Davis, "The True Function of the Normal Woman," in *Anti-Suffrage Essays by Massachusetts Women*, pp. 123–127.
22. Anna Howard Shaw accused the liquor interests of financing this ad. See "'Rum Men Fighting Suffrage': Liquor Interests Financed Anti-Suffrage Campaigns, Dr. Anna Shaw Asserts—Reads 'Ads.,'" *Wichita Eagle* (Kansas), April 20, 1913, p. 6.

23. Quoted in Candace Falk, et al., *Emma Goldman: A Documentary History of the American Years*, vol. 1: *Made for America, 1890–1901* (Berkeley: University of California Press, 2003), p. 43.
24. Emma Goldman, "Woman Suffrage" (1910), in Emma Goldman, *Anarchism and Other Essays* (London: Mother Earth Publishing Association, 1911), pp. 209–210, 213. Goldman's anti-suffragist sentiments were shared by several women who had made a place for themselves in a man's world, such as Ida Tarbell, a pioneering muckraking journalist. Tarbell had joined the New York State Association Opposed to the Extension of Suffrage to Women in 1903 and became a member of its executive board in 1908. In an astonishing disconnect, she believed that woman's participation in politics was counter to her "true nature." See Ida M. Tarbell, "The Irresponsible Woman and the Friendless Child," in *Anti-Feminism in America: A Reader*, ed. Angela Howard and Sasha Tarrant (New York: Routledge, 2000), pp. 114–115; and Kathleen Brady, *Ida Tarbell: Portrait of a Muckraker* (Pittsburgh: University of Pittsburgh Press, 1989), chapter 10.
25. Goldman, "Woman Suffrage," pp. 215–216.
26. Goldman, "Woman Suffrage," p. 217.
27. Anna Howard Shaw, "The New Man," reprinted in Wilmer A. Linkugel, "The Speeches of Anna Howard Shaw," Ph.D diss., University of Wisconsin, 1960, vol. 2, p. 969.
28. Stanton et al., *History of Woman Suffrage*, 1:72.
29. Quoted in Amy Aronson, *Crystal Eastman: A Revolutionary Life* (New York: Oxford University Press, 2019), p. 107.
30. Anna Howard Shaw, "The Great Defect in Our Government," reprinted in Linkugel, "The Speeches of Anna Howard Shaw," 2:147–178.
31. NAWSA was formed when the National Woman Suffrage Association and the American Woman Suffrage Association merged. On Shaw's reach and prominence, see James R. McGovern, "Anna Howard Shaw, New Approaches to Feminism," *Journal of Social History*, 3/2 (Winter 1969), p. 139, and for example, "Fine Program," *Messenger-Inquirer* (Owensboro, Kentucky), March 15, 1903, p. 1; "Shaw—'The New Man'," *Iola Daily Record* (Kansas), July 25, 1907, p. 2; "Anna Howard Shaw Gave a Spendid Address Yesterday," *Emporia Gazette* (Kansas), July 26, 1907, p. 4.
32. I discuss the relationship between Shaw and Lucy Anthony at greater length in Lillian Faderman, *To Believe in Women: What Lesbians Have Done for America—A History* (Boston: Houghton Mifflin, 1999), chapter 3; letter, Anna Howard Shaw to Clara Osburn, August 19, 1902, microfilm reel 17, Anna Howard Shaw Papers, Schlesinger Library, Radcliffe Institute for Advanced Study, Cambridge, MA (hereafter Shaw Papers).
33. Anna Howard Shaw, *The Story of a Pioneer* (New York: Harper and Bros., 1915), p. 240.
34. Anna Howard Shaw, "Inveterate Optimist of the Suffragist Movement," *Current Opinion*, December 1915, p. 398. Early in Shaw's suffrage career, an article in the Sunday edition of *New York World* (August 6, 1895, p. 23) reported that Shaw welcomed women in pants to her summer home. The headlines and subheadings

were intended to shock: "AN ADAMLESS EDEN OF WOMEN IN BLOOMERS"; "Summer Suffragists Who Discard Skirts and Wear Bathing Suits Just Like a Man"; "THE REV. ANNA SHAW'S INTERESTING COLONY AT SELECT WIANNO." Shaw was upset about the article and called it "almost libelous" (*The Story of a Pioneer*, p. 288). But she was careful never again to give reporters such fodder. Shaw's womanly appearance in "Women and Religion," *The Times* (Philadelphia), May 27, 1893, p. 3; "A Woman Preacher," *St. Paul Globe* (Minnesota), January 21, 1893, p. 9; *Pomona Weekly Times* (California), June 18, 1895, clipping, folder 18, box 1, Susan B. Anthony Papers, Sophia Smith Collection, Smith College, Northampton, MA.

35. "Mother heart": Shaw, *The Story of a Pioneer*, p. 124; "Call not": "Louisiana in War Times," *Times-Picayune* (New Orleans), January 15, 1893, p. 20.

36. "The same old woman" in Anna Howard Shaw, "The New Man," reprinted in Linkugel, "The Speeches of Anna Howard Shaw," 2:969; she slipped in: article on Anna Howard Shaw's "The Fundamental Principle of a Republic," quoted in an unidentified newspaper clipping, July 1, 1915, box 20, Shaw Papers; "She wins over" in "At the Chautauqua Tonight," *Sedalia Democrat* (Missouri), July 26, 1907, p. 1.

37. Willard writes openly about her masculine persona and her domestic life with Jackson and then Gordon in *Glimpses of Fifty Years: The Autobiography of an American Woman* (Chicago: H. J. Smith, 1889). See also my discussion of Willard's masculine persona and domestic life in Faderman, *To Believe in Women*, pp. 30–35; "never abrupt" in *Boston Times-Democrat*, clipping, Willard Scrapbook 57, p. 63, reel 39, WCTU Library, Evanston, Illinois; "Womanliness first": quoted in Anna Adams Gordon, *The Beautiful Life of Frances E. Willard: A Memorial Volume* (Chicago: Woman's Temperance Publishing Association, 1898), p. 13. In 1888, Shaw had been hired by Willard to be the head of the suffrage department of the WCTU. Shaw took Willard as her mentor in "womanliness."

38. Adella Hunt Logan, "Colored Women as Voters," *The Crisis*, 4/5 (September 1912), pp. 242–243.

39. Elizabeth Cady Stanton, "Universal Suffrage," *National Anti-Slavery Standard*, July 29, 1865, reprinted in Gordon, *The Selected Papers of Elizabeth Cady Stanton and Susan B. Anthony*, 1:551.

40. Susan B. Anthony, address delivered at Ottumwa, Kansas, July 4, 1865, quoted in Harper, *The Life and Work of Susan B. Anthony*, 1:220–221.

41. Quoted in Lori D. Ginzberg, *Elizabeth Cady Stanton: An American Life* (New York: Hill and Wang, 2009), p. 119.

42. Quoted in Faye E. Dudden, *Fighting Chance: The Struggle over Woman Suffrage and Black Suffrage in Reconstruction America* (New York: Oxford University Press, 2011), p. 71.

43. Douglass quoted in "Document 30: Debates at the American Equal Rights Association Meeting, New York City, May 12–14, 1869," in *The Concise History of Woman Suffrage: Selections from History of Woman Suffrage*, ed. Mari Jo Buhle and Paul Buhle (Champaign: University of Illinois Press, 2005), p. 284; Truth quoted in "Document 26: Sojourner Truth, Address to the First Annual Meeting of the American Equal Rights Association, New York City, New York, May 9,

1867," in Buhle and Buhle, *The Concise History of Woman Suffrage*, p. 261. The split would continue until 1890, when the two groups finally merged to form NAWSA.

44. "Justice is not" quoted in Margaret Hope Bacon, "One Great Bundle of Humanity: Frances Ellen Watkins Harper (1825–1911)," *Pennsylvania Magazine of History and Biography*, 113/1 (January 1989), pp. 21, 34; "The white women" quoted in Jane Rhodes, *Mary Ann Shadd Cary: The Black Press and Protest in the Nineteenth Century* (Bloomington: Indiana University Press, 1999), p. 193. Mary Ann Shadd Cary, the first Black woman to go to law school in America, joined the National Woman Suffrage Association and appeared with other members in front of the House Judiciary Committee in January 1874, representing 600 Washington, DC, women who were petitioning to get the vote as taxpayers. See "Argument before the Judiciary Committee of the House of Representatives upon the Petition of 600 Citizens Asking for the Enfranchisement of Women of the District of Columbia, January 21, 1874" (Washington, DC: Gibson Brothers, 1874); "No longer sold" quoted in Stanton et al., *The History of Woman Suffrage*, 2:833–834.

45. Mary Church Terrell, "The Progress and Problems of Colored Women," Speeches and Writings, 1866–1920, Mary Church Terrell Papers, Library of Congress, Washington, DC. The speech was given several times between 1898 and 1920. Mary Church Terrell, *A Colored Woman in a White World* (1940; rpt., Lanham, MD: Rowman and Littlefield, 2020), p. 180. Rosalyn Terborg-Penn observes that "just as the majority of white women who actively participated in the organized movement were among the middle class, the majority of the Black women who were suffragists appear to have enjoyed higher status than the masses of women of their race" (*African-American Women and the Struggle for the Vote, 1850–1920* [Bloomington: Indiana University Press, 1998], p. 2). See Paula Giddings's discussion of the National Association of Colored Women in *When and Where I Enter: The Impact of Black Women on Race and Sex in America* (New York: William Morrow, 1984).

46. Robert Terrell quoted in Terrell, *A Colored Woman in a White World*, p. 180; "Ought to be at home" quoted in Terborg-Penn, *African-American Women and the Struggle for the Vote*, p. 99; "The Justice of Woman Suffrage," a keynote address at a National Suffrage Convention, *Wyandotte Chief* (Kansas City, Kansas), February 15, 1900, p. 2. The speech was reprinted for years in other Black newspapers and magazines, including the *Washington Bee*, February 17, 1900. Even twelve years later it was reprinted in full in *The Crisis*, 4/5 (September 1912), pp. 243–245.

47. Quoted in Jacqueline Bacon, *Freedom's Journal: The First African American Newspaper* (Lanham, MD: Lexington Books, 2007), p. 142.

48. Pauline E. Hopkins, "Women's Department," *The Colored American Magazine*, 1/2 (June 1900), p. 122. Hopkins's view of woman's role evolved. A couple of years later, she wrote that "the Negro woman feels womanhood stir within her and boldly advances to scale the heights of intellectual advancement, feeling that the door has been opened for her to take an active, intelligent, and resolute part in the march of human progress" ("Higher Education of Colored Women in White

Schools and Colleges," *The Colored American Magazine*, 5/6 [October 1902], p. 447); "woman suffrage convert": see, for example, the reprint of Lurana W. Sheldon's poem titled "Suffrage" in *The Colored American Magazine*, 14/9 (October 1908), p. 553.

49. "Vast Suffrage Host Is on Parade Today . . . Chinese Women to Ride," *New York Times*, May 4, 1912, p. 22.

50. Poem quoted in Judy Yung, "The Social Awakening of Chinese-American Women as Reported in *Chung Sai Yat Po*, 1900–1911," in *Unequal Sisters: A Multicultural Reader in U.S. Women's History*, ed. Vicki L. Ruiz and Ellen Carol DuBois, 2nd ed. (New York: Routledge, 1994), p. 275.

51. Editorials quoted in Yung, "The Social Awakening," pp. 273, 279; "made speeches" in Judy Yung, *Unbound Feet: A Social History of Chinese Women in San Francisco* (Berkeley: University of California Press, 1995), p. 117.

52. *New York Tribune*, April 11, 1912, quoted in Cathleen D. Cahill, *Recasting the Vote: How Women of Color Transformed the Suffrage Movement* (Chapel Hill: University of North Carolina Press, 2020); "Government of all the people" quoted in Kimberley Jensen, "'Neither Head nor Tail to the Campaign': Esther Pohl Lovejoy and Oregon Woman Suffrage Victory, 1912," *Oregon History Quarterly*, 108/3 (Fall 2007), p. 74; Shaw quoted in Cahill, *Recasting the Vote*, p. 40; "Vast Suffrage Host is on Parade To-day," *New York Times*, May 4, 1912, p. 22; "20,000 Women, All Hats Alike, In Suffrage Parade," *Evening World* (New York), May 4, 1912, p. 1. Unfortunately, the parade's celebration of woman suffrage in China was premature. When the new constitution of the Chinese Republic was written, it contained no provision for woman suffrage, and the electoral laws that were passed in August 1912 specifically excluded women from voting. Yet the heady conviction that women would be able to vote in China had stirred Chinese women in America to take a public stance on suffrage for the first time, while also reenergizing white suffragists for the still-long battle ahead.

53. Beth Jeffries, "Indian Women the First Suffragists, and Used Recall, Chippewa Avers," *Washington Times*, August 3, 1914. See also "Squaws Beat Militants to Right of Franchise," *Los Angeles Times*, January 31, 1913, p. 11.

54. Elizabeth Cady Stanton, "The Matriarchate, or Mother-Age," address to the National Council of Women, *National Bulletin*, February 25, 1891, rpt. in Speaking While Female Speech Bank, https://speakingwhilefemale.co/womens-lives-stanton2/. See also Gail H. Landsman, "The 'Other' as Political Symbol: Images of Indians in the Woman Suffrage Movement," *Ethnohistory*, 39/3 (Summer 1992), pp. 259; "The sisterhood" in *Geneva Advertiser-Gazette* (New York), February 27, 1913, p. 4.

55. Cathleen Cahill points out that in Baldwin's employment identification photograph for the Office of Indian Affairs, she wore the traditional dress of the Chippewa woman, defying the office's policy of assimilating Indians. Cahill speculates that Baldwin was merely too busy to organize the Indian float ("Marie Louise Bottineau Baldwin: Indigenizing the Federal Indian Service," *American Indian Quarterly*, 37/3 [Summer 2013], pp. 65–86).

56. "Suffragists to Make Final Plans at Session Monday," *Washington Times*, February 18, 1913, p. 5.
57. Florence Kelley quoted in Ellen Carol DuBois, *Suffrage: Women's Long Battle for the Vote* (New York: Simon and Schuster, 2020), p. 160.
58. NAWSA membership in Wil[mer] A. Linkugel and Martha Solomon, *Anna Howard Shaw, Suffrage Orator and Social Reformer* (Westport, CT: Greenwood Press, 1991), p. 9; Florence Kelley, 1906, quoted in DuBois, *Suffrage*, p. 160.
59. Quoted in Sidney R. Bland, "New Life in an Old Movement: Alice Paul and the Great Suffrage Parade of 1913 in Washington, D.C.," *Records of the Columbia Historical Society, Washington, D.C.* (1971/1972), p. 664.
60. "Modern Chivalry: Excoriate Policemen: Women Pour out Their Wrath," *Los Angeles Times*, March 7, 1913; Associated Press, "Capitol Ablaze over Insults to Suffragists," *Buffalo Evening News* (New York), March 4, 1913, p. 17.
61. Logan, "Colored Women as Voters"; Terborg-Penn, *African-American Women and the Struggle for the Vote*; "Illinois Women Feature Parade . . . Question of Color Line Threatens for While [sic] to Make Trouble in Ranks," *Chicago Tribune*, March 4, 1913, p. 3.
62. Marjorie Julian Spruill discusses NAWSA's "southern strategy" in "Race, Reform, and Reaction at the Turn of the Century: Southern Suffragists, the NAWSA, and the Southern Strategy," in *Votes for Women: The Struggle for Suffrage Revisited*, ed. Jean H. Baker (New York: Oxford University Press, 2002), pp. 102–117. As Ida B. Wells, Wells-Barnett had written *Southern Horrors: Lynch Law in All Its Phases* (1892; rpt., Boston: Bedford Books, 1997), in which she pointed out that Black men were often lynched for rape when in fact they had had consensual relations with white women. Because her exposé reached few white readers, she took her case to Britain, where her audiences vowed to form investigative committees. Her anti-lynching campaign finally received attention in America when the *New York Times* published an outraged article—not about the horrors of lynching but about the British interfering with what went on in America. The article referred to Wells-Barnett as "a slanderous and nasty-minded mulatress, who does not scruple to represent the victims of black brutes in the South as willing victims" ("British Anti-Lynchers," *New York Times*, August 2, 1894, p. 4); W. E. B. Du Bois, "Politics," *The Crisis*, 5/6 (April 1913), p. 1.
63. "We will never win": letter, Anna Howard Shaw to Dr. Esther Phol-Lovejoy, March 12, 1914, folder 46, Shaw Papers. "Votes for women": Anna Howard Shaw, "Militancy," *Trend*, October 10, 1913, p. 31.
64. "Nurtured a deep resentment": Sylvia D. Hoffert, *Alva Vanderbilt Belmont: Unlikely Champion of Women's Rights* (Bloomington: Indiana University Press, 2011), p. 71.
65. Hoffert, *Alva Vanderbilt Belmont*, p. 74; E[stelle] Sylvia Pankhurst, *The Suffragette: A History of the Women's Militant Suffrage Movement, 1905–1910* (1911; rpt., Boston: The Woman's Journal, 1912), p. 46; "Suffragette Hits Churchill," *Dundee Courier*, November 15, 1909, quoted in Fern Riddell, *Death in Ten Minutes: Kitty Marion: Activist, Arsonist, Suffragette* (London: Hodder and Stoughton, 2018).

66. Harriot Stanton Blatch and Alma Lutz, *Challenging Years: The Memoirs of Harriot Stanton Blatch* (New York: G. P. Putnam's Sons, 1940), p. 92; Meredith Tax, *The Rising of the Women: Feminist Solidarity and Class Conflict, 1880–1917* (Champaign: University of Illinois Press, 2001), p. 170. See also Ellen DuBois, "Working Women, Class Relations, and Suffrage Militance," in Ruiz and DuBois, *Unequal Sisters*, pp. 271–288. Other suffrage groups had by now taken up the battle too. The president of the 2-million-member National Federation of Women's Clubs, which had been devoted largely to literary discussions, announced, "Ladies, Dante is dead. He died several centuries ago, and a great many things have happened since then. Let us drop the study of his Inferno and proceed in earnest to contemplate our own social order." In 1910, the federation made suffrage its main concern. See Rhett Child Dorr, *What Eight Million Women Want* (Boston: Small, Maynard, 1910), pp. 56, 323. Working-class women formed the Wage Earners Suffrage League.
67. Quoted in Eleanor Flexner and Ellen Fitzpatrick, *Century of Struggle: The Woman's Rights Movement in the United States*, enlarged ed. (Cambridge, MA: Belknap Press of Harvard University Press, 1975), p. 267.
68. "How long must women wait?": Alva E. Belmont, "Excuses for White House Picketing: A Statement in Extenuation from Mrs. O. H. P. Belmont, of the National Woman's Party," *New York Times*, July 9, 1917, p. 7; "Free 23 Suffragists after Six-Day Fast," *New York Times*, August 21, 1918.
69. President Woodrow Wilson, "Address to the Senate on the Nineteenth Amendment," September 30, 1918, The American Presidency Project, https://www.presidency.ucsb.edu/documents/address-the-senate-the-nineteenth-amendment.
70. "Kaiser Wilson," *The Suffragist*, August 18, 1915, p. 6.
71. "Women of U.S. to Work in Munition Plants Is Urged: Suffrage Leader Calls Conference to Decide on Action in Case of War," *Austin American* (Texas), February 6, 1917, p. 1; "Red Cross Call Brings Women to Nation's Aid," *Chicago Tribune*, February 7, 1917, p. 3.
72. Eleanor Flexner interviewed Paul in 1956 and wrote that almost forty years later Paul continued to make this charge. Despite Flexner's "attempt to point out the mountain of evidence for continuous suffrage work by the 'National,' she [Paul] refused to budge from her position" (Flexner and Fitzpatrick, *Century of Struggle*, p. 377n16).
73. Alice Kessler-Harris, *Out to Work: A History of Wage-Earning Women in the United States* (New York: Oxford University Press, 1982), p. 219; Alice Dunbar Nelson, "The Negro Woman in War Work," in Emmett J. Scott, *The American Negro in the World War* (1919; rpt., New York: Arno Press, 1969), pp. 374–397.
74. Harriot Stanton Blatch, *Mobilizing Woman-Power* (New York: National Board of the Young Woman's Christian Association, 1918), p. 86.
75. The Marines enlisted women too, primarily to take over men's clerical jobs so the men could be sent to battle. See Captain Linda L. Hewitt, *Women Marines in World War I* (Washington, DC: History and Museums Division, U.S. Marine Corps, 1974). The Army enlisted several hundred women to go to France and become part of the Signal Corps as specialists in the new technology of telephone

switchboard operations. See Elizabeth Cobbs, The *Hello Girls: America's First Women Soldiers* (Cambridge, MA: Harvard University Press, 2017). See also Jean Ebbert and Mary-Beth Hall, *The First, the Few, the Forgotten: Navy and Marine Corps Women in World War I* (Annapolis, MD: Naval Institute Press, 2002); "a woman who works" quoted in Lettie Gavin, *American Women in World War I: They Also Served* (Niwot: University Press of Colorado, 1997).

76. Anna Howard Shaw, speech, "Select Your Own Principle of Life," folder 546, box 23, Shaw Papers.
77. Letter, Woodrow Wilson to Anna Howard Shaw, August 22, 1918, reel 17, Shaw Papers.
78. "More converts" quoted in Trisha Franzen, *Anna Howard Shaw: The Work of Suffrage* (Champaign: University of Illinois Press, 2014); "perhaps the strongest" quoted in "Dr. Anna Howard Shaw Loved Peace but Spent Much Time in Fighting," *Literary Digest*, August 16, 1919, p. 54; Anna Howard Shaw obituary, *New York Times*, July 4, 1919, p. 8; Anna Howard Shaw obituary, *The Nation*, July 12, 1919, p. 33.
79. Crystal Eastman, "Now We Can Begin," speech given December 1, 1920, and published in *The Liberator* (December 1920).

8.
THE "NEW WOMAN" AND "NEW WOMEN" IN A NEW CENTURY

1. "Feminists Debate Plans for a House," *New York Times*, April 22, 1914, p. 12.
2. Marie Jenney Howe, quoted in "Feminists Ask for Equal Chance: Leaders in Movement Discuss 'Breaking into the Human Race' at Cooper Union," *New York Times*, February 21, 1914, p. 18.
3. Women in the labor force: Sophonisba P. Breckinridge, *Women in the Twentieth Century: A Study of Their Political, Social, and Economic Activities* (New York: McGraw-Hill, 1933), p. 112. "Typewriters" was the original term for typists. Around the beginning of the twentieth century, women accounted for about 60 percent of stenographers and typewriters. Roslyn L. Feldberg discusses the initial prejudice against women clerical workers in "Union Fever: Organizing among Clerical Workers, 1900–1930," *Radical America*, 14/3 (May–June 1980), pp. 53–70.
4. "Imbided": Lydia Kingsmill Commander, *The American Idea: Does the National Tendency toward a Small Family Point to Race Suicide or Race Development?* (New York: A. S. Barnes, 1907), pp. 166, 165; Marion Harland, "The Passing of the Home Daughter," *The Independent*, 71 (July 13, 1911).
5. "I am trying": quoted in Nancy Cott, *The Grounding of Modern Feminism* (New Haven, CT: Yale University Press, 1987), p. 44; Dee Garrison, *Mary Heaton Vorse: The Life of an American Insurgent* (Philadelphia: Temple University Press, 1989), p. 87.
6. In the first U.S. sex survey, conducted between 1892 and 1920 (though it remained unpublished until 1980), Clelia Duel Mosher suggests that New Women

were not alone among women born in the Victorian era in valuing sexual pleasure (*The Mosher Survey* [New York: Arno Press, 1980]). Mosher, who interviewed forty-five women born in that era, quotes respondents' statements such as "a rational use of [sex] tends to keep people healthier." However, unlike New Women, Mosher's anonymous respondents did not make public pronouncements about sex. See also Carl Degler, "What Ought to Be and What Was: Women's Sexuality in the Nineteenth Century," *American Historical Review*, 79/5 (December 1974), pp. 1467–1490; *Ladies Home Journal*, 1918, quoted in James R. McGovern, "The American Woman's Pre–World War I Freedom in Manners and Morals," *Journal of American History*, 4/2 (September 1968), pp. 315–333; Ellen Carol DuBois and Linda Gordon, "Seeking Ecstasy on the Battlefield: Danger and Pleasure in Nineteenth-Century Feminist Thought," in *Pleasure and Danger: Exploring Female Sexuality*, ed. Carole S. Vance (Boston: Routledge and Kegan Paul, 1984), pp. 31–49.

7. Charlotte Perkins Gilman, *Women and Economics: A Study of the Economic Relation between Men and Women as a Factor in Social Evolution* (Boston: Small, Maynard, 1898), p. 32; Edward Carpenter, *Love's Coming of Age: A Series of Papers on the Relation of the Sexes* (1894), https://www.gutenberg.org/files/63081/63081-h/63081-h.htm.

8. Hutchins Hapgood, *A Victorian in the Modern World* (New York: Harcourt, 1939), p. 320.

9. "Furtiveness": Lois Palken Rudnick, *Mabel Dodge Luhan: New Woman, New Worlds* (Albuquerque: University of New Mexico Press, 1987), p. 90; "sexual freedom": Linda J. Lumsden, *Inez: The Life and Times of Inez Milholland* (Bloomington: Indiana University Press, 2014), p. 111.

10. William Lee Howard, "Effeminate Men and Masculine Women," *New York Medical Journal* (May 5, 1900), pp. 686–687. See also Lillian Faderman, *Surpassing the Love of Men: Romantic Friendship and Love between Women from the Renaissance to the Present* (New York: William Morrow, 1981), part 3A, chapter 3; Carroll Smith-Rosenberg, "The New Woman as Androgyne: Social Disorder and Gender Crisis, 1870–1936," in *Disorderly Conduct: Visions of Gender in Victorian America* (New York: Knopf, 1985), pp. 245–296.

11. Margaret Deland, "The Change in the Feminine Ideal," *Atlantic Monthly*, 105 (March 1910), pp. 290–302. See also Ruth Maxa Filer, *Margaret Deland: Writing toward Insight* (Bloomington, IN: Balboa Press, 2014).

12. Ann Marie Nicolosi suggests that feminist leaders thrust Milholland forward because her physical attractiveness disarmed even the enemies of woman suffrage and would "bring women into the movement who might fear the taint of masculinity and gender transgression" ("'The Most Beautiful Suffragette': Inez Milholland and the Political Currency of Beauty," *Journal of the Gilded Age and Progressive Era*, 6/3 [July 2007], pp. 286–309). Max Eastman, *Enjoyment of Living* (New York: Harper, 1948), pp. 298, 320.

13. "Vassar Girls in Two Plays," *New York Times*, December 13, 1908, p. 5; "Vassar Girls Aid Police," *The Sun* (New York), February 16, 1908, p. 1. See also, for example, "Vassar Girls Take Charge of Truants," *Oregon Daily Journal*, February 23,

1908, p. 15; "Vassar Girls Aid Police," *Baltimore Sun*, February 17, 1908, p. 2; "Vassar Girls Study Boys," *Brewster Record* (Kansas), March 13, 1908, p. 2; "Vassar Suffragist to Work in Japan," *Des Moines Register*, June 28, 1908, p. 23.

14. Taylor quoted in *The Outlook*, May 8, 1909, pp. 68–69; Dale Mezzacappa, "Vassar College and the Suffrage Movement," *Vassar Quarterly*, 69/3 (March 1, 1973), p. 108.

15. "No doubt": "Has Trained for Work," *St. Louis Globe-Democrat*, August 4, 1909, p. 6; "Society spell-binders": *South Bend Tribune*, December 29, 1909, p. 2; "Ardent Suffragette and Her Methods," *Miami News*, February 15, 1912, p. 1. "Sidelights," *Nebraska State Journal* (Lincoln), January 4, 1914, p. 43.

16. "Eastman, *Enjoyment of Living*, p. 324; "The American Joan of Arc Startles Her Many Admirers by Marrying a Mere Man," *Buffalo Sunday Morning News*, July 27, 1913, p. 18; "Just Like a Woman after All!," *St. Louis Post-Dispatch*, August 3, 1913, p. 46.

17. Lumsden, *Inez*, pp. 97–99.

18. "Her frequent speeches": "Mrs. Boissevain Very Ill," *New York Times*, October 26, 1916; "in the bloom": "Inez Boissevain," *Los Angeles Evening Express*, December 1, 1916, p. 12; "Men and Affairs," *Morning Call* (Altoona, Pennsylvania), December 1, 1916, p. 6.

19. Baron de Lahontan, *Nouveaux voyages dans l'Amerique* (1703), quoted in Richard White, *The Middle Ground: Indians, Empires, and Republics in the Great Lakes Region, 1650–1815* (1981; rpt., Cambridge: Cambridge University Press, 2010), p. 63; "half of humanity": quoted in Tadeusz Lewandowski, *Red Bird, Red Power: The Life and Legacy of Zitkala-Sa* (Norman: University of Oklahoma Press, 2016), p. 21.

20. The 1901 letters of Zitkala-Sa to Dr. Carlos Montezuma are reprinted in Doreen Rappaport, *The Flight of Red Bird: The Life of Zitkala-Sa* (New York: Puffin Books, 1999), pp. 113, 122. See also Ruth Spack, "Dis/Engagement: Zitkala-Sa's Letters to Carlos Montezuma," *MELUS: Multi-Ethnic Literature of the United States*, 26/1 (Spring 2001), pp. 173–204.

21. Reprinted in Rappaport, *The Flight of Red Bird*, pp. 91–92. See also Dorothy Ann Nason, "Red Feminist Literary Analysis: Reading Violence and Criminality in Contemporary Native Women's Writing," PhD diss., University of California, Berkeley, 2010, chapter 3.

22. Zitkala-Sa, "A Warrior's Daughter," *Everybody's Magazine* (April 1902), pp. 346–352.

23. Anna J. Cooper, *A Voice from the South by a Black Woman of the South* (Xenia, OH: Aldine, 1892), p. 21.

24. Treva Blaine Lindsey, "Configuring Modernities: New Negro Womanhood in the Nation's Capital, 1890–1940," PhD diss., Duke University, 2010, p. 51. The New Negro Woman is also discussed in Ann Heilmann, ed., *Feminist Forerunners: New Womanism and Feminism in the Early Twentieth Century* (Chicago: Pandora, 2003), part 2.

25. Fanny Barrier Williams, "The Woman's Part in a Man's Business," *Voice of the Negro*, 1/11 (November 1904), p. 545. Despite enchantment with such trappings of

True Womanhood, Williams was a well-known suffragist and the only Black woman invited to give a eulogy at the National American Woman Suffrage Association's memorial service for Susan B. Anthony.

26. Quoted in Malinda Alaine Lindquist, "'The World Will Always Want Men': Anna Julia Cooper, Womanly Black Manhood, and Predominant Man-Influence," *Left History*, 11/2 (Fall 2006), p. 42, n. 40.

27. Scholars have also called Cooper a "womanist," a preferred term for Black feminists since Alice Walker coined it in *In Search of Our Mother's Garden: Womanist Prose* (New York: Harcourt Brace, 1984), p. 15. "Womanist" is cognizant of the intersectional effect on Black women of race, sex, and class. See, for example, Mark S. Giles, "Dr. Anna Julia Cooper, 1858–1964: Teacher, Scholar, and Timeless Womanist," *Journal of Negro Education*, 75/4 (Fall, 2006), pp. 621–634; "seem thoroughly abreast": Cooper, *A Voice from the South*, p. 75; "blue-stocking debate": Cooper, *A Voice from the South*, p. 123; "impoverished": Cooper, *A Voice from the South*, p. 28.

28. "Mother heart" in Anna Howard Shaw, *The Story of a Pioneer* (New York: Harper and Bros., 1915), p. 124; Anna Julia Cooper, "The Status of Woman in America" (1892), in *Words of Fire: An Anthology of African-American Feminist Thought*, ed. Beverly Guy-Sheftall (New York: New Press, 1995), p. 44. Vivian M. May is critical of historians who present Cooper as a "pawn of true womanhood." She suggests that Cooper's "borrowing from True Womanhood discourse" is "a form of strategic redeployment," which put the members of her "privileged" audience at ease "by reassuring them of her confidence in their venerated beliefs" (*Anna Julia Cooper, Visionary Black Feminist: A Critical Introduction* [New York: Routledge, 2007] p. 69). Brittney C. Cooper develops a similar argument in *Beyond Respectability: The Intellectual Thought of Race Women* (Urbana: University of Illinois Press, 2017).

29. Anna J. Cooper, "Colored Women as Wage-Earners," *Southern Workman and Hampton School Record*, 28 (August 1899), pp. 295–298. For a discussion of Cooper's essay, see Shirley Wilson Logan, "What Are We Worth? Anna Julia Cooper Defines Black Women's Worth at the Dawn of the Twentieth Century," in *Sister Circle: Black Women and Work*, ed. Shirley Harley and the Black Women and Work Collective (New Brunswick, NJ: Rutgers University Press, 2002), pp. 146–161.

30. Claudia Goldin, "The Work and Wages of Single Women, 1870–1920," *Journal of Economic History*, 40/1 (March 1980), p. 81.

31. J. Clay Smith, "Black Women Lawyers: 125 Years at the Bar; 100 Years in the Legal Academy," *Howard Law Journal*, 40/2 (Winter 1997), pp. 366–372; J. Clay Smith, "Charlotte E. Ray Pleads before Court," *Howard Law Journal*, 43/2 (Winter 2000), pp. 121–139; Cecily Barker McDaniel, "'Fearing I Shall Not Do My Duty to My Race If I Remain Silent': Law and Its Call to African American Women, 1872–1932," PhD diss., Ohio State University, 2007, p. 105; U.S. Census, "Comparative Occupation Statistics, 1870–1930: A Comparable Series of Statistics Representing a Distribution of the Nation's Labor Force . . . ," part 2, table 15, p. 172, https://www2.census.gov/library/publications/decennial/1940/population

-occupation/00312147ch2.pdfhttps://www2.census.gov/library/publications/decennial/1940/population-occupation/00312147ch2.pdf.

32. From 1937 to 1945, Alexander served as a medical advisor for Howard University. See Virginia Margaret Alexander Papers, UPT 50 A374V, University of Pennsylvania Archives and Record Center, Philadelphia. See also W. E. B. DuBois, "Can a Colored Woman Be a Physician?," *The Crisis* (February 1933), pp. 33–34; Vanessa Northington Gamble, "Outstanding Services to Negro Health: Dr. Dorothy Boulding Ferebee, Dr. Virginia M. Alexander, and Black Women Physicians' Public Health Activism," *American Journal of Public Health*, 106/8 (August 2016), pp. 1397–1404.

33. Northward migration in Eddie S. Glaude Jr., *African American Religion* (New York: Oxford University Press, 2014), p. 58. See also Isabel Wilkerson, *The Warmth of Other Suns: The Epic Story of America's Great Migration* (New York: Vintage, 2011). Several scholars have argued that the rural Black women migrants to northern cities were the object of uplift attempts by middle-class Black women, who tried to inculcate in the rural women the Black True Women values of respectability. See Victoria W. Wolcott, *Remaking Respectability: African American Women in Interwar Detroit* (Chapel Hill: University of North Carolina Press, 2001); Jane Rhodes, "Pedagogies of Respectability: Race, Media, and Black Womanhood in the Early 20th Century," *Souls: A Critical Journal of Black Politics, Culture, and Society*, 18/2–4 (2016), pp. 201–214; Addie Hunter quoted in Jacqueline Jones, *Labor of Love, Labor of Sorrow: Black Women, Work, and the Family, from Slavery to the Present* (New York: Basic Books, 1985), p. 148; Martha H. Patterson, "'Chocolate Baby, A Story of Ambition, Deception, and Success': Refiguring the New Negro Woman in the *Pittsburgh Courier*," in *The New Woman International: Representations in Photography and Film from the 1870s through the 1960s*, ed. Elizabeth Otto and Vanessa Rocco (Ann Arbor: University of Michigan Press, 2011), p. 195.

34. Jacqueline Najuma Stewart discusses the impact of early twentieth-century movies on the Black community in *Migrating to the Movies: Cinema and Black Urban Modernity* (Berkeley: University of California Press, 2005).

35. "When we began" quoted in A'Lelia Perry Bundles, *On Her Own Ground: The Life and Times of Madam C. J. Walker* (New York: Washington Square Press, 2001), p. 137; "She hungered": Ruth Queen Smith, "Madame C. J. Walker (1867–1919): African American Entrepreneur, Philanthropist, Social Change Activist, and Educator of African-American Women," PhD diss., University of Tennessee, Knoxville, 2007, p. 69.

36. "Go back": "Madam Walker," *Pittsburgh Press*, October 10, 1909, p. 31; untitled biographical sketch, Madame C. J. Walker Papers, Indiana Historical Society, Indianapolis.

37. "Madam C. J. Walker, Noted Philanthropist, Lecturer, Traveler, and Most Wonderful Business Woman in the World," *Kansas City Sun* (Missouri), February 23, 1918, p. 1.

38. Quoted in Annalise Orleck, *Common Sense and a Little Fire: Women and Working-Class Politics in the U.S., 1900–1965* (Chapel Hill: University of North Carolina Press, 1995), p. 6.

39. Of the workers in the ladies' garment trade, 55 percent were eastern European Jewish immigrants, 35 percent were Italian, and 7 percent were native-born Americans. Of the participants in the Uprising of 20,000 (discussed below), 70 percent were Russian Jewish women, 20 percent were Russian Jewish men, and only 6 percent were Italian women. Meredith Tax suggests that so few Italian women participated in the strike because the organizers spoke mainly Yiddish (*The Rising of the Women: Feminist Solidarity and Class Conflict, 1880–1917* [1980; rpt., Champaign: University of Illinois Press, 2001], p. 211); "satisfied" quoted in "Teachers Scorned Idea of a Union," *New York Times*, April 5, 1907, p. 7. In 1903, two upper-middle-class sisters-in-law, Marie and Bessie Van Vorst, published an investigative study that seemed to confirm the union leaders' prejudices (*The Woman Who Toils: Being the Experiences of Two Gentlewomen as Factory Girls* [New York: Doubleday, 1903]). The Van Vorsts, disguised as working-class women, took jobs in a shoe factory, a textile mill, and a pickling factory. They claimed to have found that though the women's highest wages were lower than the men's lowest, their salary was not essential to them, as it was to the men: many of the women lived with their parents and made only small contributions to the household; some worked for luxuries such as nice clothes; and some were only semi-breadwinners. The authors concluded that "There will be no strikes among them as long as the question of wages is not vital to them" (p. 78). But as events proved, wages were vital to the self-supporting immigrant women who continued to come into the country. They were soon walking picket lines.

40. Clara Lemlich, "'Life in the Shop': The Story of an Immigrant Garment Worker," *New York Evening Journal*, November 28, 1909, https://shec.ashp.cuny.edu/items/show/507.

41. "Arrest Strikers for Being Assaulted," *New York Times*, November 5, 1909, p. 1; "Rowdies Attack and Seriously Injure Girls," *Arizona Daily Star* (Tucson), September 15, 1909, p. 1.

42. Louis Levine, *The Women's Garment Workers: A History of the International Ladies Garment Workers Union* (New York: B. W. Huebsch, 1925), p. 154; Clara Lemlich Shavelson, "Remembering the Waistmakers General Strike, 1909," ed. Morris U. Schappes, *Jewish Currents*, November 1982: https://archive.jewishcurrents.org/remembering-the-waistmakers-general-strike-1909/; Howard M[orley] Sachar, *A History of the Jews in America* (New York: Random House, 1992), p. 183.

43. "Girl Strikers Tell the Rich Their Woes," *New York Times*, December 16, 1909, p. 3; "Striking Girls Are Obdurate," *Evening Republican* (Meadville, Pennsylvania), November 24, 1909, p. 3; "Ah," quoted in Orlick, *Common Sense and a Little Fire*, p. 6.

44. The term "industrial feminists" was coined in 1915 to describe the college-educated women of the WTUL. See Mildred Moore, "A History of the Women's Trade Union League of Chicago," master's thesis, University of Chicago, 1915, p. 3. But it applies equally well to wage-earning women who demanded their rights as women and as workers, who were among the first intersectionalists; "We are learning" quoted in "Feminists Ask for Equal Chance," *New York Times*, Feb-

ruary 21, 1914, p. 18; "Why are you paid" quoted in Orleck, *Common Sense and a Little Fire*, p. 100.
45. See, for example, "Girl Strikers in Plymouth Church," *Standard Union* (Brooklyn, New York), January 21, 1910, p. 14.
46. "Something better" quoted in Alfred Allan Lewis, *Ladies and Not-So-Gentle Women: Elisabeth Marbury, Anne Morgan, Elsie de Wolf, Anne Vanderbilt, and Their Times* (New York: Penguin, 2000), p. 55; "born rebel" in Sylvia D. Hoffert, *Alva Vanderbilt Belmont: Unlikely Champion of Women's Rights* (Bloomington: Indiana University Press, 2012), p. 74; stirred by the strikers in Hoffert, *Alva Vanderbilt Belmont*, p. 79; "Upward of 100 Striking New York Shirt-Waist Workers and Non-Union Girls Engage in a Riot," *Boston Globe*, January 26, 1910, p. 16; "mink coat brigade" in Rose Schneiderman, *All for One* (New York: P. S. Eriksson, 1967), p. 8; David Von Drehle, *Triangle: The Fire That Changed America* (New York: Atlantic Monthly Press, 2003), pp. 52–53. The arrest of Inez Milholland while she was supporting the strikers is reported in "Girl Strikers Tell the Rich Their Woes." "Women to Rescue," *New York Tribune*, December 20, 1909, p. 2. I discuss several of the elite women of the WTUL in Lillian Faderman, *To Believe in Women: What Lesbians Have Done for America—A History* (Boston: Houghton Mifflin, 1999), chapter 6.
47. Colony Club in "Girl Strikers Tell the Rich Their Woes" and Rheta Childe Dorr, *What Eight Million Women Want* (Boston: Small, Maynard, 1910), p. 172; bail in Von Drehle, *Triangle*, p. 76; "Miss Taft and Girl Strikers," *The Sun* (New York), January 16, 1910, p. 1.
48. Ellen Carol DuBois, "Working Women, Class Relations, and Suffrage Militance: Harriot Stanton Blatch and the New York Woman Suffrage Movement, 1894–1909," *Journal of American History*, 74/1 (June 1987), pp. 34–58.
49. It was not until 1922 that the WTUL elected its first president not to have a college education, Maud O'Farrell Swartz. She was an Irish immigrant, proofreader, member of the International Typographical Union, and Schneiderman's life partner.
50. The strike was not entirely successful. The Triangle Shirtwaist Factory famously continued its inhumane treatment of workers. Doors were locked during the workday, supposedly to keep the workers from stealing the merchandise on which they worked. In 1911, a fire killed 146 women workers who could not escape the burning factory.
51. Orleck, *Common Sense and a Little Fire*, p. 53.
52. Felicity Barringer, "Journalism's Greatest Hits: Two Lists of a Century's Top Stories," *New York Times*, March 1, 1999, section C, p. 1.
53. Steve Weinberg, *Taking on the Trust: The Epic Battle of Ida Tarbell and John D. Rockefeller* (New York: W. W. Norton, 2008), pp. 69–70.
54. Ida M. Tarbell, "Woman as Inventor," *The Chautauquan*, 7/6 (March 1887), pp. 355–357.
55. Ida M. Tarbell, *The Business of Being a Woman* (New York: Macmillan, 1912). See also Robert Stinson, "Ida M. Tarbell and the Ambiguities of Feminism," *Pennsylvania Magazine of History and Biography*, 101/2 (April, 1977), pp. 217–239.

56. Ida M. Tarbell, *All in a Day's Work: An Autobiography* (New York: Macmillan, 1939), p. 32.
57. Tarbell, *The Business of Being a Woman*, p. 28.
58. Tarbell, *All in a Day's Work*, p. 36.
59. Quoted in Elaine Weiss, *The Woman's Hour: The Great Fight to Win the Vote* (New York: Penguin, 2019), p. 122.

9.
"IT'S SEX O'CLOCK IN AMERICA"

1. Peter Clark Macfarlane, "Diagnosis by Dreams," *Good Housekeeping*, 60/2 (February 1915), pp. 280–281; "Freud Declares That the Dream Is the Guardian of Sleep," *New York Tribune*, June 18, 1920, p. 6; "Glands and Emotions," *Tampa Tribune*, March 20, 1922, p. 6; *Dayton Daily News*, December 31, 1922, p. 64; "Freud Held Majority of Ills Mental," *Leader-Telegram* (Eau Claire, Wisconsin), July 28, 1929, p. 15.
2. Reedy's *St. Louis Mirror* article was quoted in "Sex O'Clock in America," *Current Opinion* (August 1913), p. 113.
3. "The Coming Woman," *New York Daily Herald*, April 2, 1870, p. 6.
4. "The time is approaching" is quoted in "The Woman Question," *Oskaloosa Independent* (Kansas), June 3, 1871, p. 2, in which the editors complain that Woodhull "reduces women (and men too) square down to the level of the beasts." "A Shameless Avowal," *Detroit Free Press*, May 27, 1871, p. 4; "Mistress Victoria Woodhull—Free Love Candidate," *Quad Times* (Davenport, Iowa), May 29, 1871, p. 4.
5. Thomas Nast cartoon in *Harper's Weekly*, February 17, 1872, p. 140.
6. "The principles" in Victoria Claflin Woodhull, "And the Truth Shall Make You Free: A Speech on the Principles of Social Freedom" (1871), reprinted in *Selected Writings of Victoria Woodhull: Suffrage, Free Love, and Eugenics*, ed. Cari M. Carpenter (Lincoln: University of Nebraska Press, 2010), pp. 51, 52; reports on the audience response to Woodhull's speech in "Mrs. Woodhull's Lecture," *New York Tribune*, November 21, 1871, and "Mrs. Woodhull's Lecture," *Chicago Tribune*, November 22, 1871. Woodhull and the Comstock Act: Helen Lefkowitz Horowitz, "Victoria Woodhull, Anthony Comstock, and the Conflict over Sex in the United States in the 1870s," *Journal of American History*, 87/2 (September 2000), pp. 403–434.
7. Joanne E. Passet, *Sex Radicals and the Quest for Women's Equality* (Champaign: University of Illinois Press, 2003), pp. 5, 57.
8. Angela Heywood, "The Ethics of Touch—Sex Unity," *The Word* (June 1889), p. 3; see also "Penis Literature—Onanism or Health?," *The Word* (April 1884), p. 2; Marshal Henry Cushing, *The Story of Our Post Office: The Greatest Government Department in All Its Phases* (Boston: A. M. Thayer, 1893), p. 613.
9. Angela Heywood, "Sex-Nomenclature—Plain English," *The Word* (April 1887), pp. 2–3. The Heywoods are discussed in Hal D. Sears, *The Sex Radicals: Free Love in Victorian America* (Lawrence: University Press of Kansas, 1977); Jesse F.

Batten, "The Word Made Flesh: Language, Authority, and Sexual Desire in Late Nineteenth-Century America," in *American Sexual Politics: Sex, Gender, and Race Since the Civil War*, ed. John C. Fout and Maura Shaw Tantillo (Chicago: University of Chicago Press, 1993), pp. 101–122; and Passet, *Sex Radicals and the Quest for Women's Equality*.

10. Clelia Duel Mosher, *The Mosher Survey: Sexual Attitudes of Forty-Five Victorian Women*, ed. James MaHood and Kristine Wenburg (New York: Arno Press, 1980), pp. 277, 416, 328, 138, 340.
11. See Carl Degler, "What Ought to Be and What Was: Women's Sexuality in the Nineteenth Century," *American Historical Review*, 79/5 (December 1974), pp. 1467–1490. Dr. Degler discovered Dr. Mosher's study in 1973.
12. Reedy quoted in "Sex O'Clock in America," 113.
13. "About eight thousand": William Marion Reedy, "The Daughter of the Dream," *St. Louis Mirror*; rpt. in *St. Louis Medical Review*, 57 (November 1908), pp. 401–402; "depth and glory": Emma Goldman, "Marriage and Love," in Emma Goldman, *Anarchism and Other Essays* (New York: Mother Earth Publishing, 1911), p. 10. Goldman originally presented the gist of these ideas in "What I Believe," *New York World*, July 19, 1908.
14. "Sex O'Clock in America," p. 113.
15. Clara E. Laughlin, *The Work-a-Day Girl: A Study of Some Present Conditions* (1913; rpt. New York: Arno Press, 1974), p. 62.
16. See Claudia Goldin, "The Work and Wages of Single Women, 1870–1920," *Journal of Economic History*, 40/1 (March 1980), pp. 81–88; and Kathy Peiss, *Cheap Amusements: Working Women and Leisure in Turn-of-the-Century New York* (Philadelphia: Temple University Press, 1986). Joanne J. Meyerowitz suggests that it was early twentieth-century working women who "helped chart the modern sexual terrain," even teaching bohemians "new sexual possibilities" (*Women Adrift: Independent Wage Earners in Chicago, 1880–1930* [Chicago: University of Chicago Press, 1991], p. 116).
17. Barbara Meil Hobson, *Uneasy Virtue: The Politics of Prostitution and the American Reform Tradition* (New York: Basic Books, 1987), p. 140.
18. Ruth M. Alexander discusses the enforcement by middle-class elites of laws that punished working girls perceived to be wayward (*The "Girl Problem": Female Sexual Delinquency in New York, 1900–1930* [Ithaca, NY: Cornell University Press, 1995]).
19. Peiss discusses various other sexualized retreats for turn-of-the-century working-class women, including amusement parks that featured rides such as the Barrel of Love, which forced participants' bodies into contact, and the Dew Drop, which caused skirts to fly up and reveal thighs (*Cheap Amusements*, pp. 134–135).
20. "The dance hall" in Rheta Childe Dorr, *A Woman of Fifty* (New York: Funk and Wagnalls, 1924), p. 101. As a muckraking journalist, Dorr had gone undercover to work as a salesclerk, laundress, seamstress, and assembly line worker, as she reported in a six part series coauthored with William Hard, titled "The Woman's Invasion," in *Everybody's Magazine* (part I: October 1908, pp. 579–591; part II: December 1908, pp. 798–810; part III: January 1909, pp. 73–85; part IV:

February 1909, pp. 236–248; part V: March 1909, pp. 372–385; part VI: April 1909, pp. 521–532.) The experiences did not give her confidence in the ability of young women of the laboring class to control their sexuality; "a straight chute" in Rheta Childe Dorr, *What Eight Million Women Want* (Boston: Small, Maynard and Company, 1910), p. 209; "There are very few" in E. Norine Law, *The Shame of a Great Nation: The Story of the "White Slave Trade"* (Harrisburg, PA: United Evangelical Publishing House, 1909), pp. 192–193. The silent movies took up the theme, too. One example is George Loane, dir., *Traffic in Souls* (New York: Universal Film Manufacturing Company, 1913), in which an irresponsible young woman is taken by a villain to a dance hall where he plies her with liquor, encourages her to dance with a stranger, and then abducts her to a brothel.

21. Charles Nesbitt describes "slumming" in New York City in the 1880s and 1890s in his unpublished autobiography, including visits to hangouts for "perverts of both sexes" such as Walhalla Hall (quoted in Jonathan Katz, *Gay/Lesbian Almanac: A New Documentary* [New York: Harper and Row, 1983], pp. 218–219).

22. Mary Casal [Ruth Fuller Field], *The Stone Wall: An Autobiography* (Chicago: Eyncourt Press, 1930), pp. 165, 185.

23. I discuss the sexologists' pathologizing of female same-sex relations in Lillian Faderman, *Surpassing the Love of Men: Romantic Friendship and Love between Women from the Renaissance to the Present* (New York: William Morrow, 1981), pp. 239–253.

24. Louise DeKoven Bowen and the Juvenile Protective Association of Chicago, *The Girl Employed in Hotels and Restaurants* (Chicago: Hale-Crossely, 1912), pp. 7, 9. Official government reports also emphasized that working girls were exposed to advances they did not welcome but might feel forced to accept. The reports presented story after story of working women's vulnerability: bosses who were married but promised their girl workers a raise in return for a date; waitresses who were constantly subjected to familiarities by customers and finally felt that unless they permitted such familiarities, they "stood no show of getting any tips" (*Wage-Earning Women in Stores and Factories*, vol. 5 of *Report on the Condition of Women and Child Wage-Earners in the United States*, prepared under the direction of Charles P. Neill [Washington, DC: Government Printing Office, 1910], pp. 75–76).

25. Laughlin, *The Work-a-Day Girl*, p. 62.

26. Laughlin, *The Work-a-Day Girl*, p. 50. It was true that working girls could seldom afford diversions on their own. A female sweatshop worker or salesgirl might earn as little as $3.50 a week. Room and board in a shabby boardinghouse or a YWCA cost at least $2.50 a week. If she had to take a streetcar to work or save up to buy a hat or winter coat, she had little left to spend on fun. A male sweatshop worker might earn as much as $16 a week, and he could afford to be generous with a compliant date. See Sadie Frowne, "The Story of a Sweatshop Girl," *The Independent*, 54 (September 25, 1902), pp. 2279–2282; "A Salesgirl's Story," *The Independent*, 54 (May–August 1902), pp. 1818–1821.

27. Neill, *Wage-Earning Women*, p. 76.

28. Evelyn Brooks Higginbotham writes about the "bourgeois vision" of Black women reformers, particularly within the church, who cleaved to a "politics of respectability" not only to promote racial uplift but also to counter negative stereotypes of Black people among whites (*Righteous Discontent: The Women's Movement in the Black Baptist Church, 1880–1920* [Cambridge, MA: Harvard University Press, 1994], p. 15); "Politics of Respectability," chapter 7, pp. 185–230; "developing the best": quoted in "Negro Conference Ended," *New York Times*, July 24, 1897, p. 5; "watch over": quoted in Steve Kramer, "Uplifting Our 'Downtrodden Sisterhood': Victoria Earle Matthews and New York City's White Rose Mission, 1897–1907," *Journal of African American History*, 91/3 (Summer 2006), 243. White women reformers were also concerned with young Black women from the South coming north and being lured into prostitution. Frances A. Kellor, a prominent investigator into abuses of women, wrote in 1905 about the need for preventive measures regarding the naïve and helpless southern negro woman brought north on promises of easy work, lots of money, and good times. Kellor laments that such a woman very soon ends up working in a sporting house: "Southern Colored Girls in the North," *Bulletin of the Inter-Municipal Committee on Household Research*, 1/7 (May 1905), pp. 5–9.
29. Quoted in Hallie Q. Brown, *Homespun Heroines and Other Women of Distinction* (Xenia, OH: Aldine, 1926), p. 214.
30. Hunter quoted in Hazel V. Carby, "Policing the Black Woman's Body in an Urban Context," *Critical Inquiry*, 18/4 (Summer 1992), p. 745.
31. New York State Reformatory for Women at Bedford Hills case file: quoted in Saidiya Hartman, *Wayward Lives, Beautiful Experiments: Intimate Histories of Riotous Black Girls, Troublesome Women, and Queer Radicals* (New York: Norton, 2019), p. 63.
32. Quoted in Frederick Lewis Allen, *Only Yesterday: An Informal History of the 1920s* (New York: Harper and Row, 1931), p. 88.
33. Alyse Gregory, "The Changing Morality of Women," *Current History* (November 1923), 298–299; "A Dissent from Mrs. Elizabeth Tilton, Chairman of the Legislative Committee of the Parents' and Teachers' Association," *Current History* (March 1924), p. 1126. Commentary on "The Changing Morality of Women," *Social Hygiene Bulletin*, 10 (1924), pp. 57–58.
34. Paula S. Fass discusses the shift in concern to middle-class young women in *The Damned and the Beautiful: American Youth in the 1920s* (New York: Oxford University Press, 1977), chapter 1; Charlotte Perkins Gilman, "The New Generation of Women," *Current History* (August 1923), pp. 736–737.
35. Donald Ramsey Young, "Motion Pictures: A Study in Social Legislation," PhD diss., University of Pennsylvania, 1922, p. 31; ads quoted in Allen, *Only Yesterday*, p. 88.
36. "A Sensational Story of Jazz-Mad Youngsters," *Daily Times* (Davenport, Iowa), December 1, 1923, p. 9; "Plays and Players," *Weekly Iberville South News* (Plaquemine, Louisiana), February 23, 1924, p. 3; *Demopolis Times* (Alabama), February 21, 1924, p. 5. In the midst of the Depression, under the pressure of government censorship and boycotts by the Catholic Church, Hollywood agreed to

adopt the Motion Picture Production Code, promising that films would cease to "lower the moral standards of those who see [them]" and that the audience's sympathy would never "be thrown on the side of crime, wrongdoing, evil, or sin" ("Ethical Code to Be Enforced," *Congressional Record—House*, June 13, 1933, pp. 5906–5907). Joshua Zeitz, looking at the documented behavior of girls from small towns in the 1920s, argues that the flapper, who epitomized the new morality, "was every bit as much a small town as a big city phenomenon" (*Flapper: A Madcap Story of Sex, Style, Celebrity, and the Women Who Made America Modern* [New York: Three Rivers Press, 2006], p. 79). For a study of flappers in conservative Salt Lake City, Utah, see Bree Ann Romero, "Sinners in the City of Saints: Flappers in Salt Lake City," MA thesis, Utah State University, 2014.

37. Vicki Ruiz, *From out of the Shadows: Mexican Women in Twentieth-Century America* (New York: Oxford University Press, 1998), chapter 3.
38. "How Do You Kiss," *La Opinion*, May 9, 1927, quoted in Ruiz, *From out of the Shadows*, p. 67.
39. Judy Yung, *Unbound Feet: A Social History of Chinese Women in San Francisco* (Berkeley: University of California Press, 1995), chapter 3.
40. Quoted in Yung, *Unbound Feet*, p. 171.
41. Quoted in James R. McGovern, "The American Woman's Pre–World War I Freedom in Manners and Morals," *Journal of American History*, 55 (September 1968), p. 324.
42. Sigmund Freud, Lecture V, "Five Lectures Given at the Twentieth Anniversary of the Founding of Clark University" (1909), *American Journal of Psychology*, 21/2 (April 1910), p. 218; "a giant": quoted in Vivian Gornick, *Emma Goldman: Revolution as a Way of Life* (New Haven, CT: Yale University Press, 2011), p. 56.
43. Mari Jo Buhle, *Feminism and Its Discontents: A Century of Struggle with Psychoanalysis* (Cambridge, MA: Harvard University Press, 1998), p. 24.
44. Candace Falk, *Love, Anarchy, & Emma Goldman: A Biography* (New Brunswick, NJ: Rutgers University Press, 1984).
45. Margaret Sanger, "Suppression," *The Woman Rebel*, 1/4 (June 1914), p. 25.
46. Dennis Wepman, "No Gods, No Masters," in *Big Town, Big Time: A New York Epic: 1898–1998*, ed. Jay Maeder (New York: Daily News, 1999), p. 42.
47. Margaret H. Sanger, *Family Limitation* (New York: self-published, 1914), p. 2.
48. In her autobiography, Sanger says that she returned to New York after her husband, tricked into giving a copy of *Family Limitation* to an undercover policeman, had been arrested and sentenced to prison (*Margaret Sanger: An Autobiography* [New York: W. W. Norton, 1938], chapter 14).
49. "Clinic Opened Here for Birth Control; Challenges Police," *Brooklyn Daily Eagle*, October 22, 1916, p. 1.
50. "Large of build": Sanger, *Margaret Sanger*, p. 227; "Mrs. Sanger Fights as Police Seize Her in Raid on 'Clinic,'" *Brooklyn Daily Eagle*, October 26, 1916, p. 1.
51. Quoted in "A Birth Control Decision," *Medical Times* (May 1917), p. 142.
52. Quoted in "A Birth Control Decision," *Medical Times* (May 1917), p. 142.

53. "I feel ready" quoted in Vicki Cox, *Margaret Sanger: Rebel for Women's Rights* (Philadelphia: Chelsea House, 2005), p. 66; Margaret Sanger, *Woman and the New Race* (New York: Eugenics Publishing, 1920), pp. 25–26, 204, 191.
54. "A glorious 'chain'": Margaret Sanger, *My Fight for Birth Control* (New York: Farrar and Rinehart, 1931), p. 136; Katharine Bement Davis, *Factors in the Sex Life of Twenty-Two Hundred Women* (New York: Harper and Brothers, 1929), pp. 374, 377; Peter C. Engleman, *A History of the Birth Control Movement in America* (Santa Barbara, CA: ABC-CLIO, 2011), p. 144; "Margaret Sanger Dares to Tell the Truth about Birth Control," *Montgomery Advertiser* (Alabama), April 29, 1923, p. 31; "Margaret Sanger Dares to Speak Frankly about Birth Control," *Capper's Weekly* (Topeka, Kansas), February 24, 1924, p. 21; "Sees Birth Control Movement Increasing Here: Family Limitation Favored by Many Doctors, Says Founder," *Ogden Standard-Examiner* (Utah), December 9, 1928, p. 17.
55. Dorothy Parker, "The Flapper," *The New York Life*, January 26, 1922, p. 22.
56. "The corset" quoted in Bruce Bliven, "Flapper Jane," *New Republic*, September 9, 1925, http://arcadiasystems.org/academia/flapperjane.html. James McGovern contrasts the flapper to the Gibson Girl of the previous generation in "The American Woman's Pre–World War I Freedom in Manners and Morals," p. 324.
57. Student quoted in "The Case against the Younger Generation," *Literary Digest*, June 17, 1922, p. 51; *Life* magazine cover by John Held Jr., October 1, 1925.
58. Joanne J. Meyerowitz, *Women Adrift: Independent Wage Earners in Chicago, 1880–1930* (Chicago: University of Chicago Press, 1991), p. xxiii; Ade quoted in Moira Weigel, *Labor of Love: The Invention of Dating* (New York: Farrar, Straus and Giroux, 2016), p. 12.
59. A rare exception among Chinese American women in the 1920s was Flora Belle Jan, a journalist and self-identified flapper who learned flapper ways as a student at the University of California, Berkeley, and the University of Chicago (*Unbound Spirit: Letters of Flora Belle Jan*, ed. Fleur Yano and Saralyn Daly [Champaign: University of Illinois Press, 2010]). At her death in 1950, her daughters had inscribed on her gravestone that she was a "feminist before her time" (*Unbound Spirit*, p. xviii). "The 'Flapper' Age" and "Not a Flapper Mother," *Chicago Defender*, July 29, 1922.
60. "Sex-race marketplace": Erin D. Chapman, *Prove It on Me: New Negroes, Sex, and Popular Culture in the 1920s* (New York: Oxford University Press, 2012), p. 7; "synonym": John B. Kennedy, "So This Is Harlem," *Collier's*, October 28, 1933, p. 27.
61. Trixie Smith, "My Man Rocks Me" lyrics, https://davidsuisman.net/?page_id=437.
62. "Mama's Gone, Goodbye," https://adp.library.ucsb.edu/index.php/matrix/detail/2000029819/140053-Mamas_gone_goodbye.
63. Davis, *Factors in the Sex Life of Twenty-Two Hundred Women*, p. 247. See also my analysis of Davis's findings in Faderman, *Surpassing the Love of Men*, pp. 326–327.
64. Ma Rainey, "Down in the Basement," https://www.youtube.com/watch?v=g1FwWhBj7hY; Rainey, "Southern Blues," https://www.youtube.com/watch?v

=zkpJFSsR1a0; Rainey, "Prove It on Me Blues," https://www.youtube.com/watch?v=yRyaUcVfhak. Angela Davis points to Rainey's "Prove It on Me Blues" as a prime example of a Black woman affirming her independence from her community's "orthodox norms of womanhood" (*Blues Legacies and Black Feminism: Gertrude "Ma" Rainey, Bessie Smith, and Billie Holiday* [New York: Vintage Books, 1998], pp. 39–40). Lucille Bogan, "Coffee Grindin' Blues," https://www.youtube.com/watch?v=BVbtxztXUks; Bogan, "B.D. Woman's Blues," https://www.youtube.com/watch?v=_nmrWB1ovQo. See also my discussion of lesbian sexuality in Harlem and Greenwich Village in Lillian Faderman, *Odd Girls and Twilight Lovers: A History of Lesbian Life in Twentieth-Century America* (New York: Columbia University Press, 1991), chapter 3.

65. "Mere presence" quoted in Jill Norgren, *Belva Lockwood: The Woman Who Would Be President* (New York: New York University Press, 2007), p. 42; College administrators quoted in "The Case against the Younger Generation," pp. 59, 51, 52; "Flapper Daughters Cause of Suicide," *Urbana Daily Courier* (Illinois), December 16, 1925.

66. Mildred Adams, "Now We Can Say Farewell to the Flapper," *New York Times*, January 20, 1929, p. 10; *Ladies' Home Journal* quoted in Kathy Peiss, *Hope in a Jar: The Making of America's Beauty Culture* (1998; rpt., Philadelphia: University of Pennsylvania Press, 2011), p. 130.

67. Cardinal O'Connell quoted in "Cardinal Raps Public Filth," *Los Angeles Times*, April 28, 1938, p. 9; Emily Post, *Etiquette in Society, in Business, in Politics, and at Home*, rev. ed. (New York: Funk and Wagnalls, 1937), p. 355. See also Cas Wouters, *Sex and Manners: Female Emancipation in the West, 1890–2000* (Thousand Oaks, CA: Sage, 2004), pp. 98–100.

68. Robert S. Lynd and Helen Merrell Lynd, *Middletown in Transition* (New York: Harcourt Brace Jovanovich, 1937), pp. 170–175.

69. Engleman, *A History of the Birth Control Movement in America*, p. 167; Andrea Tone, *Devices and Desires: A History of Contraceptives in America* (New York: Hill and Wang, 2001), pp. 151–152.

10.

WOMAN ON A SEESAW

1. Norman Cousins, "Will Women Lose Their Jobs?," *Current History and Forum* (September 1939), p. 14.

2. Katherine Gauss Jackson, "Must Married Women Work?," *Scribner's* (April 1935), pp. 240–241.

3. Phyllis Blanchard and Carolyn Manasses, *New Girls for Old* (New York: Macaulay Company, 1930), pp. 237–238. Retrograde as their views of working women were, Blanchard and Manasses, good Freudians, were able to acknowledge that "after hundreds of years of mild complaisance to wifely duties, modern women have awakened to knowledge that they are sexual beings" (p. 196). See also Frank Stricker's critique of Blanchard and Manasses in "Cookbooks and Law Books:

4. "Narrow": Jane Allen, "You May Have My Job: A Feminist Discovers Her Home," *The Forum*, 87 (April 1932), p. 228; Jackson, "Must Married Women Work?," pp. 240, 241; Frank L. Hopkins, "Should Wives Work?," *American Mercury*, 39 (December 1936), pp. 409–416.
5. Quoted in Jennifer Barker-Devine, "'Make Do or Do Without': Women during the Great Depression," in *Great Depression: People and Perspectives*, ed. Hamilton Cravens and Peter C. Mancall (Santa Barbara, CA: ABC-CLIO, 2009), p. 56.
6. "Wages and Hours of Labor," in *Handbook of Labor Statistics*, Bulletin no. 616 (Washington, DC: Department of Labor, 1936), p. 876. Alice Kessler-Harris discusses the benefits for white women of labor segregation by gender in *Out to Work: A History of Wage-Earning Women in the United States* (New York: Oxford University Press, 1982), chapter 9.
7. Janet M. Hooks, "Women's Occupations through Seven Decades," Women's Bureau Bulletin 218 (Washington, DC: U.S. Department of Labor, 1947).
8. Susan Ware, *Holding Their Own: American Women in the 1930s* (Boston: Twayne, 1982), p. 7.
9. Single women: Ware, *Holding Their Own*, p. 7; "a fanatical pride": Willis J. Ballinger, "Spinster Factories: Why I Would Not Send a Daughter to College," *The Forum and Century*, 87/5 (May 1932), p. 303.
10. Ballinger, "Spinster Factories," pp. 304–305.
11. Mary Woolley, "Inaugural Address," May 15, 1901, Compass, https://compass.five colleges.edu/object/mtholyoke:20734.
12. Tiziana Rota, "Between 'True Women' and 'New Women': Mount Holyoke Students, 1837–1908," PhD diss., University of Massachusetts, Amherst, 1983; Mary E. Cookingham, "Bluestockings, Spinsters and Pedagogues: Women College Graduates, 1865–1910," *Population Studies*, 38 (1984), 349–364; Barbara Miller Solomon, *In the Company of Educated Women: A History of Women and Higher Education in America* (New Haven, CT: Yale University Press, 1985), p. 120. I discuss Woolley's presidency at greater length in Lillian Faderman, *To Believe in Women: What Lesbians Have Done for America—A History* (Boston: Houghton Mifflin, 1999), chapter 12.
13. Newton D. Baker, et al., "The Complete Roster of America's Greatest Women," *Good Housekeeping* (March 1931), p. 17.
14. "What Would Mary Lyon Say?," *Boston Sunday Globe*, February 7, 1937, p. 1. "Dr. Woolley Opposes Male Successor," *Newsweek*, February 13, 1937; "There are too many" quoted in Penina Migdal Glazer and Miriam Slater, *Unequal Colleagues: The Entrance of Women into the Professions, 1890–1940* (New Brunswick, NJ: Rutgers University Press, 1987), pp. 259–260.
15. Eleanor Roosevelt, "Women Must Learn to Play the Game as Men Do," *Redbook*, 50 (April 1928), p. 78.
16. Anna Howard Shaw, *The Story of a Pioneer* (New York: Harper and Brothers, 1915), p. 124; ER's ambition for mother heart values to become part of mainstream

politics was encouraged by several politically savvy women couples with whom ER became close friends in the early 1920s. See Blanche Wiesen Cook, *Eleanor Roosevelt*, vol. 1, *The Early Years, 1884–1933* (New York: Viking Penguin, 1992), pp. 319–328, 383–386.

17. "Champion of the underdog": Eleanor Roosevelt, "The Seven People Who Shaped My Life," *Look*, 15 (July 19, 1951), p. 54; "anti-suffragette" in Joseph P. Lash, *Eleanor and Franklin: The Story of Their Relationship* (New York: Norton, 1971), p. 192.
18. Quoted in Zoe Beckley, "Mrs. F. D. Roosevelt, T.R.'s Niece, Democratic Convert," *The Times* (Shreveport, LA), August 22, 1920, p. 17.
19. Cook, *Eleanor Roosevelt*, 1:349–350.
20. 1924 Democratic Party Platform, https://www.presidency.ucsb.edu/documents/1924-democratic-party-platform.
21. Eleanor Roosevelt, "Women Must Learn to Play the Game as Men Do," *Redbook*, 50 (April 1928), pp. 78–79.
22. Statistics in Martin Gruberg, *Women in American Politics: An Assessment and Sourcebook* (Oshkosh, WI: Academia Press, 1968), p. 9; "Fisher Analyzes Hoover's Victory," *New York Times*, November 25, 1928, section 2, p. 1.
23. The intimate relationship between ER and Hickok has been widely discussed since the publication of Doris Faber's *The Life of Lorena Hickok, E.R.'s Friend* (New York: William Morrow, 1980). See, for example, Lillian Faderman, *Surpassing the Love of Men: Romantic Friendship and Love between Women from the Renaissance to the Present* (New York: William Morrow, 1981), pp. 310–311; and Susan Quinn, *Eleanor and Hick: The Love Affair That Shaped the First Lady* (New York: Random House, 2016); "the final one" in Maurine H. Beasley, *Women of the Washington Press: Politics, Prejudice, and Persistence* (Evanston, IL: Northwestern University Press, 2012), pp. 57–58.
24. Eleanor Roosevelt, "Women in Politics," *Good Housekeeping*, three-part article: January, pp. 19, 150; March, pp. 45, 68; and April 1940, pp. 45, 201.
25. Elsie L. George, "The Women Appointees of the Roosevelt and Truman Administrations: A Study of Their Impact and Effectiveness," PhD diss., American University, 1972; "the General" quoted in Frances M. Seeber, "Eleanor Roosevelt and Women in the New Deal: A Network of Friends," *Presidential Studies Quarterly*, 20/4 (Fall 1990), p. 708; "America's first female boss": Susan Ware, *Partner and I: Molly Dewson, Feminism, and New Deal Politics* (New Haven, CT: Yale University Press, 1987), xi. See also John Thomas McGuire, "'Beginning an Extraordinary Opportunity': Eleanor Roosevelt, Molly Dewson, and the Expansion of Women's Boundaries in the Democratic Party, 1924–1934," *Women's History Review*, 23/6 (2014), 922–937; "The matter" quoted in Ware, *Holding Their Own*, p. 91.
26. Perkins quoted in Cook, *Eleanor Roosevelt*, 1:385; "Do something" quoted in George Martin, *Madam Secretary: Frances Perkins* (Boston: Houghton Mifflin, 1976), p. 64; Drew Pearson, "Merry-Go-Round," *Miami Herald*, January 17, 1938, p. 6.
27. Blanche Wiesen Cook, *Eleanor Roosevelt*, vol. 2, *The Defining Years, 1933–1938* (New York: Viking, 1999), p. 161.

28. Quoted in Elaine M. Smith, "Mary McLeod Bethune and the National Youth Administration," in *Clio Was a Woman: Studies in the History of American Women*, ed. Mabel E. Deutrich and Virginia C. Purdy (Washington, DC: Howard University Press, 1980), pp. 149–177.
29. Ronald W. Walters and Robert C. Smith, *African American Leadership* (Albany: State University of New York Press, 1999), p. 112.
30. Perkins even had a health-care-for-all proposal, which was defeated by the powerful American Medical Association because such a system of care would have intruded into private medical practices.
31. Geraldine Sartain and Evelyn Seeley, "The Forgotten Woman," *New York World-Telegram*, October 18, 1932.
32. "The forgotten man" quoted in Amity Shlaes, *The Forgotten Man: A New History of the Great Depression* (New York: HarperCollins, 2007), p. 127; "Hardest time of all" quoted in Michael Golay, *America 1933: The Great Depression, Lorena Hickok, Eleanor Roosevelt, and the Shaping of the New Deal* (New York: Simon and Schuster, 2013), p. 190.
33. Jane Kahramanidis, "The She-She-She Camps of the Great Depression," *History* (February–March 2008), pp. 13–16.
34. Cartoon in *Tampa Tribune*, November 26, 1936, p. 9; "Come and Get It," *Times-News* (Hendersonville, NC), December 7, 1936, p. 2.
35. Hilda W. Smith, "Relief Camps Aid Women," *New York Times*, June 14, 1936.
36. Samuel Milton Elam, "Lady Hoboes," *New Republic* (January 1930), pp. 164–169.
37. Jeane Westin, *Making Do: How Women Survived the '30s* (Chicago: Follett Publishing, 1976), pp. 157–159. Westin includes interviews with several women who were hoboes; "Men on the road" quoted in Walter C. Reckless, "Why Women Become Hoboes," *American Mercury*, 31 (February 1934), p. 178. See also Thomas Minehan, "Girls of the Road," *Independent Woman*, 13 (October 1934), pp. 316–317.
38. See William N. Eskridge Jr., *Gaylaw: Challenging the Apartheid of the Closet* (Cambridge, MA: Harvard University Press, 1999), chapter 1; J. R. Roberts identified these hoboes as "lesbian" ("Lesbian Hoboes: Their Lives and Times," *Dyke* [1977], pp. 36–50). Terms such as "transgender," "transman," and "genderqueer" were not yet in use in the 1970s.
39. Ben Reitman claimed that there were well over 13,000 women hoboes (*Sister of the Road: The Autobiography of Boxcar Bertha* [1937; rpt., Chico, CA: AK Press, 2002], p. 8). Despite the title, this "autobiography" was written by Reitman and was based on a composite of the lives of three women hoboes that Reitman, a physician, met during his own hobo years. The theory that unemployment was the main reason women become hoboes was challenged by Reckless, a criminologist, in "Why Women Become Hoboes." Unemployment statistics in William A. Sundstrom, "Last Hired, First Fired? Unemployment and Urban Black Workers during the Great Depression," *Journal of Economic History*, 52/2 (June 1992), p. 417. Female hoboes were not unknown in the late nineteenth century. Some had been anarchists and were escaping from the social strictures they despised. They often traveled with like-minded men and set up temporary homes in hobo

camps, or "hobohemias"—where, ironically, they did the cooking and the laundry, just as women did who seldom crossed the threshold of their domestic sphere. Other nineteenth-century female hoboes were like Mountain Charley, the gold prospector of the mid-nineteenth century (see chapter 5). They craved freedom to live their lives as men, which they could do more easily on the road, incognito, than they could at home. When they worked it was as migrant laborers, in men's jobs. Cities and towns across America already had "cross-dressing" laws, and if these female hoboes were discovered, they were in trouble, as the *Minneapolis Tribune* reported in the 1886 case of a twenty-three-year-old "poor Swede girl," hired by a dairyman to herd cattle and "do men's work." When arrested the "Swede" claimed to be wearing men's clothes "without knowing that she was offending against the law (Tim Cresswell, *The Tramp in America* [London: Reaktion Books, 2001], p. 88).

40. "Sense of power" quoted in Reckless, "Why Women Become Hoboes," p. 179.
41. Poster, "The More Women at Work the Sooner We Win!" (c. 1943), Library of Congress Prints and Photographs Division, https://www.loc.gov/pictures/item/2017872004/.
42. Eleanor F. Straub, "Women in the Civilian Labor Force," in Deutrich and Purdy, *Clio Was a Woman*, pp. 206–226; In practice, equal pay could be elusive. Despite the Rosie the Riveter image, even during the war there was often labor segregation by gender. In the factories of major industrial cities such as Detroit, for example, more than half of the women workers were clustered in only five of seventy-two job classifications, and only 11 percent of the men workers were employed in the predominantly female classifications. See Ruth Milkman, *Gender at Work: The Dynamics of Job Segregation by Sex during World War II* (Champaign: University of Illinois Press, 1987), p. 56; Women in the work force: Kessler-Harris, *Out to Work*, p. 274; and Susan M. Hartmann, *The Homefront and Beyond: American Women in the 1940s* (Boston: Twayne, 1982), p. 42.
43. "GARBO IN PANTS!," quoted in Mercedes de Acosta, *Here Lies the Heart* (1968; rpt., New York: Arno Press, 1975), p. 229; Associated Press, "Dietrich Defends Use of Pants to Hide Legs," *Charlotte Observer* (North Carolina), June 24, 1937, p. 7; "Fair Pantists to Feel Kick," *Pittsburgh Post-Gazette*, March 3, 1933, p. 24.
44. United States Employment Service, "COME ON, WOMEN . . . ," n.d., Calisphere, https://calisphere.org/item/e62fc644218249791150e655f3322def/; J. Howard Miller, "We Can Do It!," ca. 1942, National Museum of American History, https://americanhistory.si.edu/collections/search/object/nmah_538122.
45. Redd Evans and John Jacob Loeb, "Rosie the Riveter," 1942, https://www.youtube.com/watch?v=55NCElsbjeQ.
46. Richard Santillan, "Rosita the Riveter: Midwest Mexican American Women during World War II, 1941–1945," *Perspectives in Mexican American Studies*, 2 (1989), pp. 115–146.
47. Naomi Quinonez, "Rosita the Riveter: Welding Tradition with Wartime Transformations," in *Mexican Americans and World War II*, ed. Maggie Rivas-Rodriguez (Austin: University of Texas Press, 2005), pp. 245–268.

48. Jean Reynolds, "Mexican American Women in 1930s' Phoenix: Coming of Age during the Great Depression," *Journal of Arizona History*, 47/3 (Autumn 2006), p. 229; "Who's going to hire you?" quoted in Vicki L. Ruiz, "The Acculturation of Young Mexican American Women," in *Major Problems in Mexican American History*, ed. Zaragosa Vargas (Boston: Houghton Mifflin, 1999), p. 266.

49. Time-and-a-half: Santillan, "Rosita the Riveter," pp. 126–127; Morales quoted in Sherna Berger Gluck, *Rosie the Riveter Revisited: Women, the War, and Social Change* (Boston: Twayne, 1987), pp. 226, 228. Patricia Portales finds a similar impact on Mexican American women who worked in the defense industry in San Antonio: "Tejanes on the Homefront: Women, Bombs, and the (Re)Gendering of War in Mexican American World War II Literature," in *Latinas/os and World War II: Mobility, Agency, and Ideology*, ed. Maggie Rivas-Rodriguez and B. V. Olguin (Austin: University of Texas Press, 2014), pp. 175–178; Salazar quoted in Gluck, *Rosie the Riveter Revisited*, pp. 71, 74.

50. Leti Volpp, "Divesting Citizenship: On Asian American History and the Loss of Citizenship through Marriage," *UCLA Law Review*, 53 (2005), pp. 405–483.

51. Xiaojian Zhao, "Chinese American Women Defense Workers in World War II," *California History*, 75/1 (Summer 1996), pp. 138–153. "For centuries": Louise Purwin, "Chinese Daughters of Uncle Sam," *Independent Woman*, 21 (Spring 1942), p. 336.

52. Jade Snow Wong, *Fifth Chinese Daughter* (New York: Harper and Row, 1940), chapter 22. K[evin] Scott Wong discusses the contributions of other middle-class Chinese American women to the war effort in *Americans First: Chinese Americans and the Second World War* (Cambridge, MA: Harvard University Press, 2005), chapter 2.

53. Zhao, "Chinese American Women Defense Workers in World War II," p. 149.

54. Valerie Matsumoto, "Japanese American Women during World War II," *Frontiers: A Journal of Women's Studies*, 8/1 (1984), pp. 6–14. About 500 Japanese American women were accepted as enlistees in the Women's Army Corps. See Brenda L. Moore, *Serving Our Country: Japanese American Women in the Military during World War II* (New Brunswick, NJ: Rutgers University Press, 2003); "pretty free": transcript, interview with Sue Kunitomi [Embrey] by Arthur A. Hansen, David A. Hacker, and David J. Bertagnoli, August 24 and November 15, 1973, California State University, Fullerton, Oral History Program, Japanese American Project, p. 115, UCLA Library, Special Collections, Los Angeles.

55. Kunitomi [Embrey] interview, pp. 141, 133.

56. Kunitomi [Embrey] interview, pp. 143–144.

57. Jean Collier Brown, "The Negro Woman Worker," Women's Bureau Bulletin 165 (Washington, DC: U.S. Department of Labor, 1938), p. 2; Sundstrom, "Last Hired, First Fired?," table 1, p. 417.

58. Executive order 8802, https://www.ourdocuments.gov/doc.php?flash=false&doc=72&page=transcript; Consolidated-Vultee quoted in Paul Spickard, "Work and Hope: African American Women in Southern California during World War II," *Journal of the West*, 32/3 (July 1993), pp. 71–72.

59. Kathryn Blood, "Negro Women War Workers," Women's Bureau Bulletin 205 (Washington, DC: U.S. Department of Labor, 1945); Karen Tucker Anderson, "Last Hired, First Fired: Black Women Workers during World War II," *Journal of American History*, 69/1 (June 1982), pp. 82–97; race prejudice: Cheryl Mullenbach, *Double Victory: How African American Women Broke Race and Gender Barriers to Help Win World War II* (Chicago: Chicago Review Press, 2013), p. 16; "as toothless" quoted in Mullenbach, *Double Victory*, p. 14.

60. "The American way" quoted in Anna M. Rosenberg, "Womanpower and the War," *Opportunity: Journal of Negro Life*, 21/2 (April 1943), pp. 35–36; "We have our percentage" quoted in George E. DeMar, "Negro Women Are Workers, Too," *Opportunity: Journal of Negro Life*, 21/2 (April 1943), p. 41; "Whatever the hierarchies": Anderson, "Last Hired, First Fired," p. 84. Anderson observes that the Fair Employment Practices Commission did take cases of discrimination against Black women seriously, yet it had little success in enforcing compliance (pp. 92–93). "Hitler was the one" quoted in Gluck, *Rosie the Riveter Revisited*, p. 42; Maureen Honey, ed., *Bitter Fruit: African American Women in World War II* (Columbia: University of Missouri Press, 1999), p. 2.

61. Alison R. Bernstein, *American Indians and World War II: Toward a New Era in Indian Affairs* (Norman: University of Oklahoma Press, 1991), p. 73.

62. "Indian Women Harness Old Talents to New War Jobs," *Los Angeles Times*, October 22, 1942, p. 13; "Indians on Warpath: More Than 50,000 Redskins under Arms," *Alabama Journal* (Montgomery), March 9, 1944, p. 4; "Indians All Out to Scalp the Axis," *The Mercury* (Pittstown, PA), March 16, 1943, p. 4; "Indians Again on the Warpath," *The Morning Call* (Allentown, PA), April 16, 1944, p. 6.

63. Quoted in "Indian Girls Now at War Jobs," *New York Times*, February 6, 1943, p. 16.

64. "Petticoat Rule," *Daily Mail* (Hagerstown, Maryland), May 12, 1943, p. 1; "Efficiency," *Ludington Daily News* (Michigan), May 12, 1943, p. 6; "Petticoats Rule Change," *Ogden Standard-Examiner* (Utah), May 14, 1943, p. 14.

65. Grace Mary Gouveia, "We Also Serve: American Indian Women's Role in World War II," *Michigan Historical Review*, 20/2 (Fall 1994), pp. 153–182.

66. Congresswoman Frances Bolton (R-Ohio) to the League of Republican Women, quoted in "Says Waacs Retain Femininity," *New York Times*, January 5, 1943, p. 16.

67. The military needed all the able-bodied women it could get, but the military's racialist policies reflected the country's. In 1941, for example, only fifty-six Black women were allowed in the nursing corps—to work with the segregated Black troops. In 1943, when more Black nurses were needed to tend to the casualties, a nurse training bill lifted the quota. However, by 1944 the need for Black nurses to work with Black servicemen was so great that the U.S. Cadet Nurse Corps ran ads in *The Crisis*, calling for "Ladies 17 to 35 Years of Age" and showing a sketch of a Black women in uniform alongside copy promising "Free education, snappy nurse's uniform, your complete tuition, room and board, and regular allowance of $15 to at least $30 a month" (ad in *The Crisis*, July 1944); "Who will then": Rep. Clare Eugene Hoffman, "Women Should Not Be Recruited for the Armed

Forces," March 17, 1942, quoted in William Dudley, *World War II: Opposing Viewpoints* (San Diego, CA: Greenhaven Press, 1997), p. 169; "Women and War," *Commonweal*, 35 (March 27, 1942), p. 549.

68. "Address by Mrs. Oveta Culp Hobby . . . Women's National Press Club, September 6, 1942," reprinted in *Congressional Record—House*, September 14, 1942, pp. 7150–7152; "Skirts" in Mattie E. Treadwell, *The Women's Army Corps* (1954; rpt., Washington, DC: U.S. Government Printing Office, 1971), p. 63; "Says Waacs Retain Femininity," *New York Times*, January 5, 1943, p. 16; "Says Wacs Will Be Fine Wives," *New York Times*, May 5, 1944, p. 14; "Wac's Femininity Is Increased by Service: She 'Will Always Remain a Civilian at Heart,'" *New York Times*, January 19, 1945, p. 20.

69. Jacqueline Cochran, *The Stars at Noon* (Boston: Little, Brown, 1954), p. 106; Eleanor Roosevelt, "My Day" (syndicated), *Pittsburgh Press*, September 1, 1942, p. 21. ER would not have approved, had she known, of the treatment of Black women applicants to the Women Airforce Service Pilots (WASP). Janet Harmon Waterford, for instance, graduated from Spelman College in 1929, began flying in 1933, and helped form a Black air pilots' association. A white woman whom she was teaching to fly in 1943 encouraged her to apply to become a WASP. When Waterford showed up for her interview, she was told by the recruiter, "Well, I've never interviewed a colored girl for flying," and he refused to do it. Sadie Lee Johnson, a Black woman from Mississippi, also applied to the WASP and received a letter directly from Cochran, head of the WASP, who feared that admitting Blacks would make the already controversial program even more controversial: "Unfortunately, there is no provision for the training of colored girls in the Women's Flying Training Program. However, I would suggest you investigate the Women's Army Corps, since they enlist colored girls for various types of work" (Kimberly Enderle, "On Shifting Ground: The Women Airforce Service Pilots of WWII—Public Images, Private Realities, and the Burdens of Lasting Progress," MA thesis, San Diego State University, 2018, pp. 181, 274–275). In her autobiography, Cochran recalls that early in the program she received an application from a New Jersey school teacher who was a pilot and "a fine specimen." Cochran traveled to meet with her in person and tell her that the program was highly controversial and that admitting Black women into it would be its death knell (*The Stars at Noon*, pp. 127–128).

70. Rita Victoria Gomez, "Angels Calling from the Sky: The Women Pilots of World War II," in *A Woman's War Too: U.S. Women in the Military in World War II*, ed. Paula Nassen Poulus (Washington, DC: National Archives and Records, 1996), pp. 98–111.

71. "Army & Navy—Unnecessary and Undesirable?," *Time*, May 29, 1944; *Congressional Record, Proceedings and Debate of the 78th Congress, 2nd Session*, vol. 90, part 9, June 3, 1944, p. A-2766.

72. "You should try" in *The White House Press Conferences of Eleanor Roosevelt*, ed. Maurine Hoffman Beasley (New York: Garland, 1983), p. 288.

73. Harold L. Ickes, "Watch Out for the Women," *Saturday Evening Post*, 215/34 (February 20, 1943), p. 19.

74. Quoted in Margaret Mead, "The Women in the War," in *While You Were Gone: A Report on Wartime Life in the United States*, ed. Jack Goodman (New York: Simon and Schuster, 1946), p. 278.

11.
SENDING HER BACK TO THE PLACE WHERE GOD HAD SET HER

1. Quoted in Andrea S. Walsh, *Women's Film and Female Experience, 1940–1950* (New York: Praeger, 1984), p. 77.
2. Laura Bergquist, "A New Look at the American Woman," *Look* (October 16, 1956), p. 3.
3. Alyse Gregory, "The Changing Morality of Women," *Current History* (November 1923), pp. 298–299.
4. See Elaine Tyler May's discussion of what accounted for young adults' endorsement of "traditional" family roles in the years after World War II. May concludes that it was rooted in factors such as Cold War insecurities and insulated suburban life, but she also argues that postwar family life was less a return to tradition than a new vision about creating a home that would fulfill all its members' requirements for "the good life" (*Homeward Bound: American Families in the Cold War Era* [New York: Basic Books, 1999], p. 25).
5. Mudd's early feminism and career are discussed in Kristin Celello, *Making Marriage Work: A History of Marriage and Divorce in the Twentieth-Century United States* (Chapel Hill: University of North Carolina Press, 2009); Rebecca L. Davis, *More Perfect Unions: The American Search for Marital Bliss* (Cambridge, MA: Harvard University Press, 2010); Ian R. Dowbiggin, *The Search for Domestic Bliss: Marriage and Family Counselling in Twentieth-Century America* (Lawrence: University of Kansas Press, 2014); and Helen Hunter, "Redefining American Motherhood: Emily Mudd's Mission at Home and Abroad" (Philadelphia: University of Pennsylvania Humanities Forum, 2016).
6. Men must learn to adapt: in Emily Hartshorne Mudd, "Youth and Marriage," *Annals of the American Academy of Political and Social Science* (November 1937), pp. 111–118; a contributor to the world's work in Mrs. Emily H. Mudd, "Women's Conflicting Values," *Marriage and Family Living*, 8/3 (August 1946), pp. 58–61.
7. "Susan B. Anthony, Florence Nightingale": Mudd, "Women's Conflicting Values," p. 59. "In these modern days": Emily Hartshorne Mudd, "Woman's Finest Role," *Reader's Digest*, 67 (September 1955), pp. 21–23.
8. Lead Belly (Huddie Ledbetter), "National Defense Blues," c. 1946, in *Smithsonian Folkways Collection* (2015), https://www.youtube.com/watch?v=yuwnYGSZS3I.
9. Mitra Toossi, "A Century of Change: The U.S. Labor Force, 1950–2050," *Monthly Labor Review* (May 2002), table 3, p. 19. In 1934, near the height of the Depression, the birth rate was 18.4 per 1,000 women; in the 1950s it was 25.3 per 1,000 women. See James R. Wetzel, "American Families: 75 Years of Change," *Monthly Labor Review*, 113/3 (March 1990), p. 8.

10. Patricia Albjerg Graham, "Expansion and Exclusion: A History of Women in Higher Education," *Signs*, 3/4 (Summer 1978), p. 766; "a girl": Charles W. Cole, "American Youth Goes Monogamous," *Harper's* (March 1957), p. 32.
11. Lynn White Jr., *Educating Our Daughters: A Challenge to the Colleges* (New York: Harper and Brothers, 1950), p. 32.
12. Bergquist, "A New Look at the American Woman," p. 3.
13. Rosa Parks with Jim Haskins, *Rosa Parks: My Story* (New York: Dial, 1992), p. 116.
14. Parks, *Rosa Parks*, pp. 136, 139.
15. Chester Higgins, "Why Mrs. Parks Left Ala.," *Pittsburgh Courier*, August 31, 1957, p. 39.
16. Quoted in Barbara Ransby, *Ella Baker and the Black Freedom Movement: A Radical Democratic Vision* (Chapel Hill: University of North Carolina Press, 2003), pp. 189–190. The contrast between Baker's and King's leadership styles is discussed in Marilyn Bordwell DeLaure, "Planting Seeds of Change: Ella Baker's Radical Rhetoric," *Women's Studies in Communication*, 31/1 (Spring 2008), pp. 1–28.
17. Paradoxically, the 1950s' spiritual heirs to the "antis" established a movement of conservative women deeply involved in political issues, which culminated in Phyllis Schlafly's campaign against the Equal Rights Amendment in the 1970s. See Michelle M. Nickerson, *Mothers of Conservatism: Women and the Postwar Right* (Princeton, NJ: Princeton University Press, 2012).
18. Benjamin Spock, *Baby and Child Care* (New York: Duell, Sloane, and Pearce, 1957), p. 570.
19. Cotton Mather, *Ornaments for the Daughters of Zion . . .* (1692; rpt., Oxford: University of Oxford Text Archive, 2005), p. 10; Rodman's proposal in "Feminists Debate Plans for a House," *New York Times*, April 22, 1914, p. 12; Spock, *Baby and Child Care*, p. 569.
20. Violet Brown Weingarten, "Case History of an Ex-Working Mother," *New York Times*, September 20, 1953, section SM, p. 54.
21. Talcott Parsons and Robert F. Bales, *Family Socialization and Interaction Process* (Glencoe, IL: Free Press, 1955), p. 24.
22. Ferdinand Lundberg and Marynia Farnham, *Modern Woman: The Lost Sex* (New York: Harper and Brothers, 1947), pp. 143, 366; Mari Jo Buhle discusses Lundberg's and Farnham's misinterpretation of Freud's theory of penis envy in *Feminism and Its Discontents: A Century of Struggle with Psychoanalysis* (Cambridge, MA: Harvard University Press, 1998), p. 176.
23. "If you're born" quoted in Dorothy Doan, "Today's Women Lost, Says Psychiatrist," *St. Louis Post-Dispatch* (Missouri), July 31, 1947, p. 2D. The newsreel, titled "Strongly against Careers for Women Is Dr. Marynia Farnham," is available at https://www.youtube.com/watch?v=UOH-PyZecVM.
24. "Some kind" quoted in "If I Were Twenty Again . . . Psychiatrist Wanted Glamour," *St. Louis Post Dispatch*, September 9, 1957, p. 57; "deviant" quoted in Dorothy Doan, "Today's Woman Is Frustrated," *Miami Herald*, July 30, 1947, p. 10.
25. Laura D. Hirshbein, "History of Women in Psychiatry," *Academic Psychiatry*, 28/4 (February 2004), pp. 337–343.

26. "Conditioned by forces" quoted in "If I Were Twenty Again," p. 57; "crusaders" quoted in Doan, "Today's Woman Is Frustrated," p. 10; "nurtured on talk" quoted in Doris Lockerman, "Let's See Now," *Atlanta Constitution*, July 29, 1947, p. 14.
27. "Loneliness" in "If I Were Twenty Again," p. 57.
28. Linda Nison Charlton began writing for the *New York Times* in 1969. She married in 1972 and had two children, but she continued to be a reporter until her death in 1986 at the age of forty-nine.
29. Gallup poll in Stephanie Coontz, *The Way We Never Were: American Families and the Nostalgia Trap* (New York: Basic Books, 1992), p. 186. "Men Dislike Women Who . . . ," *Austin American* (Texas), December 4, 1955, p. 72; Clifford R. Adams, "How to Be Marriageable," *Ladies' Home Journal*, part 1: March 1954, pp. 46–47; part 2: April 1954, pp. 48–49; part 3: May 1954, pp. 54–55; part 4: June 1954, pp. 50–51.
30. Clifford R. Adams, "Making Marriage Work," *Ladies' Home Journal* (June 1951), p. 28. Joanne Meyerowitz in "Beyond the Feminine Mystique: A Reassessment of Post War Mass Culture," in *Not June Cleaver: Women and Gender in Post-War America, 1945–1960*, ed. Joanne Meyerowitz (Philadelphia: Temple University, 1994), chapter 11, shows that women's magazines frequently included articles about much admired independent women. However, a reader taking in the preponderance of ads, short stories, and articles in those magazines, such as "Everything to Make Him Happy" (Gertrude Schweitzer, *Ladies Home Journal*, 64/7, July 1947), could not have concluded that their dominant message promoted woman's independence.
31. See Gerard Jones's discussion of social instruction on proper family conduct in *Father Knows Best* in *Honey, I'm Home! Sitcoms: Selling the American Dream* (New York: St. Martin's Press, 1992), chapter 7. See also Mary Beth Haralovich, discussion of the role of *Father Knows Best* and *Leave It to Beaver* in social formation that naturalized woman's place in the home in "Sitcoms and Suburbs: Positioning the 1950s Homemaker," *Quarterly Review of Film and Video*, 11/1 (1989), pp. 61–83.
32. Austin C. Wehrwein, "Minnesota Says 'Coya, Come Home': Voters and Husband Agree That It's the Place for Congresswoman," *New York Times*, November 6, 1958, p. 23.
33. "70 percent" in Associated Press, "Ladies Like Derbies," *Logan Daily News* (Ohio), June 5, 1950, p. 4; Michella M. Marino interview with Loretta Behrens, Michella Marino Oral History Collection, Special Collections and University Archives, University of Massachusetts, Amherst, https://credo.library.umass.edu/view/full/mums812-s02-i001. See also Suzanne R. Becker, "Contesting and Constructing Gender, Sexuality, and Identity in Women's Roller Derby," PhD diss., University of Nevada, Las Vegas, 2018; Associated Press, "Girls' Roller Derby Is Big League Sport," *Evening Sun* (Baltimore, Maryland), March 17, 1950, p. 37; "Income of Families and Persons in the United States: 1950," United States Census Bureau, Report Number P60-09 (March 25, 1952), p. 1.
34. "Usually prefer" in Associated Press, "Girls' Roller Derby Is Big League Sport," p. 37; "I want" quoted in Alan Ebert, "Skaters Can Be Ladies Too, Gloria Mack

(a Lady) Insists," *Roller Derby News*, January 1959, quoted in Michella Mary Marino, "Sweating Feminists: Women Athletes, Masculine Culture, and American Inequality from the 1930s to the Present," PhD diss., University of Massachusetts, Amherst, 2013, p. 158; "Queen of queens" in "Virginia Rushing of New York Roller Derby . . . Shows Good Form on or off the Rink," *Daily News* (New York), January 1, 1950, p. 23; Associated Press, "Monta Jean Payne, Prettiest of All Roller Derby Girls," *Herald-News* (Passaic, New Jersey), June 2, 1950, p. 24.

35. "The media presented these girls": see, for example, "Zoot Suit Gangs Draw Ire of Sheriff," *Arizona Daily Star* (Tucson), March 16, 1943, p. 7; and "'Pachuca' Girls and Zoot-Suit Victim," *Herald-Journal* (Logan, Utah), June 12, 1943, p. 1. The latter article was about three pachucas slashing and beating a twenty-two-year-old white waitress in Los Angeles. Pachuco or pachuca gangs had formed in the United States as early as the 1930s, but they made headlines all over the country in 1942, when gang members in Los Angeles were held responsible for the death of a young Mexican American man, and again in 1943, when white servicemen on leave in Los Angeles attacked and brutalized pachucos who were dressed in their distinctive "zoot suit" style. Pachucas were implicated in both events. See Gerardo Licon, "Pachucas, Pachucos, and Their Culture: Mexican American Youth Culture of the Southwest," PhD diss., University of Southern California, 2010, and Catherine S. Ramirez, *The Woman in the Zoot Suit: Gender, Nationalism, and the Cultural Politics of Memory* (Durham, NC: Duke University Press, 2009). For postwar newspaper coverage of pachucas, see, for example, International News Service, "Auxiliary to Hoodlum Gangs Bared," *Minneapolis Star* (April 28, 1954), p. 2; United Press International, "G.I.'s Gun Death Linked to Pachucos," *Arizona Republic*, August 25, 1954, p. 1; "Detectives Press Inquiry into Teenager Sex Club," *Nashville Banner*, April 28, 1956, p. 1; Rosa Linda Fregoso, "Homegirls, Cholas, and Pachucas in Cinema," *California History*, 74/3 (1995), p. 318; "Origenes de 'Pachucos' y 'Malinches,'" *La Opinion*, August 26, 1942, p. 3, quoted in Catherine S. Ramirez, "Crimes of Fashion: The Pachuca and Chicana Style Politics," *Meridians*, 2/2 (2002), p. 12.

36. "Dr. Van Arsdale Addresses Club on Girl Delinquency," *Press-Democrat* (Santa Rosa, California), March 15, 1946, p. 10.

37. Tattoos: Laura L. Cummings, "Cloth-Wrapped People, Trouble, and Power: Pachuco Culture in the Greater Southwest," *Journal of the Southwest*, 45/3 (Autumn 2003), p. 343; Spanglish: Catherine S. Ramirez, "Pachucas and the Languages of Resistance," *Frontiers: A Journal of Women's Studies*, 27/3 (2006), p. 6; media accounts: Licon, "Pachucas, Pachucos, and Their Culture," p. 3.

38. Licon, "Pachucas, Pachucos, and Their Culture," p. 182.

39. Miroslava Chavez-Garcia, *States of Delinquency: Race and Science in the Making of California's Juvenile Justice System* (Berkeley: University of California Press, 2012), pp. 10, 2.

40. Los Guilucos: Dilys Jones, "Honor System Success in State Girl School," *San Francisco Examiner*, December 14, 1947, p. 40; In New York, too, the resources of the state were spent on trying to transform girl gang members, mostly Puerto Rican and Black, into acceptable versions of woman. Social workers were trained to

introduce gang girls "to the finer points of hairstyling, cooking, dressmaking, and etiquette" and to hold "charm clinics" for them. See Anne Campbell, *The Girls in the Gang*, 2nd ed. (Cambridge, MA: Blackwell, 1991), pp. 16–19. Newspaper accounts presented New York gangs as having been influenced in style by the pachucas and pachucos of the West Coast. See Robert S. Bird, "Teen-Age Gangs in New York," *Daily Times-News* (Burlington, North Carolina), March 31, 1958, p. 18. Like pachucas on the West Coast, Puerto Rican and Black girl gang members on the East Coast were sensationalized in the media as, for example, being "as quick as the boys to flip the blade of a switch knife, or draw an ice pick" (James McGlincy, "Angels with Dirty Faces Boast Molls Nowadays," *Daily News* [New York], June 17, 1954, p. 12).

41. Associated Press, "Female Lawmakers: Two New Congresswomen Take Oath of Office," *Fort Lauderdale News*, June 4, 1957, p. 2.
42. Quoted in Gretchen Urnes Beito, *Coya Come Home: A Congresswoman's Journey* (Los Angeles: Pomegranate Press, 1990), p. 65.
43. Barbara Flanagan, "Coya Knutson, Woman Legislator," *Star Tribune* (Minneapolis), December 10, 1950, p. 40.
44. First bill: Earl Wingard, "Sentiment Grows for Pruning State Budget," *Minneapolis Star*, February 9, 1951, p. 11; highest number of votes: Gretchen Urnes Beito, "The Constituency of Coya Knutson, 1954," MA thesis, University of North Dakota, 1982, p. 19.
45. Elizabeth Kastor, "A Woman's Place," *Washington Post*, November 17, 1996.
46. John C. McDonald, "How Coya Stormed the Capitol," *Minneapolis Morning Tribune*, September 30, 1955, p. 18.
47. Andy Knutson claimed that he was inebriated when he signed the letter that was penned either by those supporting his wife's political rival or by members of the Democratic Farm Labor Party, whom Coya had displeased by refusing to back Adlai Stevenson, their pick for the 1956 Democratic presidential nomination.
48. Quoted in Annette Atkins, *Creating Minnesota: A History from the Inside Out* (St. Paul: Minnesota Historical Society Press, 2008), p. 229.
49. "Out of Andy's Inn," *Time*, 71/20 (May 19, 1958), pp. 17–18.
50. Wehrwein, "Minnesota Says 'Coya, Come Home'"; New Jersey woman quoted in Kendall Anderson, "First Minnesota Congresswoman Faced Tough Test," *Session Weekly* (Minnesota Legislature), May 29, 1996, p. 25. Betty McCullum became a representative from Minnesota in 2001.
51. Pitirim A. Sorokin, *The American Sex Revolution* (Boston: Porter Sargent, 1956), p. 19.
52. Elaine Tyler May suggests in *Homeward Bound* that post–World War II suspicion of sex outside of marriage was less a relic of Victorian times than it was the obsession with domestic containment that kept the family safe from threatening social forces, analogous to foreign policy containment that kept America safe from Communism. Sex manuals aimed at married couples in the 1950s decried premarital sex for women not only because it was morally wrong but also because it was "highly detrimental to good marital sexual adjustment." It was incumbent on a midcentury wife to bolster her husband's sexual confidence, and her prior sex-

ual experience would not be productive to that end. See Jessamyn Neuhaus, "The Importance of Being Orgasmic: Sexuality, Gender, and Marital Sex Manuals in the United States, 1920–1963," *Journal of the History of Sexuality*, 9/4 (October 2000), p. 462; Howard Whitman, "The Slavery of Sex Freedom: America's Moral Crisis," *Better Homes and Gardens* (June 1957), p. 59.

53. Sorokin, *The American Sex Revolution*, p. 19; Little Richard, "Good Golly, Miss Molly" (Los Angeles: Specialty Records, 1958); The Dominoes, "Sixty-Minute Man" (Cincinnati, Ohio: Federal Records, 1951).
54. Elizabeth Fraterrigo, *Playboy and the Making of the Good Life in Modern America* (New York: Oxford University Press, 2011), p. 25. Bettie Page was arrested at a photo shoot and told by a policeman that if she pleaded guilty to "creating pornography," the charges against her would be lowered to "indecent exposure." She was livid. "I am not indecent. I will not plead guilty to it!" she informed him. In court she was fined five dollars and released. See Richard Foster, *The Real Bettie Page: The Truth behind the Queen of the Pinups* (New York: Birch Lane Press, 1997), p. 45.
55. Granahan quoted in Joanne Meyerowitz, "Women, Cheesecake, and Borderline Material," *Journal of Women's History*, 8/3 (Fall 1996), p. 24; "Smut Held Cause of Delinquency," *New York Times*, June 1, 1955, p. 35.
56. Helga Moray, *Untamed* (New York: Dell, 1950); J. C. Priest, *Forbidden* (New York: Woodford Press, 1952).
57. Margaret Culkin Banning, "Filth on the Newsstands," *Reader's Digest* (October 1952), p. 116; Ezekiel Candler Gathings, *Report of the Select Committee on Current Pornographic Materials, House of Representatives, 82nd Congress* (Washington, DC: Government Printing Office, 1952). Regarding magazines and books with sexually explicit material, Banning testified, "I have been told by the heads of various homes for delinquent girls that the girls come in with their suitcases practically full of them" (pp. 64–66).
58. Alice J. Clague and Stephanie J. Ventura, *Trends in Illegitimacy, United States: 1940–1965* (Washington, DC: Government Printing Office, 1968). The "illegitimacy ratio" continued to rise, increasing by 49 percent from 1959 to 1965. The increase was significantly greater among white women than among nonwhite women during these years (pp. 5, 11). Of the forty-nine Florence Crittenton maternity homes in the early 1950s, one-third provided services for Black women, and three were "solely for Negro girls." Ann Fessler, *The Girls Who Went Away: The Hidden History of Women Who Surrendered Children for Adoption before Roe v. Wade* (New York: Penguin, 2006), pp. 108–109. Fessler also shows that young Black women from middle-class or upwardly striving families faced stigma similar to that faced by young white women in the same socioeconomic classes. See also Rickie Solinger, *Wake Up Little Susie: Single Pregnancy and Race before Roe v. Wade* (New York: Routledge, 2000).
59. Marian J. Morton, "Fallen Women, Federated Charities, and Maternity Homes, 1913–1973," *Social Service Review*, 62/1 (March 1988), pp. 61–82.
60. On Rev. Buckminster, see chapter 4. Wini Breines discusses the confusion inherent in the double standard in *Young, White, and Miserable: Growing Up Female*

in the Fifties (Chicago: University of Chicago Press, 2001), chapter 3. See also Breines's discussion of beatnik girls in the 1950s and the complications in their efforts to claim a freer sexuality in "The 'Other' Fifties: Beats and Bad Girls," in Meyerowitz, *Not June Cleaver*, pp. 382–408.

61. Alfred C. Kinsey et al., *Sexual Behavior in the Human Female* (Philadelphia: W. B. Saunders, 1953), p. 204.
62. I discuss midcentury psychiatric and social attitudes about female homosexuality, as well as the proliferation of a lesbian subculture, in Lillian Faderman, *Odd Girls and Twilight Lovers: A History of Lesbian Life in Twentieth-Century America* (New York: Columbia University Press, 1991), pp. 130–187; Martin S. Weinberg et al., "Sexual Autonomy and the Status of Women: Models of Female Sexuality in U.S. Sex Manuals from 1950 to 1980," *Social Problems*, 30/3 (February 1983), pp. 312–324.
63. Responses to Kinsey's work: "Report Is 'Bunk Plus Arrogance,'" *The Tablet* (Brooklyn, New York), August 29, 1953, p. 4; Phyllis Battelle, "Fannie Hurst Says, 'Women Exaggerate,'" *Muncie Evening Press* (Indiana), August 20, 1953, p. 21; "Move on Kinsey Decried," *New York Times*, September 2, 1953, p. 15; "House May Call Kinsey; Unit Is Asked to Investigate His Financial Backing," *New York Times*, January 7, 1954, p. 21; Edmund Bergler and William S. Kroger, *Kinsey's Myth of Female Sexuality: The Medical Facts* (New York: Grune and Stratton, 1954), p. 2.
64. Hans Zeisel, review of *Sexual Behavior in the Human Female*, *University of Chicago Law Review*, 21 (1954), p. 519. Black women had been interviewed for Kinsey's study, but the results of their interviews were not included in the book. Kinsey had sought funding from the Committee for Research in Problems with Sex, headed by the psychologist Robert Yerkes, whose own work was based on racialist theories. Yerkes advised Kinsey to "postpone research into human variants—racial, cultural, degree of typicalness." The biographer James H. Jones suggests that Kinsey initially rejected the advice: he interviewed Black men for his 1947 *Sexual Behavior in the Human Male* as well as Black women for his 1953 volume on females. But ultimately he did follow Yerkes's advice in excluding the results of the interviews with Black men and women for both books. See James H. Jones, *Alfred C. Kinsey: A Life* (New York: Norton, 1997), p. 440. Jonathan Gathorne-Hardy quotes Kinsey as saying that he decided not to include Black men in *Sexual Behavior in the Human Male* because the interviews with "many lower-level Blacks conformed too closely to the vulgar stereotypes" (*Sex the Measure of All Things: A Life of Alfred Kinsey* [Bloomington: Indiana University Press, 2000], pp. 261–262).

12.
A NEW "NEW WOMAN" EMERGES (CARRYING BAGGAGE)

1. Quoted in Betty Reale, "Capital Comments," *Indianapolis Star*, June 3, 1962, p. 81.
2. Helen Gurley Brown, *Sex and the Single Girl* (New York: Bernard Geis, 1962), p. 225.

3. "Move, run" quoted in Juliet Nicolson, "Mary Quant: Life, Love, and Liberty," *Harper's Bazaar* (February 11, 2020), https://www.harpersbazaar.com/uk/fashion/shows-trends/a30873182/mary-quant-designer/; "much more in charge" quoted in David Wills, *Switched On: Women Who Revolutionized Style in the '60s* (San Francisco: Weldon Owen, 2017), p. 250.
4. Featured in *Seventeen*: Edward J. Rielly, *The 1960s: American Popular Culture through History* (Westport, CT: Greenwood Press, 2003), p. 81; Retailers' reports: Isadore Barmash, "Is Miniskirt Vogue Just a Fad?," *Democrat and Chronicle* (Rochester, NY), December 9, 1966, p. 29; "If a girl" quoted in John H. Lyst, "Miniskirts Lift Eyebrows but May Lower Job Chances," *Indianapolis Star*, December 10, 1967, p. 42; Joe Brown, "Conservative Line: No Minis," *Atlanta Constitution*, June 2, 1967, p. 1.
5. *Family Planning Program: Hearing before the Subcommittee on Employment, Manpower, and Poverty, S. 2939, United States Senate, May 10, 1966* (Washington, DC: U.S. Government Printing Office, 1966), p. 21.
6. Pearl S. Buck, "The Pill and the Teen-Age Girl," *Reader's Digest* (April 1968), p. 111; "The Pill: How It Is Affecting U.S. Morals, Family Life," *U.S. News and World Report*, July 11, 1966. The term "wife-swapping" itself is revealing of the old notion that a husband had jurisdiction over the doings of his wife.
7. Betsy Marvin McKinney, "Is the Double Standard out of Date?," *Ladies' Home Journal* (May 1961), p. 10.
8. The article caught the attention: Gail Collins, *When Everything Changed: The Amazing Journey of American Women from 1960 to the Present* (New York: Little, Brown, 2009), p. 154; Brown, *Sex and the Single Girl*, p. 225.
9. Sold 2 million copies: Jennifer Scanlon, *Bad Girls Go Everywhere: The Life of Helen Gurley Brown* (New York: Oxford University Press, 2009), p. 58; Brown, *Sex and the Single Girl*, p. 246.
10. "The marriage act": Ann Fessler, *The Girls Who Went Away: The Hidden History of Women Who Surrendered Children for Adoption in the Decades before Roe v. Wade* (New York: Penguin, 2006), p. 41.
11. Brown, *Sex and the Single Girl*, pp. 84, 155, 153.
12. See chapter 9.
13. Barbara Ehrenreich, Elizabeth Hess, and Gloria Jacobs, *Re-Making Love: The Feminization of Sex* (New York: Doubleday, 1986), p. 56. However, Gloria Steinem criticized Brown's book for conveying to young women the idea "that if they look good, smell good, [and] wear the right perfume and underwear, wonderful things will happen to them. It's the hope of all discriminated against groups that if we just behave nicely somehow the world will accept us" (quoted in Carol Krucoff, "Wanting It All!," *Washington Post*, November 10, 1982).
14. *American Women: The Report of the President's Commission on the Status of Women* (Washington, DC: Government Printing Office, 1963), p. 25.
15. Peterson quoted in Christine Stansell, *The Feminist Promise, 1792 to the Present* (New York: Modern Library, 2010), p. 198. In the 1980s, after two decades of the second

wave of feminism, Peterson, attributing her condemnation of feminism to "twenty years ago," acknowledged that "today, feminism as a philosophy has been granted the legitimacy it deserves" ("The Kennedy Commission," in *Women in Washington: Advocates for Public Policy*, ed. Irene Tinker [Beverley Hills, CA: Sage, 1983], p. 21).

16. Esther Peterson, "You Can't Giddyup by Saying Whoa," in *Rocking the Boat: Union Women's Voices, 1915–1975*, ed. Brigid O'Farrell and Joyce L. Kornbluh (New Brunswick, NJ: Rutgers University Press, 1996), pp. 58–83; Esther Peterson, interview by Jewell Fenzi, December 16, 1992, Association for Diplomatic Studies and Training, Foreign Affairs Oral History Program, Foreign Service Spouse Series, Library of Congress, Washington, DC; Esther Peterson with Winifred Conkling, *Restless: The Memoirs of Labor and Consumer Activist Esther Peterson* (Washington, DC: Caring Publishing, 1995).

17. Esther Peterson, oral history interview by Ronald J. Grele, interview 1, May 18, 1966, pp. 17–18, John F. Kennedy Presidential Library and Museum, Boston, MA (hereafter Kennedy Presidential Library).

18. Esther Peterson, oral history interview by Ann M. Campbell, interview 2, January 20, 1970, pp. 36–37, Kennedy Presidential Library.

19. Rebecca DeWolf, "The Equal Rights Amendment and the Rise of Emancipationism, 1932–1946," *Frontiers: A Journal of Women's Studies*, 38/2 (2017), pp. 47–80.

20. The National Woman's Party in the 1950s: Carl M. Brauer, "Women Activists, Southern Conservatives, and the Prohibition of Sex Discrimination in Title VII of the 1964 Civil Rights Act," *Journal of Southern History*, 49/1 (February 1983), p. 39; Peterson, oral history interview by Campbell, p. 32; Peterson, oral history interview by Grele, p. 22.

21. John F. Kennedy, "Executive Order 10980—Establishing the President's Commission on the Status of Women," December 14, 1961, the American Presidency Project, https://www.presidency.ucsb.edu/documents/executive-order-10980-establishing-the-presidents-commission-the-status-women; Peterson, oral history interview by Campbell, p. 58; Macy quoted in Cynthia Harrison, *On Account of Sex: The Politics of Women's Issues, 1945–1968* (Berkeley: University of California Press, 1988), p. 132.

22. Peterson, oral history interview by Campbell, p. 63.

23. Moynihan quoted in Alice Kessler-Harris, *In Pursuit of Equity: Women, Men, and the Quest for Economic Citizenship in Twentieth Century America* (New York: Oxford University Press, 2001), p. 218; Neuberger quoted in Stansell, *The Feminist Promise*, p. 202.

24. *American Women*.

25. Edward Eddy, "On Being Female," *New York Times*, August 1, 1965.

26. John Fitzgerald Kennedy interviewed by Eleanor Roosevelt, *Prospects of Mankind*, National Educational Television, April 18, 1962; Esther Peterson, oral history interview by Ann M. Campbell, interview 3, February 11, 1970, pp. 75–76, Kennedy Presidential Library.

27. Paul in Brauer, "Women Activists, Southern Conservatives," p. 39; Smith in Louis Menand, "How Women Got in on the Civil Rights Act," *New Yorker*, July 14, 2014, https://www.newyorker.com/magazine/2014/07/21/sex-amendment.
28. Don Oberdorfer, "'Judge' Smith Moves with Deliberate Drag," *New York Times*, January 12, 1964; Menand, "How Women Got in on the Civil Rights Act."
29. Letter in *Congressional Record, 88th Congress, 2nd Session*, February 8, 1964, p. 2577; Celler quoted in *Congressional Record, 88th Congress, 2nd Session*, p. 2577. See also Robert C. Bird's discussion of the proceedings in "More than a Congressional Joke: A Fresh Look at the Legislative History of Sex Discrimination of the 1964 Civil Rights Act," *William and Mary Journal of Women and the Law*, 3/1 (April 1997), pp. 137–161.
30. St. George quoted in *Congressional Record*, February 8, 1964, p. 2581; Griffiths quoted in *Congressional Record*, February 8, 1964, p. 2578. In what may have been a ploy to ensure the southern vote, Griffiths declared that she supported the amendment "primarily because I feel as a white woman when this bill [without the proposed amendment] has passed the House and the Senate and has been signed by the President that white women will be the last at the hiring gate." In a 1966 speech to the House, Griffiths championed Black women workers, pointing out that "they are victims of both race discrimination and sex discrimination, and have the highest unemployment rate and the lowest average earnings" (*Congressional Record—House*, June 20, 1966, p. 13689).
31. Ballot vote in *Congressional Record—House*, February 8, 1964, p. 2584; interview in Brauer, "Women Activists, Southern Conservatives," p. 51.
32. Quoted in Jo Freeman, *We Will Be Heard: Women's Struggles for Political Power in the United States* (Lanham, MD: Rowman and Littlefield, 2008), p. 183.
33. *Congressional Record—House*, June 20, 1966, p. 13689.
34. Quoted in Marjorie J. Spruill, *Divided We Stand: The Battle over Women's Rights and Family Values That Polarized America* (New York: Bloomsbury, 2017), p. 18.
35. *Congressional Record—House*, June 20, 1966, pp. 13689–13690.
36. Betty Friedan, *The Feminine Mystique* (1963; rpt., New York: Norton, 2013), p. 78.
37. "Replaced" in Friedan, *The Feminine Mystique*, p. 93.
38. Friedan, *The Feminine Mystique*, pp. 80, 121–122.
39. "Bitterly humiliating" quoted in Carol Giardina, "M[arch]O[n]W[ashington] to NOW: Black Feminism Resets the Chronology of Modern Feminism," *Feminist Studies*, 44/3 (2018), p. 741. Myrlie Evers missed her flight to Washington, and the lawyer Daisy Bates delivered a one-minute tribute to women" in her place. The entertainer Josephine Baker spoke before the official program began. "Jane Crow" in Pauli Murray and Mary O. Eastwood, "Jane Crow and the Law: Sex Discrimination and Title VII," *George Washington Law Review*, 34/2 (December 1965), pp. 235–256.
40. "Statement of Purpose," National Organization for Women, October 1966, https://now.org/about/history/statement-of-purpose/.
41. "Eleven Picket Times Classified Office to Protest Male-Female Labels," *New York Times*, August 31, 1967, p. 66.

42. Pittsburgh Press Company v. Pittsburgh Commission on Human Relations, 413 U.S. 376 (1973).
43. Janet L. Yellen, "The History of Women's Work and Wages and How It Has Created Success for Us All," Brookings, May 2020, https://www.brookings.edu/essay/the-history-of-womens-work-and-wages-and-how-it-has-created-success-for-us-all/. In 1970, close to a hundred women working at Time Inc. filed a sex discrimination complaint. Women at other newsmagazines such as *Newsweek* followed suit. See Lynn Povich, *The Good Girls Revolt: How the Women of Newsweek Sued Their Bosses and Changed the Workplace* (New York: PublicAffairs, 2012). In the 1950s, 34 percent of American women worked outside the home; by the end of the 1960s, 43 percent did. See Mitra Toossi, "A Century of Change: The U.S. Labor Force, 1950–2050," *Monthly Labor Review* (May 2002), p. 18. In terms of wages, women actually lost ground from 1955, when they earned 63.9 percent of what men earned; in 1967, at their lowest point in the 1960s, women's wages sank to 57.8 percent of men's wages. See *U.S. Working Women: A Databook* (Washington, DC: U.S. Department of Labor, 1977), p. 37; Harry Ferguson, "It's Still a Man's World," *Boston Globe*, February 12, 1963, p. 8.
44. Betty Friedan, "Up from the Kitchen Floor," *New York Times*, March 4, 1973, p. 8.
45. "Everyone has a right": Friedan, "Up from the Kitchen Floor," p. 8; "Warping the issue" quoted in Susan Brownmiller, "Sisterhood Is Powerful," *New York Times*, March 15, 1970, p. 140; Murray's description of her "inverted sexual instincts" included "wearing pants, wanting to be one of the men, doing things that fellows do, [and experiencing] very natural falling in love with the female sex": quoted in Rosalind Rosenberg, *Jane Crow: The Life of Pauli Murray* (New York: Oxford University Press, 2017), p. 58. In the mid-twentieth century, when sexuality and gender behavior were conflated, Murray—disturbed by the idea that she was "homosexual" and baffled by her gender identification—sought psychiatric treatment and was for a time willingly institutionalized. In contemporary terms, she was probably transgender, as recent writers have speculated. See also Naomi Simmons-Thorne, "Pauli Murray and the Pronominal Problem: A De-Essentialist Trans Historiography," *Activist History Review* (May 30, 2019), https://activisthistory.com/2019/05/30/pauli-murray-and-the-pronominal-problem-a-de-essentialist-trans-historiography/; Murray's defense of Friedan: Pauli Murray, letter to the editor, *New York Times*, March 25, 1973, p. 22.
46. Friedan, "Up from the Kitchen Floor," p. 8; Ti-Grace Atkinson, "Vaginal Orgasm as a Mass Hysterical Survival Response" (1968; rpt. in *Amazon Odyssey* [New York: Links Books, 1974], pp. 5–8). See also Breanne Fahs, "Ti-Grace Atkinson and the Legacy of Radical Feminism," *Feminist Studies*, 37/3 (Fall 2011), pp. 561–590.
47. Author interview with Ivy Bottini, August 19, 2004, Los Angeles; Ivy Bottini (as told to Judith Branzburg), *The Liberation of Ivy Bottini: A Memoir of Love and Activism* (Fairfield, CA: Bedazzled Ink, 2018); Alice Echols, *Daring to Be Bad: Radical Feminism in America, 1967–1975* (Minneapolis: University of Minnesota Press, 1989), p. 219.

48. "Oh, God" quoted in Arlene Van Breems, "NOW to Parley on West Coast," *Los Angeles Times*, September 3, 1971, p. 15. NOW's Lesbian Rights Resolution: "Lesbian Rights—1971," Feminist Majority Foundation, https://feminist.org/resources/feminist-chronicles/part-iii-the-early-documents/lesbian-rights-1971/. For a more extensive discussion of NOW's lesbian resolution, see Lillian Faderman, *The Gay Revolution: The Story of the Struggle* (New York: Simon and Schuster, 2015), pp. 304–306.
49. Frances M. Beal, *Double Jeopardy: To Be Black and Female* (1969; reprinted in *Meridians*, 8/2 [2008]), p. 174.
50. Susan M. Hartmann has shown that in the 1940s and 1950s, women of color were successful in forcing some mixed-sex organizations as well as unions to comply with their demands, though they were not organized as feminists (*The Other Feminists: Activists in the Liberal Establishment* [New Haven, CT: Yale University Press, 1998]).
51. Quoted in Robert O. Self, *All in the Family: The Realignment of American Democracy since the 1960s* (New York: Hill and Wang, 2012), p. 115.
52. See Cecilia Conrad, "Black Women: The Unfinished Agenda," *The American Prospect*, September 21, 2008, https://prospect.org/special-report/black-women-unfinished-agenda/; Norton quoted in Charlayne Hunter, "Many Blacks Wary of 'Women's Liberation' Movement in the U.S.," *New York Times*, November 17, 1970, p. 47.
53. Daniel Patrick Moynihan, *The Moynihan Report: The Negro Family, The Case for National Action* (1965), BlackPast.org, https://www.blackpast.org/african-american-history/moynihan-report-1965/. As Joyce A. Ladner, a Black sociologist, pointed out, not only did Moynihan neglect the effects of systemic racism on the Black family dynamic, but his misguided valorization of the white middle-class nuclear family was absurd in view of the 1960s eruption of white hippies, swingers, and others who were trying desperately to escape its limitations (Ladner, *Tomorrow's Tomorrow: The Black Woman* [Garden City, NY: Doubleday, 1971], p. 168).
54. There were a few exceptions to "acknowledged power" that proved the rule. Fannie Lou Hamer, a plantation worker who became an activist after she was repeatedly denied the right to vote, drew national attention when delegates from the Mississippi Freedom Democratic Party she helped found were refused seats at the 1964 National Democratic Convention. Hamer, who appeared before the credentials committee to argue that her party had a right to be seated, spoke so eloquently about abuse by police who had tried to keep her from voting that her speech, played on nightly television news programs all over the country, made her for a time a household name. But she and Rosa Parks in the 1950s were among the few women figures in the struggle for Black civil rights who were given wide recognition—until the advent of Angela Davis, who also became an iconic figure. For a discussion of Hamer at the 1964 convention, see Kay Mills, *This Little Light of Mine: The Life of Fannie Lou Hamer* (New York: Plume, 1993), pp. 121–125; Ella Baker, "Bigger than a Hamburger," *Southern Patriot*, 18 (June 1960), https://www.crmvet.org/docs/sncc2.htm. See my discussion of Baker

in chapter 11. Baker is finally being recognized as a major figure in the Black civil rights movement. See, for example, Mark Engler, "It's Time We Celebrate Ella Baker Day," *The Nation*, January 17, 2020, https://www.thenation.com/article/activism/ella-baker/ Ella Baker, "Developing Community Leadership," interview with Gerda Lerner, December 1970, https://americanstudies.yale.edu/sites/default/files/files/baker_leadership.pdf.

55. SNCC and women: Joyce Ladner, "Mississippi Movement Set Example for Female Leaders," *Jackson Clarion Ledger*, June 29, 2014. See also Charles Payne, "Men Led, but Women Organized: Movement Participation of Women in the Mississippi Delta," in *Women in the Civil Rights Movement: Trailblazers and Torchbearers, 1941–1965*, ed. Vicki L. Crawford, Jacqueline Anne Rouse, and Barbara Woods (Bloomington: Indiana University Press, 1993), pp. 1–11. Ruby Smith Robinson is discussed in Carol Giardina, "The Making of a Modern Feminist Vanguard, 1964–1973: Southern Women Whose Leadership Shaped the Movement and the Nation—a Synthetic Analysis," *Journal of Southern History*, 85/3 (August 2019), pp. 611–652.

56. King and Hayden discussed in Susan Brownmiller, *In Our Time: Memoir of a Revolution* (New York: Dial Press, 1999), p. 13; [Casey Hayden et al.], "Position Paper: Women in the Movement," November 1964, Civil Rights Movement Archive, https://www.crmvet.org/docs/sncfem.htm; "caused hardly a ripple" quoted in Dorothy Dawson Burlage et al., *Deep in Our Hearts: Nine White Women in the Freedom Movement* (Athens: University of Georgia Press, 2000), p. 365.

57. Mary King has described the context of the "prone" comment, writing that she understood Carmichael to be joking (*Freedom Song: A Personal Story of the 1960s Civil Rights Movement* [New York: William Morrow, 1988], pp. 451–452). Frances Beal, cofounder of SNCC's Black Women's Liberation Committee, has said that Carmichael never meant the words the way they came out, and "he lived with the shame of his comment for years" (quoted in Teshima Walker, "Memory Swap Meet," *Tell Me More*, NPR, April 16, 2010, https://www.npr.org/sections/tellmemore/2010/04/16/126063465/memory-swap-meet).

58. Cynthia Griggs Fleming, *Soon We Will Not Cry: The Liberation of Ruby Doris Smith Robinson* (Lanham, MD: Rowman and Littlefield, 1998), p. 96.

59. "Feminist": Frances Beal, interview by Loretta J. Ross, March 18, 2005, Voices of Feminism Oral History Project, Sophia Smith Collection, Smith College, Northampton, MA; Cleaver quoted in Charles E. Jones and Judson L. Jeffries, "Don't Believe the Hype," in *The Black Panther Party [Reconsidered]*, ed. Charles E. Jones (Baltimore, MD: Black Classic Press, 1998), p. 49; Mary Dore, dir., *She's Beautiful When She's Angry* (New York: International Film Circuit, 2014). Angela Davis complained of similar experiences in the Los Angeles branch of SNCC, where the men accused the women of being "too domineering and trying to control everything, including the men . . . trying to rob them of their manhood" (*Angela Davis: An Autobiography* [1974; rpt., New York: International Publishers, 1988], p. 181). Davis claimed that such sexism in the movement was "a constant problem in my political life" (pp. 161–162).

60. Beal, *Double Jeopardy*, 167–168.
61. Coalitions: Kristen Anderson-Bricker, "Triple Jeopardy: Black Women and the Growth of Feminist Consciousness in SNCC, 1964–1975," in *Still Lifting, Still Climbing: Contemporary African-American Women's Activism*, ed. Kimberly Springer (New York: New York University Press, 1999), pp. 49–69; Kimberle Crenshaw, "Demarginalizing the Intersection of Race and Sex: A Black Feminist Critique of Antidiscrimination Doctrine, Feminist Theory and Antiracist Politics," *University of Chicago Legal Forum*, 1 (1989), pp. 139–167; "History of the Organization," *Triple Jeopardy*, 1/4 (February–March 1972), p. 8. The militant rhetoric of the Black women's movement had effect even on Black women leaders who had found a home in NOW. For instance, Congresswoman Shirley Chisholm, the first Black women to be elected to congress and to run for president of the United States, declared to Congress that she had been "far oftener discriminated against because I am a woman than because I am Black": *Congressional Record*, May 21, 1969, Extensions of Remarks, E4165-6, Duke University Digital Repository. But by 1973 Chisholm began speaking of Black women's "twin jeopardy" of oppressions: see Anastasia Curwood, "Black Feminism on Capitol Hill: Shirley Chisholm and Movement Politics, 1968–1984," *Meridians*, 13/1 (2015), p. 215.
62. Interview with Jessie de la Cruz in Ellen Cantarow, Susan Gushee O'Malley, and Sharon Hartman Strom, *Moving the Mountain: Women Working for Social Change* (New York: Feminist Press, 1980), p. 162.
63. "The old customs" and "It's way past" in interview with de la Cruz in Cantarow, O'Malley, and Strom, *Moving the Mountain*, pp. 180, 178. See also Linda K. Kerber and Jane De Hart Matthews, eds., "Jessie Lopez de la Cruz: the First Woman Farmworker Organizer out in the Fields," in *Women's America: Refocusing the Past* (New York: Oxford University Press, 1982), pp. 406–414.
64. "No place for a woman" quoted in Margaret Rose, "Traditional and Nontraditional Patterns of Female Activism in the United Farm Workers of America, 1962 to 1980," *Frontiers*, 11/1 (1990), pp. 26–32. See also Peter Bratt, dir., *Dolores* (Boston: PBS Distribution, 2017).
65. FBI file, Cesar Chavez and United Farm Workers et al., part I, Communist Infiltration of the National Farm Workers Association, https://vault.fbi.gov/Cesar%20Chavez/Cesar%20Chavez%20Part%201%20of%2017; Barbara L. Baer, "Stopping Traffic: One Woman's Cause," in *A Dolores Huerta Reader*, ed. Mario T. Garcia (Albuquerque: University of New Mexico Press, 2008), p. 39.
66. "Unwritten policy": author interview with Irma Cota, UFW strike participant in the Salinas Valley, San Diego, California, July 31, 2020; Bratt, *Dolores*.
67. Interview with Dolores Huerta by Jason M. Breslow, *Frontline* (PBS), June 25, 2013, https://www.pbs.org/wgbh/frontline/article/dolores-huerta-an-epidemic-in-the-fields/; Carol Kleiman, "Bringing the Farmworkers' Plight to the City," *Chicago Tribune*, April 19, 1975, p. 254.
68. Chicanas in Brown Berets: Ernesto Chavez, *Mi Raza Primero! (My People First!): Nationalism, Identity, and Insurgency in the Chicano Movement in Los Angeles*,

1966–1978 (Berkeley: University of California Press, 2002), p. 58; Dionne Espinoza, "Revolutionary Sisters: Women's Solidarity and Collective Identification among Chicana Brown Berets in East Los Angeles, 1967–1970," *Aztlan*, 26/1 (November 2001), pp. 15–58; Juan Herrera, "La Lucha Continua! Gloria Arellanes and the Women of the Chicano Movement," in *East of East: The Making of Greater El Monte*, ed. Romeo Guzman et al. (New Brunswick, NJ: Rutgers University Press, 2020), pp. 102–111; Alma M. Garcia, "Introduction," in *Chicana Feminist Thought: The Basic Historical Writings*, ed. Alma M. Garcia (London: Routledge, 1997), pp. 1–16. "Big mouth": Gloria Arellanes, untitled essay on the history of the Chicana-run free clinics, folder 1, box 1, Gloria Arellanes Collection, Archives and Special Collections, John F. Kennedy Memorial Library, California State University, Los Angeles (hereafter Gloria Arellanes Collection).

69. Resignation letter: All ex-members of the Brown Beret female segment to Aron Mangancilla, February 25, 1970, box 1, folder 1, Gloria Arellanes Collection.
70. "Chicanas, find yourself!" quoted in Espinoza, "Revolutionary Sisters," p. 20. "*Vendidas*" quoted in Herrera, "La Lucha Continua!," p. 109.
71. Quoted in Vicki L. Ruiz, *From out of the Shadows: Mexican Women in Twentieth-Century America*, 10th anniversary ed. (New York: Oxford University Press, 2008), p. 108.
72. "Has rejected" quoted in Elizabeth Martinez, "La Chicana," in Garcia, *Chicana Feminist Thought*, p. 34. See also Alma M. Garcia, "The Development of Chicana Feminist Discourse, 1970–1980," *Gender and Society*, 3/2 (June 1989), pp. 217–218; Enriqueta Vasquez, *Enriqueta Vasquez and the Chicano Movement: Writings from El Grito del Norte*, ed. Lorena Oropeza and Dionne Espinoza (Houston, TX: Arte Publico Press, 2006), p. 183.
73. "Divisive" quoted in Maylei Blackwell, *Chicana Power! Contested Histories of Feminism in the Chicano Movement* (Austin: University of Texas Press, 2011), p. 177. There was no second national Chicana women's conference because the walkout created an immense rift in the incipient Chicana feminist movement; "Chicana motherhood" quoted in Mirta Vidal, "Chicanas Speak Out," *International Socialist Review* (October 1971), p. 7.
74. "Peace March Gals" quoted in Amy Swerdlow, "Ladies Day at the Capital: Women Strike for Peace Versus HUAC," *Feminist Studies*, 8/3 (Autumn 1982), p. 505.
75. Marjorie Hunter, "5,000 Women Rally in Capital against War," *New York Times*, January 16, 1968, p. 3.
76. "Corpse" and "You are joyfully" quoted in Elizabeth Currans, *Marching Dykes, Liberated Sluts, and Concerned Mothers: Women Transforming Public Space* (Champaign: University of Illinois Press, 2017), p. 87; "synonymous with powerlessness" quoted in Say Burgin, "Understanding American Activism as a Gendering Activity: A Look at the U.S.'s Anti-Vietnam War Movement," *Journal of International Women's Studies*, 13/6 (2012), p. 23.

13.
RADICAL WOMEN AND THE RADICAL WOMAN

1. Joreen [Jo Freeman], "The Bitch Manifesto," in *Notes from the Second Year: Women's Liberation; Major Writings of the Radical Feminists*, ed. Shulamith Firestone and Anne Koedt (New York: New York Radical Feminists, 1970), p. 5.
2. This feminist maxim, coined by the Australian activist Irina Dunn, was popularized by Gloria Steinem. See "Origin of That Fish Line," *Duluth News Tribune*, August 17, 2014, https://www.duluthnewstribune.com/lifestyle/3325954-origin-fish-line.
3. Vivian Gornick, "Women's Liberation: The Next Great Moment in History Is Theirs," *Village Voice*, November 27, 1969, pp. 11–12.
4. Che Guevara, *Guerrilla Warfare* (New York: Monthly Review Press, 1961), p. 93; Susan Brownmiller, "'Sisterhood Is Powerful': A Member of the Women's Liberation Movement Explains What It's All About," *New York Times Magazine*, March 15, 1970, p. 230; Alice Echols, *Daring to Be Bad: Radical Feminism in America, 1967–1975* (Minneapolis: University of Minnesota Press, 1989), chapter 3.
5. Anne Koedt, "The Myth of the Vaginal Orgasm," in Firestone and Koedt, *Notes from the Second Year*, pp. 37–41. Koedt was influenced by the scientific study of William H. Masters and Virginia E. Johnson, who found that physiological markers showed that women received far more sexual pleasure through clitoral stimulation than through vaginal intercourse (*Human Sexual Response* [Boston: Little, Brown, 1966]). Shere Hite, whose book *The Hite Report: A Nationwide Study on Female Sexuality* (New York: Macmillan, 1976) was based on interviews of 3,000 women, confirmed for masses of readers what Masters and Johnson and Koedt had written about the superior efficacy of clitoral stimulation. Hite's book sold over 48 million copies worldwide.
6. Norman Nadel, "Girls Want Equality—Now!," *Pittsburgh Press*, May 15, 1970, p. 26; Marilyn Bender, "Books to Liberate Women," *New York Times*, March 8, 1970, Book Review, p. 6; Shulamith Firestone, *The Dialectic of Sex: The Case for Feminist Revolution* (1970; rpt., New York: Quill, 1993), pp. 46, 91.
7. Aldous Huxley, *Brave New World* (London: Chatto and Windus, 1932).
8. Grace Lichtenstein, "Women's Lib Wooed by Publishers, *New York Times*, April 17, 1970, p. 32.
9. The work of the openly homosexual writer Jean Genet is also analyzed in Kate Millett, *Sexual Politics* (New York: Doubleday, 1970), by way of contrast to the work of Lawrence, Miller, and Mailer.
10. Kate Millett, *Flying* (New York: Knopf, 1974).
11. "It grabs the male ego" in John Locken, "'Sexual Politics' Is Revolution's 'Bible,'" *Minneapolis Star*, August 27, 1970, p. 80; "a farrago" in Irving Howe, "The Middle-Class Mind of Kate Millett," *Harper's*, December 1970, p. 110. See also Marilyn Bender, "Sexual Politics Called 'Women's Lib Bible,'" *Miami Herald*,

July 23, 1970, p. 23; Frank J. Prial, "Feminist Philosopher Katharine Murray Millett," *New York Times*, August 27, 1970, p. 30.

12. "Women's Lib: A Second Look," *Time*, December 14, 1970, p. 68; "lavender menace" quoted in Susan Brownmiller, "Sisterhood Is Powerful," *New York Times*, March 15, 1970, p. 230.
13. "Sexual McCarthyism" quoted in Judy Klemesrud, "The Lesbian Issue and Women's Lib," *New York Times*, December 18, 1970, p. 47; lavender armband in Rachel Shteir, "A Last Interview with Kate Millett," *New Yorker*, September 13, 2017, https://www.newyorker.com/books/page-turner/a-last-interview-with-kate-millett.
14. "The time" in Associated Press, "Women's Lib Defends Lesbians from 'Sexism,'" *Miami News* (Florida), December 18, 1970, p. 8; "struggling" in Associated Press, "Activists in Women's Liberation Say Lesbians Part of Movement," *Arizona Republic*, December 18, 1970, p. 26.
15. "Whenever the enemy" in Ti-Grace Atkinson, "Lesbianism and Feminism," in *Amazon Expedition: A Lesbian-Feminist Anthology*, ed. Phyllis Birkby et al. (Washington, NJ: Times Change Press, 1973), p. 15; "serving" in Birkby et al., *Amazon Expedition*, p. 16.
16. Carol Hanisch, "The Personal Is Political," in Firestone and Koedt, *Notes from the Second Year*, pp. 76–77; Sarah Schulman, *The Sophie Horowitz Story* (Tallahassee, FL: Naiad Press, 1984), p. 126.
17. Radicalesbians, "The Woman-Identified Woman" (1970), reprinted in *Lesbians Speak Out*, ed. Carol Wilson (Oakland, CA: Women's Press Collective, 1974), pp. 87–89; Rita Mae Brown, "Take a Lesbian to Lunch," *The Ladder*, 16/7–8 (April–May 1972), p. 17.
18. Albert Ellis, introduction to Donald Webster Cory, *The Lesbian in America* (New York: Tower, 1964), p. 13.
19. "If men" quoted in Sherie M. Randolph, *Florynce "Flo" Kennedy: The Life of a Black Feminist Radical* (Chapel Hill: University of North Carolina Press, 2015), p. 263;"There are very few" quoted in Gloria Steinem, "The Vebal Karate of Florynce R. Kennedy," *Ms.*, August 19, 2011, https://msmagazine.com/2011/08/19/the-verbal-karate-of-florynce-r-kennedy-esq/.
20. Randolph, *Florynce "Flo" Kennedy*, p. 206. For examples of widespread coverage of the National Black Feminist Organization announcement, see United Press International, "Black Women Start Lib Unit," *News Journal* (Wilmington, Delaware), August 16, 1973, p. 3; Associated Press, "Black Feminists Form Organization," *Hawaii Tribune-Herald* (Hilo), August 19, 1973, p. 15; Associated Press, "Black Feminists Form Their Own Group," *Reno Gazette-Journal* (Nevada), August 28, 1973, p. 9; Karla Jay, "Double Trouble for Black Women: An Interview with Margaret Sloan," *The Tide*, 3/9 (July 1974), p. 24.
21. "National Black Feminist Organization Statement of Purpose," in *Feminism in Our Time: The Essential Writings, World War II to the Present*, ed. Miriam Schneir (New York: Vintage Books, 1994), pp. 171–174.
22. Lorraine Bethel, "What Chou Mean We, White Girl? Or The Cullud Lesbian Feminist Declaration of Independence," *Conditions: The Black Women's Issue*, 5/2 (November 1979), p. 86.

23. "Combahee River Collective Statement," BlackPast, https://www.blackpast.org/african-american-history/combahee-river-collective-statement-1977/. See also Kimberly Springer, *Living for the Revolution: Black Feminist Organizations, 1968–1980* (Durham, NC: Duke University Press, 2005).
24. "Onus" in Gloria Anzaldúa, *Borderlands/La Frontera: The New Mestiza* (San Francisco: Aunt Lute Books, 1987), p. 17; "rape of our tongue" in Anzaldúa, "La Prieta," in *This Bridge Called My Back: Writings by Radical Women of Color*, ed. Cherríe L. Moraga and Gloria E. Anzaldúa (Boston: Persephone Press, 1981), p. 226; Sufi story in Anzaldúa, "La Prieta," p. 229.
25. "Coils" in Anzaldúa, "La Prieta," p. 198; "I belong" in Anzaldúa, "La Prieta," p. 209.
26. Alice Walker, *In Search of Our Mothers' Gardens: Womanist Prose* (New York: Harcourt Brace, 1983), pp. xi–xii.
27. Quoted in Jonathan Black, "Report from Chicago: The Expectation of Rising Revolutions," *Village Voice*, October 16, 1969, p. 64.
28. Choonib Lee, "Women's Liberation and Sixties Armed Resistance," *Journal for the Study of Radicalism*, 11/1 (Spring 2017), pp. 25–52.
29. "Boston Bard," *United States Gazette* (Philadelphia), March 10, 1826, p. 4; accomplished some feat: see, for example, "Ladies Welcome," *Ada Weekly News* (Oklahoma), October 10, 1957, p. 3; "She Knows the Joy of Conquest," *Spokane Chronicle*, September 22, 1952, p. 8.
30. *Women Rise Up* reprinted in Louis G. Heath, *Vandals in the Bomb Factory: The History and Literature of the Students for a Democratic Society* (Metuchen, NJ: Scarecrow Press, 1976), pp. 365–366; uniforms in Jo B. Paoletti, *Sex and Unisex: Fashion, Feminism, and the Sexual Revolution* (Bloomington: Indiana University Press, 2015).
31. The FBI identified Bernardine Dohrn, Susan Saxe, and Katherine Ann Power as Weathermen. See, for example, "The Weather Underground: Report of the Subcommittee to Investigate the Administration of the Internal Security Act and Other Internal Security Laws," Committee of the Judiciary, U.S. Senate, 94th Congress, 1st Session (Washington, DC: U.S. Government Printing Office, 1975), pp. 33, 36. Bill Ayers, the founder of the Weathermen, later denied that Saxe and Power were members of his group. See Scott Jaschik, "Banned in Boston," *Inside Higher Ed*, March 30, 2009, https://www.insidehighered.com/news/2009/03/30/banned-boston.
32. "Armed struggle" in Bernardine Dohrn et al., Students for a Democratic Society magazine, *Prairie Fire*, in *The Weather Underground: Report of the Subcommittee to Investigate the Administration of the Internal Security Act*, Committee of the Judiciary, United States Senate (Washington, DC: Government Printing Office, 1975), appendix 1, p. 122; Dee Wedemeyer and John Barbour, "How Did It Happen? Honor Girl Student Now on FBI List," *Los Angeles Times*, November 1, 1970, p. B6; Lucinda Franks, "Return of the Fugitive," *New Yorker*, June 13, 1994, p. 42.
33. Richard L. Abel, *American Lawyers* (New York: Oxford University Press, 1989), p. 96; Patricia Lear, "Rebel without a Pause," *Chicago Magazine*, May 1, 1993, https://www.chicagomag.com/chicago-magazine/may-1993/rebel-without-a-pause/.

34. J. Edgar Hoover, testimony before the House Subcommittee on Appropriations, March 17, 1971, 92nd Congress, 1st Session, quoted in Bryan Burrough, *Days of Rage: America's Radical Underground, the FBI, and the Forgotten Age of Revolutionary Violence* (New York: Penguin, 2015), p. 57; Dolores Ibárruri, "Women at the Front," September 4, 1936, in Marxists Internet Archive, https://www.marxists.org/archive/ibarruri/1936/09/04.htm.
35. "Guerrilla strategy" quoted in Lindsey Blake Churchill, "Exploring Feminism's Complex Relationship with Political Violence," MA thesis, University of South Florida, 2005, p. 22; "street fighting" and "ruling class" in Echols, *Daring to Be Bad*, p. 125; "Dig it" quoted in David Barber, *A Hard Rain Fell: SDS and Why It Failed* (Jackson: University Press of Mississippi, 2008), pp. 210–211.
36. John Kifner, "That's What the Weathermen Are Supposed to Be: Vandals in the Mother Country," *New York Times*, January 4, 1970, pp. 15–19; "incredible fury" in Peter Babcox, "Meet the Women of the Revolution," *New York Times*, February 9, 1969, p. 34.
37. Kifner, "That's What the Weathermen Are Supposed to Be," p. 18.
38. *The Weather Underground*, p. 16; see also Cathy Collis, "Women and the Weathermen," *Western Tributaries*, 4 (2017), pp. 1–12.
39. *The Weather Underground*, pp. 62–63. Though Dohrn had faced a prison sentence of up to eight years, by the time she gave herself up, federal charges against her had been dropped. She was sentenced to three years probation and a $1,500 fine. From 1991 to 2013 she was a professor of law at Northwestern University.
40. Angela Davis, *Angela Davis: An Autobiography* (1974; rpt., New York: International Publishers, 1988), pp. 109–110. There had been no women tenured faculty members in the Philosophy Department. See *UCLA General Catalog, 1968–69*, p. 383, https://registrar.ucla.edu/file/6712b8c2-8bee-45b8-92b1-3727a0c3287a.
41. "A national conspiracy" in Yolanda du Luart, dir., *Angela Davis: Portrait of a Revolutionary* (London: Contemporary Films, 1972). See also the American Association of University Professors' extensive report, sympathetic to Davis, in "Academic Freedom and Tenure: The University of California at Los Angeles," *AAUP Bulletin* (Autumn 1971), pp. 382–422.
42. John Lennon, "Angela," track B4 on *Some Time in New York City*, Apple Records SVBB3392, 1972, vinyl.
43. "Reds Hoping to Make Martyr of Angela to Raise Funds," *Chicago Tribune*, January 7, 1971, p. 6.
44. Kathleen Cleaver, wife of the Black Panther leader Eldridge Cleaver, had been the communications secretary for the Panthers. In 1974, when Huey Newton, cofounder and head of the Panthers, fled to Cuba to avoid arrest, he appointed Elaine Brown to head the Panthers in his absence. Brown writes in her memoir of experiences that were similar to those of Davis: in the Panthers, she says, "a woman asserting herself was a pariah" (*A Taste of Power: A Black Woman's Story* [New York: Doubleday, 1993], p. 357); "matriarchal" in Davis, *Angela Davis*, p. 201.

45. Quoted in "The Making of a Fugitive," *Life*, 69/11 (September 11, 1970), p. 27.
46. Quoted in Bart Barnes and Nancy Scannell, "No Sporting Chance: The Girls in the Locker Room," *Washington Post*, May 12, 1974, p. A14; Lesley Visser, "The Battle Is over the Law's Interpretation," *Boston Globe*, June 15, 1978, p. 46.
47. Janice Berman, "Martyr for Abortion Reform," *San Francisco Examiner*, October 22, 1971, p. 26; Jon Nordheimer, "She's Fighting Conviction for Aborting Her Child," *New York Times*, December 4, 1971; Martin Abramson, "One Case Gains National Attention," *Lowell Sun* (Massachusetts), September 5, 1972, p. 19.
48. Harry Blackmun, William J. Brennan, Lewis F. Powell, Potter Stewart, and Warren Burger (all Republicans) joined Democrats William O. Douglas and Thurgood Marshall in voting yes. Byron White, a Democrat, joined William Rehnquist, a Republican, in voting no.
49. Phyllis Schlafly, "What's Wrong with Equal Rights for Women?," *Phyllis Schlafly Report*, February 1972, https://eagleforum.org/wp-content/uploads/2017/03/PSR-Feb1972.pdf.
50. Jennifer L. Holland, *Tiny You: A Western History of the Anti-Abortion Movement* (Berkeley: University of California Press, 2020).
51. "What would become" quoted in Carl M. Brauer, "Women Activists, Southern Conservatives, and the Prohibition of Sex Discrimination in Title VII of the 1964 Civil Rights Act," *Journal of Southern History*, 49/1 (February 1983), pp. 48–49; Celler in *Congressional Record—House*, August 10, 1970, p. 28001, https://www.govinfo.gov/content/pkg/GPO-CRECB-1970-pt21/pdf/GPO-CRECB-1970-pt21-1-2.pdf.
52. Ervin's opposition to the ERA in "The Senate Passes the Equal Rights Amendment," March 22, 1972, United States Senate, https://www.senate.gov/artandhistory/history/minute/Senate_passes_ERA.htm; letter to the Senate Minority Leader about the Proposed Constitutional Amendment on Equal Rights for Men and Women," in *Public Papers of the Presidents of the United States, Richard Nixon, 1972* (Washington, DC: Government Printing Office, 1972), p. 444, https://quod.lib.umich.edu/p/ppotpus/4731812.1972.001?rgn=main;view=fulltext.
53. Mark Lieberman and Gene Spagnoli, "Liz Holtzman, Celler's Nemesis, Keeps Her Cool," *Daily News* (New York), June 22, 1972, p. 33; Elizabeth Holtzman, "Not a Job for a Woman," *Politico*, June 29, 2016, https://www.politico.com/magazine/story/2016/06/2016-hillary-clinton-woman-women-politics-feminist-feminism-history-sexism-leadership-214000/; "Liz the Lion Killer," *Time*, July 3, 1972, http://content.time.com/time/subscriber/article/0,33009,877856,00.html.
54. Quoted in Kirsten Marie Delegard, *Battling Miss Bolsheviki: The Origins of Female Conservatism in the United States* (Philadelphia: University of Pennsylvania Press, 2012), p. 214.
55. The Daughters of the American Revolution's role in the radical right is discussed in Seymour Martin Lipset, "The Radical Right: A Problem for American Democracy," *British Journal of Sociology*, 6/2 (June 1955), pp. 176–209; and Randall J. Hart, "The Greatest Subversive Plot in History? The American Radical Right

and Anti-UNESCO Campaigning," *Sociology*, 48/3 (2014), pp. 554–572. The Birch Society's view of the ERA is discussed in William E. Dunham, "The Equal Rights Amendment," December 1974, folder 9, box 86, Diane D. Blair Papers, MC 1632, Special Collections, University of Arkansas Libraries, Fayetteville; Gallup poll in Mark R. Daniels, Robert Darcy, and Joseph W. Westphal, "The ERA Won—At Least in the Opinion Polls," *PS*, 15/4 Autumn 1982, table 1, p. 579.

56. Donald T. Critchlow, *Phyllis Schlafly and Grassroots Conservatism: A Woman's Crusade* (Princeton, NJ: Princeton University Press, 2008), p. 33.

57. Phyllis Schlafly, *A Choice Not an Echo* (Alton, IL: Pere Marquette Press, 1964); "I would remind you": "Goldwater's 1964 Acceptance Speech," *Washington Post*, https://www.washingtonpost.com/wp-srv/politics/daily/may98/goldwaterspeech.htm.

58. Phyllis Schlafly, "What's Wrong with 'Equal Rights' for Women?," *Phyllis Schlafly Report*, February 1972, https://www.phyllisschlafly.com/family/whats-wrong-with-equal-rights-for-women-february-1972/; Schlafly, "The Fraud Called the Equal Rights Amendment," *Phyllis Schlafly Report*, May 1972, https://www.phyllisschlafly.com/constitution/the-fraud-called-the-equal-rights-amendment-may-1972/; and Schlafly, "The Right to Be a Woman," *Phyllis Schlafly Report*, November 1972, https://www.phyllisschlafly.com/constitution/the-right-to-be-a-woman/.

59. "Congress will be" quoted in Critchlow, *Phyllis Schlafly and Grassroots Conservatism*, p. 212. Schlafly was not alone in spreading panic about the dangers of conscription that would be triggered by the ERA. Lottie Beth Hobbs, a Christian fundamentalist in Texas, published the *Pink Sheet*, an anti-ERA screed, in which she warned her women readers, "DO YOU WANT YOUR HUSBAND TO SLEEP IN THE BARRACKS WITH WOMEN?," (quoted in Nancy L. Cohen, *Delirium: The Politics of Sex in America* [Berkeley, CA: Counterpoint, 2012], p. 50). Around the country, anti-ERA groups mushroomed, such as Happiness of Womanhood and the League of Housewives. See United Press International, "They're Housewives and Proud of It," *New York Times*, April 3, 1972, p. 44. See also my discussion of Schlafly's battle against the pro-ERA International Women's Year Conference in 1977 in Lillian Faderman, *The Gay Revolution: The Story of the Struggle* (New York: Simon and Schuster, 2015), pp. 309–317.

60. Associated Press, "Bread Used as a Symbolic Gesture," *Dixon Evening Telegraph* (Illinois), March 14, 1973, p. 24; "ERA Loss," *Albany Democrat-Herald* (Oregon), June 30, 1982, p. 1.

61. Quoted in Earni Young, "NOW Leader: Women Haven't Lost War Yet," *Philadelphia Daily News*, June 30, 1982, p. 14.

62. "What Next for US Women," *Time*, December 5, 1977, p. 39; Phyllis Schlafly, Ed Martin, and Brett M. Decker, *The Conservative Case for Trump* (Washington, DC: Regnery Publishing, 2016), chapter 6.

63. Ronald Reagan, *Abortion and the Conscience of the Nation* (New York: Thomas Nelson, 1984), p. 40. Reagan must be credited with appointing the first woman to the Supreme Court, Sandra Day O'Connor, and the second woman to be secre-

tary of health and human services, Margaret Heckler. Susan Faludi, *Backlash: The Undeclared War against Women* (New York: Crown, 1991).

64. Dena Kleiman, "Many Young Women Now Say They'd Pick Family over Career," *New York Times*, December 28, 1980; Barbara Bassler, "Putting a Career on Hold," *New York Times*, December 7, 1986; Brenda Lane Richardson, "Professional Women Do Go Home Again," *New York Times*, April 20, 1988; George Gilder, "Women in the Work Force," *Atlantic*, September 1986, https://www.theatlantic.com/magazine/archive/1986/09/women-in-the-work-force/304924/; George Gilder's *Sexual Suicide* was reissued in 1986 as *Men and Marriage* (New Orleans: Pelican).

65. David E. Bloom and Neil G. Bennett, "Marriage Patterns in the United States," *National Bureau of Economic Studies: Labor Research*, September 1985, https://www.nber.org/system/files/working_papers/w1701/w1701.pdf; Eloise Salholz, "The Marriage Crunch," *Newsweek*, June 2, 1986, p. 55.

66. Mitra Toossi, "A Century of Change: The U.S. Labor Force, 1950–2025," *Monthly Labor Review* (May 2002), p. 18. See also the tables in "Women at Work: A Visual Essay," *Monthly Labor Review* (October 2003), pp. 47–49; Daniel Borzelleca, "The Male-Female Ratio in College," *Forbes*, February 16, 2012, https://www.forbes.com/sites/ccap/2012/02/16/the-male-female-ratio-in-college/?sh=7806f8e4fa52; Marjorie A. Bowman, "Historical Context," in *Women in Medicine: Career and Life Management*, 3rd ed., ed. Marjorie A. Bowman, Erica Frank, and Deborah I. Allen (New York: Springer, 2002), p. 2; Rhoda Wynn, "Saints and Sinners: Women and the Practice of Medicine throughout the Ages," *JAMA*, 283/5 (2000), pp. 668–669.

67. Susan Bolotin, "Voices from the Post-Feminist Generation," *New York Times*, October 17, 1982, section 6, p. 29.

14.

HOW SEX SPAWNED A NEW "WOMAN"

1. "How to Be as Horny as a Guy," in *The Bust Guide to the New Girl Order*, ed. Marcelle Karp and Debbie Stoller (New York: Penguin, 1999), p. 104. The book is an anthology of six years of *Bust* articles. *Bust* continued to attract huge numbers of readers into the new millennium, including 500,000 unique visitors to its website every month. See also Alix Strauss, "Bust Magazine Is on a Mission," *New York Times*, October 31, 2018, p. MB5.

2. Camille Paglia, "Perspective Needed—Feminism's Lie," *Seattle Times*, February 17, 1991.

3. Camille Paglia, *Sexual Personae: Art and Decadence from Nefertiti to Emily Dickinson* (New Haven, CT: Yale University Press, 1990), pp. 20–21, 38.

4. Camille Paglia, *Vamps and Tramps: New Essays* (New York: Penguin, 1995), p. xvi; Katie Roiphe, *The Morning After: Sex, Fear, and Feminism on Campus* (Boston: Little, Brown, 1993).

5. See Catharine A. MacKinnon and Andrea Dworkin, eds., *In Harm's Way: The Pornography Civil Rights Hearings* (Cambridge, MA: Harvard University Press, 1997).

6. "Rape Hype Betrays Feminism," *New York Times Magazine*, June 13, 1992, pp. 26–30.
7. N.O.W. Women's Sexuality Conference, "Speak Out" Portion, Produced by Nanette Rainone, June 9 or 10, 1973, 46 min., tape no. BC 1580, Pacifica Radio Archives, https://www.pacificaradioarchives.org/recording/bc1580; Laurie Johnston, "Women's Sexuality Conference Ends in School Here," *New York Times*, June 11, 1973, p. 10; "limited and limiting" in Ellen Carol DuBois and Linda Gordon, "Seeking Ecstasy on the Battlefield: Danger and Pleasure in Nineteenth-Century Feminist Sexual Thought," in *Pleasure and Danger: Exploring Female Sexuality*, ed. Carole S. Vance (Boston: Routledge and Kegan Paul, 1984), p. 67. Vance's book is a collection of papers delivered at the Barnard conference "Toward a Politics of Sexuality" on April 24, 1982.
8. Alan K. Simpson to Anita Hill in *Nomination of Judge Clarence Thomas to Be Associate Justice of the Supreme Court of the United States: Hearings before the Committee on the Judiciary, U.S. Senate, October 11, 12, 13, 1991* (Washington, DC: U.S. Government Printing Office, 1993), p. 128.
9. Anita Hill, *Speaking Truth to Power* (New York: Doubleday, 1997), pp. 50, 51.
10. Hill, *Speaking Truth to Power*, p. 61.
11. Anita Hill to Dennis DeConcini in *Nomination of Judge Clarence Thomas*, p. 123.
12. Testimony of Anita F. Hill in *Nomination of Judge Clarence Thomas*, pp. 36–40.
13. "Let's get my guy in" quoted in Lisa Chase, "An Oral History of the Day Women Changed Congress," *Elle*, September 9, 2014, https://www.elle.com/culture/career-politics/a14737/history-of-nytimes-photo-house-of-representatives-1991/; "a closet liberal" in David Margolick, "Questions to Thomas Fall Short of the Mark," *New York Times*, September 15, 1991, p. 1.
14. Hill, *Speaking Truth to Power*, p. 352.
15. "Nina Totenberg's NPR Report on Anita Hill's Charges of Sexual Harassment by Clarence Thomas," October 6, 1991, NPR *Weekend Edition*, Jewish Women's Archive, https://jwa.org/media/transcript-of-nina-totenbergs-npr-report-on-anita-hills-charges-of-sexual-harassment-by-0.
16. Maureen Dowd, "Seven Congresswomen March to Senate to Demand Delay in Thomas Vote," *New York Times*, October 9, 1991; Annys Shin and Libby Casey, "Anita Hill and Her 1991 Congressional Defenders to Joe Biden," *Washington Post*, November 22, 2017; Chase, "An Oral History of the Day Women Changed Congress."
17. Hill, *Speaking Truth to Power*, p. 13.
18. *Nomination of Judge Clarence Thomas*, pp. 81–83, 97; David Brock, *Blinded by the Right: The Conscience of an Ex-Conservative* (2001; rpt., New York: Broadway Books, 2003), 107; David Brock, "The Real Anita Hill," *American Spectator* (March 1992), pp. 18–31.
19. *Nomination of Judge Clarence Thomas*, p. 254. Simpson's accusation that Hill was a lesbian was so disquieting that the conservative journalist William Safire sided briefly with her, writing that instead of innuendo, if Simpson had evidence that Hill's sexual preference had any bearing on her charge of sexual harassment, "let

him make his case or shut up" ("The Plot to Savage Thomas," *New York Times*, October 14, 1991). Tabloid reporter in Hill, *Speaking Truth to Power*, p. 3.
20. *Nomination of Judge Clarence Thomas*, p. 157.
21. John Danforth, Thomas Confirmation Debate, October 8, 1991, C-Span, https://www.c-span.org/video/?21886-1/thomas-confirmation-debate.
22. Forty-one Republicans voted yes and forty-six Democrats voted no.
23. *Nomination of Judge Clarence Thomas*, p. 118.
24. Michael X. Delli Carpini and Bruce A. Williams, "The Year of the Woman? Candidates, Votes, and the 1992 Elections," *Political Science Quarterly*, 108 (1993), pp. 29–36.
25. Quoted in Danielle Service, "Second-Generation Walker Makes Her Own Stand for Feminism," *Emory Report*, 49/23 (March 17, 1997), https://www.emory.edu/EMORY_REPORT/erarchive/1997/March/ermarch.17/3_17_97Walker.html. Walker elaborated on these ideas in "Being Real: An Introduction," in *To Be Real: Telling the Truth and Changing the Face of Feminism*, ed. Rebecca Walker (New York: Anchor Books, 1995), pp. xxix–xxxix.
26. Rebecca Walker, "Becoming the Third Wave," *Ms.* (January–February 1992), pp. 39–41.
27. Nancy Friday, *Women on Top: How Real Life Has Changed Women's Sexual Fantasies* (New York: Simon and Schuster, 1991), p. 13.
28. Some scholars conflate postfeminism and third-wave feminism. See Fien Adriaens and Sofie Van Bauwel, "*Sex and the City*: A Postfeminist Point of View? Or How Popular Culture Functions as a Channel for Feminist Discourse," *Journal of Popular Culture*, 47/1 (February 2014), pp. 174–195. The distinction I have tried to highlight is based on third-wave feminists' understanding of their connection to the second wave, compared to postfeminists' hostility toward the second wave; "these days" in JeeYuen Lee, "Beyond Bean Counting," in *Listen Up: Voices from the Next Feminist Generation*, ed. Barbara Findlen (1995; rpt., Seattle: Seal Press, 2001), p. 92.
29. See also R. Claire Synder, "What Is Third-Wave Feminism?," *Signs*, 34/1 (Autumn 2008), pp. 175–196.
30. Nancy Friday, *My Secret Garden: Women's Sexual Fantasies* (New York: Simon and Schuster, 1973); "tentative" in Friday, *Women on Top*, p. 15; "sound like a new race," in Friday, *Women on Top*, p. 9.
31. Friday, *Women on Top*, pp. 4–5, 64–65.
32. Candace Bushnell, *Sex and the City* (New York: Grand Central Publishing, 1997), pp. 35–36.
33. Jennifer Keishin Armstrong, *Mary and Lou and Rhoda and Ted: And All the Brilliant Minds Who Made the* Mary Tyler Moore Show *a Classic* (New York: Simon and Schuster, 2013), chapter 11.
34. "Vice President Quayle and the Murphy Brown Speech," *The Forerunner*, August 1, 1992, https://www.forerunner.com/forerunner/x0406_quayles_murphy_brown.html. The cultural uproar that resulted from the episode is reflected in Barbara Dafoe Whitehead, "Dan Quayle Was Right," *Atlantic*, April 1993; and Rick Du Brow, "The Unwed Mother of All TV Battles: Television: The Furor

Involving Vice President Dan Quayle and 'Murphy Brown' Illustrates the Impact That TV Can Have as a Social Force," *Los Angeles Times*, May 21, 1992.

35. "Threesomes are huge": *Sex and the City*, episode "Three's a Crowd," July 26, 1998, https://www.imdb.com/title/tt0698692/characters/nm0000326; "I'm a trisexual": *Sex and the City*, episode "Boy, Girl, Boy, Girl," June 25, 2000, https://www.imdb.com/title/tt0698620/characters/nm0000326.

36. Tanya Gold, "Sorry, Sisters, But I Hate *Sex and the City*," *The Telegraph*, May 21, 2010; Joan Swirsky, "The Death of Feminism, II: *Sex and the City* Is a Pity," *Newsmax*, July 23, 2003. For a feminist reading of *Sex and the City*, see Astrid Henry, "Orgasms and Empowerment," in *Reading Sex in the City*, ed. Kim Akass and Janet McCabe (New York: I. B. Taurus, 2004), pp. 65–83. "20 percent" in Tamala M. Edwards, "Flying Solo," *Time*, August 20, 2000, http://content.time.com/time/magazine/article/0,9171,52954-4,00.html. Edwards's information came from Barbara Dafoe Whitehead, codirector of Rutgers University's National Marriage Project.

37. James Poniewozik, "All-TIME 100 TV Shows," *Time*, https://time.com/collection/all-time-100-tv-shows/.

38. Bikini Kill, "White Boy," from the album *Yeah, Yeah, Yeah, Yeah* (Olympia, WA: Kill Rock Stars, 1993), vinyl.

39. Underground subcultures in Wini Breines, "The 'Other' Fifties: Beats and Bad Girls," in *Not June Cleaver: Women and Gender in Postwar America, 1945–1960*, ed. Joanne Meyerowitz (Philadelphia: Temple University Press, 1994), pp. 382–408; Tom McCarthy, "Patti: Poet as Macho Woman," *Village Voice*, February 7, 1974, p. 47; "Female," in Patti Smith, *Seventh Heaven* (New York: Telegraph Books, 1972), p. 44. Some of the earliest punk icons expressly disdained machismo and experimented with androgyny. Iggy Pop, known as the "godfather of punk," even appeared on stage in semidrag. For a discussion of Iggy Pop's gender-bending, see Sasha Geffen, *Glitter Up the Dark: How Pop Music Broke the Binary* (Austin: University of Texas Press, 2020), chapter 3; "a little Brando" in Amy Gross, "Introducing Rock 'n' Roll's Lady Raunch: Patti Smith," *Mademoiselle* (September 1975), http://www.oceanstar.com/patti/intervus/7509made.htm; Debbie Harry, the female lead singer for the otherwise all-male band Blondie, was an exception to the secondary roles of women in the 1970s. With her peroxided blonde hair, Harry created an onstage persona of "an inflatable doll, but with a dark, provocative, aggressive side" (Debbie Harry, *Face It: A Memoir* [New York: Dey Street Books, 2019]). Courtney Love, inspired by male punk bands such as Big Black in the 1980s, was dismissive in the 1990s of riot grrrls as "teensy, weensy." She resented being associated with them and their style of radical-feminist politics, shouting at an audience of women, "I'M NOT POLITICALLY CORRECT. AND I'M NOT THE VOICE OF A GENERATION. SO FUCK YOU!!!!" (Poppy Z. Brite, *Courtney Love: The Real Story* [London: Orion, 1997], pp. 131, 176).

40. Tobi Vail, "The Jigsaw Manifesto," *Jigsaw*, 4 (1991), quoted in Alison Piepmeier, *Girl Zines: Making Media, Doing Feminism* (New York: New York University Press, 2009), p. 1.

41. Quoted in Celina Hex, "Fierce, Funny, Feminists: Gloria Steinem and Kathleen Hanna Talk Shop," *Bust* (Winter 2000), pp. 52–56.
42. Sara Marcus, *Girls to the Front: The True Story of the Riot Grrrl Revolution* (New York: HarperCollins, 2010).
43. "News cycle": see, for example, Bob Dart, "Hispanic Anger, Frustration, Boil over in Nation's Capital," *Atlanta Constitution*, May 8, 1991, p. 10; the start of "riot grrrls" in Elke Zobl and Kristen Schilt, "Connecting the Dots: Riot Grrrls, Ladyfests, and the International Grrrl Zine Network," in *Next Wave Cultures: Feminism, Subcultures, Activism*, ed. Anita Harris (New York: Routledge, 2007), p. 174; "That's girl" in Ann Japenga, "Punk Feminists Band Together as Riot Girls," *San Francisco Examiner*, November 22, 1992, p. 215.
44. "New-Style Female Bands Are a Riot, Grrrl," *Daily Tar Heel* (Chapel Hill, North Carolina), September 24, 1992, p. 14.
45. "Rallying cry": see interview with Kathleen Hanna, *The Laura Flanders Show*, GRITtv, April 8, 2015, https://www.youtube.com/watch?v=owMzgJZRjAA.
46. Michael Jackson, "Bad" (official video), https://www.youtube.com/watch?v=Sd4SJVsTulc; Madonna, "Express Yourself" (official video), https://www.youtube.com/watch?v=GsVcUzP_O_8; Bikini Kill, "Resist Psychic Death," from the album *Yeah, Yeah, Yeah, Yeah*, https://www.youtube.com/watch?v=6NnJkJWhooE.
47. Lindsay Shonteff, dir., *The Million Eyes of Sumuru* (Los Angeles: American International Pictures, 1967); 7 Year Bitch, "Dead Men Don't Rape," from the album *Sick 'Em*, 1992, https://www.youtube.com/watch?v=j2ybKzN869A.
48. Madonna, "Material Girl" (official video), https://www.youtube.com/watch?v=6p-lDYPR2P8; "REAL BOYZ" quoted in Geffen, *Glitter Up the Dark*, p. 188.
49. Gannett News Service, "The Look: Anything but Cute," *Burlington Free Press* (Vermont), August 10, 1992, p. 22; Lauren Spencer, "Grrrls Only," *Washington Post*, January 3, 1993, p. C2.
50. Angela Heywood, "Sex-Nomenclature," *The Word* (April 1887), pp. 2–3; Joreen [Jo Freeman], "The Bitch Manifesto," in *Notes from the Second Year: Women's Liberation; Major Writings of the Radical Feminists*, ed. Shulamith Firestone and Anne Koedt (New York: New York Radical Feminists, 1970), p. 5; "Revolution, Girl Style," *Newsweek*, November 22, 1992, https://www.newsweek.com/revolution-girl-style-196998.
51. Bratmobile, "Bitch Theme," from the album *Pottymouth*, https://www.youtube.com/watch?v=Qpvh8a3EeYo; Bikini Kill, "Lil' Red Riding Bitch" lyrics quoted in Emily White, "Revolution Girl-Style Now!," *Chicago Reader*, September 24, 1992, https://chicagoreader.com/news-politics/revolution-girl-style-now/.
52. Bratmobile, "Juswanna," from the album *Pottymouth*, https://www.youtube.com/watch?v=n4Y7VA3whXo; Bikini Kill, "Don't Need You" and "This Is Not a Test," from the album *Yeah, Yeah, Yeah, Yeah*, https://www.youtube.com/watch?v=3xEhindB900; The Frumpies, "Fuck Yr. Frumpies," from the album *Frumpie One-Piece*, https://www.youtube.com/watch?v=vgUTFRJKivs.
53. White, "Revolution Girl-Style Now!"

54. Cold Cold Hearts, "Broken Teeth," from the album *Cold Cold Hearts*, https://www.youtube.com/watch?v=kaa48nKrWCI.

15.
"WOMAN" IN A NEW MILLENNIUM

1. S. Josephine Baker, *Fighting for Life* (New York: Macmillan, 1939), p. 64.
2. Amy Coney Barrett Senate Confirmation Hearing, Day 1 Transcript, October 12, 2020, Rev Transcript Library, https://www.rev.com/blog/transcripts/amy-coney-barrett-senate-confirmation-hearing-day-1-transcript; nomination acceptance speech transcript in *Epoch Times*, September 26, 2020, https://www.theepochtimes.com/read-full-transcript-of-acceptance-speech-by-supreme-court-nominee-amy-coney-barrett_3515776.html.
3. Quoted in Lisa Belkin, "The Opt-Out Revolution," *New York Times Magazine*, October 26, 2003, https://www.nytimes.com/2003/10/26/magazine/the-opt-out-revolution.html.
4. S. J. Hanson and Anne E. Burke, "Fertility Control: Contraception, Sterilization, and Abortion," in *The Johns Hopkins Manual of Gynecology and Obstetrics*, 4th ed., ed. K. Joseph Hurt et al. (Philadelphia: Lippincott Williams and Wilkins, 2012), pp. 382–395; Stanley K. Henshaw, "Abortion Incidence and Services in the United States, 1995–1996," *Family Planning Perspectives*, 30/6 (November–December 1998), pp. 263–270, 287; Erin Duffin, "Percentage of the U.S. Population Who Have Completed Four Years of College or More from 1940 to 2019," *Statista*, March 2020, https://www.statista.com/statistics/184272/educational-attainment-of-college-diploma-or-higher-by-gender/; Michelle J. Chang et al., "Beyond Myths: The Growth and Diversity of Asian American College Freshmen, 1971–2005" (Los Angeles: University of California, Los Angeles Higher Education Research Institute, 2007); Patricia Gandara, "Fulfilling America's Future: Latinas in the U.S.," in *The White House Initiative on Educational Excellence for Hispanics*, 2015, https://permanent.fdlp.gov/gpo64749/Fulfilling-Americas-Future-Latinas-in-the-U.S.-2015-Final-Report.pdf. The report includes comparative discussions of Black, Asian, and white women.
5. Richard K. Neumann Jr., "Women in Legal Education: What the Statistics Show," *Journal of Legal Education*, 50/3 (August 2000), table 1, p. 315; Edward S. Salsberg and Gaetano J. Forte, "Trends in the Physician Workforce, 1980–2000," *Health Affairs*, 21/5 (September/October 2002), pp. 165–173; Dottie Lamm, "Gender Isn't the Barrier It Once Was," *Denver Post*, October 6, 2011; business majors in Belkin, "The Opt-Out Revolution"; Yilu Zhao, "Women Soon to Be the Majority of Veterinarians," *New York Times*, June 9, 2002; Zena Burgess and Phyllis Tharenou, "Women Board Directors: Characteristics of the Few," *Journal of Business Ethics*, 37 (April 2002), pp. 39–49. The authors point out that the number represents only a little over 11 percent of board members. Nevertheless, the trend was an increase over preceding years. Peter Fronczek and Patricia Johnson, "Occupations: 2000," August 2003, https://www.census.gov/prod/2003pubs/c2kbr-25.pdf.

6. Dena Kleiman, "Many Young Women Now Say They'd Pick Family over Career," *New York Times*, December 28, 1980; Brenda Lane Richardson, "Professional Women Do Go Home Again," *New York Times*, April 20, 1988; Iris Krasnow, *Surrendering to Motherhood: Losing Your Mind, Finding Your Soul* (New York: Miramax Books, 1997); "Washington Post–Kaiser Foundation–Harvard University Gender Poll Results," *Washington Post*, March 26, 1998. Fewer of the men respondents (35 percent) longed for a return to the era of the happy housewife, which suggested that many men no longer felt that being the family's sole breadwinner affirmed their manhood; James T. Bond, Ellen Galinsky, and Jennifer E. Swanberg, 1997 *National Study of the Changing Workforce* (New York: Families and Work Institute, 1998), p. 54. Men continued to evolve consistently away from an attachment to sex-role divisions, at least in response to polling questions. For instance, in a 1977 poll that asked whether men should earn the money and women stay home and take care of house and family, 74 percent of men said yes; only 40 percent of men said yes to the same question in 2008. See Brian Heilman et al., "State of America's Fathers" (Washington, DC: Promundo, 2016), p. 58.
7. Sharon R. Cohany and Emy Sok, "Trends in Labor Force Participation of Married Mothers of Infants," *Monthly Labor Review* (February 2007), p. 9; Linda Hirshman, "Homeward Bound," *The American Prospect*, November 21, 2005, https://prospect.org/article/homeward-bound-d2/.
8. The essentialism of these respondents' views about women's cognitive differences from men is reminiscent of Carol Gilligan's popular study *In a Different Voice: Psychological Theory and Women's Development* (Cambridge, MA: Harvard University Press, 1982); women's book club members quoted in Belkin, "The Opt-Out Revolution." Arielle Kuperberg and Pamela Stone have shown statistically that college-educated professional women, who were usually the demographic featured in media pieces on women "opting out" of the workforce, were actually somewhat less likely than women in other demographics to have left the workforce during these years ("The Media Depiction of Women Who Opt Out," *Gender and Society*, 22/4 [August 2008], pp. 497–517).
9. Lauren Key Burns, "The Ultimate Dance," in *Choosing Home: 20 Mothers Celebrate Staying Home, Raising Children, and Changing the World*, ed. Rachel Chaney and Kerry McDonald (n.p., 2015).
10. Caitlin Flanagan, "To Hell with All That," *New Yorker*, July 5, 2004, p. 38. See also Flanagan, *To Hell With All That: Loving and Loathing Our Inner Housewife* (New York: Little, Brown, 2006), in which she later admitted that she was "far too educated and uppity to have knuckled down and learned anything about stain remover" (pp. 52–53), but she waxed poetic, with a fair degree of seriousness, over old-fashioned books of housewifery that offer tips about "wiping down an empty refrigerator once a month" (p. 46); Benjamin Spock, *Baby and Child Care* (New York: Pocket Books, 1957), p. 569.
11. Daphne de Marneffe, *Maternal Desire: On Children, Love, and the Inner Life* (New York: Little, Brown, 2004), p. 15.
12. Quoted in Louise Story, "Many Women at Elite Colleges Set Career Path to Motherhood," *New York Times*, September 20, 2005. See also Leslie Bennetts,

The Feminine Mistake: Are We Giving Up Too Much? (New York: Hachette, 2007), chapter 1.

13. Richard Posner, "Elite Universities and Women's Careers," *The Becker-Posner Blog*, September 25, 2005. See also Richard A. Posner, "Conservative Feminism," *University of Chicago Legal Forum* (1989), pp. 191–217, in which Posner argued against feminist proposals such as comparable worth, affirmative action for women, and government-sponsored day care.
14. Leslie Stahl, "Staying at Home," *60 Minutes*, CBS, October 10, 2004.
15. See Judith Warner's discussion of how all forms of media encourage the disproportionate cultural influence of the upper-middle-class—including, in the early twenty-first century, the resurgence of the "mommy mystique" (*Perfect Madness: Motherhood in the Age of Anxiety* [New York: Riverhead Books, 2005], chapter 1); "sell cars" quoted in Chaney and McDonald, *Choosing Home*; "psychological well-being" in Leslie Morgan Steiner, ed., *Mommy Wars: Stay-at-Home and Career Moms Face Off on Their Choices, Their Lives, Their Families* (New York: Random House, 2006), p. xxiv.
16. Since on average lesbians had more consistent work histories and higher levels of education than heterosexual women did, in 2007—at the height of the opt-out revolution—they were earning 26 percent more than heterosexual women workers (though they were earning 13 percent less than heterosexual men workers). See Marieka Klawitter, "Meta-Analysis of the Effects of Sexual Orientation on Earnings," *Industrial Relations*, 54/1 (January 2015), https://onlinelibrary.wiley.com/doi/full/10.1111/irel.12075; Black women MBAs in Belkin, "The Opt-Out Revolution"; Lonnae O'Neal Parker, *I'm Every Woman: Remixed Stories of Marriage, Motherhood, and Work* (New York: Amistad, 2005), p. 12.
17. Quoted in Lynette Clemetson, "Work vs. Family, Complicated by Race," *New York Times*, February 9, 2006, https://www.nytimes.com/2006/02/09/fashion/thursdaystyles/work-vs-family-complicated-by-race.html. Black women with college degrees were also earning more than white women with college degrees because, like lesbians, Black women were more likely than white women to stay employed and to work longer hours.
18. Quoted in Kate Shatzkin, "Mutual Support," *Baltimore Sun*, February 6, 2005, pp. N1, N5.
19. Sheryl Sandberg, *Lean In: Women, Work, and the Will to Lead* (New York: Knopf, 2013), p. 118.
20. Derek Thompson, "It's Not Just a Recession. It's a Mancession!," *Atlantic*, July 9, 2009, https://www.theatlantic.com/business/archive/2009/07/its-not-just-a-recession-its-a-mancession/20991/. In 2005, 63 percent of mothers of preschool children worked. By 2010, 68 percent were working. See Diana Lavery, "More Mothers of Young Children in U.S. Workforce," Population Reference Bureau, November 7, 2012, https://www.prb.org/resources/more-mothers-of-young-children-in-u-s-workforce/; Judith Warner, "The Opt-Out Generation Wants Back In," *New York Times*, August 7, 2013. O'Donnel's fate is also discussed in "Opt-Out Over? Stay at Home Moms Look to Rejoin Workforce," CBS News, August 8, 2013, https://www.youtube.com/watch?v=fTyVu_u24j0. For earlier dis-

cussions of the difficulties opt-out women had in rejoining the workforce, see Sylvia Ann Hewlett and Carolyn Buck Luce, "Off-Ramps and On-Ramps: Keeping Talented Women on the Road to Success," *Harvard Business Review* (March 2005), https://hbr.org/2005/03/off-ramps-and-on-ramps-keeping-talented-women-on-the-road-to-success; and Linda Hirshman, "Bumpy Ride," *The American Prospect*, May 24, 2007, https://prospect.org/article/bumpy-ride/. Both articles reported that only a fraction of the highly qualified women who wanted to opt in again were able to find satisfactory jobs.

21. Cohany and Sok, "Trends in Labor Force Participation," charts 1 and 2, p. 10; Arlie Hochschild with Anne Machung, *The Second Shift: Working Families and the Revolution at Home* (New York: Viking Penguin, 1989).

22. Joan Williams, *Unbending Gender: Why Family and Work Conflict and What to Do about It* (New York: Oxford University Press, 2000); Susan Cheever, "Baby Battles," in Steiner, *Mommy Wars*, p. 42.

23. The term "mommy track" was coined by Felice N. Schwartz in "Management Women and the New Facts of Life," *Harvard Business Review* (January 1989), https://hbr.org/1989/01/management-women-and-the-new-facts-of-life; "mommy trap" quoted in Beverly Beyette, "A New Career Flap: What's a Mommy Track and Why Are So Many Women Upset about It?," *Los Angeles Times*, March 17, 1989.

24. "American Time Use Survey," Bureau of Labor Statistics, June 25, 2020, table 3, https://www.bls.gov/news.release/atus.nr0.htm; "tend the home" in Colette A. Allred, "Attitudes on Women's Roles in the Home, 1986–2016," *Family Profiles*, FP-18-10 (2018), National Center for Family and Marriage Research, Bowling Green State University, https://www.bgsu.edu/ncfmr/resources/data/family-profiles/allred-attitudes-womens-roles-home-fp-18-10.html; Kim Parker et al., "On Gender Differences, No Consensus on Nature vs. Nurture," Pew Research Center, December 5, 2017, https://www.pewresearch.org/social-trends/2017/12/05/on-gender-differences-no-consensus-on-nature-vs-nurture/; Danielle Paquette, "The Stark Difference between Millennial Men and Their Dads," *Washington Post*, May 26, 2016. Paquette discusses a 2016 YouGov survey of 1,000 American men, "The Decline of the Manly Man," which found that less than one-third of millennials felt "completely masculine," compared to double that number in the boomer generation. See also Claire Cain Miller, "Millennial Men Aren't the Dads They Thought They'd Be," *New York Times*, July 30, 2015. In a Family and Work Institute Study that Miller cites, only 35 percent of millennial men thought that men should be the breadwinners and wives the caregivers.

25. Joan C. Williams and Amy J. C. Cuddy, "Will Working Mothers Take Your Company to Court?," *Harvard Business Review* (September 2012), https://hbr.org/2012/09/will-working-mothers-take-your-company-to-court; Erika Janes, "Yes, Being 'Mommy Tracked' Is a Real Thing—But You Don't Have to Put Up with It," *The Muse* (2016), https://www.themuse.com/advice/mommy-track-what-to-do; Jonathan Stempel, "Ex-VP Sues Goldman over 'Mommy Track,'" Reuters, March 24, 2010; Debra Cassens Weiss, "'Mommy Track Is a Dead End' at Morrison and Foerster, Associates Allege in $100M Suit," *ABA Journal*, April 30, 2018,

https://www.abajournal.com/news/article/mommy_track_is_a_dead_end_at_morison_foerster_associates_allege_in_100m_su.

26. Sandberg, *Lean In*, pp. 120, 111. Along with the publication of her book, Sandberg founded and funded the Lean In Foundation to advocate for gender equality and help women start "lean-in circles" through which they could encourage one another to be "unapologetically ambitious." Forty-four thousand circles were established in the United States and in 170 countries abroad. Diverse by design, the foundation aimed to pull in every demographic of women, such as Latina immigrants, women in the military, women of color, and so-called left over women in China.

27. "The risk" in Sandberg, *Lean In*, p. 118.

28. Anne-Marie Slaughter, "Why Women Still Can't Have It All," *Atlantic*, 310/1 (July–August 2012), p. 21; Kathy Caprino, "Why the Concept behind 'Lean In' Needs to Be Modified," *Forbes*, March 12, 2015, https://www.forbes.com/sites/kathycaprino/2015/03/12/why-the-concept-behind-lean-in-needs-to-be-modified/?sh=7d8f774668b6; Caitlin Flanagan, "What about the Children?," *Time*, March 7, 2013, https://ideas.time.com/2013/03/07/what-about-the-children/.

29. Michelle Obama quoted in Emily Alford, "Michelle Obama on Lean In: 'That Shit Doesn't Work All the Time,'" *Jezebel*, December 2, 2018, https://jezebel.com/michelle-obama-on-lean-in-that-shit-doesnt-work-all-th-1830807096. Shortly after Obama's attack on the Lean-In movement, Sandberg was caught up in a scandal that held her responsible for Russia's use of Facebook to influence the 2016 election. Some media evinced a puzzling amount of schadenfreude about the downfall of Sandberg and her movement. See, for example, Caitlin Gibson, "The End of Leaning In: How Sheryl Sandberg's Message of Empowerment Fully Unraveled," *Washington Post*, December 20, 2018; Mike Dorning, "Employer: Michelle Obama's Raise Well-Earned," *Chicago Tribune*, September 27, 2006.

30. Judith Newman, "Lean In: Five Years Later," *New York Times*, March 16, 2018; Kelsey Snell, "Tammy Duckworth Brings Her Baby to Senate Floor after Rule Change," NPR, April 18, 2018, https://www.npr.org/2018/04/18/603354839/after-lawmaker-gives-birth-senate-poised-to-allow-infants-in-for-votes.

31. Chant at a Me Too rally, quoted in Brittny Mejia, "Sparked by MeToo Campaign, Sexual Assault Survivors Rally and March in Hollywood," *Los Angeles Times*, November 12, 2017.

32. Louise DeKoven Bowen: see chapter 9; Claire Safran, "What Men Do to Women on the Job: A Shocking Look at Sexual Harassment," *Redbook* (November 1976), pp. 217–223; Elizabeth Kolbert, "The Thomas Nomination; Sexual Harassment at Work Is Pervasive, Survey Suggests," *New York Times*, October 11, 1991.

33. Florence Rush, *The Best-Kept Secret: The Sexual Abuse of Children* (Englewood Cliffs, NJ: Prentice-Hall, 1980); Jeffrey Moussaieff Masson, *The Assault on Truth: Freud's Suppression of the Seduction Theory* (New York: Farrar, Straus and Giroux, 1984); Charles C. Mapes, "A Pracitical Consideration of Sexual Assault," in *The Medical Age*, vol. 24, ed. Frederick W. Mann (Detroit: E. G. Swift, 1906), p. 937; Gurney Williams, "Rape in Children and in Young Girls," *International*

Clinics, 23 (1913), pp. 245–267; F. R. Bronson, "False Accusations of Rape," *American Journal of Urology and Sexology*, 15/3 (March 1919), pp. 101–109.

34. Akin quoted in Kevin McDermott, "Akin Says 'Legitimate' Rape Won't Cause Pregnancy," *St. Louis Post-Dispatch*, August 20, 2012; Mourdock quoted in "Mourdock Talks Rape, Pregnancy, and God's Plan," Associated Press, October 23, 2012; Jessica Valenti, "Ending Rape Illiteracy: Why the Next Feminist Battle Should Be Defining Rape for the Masses," *The Nation*, October 23, 2012.
35. "No means no" quoted in Karen Anderson, "Biden Discusses Sexual Assault Prevention at UNH," WBZ-TV (CBS Boston), April 4, 2011, https://boston.cbslocal.com/2011/04/04/biden-discusses-sexual-assault-prevention-at-unh/. As a senator in 1993, Biden, perhaps mindful of his failings in the Thomas hearings, had sponsored the Violence against Women Act—which, among other things, prohibited an accused rapist from introducing his accuser's sexual history in court as a way to discredit her; Garance Franke-Ruta, "Richard Mourdock, Mitt Romney, and the GOP Defense of Coerced Mating," *Atlantic*, October 26, 2012, https://www.theatlantic.com/politics/archive/2012/10/richard-mourdock-mitt-romney-and-the-gop-defense-of-coerced-mating/264035/.
36. Vanessa Grigoradis, "A Very Different Kind of Sexual Revolution on Campus," *New York*, September 22, 2014; Emma Sulkowicz, "My Rapist Is Still on Campus," *Time*, May 15, 2014; Andie Linker et al., "Carry That Weight," *Chicago Tribune*, October 16, 2014, p. 34.
37. Paul Nungesser v. Columbia University et al., S.D.N.Y. (2016), 1:15-cv-3216-GHW, March 11, 2016; Max Kutner, "'Mattress Project': Columbia Grad Settles Lawsuit over Emma Sulkowicz's Protest Art," *Newsweek*, July 13, 2017, https://www.newsweek.com/paul-nungesser-columbia-lawsuit-settlement-emma-sulkowicz-633708.
38. "Different kind" in Linda Hirshman, *Reckoning: The Epic Battle against Sexual Abuse and Harassment* (Boston: Houghton Mifflin Harcourt, 2019), p. 5; Catharine MacKinnon, *Sexual Harassment of Working Women: A Case of Sex Discrimination* (New Haven, CT: Yale University Press, 1979).
39. "'Just like I hired you'" quoted in DeNeen L. Brown, "She Said Her Boss Raped Her in a Bank Vault," *Washington Post*, October 13, 2017, https://www.washingtonpost.com/news/retropolis/wp/2017/10/13/she-said-her-boss-raped-her-in-a-bank-vault-her-sexual-harassment-case-would-make-legal-history/; "Without question" in Meritor Savings Bank v. Vinson, 477 U.S. 57 (1986), p. 477; Mary Battiata, "Mechelle Vinson's Long Road to Court, *Washington Post*, August 12, 1986; Augustus B. Cochran III, *Sexual Harassment and the Law: The Mechelle Vinson Case* (Lawrence: University Press of Kansas, 2004).
40. "Younger, College-Educated and Democratic Women Most Likely to Say 'Feminist' Describes Them Very Well,'" Pew Research Center poll, July 6, 2020, https://www.pewresearch.org/fact-tank/2020/07/07/61-of-u-s-women-say-feminist-describes-them-well-many-see-feminism-as-empowering-polarizing/ft_2020-07-07_feminism_01/.
41. Valerie Jarrett, "A Renewed Call to Action to End Rape and Sexual Assault," U.S. Department of Health and Human Services, January 23, 2014, https://obama

whitehouse.archives.gov/blog/2014/01/22/renewed-call-action-end-rape-and-sexual-assault; Caroline Kitchens, "It's Time to End 'Rape Culture' Hysteria," *Time*, March 20, 2014, https://time.com/30545/its-time-to-end-rape-culture-hysteria/.

42. Jillian Rayfield, "Political Must-Reads: Salon's Twitter 50," *Salon*, October 4, 2012; #RapeCultureIsWhen: https://twitter.com/zerlinamaxwell/status/1041756185882505219?lang=en.

43. Alex Tresniowski, "Cosby under Fire," *People*, December 18, 2006; Ed Pilkington, "Bill Cosby's Lawyers Strong-Armed Tabloid into Ditching Story on Rape Claims," *The Guardian*, November 21, 2014.

44. "Google 'Bill Cosby'": "Hannibal Buress on Bill Cosby: 'You're a Rapist,'" *Philadelphia*, October 17, 2014, https://www.phillymag.com/things-to-do/2014/10/17/hannibal-buress-bill-cosby-rapist/.

45. Noreen Malone, "'I'm No Longer Afraid': 35 Women Tell Their Stories about Being Assaulted by Bill Cosby, and the Culture That Wouldn't Listen," *New York*, July 26, 2015, https://nymag.tumblr.com/post/125179609945/im-no-longer-afraid-35-women-tell-their.

46. "Trump's Uncensored Lewd Comments about Women from 2005," CNN/YouTube, https://www.youtube.com/watch?v=FSC8Q-kR44o; "FUCK YOU" quoted in Rebecca Traister, *Good and Mad: The Revolutionary Power of Women's Anger* (New York: Simon and Schuster, 2018), p. xxii.

47. Clarence Page, "What Next for #MeToo, America?," *Chicago Tribune*, December 8, 2017; Zahara Hill, "A Black Woman Created the 'Me Too' Campaign against Sexual Assault Ten Years Ago," *Ebony*, October 8, 2017, https://www.ebony.com/news/black-woman-me-too-movement-tarana-burke-alyssa-milano/#axzz4vjZwLmqd.

48. "More Than 12M 'Me Too' Facebook Posts, Comments, Reactions in 24 Hours," CBS News, October 17, 2017, https://www.cbsnews.com/news/metoo-more-than-12-million-facebook-posts-comments-reactions-24-hours/; "Open Letter: Alianza Nacional de Campesinas," Latino USA, November 15, 2017, https://www.latinousa.org/2017/11/15/open-letter-latina-farmworkers-wrote-hollywood-sexual-assault/; "$22 milllion" in Joanna Walters, "#MeToo: A Revolution That Can't Be Stopped," *The Guardian*, October 21, 2018.

49. Juliana Menasce Horowitz and Ruth Igielnik, "A Century after Women Gained the Right to Vote, Majority of Americans See Work to Do on Gender Equality," Pew Research Center, July 7, 2020, https://www.pewresearch.org/social-trends/2020/07/07/a-century-after-women-gained-the-right-to-vote-majority-of-americans-see-work-to-do-on-gender-equality/.

50. Melissa Gira Grant, "The Elite Sisterhood of Amy Coney Barrett," *The New Republic*, September 29, 2020, https://newrepublic.com/article/159520/elite-sisterhood-amy-coney-barrett.

51. Bill Clinton, *My Life* (New York: Knopf, 2004), 255, 286, 296.

52. "I suppose" quoted in Kathleen Hall Jamieson, *Beyond the Double Bind: Women and Leadership* (New York: Oxford University Press, 1995), p. 27; campaign man-

agers in Associated Press, "Hillary Sees Silver Lining in Crowded Campaign," *The Tennessean* (Nashville), October 27, 1992, p. 6.

53. Laura Parker, "Tipper Balances Hillary Factor on Party Ticket," *Green Bay Press-Gazette* (Wisconsin), July 10, 1992, p. 2; "The Homemaker and the Career Wife," *The Tennessean* (Nashville), July 10, 1992, p. 7; "Hillary: Wife's Strong Role Draws Verdict on '90s Women," *Los Angeles Times*, July 14, 1992, p. A8; Tipper Gore, *Raising PG Kids in an X-Rated Society* (Nashville, TN: Parthenon Press, 1987).
54. Mary McGrory, "Barbara vs. Hillary: 1992's Real Contest," *St. Louis Post-Dispatch*, April 16, 1992, p. 32.
55. Mary Vorbil, "Hillary Clinton Bakes Up a Batch of Cookies and Then Goes to a Tea," *Miami Herald*, July 14, 1992, p. 86. Clinton's oatmeal chocolate chip recipe won by 55.2 percent of the votes to 44.8 percent.
56. Amy Robach, *Today Show*, NBC, September 3, 2008; John Roberts quoted in Ben Smith, "CNN's Roberts Asks Whether Palin's Nomination Will Cut into Time with Baby," *Politico*, August 29, 2008, https://www.politico.com/blogs/ben-smith/2008/08/cnns-roberts-asks-whether-palins-nomination-will-cut-into-time-with-baby-011454; "You can juggle" quoted in Jodi Kantor and Rachel L. Swarns, "A New Twist in the Debate on Mothers," *New York Times*, September 1, 2008.
57. O'Reillly quoted in "GOP Convention Wrap-Up," *Reliable Sources*, CNN, September 7, 2008, http://www.cnn.com/TRANSCRIPTS/0809/07/rs.01.html.
58. "Revisiting the Mommy Wars," Pew Research Center, September 15, 2008, https://www.pewresearch.org/social-trends/2008/09/15/revisiting-the-mommy-wars; "thrilled to see" in Kantor and Swarns, "A New Twist in the Debate on Mothers."
59. Daniel Nasaw, "Enthusiastic Republicans Praise Sarah Palin's Attacks on Barack Obama and the Media," *The Guardian*, September 4, 2008; Associated Press, "McCain Moves ahead of Obama in New Poll," September 8, 2008; Michael Falcone et al., "Palin Asset for Republicans in Rural Vote," Reuters, September 12, 2008; "McCain's Image Improves—With Big Assist from Palin," Pew Research Center, September 10, 2008, https://www.pewresearch.org/politics/2008/09/10/mccains-image-improves-with-big-assist-from-palin/; Michael Falcone and Zachary Abrahamson, "GOP Base Still Wild about Palin," *Politico*, September 29, 2009, https://www.politico.com/story/2009/09/gop-base-still-wild-about-palin-026236.
60. See, for example, Jessica Estepa, "Donald Trump on Carly Fiorina: 'Look at That Face!,'" *USA Today*, September 10, 2015. See also Linda Beail, Lilly J. Goren, and Mary A. McHugh, "Madame President? Female Candidates, Masculine Norms of Executive Power, and the 2020 Nomination Contest," in *The Making of the Presidential Candidates 2020*, ed. Jonathan Bernstein and Casey B. K. Dominguez (Lanham, MD: Rowman and Littlefield, 2019), pp. 1–24.
61. Quoted in Cleve R. Wootson Jr. and Amy B. Wang, "Hillary Clinton Calls Donald Trump a Creep," *Washington Post*, August 23, 2017.
62. "To stay focused" quoted in Jessie Hellmann, "Clinton: Trump Stalked Me around Debate Stage," *The Hill*, October 14, 2016; Amie Parnes, "Hillary Clin-

ton's Likability Problem," *The Hill,* December 2, 2015; Susan Bordo, *The Destruction of Hillary Clinton* (Brooklyn, NY: Melville House, 2017).

63. Transcript, Joe Biden interview, *Face the Nation,* CBS, October 30, 2016, https://www.cbsnews.com/news/face-the-nation-transcript-october-30-2016-biden-pence-benenson/.

64. Debra Cassens Weiss, "Amy Coney Barrett Signed 2006 Ad Calling for End to 'Barbaric Legacy of Roe v. Wade,'" *ABA Journal,* October 2, 2020, https://www.abajournal.com/news/article/barrett-signed-2006-add-calling-for-end-to-barbaric-legacy-of-roe-v.-wade.

65. Transcript, Amy Coney Barrett nomination acceptance speech, in *Epoch Times,* September 24, 2020, https://www.theepochtimes.com/read-full-transcript-of-acceptance-speech-by-supreme-court-nominee-amy-coney-barrett_3515776.html.

66. Lydia Kiesling, "Amy Coney Barrett and the Myth of the Working Mother," *Harper's Bazaar,* October 22, 2020, https://www.harpersbazaar.com/culture/politics/a34450007/amy-coney-barrett-myth-of-the-working-mother/.

67. Barrett Senate Confirmation Hearing, Day 1 Transcript.

68. "What does she have" quoted in Ruth Graham, "Amy Coney Barrett's Supreme Court Nomination Is Personal for Conservative Christian Women," *New York Times,* September 28, 2020; "it's possible" quoted in Graham, "Amy Coney Barrett's Supreme Court Nomination Is Personal for Conservative Christian Women."

69. Ruth Marcus, "The Micro-Thin Silver Lining in the Amy Coney Barrett Nomination," *Washington Post,* September 27, 2020.

70. Quoted in Michael S. Rosenwald, "Kamala Harris and the Shameful History of Slamming Women as 'Unlikable,'" *Washington Post,* October 9, 2020.

71. Quoted in Karen Tumulty et al., "How Sexist, Racist Attacks on Kamala Harris Have Spread Online—A Case Study," *Washington Post,* October 7, 2020.

72. "Transcript, Kamala Harris' DNC Speech," CNN, August 20, 2020, https://www.cnn.com/2020/08/19/politics/kamala-harris-speech-transcript/index.html.

73. "Employment Characteristics of Families—2019," Bureau of Labor Statistics, April 21, 2020; "Conservative College Woman Attracts Like-Minded," *Washington Times,* September 24, 2006; Joy Pullmann, "The Left Hates Amy Coney Barrett Because She Disproves All Their Lies about Women," *The Federalist,* September 28, 2020, https://thefederalist.com/2020/09/28/the-left-hates-amy-coney-barrett-because-she-disproves-all-their-lies-about-women/.

74. Karin A. Lips, "Conservative Women Know What It's Like to Be Mocked: We'll Defend Amy Coney Barrett," *USA Today,* September 29, 2020.

EPILOGUE

1. "Female Lawmakers: Two New Congresswomen Take Oath of Office" (AP), *Fort Lauderdale News* (Florida), June 4, 1957, p. 2; on "superhero," see, for example, "Boss Lady! U.S. Impeachment Manager Stacey Plaskett's Cape Dress Is Taking the Internet by Storm," MSN News, February 11, 2021; Luke Broadwater, "Stacey Plaskett Takes Trump Lawyers to Task for Use of 'Clip after Clip of Black

Women' as Part of the Defense," *New York Times*, February 12, 2021; Anoush Gomes, "Stacey Paskett's Cape Dress Steals Show as Rep. Makes History at Trump Impeachment Trial: 'Power Statement,'" *Media, Arts, Entertainment World Wide*, February 13, 2021; Akanksha Saxena, "'Power Statement: U.S. Impeachment Manager Stacey Plaskett's 'Fierce' Cape Look Bowled Netizens Over," *Times Now*, February 11, 2021.

2. Rev. John Cotton Jr., *A Meet Help, or, A Wedding Sermon Preached at New-Castle in New-England, June 19, 1694* (Boston: B. Green and J. Allen, 1699), pp. 21–23.

3. Thomas Jefferson to Anne Willing Bingham, May 11, 1788, in *The Papers of Thomas Jefferson*, vol. 13, ed. Julian P. Boyd (Princeton, NJ: Princeton University Press, 1956), p. 151.

4. Lorenzo D. Johnson, *Martha Washingtonianism, or a History of the Ladies' Temperance Benevolent Societies* (New York: Saxton and Miles, 1843), p. 41.

5. *Gangsta Bitch Music* cover, https://www.newburycomics.com/products/cardi_b-gangsta_bitch_music_vol_1_lp?variant=31670026403945; "WAP" video, https://www.youtube.com/watch?v=hsm4poTWjMs.

6. John Caramanica, "Cardi B and Megan Thee Stallion Take Control," *New York Times*, August 7, 2020; Maija Kappler, "WAP Is Making People Uncomfortable Because It's about Female Pleasure," *Huffington Post*, August 16, 2020; Brianna Holt, "Why Cardi B and Megan Thee Stallion's Empowering Anthem WAP Is So Important," *Complex*, August 9, 2020; Hannah Sparks, "Doctors Slam Critics of Cardi B's WAP Song," *New York Post*, August 12, 2020; "The 20 Best Rap Songs of 2020," *Billboard*, December 10, 2020; Lucas Shaw, "Cardi B's Sexy 'WAP' Rides Controversy to the Top," *Bloomberg*, September 9, 2020, https://www.bloomberg.com/graphics/pop-star-ranking/2020-september/cardi-b-s-sexy-wap-rides-controversy-to-the-top.html.

7. Johnson, *Martha Washingtonianism*, p. 41.

8. "My faith" quoted in "Watch: Marjorie Taylor Greene Gropes a Lifesize Trump Cut-Out," *Edge Media Network*, February 5, 2021, https://www.edgemedianetwork.com/story.php?301780; Phyllis Schlafly, "Second Amendment Rights in Reality and in Court," *Eagle Forum*, October 31, 2001, https://eagleforum.org/column/2001/oct01/01-10-31.shtml; "Squad's Worst Nightmare": Julia Reinstein, "A QAnon-Supporting Congressional Candidate Posted a Pic of Herself Holding a Gun Next to the "Squad," *Buzzfeed News*, September 4, 2020, https://www.buzzfeednews.com/article/juliareinstein/marjorie-taylor-greene-qanon-gun-facebook-squad.

9. Charles Bethea, "How the QAnon Candidate Marjorie Taylor Greene Reached the Doorstep of Congress," *New Yorker*, October 9, 2020, https://www.newyorker.com/news/us-journal/how-the-qanon-candidate-marjorie-taylor-greene-reached-the-doorstep-of-congress; Jordan Williams, "Marjorie Taylor Greene Expressed Support on Facebook for Violence against Democrats," *The Hill*, January 26, 2021; Alan Feuer, "AR-15 Rifles Are Beloved, Reviled and a Common Element in Mass Shootings," *New York Times*, January 13, 2016; Paul Bedard, "Marjorie Taylor Greene, with New Gun Giveaway, Vows No Gun Ban 'On My Watch,'" *Washington Examiner*, February 25, 2021, https://www.washingtonexaminer.com

/washington-secrets/marjorie-taylor-greene-with-new-gun-giveaway-vows-no-ban-on-my-watch.

10. Quoted in Susan B. Anthony, "The New Century's Manly Woman," *Leslie's Weekly*, March 3, 1900, p. 170.
11. Anne M. Peterson, "Megan Rapinoe Is Being, Well, Megan Rapinoe at the World Cup," *Akron Beacon Journal* (Ohio), June 30, 2019, p. C7; "no caveat" in Megan Rapinoe with Emma Brockes, *Megan Rapinoe: One Life* (New York: Penguin Press, 2020), p. 203.
12. Quoted in "You Can't Win Championship without Gays on Your Team, says Megan Rapinoe," *Business Standard*, June 29, 2019; see also Ross Forman, "Soccer Star Megan Rapinoe Comes Out," *Windy City Times*, July 3, 2012.
13. Jenna Amatulli, "Megan Rapinoe Holding World Cup Trophy and Screaming 'I Deserve This' Is a Mood," *Huffington Post*, July 10, 2019, https://www.huffpost.com/entry/megan-rapinoe-i-deserve-this-ashlyn-harris-womens-soccer_n_5d26016de4b0583e482a870a.
14. "Culture has evolved" quoted in Taylor Telford, "No More 'Mr.' Potato Head: Hasbro Makes Classic Toy Gender Neutral," *Washington Post*, February 25, 2021; Joseph Chamie, "America's Single-Parent Families," *The Hill*, March 19, 2021; Danielle Taylor, "Same-Sex Couples Are More Likely to Adopt or Foster Children," United States Census Bureau, September 17, 2020, https://www.census.gov/library/stories/2020/09/fifteen-percent-of-same-sex-couples-have-children-in-their-household.html. "They": Merriam-Webster, "Merriam-Webster's Words of the Year: 2019," https://www.merriam-webster.com/words-at-play/word-of-the-year-2019-they; Glenn Beck quoted in Ryan Nagelhout, "Glenn Beck Is Ranting Wildly about the Mr. Potato Head Nontroversy: 'It Is the End of Freedom in America,'" *Uproxx*, March 3, 2021, https://uproxx.com/viral/glenn-beck-mr-potato-head-end-of-freedom-in-america-video/; Mark Dice, https://twitter.com/markdice/status/1364991938701660166?lang=en.
15. Jeffrey M. Jones, "LGBT Identification Rises to 5.6% in Latest U.S. Estimate," Gallup News, February 24, 2021; Justin Ramb, "Gender: Beyond the Binary," Bigeye 2021 National Study, https://lp.bigeyeagency.com/hubfs/Gender_BeyondtheBinary.pdf; Will Oremus, "Here Are All the Different Genders You Can Be on Facebook," *Slate*, February 13, 2014.
16. Katy Steinmetz, "The Transgender Tipping Point: America's Next Civil Rights Frontier," *Time*, May 29, 2014, https://time.com/135480/transgender-tipping-point/.
17. Author interview with Olivia Dunning (pseud.), October 17, 2020, San Diego, CA.
18. "Transman": author interview with Zachary Shattuck, March 23, 2021, San Diego, CA; Hannah Rossiter, "She's Always a Woman: Butch Lesbian Trans Women in the Lesbian Community," *Journal of Lesbian Studies*, 20/1 (2016), pp. 87–96; Tobi Hill-Meyer, panel: "Butch Trans Women," Oakland, CA, December 9, 2011 (Handbasket Productions), https://www.youtube.com/watch?v=_xfTN-dKqO4.
19. "Economic and societal burden" in Hagai Levine et al., "Temporal Trends in Sperm Count," *Human Reproduction Update*, 23/6 (November–December 2017),

https://www.ncbi.nlm.nih.gov/pmc/articles/PMC6455044/; Nicholas Kristof, "What Are Sperm Telling Us?," *New York Times*, February 20, 2021, p. SR7; Shanna H. Swan with Stacey Colino, *Count Down: How Our Modern World Is Threatening Sperm Counts, Altering Male and Female Reproductive Development, and Imperiling the Future of the Human Race* (New York: Simon and Schuster, 2021); Ashley Fetters, "Sperm Counts Continue to Fall," *Atlantic*, October 12, 2018, https://www.theatlantic.com/family/archive/2018/10/sperm-counts-continue-to-fall/572794/; "among white people" quoted in Maya Salam, "Sperm Count in Western Men Has Dropped over 50 Percent since 1973," *New York Times*, August 16, 2017, https://www.nytimes.com/2017/08/16/health/male-sperm-count-problem.html?searchResultPosition=1; Alexander Borsa et al., "The Doomsday Sperm Theory Embraced by the Far Right," *Slate*, May 14, 2021. Swan quoted in Brian Walsh, "Falling Sperm Counts Could Threaten the Human Race," *Axios*, February 24, 2021, https://www.axios.com/falling-sperm-count-endocrine-disruption-59c8be98-bfad-4e9b-8738-985ece67a21d.html. Some reproductive experts have begun questioning the theory that a high sperm count means that a male is more fertile. See Marion Boulicault et al., "The Future of Sperm: A Biovariability Framework for Understanding Global Sperm Count Trends," *Human Fertility*, May 10, 2021, https://pubmed.ncbi.nlm.nih.gov/33969777/.

20. John Cotton, *A Meet Help*, p. 21.
21. Elise Gould, "The Labor Market Continues to Improve in 2019 as Women Surpass Men in Payroll Employment, But Wage Growth Slows," Economic Policy Institute, *Working Economics Blog*, January 10, 2020, https://www.epi.org/blog/the-labor-market-continues-to-improve-in-2019-as-women-surpass-men-in-payroll-employment-but-wage-growth-slows/; Maggie McGrath, "American Women Lost More than 5 Million Jobs in 2020," *Forbes*, January 12, 2021, https://www.forbes.com/sites/maggiemcgrath/2021/01/12/american-women-lost-more-than-5-million-jobs-in-2020/?sh=750f391d2857; Anthony P. Carnevale, Nicole Smith, and Artem Gulish, *Women Can't Win: Despite Making Educational Gains and Pursuing High-Wage Majors, Women Still Earn Less than Men*, Georgetown University Center on Education and the Workforce, 2018, https://cew.georgetown.edu/cew-reports/genderwagegap/. On average, women earned 81 percent of what men did, up from 57 percent in 1975; Helaine Olen, "The Pandemic Is Devastating a Generation of Working Women," *Washington Post*, February 5, 2021.
22. Amanda Fins, "Women in Leisure and Hospitality Are among the Hardest Hit by Job Losses and Most at Risk of Covid-19 Infection," National Women's Law Center, November 2020, https://nwlc.org/wp-content/uploads/2020/11/LeisureFS.pdf; Eleni X. Karageorge, "Covid-19 Recession Is Tougher on Women," *Monthly Labor Review*, September 2020, https://www.bls.gov/opub/mlr/2020/beyond-bls/covid-19-recession-is-tougher-on-women.htm; Amanda Holpuch, "The Shecession: Why Economic Crisis Is Affecting Women More than Men," *The Guardian*, August 4, 2020; Daniel L. Carlson, Richards Petts, and Joanna Pepin, "Changes in Parents' Domestic Labor during the Covid-19 Pandemic," SocArXiv Papers, May 6, 2020, https://osf.io/preprints/socarxiv/jy8fn/; Misty L. Heggeness

and Jason M. Fields, "Working Moms Bear Brunt of Home Schooling While Working during Covid-19," US Census Bureau, Research Connections, August 18, 2020, https://www.researchconnections.org/childcare/resources/38452.

23. Steven Jessen-Howard and Simon Workman, "Corona Virus Pandemic Could Lead to Permanent Loss of Nearly 4.5 Million Child Care Slots," Center for American Progress, April 24, 2020, https://www.americanprogress.org/issues/early-childhood/news/2020/04/24/483817/coronavirus-pandemic-lead-permanent-loss-nearly-4-5-million-child-care-slots/.

24. Rebecca Dickinson, diary extracts, in Daniel White Shells and Reuben Field Wells, *A History of Hatfield, Massachusetts, in Three Parts* (Springfield, MA: F. C. H. Gibbons, 1910), pp. 206–207; Rebecca Traister, *All the Single Ladies: Unmarried Women and the Rise of an Independent Nation* (New York: Simon and Schuster, 2016); Pew Research Center, "Survey of U.S. Adults, Conducted June 25–July 8, 2019," https://www.pewresearch.org/wp-content/uploads/2020/02/PSDT_11.06.19_cohabitation_TOPLINE.pdf; "The State of American Households: Smaller, More Diverse and Unmarried," *U.S. News and World Report*, February 14, 2020, https://www.usnews.com/news/elections/articles/2020-02-14/the-state-of-american-households-smaller-more-diverse-and-unmarried; "Marital Status of the U.S. Population, by Sex 2020," Statista, January 20, 2021, https://www.statista.com/statistics/242030/marital-status-of-the-us-population-by-sex/.

25. Charlotte Perkins Gilman, *Women and Economics: A Study of the Economic Relation between Men and Women as a Factor in Social Evolution* (Boston: Small, Maynard, 1898), p. 32.

ACKNOWLEDGMENTS

A writer labors alone to get her words down, but no book can come to fruition without the support of countless others. I could not have written *Woman* had I not had the help of the many friends who cheered me on, read numerous drafts of chapters, and made invaluable suggestions. I am grateful to the colleagues who offered materials, assisted me in getting access to collections, and gave me good advice on many occasions. This book has been greatly enriched by the individuals who were willing to share their own contemporary woman stories with me. And I do not know what I would have done during the hard times of the COVID-19 pandemic had it not been for the archivists and librarians who went the extra mile to give me access to materials that were vital to this project.

My thanks to Irma Cota, Lorena Young, Deborah Hertz, April Sanchez, Oliva Espin, Ethan Carter, Olivia Dunning (pseud.), Janice Steinberg, Sue Reynolds, Sharon Young, Allison Rossett, Kimberly Enderle, Linda Garber, Mary Meriam, Walt Meyer, Zach Shattuck, Martha Barnett, and Lydia Stryker. I am especially grateful to Anne Marie Welsh, not only for her remarkable insights but also for being "the reader in my head" all through the writing of this book.

I am deeply appreciative of the invaluable research help I received from Olga Tsapina, the American history curator at the Huntington Library; Meg Metcalf, the Women's Gender and LGBTQ+ collection specialist at the Library of Congress; Sarah Horowitz, the curator of rare books and manuscripts, Quaker and Special Collections, at Haverford College; Kathleen Shoemaker, the reference coordinator at the Stuart A. Rose Manuscript, Archives and Rare Book Library at Emory University; Holly Smith and Kassandra Ware, archivists at the Spelman College Archives; Azalea Camacho, the archivist and special collections librarian at the John F. Kennedy Memorial Library, California State University, Los Angeles; Jackson Bui of the Access Services Department, Special

Collections, University of California, Irvine; William McCarthy, the reference archivist at the Congregational Library and Archives; and Meaghan Wright, the assistant reference librarian at the Phillips Library, Peabody Essex Museum. Thank you for your dedication to historical research.

I am grateful to Yale University Press for having faith in this book from the start. My special thanks go to my editor, Adina Berk, and her wonderful assistant, Ash Lago. Thank you to John Donatich, director of Yale University Press, and Mary Pasti, the production editor, for cheering me on. I consider myself fortunate to have had eagle-eyed copy editors, John Donohue and Jeanne Ferris of Westchester Publishing Services. Thank you for your meticulous work.

For more than four decades I have been blessed to have Sandra Dijkstra as my extraordinary agent and dear friend. Thank you, Sandy, for seeing me through a dozen books and for having faith in this one.

My lifelong gratitude goes to Phyllis Irwin. She is the spouse any writer would be fortunate to have.

ILLUSTRATION CREDITS

Mary Dyer Led to Execution on Boston Common, 1 June 1660. Unknown artist, nineteenth century. Brooklyn Museum. Wikimedia Commons.

"A Society of Patriotic Ladies, at Edenton in North Carolina." Unknown artist, 1775. Library of Congress, British Cartoon Prints Collection. Wikimedia Commons.

The murder of Sarah Cornell: "A Minister Extraordinary Taking Passage & Bound on a Foreign Mission to the Court of His Satanic Majesty!" Lithograph by Henry R. Robinson, 1833. Library of Congress, Prints and Photographs Division. Wikimedia Commons.

Loreta Janeta Velázquez. Photograph by a U.S. Army employee, c. 1870. Wikimedia Commons.

Victoria Woodhull and "free love." Cartoon by Thomas Nast. *Harper's Weekly*, February 17, 1872. Wikimedia Commons.

Vassar College Resolutes. Archives and Special Collections, Vassar College Library. ID 08.17.

Carrie Nation. "G. Washington to Date." Cartoon by Charles L. Bartholomew. *Minneapolis Journal*, February 6, 1901. Hennepin County Library.

Harriet Tubman. Unknown photographer, c. 1860–1880. Wikimedia Commons.

Anna Julia Cooper, c. 1902. Library of Congress, C. M. Bell Studio Collection. Wikimedia Commons.

Anti-suffrage postcard. "Where Oh Where Is My Wandering Wife Tonight?" Dunston-Weiler Lithograph Company, New York, 1909. Wikimedia Commons.

Zitkala-Sa. Photograph by Gertrude Käsebier, 1898. Wikimedia Commons.

Madam C. J. Walker. Unknown photographer, 1911. Wikimedia Commons.

The Flapper. Magazine cover by John Held Jr. *Life*, October 1, 1925.

[Mary McLeod Bethune], "Mrs. Eleanor Roosevelt and others at the opening of Midway Hall, one of two residence halls built by the Public Buildings Administration of FWA for Negro government girls . . . ," May 1943. Photographs Illustrating the Activities of the Public Buildings Administration, 1939–1943, General Records of the Federal Works Agency, 1930–1950.

Teletypist interned in Jerome Relocation Center, Denson, Arkansas, March 11, 1943. Photograph by Tom Parker, War Relocation Authority, Department of the Interior. National Archives and Records Administration. Wikimedia Commons.

Housewives. "Washington, D.C. Dusting mits with which dusting can be done with both hands develops speed and efficiency. Dusting mit or dust cloth in the pocket, dusting as you clean, eliminates travel time." Unknown photographer, between 1924 and 1950. National Archives at College Park, National Archives and Records Administration. Wikimedia Commons.

Roller derby players. Photograph by Al Aumuller. *New York World-Telegram and Sun*, March 10, 1950. Library of Congress. Wikimedia Commons.

Dolores Huerta, c. 1965. Jon Lewis photograph of Dolores Huerta © Yale University. All rights reserved.

Wanted poster. FBI director J. Edgar Hoover listed Angela Davis on the Ten Most Wanted Fugitive List on August 18, 1970. Federal Bureau of Investigation. Wikimedia Commons.

Women's March 2017, San Diego. Photograph by Bonzo McGrue. Creative Commons.

INDEX

abolitionists, 105–113
abortion: Amy Coney Barrett and, 410; pro-family conservatives and, 351–352; public opinion on, in the 1920s, 242; Reagan on, 357; *Roe v. Wade*, 339, 351, 357, 366, 385, 410; Shirley Ann Wheeler case (1971), 350–351
Abzug, Bella, 378
Act for the Suppression of Drinking Houses and Tippling Shops (1851), 102
Act for the Suppression of Trade in, and Circulation of, Obscene Literature and Articles of Immoral Use (Comstock Act). *See* Comstock Act (1873)
Adam (Old Testament), 13–14
Adams, Abigail, 55–56, 63–64, 74
Adams, Clifford R., 287
Adams, John: idea of woman, 75; letters from Abigail Adams to, 55–56, 74; Mercy Otis Warren and, 75; on woman suffrage, 195; on women's voice in government, 63, 75, 390
Addams, Jane, 158, 159–160, 161, 223, 254, 278
Adelitas, the, 328–329
adultery, 27, 40, 202
The Adventures of Ozzie and Harriet (television show), 287
Advocate of Moral Reform (journal), 92, 93, 94
Afric-American Female Intelligence Association, 107–108, 109
African Methodist Episcopal (AME) Church, 73, 74
Against Fornication Act (1662), 30–31
Against Our Will: Men, Women and Rape (Brownmiller), 337

agency. *See* women's agency
agricultural work, by women during World War I, 194–195. *See also* farmworkers
Agricultural Workers Association, 325
Ahhaton, Sarah, 27
Akin, Todd, 399
alcohol consumption: Native Americans, 99; nineteenth-century, 95; temperance movement, 95–101
Alexander, Virginia, 211
Algonquin Indians, 26, 27
Alianza Nacional de Compesinas, 404
Allen, Richard, 73
Alpha Suffrage Club, 191
Amalgamated Clothing Workers of America, 307
Amatulli, Jenna, 418
"Amazon(s)," 8, 61, 164, 318
American Anti-Slavery Society, 108, 111, 182–183; convention (1833), 107
American Association for the Advancement of Science, 145
American Association of University Women, 253
American Civil Liberties Union (ACLU), 253
American Enterprise Institute, 402
American Equal Rights Association, 182
American Federation of Labor, 217
American Female Moral Reform Society, 94
American Indians. *See* Native Americans
American Institute of Family Relations, 287
American Magazine, 38, 39, 79
American Medical Association, 248

American Mercury, 250
American Museum, 80
American Red Cross, 135
American Revenue Act of 1764, 67
American Revolution. *See* Revolutionary War (1775–1783)
American Spectator, 368–369
American Woman Suffrage Association, 183, 184
"An Appeal in Favor of That Class of Americans Called Africans" (Child), 106
anatomical sex: changing, among Native Americans, 27–28; gender complexities and, 420; gendered behavior and, 7–8. *See also* females (assigned at birth), "posing as men"
Anderson, Mary, 467n10
Andrews, John, 137
androgyny, 8, 173, 332
"The Angel in the House" (Patmore), 453n4
Anthony, Lucy, 179, 192
Anthony, Susan B., 100, 135, 278; American Equal Rights Association and, 182; Elizabeth Cady Stanton and, 170; gender-shaming, 172–173; Horace Greeley and, 174; illegal voting by, 168–169, 171–172, 467n10; "The New Century's Manly Woman" essay (1900), 173; New York Sons of Temperance convention (1852) and, 102; "The True Woman" lecture (1857), 170–171; universal suffrage and, 182, 183, 184; Victoria Woodhull and, 226; World's Temperance Convention (1853) and, 102–103
anti-establishment punk subculture, 377
anti-Semitism, Bryn Mawr and, 152
Anti-Slavery Convention of American Women, 106
anti-slavery societies/movement, female, 105–113
anti-suffrage movement, 5, 174–178, 179, 469n24
Anzaldúa, Gloria, 341–342
Apache women, 133–134
Appeal to the Christian Women of the South (Grimké), 111

apprenticeships, 54
Arellanes, Gloria, 328
Armory Show (1913), 202
Arnold, Henry, 273
Arrington, Marie, 343
Arthur, Timothy Shay, 96
arts, becoming a lady and the, 44–48
Asian American women, 385–386. *See also* Chinese American women/immigrants; Japanese American women
Aspiranto Health Home, 212
Atherton, Humphrey, 20
athletes, female, 350
Atkinson, Ti-Grace, 318–319, 337
Atlanta Baptist Female Seminary, 153
Atlanta Constitution, 9
Atlantic Monthly, 203
attire/clothing: female hoboes, 262; flapper, 243–244; of impeachment manager (2021), 415; media reporting on women in politics, 292; of pachucas, 290, 291; Puritanism and, 23–24; ultraradicals of the 1970s, 344; on westward trails, 456n42; women in the workforce during World War II, 265; of women serving in the military, 273; during World War II, 264. *See also* fashion
automobile, as sex site, 238–239
Avery, Elizabeth, 15–16
Avery, Rev. Ephraim, 118

baby boom, 279
Bad (music video), 380
Bagley, Sarah, 122, 123
Baker, Ella, 281–282, 321–322
Baker, Sarah Josephine, 384
Baldwin, Marie Louise Bottineau, 187, 188, 472n55
Ballinger, Willis J., 252
Banning, Margaret Culkin, 298, 501n57
Baptist preachers, 57
Bardot, Brigitte, 299
Barnard College, 152, 363
Barrett, Amy Coney, 384–385, 410–412
Barrett, Jesse, 410
Barrow, Clyde, 343

Barton, Clara, 135
Barton, William, 66
bastardy laws, 29, 30–31, 234, 298, 424
Baudelaire, Charles, 164
Beal, Frances, 323
Bean, Mary (Berengera Caswell), 453–454n11
Beate, Native American story of, 99–100
beauticians, 215
Beauvoir, Simone de, 8
Beck, Glenn, 419
Beecher, Catharine, 142, 175, 177, 452n66
Beecher, Rev. Henry Ward, 226
Beecher, Rev. Lyman, 143
Belmont, Alva, 191–192, 219, 220
Beloved Woman, 26, 41
Bennington College, 317
Bergler, Edmund, 300
Bethel, Lorraine, 340
Bethune, Mary McLeod, 155–156, 258–259
Bethune-Cookman College, 259
Betty Crocker Homemaker Award, 344
Bible, the, 91
Biden, Joe, 366, 367, 368, 399–400, 409, 527n35
Bikini Kill, 377–379, 380, 382
binary genders, 419
Biographical Sketches and Interesting Anecdotes of Persons of Color (Mott), 94
birth control: birthrate and, 251–252; during the Great Depression, 248; Margaret Sanger and, 239–242; the Pill, 303–305; used by women in twenty-first century, 385; after World War II, 277–278
birthrate, 251–252
Bishop, Bridget, 25
"bitch," 381–382
"The Bitch Manifesto" (Freeman), 322, 381
"Black Cabinet," 259
Black civil rights movement. *See* civil rights movement
Black feminism/feminists: Anna Julia Cooper, 209–210; Combahee River Collective, 340–341; National Black Feminist Organization, 339–340; "womanist" and, 342, 478n27; Zerlina Maxwell (tweeter), 402

Black matriarchy, 321
Black men: Black matriarchy and, 321; given right to vote, 76; reaction to female participation in anti-slavery movement, 108–110; sex study and, 502n64; Student Nonviolent Coordinating Committee and, 349; universal suffrage and, 182–183
Blackmun, Harry, 351
Black Panthers, 323, 327, 345, 347, 514n44
Black people: Great Northward Migration and, 212; Kinsey study and, 502n64; Mary McLeod Bethune's work for, 259; temperance movement and, 97–100. *See also* Black men; Black women; enslaved females
"Black Power," 323
Blackwell, Elizabeth, 161–162
Blackwell, Emily, 161, 162–163
Blackwell, Henry, 183
Black women: blues music and, 245; business empire by, 214–216; Daniel Patrick Moynihan on, 321, 507n53; early Black women's colleges for, 152–156; Eleanor Roosevelt and leadership by, 258–259; first in the Senate, 370–371; flappers, 244; Florence Crittenton maternity homes and, 501n58; Kinsey study and, 502n64; moral reform movement, nineteenth-century, 92–94, 97–99; National Association of Colored Women, 184; as "new women," 208–216; in nineteenth-century battle against social evils, 88; opting-out trend and, 391–392; portrayed in race films, 212–213; postrevolutionary education of, 82; preachers after Revolutionary War, 73–74; pregnant out of wedlock, 298–299, 501n58; prostitutes, 93; racism of early elite colleges, 152; radical feminism of the 1970s and, 339–341; role in civil rights movement, 280–282, 321–324; sexuality of twentieth-century working class, 233–234, 485n28; suffrage for, 184–186, 471n44; suffrage parade (1913) and, 190–191; temperance movement, 97–99, 448–449n31; ultradical, 347–350; wages of, compared with

Black women (cont.)
  white women, 524n17; white women compared with, 320–321, 323; Women Airforce Service Pilots (WASP) and, 495n69; women's movement, 323–324, 509n61; in the workforce during the Depression, 269–270. *See also* Black feminism/feminists; enslaved females; free Black women; women of color; *individual names of Black women*
Black Women's Alliance, 324, 341
Black Women's Liberation Committee, 323
Blair, James, 31
Blair, Sarah Harrison, 31
Blanchard, Phyllis, 488n3
Blatch, Harriot Stanton, 192, 195, 204
Blondie, 520n39
Bloomer, Amelia, 96–97, 100, 101–102, 450n43
bloomers, 180, 264, 450n43
Blue Anchor (Boston tavern), 21
blues music, 244–245
"Bluestocking of Susquehana," 59
boardinghouses and boardinghouse keepers, 21, 100, 124, 152, 160
Bogan, Lucille, 245–246
Boissevain, Eugen, 205
Bond, Stanley, 344–345
Bork, Robert, 366
Boston, Massachusetts, 16, 23
Boston Courier, 118
Boston Globe, 253–254, 317
Boston Latin School, 83
Boston marriages, 164, 465n60
Boston Times-Democrat, 181
Boston University, 461n21
Bottini, Ivy, 319
Boudin, Kathy, 347
Bourne, Dorothea, 53–54
Bourne, Louis, 53, 54
Bowen, Louise DeKoven, 232, 397–398
Boxer, Barbara, 368
boycotts, Revolutionary War, 68
Boyd, Kimberly, 418–419
Bradbury, Mary, 25–26
Bradford, William, 17
Bradley, Justice Joseph, 165, 167
Bradstreet, Anne, 15

Bradwell, James, 163
Bradwell, Myra, 163, 165
Bradwell v. State of Illinois (1873), 165
Brandeis University, 344, 347
Bratmobile, 378, 381–382
Braun, Carol Moseley, 370–371
Breedlove, Sarah, 213–214. *See also* Madam C. J. Walker products
Brent, Margaret, 31–33
Brewster, Margaret Wadsworth, 61
Bronson, F. R., 398–399
Brooksop, Joan, 33
Brown, Antoinette, 172
Brown, Elaine, 514n44
Brown, Helen Gurley, 305–306, 376, 503n13
Brown, Jerry, 406
Brown, John, 137
Brown, Mary Ann Brigham, 87, 106–107
Brown, Rita Mae, 338
Brown, Willie, 412
Brown Berets, 327–328
Brownmiller, Susan, 337
Brownsville Clinic, Brooklyn, 240–241
Bryn Mawr, 150–152, 285, 461–462n25
Bryn Mawr Summer School for Women Workers in Industry, 151
Buck, Pearl, 304
Buckminster, Joseph, 87, 299
Buford, Harry T. (Loreta Janeta Velazquez), 136
Bureau of Labor Statistics, 394
Buress, Hannibal, 403
Burke, Tarana, 404
Burlend, Rebecca, 125
Burlington, New Jersey, 66–67
Burns, Lauren, 388
Burns, Lucy, 189–190, 192
Burton, Evelena, 244
Bush, Barbara, 406–407
Bush, George H. W., 364
The Business of Being a Woman (Tarbell), 222
Bust (zine), 360
butch lesbians, 420–421
Butler, Judith, 8

CAA. *See* Civil Aeronautics Administration (CAA)
cabinet member, first female, 258

Cady, Elizabeth. *See* Stanton, Elizabeth Cady
Callender, Hannah, 46, 56
Calvert, Leonard, 32
Calvillo, Maria del Carmen (ranch owner), 131–132
Cardi B (rap singer), 416
career(s): Black women, 211–212; Bryn Mawr graduates, 151; chosen over domestic role of women, 199–200; combining marriage with, 278; Great Depression and, 250–251; Hillary Clinton and, 406; increasing desire of nineteenth-century young girls for, 167; in medicine, 161–163; Mount Holyoke women choosing over marriage, 253; opting out of, 386–392, 393, 415, 523n8; social work, 157–158; teaching, 156–157; of women in early twenty-first century, 386; women leaving their, 6, 387–388. *See also* workforce, women in
Carmichael, Stokely, 322, 323, 508n57
Carpenter, Edward, 201
Carroll, Anna Ella, 135135
Cary, Mary Ann Shadd, 467n10, 471n44
Casiano, Inez, 320
Castle, Irene, 213
Caswell, Berengera (Mary Bean), 453–454n11
Catt, Carrie Chapman, 193–194, 426n5
celibacy, 58
Celler, Emanuel, 312, 352, 353
"The Changing Morality of Women" (Gregory), 235
Charles I, king of England, 23
Charlotte, queen of England, 59
Charlton, Anna, 116
Charlton, Linda, 286, 498n28
Chatham College, 310–311
Chatham Street Chapel, New York City, 91
Chavez, Cesar, 324, 325, 326, 327
Cheever, Susan, 394
Cherokee Female Seminary, 146–147
Cherokee National Council, 146
Cherokee Nation/women, 4–5, 26, 41–42, 132, 146–147, 431n49, 435–436n15
Cherokee Rose Buds, 147
Chestnut, Mary Boykin, 52

Chicago Defender, 244
Chicago Record, 243
Chicana women, 324; Adelitas, 328–329; feminism of, 329; radical feminism, 341–342. *See also* Mexican American women/immigrants
Child, Lydia Maria, 106
childbearing: colonial America, 12–13; enslaved women, 50–51; in the 1950s, 279
child care, 422–423
children: opinions for political candidates with small, 407–408; women choosing to stay home with, 388–389; of working mothers, 302, 309
Chilocco Indian School, Newkirk, Oklahoma, 271
China, 186–187, 471n52
Chinese American women/immigrants: flapper age, 243–244, 487n59; in the 1920s, 237–238; revolutionary China and, 186–187; working during World War II, 267–268
Chinese Exclusion Act of 1882, 267
Chiricahua Apaches, 133–134
Chisholm, Shirley, 320, 509n61
A Choice Not an Echo (Schlafly), 354–355
Chopin, Kate, 44
Christian Indians, 26–27
Christianity, early Black woman's colleges and, 154–155
Christian missionaries, 39–41
Christian schooling, 40–41
Chung Sai Yat Po (newspaper), 186–187
Church, Mary. *See* Terrell, Mary Church
Churchill, Winston, 191–192
cisgender males, 421
cities. *See* urban areas
Civil Aeronautics Administration (CAA), 274
civil disobedience by women, 171–172, 467n10
Civilian Conservation Corps (CCC), 260–261
Civil Rights Act, Title VII, 311–312, 313, 317, 401
Civil Rights Act of 1875, 165
Civil Rights Act of 1964, 311–313, 316

civil rights movement, 71; Black women's role in, 280–282, 321–322, 507–508n54; feminist sit-in, 322; Rosa Parks and, 280–281
Civil War (1861–1865), 134–141
Claflin, Tennessee, 225
Clarke, Edward, 149
Clark University, 239
Clatsop Plains, Oregon, 127
Cleaver, Eldridge, 323
Cleaver, Kathleen, 514n44
clerical jobs, 199, 475n3
clinic, first birth control, 240–241
Clinton, Bill, 405–406
Clinton, Hillary Rodham, 405–407, 409
Clinton, Mississippi, 153
Clinton, Rachel, 25
clothing. *See* attire/clothing
Coast Guard Women's Reserve (SPAR), 272
Cochran, Jacqueline, 273–274
"cock," 227, 381
"Code of Handsome Lake," 42–43
coeds, on college campuses, 246
Cold Cold Hearts, 382
collectives/collective housing, 282, 334
college(s): Chinese American middle-class daughters, 267–268; coed, during flapper age, 246; Equal Opportunity in Education Act, 350; female seminaries, nineteenth-century, 143–148; during the Great Depression, 252–253; in the South, 147–149; women's leadership in, 150–151. *See also* higher education for women
college campuses, sexual assault on, 399–401
college-educated women: birthrate and, 251–252; in Boston marriages, 164; choosing motherhood instead of careers, 386–389; early twentieth century, 199–200; during the Great Depression, 251–252; Hull House and, 159, 160; marriage during the Depression and, 252; in the 1950s, 279–280; in social service professions, 157
College of William and Mary, 4
college sports, 350

Collins, Rebecca Singer, 93–94
colonial America: Anne Hutchinson, 16–17; dismissal of Pequot women, 11; freedoms of women in New Amsterdam settlement, 34; idea of woman in, 3–4, 415; laws of coverture, 13; marriage, 13, 29; Mary Dyer and, 18–20; publications by women, 15–16; Puritan thought, 13–14; Quaker women preaching, 14; role of woman, 12–13; upper-class women, 43–44; women banished from Massachusetts Bay Colony, 17–18; women exercising agency during, 5. *See also* Revolutionary War (1775–1783)
Colony Club, 192, 220
The Colored American Magazine, 109, 185–186
Colored Section of the Women's Christian Temperance Union, 98
A Colored Woman in a White World (Terrell), 184, 471n45, 471n46
Colored Woman's League, 209
Colored Women's League of Washington, DC, 184
The Color Purple (Walker), 342, 371
Columbian College of Law, 165
Columbia University, 400–401
Combahee River Collective, 340–341, 359
Common Sense (Paine), 63
Commonweal, 273
Communist Party USA, 204, 347, 348
Community Service Organization, 325–326
Comstock, Anthony, 244
Comstock Act (1873), 226–227, 240
condoms, 248
Congress: ERA in, 352–354; first Black women in the Senate, 370–371; Hill–Thomas hearings and, 367; "lean-in" movement and, 397; women serving in, 256–257, 291, 292, 294, 312, 313, 317
Congressional Union for Woman Suffrage, 192
conquistadors, 133
conservatism: Amy Coney Barrett and, 410–411; ERA and, 352–354; gender-neutral Potato Heads and, 419; Phyllis

Schlafly, 354–355; "pro-family," 351–352; Sarah Palin and, 407–408
The Conservative Case for Trump (Schlafly), 356
contraception. *See* birth control
conversions to Christianity, 26–27
Cooper, Anna Julia, 209–210, 214, 478n27
cooperative housing, 198–199
Cooper Union labor meeting, 217–218
Cornell, Sarah, 118–119, 453–454n11
Cornell University, 149, 152, 162
Cornish, Rev. Samuel, 108, 185
corset makers, 100
Cosby, Bill, 402–403
Cotton, Charles, 147–148
Cotton, Eliza, 148
Cotton, Rev. John, 16–17, 21, 24
cotton gin, 72
Council on National Defense, Women's Section, 195
courting, flappers and, 243
court trials, eighteenth-century pirate, 38
Cousins, Norman, 249
coverture laws, 13, 31, 51, 76–78, 131, 267
COVID-19 pandemic, 422
Cox, James M., 255
Crandall, Prudence, 82–83
Crapo, Michael, 411
Crawford, T. Harley, 4–5, 132
creation stories, 28, 42–43
Cree Indians, 27
Crenshaw, Kimberlé, 324
The Crisis, 191
Crittenton, Charles, 299
Crittenton, Florence, 298–299
Cromwell, Oliver, 23
"cross-dressing," 491–492n39
crotch clutching, 379–380
The Culled Lesbian Feminist Declaration of Independence, 340
Cumming, Kate, 139
"cunt," 227, 381
Current Opinion, 229
Cushier, Elizabeth, 162, 163

Daily Times (Davenport, Iowa), 237
dame schools, 23

dance(s): becoming a lady and, 44, 47; dance halls, 7, 230–231, 234; flappers, 243, 244
Danforth, John, 366, 369–370
Daniels, Josephus, 195
date rape, 362
dating, flapper age and, 243
Daughters of Liberty, 61, 67–69
Daughters of Temperance, 98, 100, 102
Daughters of the American Revolution, 354
David, Katharine Bement, 245
Davis, Angela, 4, 347–350
Dawn Mist, Princess, 188
Days of Rage, 346
DeBlasio, Bill, 340
Declaration of Independence preamble, 43
"Declaration of Sentiments," at Seneca Falls women's rights convention (1848), 169, 178
DeConcini, Dennis, 367
defense industry, 264, 266, 268, 269, 270–271, 279
de Gardoqui, Diego, 63
Degler, Carl, 228
de la Cruz, Jessie Lopez, 324–325
Deland, Margaret, 202–203
Delaware Indians, 27, 99
de Marneffe, Daphne, 389
Democratic National Committee, 255, 258
Democratic Party, women's political participation and, 255–256
demonstrations: New York Radical Women at antiwar (1968), 330–331; by "pro-family" conservatives, 352; Women Strike for Peace (1962), 330. *See also* protests
Department of Labor, 195, 308
Depression. *See* Great Depression
Devons, Bridget, 136
de Vries, Peter, 34
Dew, Thomas Roderick, 4, 115–116
Dewson, Molly, 258
The Dial (magazine), 143
The Dialects of Sex: The Case for a Feminist Revolution (Firestone), 334
diary(ies): of Emily Blackwell, 163; unmarried women in eighteenth

diary(ies) (cont.)
century, 55, 56; on westward expansion trip, 126; of women during Revolutionary War, 66
Diary from Dixie (Chestnut), 52
Dice, Mark, 419
Dickens, Charles, 454n12
Dickey, Sarah, 153
Dickinson, Anna, 149
Dickinson, Rebecca, 55
Dietrich, Marlene, 264
Dinsmoor, Silas, 42
Dior, Christian, 276, 301, 303
Dirksen, Everett, 312
discrimination(s): admission of Black women into colleges, 152; of Black women during World War II, 494n60; employment, 311, 312–313, 315; in hiring practices during World War II, 269–270; intersection of, 324; sex discrimination, 310, 313, 315, 506n43; Title VII banning, 311. *See also* prejudice
divorce/divorce laws, 29, 48, 170, 396
Dix, Dorothea, 135, 140, 238
doctorate programs for women. *See* PhD programs for women
doctors. *See* medicine, women's careers in
Dodge, Mabel, 201–202
Dohrn, Bernardine, 345–346, 514n39
domestic role of women: Black woman's suffrage and, 185; of Black women, 152–153; Catharine Beecher on, 143; education for women and, 85, 145–146; *Godey's Lady's Book* promoting, 116–117; Hillary Clinton contrasted with Barbara Bush, 406–407; homemaker role of women in the 1950s, 282–287; John Adams on, 75; ladydom training and, 44; opposition to woman suffrage and, 172; Phyllis Schlafly and, 354–356; postrevolutionary schools and, 82; post–World War II attitudes toward, 277; women choosing careers over, 199–200. *See also* mothers and motherhood; stay-at-home mothers; "traditional" family roles
domestic servants, 50, 131, 211, 212, 234
dominant idea of woman/womanhood. *See* idea of woman/womanhood

The Donna Reed Show (television show), 287, 289
Dorr, Rheta Childe, 230, 483n20
Double Jeopardy: To Be Black and Female (Beal), 323
Douglass, Frederick, 169–170, 183
Douglass, Sarah Mapps, 93, 108
Dover, New Hampshire, textile factory, 120
dress. *See* attire/clothing
dressmakers, 100
dress reform, 129, 180, 264
drunkenness, 95–96, 99, 101, 449n32
Dubois, Frank, 9, 136, 420, 426–427n12
Du Bois, W. E. B., 191
Duke University, 148
Dunmore, Earl of, 72
Dunning, Olivia, 420
Dworkin, Andrea, 362
Dwyer, Florence, 292
Dyer, Mary, 18–20, 429n29

Eagle Forum, 356, 411
Earhart, Amelia, 273
East Los Angeles Free Clinic, 327–328
Eastman, Crystal, 197
Eastman, Max, 203, 205
Eckert, Bertha, 271
Edelsberg, Herman, 313
Edenton Ladies Patriotic Guild of North Carolina, 68
Edmonds, Sarah Emma (Franklin Thompson), 136
Educating Our Daughters (White), 280
education: colonial women, 22; Fuller vs. Beecher camp on women's, 144; Margaret Fuller and, 44; postrevolutionary era, 78–85. *See also* college(s); higher education for women; schools
EEOC. *See* Equal Employment Opportunity Commission (EEOC)
eighteenth century: Black females in, 48–54; class differences, 43, 436n20; education and, 6; end of witch hysteria in, 37; idea of woman in, 36–37, 38, 63; ladydom, 44–48; Native Americans in, 29, 39–43; in the public sphere, resentment of, 38–39; spinsters in, 54–61; women in combat, 6
eight-hour workday, 160

Eisemann-Schier, Ruth, 343
Eisenhower, Dwight, 351
Ekberg, Anita, 299
Eleventh National Women's Rights Convention (1866), 182
El Grito del Norte (newspaper), 329
Elisabeth Irwin High School, 347
Ellis, Albert, 338–339
Ellis, Havelock, 57, 164, 202
Emerson, Ralph Waldo, 119
Emily's List, 370
employment: discrimination, 311, 312–313, 315; eight-hour workday, 160; late nineteenth-century changes and, 166–167; in New Amsterdam settlement, 34; recession of 2008–2009 and, 392–393; sex-segregated help-wanted ads, 316–317; social reform work, nineteenth century, 157–161; for unmarried women in eighteenth century, 54, 55. *See also* workforce, women in; working women
encephalitis, 24
English-Figaro, Cheli, 392
enslaved females: ignoring womanhood of, 4, 48–49, 50; impact of Revolutionary War on, 72–73; mothers/motherhood, 50–51; serving in Revolutionary War, 72; sexual exploitation of, 52–53, 438–439n47; sexual functions of, 50; treatment of, 49–50; work by, 50
enslaved men, 51, 53–54
enslaved people: doing work of colonial wives and daughters, 44; "mulatto," 52; Revolutionary War and, 72; universal suffrage and, 182; white women's ownership of, 51–52
Equal Employment Opportunity Commission (EEOC), 313, 315, 316–317, 365, 366, 369
Equality League of Self-Supporting Women, 192
Equal Opportunity in Education Act, 350
Equal Protection Clause, Fourteenth Amendment, 410
Equal Rights Amendment (ERA), 5, 308–309, 311–312, 352–358
ERA. *See* Equal Rights Amendment (ERA)

erotica, 363
Ervin, Sam, 352–353
essentialist notion of woman, 180, 420
evangelical revivalist movements, 57, 90
evangelicals, on drunkenness, 95
Eve (Old Testament), 13–14
Evers, Medgar, 315
Eve's Garden, New York, 363
Excuse 17, 378
executions, 20, 21, 43
Executive Order 8802, 269, 270
Executive Order 10980, 309
The Exploits of Elaine (film), 213
Express Yourself (Madonna), 380

Facebook, 403, 405, 412, 419
Face the Nation (television show), 409
Factors in the Sex Life of Twenty-Two Hundred Women (Davis), 245
Factory Girls' Association, 121–122
Fair Employment Practices Commission (FEPC), 269, 270, 494n60
Fairhill estate, Pennsylvania, 60
Falwell, Jerry, 356
Families and Work Institute poll, 386, 392
Family Circle (magazine), 407
Family Limitation (Sanger), 240
Family Weekly Magazine, 286–287
Farley, Jim, 258
farmer's daughters, textile factories and, 118
Farm Labor Party, 293
farmworkers: sexual harassment of, 404; unionizing, 324–326
Farnham, Marynia, 284–286
fashion: miniskirt, 303; New Look (1940s and 1950s), 276, 301; of the 1950s, 279; Puritan, 23–24. *See also* attire/clothing
Father Knows Best (television show), 287, 289
A Father's Legacy to His Daughters (Gregory), 46
FBI (Federal Bureau of Investigation): Hill–Thomas hearings and, 366–367; report on Dolores Huerta, 326; women on most-wanted list of, 343–349, 345, 347, 348
The Federalist, 413

Female Academy of Portsmouth, New Hampshire, 82
female anti-slavery societies/movement, 105–113
Female Anti-Slavery Society of Salem, 105–106, 450n50
Female Collegiate Institute, Virginia, 147
"Female Influence," 86
Female Labor Reform Association, 122–123
female literary societies, 107–108
Female Moral Reform Society, 91–93, 94–95, 330
"The Female Patriots" (Griffitts), 61
females (assigned at birth), "posing as men": during Civil War, 135–136; hoboes and, 262; identifying as transmen, 420; during Revolutionary War, 66; seventeenth-century, 28. *See also* transgender/transgender people
female seminaries, 142, 143–148, 153
"Female Sexual Inversion" (Ellis), 57
female slave owners, 51–52
feme covert laws, 33
The Feminine Mystique (Friedan), 314–315, 362
femininity: of Amy Coney Barrett, 384–385; women serving during World War II and, 265, 273
Feminist Alliance, 198–199, 282
feminist(s)/feminism, 201; on Amy Coney Barrett, 410–411; Black culture and, 342; Black feminists, 209–210; Black Women's Liberation Committee and, 323; Chicana, 324–329; of Chicanas, 329; criticism of, in the 1950s, 284; of Emma Goldman, 176; ERA and, 308; Esther Peterson and, 307, 309; fourth wave of, 402–404; Ida Tarbell on, 222–223; image of, in the 1960s, 318; lesbianism and, 336–338; millennial women returning to traditional roles and, 387–390; in the 1980s, 8, 357–359; radical (1970s), 333–342; revival of, early 1990s, 363; on the right, 413; sex-positive, 363; SNCC feminist sit-ins, 322; ultradicals and moderate, 349–350; women of color in the 1960s, 320–331; women's involvement in Revolutionary War and, 71. *See also* Black feminism/feminists; New Woman; third-wave feminism
fertility rate, 421–422
Field, Ruth Fuller, 231–232
Fifteenth Amendment, 76, 184
films. *See* movies
Finch, Katherine, 17–18
Finney, Charles, 90–91
Finney, Lydia, 90–92
Fiorina, Carly, 408–409
Firestone, Shulamith, 333, 334
First African Baptist Church, Boston, 97
First Great Awakening, 57
first ladies, 406–407. *See also* Roosevelt, Eleanor
Fisk, Thomas, 37
Five Points, New York City, 91
Flaming Youth (film), 236, 237
Flanagan, Caitlin, 388–389, 396
flappers (1920s), 7, 238, 242–244, 246–247, 487n59
Flexner, Eleanor, 474n72
Florence Crittenton homes, 298–299, 501n58
Flynn, Elizabeth "Rebel Girl" Gurley, 204
Font, Father Pedro, 431n52
Food and Drug Administration, 301, 304
Forten, James, 108
Forten, Sarah, 106
Fortune magazine, 251
Founding Fathers, 63
Fourteenth Amendment, 171, 183, 351, 410
fourth wave of feminism, 402–404
Fox, George, 33–34
Francisco de Lasuen, Fermin, 133
Frankfurter, Felix, 160
Franklin, Benjamin, 5, 59, 77; Cherokee women and, 435–436n15; Polly Stevenson and, 36–37; on women in the public sphere, 38, 39
Fraye Arbiter Shtime (newspaper), 221
Free African Society, 73
free Black women: anti-slavery movement and, 105–106, 108–109; moral reform movement, nineteenth-century, 92–94;

nineteenth-century literary societies, 107–108; temperance groups, 97
Freedom's Journal, 108
free love, 205, 225–226
Freeman, Jane, 302
Freeman, Jo, 381
French, learning, 45, 47
French nuns, 40–41
Freud, Sigmund, 224, 239, 398
Friday, Nancy, 373–374
Friedan, Betty, 314–316, 317–319, 337, 351
Friend of Virtue (journal), 87, 95
Friendship Baptist Church, Atlanta, 153
Frumpies, the, 381
"fuck," 227, 382
Fuller, Gertie, 9, 426–427n12
Fuller, Margaret, 112, 143–144, 151, 468n18
"Future Prospects of Women in the 'Enlightened Age,'" 84

Gadley, Martha, 211
Gadley v. Gadley (1875), 211
Gage, Matilda Joslyn, 135
Gage, Thomas, 72
Galloway, Joseph, 76–78
Gallup Poll, on support for the ERA, 354
gang girls, 499–500n40. *See also* pachucas (gang girls)
Gangsta Bitch Music (Cardi B), 416
Gannett, Benjamin, 66
Garbo, Greta, 264
Gardiner, John, S.J., 80
garment industry, 216–218, 251, 307, 480n39
Garrett, Mary, 461–462n25
Garrison, William Lloyd, 105
"gender," sex *vs.*, 8
gender complexities, 419–420
gendered behavior, 7–8
gender essentialism, 420–421
genderfluid, 136, 174, 419
gender-neutral Potato Heads, 418–419
gender-neutral pronouns, 9–10
gender nonbinary, 8–9, 66, 174, 419. *See also* transgender/transgender people
gender nonconforming, 419
"genderqueer," 9, 129, 174, 262, 419, 491n38
gender roles: Generation Z on traditional, 419; westward expansion and, 125–126

gender-shaming, 8, 39, 172–173
General Association of Congregational Ministers in Massachusetts, 111
General Court of Massachusetts, 12, 37
Generation Z, 419
Geneva Medical College, New York, 161–162
Georgetown Law School, 165
Georgia Female Seminary, 147–148
Gerry, Elbridge, 75
Gilder, George, 357–358
Giles, Harriet, 153, 154–155, 463n36
Gillibrand, Kirsten, 400, 401
Gilman, Charlotte Perkins, 166–167, 201, 204, 236, 423
Ginsburg, Ruth Bader, 165, 372, 410
The Girl Employed in Hotels and Restaurants (Bowen), 232
girlie magazines, 297
Godey's Lady's Book, 116, 141, 175, 453n4
The Golden Rule (journal), 87, 106–107
Goldman, Emma, 176–178, 228, 239, 326, 469n24
Goldman Sachs, 395
gold rush/gold mining, 124, 129
Goldwater, Barry, 354–355
Good, Sarah, 25
Good Housekeeping magazine, 224, 253
Good Vibrations, San Francisco, 363
Gordon, Anna, 181
Gore, Al, 406
Gore, Tipper, 406
Graham, Richard, 315, 316
Granahan, Kathryn, 292, 297
Grant, Abigail, 62, 64
Grant, Azariah, 62
Grant, Ulysses, 166
Grassley, Chuck, 411
"Graveyard Rally," Vassar College, 204
Great Awakenings, 57, 90
Great Depression: birth control during, 248; Civilian Conservation Corps (CCC) and, 260–261; hoboes during, 261–263; marriage among college-educated women during, 252; women in the workforce during, 249, 250–251; women's sexual behavior during, 247–248

Great Migration of Native Americans, 272
Great Northward Migration, 212
Greeley, Horace, 123, 174–175, 468n18
Green, Beriah, 90
Greene, Marjorie Taylor, 416–417
Greene, Thomas, 32
Greenham, Richard, 13
Greenwich Village, New York City, 202
Gregory, Alyse, 235, 277
Gregory, John, 46, 148
Griffiths, Martha, 312, 313, 352, 354, 505n30
Griffitts, Hannah, 60–61, 68, 442n14
Grimké, Angelina, 110–112, 452n66
Grimké, Judge John, 110
Grimké, Sarah, 110–112, 450n48, 452n66
Griswold, Clarissa, 130
Griswold v. Connecticut (1965), 304
Growden, Grace, 76–78
"grrrl power," 377, 379
Guerilla Warfare (Guevara), 333
Guerin, E. J. [Elsa Jane] (Mountain Charley), 128
Guevara, Che, 333

Hachard, Marie-Madeleine, 40
Hale, Mary, 21, 453n4
Hale, Sarah Josepha, 116–117, 143, 175
Hall, G. Stanley, 151
Hall, Thomas (Thomasine), 429–430n31
Ham, Roswell, 253–254
Hamer, Fannie Lou, 507n54
Hamilton, Gail, 175
Hammond, James Henry, 438–439n47
Hammond, Philipa, 18
Hampton Negro Conference (1898), 233
Handsome Lake, 42–43
hangings, witch hysteria and, 20, 22, 25
Hanley, Rev. Dexter L., 304
Hanna, Kathleen, 378–379, 380
Hapgood, Hutchins, 201
Hardenbroeck, Margaret, 34–35
Harding, Warren, 221
Harper, Frances, 98, 182, 184
Harper's Bazaar, 410
Harper's Weekly, 226
Harrington, Henry F., 149
Harris, Kamala, 412–413
Harris, Sarah, 82

Harrison, Sarah, 31
Harry, Debbie, 520n39
Hartford Female Seminary, 142, 143
Harvard College, 83
Harvard University, 296, 386
Hasbro, 418–419
Hatch, Orrin, 369
Hatfield, Massachusetts, 55
Haun, Catherine, 125–126
Hawkins, Jane, 17, 18
Hawley, Emily, 96
Hayden, Casey, 322
Heavens to Betsy, 378
Heckler, Margaret, 516–517n63
help-wanted ads, sex-segregated, 316–317
Hemings, Sally, 438n47
"hermaphrodites," 39
Hernandez, Aileen, 315, 316, 320
Hewitt, Rev. Dr., 103
Heywood, Angela, 227, 381
Heywood, Ezra, 227
Hibbins, Ann, 20, 21–22
Hickok, Lorena, 257, 490n23
Higginbotham, Evelyn Brooks, 448n31, 485n28
higher education for women: at beginning of twenty-first century, 385–386; Black women in early, 151, 152; at Cornell University, 149; early Black woman's colleges, 152–156; expansion of women in, 156, 464n42; female seminaries, 144–147; Georgia Female Seminary, 147–148; law school, 165, 204; medical school, 161–163; as a misuse of resources, 390; MRS degree and, 379, 389; nineteenth century, 144–147; opposition to, 148–149; PhDs, 3, 149–150, 461n21. *See also* college(s)
Hill, Anita (Hill–Thomas hearings), 364–365, 371, 372, 398, 518–519n19
Hirshman, Linda, 387
Hispanic women, 131–132. *See also* Mexican American women/immigrants
Historical Chronicle, 39
History of the American Indians (Adair), 41
History of the Rise, Progress, and Termination of the American Revolution (Warren), 75

History of Woman Suffrage (Stanton, Anthony, and Gage), 135, 137
Hite, Shere (Hite Report), 511n5
Hobby, Oveta Culp, 273
hoboes, 261–263, 491–492n39
Hochschild, Arlie, 393
Hoffman, Clare Eugene, 272–273
Hollenbeck Junior High School, Los Angeles, 1
Hollingsworth, Elinor, 21
Hollywood films, 213, 485–486n36
Holtzman, Elizabeth, 353
"Holy Woman" (Lozen), 133–134
Home Mission (magazine), 154
Homestead Act (1862), 129–130, 132
homesteading, 129–130
homosexual, coining of term, 164
homosexual relationships. *See* lesbian(s)/lesbianism
Hooten, Elizabeth, 33
Hoover, Herbert, 156, 253, 256
Hoover, J. Edgar, 345
Hopkins, Edward, 12
Hopkins, Harry, 262
Hopkins, Pauline, 185–186, 471n48
House Committee on Agriculture, 294
"housekeepers/housekeeping for the public good" jobs, 5, 459n4; municipal housekeeping in late nineteenth century, 158–161. *See also* moral reform movement, nineteenth-century
House Rules Committee, 311
House Un-American Activities Committee, 330
housework/household tasks, 44, 393, 394, 436n21
Howard, William Lee, 8, 202
Howard University Law School, 211
Hudson, Della, 8–9, 136
Hudson, Elizabeth, 60
Hudson, Samuel J., 9
Huerta, Dolores, 325–326
Hull, Charles, 160
Hull, Gloria, 340
Hull House, 159, 161, 258, 465n50
Hunter, Addie, 212
Hunter, Jane Edna, 234
Hutchinson, Anne, 16–17, 18

Hutchinson, Kay Bailey, 371
Hyde Amendment (1976), 352

Ibarruri, Dolores, 345
Ickes, Harold L., 275
idea of woman/womanhood: attitude toward those who did not fit, 7–8; changing in late nineteenth century, 166–167; in colonial New England, 3–4, 415; dependence on men, 115–116; in eighteenth century, 36–37, 38, 63; factors influencing shifts in, 6–7; as "the gentler sex," 343, 344; militancy's impact on, 199; nineteenth-century southerners concerned about the new, 116–117; prescriptions defined by men, 3–5; return to old dominant notions of, 7, 421–422, 424; after Revolutionary War, 74–78; sex and, 225; in "The True Woman" lecture (Anthony), 170–171; twentieth-century "New Woman," 200–223; Ventura School for Girls and, 2–3; westward migration trip and, 125–127; women's role in maintaining tyranny of, 5–6
identity politics, 341–342
Iggy Pop, 520n39
"illegitimate births/children," 30–31, 298–299, 501n58
Illinois Factory Act (1893), 160, 465n50
immigrants: at Hollenbeck Junior High School in the 1950s, 1–2; labor strikes, 217–221; pachucas, 289; popular culture of the 1920s, 237–238; Uprising of 20,000 and, 480n39. *See also* Chinese American women/immigrants; Jewish population/immigrants; Mexican American women/immigrants
immigration (1880–1920), 157
"Improvement Circles," 119
incarceration, 234, 291, 350
indentured servants, 30, 31, 44
Indiana Married Woman's Property Act, 215
Indian Citizenship Act of 1924 (Snyder Act), 188
indoctrination, 2

"industrial feminists," 218–219, 480n44
Industrial Workers of the World, 204
infidelity. *See* adultery
Instagram, 405
International Ladies Garment Workers Union, 216, 217
intersectionality, 184, 324, 341–342
"intersex," 429–430n31
inventor, woman as, 222
inverts. *See* sexual inverts/"inverts"
Iroquois culture, 28–29, 42–43
Italian immigrants, Uprising of 20,000 and, 480n39

Jackson, Jonathan, 348
Jackson, Kate, 181
Jackson, Michael, 380
Jacobs, Harriet, 52, 53
Jan, Flora Belle, 487
Jane Club, 160
Japanese American women, 268–269
Jarrett, Valerie, 402
Jay, John, 63
Jay, Sarah, 63
Jefferson, Thomas: Handsome Lake and, 42; ladydom and, 44–45, 47, 49–50; on role of women, 4, 46, 172; Sally Hemings and, 438n47
Jeffords, Mary Price, 130
Jerusalem, New York, 58
Jewish population/immigrants: Bryn Mawr and, 153; labor activism, 218–219; Uprising of 20,000 and, 480n39; working in garment factories, 216, 218–219
Jigsaw (zine), 377
Jim Crow public schools, training Black teachers for, 153
Joan of Arc, 149
John Birch Society, 354
Johns Hopkins University, 149–150, 162
Johnson, Elizabeth, 20
Johnson, Robert Ward, 129–130
Johnson, Sally, 438–439n47
Johnson, Samuel, 109
Johnson, Virginia E., 511n5
Jones, Diana, 31
Jones, Margaret, 20
Jones-Rogers, Stephanie, 52

journalists, female, 221–222, 257
Juilliard School, 292
Jumper, Hannah, 104
Just Be (nonprofit), 404
"The Justice of Woman Suffrage" (Terrell), 185
juvenile delinquents (1950s), 1–2

Kaiser Family Foundation, 386
Kansas City Sun, 216
Kantor, Jodi, 407
Kee, Elizabeth, 292
Kefauver, Estes, 297
Kelley, Florence, 160–161, 465n50
Kennedy, Florynce, 320, 337, 339
Kennedy, John F., 307–308, 309, 311
Kennedy, Ted, 368, 370
Kent State shootings (1970), 344
Ketcham, Rebecca, 126
Kiesling, Lydia, 410
King, Martin Luther, Jr., 281, 282, 315
King, Mary, 322
King Philip's War (1675–1676), 22
Kinsey, Alfred (study), 299–301, 420, 502n64
Kitchens, Caroline, 402
Kjeldahl, Bill, 295
Klobuchar, Amy, 397
Knutson, Andy, 293
Knutson, Coya, 292–295, 500n47
Koedt, Anne, 333–334, 511n5
Krafft-Ebing, Richard von, 134, 202, 232
Krasnow, Iris, 386
Kroeber, Alfred L., 432n52
Kroger, William S., 300
Ku, Angie, 389
Ku Klux Klan, 153
Kunitoi, Sue, 268–269

labor activism and labor unions: ERA and, 308; Factory Girls' Association, 121–122; farmworkers, 324–326; first working-women's, 121; International Ladies Garment Workers Union, 216; New Woman, 204. *See also* strikes
Labor Women for Kennedy, 308
Ladies Associations, during Revolutionary War, 69–71

Ladies' Home Journal, 246–247, 287, 288, 305
Lady Chatterley's Lover (Lawrence), 335
"ladydom," eighteenth-century, 44–48
Lafitau, Joseph-François, 29
Lahontan, Baron de, 27, 29–30, 133
landowners, female, 31–32
land ownership, 31–32, 35; Homestead Act and, 129–130; upper-class Hispanic women, 131
Langen, Odin, 295
Langston, John Mercer, 439n47
Langston, Lucy, 439n47
La Opinion (newspaper), 290
Larcom, Lucy, 119, 123
Lash, Joseph, 255
Latinas, working during World War II, 266–267. *See also* Mexican American women/immigrants
Laughlin, Clara, 232–233
lavender armbands, 337
law, Black women, careers in, 211
Law, E. Norine, 231
Lawrence, D. H., 335
law schools/law degrees, 165, 204
laws of coverture. *See* coverture laws
lawyers: Black women, 211; Charlotte E. Ray, 211
Lead Belly, 279
leadership, Sheryl Sandberg on, 396
leadership, women in: of Black women in civil rights movement, 321–322; Chicano women in the 1960s, 324–327; Mount Holyoke and, 252–254; of NOW, 318–319; during Roosevelt administration, 257–259
Lean In: Women, Work, and the Will to Lead (Sandberg), 395–397, 410
"lean-in" movement, 395–397, 526n26
Leave It to Beaver (television show), 287
Leavenworth Weekly Times (Kansas), 172
Lee, Arthur, 48
Lee, Jarena, 73–74
Lee, JeeYuen, 372
legal powers, of colonial women, 13
legislation: civil rights, 311–312, 311–313; Eleanor Roosevelt and social-welfare, 255. *See also* petitioning lawmakers

legislature, prohibition, 102
Leiserson Company, 217
Lemlich, Clara, 217–218
Lennon, John, 348–349
Leopold, Alice, 308
Le Petit, Mathurin, 39–40
Lerner, Gerda, 321–322
"lesbian," use of term, 318
lesbian(s)/lesbianism: Black radical feminists, 340; Chicana, 341; Kate Millett, 336; Kinsey report and, 300; Megan Rapinoe, 418; of the New Women vs. working-class girls, 231–232; not opting out of their careers in twenty-first century, 391; in NOW, 318; NOW and, 318–320, 319; Radicalesbians, 338; radical feminism of the 1970s and, 336–339; in seventeenth century, 440n58; wages, 524n16; working-class twentieth-century women, 231–232
lesbian behavior, first court case in American dealing with, 20
lesbian blues music, 245–246
"Lesbianism and Feminism" (Atkinson), 337
The Liberator (newspaper), 97, 98, 105, 111
"Liberty Teas," 68
libido, 224, 239
Life magazine, 243
The Lily (journal), 96
Limbaugh, Rush, 412
Lincoln, Abraham, 129, 132
literary societies, female, 107–108
Liu, Cynthia, 389
Livermore, Mary, 136, 223
Livingston, Henry Beekman, 47–48
Lockwood, Belva, 165–166, 246
Logan, Deborah, 60
Longe, Alexander, 26
Lorde, Audre, 340
Loren, Sophia, 299
Los Angeles, California, 237; Ventura School for Girls, 2–3
Los Angeles Times, 271
Los Guilucos (reform school), 291
Loudoun County, Virginia, 52
Love, Courtney, 520n39
Love's Coming of Age (Carpenter), 201

Lowell, Francis Cabot, 117–118; textile mills, 117–123
Lowell, Massachusetts, 118
Lowell Offerings (magazine), 119
lower-class women: leaving their jobs to stay at home, 390–391; postrevolutionary education, 82; prostitution and, 89; temperance movement and, 100–101. *See also* working-class girls/women
Lozen (Chiricahua Apache woman), 133–134
Luckenbach, Abraham, 99–100
Lugar, Richard, 399
lunch-counter sit-ins, 321
Lundberg, Ferdinand, 284
Luttrell, Narcissus, 30
Lynd, Helen and Robert, 247–248
Lyon, Mary, 4, 146, 253

Mack, Gloria, 288
MacKinnon, Catharine, 362, 401
Macy, John, 309
Madam C. J. Walker products, 214–216
Maddox, Lester, 303
Madonna, 380
"Magdalen" asylums, 89
Mailer, Norman, 335
mail-order brides, 30, 432n61
makeup, 265, 290
Malone, Annie, 214–216
Manasses, Carolyn, 488n3
manhaters, feminists condemned as, 318
"manly," calling women, 8, 173–174, 318
Mansfield, Jayne, 299
Manson, Charles, 346
Manypenny, George W., 133
Manzanar Free Press, 268–269
Mapes, Charles, 398
Marcus, Ruth, 412
Marcuse, Herbert, 347
Marine Corps Women's Reserve, 272
Marks, Jeannette, 253
Mark Twain Prize for American Humor, 403
marriage(s): age of women, in the 1950s, 279; Anna Howard Shaw on heterosexual, 179; attitudes about, in the 1980s, 358; babies born out of, 298–299; 501n58; Benjamin Franklin on, 36–37; Boston marriages, 164, 465n60; colonial woman, 13, 29; combining career with, 278; during the Depression, 250, 252; eighteenth-century, 38, 56; of Inez Milholland, 204–205; Iroquois culture, 29; John and Abigail Adams, 55–56; ladydom training and, 47; and New Woman, 200–201; in the 1950s, 279, 286–287; nineteenth-century pioneering professions and, 163; in the 1930s, 252; no longer defining and confining women, 423; Quaker, 33–34, 59; revised eighteenth-century idea of, 38; Sarah Josepha Hale on, 117; taking husband's last name in, 200
married women: birth control and, 242, 248; the Pill and, 304; working, 250–251, 386–387, 392
Married Women's Property Acts, 213
Marshall, Thurgood, 366
Martha Washingtonians, 100–101, 105, 449n38
Maryland, 31–32
Mary Tyler Moore Show (television show), 374
Massachusetts Association Opposed to the Further Extension of Suffrage to Women, 175–176
Massachusetts Bay Colony, 12–26
Massachusetts General Court, 3
Masters, William H., 511n5
Mateen, Omar, 417
Maternal Desire (de Marneffe), 389
Mather, Cotton, 17, 24–25, 282
Mather, Increase, 24
"The Matriarchate, or Mother-Age" (Stanton), 187–188
Matthews, Victoria Earle, 233–234
Maxwell, Zerlina, 402
May, Elaine Tyler, 500–501n52
McCain, John, 407
McCaskill, Claire, 399, 400
McClure's Magazine, 221
McCray, Chirlane, 340
McCrummel, James, 107
McCullough, Father Thomas, 325
McDougal, Alexander, 65

McDowall, Rev. John R., 89–90
McNamara, Margaret, 302
Mead, Margaret, 275
media: on feminism in the 1980s, 357–358; Frank Dubois story, 9; on Freudian theories, 224; Hill–Thomas hearings and, 367; on Kate Millett, 335; labor strikes and, 217; on millennial women opting out, 6, 387, 388–390, 393; race films, 212–213; reporting on women in politics, 292, 293, 294; on riot grrrls, 379; on Sarah Palin, 407–408; on women in the workforce, 6; women reporters during FDR's administration, 257
medicine, women's careers in, 161–163, 165, 211–212
Megan Thee Stallion, 416
Megquier, Mary Jane, 124
men: accusations of sexual assault by, 398–399; affairs with married, 306; blamed for prostitution, 92; continuing to hold power in the 1990s, 383; decline in sperm count of, 421–422; as defining idea of woman, 3–4; describing and prescribing who woman should be, 4; household duties and, 393–394, 395–396; ideas about gender behavior by millennial, 394; identifying with brand of masculinity, 394; "New Man," 200–201; radical feminism of the 1970s and, 333–334; on a return to traditional gender roles, 523n6; sexual exploitation by slave owners, 52–53; weaponizing of sex, 371–373; westward expansion and "posing" as, 127–129; woman's moral superiority over, 87–88. *See also individual men*
ménage à trois, 19
merchants, female, 55
"Me Too" movement, 404
Mexican American women/immigrants, 237–238, 266; activist leadership in the 1960s, 324–326; Brown Berets, 327–328; flapper age, 243–244; pachucas, 289–290; popular culture of the 1920s, 237–238; Young Citizens for Community Action, 327
Mexico, 130

Micheaux, Oscar, 212
Middlebury College, 145
middle class: flappers and, 243–244; leaving their jobs to stay at home, 390–391; westward expansion, 124
Middletown in Transition (Lynd and Lynd), 247
"middling" class, 44, 49, 81, 124
midwives and healers, 16, 17, 21, 54
migrant women, nineteenth-century, 124–125
Mikulski, Barbara, 367
Milano, Alyssa, 404
Milholland, Inez, 189–190, 203–206, 476n12
militancy, in suffrage movement, 189–193
military, women in: Civil War, 135–136; "posing as men" during Revolutionary War, 66; during World War II, 272–275; Yeomanettes during World War I, 195, 197
millennial women: choosing traditional role of women vs. career, 386–391; Me Too movement, 404; political involvement, 415–416; protest against Donald Trump, 403–404; in the public sphere, 405–413; sexual harassment/assault and, 397–403, 404–405
Miller, Henry, 335
Miller, Rachel, 58
Millett, Kate, 334–337, 361
"mill girls," 118–123, 453–454n11
Mills College, 267, 280
miners, boardinghouses for, 124
mining, 128, 129
Minnesota House of Representatives, 293
Minor, Virginia, 467n10
missionaries, 39–41
Mitchell, George, 367
Mitchellville, Maryland, 392
Mocha Moms, 392
Modern Woman: The Lost Sex (Lundberg and Farnham), 284, 285
mommy mystique, 391–392, 395
"mommy track," 394, 395, 525n23
"mommy trap," 394
Mommy Wars (Steiner), 391
Monahan, Joe, 127–128, 456n39

monogamy, 202
Monroe, Marilyn, 297, 299
"monsters," calling women, 8, 412
Montezuma, Carlos, 207
Montgomery Bus Boycott, 280
Moore, Milcah Martha, 61
Morales, Bertha, 266
moral reform movement, nineteenth-century: abolitionist movement, 105–113; free Black women participating in, 92–94, 97–99; moral superiority of woman and, 87–88, 113–114; prostitution and, 89–95, 447n18; temperance movement, 95–101
Moral Reform Retreat for Black "victims of vice," 93
Morgan, Anne, 219, 220
Morgan, J. P., 219
The Morning After: Sex, Fear, and Feminism on Campus (Roiphe), 361–362
Morris, Margaret Hill, 66–67
Morris, Robert, 45–46
Morrison and Foerster law firm, 395
Moses (code name of Harriet Tubman), 137
Mosher, Clelia Duel, 227–228, 475–476n6
"most-wanted" list of the FBI, women on, 343, 348
mother heart values, 157–158, 180, 254, 489–490n16
mothers and motherhood: advising child on being a lady, 45; Chicana, 329; children of working, 302, 309; choosing over a career, 386–389; defense of stay-at-home, 302–303; enslaved females, 50–51; having a career and, 411–412; Kamala Harris on, 412–413; millennial women choosing over careers, 386–391; Mocha Moms, 392; in the 1950s, 278, 279, 282–283; radical feminism of the 1970s on, 334; stay-at-home, 387–391; unwed, 298–299. *See also* "traditional" family roles; working mothers
Motion Picture Production Code, 485–486n36
Mott, Abigail, 94, 113

Mott, Lucretia, 107, 169
Mountain Charley (Mrs. E. J. [Elsa Jane] Guerin), 128
Mount Hermon Female Seminary, 153
Mount Holyoke College, 252–254, 258
Mount Holyoke Female Seminary, 146–147
Mourdock, Richard, 399
movies: New Woman in, 213; of the 1920s, 236; race films, 212–213; sex in the 1950s, 299
Movimiento Estudiatil Chicano de Aztlan (MEChA), 329
Moynihan, Daniel Patrick, 310, 321, 507n53
Mr. Potato Head, 418
"MRS degree," 279, 389
Ms. magazine, 336, 359
Mudd, Emily Hartshorne, 277–278
"mulatto" enslaved people, 52
"municipal housekeeping" professions, 5, 158–161, 464n47
Murphy Brown (television show), 375
Murray, Judith Sargent, 83–85
Murray, Pauli, 315, 318, 320, 506n45
music: punk, 377–379, 520n39; riot grrrls, 379–380; rock 'n' roll, 296; Rosie the Riveter song, 264–265
My Secret Garden (Friday), 373, 374
My Story of the War: A Woman's Narrative of Four Years Personal Experience as Nurse in the Union Army (Livermore), 136

NAACP, 280, 281, 323; for women, 315–316
Nanye'hi, 41
Nast, Thomas, 226
Natchez Indians, 39–40
The Nation (magazine), 197
National American Woman Suffrage Association (NAWSA), 179, 189, 190–191, 192, 193–194, 469n31
National Anti-Slavery Standard, 182, 183
National Association for the Repeal of Abortion Laws, 351
National Association of Colored Women, 184, 209, 214, 259
National Association Opposed to Woman Suffrage, 176

National Black Feminist Organization, 339–340, 359
National Collegiate Athletic Association, 350
National Consumers League, 255, 260
National Council of American Indians, 207
National Council of Negro Women, 259
National Defense Education Bill, Title II, 294
National Democratic Convention (1964), 507n54
National Educational Television, 302, 309
National Enquirer, 402
National Federation of Afro-American Women of Boston, 184
National Federation of Women's Clubs, 474
National Gazette (newspaper), 120
National Guard Armory, Newburyport, Massachusetts, 344–345
National Guardsmen, 344
National Institute of Arts and Letters, 202–203
National Negro Congress, 269
National Organization for Women (NOW): Equal Opportunity in Education Act and, 350; formation of, 315–316; lesbians/lesbianism and, 317–320; March on Washington (1978), 357; *New York Times*'s sex-segregated help-wanted ads and, 316–317; women of color in, 320; Women's Sexuality Conference (1973), 363
National Public Radio (NPR), 367
National Raza Women's Conference (1971), 329
National Student Strike Force, 344
National United Committee to Free Angela Davis, 348–349
National University Law School, 165–166
National Urban League, 270
National War Labor Board, General Order No. 16, 263
National Woman's Party, 192–193, 195, 308, 309
National Woman's Rights Convention, 116

National Woman Suffrage Association, 183, 471n44
National Women's Rights Convention (1866), 184
National Youth Administration: Division of Negro Affairs, 156, 259; women's CCC and, 261
National Youth Authority, 259
Native Americans: Christian, 26–27; Christian missionaries and schools, 39–41; Code of Handsome Lake, 42–43; creation story, 28, 42–43; drunkenness among, 99; elevation of women, 26, 27; gender diversity, 431–432n52; Homestead Act and, 129; idea of women for the Iroquois, 28–29; marriage, 29; matrilineal, 28; retaliatory attack by Siwanoy Indians, 17; role of women, 26–27; sex assigned at birth, changing, 27–28, 419–420; temperance movement and, 99–100; white encroachment and, 39–42. *See also* Cherokee Nation/women
Native American women: adultery, 27; alcohol use, 99, 449n32; Christian missionaries and, 39–41; dismissed by colonists when begging for peace and mercy, 11; disrepute of old, 43; Iroquois, 28–30; Iroquois idea of, 28–29; loss of liberty in eighteenth century, 39–40; Lozen ("Holy Woman"), 133–134; matrilineal tribes, 26, 41; men's prescriptions for, 4–5; New Woman and, 206–207; as peace emissaries, 133; peace women, 27; spinning and weaving, 42; suffrage movement and, 187–189; Ursuline Academy, 40–41; westward migration and, 132–133; woman's suffrage and, 187–188; during World War II, 270–272
nature's law: subordination of women and, 39, 63; woman's moral superiority over men, 86, 88
NAWSA. *See* National American Woman Suffrage Association (NAWSA)
needlework, 44, 45, 47
The Negro Family: The Case for National Action (Moynihan), 321

Neuberger, Maurine, 310
New Amsterdam settlement, 34
"The New Century's Manly Woman" (Anthony), 173–174
New Deal, 254, 258, 260
New England colonies. *See* colonial America
New-England Courant, 38
"new feminists," 378
New Left, 333
New Look, 276, 301
New Netherlands, 17
Newsweek magazine, 506n43
Newton, Huey, 514n44
New Woman, 200–223; Black women as, 208–216; engaging in sex for pleasure, 201–202; Freud and, 239; in Hollywood studio films, 213; Inez Milholland, 189–190, 202–206; Mosher sex survey, 227–228, 475–476n6; Mount Holyoke graduates, 253; Native American women, 206–207; sexuality of working-class girls *vs.* sexuality of, 230, 231–232; in urban centers, 200; women's ambivalence about, 202–203; working-class women and, 216–223
New Women of the Feminist Alliance, 198, 334
New York chapter of NOW, 319
New York Female Moral Reform Society, 91–93, 92–93, 94–95
New York Herald, 172
New York Hippodrome, 220
New York Infirmary for Indigent Women and Children, 162
New York magazine, 403
New York Magdalen asylum, 89
New York Medical Journal, 8, 202
New York Radical Feminists, 333–334, 335, 359
New York Radical Women, 330–331
New York Sons of Temperance, 102
New York State Association Opposed to the Extension of Suffrage, 469n24
New York State Legislature, 144–145
New York State Women's Division, Democratic Party, 255
New York Sun, 103, 196
New York Times, 6, 172, 206, 273, 286, 389; sex-segregated help-wanted ads, 316
New York Times/CBS News poll (1991), 398
New York Times Magazine, 362
New York Tribune, 144
Nightingale, Florence, 278
1950s (decade): college education in, 279–280; contrast between women of the 1920s and women of, 277; home-maker role of women in, 282–287; juvenile delinquents, 1–2; marriage in, 279, 286–287; motherhood in, 278, 279, 282–283; music, 296–297; pachucas in, 1–2, 280, 289–291; political participation by women during, 291–296; reform schools, 2, 290–291; television shows in, 287, 288–289; woman's sex life in, 296–301; women in the workforce during, 283
1960s (decade), 302–331; activism and leadership by women of color during, 320–331; ERA and, 308–309, 311; *The Feminine Mystique* (Friedan), 314–315; miniskirt during, 303; President's Commission on the Status of Women, 309–311, 315; rebirth of women's movement, 314–320; rise of the second wave of feminism in the, 307–313; Title VII, Civil Rights Act, 311–313; women's sexuality in, 303–306; working *vs.* stay-at-home mothers, 302–303
1980s (decade), 8, 357–358, 378, 379–380, 386, 393
1990s (decade). *See* postfeminism/postfeminists; third-wave feminism
Nineteenth Amendment, 175, 196
nineteenth century: anti-slavery societies/movement, 105–113; Black woman's colleges, 152–156; Boston marriages in, 164; civil rights movement, 281–282; Civil War (1861–1865), 134–141; female moral reformers, 89–95; moral leadership of women, 87–88; prostitution, 89–95; seduction laws, 94–95; temperance movement, 95–101; textile factory employment, 117–123; westward

expansion during, 123–134; women rebels in, 288–296; women's colleges, 144–152; women's professions in, 157–167
Nison, Charles, 285
Nixon, Richard, 351, 353
nonbinary people. *See* gender nonbinary
Norris, Daisy, 188
Norris, Elizabeth, 60
Norton, Mary Beth, 443–444n34
Novak, Kim, 299
NOW. *See* National Organization for Women (NOW)
nuclear family, 334, 375
Nungesser, Paul, 400, 401
nurses, 139–141

Obama, Michelle, 397
Oberlin College, 152, 209
O'Brien, Joe, 200–201
O'Connell, William, 247
O'Connor, Sandra Day, 371, 516n63
Octavio-Cortez, Alexandria, 417
The Octoroon (pamphlet), 52
O'Donnel, Sheilah, 390, 393
Office of Civil Rights, 364
Office of Indian Affairs, 271
Ogden, Rev. John Cosens, 82
Old Testament, 13–14
Olivarez, Graciela, 320
Olive Plant and Ladies' Temperance Advocate (journal), 101
Oliver, Mary, 17
Omar, Ilhan, 417
"On the Equality of the Sexes" (Sargent Stevens), 84
Opportunity (magazine), 270
opting-out fever, 386–392, 393, 415, 523n8
Oread Collegiate Institute for young women, 153–154
Oregon Trail, 126
O'Reilly, Leonora, 219
The O'Reilly Factor (television news program), 407–408
orgasm, female, 228, 333–334, 511n5
Ornaments for the Daughters of Zion: Or The Character and Happiness of a Vertuous Woman (Mather), 25
O'Sullivan, John, 123

outlaws (1970s), 342–350
Overland Trail, 129
Overmyer, David, 173
Owyhee mines, 128

pachucas (gang girls), 1–2, 280, 289–291, 499n35
Packard, Sophia, 153–155, 463n36
Page, Bettie, 297, 501
Paglia, Camille, 361–362
Paine, Thomas, 63
Palin, Sarah, 407–408
Pamunkey Indians, 26
pants, women wearing, 264
paperbacks, of the 1950s, 297–298
Parker, Bonnie, 343
Parker, Dorothy, 242
Parker, Lonnae O'Neal, 391
Parker, Thomas, 15–16, 61
Parks, Rosa, 280–281, 507n54
Parsons, Talcott, 283–284, 287
Patria (film), 213
patriotism: of women during Civil War, 135–137; of women during Revolutionary War, 64–65, 67, 68, 69–70; women in the workforce during World War II and, 263
Paul, Alice, 189–190, 191, 192, 194, 196, 308, 311, 346–347
peace treaty, Native American, 41
peace women, 27
The Pearl: A Ladies' Weekly Literary Gazette, 97, 101
Pearson, Drew, 258
Pelosi, Nancy, 415, 417
Pember, Phoebe Levy, 139–141
penmanship, 45, 47
Penn, William, 33
Pennsylvania Abolition Society, 74
Penobscot Indians, 27
People magazine, 402–403
people of color, white people replaced by, 421–422
Pequot Indians, 11, 41
performing "woman," 107
The Perils of Pauline (film), 213
Perkins, Frances, 253, 258, 491n30
Peter, Rev. Hugh, 16, 428n15

Peterson, Esther, 307–309, 311
petitioning lawmakers, 94–95, 122, 174, 175, 192
"petticoat government," 41, 140
Pew Research polls, 394, 408
Pew Research Survey, 9–10
PhD programs for women, 3, 149–150, 461n21
Phelps, Almira Hart, 145–146
Philadelphia Female Anti-Slavery Society, 106
Philadelphia Female Literary Association, 107
Philadelphia General Hospital, 211
Philadelphia Magdalen Asylum, 89
Philipse, Frederick, 35
Phillips, Ann Green, 182
Phillips, Wendell, 182–183
Phips, Lady Mary, 37
Phips, Sir William, 37
physicians, female, 161–163, 165
Picquet, Louisa, 52
Pierce, George Foster, 148
Pike County, Illinois, 125
Pill, the, 301, 303–305, 385
pilots, female, 273–274, 495n69
Ping-Hua Lee, Mabel, 186
pioneer women, 124–125
pirate trials, 38
Pitcher, Molly, 65
Pittsburgh Courier, 212, 281
Pittsburgh Press, 317
Plaskett, Stacey, 414–415
Playboy magazine, 297
Poe, Edgar Allan, 119
Poems on Divers Subjects (Brewster), 61
poetry and poets, 15, 22, 60–61, 68
political opinions: eighteenth-century ladydom and, 46; by women during/about Revolutionary War, 63–65
political participation: Chinese American women, 187; Democratic Party and, 255–256; Eleanor Roosevelt and, 255, 256; under FDR's administration, 257–259; after Hill–Thomas hearings, 370–371; Judith Sargent Murray and, 85; Mary McLeod Bethune, 156; millennial political candidates, 405–409, 412–413; millennial women, 415–416; by New York Female Moral Reform Society, 94–95; in the 1950s, 291–296; in the 1960s, 317; Ronald Reagan and, 516–517n63; of Susanna Wright (eighteenth century), 59; voting statistics, 1920s, 256. *See also* woman suffrage
political power, of Native American women, 29, 187–188
political topics, women writing about, 75, 85
"politics of respectability," 98, 448n31
polls: on being transgender, 419; on gender behavior (2006 and 2016), 394; on political candidates with small children, 408; on returning to traditional gender roles, 386; on sexual harassment, 398, 399; on traditional roles of men and women, 392, 523n6
Ponkapoag Indians, 26–27
Popenoe, Paul, 287
popular culture: of the 1920s, 236–238; of the 1950s, 296–298; television shows, 287–289, 374–376. *See also* movies; music
population growth, 1880–1920, 157
pornography, 297, 363
Poro Company, 214
Porter, Moses, 79
Posner, Richard, 389–390, 391
Post, Emily, 247
posters, during World War II, 264–265
postfeminism/postfeminists, 359, 378; attitude toward sex, 360–363; impact of Hill–Thomas hearings on, 371–372; *The Morning After* (Roiphe), 362; riot grrrls, 360; *Sexual Personae* (Paglia), 361–362; third-wave feminism contrasted with, 519n28
Power, Katherine Ann, 344–345, 513n31
prairies, women's lives on, 124–125, 455n31
Praying Indian Villages for Indians, 26
preachers, women, 33, 57, 73–74
pregnant women: enslaved, 50; unmarried, 298–299, 501n58
prejudice: anti-Chinese, 267–268; called out, during abolition movement, 109;

Eleanor Roosevelt and, 258–259; hiring of Black women and, 269–270; hiring of Chinese American women and, 267–268; hiring of Mexican American women and, 266. *See also* discrimination(s); race and racism
premarital sex, 1, 300, 500–501n52
President's Commission on the Status of Women, 309–311, 315
Presley, Elvis, 296–297
press. *See* media
Princess Dawn Mist, 188:188
Princeton University alumnae, leaving the workplace, 387–388
pro-choice movement, 351
Proctor, Colonel Thomas, 29
pro-family conservatives, 351–352
pronouns, gender-neutral, 9–10
prostitution, 5, 89–95, 448n9, 485n28
protests: anti-Vietnam, 330; Days of Rage, 346; Dohrn and violence in, 345–346; by NOW, 316; against presidency of Donald Trump, 403–404; SNCC feminist sit-in (1964), 322; textile factory workers, 120; woman's suffrage movement, 192–193; by women in civil rights movement, 280–282. *See also* demonstrations; strikes
Providence, Rhode Island, 105
Providence Gazette, 69
publications: Black woman's duty depicted in, 152–153; censorship of sex radical, 226–227; on drunkenness, 96; Lowell mill girls, 119; by Margaret Sanger, 239–240, 241, 242; radical feminist of the 1970s, 334–336; temperance, 97, 101; women's rights, 171, 239. *See also individual publications*
public speaking, women: Black women in abolition movement, 109–110; Grimké sisters during anti-slavery movement, 111; Jarena Lee, 73; Susan B. Anthony, 102–103; World's Anti-Slavery Convention and, 112–113
public sphere: anti-slavery movement, 105–113; colonial era, 14; eighteenth-century women resented in the, 38–39; free Black women, nineteenth-century,

92–94, 97–99; millennial women in the, 405–413; moral reformers in nineteenth century, 91–95; temperance movement, 96–101. *See also* political participation; workforce, women in; working women
punk rock scene, 360, 377–382, 520n39
Puritanism: adultery and, 27; Anne Bradstreet, 15; Anne Hutchinson, 16–17; clothing and, 23–24; doubt cast on, 38; education for girls, 23; idea of woman, 12–13, 14; Mary Dyer and, 19–20; Native Americans and, 26; Old Testament and, 13–14; publications by women and, 15–16; Quakers and, 14, 19, 33; widows, 427n6; witch hysteria and, 37; women preaching, 16

Quakers: on drunkenness, 95; female preachers, 57; freedoms of women, 33; Grimké sisters and, 110; marriage, 33–34; marriage resisters, 59–60; Mary Dyer and, 19; permitted women to preach, 14; prayer meetings for women, 33; single women, 59; treatment of unmarried mothers, 433n70; working with Moral Reform Retreat for Black victims of vice, 93–94
Quant, Mary, 303
Quarles, Ralph, 439n47
Quayle, Dan, 375
Quincy, Josiah, 52–53

race and racism: Black women during World War II, 494n67; college admissions for Black women, 151, 152; Hill–Thomas hearings and, 369–370; U.S. Rubber Plant segregated toilet facilities, 270
race films, 212–213
Radcliffe College, 152
Radicalesbians, 338, 359
radicalism: Black feminism, 339–341; of Chicana women, 341–342; Combahee River Collective, 340–341; New Left, 333; New York Radical Feminists, 333–334; in NOW leadership, 319; radical women in the 1970s, 333–342;

radicalism (cont.)
    right-wing, 355–356, 357; STOP ERA, 355–356; ultraradical movement, 342–350
Rainey, Gertrude "Ma," 245, 487–488n64
Raleigh Register (newspaper), 148
Randolph, George Wythe, 140
Randolph, Mary, 139–140
rape, 30, 52, 362, 372, 398–399, 402; of enslaved women, 53
#RapeCultureIsWhen, 402
rape fantasies, 373
Rapinoe, Megan, 417–418
Rawalt, Marquerite, 309
Ray, Charlotte E., 211
Reader's Digest magazine, 278, 298, 304
Reagan, Ronald, 357, 365, 466, 516–517n63
recession of 2008–2009, 392–393
Reckless, Hetty, 93
Redbook magazine, 256, 257, 398
Red Cross, 194
Reddit, 405
Red Wing, Minnesota, 286
Reed, Esther de Berdt, 69–70
Reed, John, 202
Reedy, William Marion, 228
reformers, twentieth-century, on sexuality of working-class girls, 229–235
reform journals, nineteenth-century, 87
reform professions, nineteenth-century, 157–161
reform schools (1950s), 2, 290–291
Rehnquist, William, 401
Reitman, Ben, 239, 491n39
religion: of Jemima Wilkinson, 57–58; in postrevolutionary "Young Ladies Academies," 81
The Religious Magazine and Family Miscellany, 148–149
Remond, Nancy, 106
"Resist Psychic Death" (Bikini Kill), 380
The Revolution (newspaper), 171
Revolutionary War (1775–1783): idea of woman after, 74–85; impact on enslaved people, 72; Ladies Association project, 69–71; men's cowardice, 62, 65, 66; questioning of hierarchies during, 71–72; role in changing women's lives, 443–444n34; war poetry, 442n14; woman's diary during, 66–67; women attempting to become soldiers in, 66; women present at fighting in, 65–66; women's efforts and patriotism during, 62, 64–65, 67, 68; women serving as prostitutes in, 441n9; women's organizations during, 67–68
Rhoads, James, 150–151
Rhode Island, 14, 17
riot grrrls, 360, 377–383, 379–383, 520n39
Riot Grrrl (zine), 379
riots, 379
Rivington Street Settlement House, Manhattan, 254–255
Robach, Amy, 407
Roberts, John, 407
Robertson, Pat, 411
Robinson, Harriet Hanson, 118
Robinson, Ruby Smith, 322, 323
Rockefeller, John D., Jr., 242
Rockefeller, John D., Sr., 152, 155, 221
Rockefeller, Laura Spelman, 155
Rockford Female Seminary, 159
rock 'n' roll, 296
Rockport, Massachusetts, 104
Rockwell, Norman, 264–265
Rodham, Hillary, 405–406
Rodman, Henrietta, 198, 282, 334
Rodriguez, Arturo, 327
Roe v. Wade, 339, 351, 357, 366, 385, 410
Rogers, Edith, 272–273
Roiphe, Anne, 362
Roiphe, Katie, 361–362
Roller Derby (television show), 288–289
Romney, Mitt, 300
Roosevelt, Eleanor, 292; on children of working mothers, 302, 309; as first lady, 257; helping women gain power in the government, 257–260; on "keeping women out of the kitchen," 274–275; political participation and, 255–256; President's Commission on the Status of Women, 309–310; social justice and, 254–255; on woman suffrage, 255; on women pilots, 274; women's CCC and, 261; on women working, 250

Roosevelt, Franklin D., 156, 255, 257, 260, 269
Roosevelt, Theodore, 161
Rosie the Riveter, 264–265
Royal Air Force, 273
Rubyfruit Jungle (Brown), 338
Rush, Benjamin, 81
Rush Medical College, 161, 162
Russell, Jane, 299

Safire, William, 518–519n19
Salazar, Margarita, 266–267
Salem Female Anti-Slavery Society, 450n50
Salem witch hunts, 25, 37
saloons, 95, 97, 98, 101, 104–105
same-sex relations. *See* lesbian(s)/lesbianism
Sampson, Deborah, 66
Sandberg, Sheryl, 395–397, 526n26, 526n29
Sandy Hook Elementary School, 417
San Francisco Chinatown, 238
San Francisco Examiner, 351, 379
Sanger, Margaret, 239–242
Santa Fe, New Mexico, 131
Santa Fe Trail, 129
Sargent Stevens, Judith, 83–84
Saturday Evening Post, 264, 275
Saturday Review, 249
Saxe, Susan, 344–345, 513n31
Schlafly, Phyllis, 354–356, 413, 416
Schneiderman, Rose, 204, 218–219
schools: for Black females after Revolutionary War, 82–83; Cherokee Female Seminary, 146–147; first nursing, 139; girls of Hollenbeck Junior High School, Los Angeles, 1–2; postrevolutionary female schools, 80–82; reform school in the 1950s, 2, 290–291; Ursuline Academy, 40. *See also* college(s); education
Schouler, William, 122–123
Schroeder, Pat, 355, 367
Schulman, Sarah, 338
Scotia Female Seminary, 155
Scott, Hugh, 353
Sears, Roebuck, 265
Second Amendment, 416–417

Second Great Awakening, 90
The Second Shift (Hochschild), 393
Second South Carolina Volunteer Colored Regiment, 137
second wave feminists/feminism, 8; criticism of, by postfeminists, 361–363; *The Feminine Mystique*, 314–315; gradual rise of, 307–313; NAACP for women, 315–316; third-wave feminists and, 372. *See also* National Organization for Women (NOW); New Woman
secretary of labor, Frances Perkins as, 258
seduction laws, 94–95
Senate Judiciary Committee, 364, 366, 372
Seneca Falls, New York, 102. *See also* women's rights convention, Seneca Falls (1848)
Seneca Indians, 29, 42
settlement houses, 159–160
Seventeen magazine, 303
seventeenth century: bastardy laws, 30–31; fashions, 23–24; imported ideas/books in, 24; lack of women's freedom, 30, 31–33; Massachusetts Bay Colony, 12–26; Native American women, 26–30; Quakers, 33–34; white women in the South, 30–33; witch hysteria, 20–22, 24–26, 37; women in New Amsterdam, 34–35; women working during, 22–23. *See also* colonial America
Sevier, John, 41
Sewall, Samuel, 37
sex(uality): automobile ownership and, 238–239; birth control and, 239–242; blues music and, 244–246; Boston marriages and, 164; Cardi B's "WAP" and, 416; changes in moral strictures, 235–236; female orgasm, 333–334, 511n5; flappers on Black, 244; Freudian theories, 224, 239; gender vs., 8; Mosher sex survey (1892–1920), 227–228, 475–476n6; New Woman and, 201–202, 205, 206; in the 1920s, 236; in the 1950s, 296–301; in the 1960s, 303–306; *Playboy*, 297; popular culture of the 1920s and, 236–238; postfeminists, 360–363; prostitution,

sex(uality) (cont.)
nineteenth century, 89–95; of riot grrrls, 382–383; in rock 'n' roll lyrics, 296–297; television shows about, 374–376; third-wave feminism, 360–361, 372–376; Woodhull's defense of "free love," 225–226; working-class Black women, 233–234, 485n28; of working-class girls vs. New Woman, 230, 231–232; working-class women of twentieth century and, 229–235, 483–484n20

Sex and the City (television series), 374, 375–376

Sex and the Single Girl (Brown), 305–306, 503n13

sex discrimination, 310, 313, 315, 506n43
"Sex Nomenclature" (Heywood), 381
"sex o'clock in America," 228
sex-positive feminists, 363
"sex radical" movement (1870s), 225–227
sex-segregated help-wanted ads, 316–317
sex shops, woman-centered, 363
sex survey, Clelia Duel Mosher and (1892–1920), 227–228, 475–476n6. *See also* polls
sex toys, 363
Sexual Behavior in the Human Female (Kinsey), 299–301
sexual fantasies, 373–374
sexual harassment and assault, 383, 397–398, 399; Anita Hill and, 364–372; on college campuses, 399–400; disbelief about, 398–399; "Me Too" movement, 404; Obama's White House Task Force to Protect Students from Sexual Assault, 402; by slave owners, 52–53, 438–439n47; women's accusations of, 398–399; women sharing experiences of, 401–402
Sexual Harassment of Working Women (MacKinnon), 401
Sexual Inversion (Havelock), 164
sexual inverts/"inverts," 134, 164, 202, 231, 262
Sexual Personae: Art and Decadence from Nefertiti to Emily Dickinson (Paglia), 361–362

"sexual pervert," New Woman and, 202
Sexual Politics (Millett), 334–336, 361
sexual violence, against enslaved women, 52
"sexuo-economic relation," 201, 423
Shakers, 440n59
The Shame of a Great Nation (Law), 231
Shaw, Anna Howard, 157–158, 179–181, 187, 189, 192, 195–197, 411, 469–470n34
she-merchants, 34, 55
Sherman Institute, Riverside, California, 271
Shippen, Alice, 45, 47, 148
Shippen, Nancy, 47–48
Shurtleff, Robert, 66
Signal Corps, 474–475n75
silent films, 236
silver mines, 128
Simon, Paul, 367
Simpson, Alan, 369, 518–519n19
single women, 423–424; colonial New England, 31–32; eighteenth-century, 54–61; Homestead Act and, 129–130; in the 1930s, 252; in the 1950s, 286; sexual freedom of, 305–306; television shows about, 374–376; westward migration trip by, 126–127; witch hysteria and, 21
Sisters of the Order of St. Ursula, 40
Siwanoy Indians, 17
Six Nations Iroquois Confederacy, 42
60 Minutes (television news program), 390
Sky Woman (goddess), 28, 42
Slaughter, Anne-Marie, 396
slave owners, white women as, 51–53
slavery: abolitionist movement, 105–113; abolition of, 73; female sexual modesty and, 106–107; Harriet Tubman and, 137; moral leadership by women, 87. *See also* enslaved females; enslaved people
slave trade, women involved in, 31, 34–35
Sloan, Margaret, 339, 340
S&M, 363
smallpox, 24
Smith, Barbara, 340
Smith, Clara, 245
Smith, Hilda Worthington, 261

Smith, Howard W., 311–312
Smith, Margaret Chase, 312
Smith, Mary Rozet, 160
Smith, Patti, 377
Smith College graduates, survey of, 314
Snapchat, 405
SNCC. *See* Student Nonviolent Coordinating Committee (SNCC)
Snyder Act (Indian Citizenship Act of 1924), 188
Social Hygiene Bulletin, 236
social media: Bill Cosby story and, 403; Kamala Harris on, 412; "Me Too" movement and, 404; #RapeCultureIsWhen, 402
social reform professions, nineteenth-century, 157–161
Social Security Act of 1935, 258
social services, careers in, 157–158. *See also* "municipal housekeeping" professions
Soledad Brothers, 348
Sons of Liberty, 67
Sorokin, Pitirim, 296, 299
South Carolina Training School for Nurses, 139
Southern Christian Leadership Conference (SCLC), 281–282, 321
southern colleges, 147–149, 153
Southern Literary Messenger, 115
Southern Monthly, 138
southern states, eighteenth-century, 48–52
southern strategy, of NAWSA, 190–191, 473n62
southern white women: Civil War and, 138–139; dependence on men, 115–116; ladydom, 44–48; nurses, 139–140; sexual relations with enslaved men, 53–54; slave owners, 51–53; Thomas Roderick Dew's message to, 115–116
Southgate, Eliza, 78–79
Souvestre, Marie, 254
Spanish-language print media, 237–238
SPAR (Coast Guard Women's Reserve), 272
Specter, Arlen, 368
Spelman College, 153, 155, 322, 463n39

spinning bees, during Revolutionary War, 68–69
spinning and weaving, 4, 42, 117, 124–125
spinsters, 54–61
Spock, Benjamin, 282–283
The Spy (journal), 68
Stahl, Leslie, 390
Stamp Act of 1765, 67, 68
Stanton, Elizabeth Cady, 112, 135; American Equal Rights Association and, 182; on divorce laws, 170; on Native American women, 187–188; running for Congress, 170; at Troy Female Seminary, 145; universal suffrage and, 182, 183, 184; woman suffrage and, 169–170, 175, 178
Stanton, Henry, 112
Starr, Ellen Gates, 159, 160
Star Tribune (Minneapolis), 293
state commissions on the status of women, 315
State Street Bank and Trust Company, Boston, 345
stay-at-home mothers, 387–391
Steinem, Gloria, 336–337, 378, 503n13
Steiner, Leslie, 391
Stevens, John, 83
Stevenson, Brenda, 52
Stevenson, Polly, 36–37
Stewart, Maria W. Miller, 109–110
St. George, Katharine, 312
Still, Mary, 88
stillborn births, 18
St. Louis World's Fair, 214
Stone, Lucy, 183
STOP (Stop Taking Our Privileges) ERA, 5, 355, 356
strikes: Esther Peterson and, 307; farmworkers, 325, 326; garment factory, 217, 219; Inez Milholland and, 204; Leiserson Company, 217; Lowell mill girls, 120–121; Pittsburgh cotton mill workers, 122; SNCC feminist sit-ins, 322; Triangle Shirtwaist Factory, 217, 481n50; twentieth-century garment industry, 217–221, 480n39
Student Nonviolent Coordinating Committee (SNCC), 321, 322–324, 508n59

Students for a Democratic Society, 344, 345
suffrage movement. *See* woman suffrage
suffrage parade (1913), 188, 189–190
The Suffragist (newspaper), 193
Sulkowicz, Emma, 400–401
Sullivan, James, 63, 75
Sun Yat-sen, 186, 187
Supreme Court: Amy Coney Barrett and, 384–385, 410–411; on female lawyers, 165; *Gadley v. Gadley*, 211; *Griswold v. Connecticut* (1965), 304; Hill–Thomas hearings, 364–372; *Roe v. Wade*, 351; on sexual harassment, 401; woman on, 371; women permitted to plead in the, 166
Surrendering to Motherhood (Krasnow), 386
Susquehanna River area, Pennsylvania, 59
Swan, Shanna, 422

Taft, Helen, 220
Take Back the Night, 362
Tammany Hall, 256
Tarbell, Ida, 221–223, 469n24
The Tariff in Our Times (Tarbell), 221
Task Force to Protect Students from Sexual Assault, 400
Tate, Sharon, 346
Taylor, James Monroe, 204
tea, Revolutionary War and, 68
Tea Act of 1773, 68
teachers, 153, 154, 156–157
Team Dresch, 378
television: dealing with sex, 374–376; portrayals of women in the 1950s, 1, 287; *Roller Derby*, 288–289
temperance movement, 5, 95–105, 220
ten-hour workday, 122, 123
Tennent, William, III, 67, 68
Ten Nights in a Bar-Room and What I Saw There (Arthur), 96
The Tenth Muse Lately Sprung Up in America (Bradstreet), 15
Terrell, Mary Church, 152, 184–185, 214, 471n45
Terrell, Robert, 184–185
textile mills, 117–123

"they," as Merriam-Webster's 2019 "Word of the Year," 9, 419
Thiot, Charles, 116
Third Annual Convention for the Improvement of Free People of Color in Philadelphia, 95–96
third-wave feminism: assertive sexuality of, 382–383; *Bust* and, 360–361; Hill–Thomas hearings and, 371, 372, 373; postfeminism contrasted with, 519n28; riot grrrl culture, 377–383; sexuality, 372–376; on "woman," 372
Third World Women's Alliance, 324
Thomas, Clarence, 364–366, 398
Thomas, M. Carey, 149–152, 164, 285, 461n25
Thompson, Franklin (Sarah Emma Edmonds), 136
Thoreau, Henry David, 119
Thurmond, Strom, 366
TikTok, 405
Tillis, Thom, 411
Time Inc., 506n43
Time magazine, 336, 349, 356, 376, 402
Time's Up, 404
Tinder, 419
Title IX, Equal Opportunity in Education Act, 350
Title VII, Civil Rights Act (1964), 311, 313, 315, 317, 401
Tlaib, Rashida, 417
Todd, Mary Ellen, 126
Tompson, Benjamin, 22
Totenberg, Nina, 367
"Toward a Politics of Sexuality" conference (1982), 363
Townshend Act of 1767, 68
Toynbee Hall, London, 159–160
"traditional" family roles: Amy Coney Barrett and, 385; Chicana feminists and, 329; in early twentieth century, 386–389; post–World War II, 496n4; pro-family conservatives and, 351–352; public opinion poll on (1997) returning to, 386, 392, 421–422, 424; westward expansion and, 455n32. *See also* domestic role of women; mothers and motherhood

Trail of Tears, 147
transgender/transgender people: butch lesbian transwomen, 420–421; concept of gender for, 420; "female" soldier during Revolutionary War, 66; Frank Dubois, 8–9; Gallup poll on those considering themselves as (2021), 419; gender essentialism and, 420; Jemima Wilkinson (eighteenth century), 57–58; Native Americans and, 27–28, 419–420, 431–432n52; use of term, 491n38; westward migration and, 127–128, 456n39. *See also* females (assigned at birth), "posing as men"
transman/transmen, 262, 420, 491n38
transvestism, 431n52
Treaty of Guadalupe Hidalgo, 131
Trial and Triumph (Harper), 98
Triangle Shirtwaist Factory, 217, 481n50
Triple Jeopardy (newspaper), 324
Troy Female Seminary, 144–146, 156
"The True Woman" (Anthony), 170–171
"true woman/womanhood," 117, 124, 132, 133, 170, 174, 201, 203, 208, 223, 283, 420. *See also* domestic role of women; "traditional" family roles
Trump, Donald, 356, 403–404, 408–409, 412, 414
Truth, Sojourner, 172, 182, 183, 467n12
Tubman, Harriet, 137–138, 340, 458n62, 458n63
Turchin, Nadine, 136
twentieth century: baby boom, 279; birth control and, 239–242, 277–278; "The Bitch Manifesto," 332; conservative backlash in, 351–358; employment in the 1950s, 278–279, 283; ERA, 308–309, 311–312, 352–358; fashion, 276; flapper age, 242–248; Hill–Thomas hearings, 364–372; political participation of women in, 255–257, 291–296; the radical right, 354–357; radical women (1970s), 333–342; riot grrrls, 377–383; ultraradical movement, 342–350; women in combat, 6–7; women's claim to sex in, 225–239; women's freedoms in early, 7. *See also* Great Depression; 1950s (decade); 1960s (decade); New Woman; third-wave feminism; World War II
twenty-first century. *See* millennial women
Twitter, 402, 403, 405, 412
typewriters/typists, 199, 475n13

Udall, Lee, 302
UFW. *See* United Farm Workers (UFW)
ultraradical movement, 342–350
Underground Railroad, 93, 106, 110, 137, 155
United Farm Workers (UFW), 325, 327
United States Magazine and Democratic Review, 123
Universalist Church, 84
Universal Magazine, 80
universal suffrage, 182–189
University of California, Los Angeles (UCLA), 347–348
University of Chicago, 160, 345
University of Leipzig, 150
University of Michigan, 152
University of Oklahoma, 366
University of Zurich, 150
unmarried women. *See* single women
"unsexed," calling women, 8, 39, 172
upper class(es): alcohol consumption and, 95–96; eighteenth-century ladydom, 44–48; garment industry strikes and, 217, 219–220; Hispanic women, 131–132; household tasks by, 44, 436n21; New Woman and, 200, 217; panic about working girls, 230; patriotism of women, during Revolutionary War, 69–70
Uprising of the 20,000, 218, 219–221, 480n39
Up the Sandbox (A. Roiphe), 362
urban areas: Great Northward Migration to, 212; immigrants settling in (1880–1920), 157; inverts gravitating to, 231; Native Americans in, 272; New Woman ideals in, 200; women entering workforce in, 199; working-class girls in (*see* working-class girls/women)
Ursuline Academy, 40

U.S. Cadet Nurse Corps, 494n67
U.S. Constitution, 75–76, 354. *See also specific amendments*
U.S. News and World Report, 304
U.S. Office of Indian Affairs, 132
U.S. Rubber Plant, Detroit, 270

vaginal orgasm, 333–334, 511n5
Vail, Tobi, 377–378
Vanderbilt, Willie, 191
Vane, Sir Henry, 19
Van Kleeck, Mary, 195
Van Vorst, Marie and Bessie, 480n39
Vasquez, Enriqueta, 329
Vassar College, 152, 203, 204, 205
veiling of women, 14
Velazquez, Loreta Janeta (Harry T. Buford), 136
Ventura School for Girls, 2–3, 291
Vermont Chronicle, 83
Vietnam protests, 330, 344, 345
A Vindication of the Rights of Woman (Wollstonecraft), 84
Vinson, Mechelle, 401
violence: FBI's "most-wanted" fugitives, 343–349; Marjorie Taylor Greene and, 416–417; in protests, 345–347; sexual violence toward enslaved females, 52; Violence against Women Act, 527n35. *See also* sexual harassment and assault
Violence against Women Act, 527n35
Virginia, 26, 30–31
Virginia Gazette, 72
The Voice of Industry (magazine), 123
volunteers/volunteering, 139, 157, 160, 307, 325, 328
Vorse, Mary Heaton, 200
Vorwets (newspaper), 221
"Votes for Women" parade (1912), 186, 187
voting and voting rights: after Revolutionary War, 75–76; for American Indians, 188–189; illegal, spring of 1871, 467n10; Susan B. Anthony's arrest for, 168–169, 171–172, 467n10; for women in China, 186. *See also* woman suffrage
Voting Rights Act of 1965, 316

WAAC (Women's Army Auxiliary Corps), 272, 273

WAC (Women's Army Corps), 272
Wadsworth, Benjamin, 38
wage discrepancies, 199, 251, 317, 358, 418, 506n43
wages: before COVID-19 pandemic, 422; during the Great Depression, 251; of Latinas during World War II, 266; of lesbians *vs.* heterosexual women, 524n16; Lowell mill girls, 119; President's Commission on the Status of Women report on, 310; textile factory strikes and, 120–121; women in garment industry, 480n39; working-class girls, early twentieth century, 232, 484n26
Walker, Alice, 342, 371
Walker, Charles Joseph, 214
Walker, Rebecca, 371–372
Wall, Amanda, 467n10
Wallace, Nicolle, 409
Waltham, Massachusetts, 117
war(s), impacting ideas of woman, 6–7. *See also specific wars*
War Manpower Commission, 263, 270
War of Independence. *See* Revolutionary War (1775–1783)
"War Relocation Camps," 268
Warren, Mercy Otis, 63, 75
"A Warrior's Daughter" (Zitkala-Sa), 207
warrior women, 27
Washington, George, 4, 41–42, 70–71, 132
Washington Post, 386
WASP. *See* Women Airforce Service Pilots (WASP)
Waterford, Janet Harmon, 495n69
Watkins, Katherine, 53
Watts, Isaac, 61
WAVES (Women Accepted for Volunteer Emergency Service), 272
Way, Amanda, 104
WCTU. *See* Woman's Christian Temperance Union (WCTU)
Weathermen, 344, 345, 346, 347, 513n31
Weekly Iberville South News (Louisiana), 237
Weingarten, Violet, 283
Weinstein, Harvey, 404
Weld, Theodore, 111, 112
Wellesley College, 151, 317
Wells-Barnett, Ida, 191, 471n62

western prairies, white women on, 124–125
Western Reserve University, Ohio, 162
westward migration, 123–134
"What Chou Mean We, White Girl?" (Bethel), 340
What Every Girl Should Know (Sanger), 241
Wheatley, Phillis, 442n14
Wheeler, Shirley Ann, 350
whipping, of colonial women, 17–18, 23–24
whiskey riots, 104–105
White, Lynn, Jr., 280
White, Pearl, 213
Whitechapel, London, 159–160
Whitefield, George, 57
White House Conference on Child Health, 156
White House Task Force to Protect Students from Sexual Assault, 402
White Rose Home for Working-Class Negro Girls, 233–234
white women/feminists: Black feminists breaking away from, 340; Black women compared with, 320–321, 323; Gloria Anzaldúa on, 341; inspired by Chinese suffragists, 187; universal suffrage and, 183–184; wages of Black women compared with wages of, 524n17. *See also* southern white women
Whitman, Howard, 296
Whittier, John Greenleaf, 119
Whole World's Temperance Convention (1853), 103
widows, Puritan, 427n6
"wife-swapping," 304
Wilder, E. J., 130
Wilkerson, Cathlyn, 347
Wilkinson, Eliza Yonge, 64–65
Wilkinson, Jemima, 57–58
Willard, Emma, 4, 144, 150, 470n37
Willard, Frances, 181, 223
Williams, Fanny Barrier, 208–209
Williams, Gurney, 398
Williams, Joan, 393
Williams, Roger, 4, 7–8, 11, 14
Williamson, Joel, 153
Willison, Megan K., 431n52
Wilson, Emma, 155

Wilson, Joan Hoff, 443n34
Wilson, Woodrow, 192, 193, 195, 196, 221
Winchester, Indiana, 104
Winslow, Anna Green, 47
Winthrop, John: Anne Hutchinson and, 16, 17; idea of woman by, 12, 38; Mary Dyer and, 18, 19; Pequot Indians and, 11; witch hysteria and, 20; wives of, 12–13; on women's rebellion, 17
Wisconsin State Journal, 137
Witchcraft Act of 1542, 20
witch hysteria, 20–22, 24–26, 37
Within Our Gates (film), 212
Wittig, Monique, 8
Wollstonecraft, Mary, 84
woman: being female *vs.* being, 8; challenging notion of, 7–8, 173–174; essentialist notion of, 180, 420; performance of, by suffragists, 107, 180, 181–182; prescribed gender behavior and, 8; third-wave feminists on concept of, 372. *See also* idea of woman/ womanhood
Woman and the New Race (Sanger), 242
woman-centered sex shops, 363
womanhood: enslaved women and, 48–49; westward expansion travel and, 125. *See also* "true woman/ womanhood"
Woman in the Nineteenth Century (Fuller), 144
"womanist," 342, 371, 478n27
The Woman Rebel (newsmagazine), 239–240
Woman's Christian Temperance Union (WCTU), 181
woman suffrage: American Indian women and, 187–189; Anna Howard Shaw and, 179–181, 196–197; Anna Julia Cooper on, 210; in China, 186–187, 472n52; Eleanor Roosevelt and, 255; Frances Willard and, 181–182; gender-shaming of women and, 172–173; Horace Greeley opposition to, 174–175; idea of, in 1848, 169; Inez Milholland and, 205; militancy and, 189–193; militant tactics, 196; Nineteenth Amendment, passage of, 196; popular chant at rallies for, 178; radicalism and,

woman suffrage (cont.)
171–172, 178; after Revolutionary War,
75–76; women of color and, 182–189;
women's opposition to, 175–177;
women's participation in World War I
and, 193–196; working-class women
and, 219

Woman's Wrongs (Hamilton), 175

Women Accepted for Volunteer Emergency Services (WAVES), 272

Women Airforce Service Pilots (WASP), 274, 495n69

Women and Economies (Gilman), 166, 201

women of color: in NOW, 320; in suffrage movement, 182–189; Third World Women's Alliance, 324; during World War II, 265–269. *See also* Black women; Chinese American women/immigrants; Mexican American women/immigrants; Native American women

Women on Top: How Real Life Has Changed Women's Sexual Fantasies (Friday), 373–374

Women Rise Up (pamphlet), 344

women's agency: by colonial women, 5, 17–20; by nineteenth-century mill girls, 120–123. *See also* political participation; woman suffrage

Women's American Baptist Home Mission Society, 153–155

Women's Army Auxiliary Corps (WAAC), 272

Women's Army Corps (WAC), 272, 493n54

Women's Bureau of the Department of Labor, 308

women's CCC, 261–262

Women's Land Army, 194

Women's Liberation Army, 346

Women's Medical College of Pennsylvania, 211

Women's Medical College of the New York Infirmary, 162

Women's National Abortion Action Coalition, 351

Women's New York State Temperance Society, 100

women's rights: Black women's liberation vs., 323; Grimké sisters and, 111–112;
names called about pioneers in, 202; publications, 171, 239. *See also* feminist(s)/feminism; woman suffrage; workforce, women in

Women's Rights Convention (1851), 172, 182

women's rights conventions: National Women's Rights Convention (1866), 182, 184; Seneca Falls (1848), 102, 129, 169, 178, 213; Women's Rights Convention (1851), 172, 182

Women's Trade Union League (WTUL), 217, 219, 220, 255, 258, 260, 307

Women Strike for Peace (1962), 330

"womxn," 9

The Wonders of the Invisible World (Mather), 25

Wong, Jade Snow, 267–268

Woodbridge, John, 15

Woodbridge, William, 81–82

Woodhull, Victoria, 225–226

Woodhull and Claflin's Weekly, 225, 226

Woodruff, Clinton, 5

Woolley, Mary, 252–253, 252–254

The Word (magazine), 227

The Work-a-Day Girl (Laughlin), 232

workforce, women in: at beginning of twenty-first century, 386; Black women in the 1910s, 210–212; COVID-19 pandemic and, 422–423; during the Depression, 249, 250–251; events increasing, 6; in garment factories, 216–218, 480n39; increase in professional pursuits (1870–1910), 464n47; media reporting on women opting out of, 6, 389–390; Mexican American women, 237; millennial women opting out of, 386–392; in 1920, 199; in the 1950s, 278–279, 283; in the 1960s, 317; in the 1980s, 357–358; President's Commission on the Status of Women and, 309–311; after recession of 2008–2009, 392–393; schedules and programs for, 394; sexual harassment and, 397–398, 401; types of occupations, 199, 317, 464n47; tyranny of old notions about woman and, 6; women of color during World War II, 265–269; women opting

out of, 387–392, 523n8; during World War I, 194–196, 474n75; after World War II, 278–279; during World War II, 263–272, 492n42, 494n67. *See also* working conditions
working-class girls/women: Black women, 233–235, 485n28; flappers and, 243; garment industry, 307; during the Great Depression, 251; New Woman and, 216–223; same-sex relations, 231–232; sexuality and, 229–235, 483–484n20; vulnerabilities of, 232–233, 484n24; wages, 232, 484n26
working conditions: garment industry, 216–217; Lowell textile mills, 119–120, 454n12
Working Girls Home Association, 234
Working Mother (magazine), 394
working mothers: children of, 302, 309; COVID-19 pandemic and, 422–423; "lean-in" movement, 395–397; statistics on post–World War II, 386–387; stay-at-home mothers *vs.*, 302–303
working women: in early twentieth century, 7; ERA and, 308, 309; Esther Peterson helping, 307–308; in the garment industry, 307; household duties done by, 393–394; laboring class in early nineteenth century, 117; in Massachusetts Bay Colony, 22–23; mill girls fighting for their rights, 122–123; New Amsterdam settlement, 34–35; nurses during Civil War, 139–141; "posing as men," 127–129; "sexuo-economic relation" and, 201; temperance movement women, 100; in textile factories, 117–123, 454n12; westward expansion and, 124; witch hysteria and, 25–26; Women's Bureau of the Department of Labor, 308. *See also* career(s); employment; workforce, women in
workweek, 220
World's Anti-Slavery Convention, 112–113
World's Anti-Slavery Convention (1840), 182
World's Temperance Convention, 102–103
World War I, 193–197, 212, 235
World War II, 263–275, 492n42
Wright, Frances (Fanny), 108, 142
Wright, Susanna, 59–60
"wrinkle their foreheads with politics," 4, 46, 172, 415–416, 437n28
WTUL. *See* Women's Trade Union League (WTUL)

Yale Law School, 365, 406
Yale University, 315, 361, 364, 389
"Year of the Woman" (1992), 370
Yeomanettes, 195, 197
Yerkes, Robert, 502n64
Yoshimura, Fumio, 336
Young Citizens for Community Action, 327
Young Ladies Academy, Medford, Massachusetts, 81
Young Ladies Academy of Philadelphia, 81
YouTube, 405

Zapata, Emiliano, 324
Zitkala-Sa, 206–207
zoot suits, 499n35